THE CAMBRIDGE HANDBOOK OF RACE AND SURVEILLANCE

Featuring chapters authored by leading scholars in the fields of criminology, critical race studies, history, sociology, and more, *The Cambridge Handbook of Race and Surveillance* cuts across history and geography to provide a detailed examination of how race and surveillance intersect throughout space and time. The volume reviews surveillance technology from the days of colonial conquest to the digital era, focusing on countries such as the United States, Canada, the UK, South Africa, the Philippines, India, Brazil, and Palestine. Weaving together narratives on how technology and surveillance have developed over time to reinforce racial inequality, the book delves into the often-overlooked origins of racial surveillance, from skin branding, cranial measurements, and fingerprinting to contemporary manifestations in big data, commercial surveillance, and predictive policing. Lucid, accessible, and expertly researched, this handbook provides a crucial investigation of issues throughout history and at the forefront of contemporary life.

MICHAEL KWET is a Visiting Fellow at Yale Law School's Information Society Project and a postdoctoral researcher at the Centre for Social Change at the University of Johannesburg. His research focuses on digital colonialism, carceral tech, social media, digital socialism, the environment, and surveillance.

Contents

List of Figures		*page* vii
List of Contributors		ix
Acknowledgments		xv
1	The Golden Age of Racial Surveillance Michael Kwet	1
2	Sorting Identity Eric Stoddart	19
3	Imperial Mimesis: Migration of Surveillance from the Colonial Philippines to the United States Alfred McCoy	33
4	The Racialisation of British Women during the Long Nineteenth Century: How White Women's Bodies Became Tools of Control and Surveillance Toni Weller	57
5	Linking Caste and Surveillance: How Digital Governance Has Legitimised Caste Discrimination in India Amber Sinha and Shruti Trikanad	76
6	Surveillance in South Africa: From Skin Branding to Digital Colonialism Michael Kwet	97
7	Israel/Palestine, North America, and Surveillance Yasmeen Abu-Laban and Abigail B. Bakan	123

8	Colonialism's Uneasy Legacy: Topologies of Race and Surveillance in São Paulo Claudio Altenhain, Ricardo Urquizas Campello, Alcides Eduardo dos Reis Peron, and Leandro Siqueira	137
9	China's Surveillance and Repression in Xinjiang Myunghee Lee and Emir Yazici	166
10	Asian Americans as "the Perpetual Foreigner" under Scrutiny Frank H. Wu	190
11	The Great White Father and His Little Red Children: Surveillance and Race in Native America Anton Treuer	223
12	In a Most Excellent and Perfect Order: Surveillance, Racialization, and Government Practices in Colonial Canada Scott Thompson	232
13	Surveillance and Public Schools: Policing, Desegregation, and the Criminalization of Minority Youth in Charlotte-Mecklenburg Schools Erica L. Nelson and Tracey A. Benson	255
14	Surveillance and Preventing Violent Extremism: The Evidence from Schools and Further Education Colleges in England Joel Busher, Tufyal Choudhury, and Paul Thomas	267
15	Resistance and the Politics of Surveillance and Control Anthony E. Cook	288
16	Surveilled Subjects and Technologically Mediated Law Enforcement: Reflecting on Relational Concerns Alana Saulnier	304

Figures

3.1 NSA Worldwide SIGINT/Defense cryptologic platform 2013. *page* 49
12.1 Indian Agent Permit Form (1937). Indian Agent, 1937, "Permit – To Sell Native Pony," H2c 156B Control of Indian Reserves by Indian Agents, Catalogue #H89.55.13, Royal Alberta Museum. 243
12.2 Pencil issued at a Northern Ontario Residential School. 245
12.3 Purchase Order Form (Québec 1958) and Liquor Permit Book (Manitoba 1928). 249
12.4 Interdiction Notice Identifying Newly Listed Individuals (Ontario). Liquor Control Board of Ontario 1929–1975, "Interdiction List," AO: Interdiction Records of the Liquor Licence Board of Ontario 1929–1990, RG 36-13, boxes: 194, 7, 6, 5, 4, 3, 2, 1-R, 2-R, 512, 1-D, 1, 551. 251

Contributors

Yasmeen Abu-Laban is Professor of Political Science and Canada Research Chair in the Politics of Citizenship and Human Rights at the University of Alberta, and a fellow at the Canadian Institute for Advanced Research. Her published research addresses themes relating to: ethnic and gender politics; nationalism, globalization, and processes of racialization; immigration policies and politics; surveillance and border control; and multiculturalism and antiracism. With Abigail B. Bakan and the support of the Social Sciences and Humanities Research Council of Canada, she is currently undertaking research on United Nations world conferences and declarations pertaining to race, gender, and Indigeneity.

Claudio Altenhain is a PhD candidate for the Erasmus Mundus/Erasmus+ Doctorate in Cultural and Global Criminology (DCGC). His research focuses on the anthropology of urban (in)security, science and technology studies, and postcolonial approaches to policing and crime.

Abigail B. Bakan is Professor in the Department of Social Justice in Education (SJE) at the Ontario Institute for Studies in Education (OISE), University of Toronto. Her research is in the area of anti-oppression politics. Publications include: *Theorizing Anti-Racism: Linkages in Marxism and Critical Race Theories* (co-edited with Enakshi Dua, 2014); *Negotiating Citizenship: Migrant Women in Canada and the Global System* (with Daiva Stasiulis, 2003); and *Critical Political Studies: Debates and Dialogues from the Left* (co-edited with Eleanor MacDonald and Colin Leys, 2002). With Yasmeen Abu-Laban, she is co-author of *Israel, Palestine and the Politics of Race: Exploring Identity and Power in a Global Context* (2020), and is currently undertaking SSHRC-supported research on United Nations world conferences and declarations pertaining to race, gender, and Indigeneity.

Dr. Tracey A. Benson is CEO of Tracey A. Benson Consulting and founder of the Anti-Racist Leadership Institute. He received his doctorate in Education Leadership from the Harvard Graduate School of Education and Masters of School Administration from the University of North Carolina-Chapel Hill. He has served as an assistant professor of educational leadership, high school principal, middle school vice-principal, and elementary school teacher. His book, *Unconscious Bias in Schools: A Developmental Approach to Exploring Race and Racism*, was published in August 2019.

Joel Busher is Professor of Political Sociology at the Centre for Trust, Peace and Social Relations at Coventry University. Joel's main areas of research include far-right and anti-minority activism; the escalation, de-escalation, and non-escalation of political violence; and the implementation of counterterrorism policy and its societal impacts. His book, *The Making of Anti-Muslim Protest: Grassroots Activism in the English Defence League* (2015), was awarded the British Sociological Association's Philip Abrams Memorial Prize.

Ricardo Urquizas Campello is a postdoctoral researcher in the Department of Social Anthropology at the University of Campinas (PPGAS/UNICAMP), and researcher at the Center for the Study of Violence at the University of São Paulo (NEV-USP). His research interests are the current practices of control, security, and punishment; prison systems; electronic monitoring of offenders; and forensic technologies of genetic profiling.

Tufyal Choudhury is Associate Professor Durham Law School, Durham University; a senior research fellow on National Security and the Rule of Law at the Bingham Centre for the Rule of Law; and a senior research affiliate of the Canadian Terrorism, Security and Society Research Network. His research focuses on the human rights impacts of counterterrorism law and policy. His publications include, "Suspicion, Discrimination and Surveillance: The Impact of Counter-Terrorism Law and Policy on Racialised Groups at Risk of Racism in Europe" (an ENAR project report, 2021) and "The Introduction of the Prevent Duty into Schools and Colleges: Stories of Continuity and Change" (co-authored with J. Busher and P. Thomas, in J. Busher and L. Jerome (eds.) *The Prevent Duty in Education*, 2020), among other works.

Anthony Cook is a law professor at Georgetown University. He is a graduate of Yale Law School, a magna cum laude graduate of Princeton University, and is currently pursuing his doctorate at Oxford University in sustainable urban development, studying the role of worker cooperatives in building more equitable economies. Professor Cook is a nationally recognized scholar on race, law, and American history, most notably, the work and life of Dr. Martin Luther King, Jr. For his work as a scholar and community engagement practitioner, the American Bar Association honored him as One of 21 Lawyers Leading America into the 21st Century, citing his "unique synergy of thought and action."

List of Contributors

Michael Kwet received his PhD in sociology from Rhodes University in South Africa, is a postdoctoral research fellow of the Centre for Social Change at the University of Johannesburg, and is a visiting fellow of the Information Society Project at Yale Law School. His work focuses the topics of digital colonialism, police surveillance, race, political economy, the environment, and education. Michael is the author of "Digital Colonialism: US Empire and the New Imperialism in the Global South" (*Race & Class*, 2019), "The Digital Tech Deal: A Socialist Framework for the Twentieth Century" (*Race & Class*, 2022), and has been published in numerous press outlets, including the *New York Times*, *Al Jazeera*, *VICE News*, *Wired*, *Mail & Guardian*, and *Slate*. He hosts the Tech Empire podcast and is the founder of the People's Tech website (peoplestech.org).

Myunghee Lee is a postdoctoral fellow at the Nordic Institute of Asian Studies at the University of Copenhagen. Her research focuses on contentious politics, protest, and authoritarianism. Her work appears in academic journals such as *International Security*, *International Studies Review*, and *Politics & Gender*.

Alfred W. McCoy holds the Harrington Chair in History at the University of Wisconsin-Madison. He is the author of *The Politics of Heroin in Southeast Asia* (1972), the classic study of drug trafficking, which the CIA tried to suppress; *Policing America's Empire: The United States, the Philippines and the Rise of the Surveillance State* (2009), awarded the Kahin Prize by the Association for Asian Studies; and, most recently, *To Govern the Globe: World Orders and Catastrophic Change* (2021).

Erica Nelson teaches mathematics at Denmark High School in Georgia. She received her Master's degree in middle and secondary education as well as school administration from the University of North Carolina at Charlotte. During her twenty years in education, she has served as a mathematics teacher and assistant principal.

Alcides Eduardo dos Reis Peron is a postdoctoral researcher in the Department of Sociology at the São Paulo University (USP), and researcher at the Center for the Studies of Violence (NEV-USP). His research focuses on the materialities of (in)security in urban spaces and international conflicts, entangling surveillance studies, science, technology and society studies, and international political sociology (IPS).

Alana Saulnier is an assistant professor in the Sociology Department at Queen's University, associate editor of *Surveillance & Society*, and deputy director of the Surveillance Studies Centre. Alana's research focuses on relationships between legal authorities and the public with a particular emphasis on how the use of surveillance technologies augments those relationships. Her research chiefly centers on documenting, evaluating, and governing legal authorities' use of data collection and management technologies (e.g., body-worn cameras, unpiloted aerial vehicles, etc.), but she also frequently engages experimental methods to explore the nuances of public perceptions of, and reactions to, legal authorities' use of surveillance technologies.

Amber Sinha has led programs at CIS on civil liberties research, including privacy, identity, AI, cybersecurity, and free speech. Amber's research has been cited with appreciation by the Supreme Court of India and several government committees. He is a member of the Steering Committee of ABOUT ML, an initiative to bring diverse perspectives to develop, test, and implement machine learning system documentation practices. Amber is a member of the GPA Reference Panel of Global Privacy Assembly. His first book, *The Networked Public*, was released in 2019. Amber studied law and humanities at National Law School of India University, Bangalore.

Leandro Siqueira holds a PhD in social sciences (Pontifical Catholic University of São Paulo) and is Associate Professor of Political Science at Santos Metropolitan University (UNIMES). His research focuses on surveillance studies; science, technology, and society studies; and Brazilian political thought.

Eric Stoddart teaches Christian practical theology at the School of Divinity of the University of St Andrews in Scotland. He is one of the two co-founders of the international Surveillance and Religion Network which aims to advance research in the field. His major publications include *Theological Perspectives on a Surveillance Society* (2011) and *The Common Gaze: Surveillance and the Common Good* (2021).

Paul Thomas is Professor of Youth and Policy and Associate Dean (Research) in the School of Education and Professional Development at the University of Huddersfield, UK. Paul's research focuses on how state multiculturalist policies such as Community Cohesion and the Prevent counterterrorism strategy have been understood and enacted by ground-level policymakers and practitioners. It has led to books such as *Responding to the Threat of Violent Extremism: Failing to Prevent* (2012) and *Race, Space and Place in Northern England: The (M62) Corridor of Uncertainty* (with Shamim Miah and Pete Sanderson, 2020), as well as articles in many leading journals. Paul is a qualified youth and community worker, and previously worked for the Commission for Racial Equality in the North of England.

Scott Thompson is an assistant professor in the Department of Sociology at the University of Saskatchewan, research fellow of the Surveillance Studies Centre, and associate editor of the journal *Surveillance & Society*. Having been called "the genuine historian of Surveillance Studies," he primarily uses historical case studies in order to explain and address current and pressing issues in the areas of Criminology, Sociology and Surveillance Studies. His publications include work on surveillance and colonial/First Nations relationships, surveillance, and the control of liquor consumption (*Punched Drunk*, 2009), national registration and identity cards in Canada and the United Kingdom, and the taking up of "new" surveillance technologies by police services.

Shruti Trikanad is a program officer at the Centre for Internet and Society (CIS), India. At CIS, she works primarily on issues concerning digital ID, as part of which she studied the biometric ID systems of several countries, and wrote extensively about its legal and societal implications, and how they have been assessed by courts around the world. As part of this research, she drafted a framework to evaluate the legitimacy of digital ID systems, and is now working with Research ICT Africa to apply these to ID systems in ten African countries. Shruti is an India-qualified lawyer, having completed her undergraduate law studies and Bachelor of Arts in economics and political science from Gujarat National Law University, India.

Anton Treuer is Professor of Ojibwe at Bemidji State University and author of many books, including *Everything You Wanted to Know About Indians But Were Afraid to Ask* (2012), *Warrior Nation: A History of the Red Lake Ojibwe* (2015), and *Atlas of Indian Nations* (2014). His equity, education, and cultural work has put him on a path of service around the region, the nation, and the world.

Dr. Toni Weller was educated at Cambridge University and City, University of London. She is currently a visiting research fellow in History at De Montfort University, UK. For almost the last two decades her research has focused upon the field of information history, with an emphasis on society and culture in nineteenth century Britain. She has also published and lectured on the history of surveillance and the impact of history in the digital age. Her book *History in the Digital Age* (2013) is a set text for several Digital History courses across the US and Europe. She sits on several editorial boards and is a former editor of the journal *Library & Information History*.

Frank H. Wu was named President of Queens College, City University of New York, in 2020. He previously served as Chancellor and Dean of University of California Hastings College of the Law and professor at Howard University Law School. He also has taught at Michigan, Columbia, and Johns Hopkins. He is the author of *Yellow: Race in America Beyond Black and White* (2003). He practiced law with Morrison & Foerster in San Francisco.

Emir Yazici is a faculty member in the Department of International Relations at Kırklareli University and a former postdoctoral fellow in the Department of Political Science at the University of Missouri. His research focuses on political violence, human rights, nationalism, and ethnic politics.

Acknowledgments

This volume was a love of labor. I would like to thank the fantastic set of authors who contributed their time and effort to producing chapters for the book. Their work is a timely intervention into an issue critical to people across the world.

I would also like to thank Jeffrey Vagle and Khiara Bridges, who started the project in 2018. Their early work on the book got it off the ground and gave it wings. I would like to thank Frank Wu for his support in pushing the volume forward and bringing me in as editor. Big thanks to Cambridge University Press team (Becky Jackaman, Matt Gallaway, Siddharthan Indra Priyadarshini, Jem Langworthy, and Jadyn Fauconier-Herry) for moving the manuscript along smoothly. And a huge thanks to the supremely talented artist, Zoran Svilar, for drawing a brilliant cover that captures the ideas in the book in a stunning image.

A work of this scope has many hands involved that are unseen. I would like to thank my kind and loving parents, Linda and Fred Kwet, for their unwavering support throughout the years; my wonderful grandparents, Edward and Lillian Basel; as well as Nancy Amankwa, Grace Nyambosi, Ayanda Donga, Hela, and my gentle and loving dog, Lily Kwet. Without them, this book would not have been possible.

Michael Kwet

1

The Golden Age of Racial Surveillance

Michael Kwet

We are living in times of deep turmoil and rapid change. Over the past few decades, inequality has increased within and between countries.[1] Simultaneously, new developments in digital technology have spread throughout the world, reconfiguring power relations and the rhythms of everyday life. Transnational technology corporations and powerful nation states have been the primary beneficiaries of the digital revolution, and their domination of digital technology concentrates power and wealth into their hands. The United States dominates the global tech economy, an evolution of American empire.[2] Computers, wired together across the Internet, have drastically expanded the capacity to spy on and assess individuals, groups, and populations.

Surveillance has long been used a tool for the oppression and control of those being watched. As Noam Chomsky puts it, surveillance technology can be used "for making money, and you can use it for controlling people's attitudes and beliefs, directing them toward what you want them to do."[3] Throughout modern history, surveillance has been developed and used by racially dominant groups to direct them toward "what they want them to do," most often for the purpose of exploitation and profit.

This volume chronicles how surveillance (re)produces racial inequality. Across sixteen chapters, it takes a deep dive into historical and contemporary developments, crisscrossing time and space to develop a global picture of race and surveillance.

---

[1] Jason Hickel, *The Divide: Global Inequality from Conquest to Free Markets* (New York: W. W. Norton & Company, Inc., 2017).

[2] Michael Kwet, "Digital Colonialism: US Empire and the New Imperialism in the Global South," *Race & Class* 60, no. 4 (2019); Michael Kwet, "Digital Colonialism: The Evolution of American Empire," *ROAR*, March 3, 2021, https://roarmag.org/essays/digital-colonialism-the-evolution-of-american-empire.

[3] Noam Chomsky, *Global Discontents: Conversations on the Rising Threats to Democracy* (New York: Metropolitan Books, 2017), 2.

It can be read by general and scholarly audiences, and is of critical value to anyone looking to grapple with the racialized surveillance state expanding across the world.

The use of surveillance for racial control is, of course, nothing new. For example, surveillance infrastructure in America was developed through the practice of slavery and indentured servitude. As Christian Parenti remarks, white slave holders "were forced to develop not just methods of terror but also a haphazard system of identification and surveillance."[4] Written slave passes were used in conjunction with organized slave patrols and wanted posters for runaways to police the mobility of African bodies. Skin branding with marks of slave owners were also used to catalog and keep tabs on slaves. In New York City, lantern laws required people of color to carry candle lanterns in the dark. White people were deputized to police black persons traveling in the dark without a lantern, and those caught without one could be punished with lashings, to be determined by the slave owner.[5] In the domain of labor, white slaveholders recorded the activity of slave farmers and analyzed the data to predict and alter their work routines to maximize production.[6]

While these histories expose important methods of control and exploitation within the United States, racialized surveillance extends well beyond US borders.

As Amber Sinha and Shruti Trikanand show in this volume, in India, the British targeted caste and tribes for alleged "criminality" as a means to classify, discipline, and punish "criminal tribes" – that is, those deemed genetically prone to crime. Tribes could be relocated by the British colonizers or placed in a "reformatory settlement." Passes were issued to police movements, and local authorities were empowered to surveil tribe members and inspect their places of residence. Law enforcement agencies maintained "historical sheets" that put people accused of crimes on police surveillance lists.

In Victorian Britain, Toni Weller demonstrates how women were deemed categorically different than men – almost as if they were a separate race – and women themselves became platforms for surveillance. British authorities drew upon pseudoscientific theories of evolution to impose control and order over women's bodies and minds.

In South Africa, Michael Kwet details how surveillance goes hand-in-hand with racial domination in South Africa. Colonizers used pass systems, skin branding, fingerprinting, and eventually computer systems to classify, monitor, and police the bodies and labor of Africans and other people of color. In each phase of South African history, US authorities increased their support of surveillance by white supremacist authorities in the country. Today, the United States is directly

---

[4] Christian Parenti, *The Soft Cage: Surveillance in America from Slave Passes to the War on Terror* (New York: Basic Books, 2003), 14.
[5] Simone Browne, *Dark Matters: On the Surveillance of Blackness* (Athens, GA: Duke University Press, 2015), 31–88.
[6] Caitlin Rosenthal, *Accounting for Slavery: Masters and Management* (Cambridge, MA: Harvard University Press, 2018).

administering mass surveillance in South Africa, this time through the process of digital colonialism.

In Brazil, Claudio Altenhain et al. trace the history of race and surveillance, connecting today's surveillance regimes in urban spaces to early forms of surveillance arrangements used to segregate and exploit bodies according to skin color. In Israel and Palestine, Yasmeen Abu-Laban and Abigail B. Bakan show how authorities are using surveillance against those calling for boycott, divestment, and sanctions (BDS) against Israel. And in Xinjiang, Myunghee Lee and Emir Yazici detail the Chinese Communist Party's (CCP) extreme repression of the Uyghur population. A vast array of dystopian technologies is being used en masse to surveil Uyghurs, who have been subject to indoctrination and brutal treatment by CCP authorities.

Surveillance technologies often travel across borders. In South Africa and India, fingerprinting technologies were imposed by the British, and experiments in using them to police dark-skinned bodies flowed across the colonies. In Chapter 3, Alfred McCoy illustrates how surveillance technologies were first used by American imperialists to conquer the Philippines, but soon thereafter migrated back home. McCoy traces the emergence of the modern US surveillance state to "America's first information revolution" used to colonize the Philippines at the turn of the nineteenth century. Thomas Edison's quadroplex telegraph (1874), Philo Remington's commercial typewriter (1874), and Alexander Graham Bell's telephone (1876) "allowed the transmission and recording of textual data in unprecedented quantities at unequaled speed with unsurpassed accuracy."[7] Melvil Dewey's Dewey Decimal System enabled efficient encoding and the rapid retrieval of information, and Herman Hollerith's punchcard system sped up population registers for census records.[8] Meanwhile, John Gamewell's corporation wired up police telegraph/telephone call-box systems. In short time, hundreds of US municipal security networks were sending 41 million messages per year. Biometric analytics (such as fingerprinting and Alphonse Bertillon's photographic identification) and new statistical methods (such as statistical regression) were invented, which helped make sense of the surveillance data.

The policing panopticon formed abroad would soon come home to the United States. During World War I, the "father of American military intelligence," Ralph Van Deman, designed the United States' first internal security agency as head of the US Military Intelligence Section. In collaboration with the Bureau of Investigation (FBI), McCoy observes, Van Deman presided over a counterintelligence auxiliary, the American Protective League, with 350,000 civilian operatives who amassed over

---

[7] Alfred McCoy, *Policing America's Empire: The United States, the Philippines, and the Rise of the Surveillance State* (Madison, WI: The University of Wisconsin Press), 21–27; Alfred McCoy, "Policing the Imperial Periphery: The Philippine-American War and the Origins of U.S. Global Surveillance," *Surveillance & Society* 13, no. 1 (2015): 4–26, 9–10.

[8] Hollerith went on to found IBM and the technology was used by South Africa's apartheid government decades later.

a million pages of surveillance reports on German Americans in just fourteen months. New intelligence institutions rapidly expanded to suppress strikes and the socialist left in the United States. The Lusk Raids in New York City investigated the "seditious activities" of "radicals" and "radical organizations" – including the Rand School of Social Science, which aimed at socialist education. J. Edgar Hoover's Palmer Raids targeted anarchists and other socialists for activity such as labor strikes and political assassinations. Following his retirement from the army in 1929, Van Deman spent almost twenty-five years amassing detailed files on 250,000 suspected subversives.

A second wave of surveillance commenced around World War II. The FBI and California Committee on Un-American Activities pursued a new "red scare" against the US Communist Party and its alleged allies in Hollywood. When Van Deman died in 1952, his archive was secured by the US Army Counter Intelligence Corps, who used it against "communist" adversaries for the next two decades. Van Deman's surveillance tactics were also used by the FBI for wiretapping, illegal break-ins, and mail intercepts. Domestic surveillance targets included US politicians as well as academics, cultural icons, and members of the general public.

Today, a second information revolution, once again developed in the United States, brings together advances in computing, storage, processing, sensing, statistics (including so-called artificial intelligence),[9] network connectivity, and data transmission. As with the first information revolution, authorities are making use of the new tech for social control, military, and policing purposes.

During the 2000s, a succession of US whistleblowers revealed that the US government formed a surveillance dragnet designed to mop up the world's communications. In 2013, Edward Snowden leaked hundreds of thousands of files from the National Security Agency (NSA) to journalists, who exposed much of the NSA's mass surveillance programs in detail. Through the Snowden leaks, we learned how the NSA conducts dragnet and targeted surveillance all across the world. The Middle East is a primary target. As part of the so-called "War on Terror," Muslims are spied on with no legal or practical recourse. This includes mass dragnet surveillance – for instance, Wikileaks revealed that the metadata and content of phone calls in the Bahamas and Afghanistan were recorded by the NSA, via its MYSTIC program, and held for thirty days for playback on demand – as well as targeted surveillance via programs like the National Counterterrorism Center's database of

[9] For skeptical views of artificial intelligence as "intelligence" and the topic of whether machines can think, see Noam Chomsky, *New Horizons in the Study of Language and Mind* (Cambridge, MA: Cambridge University Press, 2000), 44–45. For other skeptical takes on AI and its adverse impact on race relations and other social ills, see Yarden Katz, "Manufacturing an Artificial Intelligence Revolution" (SSRN, 2017), https://papers.ssrn.com/sol3/papers.cfm?abstract_id=3078224; Gary Smith, *The AI Delusion* (Oxford University Press, 2018); Meredith Broussard, *Artificial Unintelligence: How Computers Misunderstand the World* (Cambridge, MA: 2018); Yarden Katz, *Artificial Whiteness: Politics and Ideology in Artificial Intelligence* (New York: Columbia University Press, 2020).

terrorism suspects. Other surveillance projects revealed that the United States and its allies, such as the United Kingdom's Government Communications Headquarters (GCHQ), have spied on diplomats conducting trade negotiations, as well as non-governmental organizations, activists, and corporations, in countries like South Africa and Brazil. The use of mass and targeted surveillance by the world's most powerful governments is in service of empire. People of color are disproportionately in the crosshairs.[10]

In cities, a similar dynamic is at play. The use of sensors and the means to make sense of surveillance data has increased exponentially over the past two decades. Closed-circuit television (CCTV) cameras are central to an emerging surveillance industrial complex. Where CCTVs once provided blurry images recorded to tape on a single plot of land – making it impossible to track individuals across a wide geography – city authorities now operate advanced CCTV networks that unite thousands of high-resolution cameras into a single network. Thanks to advances in computing, we now have "smart" cameras that can identify faces, objects, and behaviors so that authorities can record, index, and make sense of the data filmed by thousands of cameras across a wide area. Through a "plug-in surveillance" model, businesses and residents are increasingly adding their own cameras to police networks so that they may access more footage of public spaces.[11] Drones are also spying from up high, allowing authorities to monitor what goes on in the city down below. Police can now watch over the entire city from centralized command-and-control centers. In many cities, outside life is becoming a filmed experience.[12]

Centralized city surveillance is expanding in sophistication and use cases. In the United States, fusion centers – surveillance centers that pool information from multiple sources into one location for information sharing between agencies – proliferated in the wake of the 9/11 attacks. The model seems to have served as a template in other countries, such as South Africa, where the Free State province was reported to be building its own fusion center.[13]

In parallel, real-time crime centers (RTCC) for police emerged with the expansion of technology for used monitoring and investigations.[14] RTCCs pool data

---

[10] See Glenn Greenwald, *No Place to Hide: Edward Snowden, the NSA, and the U.S. Surveillance State* (New York: Metropolitan Books, 2014); Jennifer Stitsa Granick, *American Spies: Modern Surveillance, Why You Should Care, and What to Do About It* (Cambridge University Press); Edward Snowden, *Permanent Record* (New York: Metropolitan Books, 2019).

[11] Michael Kwet, "The Rise of Smart Camera Networks, and Why We Should Ban Them," *The Intercept*, January 27, 2020, https://theintercept.com/2020/01/27/surveillance-cctv-smart-camera-networks.

[12] Arthur Holland Michel, *Eyes in the Sky: The Secret Rise of Gorgon Stare and How It Will Watch Us All* (New York: Harcourt Publishing Company, 2019).

[13] Michael Kwet, "Apartheid in the Shadows: The USA, IBM and South Africa's Digital Police State," *Counterpunch*, May 3, 2017, www.counterpunch.org/2017/05/03/apartheid-in-the-shadows-the-usa-ibm-and-south-africas-digital-police-state.

[14] There is little available in the public record about real-time crime centers. For details on their origins and development, see Michael Kwet and Paul Prinsloo, "The 'Smart' Classroom:

from surveillance sensors and records into one pot for storage, analysis, and real-time information sharing with boots on the ground. Corporations provide the software, infrastructure, and services needed to manage the surveillance databases ingested by these twenty-first-century surveillance centers. In New York City, Microsoft partnered with the New York Police Department (NYPD) to build a Domain Awareness System (DAS) it calls Microsoft Aware – a software platform that pools surveillance, records, and other data for real-time and long-term city surveillance. Surveillance cameras, acoustic ShotSpotter sensors, chemical sensors, and license plate readers pull information from the streets into the system, which makes use of facial recognition and license plate readers. Tens of databases were pooled into the center for data analytics, including predictive policing used for criminal investigations. As part of the deal, the NYPD gets a 30 percent cut of the revenue from sales of the system to other Microsoft Aware customers. Soon after the system was unveiled in 2012, Microsoft sold its Aware solution to Atlanta; Washington DC; Singapore; Bulgaria; and São Paulo, Brazil.[15]

Microsoft has also adopted its Aware solution for prisons – currently on offer in the UK – in a move to capture the emerging market to "upgrade" and digitize the carceral pipeline using twenty-first-century technologies. Through its Public Safety and Justice division, Microsoft works with third-party vendors supplying surveillance technology to police, jails and prisons (including for juveniles), immigration authorities, the courts, services for pretrial and probation, and social media surveillance.[16] As several chapters highlight in this volume, with these systems, people of color are targeted, sentenced, and imprisoned at rates greater than the white population. Researchers have shown time and again that the deployment of solutions like facial recognition and predictive policing have racially biased and adverse effects on people of color while failing to provide the outcomes advertised by the vendors selling them.

Police and intelligence agencies are also using special software to monitor and target persons of interest. Some authorities use cell site simulators to spy on people

---

A New Frontier in the Age of the Smart University," *Teaching in Higher Education* 25, no. 4 (2020): 510–526. For a general history of police surveillance technology in the United States into the digital era, see Brian Jefferson, *Digitize and Punish: Racial Criminalization in the Digital Age* (University of Minnesota Press, 2020).

[15] For an overview of Microsoft's relationship to police, see Michael Kwet, "The Microsoft Police State: Mass Surveillance, Facial Recognition, and the Azure Cloud," *The Intercept*, July 14, 2020, https://theintercept.com/2020/07/14/microsoft-police-state-mass-surveillance-facial-recognition; Chris Gelardi, "Inside D.C. Police's Sprawling Network of Surveillance," *The Intercept*, June 18, 2022, https://theintercept.com/2022/06/18/dc-police-surveillance-network-protests.

[16] Ibid.; Michael Kwet, "Microsoft's Iron Cage: Prison Surveillance and e-Carceration," *Al Jazeera*, www.aljazeera.com/features/2020/12/21/microsofts-iron-cage-prison-surveillance-and-e-carceral-state; Michael Kwet, "ShadowDragon: Inside the Social Media Surveillance Software That Can Watch Your Every Move," *The Intercept*, September 21, 2021, https://theintercept.com/2021/09/21/surveillance-social-media-police-microsoft-shadowdragon-kaseware.

in a broad area.[17] These devices mimic cell phone towers and trick phones near them to transmit their location and identifying information. In some versions, the device can clone a target's phone and make/receive calls and text messages that will appear as if they are coming from the target's number; capture metadata about calls such as who is being called and for how long; capture text messages; listen to and record audio from the target's handset; and intercept data usage, such as websites visited.[18] Civil rights and liberties advocates have raised concerns that cell site simulators are being used in black and brown neighborhoods to target people of color and activists.[19]

Carceral authorities and intelligence agencies also target phones with specialized software used to hack into devices and exfiltrate information. The Israeli firm NSO Group produces the notorious hacking software, Pegasus, which enables almost unlimited remote monitor of target cellphones. In 2018, the Israeli news media outlet *Haaretz* published an in-depth exposé revealing that NSO Group, together with other Israeli firms, sell cybersurveillance software to scores of dictatorships and authoritarian regimes that use their software to "locate and detain human rights activists, persecute members of the LGBT community, silence citizens who were critical of their government and even to fabricate cases of blasphemy against Islam."[20] The issue reemerged in 2021 when a massive data leak suggested repressive regimes have been using NSO Group spyware to target journalists, activists, heads of state, and other persons of interest.[21]

Some of these software solutions are used to monitor social media. For example, Israeli firm Verint's product-line clients in Azerbaijan inquired about using its software to "check sexual inclinations" of Facebook users. Years later, a 2017 report

---

[17] For an explanation of how cell site simulators work, see *Electronic Frontier Foundation*, "Street-Level Surveillance: Cell-Site Simulators/IMSI Catchers," (n.d.), www.eff.org/pages/cell-site-simulatorsimsi-catchers.

[18] Shaun Swingler, "Meet the Grabber: How Government and Criminals Can Spy on You (and How to Protect Yourself)," *Daily Maverick*, September 1, 2016, www.dailymaverick.co.za/article/2016-09-01-meet-the-grabber-how-government-and-criminals-can-spy-on-you-and-how-to-protect-yourself.

[19] See Harvey Gee, "Stingray Cell-Site Simulator Surveillance and the Fourth Amendment in the Twenty-First Century: A Review of The Fourth Amendment in the Twenty-First Century: A Review of The Fourth Amendment in an Age of Surveillance, and Unwarranted Amendment in an Age of Surveillance, and Unwarranted," *St. John's Law Review* 93, no. 2 (2019): 325–364; Brian Barrett, "The Baltimore PD's Race Bias Extends to High-Tech Spying, Too," *Wired*, August 16, 2016, www.wired.com/2016/08/baltimore-pds-race-bias-extends-high-tech-spying.

[20] Hagar Shezaf and Jonathan Jacobson, "Revealed: Israel's Cyber-spy Industry Helps World Dictators Hunt Dissidents and Gays," *Haaretz*, October 20, 2018, www.haaretz.com/israel-news/.premium.MAGAZINE-israel-s-cyber-spy-industry-aids-dictators-hunt-dissidents-and-gays-1.6573027.

[21] Amnesty International, "Massive Data Leak Reveals Israeli NSO Group's Spyware Used to Target Activists, Journalists, and Political Leaders Globally," July 18, 2021, www.amnesty.org/en/latest/press-release/2021/07/the-pegasus-project.

by Human Rights Watch detailed the arrest and torture of persons presumed to be gay, bisexual, or transgender. In Indonesia, Verint was used to create a database of LGBT persons and religious minorities.[22]

Social media software has also been used to target Black Lives Matter protesters and journalists in the United States. Dataminr, *The Intercept* reported in 2020, "relayed tweets and other social media content about the George Floyd and Black Lives Matter protests directly to police, apparently across the country."[23] Another product, ShadowDragon, is being used by police in the United States and elsewhere, which has raised concerns by civil rights and liberties organizations, who are calling to ban it.[24]

The line between commercial surveillance and police surveillance has increasingly blurred during the digital era. NSA surveillance is largely reliant upon the cooperation of tech corporations, who provide access to communications streams (such as data transmitted over internet cables) and the databases they store in cloud server farms. For instance, through NSA's PRISM program, the NSA collects stored internet communications from Microsoft, Yahoo, Google, Facebook, PalTalk, YouTube, Skype, AOL, and Apple. Using XKEYSCORE, the NSA and its allies in Australia, Canada, New Zealand, Britain, Japan, and Germany can search and analyze global internet content. Snowden said that XKEYSCORE is a "one-stop shop for access to the NSA's information" that allows users to search for emails, track website traffic and laptops, and more.[25]

Indeed, a wide variety of government agencies are piggybacking on Big Tech's commercial surveillance. In the United States, police are serving tech corporations warrants for search history data, speakers, wearables, and smart home technologies like IoT devices.[26] The Internal Revenue Service, FBI, Department of Homeland

---

[22] Human Rights Watch, "Azerbaijan: Anti-Gay Crackdown: Gay Men, Transgender Women Tortured to Extort Money, Intelligence," October 3, 2017, www.hrw.org/news/2017/10/03/azerbaijan-anti-gay-crackdown.

[23] Sam Biddle, "Police Surveilled George Floyd Protests With Help From Twitter-Affiliated Startup Dataminr," *The Intercept*, July 9, 2020, https://theintercept.com/2020/07/09/twitter-dataminr-police-spy-surveillance-black-lives-matter-protests.

[24] Kwet, "ShadowDragon."

[25] NDR.de, "Snowden-Interview: Transcript," January 26, 2014, https://web.archive.org/web/20140128224439/http://www.ndr.de/ratgeber/netzwelt/snowden277_page-3.html.

[26] See, among others, Sidney Fussell, "How Your Digital Trails Wind Up in the Police's Hands," *Wired*, December 28, 2020, www.wired.com/story/your-digital-trails-polices-hands; Frank Green, "Are 'Geofence' Warrants a Legitimate Investigative Tool or an Unconstitutional 'Digital Dragnet'? Chesterfield Robbery Case Raises Privacy Questions," *Richmond Times-Dispatch*, June 24, 2021, https://richmond.com/news/local/crime-and-courts/are-geofence-warrants-a-legitimate-investigative-tool-or-an-unconstitutional-digital-dragnet-chesterfield-robbery-case/article_bf3d01a7-d9ec-5a2c-bfe2-298630e69ea7.html; Albert Fox Cahn and Justin Sherman, "Your 'Smart Home' Is Watching – and Possibly Sharing Your Data with the Police," *The Guardian*, April 5, 2021, www.theguardian.com/commentisfree/2021/apr/05/tech-police-surveillance-smart-home-devices; Lorenzo Franceschi-Bicchierai, "Here's How Police Request Data from WhatsApp and Facebook," *VICE News/Motherboard*, www.vice.com/en/

Security, and Department of Defense have all purchased cell phone data.[27] In 2020, a data analytics firm, Mobilewalla, released a report predicting the place of residence, race, age, and gender of 17,000 George Floyd protesters in four US cities. While Mobilewalla pledged not to sell the protest data to clients or policing agencies, it demonstrated the power of private firms to monitor protesters and profile them according to their identities, thereby exposing the public to racial profiling with the potential to undermine freedom of assembly.[28] And now that *Roe v. Wade* has been overturned, women seeking abortions in US states banning the practice fear their data will fall into the hands of the police and judicial authorities.[29] Women of color, who in some states have higher rates of abortion than white women and often lack access to and effective use of contraception, would be disproportionately affected.[30]

Commercial surveillance itself also (re)produces racial inequality. For example, in 2016, *Business Insider* reported that Facebook let advertisers exclude users by race using a tool called Ethnic Affinities. The feature used data points about users to categorize them into four categories: non-multicultural (ostensibly white), African American, Asian American, and Hispanic. *Ars Technica* demonstrated that different users were shown different versions of the trailer for the movie, *Straight Outta Compton*.[31] The "general population" (non-African American, non-Hispanic) was presumed unfamiliar with the music group, N.W.A., on which the film is based, and so was given a trailer which provided context. The trailer given to the African

---

article/k7q94v/heres-how-police-request-data-from-whatsapp-and-facebook; Zack Whittaker, "This Is How Police Request Customer Data from Amazon," *Tech Crunch*, September 27, 2020, https://techcrunch.com/2020/09/27/this-is-how-police-request-customer-data-from-amazon; Laura Dobberstein, "Microsoft Tells US Lawmakers Cloud Has Changed the Game on Data Privacy, Gets 10 Info Demands *a Day* from Cops," *The Register*, July 2, 2021, www.theregister.com/2021/07/02/us_government_cloud.

[27] Joseph Cox, "How the U.S. Military Buys Location Data from Ordinary Apps," *VICE News/Motherboard*, November 16, 2020, www.vice.com/en/article/jgqm5x/us-military-location-data-xmode-locate-x; Albert Fox Cahn and Jake Laperruque, "Putting a Price on Privacy: Ending Police Data Purchases," *The Hill*, May 6, 2021, https://thehill.com/opinion/technology/552105-putting-a-price-on-privacy-ending-police-data-purchases; Laura Hecht-Felella, "Federal Agencies Are Secretly Buying Consumer Data," *Brennan Center for Justice*, April 16, 2021, www.brennancenter.org/our-work/analysis-opinion/federal-agencies-are-secretly-buying-consumer-data.

[28] Caroline Haskins, "Almost 17,000 Protesters Had No Idea a Tech Company Was Tracing Their Location," *Buzzfeed News*, June 25, 2020, www.buzzfeednews.com/article/carolinehaskins1/protests-tech-company-spying.

[29] Sara Morrison, "What Police Could Find Out about Your Illegal Abortion," *Vox*, June 24, 2022, www.vox.com/recode/23059057/privacy-abortion-phone-data-roe.

[30] Anne Branigin and Samantha Chery, "Women of color Will Be Most Impacted by the End of Roe, Experts Say," *The Washington Post*, June 24, 2022, www.washingtonpost.com/nation/2022/06/24/women-of-color-end-of-roe.

[31] Analee Newitz, "Facebook's Ad Platform Now Guesses at Your Race Based on Your Behavior," *Ars Technica*, March 18, 2016, https://arstechnica.com/information-technology/2016/03/facebooks-ad-platform-now-guesses-at-your-race-based-on-your-behavior.

Americans Affinity Group was different: it assumed baseline familiarity with N.W.A. While technically any person could be categorized in any Ethnic Affinity group – the algorithm assigned categories based on data points, as Facebook users do not declare their race to the network – the assumption is that most people placed into specific Affinity Groups do indeed fit the corresponding racial category. This was the purpose of the tool, after all.[32]

By October 2016, *ProPublica* revealed that racial customization via Ethnic Affinities can be used to discriminate against racial groups.[33] Its journalists ordered housing advertisements on Facebook and targeted them to users who were house hunting, excluding African-American, Asian-American, and Hispanic Affinity Groups. Facebook approved the ads, even though discrimination in housing advertisements violates the Civil Rights Act of 1994. In response, Facebook began building new tools to disable the use of ethnic affinity marketing for certain types of ads and it removed "thousands of categories from exclusion targeting related to potentially sensitive personal attributes, such as race, ethnicity, sexual orientation and religion" – including the "multicultural affinity" category.[34] While Facebook has declared it reined in the ability for racial targeting, an investigation at *The Markup* found that advertisers could still use the platform to target users on the basis of race.[35] Facing public pressure, Facebook finally announced that it will end advertising based on politics, race, and other "sensitive" topics.[36]

Schools are another site of mass surveillance where the line between business and the state is blurred. Visual surveillance manufacturers are pushing cameras into schools on the premise that more cameras can make campus grounds safer and more efficient via smart technologies.[37] Big data surveillance is also becoming part of the educational landscape. Many students and teachers are now being forced to use surveillance-driven big data tools for the purpose of "data analytics" and

---

[32] Nathan McAlone, "Why 'Straight Outta Compton' had different Facebook Trailers for People of Different Races," *Business Insider*, March 16, 2016, www.businessinsider.com/why-straight-outta-compton-had-different-trailers-for-people-of-different-races.

[33] Julia Angwin and Terry Paris Jr., "Facebook Lets Advertisers Exclude Users by Race," *ProPublica*, October 28, 2016, www.propublica.org/article/facebook-lets-advertisers-exclude-users-by-race.

[34] Erin Egan, "Improving Enforcement and Promoting Diversity: Updates to Ethnic Affinity Marketing," *Facebook*, November 11, 2016, https://about.fb.com/news/2016/11/updates-to-ethnic-affinity-marketing; Facebook Business, "Reviewing Targeting to Ensure Advertising is Safe and Civil," April 24, 2018, www.facebook.com/business/news/reviewing-targeting-to-ensure-advertising-is-safe-and-civil; Facebook Business, "Simplifying Targeting Categories," August 11, 2020, www.facebook.com/business/news/update-to-facebook-ads-targeting-categories.

[35] Jon Keegan, "Facebook Got Rid of Racial Ad Categories. Or Did It?" *The Markup*, July 9, 2021, https://themarkup.org/citizen-browser/2021/07/09/facebook-got-rid-of-racial-ad-categories-or-did-it.

[36] Shannon Bond, "Facebook Scraps Ad Targeting Based on politics, Race and Other 'Sensitive' Topics," *NPR*, November 9, 2021, www.npr.org/2021/11/09/1054021911/facebook-scraps-ad-targeting-politics-race-sensitive-topics.

[37] Kwet and Prinsloo, "The 'Smart' Classroom."

management.[38] Two chapters will take up the presence of police and surveillance in schools, including the adverse impact it often has on children of color.

Other big data practices have been criticized for racial discrimination. In 2012, a group of researchers found that the six facial algorithms they tested have lower accuracy for black than white subjects.[39] In 2018, the issue exploded internationally when a team of researchers found that facial recognition algorithms deployed by IBM, Microsoft, and Face++ were less accurate for black subjects than for white subjects.[40] By this time, there was growing public concern about the adverse effects of algorithmic bias on marginalized groups.[41]

Despite the dangers of algorithmic discrimination and the disparate impact of surveillance on vulnerable populations, biometric profiling is on the rise. Several chapters detail how biometric identification is derived from racist Western policing practices. India is pioneering a new wave of biometric identification through its controversial Aadhaar identification system. As Sinha and Trikanad explain, what started off as a registration system for citizen identification grew into a "cradle to grave" identity system used across a multitude of government agencies that already do, or intend to, keep track of health, employment, income, religion, caste, and other economic and demographic information; issue things like arms licenses and ration cards; collect information about crime, education, employment, taxes, marital status, religion; and more. The Aadhaar identification system assigned to residents in India constitutes an infrastructure for mass surveillance.

The US military has imposed new biometric technologies on people living in the Middle East. In Iraq, the Defense Department amassed a record of iris scans, fingerprints, DNA, and other biometrics in a database of 3 million Iraqis. In Afghanistan, the US military also constructed a massive biometric database of Afghans and used giant balloons equipped with sophisticated cameras and sensors to spy on the population below. Palantir Technologies was contracted to deploy

---

[38] See Michael Kwet, "Operation Phakisa Education: Why a Secret?" *First Monday*, 22, no. 12 (2017), https://firstmonday.org/ojs/index.php/fm/article/view/8054; Cathy O'Neil, *Weapons of Math Destruction: How Big Data Increases Inequality and Threatens Our Democracy* (New York: Broadway Books, 2017), 50–67; Roxana Marachi, "The Case of Canvas: Longitudinal Datafication through Learning Management Systems," *Teaching in Higher Education* 25, no. 4 (2020): 418–434.

[39] Brendan F. Klare, Mark J. Burge, Joshua C. Klontz, Richard W. Vorder Bruegge, and Anil K. Jain, "Face Recognition Performance: Role of Demographic Information," IEEE (2012), http://openbiometrics.org/publications/klare2012demographics.pdf.

[40] See Joy Buolamwini and Timnit Gebru, "Gender Shades: Intersectional Accuracy Disparities in Commercial Gender Classification," *Proceedings of Machine Learning Research* 81, no. 1 (2018): 1–15.

[41] See, inter alia, O'Neil, *Weapons of Math Destruction*; Virginia Eubanks, *Automating Inequality: How High-Tech Tools Profile, Police, and Punish the Poor* (New York: St. Martin's Press, 2018); Emmanuel Martinez and Lauren Kirchner, "The Secret Bias Hidden in Mortgage-Approval Algorithms," *The Markup*, August 25, 2021, https://themarkup.org/denied/2021/08/25/the-secret-bias-hidden-in-mortgage-approval-algorithms.

software that could sift through the reams of data accumulated and search for "patterns of life" that would help identify "terrorists" based on the behavioral data collected.[42] Big Tech companies like Microsoft, Amazon, Google, Oracle, AT&T, Verizon, Cisco, Dell, Hewlett Packard, and IBM are also supplying the US military with technologies used for a wide variety of purposes, including surveillance.

By comparison to Global South countries like India and South Africa, in the West, biometric surveillance has been less widely accepted – perhaps due to the perception that biometrics surveillance is not for "civilized" people.[43] Yet biometric surveillance seems more commonly accepted today thanks to the rise of consumer use cases such as facial recognition and fingerprinting to unlock smartphones. As noted earlier, surveillance-driven consumer technology blurs the line between commercial and government surveillance. This is also true with new developments like "smart cities," which are often driven by sensors conducting big data surveillance of life in the city. In fact, many smart cities begin as "safe cities" projects in which smart camera networks, ShotSpotters, and other sensors are installed to monitor the streets. Once these technologies are in place, authorities aim to expand their use cases for city administration. Video cameras, for example, can be used to monitor waste disposal, cars on the road, and people flows to determine consumer foot traffic. Retail stores, airports, and other outlets are experimenting with video analytics to service, personalize, and manipulate consumer behavior.

While the development of new technologies and business models center in the Global North, the South is acutely subject to their dominance. As we see in Chapter 6, digital colonialism is the use of technology for the political, economic, and social domination of another territory.[44] The United States has pioneered the technologies and business models now pervading the global digital economy, and US-based transnational corporations are dominant in most countries outside of the United States and mainland China. Simply put, digital technology is principally used to further the interests of American empire.

To achieve technological supremacy, US power elites and intellectuals must manufacture consent and pacify the public to accept American domination. This requires "tech hegemony" whereby the conceptualization of how technology could and should function in society assumes technology is owned and controlled by

---

[42] Annie Jacobson, *First Platoon: A Story of Modern War in the Age of Identity* (New York: Dutton, 2021).
[43] Keith Breckenridge, *Biometric State: The Global Politics of Identification and Surveillance in South Africa, 1850 to the Present* (Cambridge University Press, 2014).
[44] Kwet, "Digital Colonialism: US Empire and the New Imperialism." For a take on data colonialism, a sub-component of digital colonialism, see, *inter alia*, Nick Couldry and Ulises A. Mejias, *The Costs of Connection: How Data Is Colonizing Human Life and Appropriating It for Capitalism* (Stanford University Press, 2019).

corporations and states.[45] As such, most people do not even try to imagine a fundamentally different, more egalitarian model for a tech society.[46] Western governments have so far pacified resistance to their mass surveillance programs by invoking the so-called "War on Terror" and national security interests while constraining policy to capitalist reforms. Transnational corporations branded themselves early on as fun and innovative, and as critics began questioning their power, the tech giants launched public relations campaigns professing their concern for human rights.

For example, Microsoft President Brad Smith co-authored a book on tech ethics and has made numerous public appearances attesting to Microsoft's alleged commitments to privacy and human rights. Microsoft has made press releases attesting to its "ongoing efforts toward racial equality," including donations to Black Lives Matter and other racial justice organizations, and, in 2020, pledged to stop supplying US police forces with (its own) facial recognition technology. However, Smith fails to mention in his publications and speeches that Microsoft has a Public Safety and Justice division that supplies surveillance technologies to carceral authorities and a Defense & Intelligence division that services intelligence agencies and militaries across the world.[47]

Indeed, as noted above, Microsoft supplied its custom-built Microsoft Aware "Domain Awareness System" mass surveillance software to police in multiple cities.[48] Years later, Microsoft adapted its Aware surveillance platform for prisons, what it calls the Digital Prison Management Solution (DPMS), advertised at the UK government website. With the DPMS, prisons can ingest and process CCTV cameras, body-worn cameras, and tactical system data for applications like crowd control, perimeter breaches, and recorded incidents. Using surveillance devices, authorities can "virtually patrol a custodial community 24×7." The Solution provides "geospatial analysis," and claims it will "detect threats" by "aggregating massive amounts of data," "make data-driven decisions," "eliminate investigative silos," and "enhance intelligence capabilities" for things like "collabor[ation] with detectives, patrol, and other analysts." For prisons, Microsoft's DPMS appears unprecedented in scope and sophistication. Another Microsoft product, the Microsoft Advance Patrol Platform (MAPP), was developed for police patrol vehicles. The MAPP solution has been deployed as a pilot in Cape Town and Durban, South Africa.[49]

---

[45] Ibid, 16–17.
[46] Michael Kwet, "The Digital Tech Deal: A Socialist Framework for the Twenty-First Century," *Race & Class* 63, no. 3 (2022); Michael Kwet, "People's Tech for People's Power: A Guide to Digital Self-Defense and Empowerment," *Right2Know* (2020), www.r2k.org.za/wp-content/uploads/Peoples-Tech_August-2020.pdf; James Muldoon, *Platform Socialism: How to Reclaim our Digital Future from Big Tech* (London: Pluto Press, 2022).
[47] Brad Smith and Carol Ann Browne, *Tools and Weapons: The Promise and the Peril of the Digital Age* (New York: Penguin Press, 2019).
[48] In Brazil, police kill civilians at many times the rate of US police. See César Muñoz, "Brazil Suffers Its Own Scourge of Police Brutality," *Human Rights Watch*, June 3, 2020, www.hrw.org/news/2020/06/03/brazil-suffers-its-own-scourge-police-brutality.
[49] Kwet, "The Microsoft Police State"; Kwet, "Microsoft's Iron Cage." For an overview of how South African policing retains colonial and apartheid policies and structures, is often brutal and

Microsoft is also partnered to a wide range of surveillance vendors. A small sample includes Veritone, a supplier of facial recognition technology on the Microsoft Azure cloud available on the Microsoft website; DXC technology, which deploys prison software in major US counties; Kaseware, a surveillance platform similar to Microsoft Aware that offers mass surveillance capabilities and predictive policing; Netopia Solutions, a Morocco-based firm that offers Prison Management Software and sports features like "escape management." While it is not clear exactly where Netopia Prison Management Solution is deployed, Microsoft stated that "Netopia is [a Microsoft partner/vendor] in Morocco with a deep focus on transforming digitally, Government services in North and Central Africa." Morocco has a grotesque history of locking up journalists and dissenters, and torturing its prisoners. Netopia Solutions was a Microsoft "Africa Partner of the Year" in 2017, and its prison software is currently listed at the Microsoft AppSource website.[50]

While Microsoft is far from the only company engaged in tech "ethics washing," it has been at the forefront of an effective PR campaign that has helped it escape the techlash. For decades, Microsoft has pumped money into the academic community, including major think tanks focused on tech policy and ethics, such as Data & Society and AI Now;[51] academic institutions like New York University, Cornell University, the University of Washington, Strathmore University in Kenya, and the University of Witwatersrand in South Africa, among others; and it hosts its own set of Microsoft Research Labs spanning multiple countries. Esteemed Microsoft and Microsoft-funded researchers have taken up the topic of race and police surveillance, yet much like Brad Smith, they have erased, whitewashed, and downplayed the record of Microsoft's close relationship to authorities along the carceral pipeline, having failed to mention Microsoft's entire Public Safety and Justice division, vast array of partnerships, and wide variety of its own product offerings.[52] Moreover, this same set of prominent researchers have failed to center the issues of digital colonialism and problematize the private ownership of the means of computation and knowledge, which reinforces the neocolonial domination of American empire.[53]

Yet despite the influence of corporate money and public relations campaigns, scholars and activists are fighting back on more principled grounds. In the United States, the Athena coalition is protesting Amazon's police surveillance offerings and exploitative business practices. In Hong Kong, pro-democracy protesters tore down CCTV cameras and used laser lights to disrupt facial recognition. In South Africa,

---

racist, and generally supports the neoapartheid status quo, see Ziyanda Stuurman, *Can We Be Safe? The Future of Policing in South Africa* (Cape Town: NB Books, 2021).

[50] Kwet, "The Microsoft Police State"; Kwet, "Microsoft's Iron Cage."
[51] Katz, *Artificial Whiteness*, 93–152. AI Now eventually dropped funding from Microsoft, but money from Melinda Gates's investment and incubation company, Pivotal Ventures, has also given money to Data & Society and became an AI Now funder after it stopped receiving funds from Microsoft.
[52] Ibid.
[53] Kwet, "Digital Colonialism: US Empire"; Cecilia Rikap, *Capitalism, Power and Innovation: Intellectual Monopoly Capitalism Uncovered* (New York: Routledge, 2021).

students and activists have attacked cameras and waged legal battles against smart camera networks, and are beginning to push back against digital colonialism.[54] In India, activists are also challenging digital colonialism and the expansion of police surveillance.[55] And in China, citizens have stood up to the private sector, demanding an end to invasive forms of commercial surveillance, including facial recognition.[56] These developments provide a glimmer of hope in a time of rapidly expanding high-tech repression.

This volume presents a timely intervention into the growing crisis of racial surveillance. While there are scores of valuable works on the advance of high-tech surveillance, much of it has been generated within the North and focuses on the US and Europe. This book, by contrast, takes a much-needed global approach to the matter. With contributions by twenty-four scholars from all over the world, the topic of race and surveillance is detailed across time and space. As we will see, racial surveillance spans the globe as a tool for oppression and exploitation.

In Chapter 2, Eric Stoddart sets the tone by exploring how surveillance technologies act as sociotechnological systems that construct and sort identity. Algorithms arrange people into binary categories that are resolved and discrete, rather than the fluid, messy, and multidimensional categories of real life. This creates conditions necessary to assess, predict, and control people according to their assigned identities, reinscribing unequal power relations between people of various identities in society.

In Chapter 3, Alfred McCoy lays out the historical and contemporary context of imperial electronic surveillance constructed by the United States. Starting with the conquest of the Philippines, McCoy shows the complex relationship between technological development for foreign conquest and the reuse of these technologies at home.

In Chapter 4, Toni Weller explains how surveillance was used to impose concepts of race on women in Victorian Britain. This is more than just a metaphor: British women were treated as Others of a different nature, as conceptualized according to prevailing notions of race, class, and gender/sexuality. Police were permitted to enter the houses of female persons under the guise of "hysteria" that was said to afflict women. Weller recovers oft-neglected history about the surveillance of women, who, like alleged racial groups, were said to differ in intelligence and character according to cranial measurements. A mix of pseudoscientific racism, class

---

[54] Michael Kwet, *People's Tech for People's Power: A Guide to Digital Self-Defense and Empowerment* (Right2Know, 2020), www.r2k.org.za/wp-content/uploads/Peoples-Tech_August-2020.pdf. In 2022, the Friends of a Free Internet activist group launched a campaign for digital justice; see https://freeinternet.africa."
[55] Megha Mandavia, "Activists Rally against 'Illegal' Surveillance of CAA Protests," *Economic Times*, December 31, 2019, https://economictimes.indiatimes.com/news/politics-and-nation/global-challenges-economy-up-on-rss-meet-agenda/articleshow/85930491.cms.
[56] Jiayun Feng, "Viral Video of Man Evading Facial Recognition Leads to Surveillance Bans in Chinese Cities," *SupChina*, December 3, 2020, https://supchina.com/2020/12/03/viral-video-of-man-evading-facial-recognition-leads-to-surveillance-bans-in-chinese-cities.

discrimination, and bias against female sex work and sexuality combined with technologies of surveillance for the purpose of controlling women at a time when they were demanding more political and social power.

In Chapter 5, Amber Sinha and Shruti Trikanad take up the emergence of an electronic surveillance state in modern-day India. Sinha and Trikanad map out how British colonizers maintained "history sheets" about individuals accused, but not necessarily convicted, of a crime, and put on surveillance lists. Current attempts to digitize identity via the Aadhaar identity system, alongside e-governance programs and private sector commercial surveillance threaten to reproduce caste-based sorting of the Indian population according to race, class, religion, sex, place of birth, migration status, and disability in ways that undermine equality, civil rights, and civil liberties.

In Chapter 6, Michael Kwet traces how surveillance has been used from colonial conquest to the present in South Africa. Colonial and apartheid-era rulers utilized the latest and greatest technologies – from skin branding to fingerprinting to primitive computer systems – as a means to control and exploit the African population. The United States increased its involvement by supplying technologies in each era of white supremacist order, provoking opposition to firms like IBM, Kodak, and Hewlett Packard by anti-apartheid activists. In the post-apartheid era, US surveillance firms have reemerged through the process of digital colonialism for economic, political, and social domination.

In Chapter 7, Yasmeen Abu-Laban and Abigail B. Bakan explore Israeli surveillance against boycott, divestment, and sanctions activists. In the first part of the chapter, Abu-Laban and Bakan explain the BDS movement. Drawing inspiration from the anti-apartheid movement in South Africa, BDS activists have provoked the ire of the Israeli government, which finds itself under increasing pressure for its treatment of Palestinians by the international community. In the second part, the authors place responses by the Israeli state in relation to long-standing and still evident practices of surveillance and social sorting, as well as anti-Jewish, anti-Arab, and anti-Muslim racisms. They conclude with a reflection upon US and Canadian political landscapes and implications for antiracist movements and human rights policies.

In Chapter 8, Claudio Altenhain, Ricardo Urquizas Campello, Alcides Eduardo dos Reis Person, and Leandro Siqueira take on colonialism's legacy of race and surveillance in São Paulo, Brazil. The authors begin explaining the history of the *casa-grande* (the landowner's "big house") and *senzala* (the slaves' quarters), as well as the racialized order created during colonial conquest. They set forth the conditions to understand how today's prisons and *condomínios* (closed or gated communities) intersect with surveillance technology. Like elsewhere in the world, surveillance tech in São Paulo is reproducing the "quasi-colonial pattern" of racialized segregation in Brazil's largest and most global city.

In Chapter 9, Myunghee Lee and Emir Yazici unpack events in the Xinjiang Uyghur Autonomous Region of China. Lee and Yazici tell the history of Uyghur civilization and how Han Chinese increasingly settled the cotton-producing area during the Mao era. In recent decades, the CCP has resorted to extreme forms of surveillance and repression to quell unrest in region. From facial recognition designed to detect Uyghur persons to forced "reeducation" and labor camps, the CCP has harnessed the powers of tech to maintain power and control.

In Chapter 10, we shift gears to the Global North. Frank Wu explains how Asian Americans have been treated as inassimilable into American society, whether by biology, culture, or collective choice. He tells the history of how Asian Americans have been discriminated against, Othered, and exploited for labor by systems of white supremacy. Wu brings the history up to date, using three case examples to show how Asian Americans now face renewed discrimination and surveillance due to ongoing tensions between the US government and China.

In Chapter 11, Anton Treuer brings us back to colonial America. Not surprisingly, surveillance was used by English settlers in the conquest of America. Treuer explains how tribes were surveilled, with maps drawn so the British could divide and conquer indigenous populations. By collecting census data and exploiting military intelligence, the settlers acquired the information needed for civilian and legal system expansion. By the early twentieth century, pseudoscientific cranial measurements and blood quantum standards were used to categorize indigenous people and deny them compensation for centuries of swindling. To this day, social services have maintained a close surveillance of native children, often resulting in them removed from their birth homes and placed into foster homes or adopted.

In Chapter 12, we take another look at indigenous North America, this time in Canada. Scott Thompson delineates how authorities used surveillance in colonial Canada to classify "Indian" peoples as a racialized Other and control their behavior. Recalling the history of British racial sorting in Canada, he explains how the English imposed a "natural" racial order that placed the English on top according to "God's plan." They classified indigenous persons to settle them in villages on reserves and assimilate them as inferiors in the racial hierarchy. Key programs and sites of surveillance included Indian Agents (indigenous government officials to oversee and manage the application of policy and law on reserves, using, in part, a paper permit system) and residential schools, as well as government surveillance of indigenous alcohol consumption.

In Chapter 13, Erica Nelson and Tracey Benson detail how policing in urban areas extends to Kindergarten–Grade 12 schools. Using Charlotte Mecklenburg Schools in the United States as a case example, Nelson and Benson show how the rise of mass shootings in American schools has led to a rise in federal support for school resource officers. The increased presence of police on school grounds increases the criminalization and incarceration of school-aged children for non-criminal behavior, with disparate impact on children of color.

In Chapter 14, Joel Busher, Tufyal Choudhury, and Paul Thomas explain how the UK government's strategy for preventing violent extremism, Prevent, has shaped surveillance and monitoring practices in schools and colleges in England. Drawing on original empirical data from fieldwork, the authors demonstrate how these surveillance practices intersect with race, religion, and difference, with extra focus on Muslim students.

In Chapter 15, Anthony Cook traces resistance to racialized surveillance in American history, from abolition to Black Lives Matter. Beginning with slavery, Cook provides case examples, first focusing on slave fugitive Frederick Douglass as a prime example. He continues into the industrial age, where new technologies gave rise to new forms of surveillance – and resistance to it. The final sections of the chapter cover the Jim Crow era into the present.

In Chapter 16, Alana Saulnier provides a deep dive into the subject of how technologically mediated law enforcement in the United States may strain relations between police and racial minority communities. Saulnier argues that techno-fixes will not, in themselves, solve underlying issues of fractured community–police relations.

2

Sorting Identity

Eric Stoddart

INTRODUCTION

'Stop, who goes there?' is a precursor in World War II movies to a character presenting his papers. His identity has to be established to verify that he is not out of place, that he is authorised to be in this particular area. Who he is – his rank, age, race, or ethnicity – is of little relevance; it is much more important that he has appropriate credentials, and is therefore authorised, to pass the control point. Presenting *identity* papers meets the guard's demand in this pre-digital context. Twenty-first-century digital environments still require us to submit to identification as authorisation or verification; however, these new identifications are now deeply implicated in the broader issues of *identity*.

'Who are you?' is coupled with 'Are you who *you* say you are?' This is familiar to guards over centuries, but their digital successors have access to far more extensive sources of verification. When providing services, investigating incidents, or assessing the threat you might pose to others, surveillance systems seek to establish if you are *this* rather than *that* person. You may be authorised or unauthorised with respect to services or spaces; but you may be not-yet-authorised. Authorisation may depend on projections as to your future behaviour, postulated from statistical modelling of masses of others who share some of your characteristics and past and present behaviour. Well beyond mere identification, socio-technological processes assign virtual identities with material implications. These assignments of identity ought to prompt questions from the data-subject: 'Am I who *you* say I am?' Processes of categorisation by algorithmic sorting of personal information are mechanisms in the social construction of identity.

This chapter will deploy a social model of the multiple and variable self to consider how identity is constructed within contemporary cultures of surveillance. We will attend, therefore, to biographical identity rather than to metaphysical questions. Our concern is not with establishing the necessary and sufficient conditions for being a person as opposed to a non-person.[1] Rather, we will consider identity construction as an action of individuals in, and in relation to, society, and we will consider this issue particularly with regard to surveillance technologies as socio-technological systems.

Sorting identity is meant in two senses: as categorising and resolving. Algorithmic sorting of personal data is a fundamental aspect of twenty-first-century surveillance. Less obvious is the governmentality dimension. States seek to govern identity and govern *by* identity. Complex identity, to organisations, is like a suspended chord whose tension demands to be resolved to a satisfactory harmonic conclusion. Identities that are fluid and multidimensional are much less easily contained and managed by institutional authorities than identities assumed to be composed of binary and discrete categories. Race is a particular example, but ethnicity, class, gender, and sexuality pose similar challenges because they comprise contested, sometimes indeterminate, dimensions and intersections.

MULTIPLE AND VARIABLE SELF

Social identity theory explains how the self is constructed with respect to group identities. The project of developing the self is one of active narrative-making.[2] Interaction is fundamental to the task, for it is not just 'I', 'me', 'us', and 'we', but also 'you', 'them', and 'they' that are in play. There are groups with which we identify. These groups possess characteristics, values, and behaviours that we regard positively and share, aspire to share, or at least believe we share. Other groups are juxtaposed to ours (if not actually being in conflict). We are, in effect, identifying ourselves as *like* one or more groups, and as *not like* other groups.[3] Throughout this process we rely heavily upon stereotypes because we are unable to know each group member personally. Stereotypes, whether positive or negative, always require us to assume that the attitudes and conduct that we associate with the group applies to all its members – without distinction. We are tarring everyone in a group with the same brush, particularly so for groups juxtaposed to our own.

As individuals, we practice 'a dialectical interplay between *self-identification* – which can be individual or collective – and external *categorization* by others'.[4]

---

[1] The debate around personal identity is summarised in Georg Gasser and Matthias Stefan, 'Introduction', in Georg Gasser and Matthias Stefan (eds.), *Personal Identity: Complex or Simple?* (Cambridge University Press, 2012), 1–18.

[2] Charles Taylor, *Sources of the Self: The Making of the Modern Identity* (Cambridge University Press, 1989); Alasdair C. MacIntyre, *After Virtue* (London: Duckworth, 1981); Paul Ricoeur, 'Life in Quest of Narrative', in David Wood (ed.), *On Paul Ricoeur* (London: Routledge, 1991), 20–33.

[3] Henri Tajfel, *Human Groups and Social Categories: Studies in Social Psychology* (Cambridge University Press, 1981).

[4] Richard Jenkins, 'Identity, Surveillance and Modernity: Sorting Out Who's Who', in Kirstie Ball, Kevin D. Haggerty, and David Lyon (eds), *Routledge Handbook of Surveillance Studies* (London and New York: Routledge, 2012), 159–162, 160. Emphasis in original.

In this framework, identity is not an essence, but 'something we do'.[5] External categorisation may come from those holding on to arguments for the biological reality of race. Self-identification may rely on race understood as a social construct. As a result, the dialectic interplay around race is particularly intense. As Kwame Anthony Appiah concludes, 'there is nothing in the world that can do all we ask race to do for us'.[6] Amongst people who are mixed-race there is a variety of racial self-identification. Furthermore, some people of mixed race choose to change their racial identification over their life course.[7] It is primarily in order to 'destabilise ... notions of clear-cut, fixed categories of race' that Angela Onwuachi-Willig advocates introducing 'interraciality' to the legal lexicon.[8]

Identity is not singular, but we are multiple selves because we have membership in a number of different groups. It then follows that our self is not fixed, but variable. There are contexts in which one of our membership groups is more salient than another. This model of a multiple and variable self therefore offers us 'a powerful means of understanding how social context can come to structure the ways by which we come to understand the reality that confronts us'.[9] It might be that political moves such as a ban on travel into the USA propels our membership in the group 'Muslims' to the front of our consciousness in ways not necessarily so significant to us before. We correspondingly foreground this aspect of our identity and perhaps choose to develop it by, for example, increased religious observance. We do this more acutely aware than ever of the diverse discourses about Muslims circulating in our society. We might choose to distance ourselves from some group traits, perhaps attempting to identify more obviously with a subgroup viewed to be 'moderate'. Where it is gender that is more salient for the time being, we might opt to position ourselves in solidarity with others for whom gender-fluidity is integral to their self-presentation in public campaigns.

Intersectionality

Of course, salient social identities are often not discrete. We are not foregrounding, or experiencing, only one at any given time. Here intersectionality operates,

---

[5] Ibid., 159.
[6] Kwame Anthony Appiah, *In My Father's House: Africa in the Philosophy of Culture* (Oxford University Press, 1992), 45. A paradox, perhaps irony, lies in the value of data gathered about race that demonstrates its persistent role in primary social institutions in the USA, such as the job market, neighbourhood segregation, and health: American Sociological Association, *The Importance of Collecting Data and Doing Social Scientific Research on Race* (Washington DC: American Sociological Association, 2003). This form of surveillance highlights injustice, albeit of groups categorised within an essentialist framework.
[7] K. A. Rockquemore, D. L. Brunsma, and D. J. Delgado, 'Racing to Theory or Retheorizing Race? Understanding the Struggle to Build a Multiracial Identity Theory', *Journal of Social Issues* 65, no. 1 (2009): 13–34.
[8] Angela Onwuachi-Willig, *According to Our Hearts: Rhinelander v. Rhinelander and the Law of the Multiracial Family* (New Haven and London: Yale University Press, 2013), 265.
[9] Stephen Reicher and Nick Hopkins, 'Perception, Action, and the Social Dynamics of the Variable Self', *Psychological Inquiry* 27, no. 4 (2016): 341–347, 343.

eschewing the notion that oppression occurs along only a single axis, such as race.[10] Our social identity is constructed (as are the groups with which we associate, or with which we are associated by others) at the nexus of overlapping identities – each with their own balances of privilege and subordination. It matters that someone is a poor, unemployed, Black Muslim woman vis-a-vis a poor, but employed, White Muslim woman. The permutations are vast, and *how* intersectionality matters is a unique experience for each person.[11] (The uniqueness does not preclude finding *shared* experiences when we limit our own permutation by making just one or two aspects of our intersectionality of uppermost importance.) This is, in effect, what we do when we find enough in common with others to be part of a group, notwithstanding our unique personal combination of inter-sectional identity. We do not, however, have unconstrained freedom to manage our intersectionality. Other people, through institutions, shape the categories into which we are placed and into which we might consensually place ourselves.

A model of the multiple and variable self sheds light on both categorisation and self-categorisation. It helps us acknowledge that our choice of group membership can be constrained and that perception of self might include those groups into which we are forced and of which we do not see ourselves as a part (being required to 'be Black' because of others' ascriptions).[12]

It is in this dynamic process that we are acting (alone and in cooperation with others) and constructing our social identity as a multiple and variable self. At the same time, the way we structure reality is being shaped. How we *perceive* the experiences around which we make meaning is a process itself under construction. Furthermore, this process is affected by the extent to which we believe that we are being identified adequately or unfairly.

Misrecognition

Misrecognition is the experience of being assigned to a group with which we do not identify or denied categorisation we would wish. For example, Muslims might not be heard as concerned British citizens when they speak out against prejudice towards themselves or fellow believers. Instead, because of prevailing suspicion, they

---

[10] Kimberlé Crenshaw, 'Demarginalizing the Intersection of Race and Sex: A Black Feminist Critique of Antidiscrimination Doctrine, Feminist Theory and Antiracist Politics', *University of Chicago Legal Forum* 140 (1989): 139–167.

[11] Material circumstances, networks of relationships, and each individual's psychological development and preferences suggest that we are each unique persons. For analytical and political purposes, however, it is necessary, and reasonable, to put a limit on the granularity of a study of intersectionality.

[12] Reicher and Hopkins, 'Perception, Action, and the Social Dynamics of the Variable Self', 345. For a detailed discussion see Simone Browne, *Dark Matters: On the Surveillance of Blackness* (Durham, NC: Duke University Press, 2015).

are deemed to be *not* British – 'voicing alien identity related concerns'.[13] The negative effects of misrecognition include depression, powerlessness, and withdrawal of effort. However, at the same time, misrecognition can lead to the expenditure of greater effort to achieve one's group goals in the face of adversity.[14] It may also be the case that others prematurely close down the meaning of a particular identity, restricting it to a caricature eschewed by the group itself. For example, 'all Muslims are terrorists' is the sort of undifferentiated attack that is launched against people claiming a particular religious identity. Antagonists conceive this group's claim to be an 'identity' to be a denial of differentiation. Incorrectly, the group is purported to be claiming that 'all Muslims are the same'. This denies the dual claim of a universal dimension to an identity that permits, or perhaps encourages, 'local hybridisation'.[15]

Under misrecognition group members may reply on predictive meta-stereotypes: 'how I think that they think we are like'.[16] This interpretive lens by which people attempt to anticipate how they will be treated can be triggered where there is an imbalance of power between groups. The group with low or no power engages with the more powerful through these meta-stereotypes.[17] Furthermore, minority groups may be acutely concerned with how authorities view them. The police, for example, might be viewed 'as reflecting a community's moral values and therefore are regarded as prototypical group authorities, who are defending group norms'.[18] The threat to minorities occurs when members of the public, without necessarily any negative personal experience of a group, take their cue from the police. So, the argument goes, if the police are harsh and suspicious of a minority there can be no smoke without a fire. Rather than *reflecting* a community's moral values, the police are shaping public perceptions.

Of course, the public's and the authorities' regard for a minority may diverge because neither is a monolithic category. Sections of the public may find common cause with particular authorities to confront prejudice, or in other cases to collude with injustice. The point here is that misrecognition and meta-stereotypes offers some explanatory traction for the heightened concern over authoritative perceptions that might contribute to a feedback loop in public attitudes. In other words, a

---

[13] Leda Blackwood, Nick Hopkins, and Stephen Reicher, 'From Theorizing Radicalization to Surveillance Practices: Muslims in the Cross Hairs of Scrutiny', *Political Psychology* 37, no. 5 (2016): 597–612, 606.

[14] See theoretical sources in Leda Blackwood, Nick Hopkins, and Stephen Reicher, '"Flying While Muslim": Citizenship and Misrecognition in the Airport', *Journal of Social and Political Psychology* 3, no. 2 (2015): 148–170, 151.

[15] Ibid., 151.

[16] Joris Lammers, Ernestine H. Gordijn, and Sabine Otten, 'Looking through the Eyes of the Powerful', *Journal of Experimental Social Psychology* 44, no. 5 (2008): 1229–1238, 1229.

[17] Ibid.

[18] Jason Sunshine and Tom Tyler, 'Moral Solidarity, Identification with the Community, and the Importance of Procedural Justice: The Police as Prototypical Representatives of a Group's Moral Values', *Social Psychology Quarterly* 66, no. 2 (2003): 153–165, 154.

minority is criminalised and the public take this as 'evidence' that such a group warrants disproportionate scrutiny.[19] This is a process of invoking an '"othering" of the communities concerned'.[20] In Barbara Perry's terms, it amounts to 'permission to hate'.[21]

With its attention to groups, and individuals' construction of identity in relation to those groups, social identity theory provides, as we will see, an apposite conceptual framework when surveillance is understood as processes of social sorting. Its analytical value, however, extends to other forms of the digital gaze.

IDENTITIES UNDER SURVEILLANCE

Given its thorough politicisation, particularly with regard to minority identities, it is not unreasonable to define 'surveillance' purely negatively, as does Christian Fuchs: 'surveillance is the systematic collection and use of information in order to dominate individuals and groups'.[22] For Fuchs, surveillance is 'a specific form of control that forms one dimension of domination, exploitation, class, capitalism, patriarchy, racism, and similar negative phenomena'.[23] However, it would be a mistake to ignore the benefits of surveillance, not least in terms of medical studies, detecting crime, or imposing accountability in financial services. The advantages need not obscure the ambivalent aspects of surveillance; it can be good and bad, sometimes both at the same time. It is for this reason that David Lyon offers an alternative definition of surveillance that recognises its ambivalent nature. He states that surveillance is 'any systematic and routine attention to personal details, whether specific or aggregate, for a defined purpose. That purpose, the intention of the surveillance practice, may be to protect, understand, care for, ensure entitlement, control, manage or influence individuals or groups.'[24]

That being said, identity is constructed within technological paradigms that, if not wholly encompassing, are powerfully influential in framing our understanding of reality. Using his famous notion of *la technique*, Jacques Ellul gave an account in

---

[19] Paddy Hillyard, *Suspect Community: People's Experience of the Prevention of Terrorism Acts in Britain* (London: Pluto Press in association with Liberty, 1993). Hillyard also includes, with reference to British counterterrorism strategies directed at Irish Republicanism in the 1970s and 80s, 'the terror of prevention' (terrorising suspects), normalising emergency legislation, and violation of civil liberties and human rights.

[20] Scott Poynting and Victoria Mason, '"Tolerance, Freedom, Justice and Peace"?: Britain, Australia and Anti-Muslim Racism since 11 September 2001', *Journal of Intercultural Studies* 27, no. 4 (2006): 365–391, 365, referring particularly to a radicalising effect.

[21] Barbara Perry, *In the Name of Hate: Understanding Hate Crimes* (New York and London: Routledge, 2001), 179–223.

[22] Christian Fuchs, *Social Media: A Critical Introduction*, 2nd ed. (London: Sage, 2017), 199.

[23] Ibid., 199.

[24] David Lyon, *Surveillance after Snowden* (Cambridge: Polity Press, 2015), 3.

the 1960s of how efficiency displaced all other moral evaluations of technology.[25] Within an all-encompassing technological paradigm, the capacity to question technology is profoundly hindered because people are part of, and see from the standpoint of, the technological. Securing a perspective beyond this paradigm required, for Ellul, the resources of Christian (Protestant) faith. Martin Heidegger, who took a similarly dystopic view, concluded that it is reflection upon art that offers the only possibility for questioning technology.[26] This pessimistic approach arguably disregards those moments in the technical design process when someone might break with technological thinking.[27]

Discussions, therefore, at a too-general, even abstract, level are problematic. 'Surveillance technology' is extensively variegated, including diverse practices such as facial recognition systems, analysing individuals' credit card transactions, and police intelligence gathering. However, as the concept of the multiple and variable self discloses, it matters which group deploys, legitimates, or is subject to surveillance. Differentials in power and consequent meta-stereotypes are performed within technological cultures, not least surveillance. Race, religion, ethnicity, sexuality, gender, and other characteristics matter despite any naive assumptions that a practice is neutral because it is framed as technological.

Identities under the Panopticon

Jeremy Bentham's eighteenth-century proposal of the panopticon as a design for prisons becomes, for Michel Foucault, a significant analytical tool to understand how, alongside scientific progress and cultural developments, the formation of the human subject is interwoven with practices of surveillance, social control, and punishment.[28] Bentham's central tower for the guards was surrounded, doughnut-style, by individual cells. This would allow for the supervision of many prisoners by a few guards. Significantly, the central tower would be kept in darkness so that prisoners would not know exactly when they, as individuals, were under observation. It was the *possibility* of being observed that conveyed the disciplinary power. The panoptic model has largely been superseded within surveillance studies (as we shall see below), but there are salient vestiges for considering identity.

When surveillance is panoptic (the few watching the many, with the many never being sure quite when they are being observed) the issues for identity fall under a

---

[25] Jacques Ellul, *The Technological Society*, trans. John Wilkinson (London: Jonathan Cape, 1965), 79–80.
[26] Martin Heidegger, 'The Question Concerning Technology', *The Question Concerning Technology and Other Essays* (London: Harper Torchbooks, 1977).
[27] Andrew T. Feenberg, 'Critical Evaluation of Heidegger and Borgmann', in Robert C. Scharff and Val Dusek (eds.), *Philosophy of Technology: The Technological Condition: An Anthology* (Malden, MA; Oxford: Blackwell, 2003), 327–337, 328.
[28] Michel Foucault, *Discipline and Punish: The Birth of the Prison* (London: Penguin Books, 1977).

popularised, but simplistic, understanding of *Orwellian*. Here it is scrutiny of the population and the demise of privacy that shapes the good citizen under the eye of Big Brother. This takes the internalised disciplinary gaze of the prison – more commonly experienced in older forms of schooling, but also in hospitals and the military – as shaping the compliant subject. Identity as a prisoner, pupil, patient, or soldier is inscribed as a way of behaving when in this role; but there is always the possibility that it will leak more widely into a psychological disposition towards conformity to authority.

Whilst correct and concerning, this is, however, to miss two significant elements of Orwellian panoptic surveillance. First, it is not turned towards all the population of the country – the proles are considered of insufficient importance to warrant being under Big Brother's gaze.[29] There is a class issue in play in the novel, with poorer citizens enjoying a freedom from the state's surveillance. However, for one's identity to be deemed unworthy of surveillance is a mixed blessing. There is a freedom in being inconsequential to states' or corporations' gazes; but, being invisible may mean exclusion from services or goods such as health care, education, or welfare assistance. Therefore, it may be important to draw attention to a particular element of one's identity for strategic reasons. This element may not be what one otherwise considers to be of most importance in the intersectional construction of one's identity but it is the component that offers most strategic advantage at the time.

Second, and even more significantly for approaching the novel, *Nineteen Eighty-Four* is not fundamentally about surveillance, but newspeak. The purpose of surveillance is to ensure that the Party's control of language is effected with the aim of eradicating the possibility of insurrection.[30] By desiccating language, removing multiple words (each with nuances of meaning), the Party aspires to make *imagining* rebellion impossible. Rather than people considering resistance to be futile, the contraction of language is intended to place the very idea of disobedience beyond people's mental map. Privacy is certainly important in debates about surveillance but Orwell's fiction draws our attention to the troubling modification by states and corporations of language about surveillance. As we shall see below when considering governing by, and of, identity, the terms used to explain and legitimate surveillance really matter.

Identities under Assemblage

As surveillance breaks free from the limitations of analogue (i.e. pre-digital) technologies, Gilles Deleuze argues that it shifts from a concern with discipline to one of control.[31] Previously, societies were organised as spaces of enclosure. Typically, we

---

[29] George Orwell, *Nineteen Eighty-Four* (London: The Folio Society, 2001 [1949]), 75.
[30] Ibid., 54–55.
[31] Gilles Deleuze, 'Postscript on the Societies of Control', *October* 59 (1992): 3–7.

would pass from one institution of regulation to another: from family, to school, and then perhaps to the factory. Deleuze argues that these boundaried or enclosed spaces (integral to a panoptic theory) are being replaced by flows. We become packets of information, valuable in the marketplace. As packets of information, we flow, or rather we are dispersed through cyberspace and at multiple points moulded. However, we do still encounter institutions of enclosure. Whilst most of us do have to use codes and passwords rather than our personal signature, we have not yet been wholly dissolved into 'dividuals', as Deleuze anticipated.[32] Surveillance is now very much about reassembling data abstracted from material contexts in the surveillant assemblage.[33] Assemblage is, however, 'a potentiality' not a 'stable entity with its own fixed boundaries'.[34] It occurs where sources of data (e.g. people's bodies, administrative databases, or natural environments), gathered for often quite diverse purposes (e.g. biometric identification, credit control, traffic flows), are connected and analysed for patterns and outliers. Whilst an analogue ID card presents a face, a new mode of the digital 'screen' composes a profoundly different way of seeing: through composing an identity from data traces retrieved from multiple sources that are not free of prejudices.[35] Coding is itself a political action.[36]

Mark Poster has offered a poststructuralist model in which the database (and this would include new databases constructed in assemblage) becomes a discourse.[37] By showing how databases are a way of thinking, Poster draws our attention to data-doubles. We, as people under surveillance, are objectified and become sites from which data is gathered. Through database analysis, new identities are created for us in cyberspace. In some respects, those data-doubles are dependent on who we are, but in other ways those data doubles are independent; they are constructions by systems of surveillance. Foucault's 'interiorised' subjects (carrying the disciplining teacher in their head) have given way to objectified individuals who have identities dispersed across databases. What is more, these objectified individuals are totally unaware of many of those identities.

Even this, however, is not surveillance of *everything* *every*one does *all* of the time.[38] It is, however, 'suspicionless' in the sense that it is aimed at whole

---

[32] Kirsty Best, 'Living in the Control Society: Surveillance, Users and Digital Screen Technologies', *International Journal of Cultural Studies* 13, no. 1 (2010): 5–24.
[33] Gilles Deleuze and Félix Guattari, A Thousand Plateaus, trans. Brian Massumi (Minneapolis, MN: University of Minnesota Press, 1987).
[34] Kevin D. Haggerty and Richard V. Ericson, 'The Surveillance Assemblage', *British Journal of Sociology* 51 (2000): 605–622, 609.
[35] Louise Amoore, 'Vigilant Visualities: The Watchful Politics of the War on Terror', *Security Dialogue* 38, no. 2 (2007): 215–232.
[36] Lucy Suchman, 'Do Categories Have Politics? The Language/Action Perspective Reconsidered', *Computer Supported Cooperative Work* 2, no. 3 (1994): 177–190.
[37] Mark Poster, 'Databases as Discourses (Chapter Five)', in *The Second Media Page* (Cambridge: Polity Press, 1995); Mark Poster, *The Mode of Information* (Cambridge: Polity Press, 1990).
[38] Lyon, *Surveillance after Snowden*, 44.

populations.[39] Whilst it is 'bulk' interception, some argue that it is neither 'blanket' nor 'indiscriminate' because choices are made about which data carriers to access.[40] Critics see this as 'throwing more needleless hay' on the stack within which the search for a needle (terrorist) is already difficult.[41]

Identity under the surveillance assemblage is constructed with little transparency on the part of the corporations and state institutions that protect their algorithms from scrutiny on the grounds of commercial interest and/or national security – interests that often overlap. As Frank Pasquale observes, 'in a climate of secrecy, bad information is as likely to endure as good, and to result in unfair and even disastrous predictions'.[42] When sorting is deployed transparently, it increases the likelihood of positive outcomes. At the very least, data-subjects may acquiesce to being recognised as, for example, Black or Asian despite any misgivings around others' essentialising of what are, in fact, constructed identities. Alternatively, misrecognition and misidentification might provoke positive action in claiming inclusion in a favoured group. For example, asylum-seekers aspire to recategorisation as immigrants as a step along the path to naturalisation.

GOVERNING OF, AND BY, IDENTITY

In order to govern, a state needs not only to be able to identify those within its borders, but also those traversing, or at least hoping to cross, its borders. Two existential threats arising from mobility overlap in political arguments: the terrorist who threatens national security and the (undocumented) immigrant who takes employment opportunities, puts pressure on local services, and elevates crime rates. In the face of the social construction of the dangers of mobility, states seek to ensure that people are not out of place; states attempt to govern identity and govern by identity. This is, of course, not a straightforward process as 'securability' is elusive, especially when it is a 'feigned picture of a world in which people, objects and money move smoothly'.[43]

Governments, however, whilst ostensibly promoting inclusion agendas have other requirements of identity: 'Identity is a floating signifier that this governmental discourse attempts to articulate in a specifically delimited and defined way, so as

---

[39] Glenn Greenwald, *No Place to Hide: Edward Snowden, the NSA, and the U.S. Surveillance State* (New York: Picador, 2014), 94.

[40] Intelligence and Security Committee of Parliament, *Privacy and Security: A Modern and Transparent Legal Framework*, HC 1075, 2015, para 74.

[41] Ray Corrigan, 'Mass Surveillance Not Effective for Finding Terrorists', www.newscientist.com/article/dn26801-mass-surveillance-not-effective-for-finding-terrorists.

[42] Frank Pasquale, *The Black Box Society: The Secret Algorithms That Control Money and Information* (Cambridge, MA: Harvard University Press, 2015), 216.

[43] Louise Amoore, 'Governing by Identity', in Colin J. Bennett and David Lyon (eds.), *Playing the Identity Card: Surveillance, Security and Identification in Global Perspective* (London: Routledge, 2008), 21–36, 23.

to further the *raison d'etat*, effect government and counter the proliferation of identities.'[44] Within a governance discourse, as demonstrated by David Barnard-Wills, identity is ontologically objective, unitary, and biometric, with shallow content, being behavioural (based upon probabilistic logic), and is attributed by trusted (as in government authenticated) sources rather than being controlled by the individual him/herself.[45]

Profiling

Crucial to governing of and by identity is the notion of risk, which can be applied to particular identities in at least two ways. A category of people may be at risk of being discriminated against, in the sense of being denied legitimate access to good or services. However, another (and perhaps that same category) can be designated as risky. They are deemed a potential threat to themselves (perhaps in the case of mental illness) or to others (in criminality, including terrorism).[46] Particular groups encounter the securitisation of their identity (its management by the state primarily in terms of threats to national security) by processes of profiling, usually of racial, ethnic, and religious characteristics.[47]

A narrow definition of such profiling requires race/ethnicity to be *the sole* factor in deciding to select a person for scrutiny (whether stop and search, or closer observation and/or questioning in a security context). Isolating the race/ethnicity factor in this exclusive way means it is easy for authorities to deny, and condemn, its use.[48] A broader, and more realistic, definition means that racial/ethnic profiling can be understood as including race/ethnicity within a broader 'calculus of suspicion', alongside perhaps age, class, gender, and behaviour.[49] There would be no requirement to demonstrate that race/ethnicity was 'a key factor', or even *the* key factor (rather than sole factor), in the targeting decision.[50]

---

[44] David Barnard-Wills, *Surveillance and Identity: Discourse, Subjectivity and the State* (Farnham; Burlington, VT: Ashgate, 2012), 58.
[45] Ibid., Chapter 6.
[46] Nikolas Rose, 'At Risk of Madness', in Tom Baker and Jonathan Simon (eds.), *Embracing Risk: The Changing Culture of Insurance and Responsibility* (University of Chicago Press, 2002), 209–237; Nikolas Rose, 'The Biology of Culpability: Pathological Identity and Crime Control in a Biological Culture', *Theoretical Criminology* 4, no. 1 (2000): 5–34.
[47] Given the, albeit mistaken, credence given to essentialist models of 'race' it continues to be important to discuss 'racial' profiling although ethnic markers (recognised as social constructions around culture, and perhaps geography) are similarly deployed. We will therefore use racial/ethnic to describe the categories deployed in this form of profiling.
[48] Deborah A. Ramirez, Jennifer Hoopes, and Tara Lai Quinlan, 'Defining Racial Profiling in a Post-September 11 World', *American Criminal Law Review* 40 (2003): 1195–1233, 1204.
[49] Ibid., 1204. Ramirez and colleagues offer a more precise definition: 'racial profiling is the inappropriate use of race, ethnicity, or national origin, rather than behavior or individualized suspicion, to focus on an individual for additional investigation'. Ibid., 1205.
[50] Ronald Weitzer and Steven A. Tuch, 'Perceptions of Racial Profiling: Race, Class, and Personal Experience', *Criminology* 40, no. 2 (2002): 435.

William Press argues that from a statistical analysis, racial/ethnic profiling may simply be less effective than uniform sampling of a population.[51] However, given what we know about identity construction, particularly as regards meta-stereotypes, even if racial/ethnic profiling contributes positively to crime detection (if not prevention), harms to minority groups could be inflicted. Profiling may be a focal point as well as a reminder of past hurt – either experienced personally or to one's group in the past. There does not need to be actual violence for a form of hurt to be caused. 'Expressive harm' could still be anticipated even if a neo-Nazi march were to pass off without violence. That group's *associations with* barbarity on racial/ethnic and religious grounds make it harmful to particular sectors of society.[52]

Behaviour Detection

Sitting alongside the more obviously biased racial/ethnic profiling are behaviour detection systems which are assumed to be impartial. Based largely on the work of Paul Ekman, the theory is that physiological responses to stress (such as lying to officials in an attempt to conceal nefarious intent) are involuntary cues. With the proper training, security officers are able to spot these otherwise hidden clues and pull someone aside for further investigation. Timothy Levine and colleagues at Michigan State University have cast considerable doubt over Ekman's claims.[53] The American Civil Liberties Union reports that the Transportation Security Administration's own files discredit the behaviour detection programme.[54] Hall, concludes that the Ekman model is indeed subject to ethnic bias.

From one angle, the wider social climate of suspicion towards, for example, people who supposedly 'look Muslim' may induce anxiety in passengers at an airport who carry (or suspect they might be attributed) this identity. In other words, their physiological cues may be a result of the 'terror of suspicion'.[55] With leaps of paranoia, passengers take exception to a fellow-traveller speaking Arabic whilst queuing to board a plane.[56] 'Flying while brown' parallels the injustices

---

[51] William Press, 'To Catch a Terrorist: Can Ethnic Profiling Work?', *Significance* 7, no. 4 (2010): 164–167.

[52] Mathias Risse and Richard Zeckhauser, 'Racial Profiling', *Philosophy & Public Affairs* 32, no. 2 (2004): 131–170, 147.

[53] Timothy Levine, Steven A. McCornack, and Hee Sun Park, 'Deception Research at Michigan State University', https://msu.edu/~levinet/deception.htm.

[54] ACLU, *Bad Trip: Debunking the TSA's 'Behavior Detection' Program* (New York: American Civil Liberties Union, 2017), www.aclu.org/sites/default/files/field_document/dem17-tsa_detection_report-v02.pdf.

[55] Rachel Hall, *The Transparent Traveler: The Performance and Culture of Airport Security* (Durham, NC: Duke University Press, 2015), 144.

[56] Karen Araiza, 'Philly Pizza Shop Owner Calls 911 after He Says He Was Profiled on Flight Home', *NBC*, November 21, 2015, www.nbcsandiego.com/news/national-international/philly-pizza-shop-owner-profiled-southwest-airlines/89976.

encountered by African-Americans 'guilty' of 'driving while black'.[57] Furthermore, the behaviour detection model assumes a distinction between performance and reality that is based on particular, rather than (its assumed) universal philosophy.[58] For example, practitioners of deep meditation, possibly associated with traditionally non-Western religions (such as Sufi Islam or Buddhism) may have more control over their supposed 'involuntary cues' than other people. This capacity could be a two-edged sword because the absence of cues might raise suspicion if an innocent traveller has been meditating. On the other hand, the authorities might, should they accept the possibility of their model being undermined, take it as a reason to be even more suspicious of non-Western people. Of course, a Sufi or a Buddhist might be a well-dressed White businessman. Religions do not map to ethnic (or racial) identities to anything like the extent that religiously illiterate officials might prejudicially assume.

Burdening Identity

Although not a totalising system, making 'security' the primary frame is 'dispersed and disorganized', offering 'conditional access to circuits of consumption and civility' – 'to the benefits of liberty'.[59] Having the correct identity is that condition. This places a heavy burden on minority identities, especially where fear in the dominant group is running high. The degree of actual danger facing a community need not be high for securitisation to be deployed by a particular government. Torin Monaghan, in a study of Canada, concludes that discourses of radicalisation and extremism have become decoupled from the Canadian experience and 'have become new abstractions to articulate and expand the "war on terror"'.[60]

It is not simply that a government can declare that a group is a threat. Rather, as theorists of securitisation have come to argue, such performative speech relies on audiences who concur based on their own (preconceived) perceptions of the dangerous group identity.[61] However, this may well involve, argues Didier Bigo, a 'ex post facto justification of the everyday practices that enact a governmentality of

---

[57] Charu A. Chandrasekhar, 'Flying While Brown: Federal Civil Rights Remedies to Post-9/11 Airline Racial Profiling of South Asians', *Asian American Law Journal* 10, no. 2 (2003): 215–252; David A. Harris, 'Driving While Black and All Other Traffic Offenses: The Supreme Court and Pretextual Traffic Stops', *Journal of Criminal Law and Criminology* 87, no. 2 (1997): 544–582.
[58] Hall, *The Transparent Traveler*, 152–153.
[59] Nikolas Rose, *Powers of Freedom: Reframing Political Thought* (Cambridge University Press, 1999), 243.
[60] Jeffrey Monaghan, 'Security Traps and Discourses of Radicalization: Examining Surveillance Practices Targeting Muslims in Canada', *Surveillance & Society* 12, no. 4 (2014): 485–501, 498.
[61] Matt McDonald, 'Securitization and the Construction of Security', *European Journal of International Relations* 14, no. 4 (2008): 563–587, 566. Referring to the Copenhagen School, Barry Buzan, Ole Wæver, and Jaap de Wilde, *Security: A New Framework for Analysis* (Boulder, CO: Lynne Rienner, 1998).

fear and unease'.[62] Particularly with regards to Islam, there is 'a feedback loop that simply re-circulates demands for more programs, more information gathering, more surveillance'.[63]

CONCLUSION

Protecting one's identity is a significant concern under contemporary surveillance; presently, it is not only a task for spies, but is now required of citizens as a whole. Identity can be stolen in the sense of authorisation. Credentials can be illicitly presented to online banking systems in an attempt to raid someone's bank account, for example. However, under the surveillance *assemblage*, identity can be stolen in a more fundamental sense. Through occluded categorisation, material disadvantage can accrue should a person be sorted into a riskier designation than they warrant. Denial of access to credit or international air travel may be a minor hindrance to some; but to others, this denial may be seriously detrimental to their life chances. Misrecognition might evoke acquiescence or resistance. Either response contributes to the construction of identity. The necessity of responding to meta-stereotypes becomes formative of identity. A measure of freedom to construct one's identity is stolen because individuals must devote time and energy to reacting to attempts by authorities (state and corporate) to sort identity.

Surveillance systems, as an influential dimension of a contemporary technological paradigm, privilege some identities over others. Data-doubles are constructed at the confluence of data-streams, political projects, and embedded biases. Identity is being sorted (categorised and resolved) not only within securitising regimens but as acts of commercial and political segmentation. Distinguishing the vested interests that name, value, and promote or discourage the characteristics of categories within the surveillance *assemblage* is an added, and highly significant, task of sorting our sorted identity.

---

[62] Didier Bigo, 'The (in)Securitization Practices of the Three Universes of EU Border Control: Military/Navy – Border Guards/Police – Database Analysts', *Security Dialogue* 45, no. 3 (2014): 209–225, 211.
[63] Monaghan, 'Security Traps', 495.

3

Imperial Mimesis

Migration of Surveillance from the Colonial Philippines to the United States

Alfred McCoy

From the first hours of the US colonial conquest in August 1898, the Philippines served as the site of a social experiment in the use of police surveillance as an instrument of state power. During the decade of pacification that followed, the US army plunged into a crucible of counterinsurgency, forming its first field intelligence unit, the Division of Military Information, which combined voracious data gathering with rapid dissemination of tactical intelligence. At this periphery of empire, freed from the constraints of courts, constitution, and civil society, the US imperial regime fused new technologies from America's first information revolution to fashion what was arguably the world's first full "surveillance state."

A decade later during the social crisis surrounding World War I, these illiberal lessons migrated homeward from the Philippines through the invisible capillaries of empire to foster a domestic security apparatus. In the first weeks of war, a small cadre of Philippine veterans established the Military Intelligence Division, creating a unique fusion of federal security agencies and citizen adjuncts that persisted for the next half century.

In the century that followed, this process of imperial mimesis has recurred as US pacification campaigns in Afghanistan and Iraq have dragged on for a decade or more, skirting defeat if not disaster. During each of these attempts to subjugate an Asian society, the US military has been pushed to the breaking point and responded by drawing together all extant information resources, fusing them into an infrastructure of unprecedented power, and producing new surveillance technologies – creating thereby innovative systems for both domestic surveillance and global control.

At the level of methodology, this focus on history reminds us that there is much to be learned from placing contemporary events, such as Edward Snowden's 2013 revelations of surveillance by the National Security Agency (NSA), in their historical context. By comparison of America's colonial past with its hegemonic present, we can discern the skein of continuity and discontinuity that lends import to current events. We can thereby discern a close relationship between colonial policing and political scandal that offers insight into the logic of contemporary NSA surveillance of allied leaders. With Clio, the Greek muse of history, thus whispering in our ear, such comparison can help us sort through the din of media controversy to discern a larger design in a changing array of global power.

If we were to abstract these specifics into the realm of theory, this history of US intelligence compels a revision of Max Weber's venerable hypothesis about the monopoly of physical force as the defining attribute of the modern state.[1] The state is not, I would argue, defined solely by Weber's idealized monopoly on raw physical force, but instead by its use of coercion to extract information for heightened social control, simultaneously shaping mass consciousness and penetrating private lives. The modern state is distinguished from its early-modern antecedents by its ability, not just to punish the few, but by its capacity to monitor the many. At the start of the nineteenth century, as James C. Scott has argued, the European nation-state launched bureaucratic reforms that rendered land and society "legible" by extrinsic means such as the metric standard for measurement and patronyms for conscription – a fundamental change but one that still left the state politically blind.[2] At the start of the twentieth century, however, America moved beyond such passive data collection to become the site of an accelerating information revolution whose synergies represent a second, significant phase in the perfection of state power that seeks to render its subjects not just legible but permeable.

AMERICA'S FIRST INFORMATION REVOLUTION

During one extraordinary decade, the 1870s to 1880s, America's first information revolution arose from a synergy of innovations in the management of textual, statistical, and visual data that created, for the first time, the technological capacity for surveillance of the many rather than just a few – a defining attribute, in my view, of the modern state.

Let us listen as the dates sing, *a cappella*, a song of mingled progress. During these few years, the sum of Thomas A. Edison's quadruplex telegraph (1874), Philo Remington's commercial typewriter (1874), and Alexander Graham Bell's telephone (1876) allowed the transmission and recording of textual data in unprecedented quantities, at unequaled speed, with unsurpassed accuracy.[3] With the marriage of

---

[1] H. H. Gerth and C. Wright Mills (eds.), *From Max Weber: Essays in Sociology* (New York: Oxford University Press, 1946), 77–78.
[2] James C. Scott, *Seeing Like a State: How Certain Schemes to Improve the Human Condition Have Failed* (New Haven, CT: Yale University Press, 1998), 1–3, 11–22, 24, 29–33, 44–45, 59–61, 64–72, 373.
[3] G. Tilghman Richards, *The History and Development of Typewriters* (London: Her Majesty's Stationary Office, 1964), 23–25; Lewis Coe, *The Telegraph: A History of Morse's Invention and Its Predecessors in the United States* (Jefferson, NC: McFarland, 1993), 89.

Remington's typewriter to Edison's quadruplex telegram, Reuters and the Associated Press could transmit information around the globe at forty words per minute – the news industry's standard for the next century.[4]

This dynamic decade also saw parallel progress in the management of statistical and visual data. After engineer Herman Hollerith patented the punch card (1889), the US Census Bureau adopted his Electrical Tabulating machine in 1890 to enumerate 62,622,250 Americans within a few weeks – a stunning success that later led to the founding of International Business Machines, better known by its acronym as IBM.[5] Almost simultaneously, the development of photoengraving (1881) and George Eastman's roll film (1889) extended this information revolution to visual data.[6]

With a surprising simultaneity, parallel innovations in data storage allowed reliable encoding and rapid retrieval from this rising tide of information. At opposite ends of same small state in the mid-1870s, Melvil Dewey cataloged the Amherst College Library with his "Dewey decimal system" and Charles A. Cutter worked at Boston's Athenaeum Library to create what became the current Library of Congress system – both, in effect, inventing the "smart number" for reliable alphanumeric encoding and rapid retrieval to manage this incessant torrent of information.[7]

---

[4] Coe, *The Telegraph*, 38–42, 86–87, 97–104; Richard A. Schwarzlose, *The Nation's Newsbrokers*, vol. 2: *The Rush to Institution from 1865 to 1920* (Evanston, IL: Northwestern University Press, 1990), 4–6, 10–11, 111–117; "Telegraphy," in *McGraw-Hill Encyclopedia of Science and Technology*, vol. 13 (New York: McGraw-Hill, 1997), 421–425; Menahem Blondheim, *News over the Wires: The Telegraph and the Flow of Public Information in America, 1844–1897* (Cambridge, MA: Harvard University Press, 1994), 169–195; Robert Luther Thompson, *Wiring a Continent: The History of the Telegraph Industry in the United States, 1832–1866* (Princeton University Press, 1947), 427–439.

[5] Joel D. Howell, *Technology in the Hospital: Transforming Patient Care in the Early Twentieth Century* (Baltimore, MA: Johns Hopkins University Press, 1995), 33–34, 40–42; Charles J. Austin, *Information Systems for Health Services Administration* (Ann Arbor, MI: Health Administration Press, 1992), 13–21; F. H. Wines, "The Census of 1900," *National Geographic*, January 1900, 34–36; Friedrich W. Kistermann, "Hollerith Punched Card System Development (1905–1913)," *IEEE Annals of the History of Computing* 27, no. 1 (2005): 56–66; Emerson W. Pugh, *Building IBM: Shaping an Industry and Its Technology* (Cambridge, MA: MIT Press, 1995), 1–36; "The Electric Tabulating Machine Applied to Cost Accounting," *American Machinist*, August 16, 1902, 1073–1075; S. G. Koon, "Cost Accounting by Machines," *American Machinist*, March 26, 1914, 533–536; Douglas W. Jones, "Punched Cards: A Brief Illustrated Technical History," www.cs.uiowa.edu/~jones/cards.history.html; Mark Howells, "High Tech in the 90s: The 1890 Census," www.oz.net/~markhow/writing/holl.html.

[6] Helmut Gernsheim and Alison Gernsheim, *The History of Photography from the Camera Obscura to the Beginning of the Modern Era* (New York: McGraw-Hill, 1969), 403–409.

[7] Wayne A. Wiegand, *Irrepressible Reformer: A Biography of Melvil Dewey* (Chicago, IL: American Library Association, 1996), 14–24; Wayne A. Wiegand and Donald G. Davis Jr., *Encyclopedia of Library History* (New York: Routledge, 1994), 147–150; John Comaromi and M. Satija, *Dewey Decimal Classification: History and Current Status* (New York: Envoy Press, 1988), 4–9; Leo E. LaMontagne, *American Library Classification with Special Reference to the Library of Congress* (Hamden, CT: Shoestring Press, 1961), 52–60, 63–99, 179–233.

Within a decade, US libraries, hospitals, and armed forces applied the "smart number" to create systems that reduced otherwise inchoate masses of data to alphanumeric codes for rapid filing, retrieval, and cross-referencing that allowed a modernization of the federal bureaucracy. In quick succession, the Office of Naval Intelligence created a card method for recording intelligence (1882), and the US army's Military Information Division (MID) adopted a similar system three years later. Indicative of the torrid tempo of this information revolution, MID's intelligence cards grew from just 4,000 in 1892 to over 300,000 just a decade later.[8]

In the midst of this modernization of the federal government, US policing remained the province of city governments, with the result that modern data management came to crime detection from a mix of foreign and domestic sources. At Paris police headquarters in 1882, Alphonse Bertillon developed the first biometric criminal identification system with eleven cranial and corporeal measurements as well as two facial photographs (front and side view) that was adopted, within a decade, as the American standard.[9] During the 1890s, the inspector general of police for India, Sir Edward R. Henry, finalized the modern system of fingerprint classification, bringing the method home to Scotland Yard in 1901. After a British officer demonstrated the speed of the Henry system to American police chiefs at the St. Louis World's Fair in 1904, New York and other major cities soon adopted fingerprinting as their sole standard for criminal identification. Although the Bureau of Investigation (later the FBI) did not begin collecting fingerprints until 1924, its files passed the 6 million mark within a decade and its director was soon urging compulsory fingerprinting for all citizens. Only months after a young J. Edgar Hoover became head of the Bureau's Radical Division in 1919, he could boast of 80,000 file cards "covering the activities of not only the extreme anarchists but also the more moderate radicals."[10] The fusing of these two innovations, Henry's fingerprint classification and Bertillon's biometrics, created the modern system of criminal

---

[8] Elizabeth Bethel, "The Military Information Division: Origin of the Intelligence Division," *Military Affairs* 11, no. 1 (Spring 1947): 17–24.

[9] Alphonse Bertillon, *Alphonse Bertillon's Instructions for Taking Descriptions for the Identification of Criminals and Others by the Means of Anthrometric Indications* (New York: Kessinger Publishing, 1977), 6, 17, 91–94; Frank Morn, *"The Eye That Never Sleeps": A History of the Pinkerton National Detective Agency* (Bloomington, IN: Indiana University Press, 1982), 124–127; E. R. Henry, *Classification and Uses of Fingerprints* (London: George Routledge, 1900), 61; Henry T. F. Rhodes, *Alphonse Bertillon: Father of Scientific Detection* (London: George G. Harrap, 1956), 71–109; Jürgen Thorwald, *The Century of the Detective* (New York: Harcourt, 1965), 20–26.

[10] Donald C. Dilworth, ed., *Identification Wanted: Development of the American Criminal Identification Systems, 1893–1943* (Gaithersburg, MD: International Association of Chiefs of Police, 1977), 1–3, 6–8, 60–68, 78–79, 82–83, 103–106, 131, 161–166; Henry, *Classification and Uses of Fingerprints*, 4–7, 61–69; Bertillon, *Alphonse Bertillon's Instructions*, 10–12; Police Chiefs News Letter 2, no. 3 (March 1934): 2; *Police Chiefs News Letter* 3, no. 7 (July 1936): 2; Richard Polenberg, *Fighting Faiths: The Abrams Case, the Supreme Court, and Free Speech* (New York: Cornell University Press, 1987), 165.

identification found today on the FBI wanted posters showing fugitives on Bertillon's distinctly square card with photographs of facial front view and side view along with sample fingerprints.

While an imitator in criminal identification, the US was an innovator in the field of police and fire communications. Founded in 1879, the Gamewell Corporation adapted telegraphy and telephony to create centralized fire alarms systems that became the world's standard.[11] By 1900, America's cities were wired with a total of 764 municipal fire-alarm systems and 148 police-patrol networks handling a total of 41 million messages in a single year.[12] On the eve of empire in 1898, however, Congress, courts, and constitution had restrained any national application of these innovations, leaving the federal government with only a limited capacity for law enforcement beyond the customs barrier.

COLONIAL POLICE

After 1898, the US occupation of the Philippines required a decade of pacification that strained its military capacities to the breaking point. In this crucible of counter-insurgency, the US army forged its first field intelligence service, while also creating new paramilitary police units for political control through pervasive surveillance. In retrospect, the sum of such surveillance provided the US regime with key elements of colonial control – basic intelligence on resistance to be countered with raw force and scurrilous information about derelictions of local leaders useful in inducing their political compliance.

In early 1901, Captain Ralph Van Deman, later known as the "father of US Military Intelligence," assumed command of the army's Division of Military Information at Manila and worked to pacify the country by mapping the entire Filipino elite on data cards recording physical appearance, personal finances, and kinship networks.[13] Simultaneously, the first US civil governor, William Howard Taft, elaborated these military methods into a modern surveillance state that ruled through a near-total control over information. To build a colonial police that could

---

[11] Gamewell Fire Alarm Telegraph Co., *Emergency Signaling* (New York: Gamewell, 1916), chs. 2–7; William Maver Jr., *American Telegraphy and Encyclopedia of the Telegraph: Systems, Apparatus, Operation* (New York: Maver Publishing, 1903), 440–453; Paul Ditzel, *Fire Alarm!* (New Albany, OH: Squire Boone Village, 1990), 5, 16–28, 40–42; William Werner, *History of the Boston Fire Department and Boston Fire Alarm System* (Boston, MA: Boston Sparks Association, 1974), 177–184.

[12] Robert W. Little Jr., *York City Fire Department, York, Pennsylvania* (York, 1976), 83; Richard Heath, *Mill City Firefighters: The First Hundred Years, 1879–1979* (Minneapolis, MN: Extra Alarm Association of the Twin Cities, 1981), 32, 45, 69–71; Ditzel, *Fire Alarm!* 27; US Bureau of the Census, *Abstract of the Twelfth Census of the United States, 1900* (Washington DC: Government Printing Office, 1904), 421–422.

[13] Thomas H. Barry, Brigadier General US Volunteers, Chief of Staff, to the Commanding General, Department of Northern Luzon, March 11, 1901, Entry 4337, RG 395, National Archives and Records Administration (NARA).

control Filipino leaders, Taft picked Captain Henry T. Allen, a West Point graduate who had learned about secret police as military attaché at the czar's court in St. Petersburg. With 5,000 troops for pacification, Captain Allen's colonial police, called the Philippines Constabulary, also formed an Information Division that employed some 200 Filipino spies for an intensive surveillance of active Filipino political leaders.[14]

Discovering the power of scandal for political control, the Constabulary was both systematic in its collection and selective in its release – that is, suppressing scandal to protect allies and releasing it to destroy enemies. To grasp the elusive power of scandal, let us consider examples of each practice.

Among the thousands of reports that crossed his desk as Chief of Constabulary, Henry Allen carried just one with him through the fighting in France during World War I and into retirement near Washington DC – a document titled "The Family History of M.Q." This detailed intelligence report alleged that a prominent Filipino politician had murdered a young American soldier, concealed premarital liaisons with his two half-sisters by arranging abortions, and was later guilty of corruption.[15]

Since M.Q. was a leading legislator named Manuel Quezon who also worked as a "private spy" for the Constabulary, its American commanders suppressed allegations about his sexual affairs and charges of graft.[16] With that scurrilous "Family History of M.Q." thus buried safely in General Allen's private files until his death, Quezon enjoyed an unchecked ascent to become the first Philippine president in 1935 and, after independence in 1946, the namesake for his nation's new capital – Quezon City.

On the few occasions when the Constabulary did release such reports, the effects could be quite damaging. By 1904, Archbishop Gregorio Aglipay was about to legitimize his nationalist schism – the Iglesia Filipina Independiente, which then controlled about 30 percent of the country's Catholic parishes – by gaining the all-important sacramental authority of apostolic succession from the US Episcopal Church. Regarding Aglipay as an unrepentant revolutionary, Chief Allen sent the Episcopal bishops, gathered at Boston for their national synod, an intelligence profile of Aglipay loaded with disinformation. That document alleged that, during the Philippine revolution after 1896, Aglipay, then a Catholic priest, had ordered a captured Spanish bishop flogged with 300 lashes and had prowled the corridors of a

[14] Heath Twitchell Jr., *Allen: The Biography of an Army Officer, 1859–1930* (New Brunswick, NJ: Rutgers University Press, 1974), 4–6, 19, 24, 26, 36–59, 65–67, 75–84, 86, 290.
[15] Captain Pyle, P.S., Family History of M.Q. [c.1900], Box 7, File: 1900 Oct., Henry T. Allen Papers, Library of Congress (HTA).
[16] Letter from Austin Craig to the Secretary of the Interior, April 28, 1913, Book no. 21:II, Dean C. Worcester Papers, Harlan Hatcher Library, University of Michigan; *Philippines Free Press*, January 9, 1915, 12; *Manila Times*, November 26, 1912; December 3, 1912; December 4, 1912; December 5, 1912; December 10, 1912; *Cablenews-American*, December 8, 1912.

Catholic convent with lecherous intent.[17] Apparently appalled, the episcopal bishops rejected any affiliation, contributing to the rapid decline of Aglipay's nationalist church.[18]

COLONIAL BLUEPRINT

As the United States was completing its pacification of Philippines in 1907, Mark Twain wrote an imagined history of twentieth-century America arguing that its "lust for conquest" had destroyed "the Great [American] Republic," because "trampling upon the helpless abroad had taught her, by a natural process, to endure with apathy the like at home; multitudes who had applauded the crushing of other people's liberties, lived to suffer for their mistake."[19] Indeed, just a decade after Twain wrote those prophetic words, these colonial police methods were repatriated to provide blueprints for formation of the first US internal security apparatus.

For the United States, the Philippines was the first manifestation of the repressive potential of its new information technology. On the eve of empire in 1898, the country was still what Stephen Skowronek has called a "patchwork" state with a loosely structured administrative apparatus, leaving ample room for innovation that came, with stunning speed, in these years of empire. Whatever one might think of Skowronek's general assessment of US state strength, his weak state thesis seems useful in assessing a key area he overlooks – the federal capacity for law enforcement and overall security.[20]

During the decade that the US army was building a surveillance capacity in the Philippines, the federal government had no domestic security agency nor any covert capacity before the founding of the fledgling Bureau of Investigation, later the FBI, in 1908 – effectively leaving policing to the cities and surveillance to private agencies such as the Pinkertons. In the social crisis surrounding World War I, however,

---

[17] C. H. Brent to General Allen, July 11, 1904, Box 8, File: 1904 Jun.–Aug., HTA; C. H. Brent to Gen. Henry T. Allen, October 12, 1904, Box 8, File: 1904 Sept.–Oct., HTA. Letter from Henry T. Allen to C. H. Brent, July 12, 1904; letter from Brent to Gen. Henry T. Allen, October 12, 1904, File: Jul.–Dec. 1904, Box 6, Charles Henry Brent Papers, Manuscript Division, US Library of Congress (CHB). Kenton J. Clymer, *Protestant Missionaries in the Philippines, 1898–1916: An Inquiry into the American Colonial Mentality* (Urbana, IL: University of Illinois Press, 1986), 122.

[18] Charles H. Brent, Private Addendum to Report on Religious Conditions in the Philippine Islands (For Bishops Only), Box 6, CHB; Pedro S. Achutegui, S.J., and Miguel A. Bernad, S.J., *Religious Revolution in the Philippines*, vol. 1: *1860–1940* (Quezon City: Ateneo de Manila University Press, 1961), 388–390; Clymer, *Protestant Missionaries in the Philippines*, 120–122.

[19] Mark Twain, "Passage from 'Outlines of History' (suppressed) Date 9th Century," in Jim Zwick, ed., *Mark Twain's Weapons of Satire: Anti-Imperialist Writings on the Philippine-American War* (Syracuse University Press, 1992), 78–79.

[20] Stephen Skowronek, *Building a New American State: The Expansion of National Administrative Capacities, 1877–1920* (Cambridge, MA: Harvard University Press, 1982), 8–18, 39–46.

colonial police methods migrated homeward through the invisible capillaries of empire to provide blueprints for two new US army commands – Military Intelligence and Military Police – that became the foundation for a nascent domestic security apparatus.

When the United States entered World War I in April 1917, it had the only army on the battlefield without an intelligence service of any description. Within weeks, Colonel Van Deman drew upon his Philippine experience to establish US Military Intelligence Division (MID), quickly recruiting a staff that grew from one employee (himself) to 1,700, and to design the institutional architecture for America's first internal security agency. Just as the Philippine Constabulary had used civilian operatives, so Colonel Van Deman designed US internal security as a unique fusion of federal agencies and civilian auxiliaries that would mark its operations for the next half-century. In collaboration with the FBI, Van Deman presided over creation a wartime civilian counterintelligence auxiliary, the American Protective League, with 350,000 citizen operatives who amassed over 1 million pages of surveillance reports on German-Americans in just fourteen months – arguably the world's most intensive domestic surveillance to that date.[21] With this civilian auxiliary devoting millions of man-hours to routine domestic security, MID's officers were freed for extralegal covert operations to contain a wartime surge in labor radicalism.

Similarly, in the war's final months General Harry Bandholtz, drawing on what he called his "long experience in command of the Philippine Constabulary" (1907 to 1913), established a new army security service, the Military Police or MPs, charged with managing the chaos of Europe's postwar occupation. Following the new unit's formation in October 1918, Bandholtz quickly built a corps of 31,627 men stationed in 476 cities and towns in five nations – France, Italy, Belgium, Luxemburg, and the German Rhineland. To overcome the army's haphazard selection process, Bandholtz established a specialist service school at Autun, France, that trained over 4,000 officers and men in the last months of war. A number of former Philippines Constabulary officers played formative roles in training this new service, ending early complaints of indifference, disrespect, or even "brutality," and thereby establishing a record of professionalism and "kindness ... to the native inhabitants."[22]

---

[21] Theodore Kornweibel Jr., "Seeing Red": Federal Campaigns against Black Militancy, 1919–1925 (Bloomington, IN: Indiana University Press, 1998), 7, 184; Jeffrey M. Dorwart, Conflict of Duty: The U.S. Navy's Intelligence Dilemma, 1919–1945 (Annapolis, MD: Naval Insitute Press, 1983), 7; Charles H. McCormick, Seeing Reds: Federal Surveillance of Radicals in the Pittsburgh Mill District, 1917–1921 (University of Pittsburgh Press, 1997), 3, 12–13; Rhodri Jeffreys-Jones, The FBI: A History (New Haven, CT: Yale University Press, 2007), 65–72.

[22] Washington Evening Star, February 20, 1940; Personal Name Information Files: John R. White, Entry 21, RG 350, NARA; H. H. Bandholtz, "Provost Marshal General's Department, April 30, 1919," in United States Army in the World War 1917–1919: Reports of the Commander-in-Chief, Staff Sections and Services (Washington DC: Center of Military History, US Army, 1991), 313–328; Robert Wright, Jr., Army Lineage Series: Military Police (Washington DC: Center of Military History, US Army, 1992), 8–9.

After the war as well, General Bandholtz applied lessons learned from repressing Filipino nationalist movements to lead the army in defusing a radical miners' revolt in the West Virginia coalfields – the only armed uprising that the US state faced in the twentieth century. In 1921, some 10,000 striking mine-workers armed with rifles were shooting it out with sheriffs and private security, firing off a million bullets along a battle line across Mingo and Logan Counties in the mountains of West Virginia. In the midst of this stand-off, General Bandholtz stepped off the train at Charleston depot accompanied by a single aide. In a private meeting with the state's charismatic union leader, Frank Keeney, whose fiery words had sparked the armed protest, the general said: "These are your people. I am going to give you a chance to save them, and if you cannot turn them back, we are going to snuff them out like that." Then Bandholtz reached forward and snapped his fingers right under the union leader's nose. Keeney capitulated, promising "he would act immediately." Using the psychological tactics learned from his years in the colonial Constabulary, Bandholtz had apparently projected an aura of lethal force that bent the union to his will – just as he had single-handedly forced the cancellation of an armed workers' demonstration at Manila in 1911 and repulsed a mob of Romanian military looters standing alone on the steps of Budapest's national museum in 1919 armed only with a riding crop. With the union's full cooperation, he now deployed 2,100 federal troops to demobilize some 5,400 miners, confiscate 278 firearms, and send everyone home. Sixteen men died in the five-day Battle of Blair Mountain, but none was shot by US army troops.[23]

After the Armistice in 1918, Military Intelligence and the FBI collaborated in two years of violent, largely illegal repression against the socialist left. To correct these excesses, Republican conservatives later curtailed Washington's internal security apparatus. In 1924, Attorney General Harlan Fiske Stone, worried that "a secret police may become a menace to free government," announced "the Bureau of Investigation is not concerned with political or other opinions of individuals." Five years later, Secretary Henry Stimson abolished the State Department's Crytography unit with his famous admonition, "Gentlemen do not read each other's mail."[24]

---

[23] Major General J. G. Harbord, To: Brigadier General H. H. Bandholtz, August 31, 1921; Brig. Gen. H. H. Bandholtz, Proclamation, September 2, 1921; A Proclamation by the President of the United States, n.d.; Bandholtz, Copy Telegram No. 2, To: Adjutant General, n.d.; Minutes, Twenty-Ninth Consecutive and Fourth Biennial Convention of District No. 5, United Mine Workers of America, First Day, Pittsburg, PA, September 6, 1921; Brigadier General H. H. Bandholtz, To: the Adjutant General, September 12, 1921 – all the above from, Reel 9, Harry H. Bandholtz Papers, Michigan Historical Collections. Institute for the History of Technology and Industrial Anthropology, *The Battle of Blair Mountain (West Virginia): Cultural Resource Survey and Recording Project* (Morgantown, WV: Institute for the History of Technology and Industrial Anthropology, 1992), 35–50; Clayton D. Laurie and Ronald H. Cole, *The Role of Federal Military Forces in Domestic Disorders, 1877–1945* (Washington DC: Center of Military History, US Army, 1997), 320–324.

[24] Joan Jensen, *The Price of Vigilance* (Chicago, IL: Rand McNally, 1968), 287–289; Harold M. Hyman, *To Try Men's Souls: Loyalty Tests in American History* (Berkeley, CA: University of California Press, 1959), 323–324; McCormick, *Seeing Reds*, 202; Kornweibel, "Seeing Red,"

US COUNTERINTELLIGENCE

If General Van Deman's wartime service won him the title as "father of US Military Intelligence," then his surveillance activities during retirement should earn him another honorific: father of the American blacklist. After retiring from the army in 1929, General van Deman and his wife worked tirelessly for the next quarter-century from their bungalow in San Diego, coordinating an elaborate information exchange among military intelligence, police red squads, business security, and citizen vigilante groups to amass detailed files on 250,000 suspected subversives. Indicative of his influence over internal security, Van Deman attended the confidential National Intelligence Conference in 1940 between J. Edgar Hoover and the chief of Army Intelligence who, like the pope at Tordesillas, divided the world through the "Delimitations Agreement" – assigning all counterintelligence for the Americas to the FBI and intelligence gathering for the rest of the world to the army and its later affiliate, the Office of Strategic Services (OSS).[25]

As his wartime counterintelligence work against alien subversives drew down in 1943–1944, Van Deman concentrated on exposing the Communist Party's penetration of the film industry. By the late 1930s, Van Deman's swelling archive of 40,000 file cards on suspected subversives was already focused on Hollywood. This emphasis was evident in the card for Ring Lardner, Jr., an Oscar-winning writer for MGM Studios later blacklisted, that read: "Subject reported by good authority to be a *rabid Communist* and reported to be recruiting members for the YOUNG COMMUNIST LEAGUE in Los Angeles." Indicating the general's spreading net, the source for this report noted on the card was "Commandant, Third Naval District, New York."[26]

174–175; David Kahn, *The Reader of Gentlemen's Mail: Herbert O. Yardley and the Birth of American Codebreaking* (New Haven, CT: Yale University Press, 2004), 94–103; Roy Talbert, Jr., *Negative Intelligence: The Army and the American Left, 1917–1941* (Jackson, MS: University Press of Mississippi, 1991), 208–211; Ralph Van Deman, December 15, 1928, Office of Chief of Staff, Cross Reference Card, Microform 1194, RG 350, NARA; US Senate, Select Committee to Study Governmental Operations with Respect to Intelligence Activities, 94th Congress, 2d Session, *Supplementary Reports on Intelligence Activities*, Book 6 (Washington DC: Government Printing Office, 1976), 105–106; Regin Schmidt, *Red Scare: FBI and the Origins of Anticommunism in the United States, 1919–1943* (Copenhagen: Museum Tusculanum Press, 2000), 324–328, 368; Ábrahám Vass, "Plaque Honors Hero US General Who Prevented Romanian Looting of National Museum," *Hungary Today*, October 18, 2019, https://hungarytoday.hu/plaque-honor-hero-usa-general-romanian-looting-national-museum.

[25] Talbert, *Negative Intelligence*, 255–259; US Senate, 94th Congress, 2d Session, *Final Report of the Select Committee to Study Governmental Operations with Respect to Intelligence Activities*, Book 2 (Washington DC: Government Printing Office, 1976), 33–38.

[26] Lardner, Ring, Jr. (R-1620), Box 12, Ralph Van Deman Papers, Records of the US Senate Internal Security Subcommittee, Record Group 46, NARA; Larry Ceplair and Steven Englund, *The Inquisition in Hollywood: Politics in the Film Community, 1930–60* (Urbana, IL: University of Illinois Press, 2003), 54–82.

In the aftermath of World War II, the nation's public–private security apparatus again expanded to create the mass, anticommunist movement identified with Senator Joseph McCarthy. In this anticommunist witch hunt, General Van Deman worked closely with both the FBI and the California Committee on Un-American Activities, planning the state legislature's public exposé of the Communist Party, particularly in Hollywood. In June 1949, the California committee – headed by state Senator Jack Tenney, author of the popular song "Mexicali Rose" – drew upon General Van Deman's archive to issue a sensational 709-page report denouncing hundreds of Hollywood luminaries as "red appeasers," including, Charlie Chaplin, Maurice Chevalier, Katherine Hepburn, Danny Kaye, Ring Lardner, Jr., Gregory Peck, Edward G. Robinson, Artie Shaw, Orson Welles, Frank Sinatra, and, significantly, Helen Gahagan Douglas.[27]

Exemplifying the nature of this public–private security alliance, General Van Deman's archive thus served as an informal conduit for moving security reports from closed, classified government files into the hands of citizen anticommunist groups for public blacklisting. In the 1946 congressional elections, for example, an obscure Los Angeles lawyer named Richard Nixon reportedly used Van Deman's files for red baiting to defeat the popular five-term Democratic congressman, Jerry Voorhis. Four years later, Representative Nixon reportedly used the same files and the same tactics to beat Representative Helen Gahagan Douglas in the race for the US Senate, launching Richard Nixon on a path to the US presidency.[28]

This archive did not die with its creator. Just sixty-one minutes after General Van Deman passed away at his San Diego home in January 1952, a telex with news of his death reached the desk of FBI director J. Edgar Hoover in Washington DC. Within hours, a team from the US Army Counter Intelligence Corps occupied Van Deman's home to secure and sort his voluminous files with coded name cards for a quarter-million suspected subversives before shipping them north to the Presidio in San Francisco. For the next twenty-five years, his massive files were used by the army, and then, after 1971, by the US Senate Internal Security Committee where they assisted in the investigation of suspected communists until the late 1970s.[29]

---

[27] AP, "Hundred Named as Red Appeasers," *New York Times*, June 9, 1949; "Never Were or Would Be Reds, Fredric March and Wife Assert," *New York Times*, June 10, 1949; Richard Halloran, "Senate Panel Holds Vast 'Subversives' File Amassed by Ex-Chief of Army Intelligence," *New York Times*, September 7, 1971; California Legislature, *Fifth Report of the Senate Fact-Finding Committee on Un-American Activities, 1949* (Sacramento, CA: California Legislature, 1948), 411, 448–449, 488–537; Patrick McGilligan and Paul Buhle, *Tender Comrades: A Backstory of the Hollywood Blacklist* (New York: St. Martin's Press, 1997), 368–369.

[28] Halloran, "Senate Panel Holds Vast 'Subversives' File Amassed by Ex-Chief of Army Intelligence."

[29] Talbert, *Negative Intelligence*, 270–271; Halloran, "Senate Panel Holds Vast 'Subversives' File Amassed by Ex-Chief of Army Intelligence." Letter from R. R. Roach to D. M. Ladd, July 13, 1945; D.M. Ladd to E.A. Tamm, October 29, 1945; Colonel F. W. Hein to Commanding Officer 115th CIC Detachment, March 8, 1951; A. H. Belmont to D. M. Ladd, November 9,

More broadly, General Van Deman's methods were perpetuated inside the FBI, particularly after the 1940 Intelligence Conference that gave J. Edgar Hoover's bureau full formal control of all US counterintelligence and allowed him to use wartime conditions for extralegal operations. At the war's start, the FBI drew upon "intelligence gathered by break-ins, wiretaps, and bugs" to compile an arrest list of thousands whom the bureau deemed "a menace to the public peace and safety of the Unites States Government." To curtail enemy espionage, President Franklin D. Roosevelt authorized Hoover, in May 1940, to engage in limited wiretapping that the bureau expanded into widespread bugging. During the war, the FBI planted 6,769 wiretaps and 1,806 bugs that provided President Roosevelt with phone transcripts from his domestic enemies – notably, aviator Charles Lindberg, Senator Burton K. Wheeler, and Representative Hamilton Fish. Upon taking office in early 1945, President Harry Truman soon discovered the extraordinary extent of this FBI surveillance. "We want no Gestapo or Secret Police," Truman told his diary that May. "FBI is tending in that direction. They are dabbling in sex-life scandals and plain blackmail."[30]

During a quarter-century of warrantless wiretaps, Hoover had built a veritable archive of sexual peccadilloes among the country's political elite and used it to shape the direction of US politics – distributing a dossier on Adlai Stevenson's alleged homosexuality to contribute to his defeat in the 1952 presidential elections, circulating audio tapes of Martin Luther King, Jr.'s alleged philandering, and monitoring President Kennedy's affair with mafia mistress Judith Exner.[31]

"The moment [Hoover] would get something on a senator," recalled William Sullivan, then the FBI's third-ranking official, "he'd send one of the errand boys up and advise the senator that 'we're in the course of an investigation, and we by chance happened to come up with this data on your daughter ...' From that time on, the senator's right in his pocket."[32]

During the Vietnam War, the FBI's Cointelpro and the CIA's Operation Chaos maintained surveillance against the antiwar left and mounted thousands of illegal counterintelligence operations involving black propaganda, break-ins, and *agent provocateur* violence. At the end of the Vietnam War, the Church and

1951; Colonel H. S. Isaacson to Major General A. R. Bolling, November 27, 1951; Director to SAC San Diego, December 11, 1951; V. P. Keay to A. H. Belmont, January 22, 1952; Santoiana to Director, January 22, 1952; SAC San Diego to Director, February 4, 1952; SAC SF to Director, n.d. – all above correspondence in Subject: Van Deman, Ralph Henry, Files 65-37516, 94-37515, Federal Bureau of Investigation, Washington DC.
[30] Tim Weiner, *Enemies: A History of the FBI* (New York: Random House, 2013), 77, 86–90, 134–135.
[31] Ibid., 178, 249–250; Michael O'Brien, "The Exner File – Judith Campbell Exner, John F. Kennedy's Mistress," *Washington Monthly*, December 1999. Kitty Kelly, "The Dark Side of Camelot," *People Magazine* 29, no. 8 (January 29, 1988), http://archive.people.com/people/archive/jpgs/19880229/19880229-750-113.jpg.
[32] Ronald Kessler, *The Secrets of the FBI* (New York: Crown Publishers, 2011), 37–41.

Rockefeller committees investigated these excesses, prompting formation, under the Foreign Intelligence Surveillance Act of 1978, of so-called FISA courts to issue warrants for all national security wire taps.[33]

WAR ON TERROR

The 9/11 terrorist attacks on September 11, 2001 and the subsequent Global War on Terror represent another instance of imperial mimesis, with advanced surveillance techniques developed for the pacification of Afghanistan and Iraq migrating homeward. Struggling for new weapons to fight a perceived terrorist threat at home and abroad, Washington adopted electronic surveillance and biometric identification whose sum formed a global surveillance apparatus of unprecedented power.

Confronted with a bloody insurgency in Iraq, the US occupation served as another crucible of counterinsurgency, forging a new system of biometric surveillance and digital warfare with potential domestic applications. This new biometric identification system first appeared in the smoking aftermath of "Operation Phantom Fury," a brutal, nine-day battle that US Marines fought in late 2004 to recapture the insurgent-controlled city of Falluja. Bombing, artillery, and mortars destroyed at least half of that city's buildings and sent most of its 250,000 residents fleeing into the surrounding countryside. Marines then forced returning residents to wait endless hours under a desert sun at checkpoints for fingerprints and retinal scans. Once inside the city's blast-wall maze, residents had to wear identification tags for compulsory checks to catch infiltrating insurgents.[34]

The first hint that biometrics were helping to pacify Baghdad's far larger population of 7 million came in April 2007 when the New York Times published a singular photograph of American soldiers studiously photographing an Iraqi's eyeball.[35] With only a terse caption to go by, we can still infer the technology behind this early record of a retinal scan in Baghdad: digital cameras for US patrols, wireless data transfer to a mainframe computer, and a database to record as many adult Iraqi eyes as could be gathered. Indeed, eight months later, the Washington Post reported that the Pentagon had collected over a million Iraqi fingerprints and retinal scans. By mid-2008, the US

---

[33] Seymour M. Hersh, "Huge C.I.A. Operation Reported in U.S. Against Antiwar Forces, Other Dissidents in Nixon Years," New York Times, December 22, 1974; George Tames, "Summary of Rockefeller Panel's C.I.A. Report," New York Times, June 11, 1975; Nicholas M. Horrock, "Report by C.I.A. Puzzles Capital," New York Times, July 10, 1975; UPI, "Dr. King Maligned in Death by F.B.I.," New York Times, May 6, 1976; Nicholas M. Horrock, "Senate Panel Likely to Urge Strong Curbs on Domestic Spying," New York Times, March 14, 1976; David Binder, "Carter Signs Order to Reorganize Intelligence and Curb Surveillance," New York Times, January 25, 1978; Editorial, "Agents of Change at the F.B.I.," New York Times, August 13, 1979.
[34] Ann Scott Tyson, "Increased Security in Fallujah Slows Efforts to Rebuild," Washington Post, April 19, 2005, www.washingtonpost.com/wp-dyn/articles/A64292-2005Apr18.html.
[35] "Trying to Distinguish Friend From Foe on Streets," New York Times, April 4, 2007, http://query.nytimes.com/gst/fullpage.html?res=9903E5D71F30F937A35757C0A9619C8B63.

army had also confined Baghdad's population behind blast-wall cordons and were checking Iraqi identities by satellite link to a biometric database.[36]

As these specialist forces rotated home to America, this advanced eavesdropping capacity was quickly integrated into US internal security operations. Amidst the Pentagon's ongoing emphasis on battlefield surveillance in Iraq, the army's Northern Command announced in September 2008 that one of the Third Division's brigades in Iraq would be reassigned inside the United States as a Consequent Management Response Force (CMRF), with the mission of helping civilian authorities with "civil unrest and crowd control." According to Colonel Roger Cloutier, his battalion's tactics included "a new modular package of ... non-lethal weapons designed to subdue unruly or dangerous individuals" – including, Taser guns, roadblock equipment, shields and batons, beanbag bullets, and improved interservice communications. That September, the army's chief of staff, General George Casey, flew to Fort Stewart, Georgia for the first full CMRF mission readiness exercise. With 250 officers from all services participating, the military war gamed its future coordination with the FBI, the Federal Emergency Management Agency, and local authorities in the event of a domestic terrorist threat. Within weeks, the American Civil Liberties Union filed an expedited freedom of information request for details of these deployments, arguing that it is "imperative that the American people know the truth about this new and unprecedented intrusion of the military in domestic affairs."[37]

At home, President George W. Bush ordered the NSA, in October 2001, to commence covert monitoring of private domestic communications through the nation's telephone companies without requisite warrants.[38] Since the Bush administration decided that "metadata was not constitutionally protected," the NSA also launched a sweeping attempt under Operation Stellar Wind "to collect bulk

---

[36] Laura Blumenfeld, "Spurred by Gratitude, 'Bomb Lady' Develops Better Weapons for U.S.," *Washington Post*, December 1, 2007, www.washingtonpost.com/wp-dyn/content/article/2007/11/30/AR2007113002302.html; US Government Accounting Office, *DOD Biometrics and Forensics: Progress Made in Establishing Long-term Deployable Capabilities, but Further Actions Are Needed*, GAO-17-580 (Washington DC: GAO, August 2017), 1–32, www.gao.gov/assets/690/686416.pdf.

[37] Thom Shanker, "Gates Wants to Shift $1.2 Billion to Bolster War Surveillance," *New York Times*, July 26, 2008; Elizabeth Bumiller, "From a Carrier, Another View of America's Air War in Afghanistan," *New York Times*, February 24, 2009; Mike Ferner, "The New Generation of 'Non-Lethal' Weapons," *Counterpunch*, December 8, 2008, www.counterpunch.org/2008/12/08/the-new-generation-of-quot-non-lethal-quot-weapons; "Consequent Management Response Force to Join Army Northern Command," *Army News Service*, September 15, 2008, www.army.mil/article/12422/consequence_management_response_force_to_join_army_northern_command; Patti Bielling, "Top Army Leader Visits Newly Assigned Consequence Management Force," United States Northern Command, September 15, 2008, www.northcom.mil/news/2008/091508.html; American Civil Liberties Union," ACLU Demands Information on Military Deployment within U.S. Borders," October 21, 2008, www.aclu.org/safefree/general/3727prs20081021.html.

[38] James Risen and Eric Lichtblau, "How the U.S. Delved Deeper Via Technology," *New York Times*, June 9, 2013.

telephony and Internet metadata."[39] In 2005, the *New York Times* sparked considerable controversy by exposing Bush's illegal surveillance.[40] Nonetheless, a year later, *USA Today* reported the NSA was still "secretly collecting the phone call records of tens of millions of Americans," aiming "to create a database of every call ever made."[41] Armed with expanded powers by Congressional legislation in 2007 and 2008 that legalized Bush's once illegal program, the NSA launched its PRISM program by compelling nine internet service providers – Microsoft, Yahoo, Google, Facebook, AOL, Skype, YouTube, and others – to transfer what became billions of emails to its massive data farms.[42]

The ongoing War on Terror provided technical innovation for this rapid growth in US surveillance. By the time the United States withdrew from Iraq in late 2011, the US army's Biometrics Identity Management Agency (BIMA) had collected fingerprints and iris scans from 3 million people, or 10 percent of that country's population. In Afghanistan by early 2012, US military computers held biometrics for 2 million Afghanis, again about 10 percent of this country's population.[43] Two years after the Pentagon's Homeland Security commander, General Victor Renuart, had called for the domestic application of this technology in 2009, a company called BI2 Technologies in Plymouth, Massachusetts, began marketing the Mobile Offender Recognition and Information System (MORIS), with smartphone-based iris recognition, to dozens of police forces across America.[44] Similarly, the military's experimental Biometric Optical Surveillance System (BOSS) designed to spot suicide bombers in crowds of Afghanis or Iraqis was transferred to Homeland Security in 2010, which continued to develop facial recognition by surveillance cameras for future use by local police.[45]

---

[39] National Security Agency, Office of Inspector General, "Working Draft," March 24, 2009, 7–13, http://apps.washingtonpost.com/g/page/world/national-security-agency-inspector-general-draft-report/277.

[40] James Risen and Eric Lichtblau, "Bush Let U.S. Spy on Callers Without Courts," *New York Times*, December 16, 2005. www.nytimes.com/2005/12/16/politics/16program.html?pagewanted=all&_r=0.

[41] Leslie Cauley, "NSA Has Massive Database of Americans' Phone Calls," *USA Today*, May 11, 2006, http://yahoo.usatoday.com/news/washington/2006-05-10-nsa_x.htm?csp=1.

[42] Barton Gellman and Laura Poitras, " U.S., British Intelligence Mining Data from Nine U.S. Internet Companies in Broad Secret Program," *Washington Post*, June 6, 2013, www.washingtonpost.com/investigations/us-intelligence-mining-data-from-nine-us-internet-companies-in-broad-secret-program/2013/06/06/3a0cod a8-cebf-11e2-8845-d97occb04497_story.html.

[43] Steve Mansfield-Devine, "Biometrics at War: The US Military's Need for Identification and Authentication," *Biometric Technology Today*, no. 5 (May 2012), 5–6.

[44] Zach Howard, "Police to Begin Iphone Iris Scans Amid Privacy Concerns," *Reuters*, July 20, 2011, www.reuters.com/article/2011/07/20/us-crime-identification-iris-idUSTRE76J4A120110720; Nathan Hodge, "General Wants to Scan More U.S. Irises, Fingerprints," *Wired.com*, January 29, 2009, www.wired.com/2009/01/biometrics-need.

[45] Charlie Savage, "Facial Scanning Is Making Gains in Surveillance," *New York Times*, August 21, 2013.

SURVEILLANCE UNDER OBAMA

Instead of curtailing his predecessor's wartime surveillance, as Republicans had done in the 1920s or Democrats did in the 1970s, President Barack Obama expanded the NSA's operations into a digital panopticon, remarkable for both the sheer scale of the billions of messages collected and for the selective wiretapping of leaders worldwide.

In September 2013, the *New York Times* reported that the NSA has, since 2010, applied sophisticated software to create "social network diagrams ... to unlock as many secrets about individuals as possible ... and pick up sensitive information like regular calls to a psychiatrist's office, late-night messages to an extramarital partner."[46] Beyond US borders, the centralization of all telephone and email communications into a global network of fiber-optic cables and data centers allowed the NSA to monitor the globe by penetrating just 190 data hubs – an extraordinary economy of force for both political surveillance and cyberwarfare (see Figure 3.1).[47] Through expenditures of $250 million annually under its Sigint Enabling Project, the NSA stealthily penetrated encryption designed to protect privacy. "In the future, super-powers will be made or broken based on the strength of their cryptanalytic programs," reads a 2007 NSA document. "It is the price of admission for the United States to maintain unrestricted access to and use of cyberspace."[48]

Such digital surveillance grew into "cyberwarfare" in 2009 after the formation of the US Cyber Command (CYBERCOM), with its headquarters at Fort Meade and a cyberwarfare center at Lackland Air Base initially staffed by 7,000 Air Force employees.[49] Over the next two years, the Pentagon created an enormous concentration of power by appointing the NSA's chief, General Keith Alexander, as CYBERCOM's first commander and declaring cyberspace an "operational domain" like air, land, or sea for both offensive and defensive warfare.[50] While developing this formidable cyberwarfare capacity, Washington deployed computer viruses with

---

[46] James Risen and Laura Poitras, "N.S.A. Examines Social Networks of U.S. Citizens," *New York Times*, September 29, 2013.

[47] National Security Agency, "Driver 1: Worldwide SIGINT/Defense Cryptologic Platform" (2012), in Floor Boon, Steven Derix, and Huib Modderkolk, "NSA Infected 50,000 Computer Networks with Malicious Software," *NRC.NL*, November 23, 2013, www.nrc.nl/nieuws/2013/11/23/nsa-infected-50000-computer-networks-with-malicious-software.

[48] Nicole Perlroth, Jeff Larson, and Scott Shane, "N.S.A. Able to Foil Basic Safeguards of Privacy on Web," *New York Times*, September 6, 2013.

[49] Thom Shanker and David E. Sanger, "Privacy May Be a Victim in Cyberdefense Plan," *New York Times*, June 12, 2009, www.nytimes.com/2009/06/13/us/politics/13cyber.html.

[50] Armed Forces News Service, "Gates Established US Cyber Command, Names First Commander," *The Official Site of the U.S. Air Force*, May 21, 2010, www.af.mil/News/Article-Display/Article/116589/gates-establishes-us-cyber-command-names-first-commander/; David Alexander, "Pentagon to Treat Cyberspace as 'Operational Domain'," Reuters, July 14, 2011, www.reuters.com/article/2011/07/14/us-usa-defense-cybersecurity-idUSTRE76D5FA20110714.

Imperial Mimesis 49

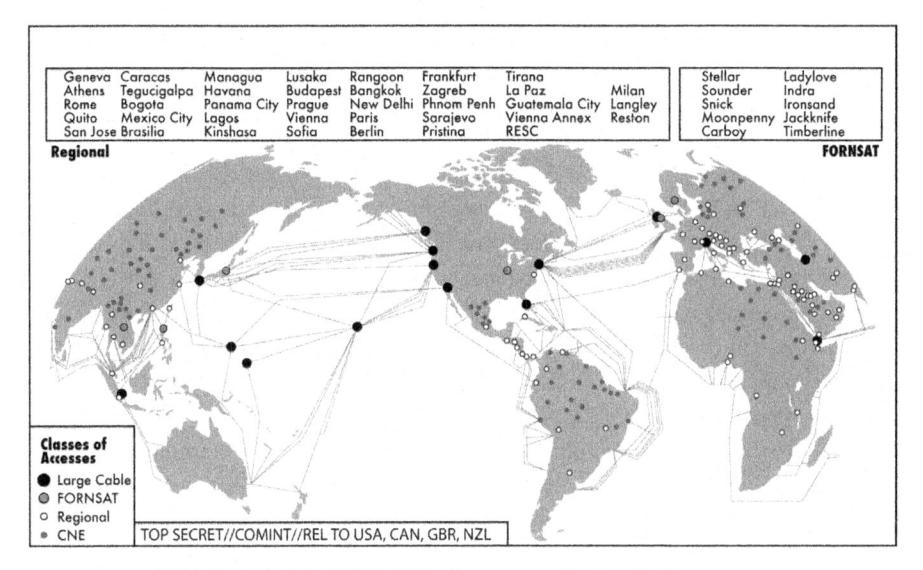

Geneva	Caracas	Managua	Lusaka	Rangoon	Frankfurt	Tirana		Stellar	Ladylove
Athens	Tegucigalpa	Havana	Budapest	Bangkok	Zagreb	La Paz	Milan	Sounder	Indra
Rome	Bogota	Panama City	Prague	New Delhi	Phnom Penh	Guatemala City	Langley	Snick	Ironsand
Quito	Mexico City	Lagos	Vienna	Paris	Sarajevo	Vienna Annex	Reston	Moonpenny	Jackknife
San Jose	Brasilia	Kinshasa	Sofia	Berlin	Pristina	RESC		Carboy	Timberline
Regional									**FORNSAT**

Classes of Accesses
● Large Cable
◉ FORNSAT
○ Regional
● CNE   TOP SECRET//COMINT//REL TO USA, CAN, GBR, NZL

FIGURE 3.1 NSA Worldwide SIGINT/Defense cryptologic platform 2013

devastating effect against Iran's nuclear facilities from 2006 to 2010, but, cautious about reactions from China and Russia, opted for conventional strikes against Libya's air defenses in 2011.[51]

Under Obama as well, the NSA cooperated with its long-time British counterpart, the Government Communications Headquarters (GCHQ), to tap the dense cluster of Trans-Atlantic Telecommunication fiber-optic cables that cross the United Kingdom. During a visit to a GCHQ facility for high-altitude intercepts at Menwith Hill in June 2008, the NSA chief, General Keith Alexander, according to a press account, asked: "Why can't we collect all the signals all the time. Sounds like a good summer project for Menwith." After two years of turning its gaze from the skies above to probe the cables below the earth at its Cornwall station, GCHQ's Operation Tempora achieved the "biggest internet access" of any partner in the

---

[51] John Markoff, "Before the Gunfire, Cyberattacks," *New York Times*, August 12, 2008; Eric Schmitt and Thom Shanker, "U.S. Debated Cyberwarfare in Attack Plan on Libya," *New York Times*, October 18, 2011; David E. Sanger, "Obama Order Sped Up Wave of Cyberattacks Against Iran," *New York Times*, June 1, 2012; Ian Traynor, "Russia accused of unleashing cyberwar to disable Estonia," *The Guardian*, May 16, 2007, www.guardian.co.uk/world/2007/may/17/topstories3.russia; Joel Brenner, *America the Vulnerable: Inside the New Threat Matrix of Digital Espionage, Crime, and Warfare* (New York: Penguin Press, 2011), Introduction; Lolita C. Baldior, "Pentagon Takes Aim at China Cyber Threat," *Associated Press*, August 19, 2010, http://archive.boston.com/news/nation/washington/articles/2010/08/19/pentagon_takes_aim_at_china_cyber_threat; Lolita C. Baldior, "U.S., China to Cooperate More on Cyber Threat," *Associated Press*, May 7, 2012, https://news.yahoo.com/us-china-cooperate-more-cyber-threat-224849178.html.

"Five Eyes" signals intercept coalition that includes the UK, United States, Australia, Canada, and New Zealand. When the project went online in 2011, GCHQ sank probes into 200 internet cables and was soon collecting 600 million telephone messages daily, accessible to 850,000 NSA employees.[52]

This close cooperation between the NSA and GCHQ dates back to the dawn of the Cold War in March 1946 when the two powers signed the top secret British–US Communication Intelligence Agreement (BRUSA) agreement, then focused on high-altitude interception of Soviet bloc radio waves. Over the next decade, this signals-intercept program expanded into a worldwide listening apparatus by adding close partners in the Five Eyes signals coalition and allies such Norway, Germany, Italy, and Turkey as adjuncts in the Echelon network.[53]

Just as colonial police once surveilled thousands of local elites, so the NSA now monitors the hundreds of national leaders who are the new "subordinate elites" in Washington's global imperium. Such surveillance provides critical information for the exercise of global power – first, operational intelligence on terrorists to be countered with covert action; next, political and economic intelligence to advantage American negotiations with allies; and, finally, scurrilous information about national leaders useful in encouraging their compliance.

In deference to the Five Eyes intelligence alliance, the NSA has, since 2007, generally exempted close "2nd party" allies from surveillance. But, says a leaked NSA document, "we can, and often do, target the signals of most 3rd party foreign partners" – meaning allies such as Germany, France, and Italy. To gain such intelligence, the NSA has tapped phones at European Council headquarters in Brussels, the European Union (EU) delegation at the UN, and the EU embassy in Washington.[54] In late 2013, the *New York Times* reported there were "more than 1,000 targets of American and British surveillance in recent years," reaching down to even mid-level actors in the international arena. Apart from obvious subjects such as Israeli Prime Minister Ehud Olmert, the NSA and GCHQ monitored the vice-president of the European Commission responsible for antitrust issues; the French

---

[52] Ewen MacAskill et al., "GCHQ Taps Fibre-Optic Cables for Secret Access to World's Communications," *The Guardian*, June 21, 2013, www.guardian.co.uk/uk/2013/jun/21/gchq-cables-secret-world-communications-nsa.

[53] Richard Norton Taylor, "Not So Secret: Deal at the Heart of UK-US Intelligence," *The Guardian*, June 24, 2010, www.guardian.co.uk/world/2010/jun/25/intelligence-deal-uk-us-released; "Minutes of the Inauguration Meeting British Signal Intelligence Conference, 11–27 March 1946," in National Security Agency, UKUSA Agreement Release 1940–1956, https://web.archive.org/web/20130910015002/http://www.nsa.gov/public_info/declass/ukusa.shtml.

[54] Stephen Castle and Eric Schmitt, "Europeans Voice Anger over Reports of Spying by U.S. on Allies," *New York Times*, July 1, 2013; Ewen MacAskill and Julian Borger, "New NSA Leaks Show How US Is Bugging Its European Allies," *The Guardian*, June 30, 2013, www.guardian.co.uk/world/2013/jun/30/nsa-leaks-us-bugging-european-allies; Laura Poitras et al., "How the NSA Targets Germany and Europe," *Der Spiegel*, July 1, 2013, www.spiegel.de/international/world/secret-documents-nsa-targeted-germany-and-eu-buildings-a-908609.html.

energy company Total; German government communications; and even benign multilateral agencies such as UNICEF and the World Health Organization.[55]

Revelations from documents leaked by former NSA employee Edward Snowden in late 2013 indicate the NSA has monitored leaders in some thirty-five nations worldwide – including, Brazilian President Dilma Rousseff; Mexican Presidents Felipe Calderon and Enrique Peña Nieto; German Chancellor Angela Merkel; Indonesian President Susilo Bambang Yudhoyono; "French diplomatic interests" during the June 2010 UN vote on Iran sanctions; and "widespread surveillance" of world leaders during the Group 20 summit meeting at Ottawa in June 2010.[56]

Such secret intelligence about its allies gives Washington a significant diplomatic advantage. During UN wrangling over the US invasion of Iraq in 2002–2003, the NSA intercepted Secretary-General Kofi Anan's conversations and monitored the "Middle Six" of Third World nations on the UN Security Council to offer inducements that would win votes. The NSA's deputy chief for Regional Targets memoed its Five Eyes allies asking "for insights as to how membership is reacting to on-going debate RE: Iraq, plans to vote on any related resolutions ... the whole gamut of information that could give US policymakers an edge in obtaining results favorable to US goals."[57]

Indicating Washington's need for incriminating information in bilateral relations, the US State Department pressed its Bahrain embassy in 2009 for details, damaging in an Islamic society, on the crown princes, asking: "Is there any derogatory information on either prince? Does either prince drink alcohol? Does either one use drugs?"[58] Indeed, the NSA's director proposed, in October 2012, that in countering Muslim radicals, their "vulnerabilities, if exposed, would likely call into question a

---

[55] James Ball and Nick Hopkins, "GCHQ and NSA Targeted Charities, German, Israeli PM and EU Chief," *The Guardian*, December 20, 2013, www.theguardian.com/uk-news/2013/dec/20/gchq-targeted-aid-agencies-german-government-eu-commissioner; James Glanz and Andrew W. Lehren, "U.S. and Britain Extended Spying to 1,000 Targets," *New York Times*, December 21, 2013.

[56] Simon Romero and Randal C. Archibold, "Brazil Angered over Report N.S.A. Spied on President," *New York Times*, September 3, 2013; Alissa J. Rubin, "French Condemn Surveillance by N.S.A.," *New York Times*, October 22, 2013; Alison Smale, "Anger Growing among Allies on U.S. Spying," *New York Times*, October 24, 2014; David E. Sanger and Mark Mazzetti, "Allegation of U.S. Spying on German Leader Puts Obama at Crossroads," *New York Times*, October 25, 2013; Alison Smale, "Data Suggests U.S. Spying on Merkel Dates to '02," *New York Times*, October 28, 2013; Editorial, "More Damage from N.S.A. Snooping," *New York Times*, October 26, 2013; Mark Mazzetti and David E. Sanger, "Tap on Merkel Provides Peek at Vast Spy Net," *New York Times*, October 31, 2013; Joe Cochrane, "N.S.A. Spying Scandal Tarnishes Relations between Two Friendly Nations," *New York Times*, November 20, 2013; Ian Austen, "Ire in Canada over Report N.S.A. Spied from Ottawa," *New York Times*, November 29, 2013.

[57] James Bamford, *The Shadow Factory: The NSA From 9/11 to the Eavsdropping of America* (New York: Anchor, 2009), 141–142.

[58] Deptel 105048, State to Embassy Manama, October 8, 2009, *Wikileaks Cablegate Archive*, Reference ID: 09STATE105048, https://wikileaks.org/plusd/cables/09STATE105048_a.html.

radicalizer's devotion to the jihadist cause, leading to the degradation or loss of his authority." The agency suggested such vulnerabilities could include "viewing sexually explicit material online" or "using a portion of the donations they are receiving ... to defray personal expenses." The NSA document identified one potential target as a "respected academic" whose "vulnerabilities" are "online promiscuity."[59]

According to James Bamford, author of authoritative books on the agency: "The NSA's operation is eerily similar to the FBI's operations under J. Edgar Hoover in the 1960s where the bureau used wiretapping to discover vulnerabilities, such as sexual activity, to 'neutralize' their targets." Jameel Jaffer, of the American Civil Liberties Union (ACLU), warned some future US president might "ask the NSA to use the fruits of surveillance to discredit a political opponent, journalist or human rights activist. The NSA has used its power that way in the past and it would be naïve to think it couldn't use its power that way in the future."[60]

Just as the Internet has centralized communications, so it has moved much commercial sex into cyberspace. With an estimated 25 million salacious sites worldwide and a combined 10.6 *billion* page views *per month* at the five top sex sites in 2013,[61] online pornography had become, as of 2006, a $97 billion global business.[62] With millions of people watching pornography and almost none admitting it, the NSA has easy access to the embarrassing habits of targets worldwide, whether Muslim militants or European leaders.

Such digital surveillance has tremendous potential for scandal, exemplified by Elliot Spitzer's forced resignation in 2008 as governor of New York after routine phone taps revealed his use of escort services;[63] and the ouster of France's budget minister Jérôme Cahuzac in 2013 following wire taps that exposed his secret Swiss bank account.[64] Although the source for such revelations is often unclear, the basis of political scandal remains sex or money, both of which the NSA can easily track.

---

[59] Glenn Greenwald, Ryan Gallagher, and Ryan Grim, "Top-Secret Document Reveals NSA Spied on Porn Habits as Part of Plan to Discredit 'Radicalizers'," *Huffington Post*, November 26, 2013, www.huffingtonpost.com/2013/11/26/nsa-porn-muslims_n_4346128.html.
[60] Ibid.
[61] David Rosen, "Is Success Killing the Porn Industry," *Alternet*, May 27, 2013, www.alternet.org/sex-amp-relationships/success-killing-porn-industry.
[62] "Top Ten Reviews Reports Worldwide Pornography Market at Least $97 Billion," CISION PR Webb, July 5, 2022, www.prweb.com/releases/pornography/toptenreviews/prweb511051.htm.
[63] Alan Feuer, "Four Charged with Running Online Prostitution Ring," *New York Times*, March 7, 2008; Nico Pitney, "Spitzer as Client 9: Read Text Messages from Spitzer to Prostitute," *Huffington Post*, March 10, 2008, www.huffingtonpost.com/2008/03/10/spitzer-as-client-9-read-_n_90787.html.
[64] Angelique Chrisafis, "French Budget Minister Accused Of Hiding Swiss Bank Account," *The Guardian*, December 27, 2012, www.theguardian.com/world/2012/dec/27/french-budget-minister-swiss-account; Angelique Chrisafis, "France's Former Budget Minister Admits Lying about Secret Offshore Account," *The Guardian*, April 2, 2013, www.theguardian.com/world/2013/apr/02/jerome-cahuzac-france-offshore-account?INTCMP=SRCH.

The whistleblower Edward Snowden has accused the NSA of actually conducting such surveillance in a December 2013 letter to the Brazilian people, saying: "They even keep track of who is having an affair or looking at pornography, in case they need to damage their target's reputation."[65] If Snowden is right, then the aim for NSA monitoring of world leaders for collection of incriminating information represents striking continuity, across the span of a century, with the Constabulary's surveillance of Filipino leaders *circa* 1901.

Indicating the acute sensitivity of executive communications, world leaders have reacted sharply to reports of NSA surveillance – with Chancellor Angela Merkel demanding Five Eyes exempt status for Germany,[66] the European Parliament voting to curtail sharing of bank data with Washington,[67] and Brazil's President Dilma Rousseff both canceling a US state visit and contracting a $560 million satellite communications system to free her country from dependence on the Internet.[68]

FUTURE OF US GLOBAL POWER

By leaking a swelling stream of NSA documents, Edward Snowden has given us a glimpse of the changing architecture of US global power. At the broadest level, Obama's digital pivot complemented his overall defense strategy, announced in 2012, of cutting conventional forces while conserving America's power for "a combined arms campaign across all domains – land, air, maritime, space, and cyberspace."[69]

While cutting costly armaments, the Obama administration invested billions to build a new architecture for global information control. If we add the $791 billion expended on the Department of Homeland Security to the $500 billion for global intelligence in the dozen years after 9/11, then Washington made a $1.2 trillion

---

[65] Edward Snowden, "An Open Letter to the People of Brazil," *Folha de S. Paulo*, December 16, 2013, www1.folha.uol.com.br/internacional/en/world/2013/12/1386296-an-open-letter-to-the-people-of-brazil.shtml.
[66] Alison Smale, "Surveillance Revelations Shake U.S.–German Ties," *New York Times*, August 26, 2013; Alison Smale, "Indignation over Spying on Merkel May Harm U.S.," *New York Times*, October 25, 2013; Smale, "Anger Growing among Allies on U.S. Spying," *New York Times*, October 24, 2013.
[67] "Arrival and Doorstep by Martin Schulz, President of the European Parliament, Prior to the European Council Taking Place on 24 October 2013 in Brussels," *TV Newsroom – European Council of the EU*, http://tvnewsroom.consilium.europa.eu/video/shotlist/arrival-and-doorstep-ep-president-schulz4.
[68] "Brazil Will Have Its Own National-Made Secure Communications Satellite by 2016," *MercoPress* (Montevideo), November 29, 2013, http://en.mercopress.com/2013/11/29/brazil-will-have-its-own-national-made-secure-communications-satellite-by-2016.
[69] Julian E. Barnes and Nathan Hodge, "Military Faces Historic Shift," *Wall Street Journal*, January 6, 2012; US Department of Defense, *Sustaining U.S. Global Leadership: Priorities for 21st Century Defense* (Washington DC: US Department of Defense, January 2012), 2–5, https://archive.defense.gov/news/Defense_Strategic_Guidance.pdf.

investment in a new apparatus for world power.[70] In the aftermath of Snowden's damaging revelations about US global surveillance, Obama's executive review recommended regularization, not reform, of current NSA practices, allowing the agency to continue monitoring foreign leaders and collecting Americans' phone calls into the foreseeable future.[71]

Reflecting a long-term downward trajectory in US global power and its inept application under President Donald Trump, Washington suffered a series of stunning reverses in cyberspace during his administration. According to the Senate Intelligence Committee, during the 2016 presidential election, Russian intelligence, working through the Internet Research Agency, "used social media to conduct an information warfare campaign destined to spread disinformation and societal division," which was, in fact, "part of a broader, sophisticated and ongoing information warfare campaign."[72] Worse was yet come. In March 2017, the hackers' website *Wikileaks* released a kit of the CIA's top-secret hacking tools, forcing the agency to notify allies of a serious breach in its security.[73] In the administration's last weeks, the private cybersecurity firm FireEye notified the US government of a possible breach that turned out to be massive. In an operation "whose sophistication stunned even experts," Russian security services had inserted a Trojan horse software upgrade into 18,000 private and government users – including Treasury, Commerce, State, Homeland Security, and the Pentagon.[74] In the modern world, a global hegemon hacks the computers of subordinate nations; a declining power, by contrast, gets hacked.

As the disparity grows between Washington's global reach and its withering mailed fist, as it struggles to maintain 40 percent of the world's armaments *circa* 2012 with only 23 percent of its economic output, the United States will need to find ways to exercise

---

[70] Mattea Kramer and Chris Hellman, "'Homeland Security', the Trillion-Dollar Concept that No One Can Define," *TomDispatch*, February 28, 2013, www.tomdispatch.com/blog/175655; Scott Shane, "New Leaked Document Outlines U.S. Spending on Intelligence Agencies," *New York Times*, August 30, 2013.

[71] David E. Sanger, "Obama Panel Said to Urge N.S.A. Curbs," *New York Times*, December 13, 2013.

[72] US Senate, 116 Congress, 1st Session, *Report of the Select Committee on Intelligence, United States Senate on Russian Active Measures Campaigns and Interference in the 2016 U.S. Election.* Volume 2: *Russia's Use of Social Media with Additional Views* (Washington DC: US Senate, 2019), 1–22, www.intelligence.senate.gov/sites/default/files/documents/Report_Volume2.pdf.

[73] Greg Miller and Ellen Nakshima, "Wikileaks Says It Has Obtained a Trove of CIA Hacking Tools," *Washington Post*, March 7, 2017, www.washingtonpost.com/world/national-security/wikileaks-says-it-has-obtained-trove-of-cia-hacking-tools/2017/03/07/c8c50c5c-0345-11e7-b1e9-a05d3c21f7cf_story.html; Ellen Nakashima and Shane Harris, "Elite CIA Unit that Developed Hacking Tools Failed to Secure Its Own Systems, Allowing Massive Leak, an Internal Report Found," *Washington Post*, June 16, 2020, www.washingtonpost.com/national-security/elite-cia-unit-that-developed-hacking-tools-failed-to-secure-its-own-systems-allowing-massive-leak-an-internal-report-found/2020/06/15/502e3456-ae9d-11ea-8f56-63f38c990077_story.html.

[74] David E. Sanger, Nicole Perlroth, and Eric Schmitt, "Scope of Russian Hacking Becomes Clear: Multiple U.S. Agencies Were Hit," *New York Times*, December 14, 2020, www.nytimes.com/2020/12/14/us/politics/russia-hack-nsa-homeland-security-pentagon.html.

its global power more economically.[75] In the early years of the Cold War *circa* 1950, the enormous cost of maintaining the US military's global presence with 500 bases worldwide was sustainable since the country controlled some 50 percent of gross world product.[76] But as its share of world output falls to 17 percent by 2016 and its social welfare costs climb from 4 percent of GDP in 2010 to 18 percent by 2050, savings become imperative for Washington's survival as a world power.[77]

Along with cyberwarfare, digital surveillance offers Washington a cost-effective means for the exercise of global power. Current computer technology allows the NSA to conduct global surveillance that is both far more pervasive and far less expensive than earlier espionage. With a few hundred cable probes and computerized decryption, the NSA can now capture the kind of gritty details of private life that J. Edgar Hoover once collected and provide the sort of comprehensive coverage of entire populations epitomized by secret police like East Germany's Stasi. Once Hoover's FBI agents had tapped thousands of phones, stenographers had typed up countless transcripts, and clerks had stored this salacious paper harvest in floor-to-ceiling filing cabinets, J. Edgar Hoover still only knew about the inner-workings of the elite in one city: Washington DC. To gain the same intimate detail for an entire country, the German Democratic Republic's Stasi had to employ one police informer for every six East Germans – an unsustainable allocation of human resources.[78] By contrast, the marriage of the NSA's technology to the Internet's data hubs *circa* 2012 allowed the agency's 37,000 employees a similarly close coverage of the entire globe at the cost-effective ratio of just one operative for every 200,000 people on the planet.[79]

Compared to the $2 trillion cost for US military intervention in Afghanistan,[80] the NSA's 2012 budget of just $11 billion for both worldwide surveillance and

---

[75] Sam Perlo-Freeman et al., *Trends in World Military Expenditure*, 2012 (Stockholm: Stockholm International Peace Research Institute, 2013), 2; Åsa Johansson et al., "Looking to 2060: Long-Term Global Growth Prospects: A Going for Growth Report," *OECD Economic Policy Papers*, no. 3 (OECD Publishing, 2012), fig. 10, 23.

[76] *Chicago Daily Tribune*, September 11, 1954 and February 14, 1955; James R. Blaker, *United States Overseas Basing: An Anatomy of the Dilemma* (New York: Praeger, 1990), table 2; Julian Go, *Patterns of Empire: The British and American Empires, 1688 to Present* (Cambridge University Press, 2011), 170.

[77] International Monetary Fund, "World Economic Outlook Database," April 2011 edition, www.imf.org/external/pubs/ft/weo/2011/01/weodata/index.aspx; Mark Weisbrot, "2016 When China Overtakes the US," *The Guardian*, April 27, 2011, www.guardian.co.uk/commentisfree/cifamerica/2011/apr/27/china-imf-economy-2016; Michael Mandelbaum, *The Frugal Superpower: America's Global Leadership in a Cash-Strapped Era* (Philadelphia: Public Affairs, 2010), 20, 46–52, 185.

[78] John O. Koehler, *Stasi: The Untold Story of the East German Police* (Boulder, CO: Westview Press, 1999), www.nytimes.com/books/first/k/koehler-stasi.html.

[79] Camille Tuutti, "Introverted? Then NSA Wants You," *FCW: The Business of Federal Technology*, April 16, 2012, https://fcw.com/blogs/circuit/2012/04/fedsmc-chris-inglis-federal-workforce.aspx.

[80] Sarah Almukhtar and Rod Nordland, "What Did the U.S. Get for $2 Trillion in Afghanistan, *New York Times*, December 9, 2019, www.nytimes.com/interactive/2019/12/09/world/middleeast/afghanistan-war-cost.html.

cyberwarfare is a cost-savings that Washington can ill afford to forego.[81] Even at the end of Obama's term in 2016, US dominance of the cyber domain was so complete, and the promise of its future yield was so enticing, that the White House refused any check on its prerogatives, even at the cost of alienating close allies.

Yet in the marketplace of military ideas, even a crushing technological advantage is soon lost. Washington was quick to weaponize the Internet, forming its Cyber Command in 2009 and deploying computer viruses against Iran's nuclear facilities. But even then, Russia was not far behind, using cyberstrikes to cripple Georgia's computers in 2008 and later disable Ukraine's electrical grid – prompting NATO's security summit in 2016 to make cyberspace a new domain for military operations.[82] Not only did that St. Petersburg "troll factory," the Internet Research Agency, try to influence the 2016 US presidential elections, but Russian hackers soon stole some of the NSA's top-secret cyber tools and later achieved a massive breach of US computer communications.[83] Showing the accessibility of cyberwar even to secondary powers, in 2011 Iranian intelligence hacked into the navigation system of the CIA's super-secret RQ-170 Sentinel drone and forced one to land for plunder of its top-secret technology.[84] The digital surveillance and cyberwarfare that seemed, as late as 2016, wonder weapons capable extending US global dominion, have quickly become just another dangerous arena for military conflict, accessible to powers large and small.

---

[81] Scott Shane, "New Leaked Document Outlines U.S. Spending on Intelligence Agencies," *New York Times*, August 30, 2013.

[82] John Markoff, "Before the Gunfire, Cyberattacks," *New York Times*, August 12, 2008, www.nytimes.com/2008/08/13/technology/13cyber.html; Andy Greenberg, "New Clues Show How Russia's Grid Hackers Aimed for Physical Destruction," *Wired*, September 12, 2019, www.wired.com/story/russia-ukraine-cyberattack-power-grid-blackout-destruction; David E. Sanger, "As Russian Hackers Probe, NATO Has No Clear Cyberwar Strategy," *New York Times*, June 16, 2016, www.nytimes.com/2016/06/17/world/europe/nato-russia-cyberwarfare.html.

[83] Neil MacFarquhar, "Inside the Russian Troll Factory: Zombies and a Breakneck Pace," *New York Times*, February 18, 2018, www.nytimes.com/2018/02/18/world/europe/russia-troll-factory.html; Scott Shane, Nicole Perlroth, and David E. Sanger, "Security Breach and Spilled Secrets Have Shaken the N.S.A. to Its Core," *New York Times*, November 12, 2017, www.nytimes.com/2017/11/12/us/nsa-shadow-brokers.html.

[84] Andrew Cockburn, *Kill Chain: The Rise of High-Tech Assassins* (New York: Picador, 2016), 256; Scott Peterson, "Exclusive: Iran Hijacked US Drone, Says Iranian Engineer," *Christian Science Monitor*, December 15, 2011, www.csmonitor.com/World/Middle-East/2011/1215/Exclusive-Iran-hijacked-US-drone-says-Iranian-engineer.

4

The Racialisation of British Women during the Long Nineteenth Century

How White Women's Bodies Became Tools of Control and Surveillance

Toni Weller

As David Hillman and Ulrika Maud note, 'the body has always been a contested site'.[1] This chapter applies Sara Ahmed's position that the racialisation of bodies occurs through a differentiation between bodies on the grounds of Otherness, and argues that the period between 1780 and the outbreak of World War I in 1914 witnessed a distinctive chapter in the racialisation of British women.[2] Racialisation is, as Ahmed asserts, a *process* that takes place in time and space, and which has 'multiple histories'.[3] Surveillance likewise can be understood as a process as much as an act, and is 'historically present not just in technology or statecraft, but also in society and culture'.[4] During this 'long' nineteenth century between 1780 and 1914, the long-standing idea that women were biologically distinct from men became, for the first time, legitimised by science and the Victorian state, and women's physical bodies themselves became platforms for surveillance. In a period which has been recognised by many as a turning point for overt information collection, women became almost literal information objects.[5]

---

[1] David Hillman and Ulrika Maud, 'Introduction', in David Hillman and Ulrika Maud (eds.), *Cambridge Companion to the Body in Literature* (Cambridge University Press, 2015), 1.
[2] Sara Ahmed, *Strange Encounters: Embodied Others in Post-Coloniality* (New York: Routledge, 2000).
[3] Sara Ahmed, 'Racialized Bodies', in Mary Evans and Ellie Lee (eds.), *Real Bodies: A Sociological Introduction* (Basingstoke: Palgrave, 2002), 46–63.
[4] Toni Weller, 'The Historical Ubiquity of Surveillance', in Andreas Maklund and Laura Skouvig (eds.), *Histories of Surveillance from Antiquity to the Digital Era: The Eyes and Ears of Power* (London: Routledge, 2021), 163.
[5] On the significance of information as a concept during the nineteenth century see Toni Weller (ed.), *Information History in the Modern World. Histories of the Information Age* (Basingstoke: Palgrave, 2011); and Ann Blair et al. (eds.), *Information: A Historical Companion* (New Jersey: Princeton University Press, 2021), amongst many others.

Over this period 'changing ideas about sexual difference between women and men informed women's experience',[6] and these challenged the ways in which constructions of race and constructions of gender interlinked. Nineteenth-century concepts of race were less fixed than we might understand them to be today – understandings of class, gender, and race were fluid across the century and fed into broader contemporary discourses of nationalism and power. As Crenshaw has asserted about the American experience of women in this period, modern feminist discussions often fail because of an assumption that race, gender, sexuality, and class are 'mutually exclusive', when they are not.[7] Others have shown that historically 'the discourse on race has been too narrowly defined in black and white terms'.[8] Gender has often been overlooked by surveillance scholars but 'gender and sexuality were intensely controlled by social and moral norms', and surveillance itself has been 'full of male assumptions'.[9] Surveillance has a historical ubiquity which feeds into the discourses of the period.[10] In taking a broader view of how gender, class, and race interlinked during the nineteenth century, it is possible to identify distinct shifts in the ways in which white British women were perceived to be the Other, an almost literal and physical race apart from men, with their very biology forming the essence of this racialisation.

As Evelyn Brooks Higginbotham has argued, race can operate as a metalanguage, speaking for other hierarchies of difference, whether of gender or class.[11] This idea of an interconnection between race and gender in particular, has been supported by other scholars who suggest that race and gender came into existence 'in and through relation to each other'.[12] During the nineteenth century, women were often regarded as so biologically and inherently different from men that they could be treated and considered, in Victorian terms, as racially different. As we shall see, the mainstream acceptance of 'hysteria' as a female malady within nineteenth-century medicine and science, combined with an emergent Victorian central state, led to surveillance techniques which could focus upon women's physical bodies and

---

[6] Lynn Abrams, *The Making of the Modern Woman: Europe 1789–1918* (London: Longman, 2002), 2.
[7] See Kimberlé W. Crenshaw, 'Mapping the Margins: Intersectionality, Identity Politics, and Violence against Women of Colour', *Stanford Law Review* 43, no. 6 (1991): 1241–1299, 1242. This idea of the fluidity of class, race, and gender is especially well discussed by theorists such as Patricia Hill Collins, Evelyn Nakano Glenn, Michael Omi, and Howard Winant.
[8] Barbara Ryan (ed.), *Identity Politics in the Women's Movement* (New York University Press, 2001), 85.
[9] Hille Koskela, '"You Shouldn't Wear that Body": The Problematic of Surveillance and Gender', in Kirsty Ball, Kevin D. Haggerty, and David Lyon (eds.), *Routledge Handbook of Surveillance Studies* (London: Routledge, 2012), 49.
[10] Weller, 'The Historical Ubiquity of Surveillance', 163–179.
[11] Evelyn Brooks Higginbotham, 'African American Women's History and the Metalanguage of Race', *Signs* 17 (1992): 251–274.
[12] Anne McClintock, *Imperial Leather: Race, Gender and Sexuality in the Colonial Context* (New York: Routledge, 1995), 4–5.

behaviours. The state's involvement further legitimised these interplaying ideas of race, gender, and power since 'the impact of state action or inaction is gendered, affecting men as a group and women as a group differently'.[13] Although the specific experience of women may have differed, the processes which allowed women's bodies to become racialised, identified as Other compared to men, were emergent throughout this period. Indeed, Sara Ahmed has shown we cannot understand the more modern notion of race without reference to embodiment.[14]

The most significant differences between women came from social class although there were, of course, more overt racial differences of colour, notably between white women of the British Empire (with their perceived moral superiority) and women from the colonies.[15] White women were certainly identified as being distinct from black women, but it is too simplistic to suggest that the racialisation of women during the nineteenth century was focused purely around this more modern notion of colour. Moreover, we 'cannot isolate the production of racial bodies from the gendering and sexualizing of bodies'.[16] Women's roles as child bearers became increasingly significant during the nineteenth century as colonialising discourses emphasised the supremacy of the (white) British race. Since it was women, and not men, who would give birth to future generations of Britons, the behaviour and bodies of women became of greater interest to science, state, and medicine. Consequently, constructions of female identity and the physical surveillance of female bodies by men and the male dominated state, had a profound impact on the way in which these drivers of identity and surveillance interwove with the racialisation of women into the twentieth century.

The notion of women having a natural place in the home had a long heritage but throughout this period there was a development of new ideas about women and their roles and behaviours.[17] As far back as the sixteenth century men and women were accepted as having natural 'separate spheres' of experience and authority, with the domestic setting believed to be the place that was best suited to a woman's natural sensibilities and strengths. The works of Jean-Jacques Rousseau popularised the ideology of domesticity and motherhood for women (although fiercely contested by some women, notably Mary Wollstonecraft).[18] However, the impact of

---

[13] Jan Jindy Pettmen, *Worlding Women: A Feminist International Politics* (New York: Routledge, 2005), 9.
[14] Ahmed, 'Racialized Bodies'.
[15] See, e.g., Catherine Hall, Keith McClelland and Jane Rendall (eds.), *Defining the Victorian Nation: Class, Race, Gender and the Reform Act of 1867* (Cambridge University Press, 2000), 53–54; Abrams, *The Making of the Modern Woman*, 243–263.
[16] Ahmed, 'Racialized Bodies', 47.
[17] For the heritage of these ideas see Amanda Vickery, 'Golden Age to Separate Spheres? A Review of the Categories and Chronology of English Women's History', *Historical Journal* 36, no. 2 (1993): 383–414; Richard Price, *British Society 1680–1880: Dynamism and Change* (Cambridge University Press, 1999); Abrams, *The Making of the Modern Woman*.
[18] See, e.g., Jean-Jacques Rousseau, *Emile, or, On Education* (London, 1783) and Mary Wollstonecraft, *A Vindication of the Rights of Woman* (London: J. Johnson, 1792).

Enlightenment thought and medical science legitimised the idea that there was a more fundamental difference 'between male and female in relation to minds, moral constructions, capacities and roles'.[19] This 'separate spheres' ideology remained a consistently powerful driver in British society during from the latter decades of the 1700s into the pre-war years of the 1900s. A woman's body was deemed to be unstable, unable to be controlled by the woman herself. Her 'wandering womb' – the belief that the womb was not fixed inside the body but moved freely if not put to its 'proper' purpose of reproduction – was believed to cause fits of hysteria that also affected the mind.[20] Derived from the Greek *hystera*, meaning womb, this 'female malady' became 'associated with the sexuality and essential nature of women'.[21] For women, it was considered inevitable that they should suffer from such disorders – their biology made it unavoidable. Men, on the other hand, with their different physiology and lack of womb, were regarded as exempt from such conditions. Science justified, therefore, that it should be men who needed to cure and control such specifically female maladies of the body and mind.

By the nineteenth century 'hysteria' was used to cover a myriad of female symptoms from fainting, dizziness, and tiredness but also, and increasingly, acts of defiance or independence. The doctor Edward Tilt was far from alone when he argued in 1851 that menstruation gave rise to monthly nervousness and hysteria.[22] As Elaine Showalter has shown in her magnificent study of madness, lunacy was associated with all parts of female reproduction from menstruation and pregnancy to lactation and menopause.[23] These were all signs of 'uterine disorder' caused, so argued the medical men such as Tilt, by a failure to follow the path intended by nature.[24] Even a woman who dutifully followed the path of marriage and children could still end up with inevitable physical and mental breakdowns due to the inherent fragility and instability of the female body and mind – an argument often applied where a woman had demonstrated a desire for autonomy or to challenge existing social norms. As Abrams has shown, the cure 'according to those doctors who chose to specialise in female nervous complaints, was either marriage and children or complete rest and deprivation of any sensory stimulation'.[25] Or, in more extreme cases where these suggestions had not worked, physicians recommended

---

[19] Abrams, *The Making of the Modern Woman*, 3.
[20] Ibid.
[21] Elaine Showalter, *The Female Malady: Women, Madness and English Culture, 1830–1980* (London: Virago, 1987), 7.
[22] Edward Tilt, *On the Preservation on the Health of Women ay the Critical Periods of Life* (London, 1851). Some other contemporary examples also on this theme: Lionel Weatherly, *The Young Wife's Own Book* (London: Griffith and Farran, 1882); George Black, *The Young Wife's Advice Book* (London: Ward, Tilt and Co., 1888); Robert Reid Rentoul, *The Dignity of Women's Health and the Nemesis of Its Neglect* (London: J. & A. Churchill, 1890).
[23] Showalter, *The Female Malady*. See also Ji Won Chung, *Picturing Women's Health* (New York: Routledge, 2015).
[24] Abrams, *The Making of the Modern Woman*, 24–25.
[25] Ibid., 25.

gynaecological surgery, which was an especially popular choice during the 1860s.[26] In 1893 one male doctor claimed that such surgery made women 'tractable, orderly, industrious and cleanly'.[27] Some public female figures such as Florence Nightingale, openly challenged being forced into the bodily confines of acceptable behaviour, such as with her 1852 essay *Cassandra*.[28] Others suffered more privately.[29] Moreover, such medical opinions easily crossed into the public consciousness as research was published not just by the scientific journals of the day but also by popular periodicals with ever-increasing circulation.[30]

This idea of female fragility was not therefore new to the nineteenth century, but the influence of Victorian science, rationality, control, and order, as applied to so many other aspects of the nineteenth-century experience, suggested that the female body and mind could, and should, also be ordered and controlled. This expectation was also reinforced by Victorian culture – from notions of women as *The Angel in the House*, as based on Coventry Patmore's titular poem of 1854, to the nineteenth-century popularity of the mythical *Pygmalion* which, as Bettany Hughes has noted, sustained 'the notion that women were moulded and made by men'.[31] Art historians have noted that even in much Victorian art 'the female body seems possessed', representing the mental and bodily psychosis that could befall women if they were not properly contained.[32] As Lyn Abrams has shown, the authority of what was happening to a woman's body 'shifted from she who experienced the bodily sensations to he who observed the symptoms'.[33] For women, surveillance became physical, biological, and racialised in a way it was not, and could never be, for men.

While surveillance and control of this kind was done under the auspices of a woman's own good, or protecting herself from herself, there was a shift in emphasis as the nineteenth century progressed. A woman's role was understood to be in the domestic sphere, protecting the home and family, producing the next generation of British citizens and soldiers. Those who transgressed this natural order most

[26] See, e.g., Barbara Ehrenreich and Deidre English, *For Her Own Good: Two Centuries of the Experts' Advice to Women* (New York: Anchor Books, 2005).
[27] G. J. Barker-Benfield, *The Horrors of the Half-Known Life: Male Attitudes Toward Women and Sexuality in 19th Century America* (New York: Routledge, 2004), 122.
[28] Florence Nightingale, *Cassandra: An Essay* (New York: The Feminist Press, 1979 [1852]).
[29] An excellent discussion of this is Victoria Glendinning, *A Suppressed Cry: Life and Death of a Quaker Daughter* (London: Routledge & Kegan Paul, 1969), which discusses the life of Winnie Seebohm during the end of the nineteenth century, and her experience at Newnham College, Cambridge.
[30] See Karen Flint, *The Woman Reader, 1837–1914* (Oxford: Clarendon Press, 1993), 53; Toni Weller, 'The Puffery and Practicality of Etiquette Books: A New Take on Victorian Information Culture', *Library Trends* 62, no. 3 (2014): 663–680.
[31] Bettany Hughes, *Venus and Aphrodite. History of a Goddess* (London: Weidenfeld & Nicolson, 2020), 185.
[32] S. P. Casteras, *The Substance or the Shadow: Images of Victorian Womanhood* (New Haven, CT: Yale Center for British Art, 1982), 169.
[33] Abrams, *The Making of the Modern Woman*, 23.

vehemently were female prostitutes who were not only neglecting their moral duties at home but who were also blamed for spreading venereal disease through the army – a transgression, it was argued, which weakened the defences of the nation and the national health as a whole.[34] In response, the government enacted the Contagious Diseases Act of 1864 which was re-enacted and expanded in 1866 and again in 1869. The Acts applied to port and garrison towns and gave police special powers to apprehend women they believed guilty of prostitution or having venereal disease. Any women arrested under the 1864 Act were thereafter legally subjected to regular medical inspections or detained in a hospital for three months until physicians believed that she was cured of any venereal disease. It was not possible to tell for sure if any venereal disease had been cured without a blood test; such tests did not become available until 1906, causing a great deal of subjective opinion over whether women should be detailed or released.[35] Contemporaries noted that male 'pests' were not subject to the same judgment or legislation as women.[36] In terms of the racialisation of woman, as Pettman argues, these 'powerful associations of the female body with sexuality suggest other uses of the woman/colonised analogy' during the long nineteenth century.[37] The unique nature of female biology made state surveillance a gendered phenomenon, but it was also inherently a racialised one. Processes of racialisation involve the use of biological criteria, in this case a women's sexual health, 'to separate people into distinct groups for the purpose of domination and exploitation'.[38] Arguably, the Contagious Diseases Acts legislated for this very construct. A woman who was using her body to fulfil her moral duty at home was not just perpetuating the British race with future citizens and soldiers, but also maintaining the (white) British Empire at home. The very 'whiteness' of women was used as a boundary, and, as Laura Brown has suggested, this resulted in gender and race identities becoming deeply connected in male colonising discourses.[39]

Since most doctors and police were male, it was by default largely men monitoring women in a 'male-administered world of state authority'.[40] Judith Walkowitz

[34] Martha Vicinus (ed.), *Suffer and Be Still: Women in the Victorian Age* (London: Methuen, 1980).
[35] E. M. Sigsworth and T. J. Wyke, 'A Study of Victorian Prostitution and Venereal Disease', in Martha Vicinus (ed.), *Suffer and Be Still. Women in the Victorian Age* (London: Methuen, 1980), 77–99.
[36] See, e.g., contemporary reports by women of being harassed by men in the street or on public transport such as *Pall Mall Gazette*, xlvi, 19 July 1887, 6969. Also L. Bland, 'Purifying the Public World: Feminist Vigilantes in Late Victorian England', *Women's History Review* 1, no. 3 (1992): 397–412.
[37] Pettmen, *Worlding Women*, 37.
[38] Joshua F. Inwood and Robert A. Yarbrough, 'Racialized Places, Racialized Bodies: The Impact of Racialization on Individual and Place Identities', *GeoJournal* 75 (2010): 299–301.
[39] Laura Brown, *Ends of Empire: Women and Ideology in Early Eighteenth Century English Literature* (Ithaca, NY: Cornell University Press, 1993), 19.
[40] M. J. D. Roberts, 'Feminism and the State in Later Victorian England', *Historical Journal* 38, no. 1 (1995): 85–110, 106.

describes the 'coarse brutality' of the male doctors doing the examinations, having no more than three minutes per exam, and using instruments still hot from boiling water, if sterilised at all.[41] The Acts mandated that women receive highly invasive tests 'on the mere suspicion of prostitution'.[42] One contemporary woman described the Acts in terms of both gender and race, stating that 'women are now treated as white slaves'.[43] Richard Price goes as far as to suggest that the Contagious Diseases Acts 'endorsed the symbolic and arbitrary rape of women by the state'.[44] Yet there was fierce opposition to the Acts by many contemporaries. Between 1870 and 1885 there were over 17,000 petitions against the Acts with over 2.6 million signatures presented to Parliament.[45] Despite this it took until 1886 for the Acts to be repealed, over twenty years after they were first introduced, and during which time over 5,000 women had been subjected to vaginal examinations with no evidence of venereal disease.[46] The Acts, argued Lynn Abrams, 'were more successful in controlling women than disease'.[47]

Richard Price suggests that the Contagious Diseases Acts 'gave the lie to the notion of the Victorian state as a laissez-faire formation. Their interventionalism transgressed the most intimate boundaries of the public and private spheres'.[48] Since police could come to a woman's home and demand that she be examined, if they suspected her of having venereal disease, it became impossible to keep public and private worlds separate. As Judith Walkowitz has suggested, a home visit was so public that everyone knew that a woman had been accused of prostitution and judged her accordingly, irrespective of actual evidence.[49] Any respectability was irrefutably damaged after such a visit. Indeed, 'public shaming was one of the principal functions of police registration and surveillance'.[50] Middle-class women were less targeted by police under the Contagious Diseases Acts, which tended to focus on working-class or poorer women who were more likely to succumb to prostitution. However, the significance of this was felt by all women since it emphasised the importance of appropriate dress

---

[41] Judith Walkowitz, 'The Making of an Outcast Group: Prostitutes and Working Women in Nineteenth Century Plymouth and Southampton' in Martha Vicinus (ed.), A Widening Sphere: Changing Roles of Victorian Women (London: Methuen, 1980), 72–93, quotation from 81.
[42] Price, British Society 1680–1880, 223.
[43] Mary Ann Godden, as told to Josephine Butler in Josephine Butler, 'The Garrison Towns of Kent', The Shield, 25 April 1870, 62.
[44] Price, British Society 1680–1880, 223.
[45] Sigsworth and Wyke, 'A Study of Victorian Prostitution and Venereal Disease', 77. See also B. Scott, A State Inequity (London, 1890).
[46] Price, British Society 1680–1880, 223.
[47] Abrams, The Making of the Modern Woman, 155.
[48] Price, British Society 1680–1880, 223.
[49] Walkowitz, 'The Making of an Outcast Group', 82.
[50] Ibid., 83.

codes and respectable behaviour – behaviour which stifled Victorian women so much that Florence Nightingale described it as 'death in life'.[51]

Sara Ahmed notes that 'racialization involves ... the constitution of both social and bodily space in the everyday encounters we have with others'.[52] For the Victorians, and for Victorian women in particular, these everyday encounters were heavily regulated in the form of behavioural etiquette, with one writer from 1834 suggested that social etiquette was a barrier that society drew around itself to protect against 'offences the "law" cannot touch'.[53] Another from 1845 suggested that etiquette was vital to 'establish a standard of one kind or another'.[54] Victorian etiquette can be understood as a way of self-regulating society and controlling behaviour, where deviation from the accepted norms resulted in others making value judgements about your character and respectability.[55] Women themselves were often, as Martha Vicinus has argued, 'the greatest enforcers of standards of moral behaviour'.[56] Anthony Giddens has termed surveillance as a form of 'social supervision', and arguably the potency of Victorian 'respectability' created an informal and cultural social surveillance amongst women themselves – a kind of social panopticon, that was enacted by society, etiquette, and social conventions.[57]

Such social respectability was essential to the Victorian frame of mind. Critically, it was also essentially linked with racial ideology in a way that is fundamentally different to twenty-first-century thought. Throughout the nineteenth century, ideas of racial difference were as much about social distinctions as they were differences in skin colour. While undoubtedly the Victorians used race as a measure of superiority and inferiority, its markers were more complex than black and white. As David Cannadine has argued, industrialisation and the dirty, overcrowded, 'masses' of the new cities were compared by many British with 'the "dark continents" overseas, and thus equate[d] the workers in factories with coloured people abroad'.[58] More than this, 'the English lower classes were to 19th-century eyes as racially different as were Africans or Asians'.[59] White middle-class Victorian women, as the bastions of the British race,

---

[51] Nightingale, *Cassandra*, 12.
[52] Ahmed, 'Racialized Bodies', 47.
[53] Charles William Day, *Hints on Etiquette and the Usages of Society* (London, 1834), 9.
[54] A Member of the Royal Household, *The Book of Fashionable Life* (London, 1845), 11.
[55] On etiquette as a social regulator see Toni Weller, *The Victorians and Information: A Social and Cultural History* (Saarbrucken: VDM Verlag, 2009), 57–86.
[56] Vicinus (ed.), *Suffer and Be Still*, xiv.
[57] Anthony Giddens, *The Consequences of Modernity* (Oxford: Polity Press, 1990), 59. On the idea of a social panopticon, see, e.g., Weller, *The Victorians and Information*, 57–86; Toni Weller, 'The Information State: An Historical Perspective on Surveillance' in Kirsty Ball, Kevin D. Haggerty and David Lyon (eds.), *Routledge Handbook of Surveillance Studies* (London: Routledge, 2012), 57–63.
[58] David Cannadine, *Ornamentalism: How the British Saw Their Empire* (London: Allen Lane, 2001), 5.
[59] Kenan Malik, 'Why the Victorians Were Colour Blind', *New Statesman*, 7 May 2001, Culture Supplement; Cannadine, *Ornamentalism*, 125.

were therefore intrinsically judged in racial terms as much as gender or societal. The way in which they *behaved*, or fell short of social standards, was considered a justifiable cause for increasing social, sexual, and corporeal surveillance.

Surveillance of any kind necessitated the collection of information on individuals and the Victorian period saw the state clearly emerge 'as a vehicle for collecting personal information on citizens'.[60] Physical identifying information on an individual formed part of this development with information largely collected at local levels until after the outbreak of war in 1914.[61] At a centralised level, the Victorian information state demonstrated nascent forms of bureaucratic and organised information collection and surveillance, under the aegis of providing both state support for its citizens (an embryonic form of welfare), and the protection of its citizens from perceived threats (or warfare).[62] With their emphasis on deviants, potential threats to the stability of the nation and their legitimised bodily surveillance of women, the Contagious Diseases Acts can be viewed as an alternate facet to the rise of the information state during this period.[63] The high mortality and poor health of the army was seen as a driver to necessitate and legitimise state action. The Times newspaper described the Act of 1864 as 'a creature of State necessity. It has particular claims on the State ... [since] the government ... is responsible for the health of the army and navy.'[64] It was, therefore, the state's duty to intervene as a matter of public safety. There was 'an echo of the utilitarian reasoning which Edwin Chadwick had earlier advanced in favour of general public health legislation'.[65] The medical journal *The Lancet* put forward a similar view:

> It is only insofar as a woman exercises trade [i.e. prostitution] which is physically dangerous to the community that Government has any right to interfere. It does so on the same grounds that it claims to interfere with a railway when in a dangerous condition.[66]

---

[60] Toni Weller, 'Conclusion', in Toni Weller (Ed.), *Information History in the Modern World. Histories of the Information Age* (Basingstoke: Palgrave, 2011), 201.

[61] See Edward Higgs, *The Information State in England: The Central Collection of Information on Citizens Since 1500* (Basingstoke: Palgrave, 2004); Paul Stiff, Paul Dobraszczyk, and Mike Esbester, 'Designing and Gathering Information: Perspectives on Nineteenth Century Forms', in Toni Weller (ed.), *Information History in the Modern World. Histories of the Information Age* (Basingstoke: Palgrave, 2011), 57–88; Craig Robertson, 'Documents, Empire and Capitalism in the Nineteenth Century', in Blair et al. (eds.), *Information: A Historical Companion*, 152–173.

[62] See Jon Agar, *The Government Machine: A Revolutionary History of the Computer* (Cambridge, MA: MIT Press, 2003); Higgs, *The Information State in England*; Toni Weller, 'The Victorian Information Age: Nineteenth Century Answers to Today's Information Policy Questions?', *History & Policy*, June 2010, www.historyandpolicy.org/policy-papers/papers/the-victorian-information-age-nineteenth-century-answers-to-todays-informat; Weller, 'The Information State', 57–63.

[63] See Weller, 'The Information State', 57–63.

[64] *The Times*, 25 August 1863, 6.

[65] Sigsworth and Wyke, 'A Study of Victorian Prostitution and Venereal Disease', 93.

[66] *The Lancet*, 27 November 1869 (II), 729.

Such comparisons between the intimate physical surveillance of women and inanimate machinery reveals much about how medical and state authorities considered women's bodies, or at least those of degenerate prostitutes. Such women were regarded as racially inferior to men, whose biologically different bodies could not be 'dangerous to the community' in the same way. However, 'state surveillance and information collection for the purposes of welfare were often precipitated by economic or political crisis and also often the desire by the state to keep a check on potential deviants'.[67] In this context, women were seen as precipitating a political crisis by undermining the health of the army through the potential spread of venereal disease, and consequently threatening the national security of the country. Prostitutes were regarded as deviants, as transgressing the moral fabric of the nation. The Contagious Diseases Acts were not alone in this justification. The Industrial Schools Amendment Act of 1880, for example, gave the police the right to enter places thought to be brothels and forcibly remove children from their mothers, on grounds of morality and protection. Even the opposition to much of this legislation, what Richard Price has called 'social purity movements' during the latter decades of the nineteenth century, supported the use of state power to identify and eliminate what was regarded as moral sin or vice.[68] These movements were focused on childhood experience and prostitution, but it was women, and not men, who were the focus of such attention. Whilst men participated in prostitution and could be directly involved with a child's upbringing, it was women, or, more specifically, women's bodies, which alone could grow a baby. It was women who were perceived as having the moral duty to stay at home and raise future generations; it was women who were the cause of poor health in the (male) army by spreading venereal disease. It was women whose bodies were differentiated from men's on the grounds of Otherness, women whose gender and biology became innately connected with race.

The growth of the Victorian information, surveillance, state therefore had a direct relationship with the racialisation of women in this period. Physical surveillance of women can be understood in terms of traditional information, or surveillance, state discourse: welfare (ensuring healthy future generations), and warfare (protecting the national security of the country).[69] To this end, women, or women's bodies, became legitimate information objects of the state, which in turn, contributed to the processes of racialisation in this period.

Such ideology became even more dominant as the century progressed. Army recruitment drives for the Boer War (1899–1902) were so poor that they catapulted

---

[67] Weller, 'The Information State', 59.
[68] Price, *British Society 1680–1880*, 224–229.
[69] Traditionally historians have dated the dual drivers of warfare and welfare to the post-1914 decades, but there is also agreement that many of the nascent forms of the modern information, or surveillance, state originated in the latter nineteenth century. See, e.g., Agar, *The Government Machine*, 201–262; Higgs, *The Information State in England*, 133–167; and Weller, 'The Information State', 57–63.

women's roles and responsibilities further into the consideration of the state. Recruitment for the army saw large proportions of men rejected on grounds of poor health; in Manchester alone over 70 per cent% of the 11,000 men considered were turned down.[70] This led to a sense of national anxiety and panic about the health of the nation at large; this anxiety and panic, in turn, led to the establishment of a governmental interdepartmental committee of enquiry to investigate the physical deterioration of the population. The results of the enquiry, published in 1904, put a particular emphasis of blame on women, particularly working-class women, noting their ignorance of hygiene and nutrition and observing that they had a declining sense of maternal responsibility.[71] Some contemporaries described the high child mortality levels as 'a degeneration of the race' – again with emphasis on the role and responsibilities of the mother, the biologically determined female.[72] The report suggested that increasing involvement outside of the home (applying to women of all social classes) whether political, professional, or intellectual, had led to a deterioration of maternal and domestic duties. According to the report, the solution was the teaching of cookery and household management in Board Schools, allowing a solid system of inspection led by, this time, female inspectors.[73] Others similarly suggested that young girls should be taught how to care for infants. In a presentation to the Association of University Women Teachers in 1908, Dr Janet Campbell, the Chief Woman Medical Advisor to the Board of Education, echoed the Victorian arguments of her male predecessors and argued that subjects such as mathematics needed too much concentration and used too much brain energy, which could damage the frail female mind. Instead, she advocated subjects such as cookery or embroidery which caused 'comparatively little mental strain'.[74]

Whilst middle-class women were expected to remain within the domestic sphere and restrict their expectations for autonomy, official concerns about the general health of the population led to a creation of a mass of health visitors and sanitary inspectors who sought to educate working-class mothers on how to care for their children. Their belief 'was that "bad" mothers could become "good" mothers if placed under scrutiny and continual supervision'.[75] Manchester Council employed welfare visitors for the first time during the 1890s, and in 1889 the Act for Prevention of Cruelty to Children gave the state new powers to enter homes on evidence of

---

[70] Carol Dyhouse, *Girls Growing up in Late Victorian and Edwardian England* (New York: Routledge, 2013), 92.
[71] *Report of the Inter-Departmental Committee on Physical Deterioration*, vol. I (London: Parliamentary Papers, 1904), 47, 53–54, 57.
[72] See comments by John Simon in G. Newman, *Infant Mortality: A Social Problem* (London: Methuen, 1906), v–vi.
[73] *Report of the Inter-Departmental Committee on Physical Deterioration*, vol. I (London: Parliamentary Papers, 1904), 43, 58, 61–62.
[74] Janet Campbell, 'The Effect of Adolescence on the Brain of a Girl', given to a meeting of the Association of Women Teachers, London, 23 May 1908, 5–6.
[75] Abrams, *The Making of the Modern Woman*, 146.

child abuse.[76] By the end of the century female sanitary inspectors could enter working-class homes to give instruction on childcare and 'to monitor behaviour'.[77] Such legislative measures formed part of a wider context of increased state responsibility for citizen's and children's health and welfare, where other legislation such as Custody Acts of the 1870s and 1880s to some extent empowered rather than examined women by giving them more rights over their children. Yet, the ingrained idea of the 'female malady' persisted. Poor working-class mothers who chose to breastfeed babies for long periods of time as a way of saving money often suffered from, what we would now understand to be malnutrition, but medical science of the day asserted that these women were suffering from 'lactational insanity'.[78] Following World War I there were a huge number of government reports about health, particularly following the creation of the Ministry of Health in 1919, and these increasingly focused on poorer women, who, as we have seen, were regarded as racially inferior, in the Victorian sense, to their middle-class counterparts. The female body, irrespective of social class, continued to be regarded as different and set apart from that of men.

Judy Giles has said that working-class women in this period 'frequently entered the public discourse ... and her "private" life were surveilled and probed by an increasing number of educationalists, social reformers, health visitors and housing officials', as the modern information state began to emerge.[79] Working-class women in their roles as housewives and mothers became 'objects of detailed scrutiny' with their needs and aspirations spoken for them often by middle-class women.[80] By the latter decades of the nineteenth century there had been somewhat of a shift, with women increasingly responsible for the surveillance and monitoring of other women in a legislative and official capacity rather than the earlier form of social panopticonic monitoring. Throughout this period, British ideas of race, gender, and class were complex and heavily intertwined, but Ahmed's notion of racialisation as a process involving 'social and bodily space in the everyday encounters we have with others' remains underlying.[81]

By the early twentieth century, the growing information state had begun to monitor working-class mothers in terms of their entitlement for state support. The feminist writer Jan Jindy Pettmen describes this growth of the welfare state and its focus on mothers, especially working-class mothers, as a 'shift from private to public patriarchy' where 'the state replaces individual men, although still with conditions for its "protection", including, often, the surveillance of women's sexual relations'.[82]

---

[76] Prevention of Cruelty to, and Protection of, Children Act 1989, Chapter 44.
[77] Price, *British Society 1680–1880*, 229.
[78] Showalter, *The Female Malady*, 54.
[79] Judy Giles, *Women, Identity and Private Life in Britain, 1900–1950* (London: Palgrave, 1995), 18.
[80] Ibid., 100.
[81] Ahmed, 'Racialized Bodies', 47.
[82] Pettmen, *Worlding Women*, 11.

In 1914, the Defence of the Realm Act, often discussed by historians in terms of the growth of the information, or surveillance, state, also had direct surveillance implications for women. Just as the Contagious Diseases Acts before it had focused on a woman's body, so too did the Act of 1914.[83] Legislation intended for defence of the country enforced a curfew on women to prevent prostitution and the spread of disease, and it made it illegal for a woman to have sex with a soldier if she actually had venereal disease. Surveillance or control of a woman's physical body and sexual behaviour was justified by the need to keep morale high and prevent infection, but it was only women who had such physical surveillance enforced on them by the state. The fluidity of Victorian notions of race and gender are significant here. As Omi and Winant note, 'the corporeal distinction between white men and the others over whom they ruled as patriarchs and masters ... links race to gender, and people of colour to women'.[84]

Social class undoubtedly played an important role in the ways in which women were surveilled, but there was an important commonality: the female body. Hysteria, the disease of the middle-class woman was, as discussed above and as Laura Briggs has argued, a racialised condition, focused upon respectable white women who had challenged the social norms by pursuing higher education or abstaining from having children.[85] Poorer or working-class women did not tend to 'suffer' from hysteria, but instead they were subject to legislation and governmental reports directed upon their methods of parenting, or their perceived lack of nurture. As Koskela has shown in relation to modern gender surveillance, a focus on the physical body has the long-term aim of reaching the mind.[86] This Foucauldian argument has relevance.[87] During this period, surveillance and control of the physical female body was legitimised by (male) medical science and the state which could intervene 'to dictate proper feminine behaviour'.[88] The impact of this on women was significant since it led to what Richard Price has described as 'a eugenically inspired interest in good mothering to build a strong race and army'.[89] Women faced a growing battle to prove that their biological potency as wives and mothers was not detrimentally affected by their increasing demands for political and intellectual rights as the century progressed. Towards the end of the century there are examples of

[83] For the surveillance or information state in 1914 see Agar, *The Government Machine*; Higgs, *The Information State in England*; Weller, 'The Victorian Information Age'; Weller, 'The Information State', 57–63.
[84] Michael Omi and Howard Winant, *Racial Formation in the United States*, 3rd ed. (New York: Routledge, 2015), 107.
[85] Laura Briggs, 'The Race of Hysteria: "Overcivilization" and the "Savage" Woman in Late Nineteenth-Century Obstetrics and Gynecology', *American Quarterly* 52, no. 2 (2000): 246–273.
[86] Koskela, '"You Shouldn't Wear That Body"', 51.
[87] See Angela King, 'The Prisoner of Gender: Foucault and the Disciplining of the Female Body', *Journal of International Women's Studies* 5, no. 2 (2004): article 4.
[88] Showalter, *The Female Malady*, 18.
[89] Price, *British Society 1680–1880*, 228.

headmistresses who would 'insure themselves' against suggestions that female education had a derogatory effect on girls' biological potency by giving regular and thorough physical examinations to their pupils.[90] Such physical assessments were undertaken by school medical officers, often female, following which 'records would be kept on file, registering in minute detail the progress of growth, state of health and medical history of each individual girl'.[91] In so doing, women could themselves perpetuate the differentiation of female bodies, contributing to the processes of bodily racialisation inherent over the century.

The tone of such information collection changed over the course of the century. By the last decades of the nineteenth century and into the twentieth, concerns over imperial status and national efficiency became increasingly evident in much of the language used. Women still needed to be observed, and their physical bodies provided the basis for this observation, but their *duties* as good mothers to maintain and preserve the (white) British race began to take increasing precedence. In the preface to *The Medical Inspection of Girls in Secondary Schools*, published in 1914 with war at the forefront of national thought, the headmistress of the Manchester High School wrote that girls tended to work too hard and be too ambitious. Such ambition 'must be kept in check for the sake of the girl's own health and also in the interests of national efficiency and the race'.[92] During the World War I period there was an increase in literature that encouraged women to, as Carol Dyhouse has put it, look after their health 'as a moral duty, a duty they owed to the Empire and the Race'.[93] By the early twentieth century, in the build-up to war, fluid Victorian ideas of race were beginning to be replaced with a more modern emphasis on colour and biological difference.[94] This was exacerbated by growing imperial tensions which often played on the ideas of unenlightened, savage colonials saved by their Western superiors: an idea powerfully illustrated by imperial advertising, aimed at a female audience, which 'took explicit shape around the reinvention of racial difference'.[95]

By the turn of the century, it was not only male doctors and scientists, or indeed the growing information state, which placed women's physical bodies under surveillance. Increasingly there was an expectation that they should do so themselves, for the eugenically driven greater good. Barbara Ryan has argued that 'women of all races, ethnicity, sexual orientation... are disadvantaged in a society that does not

---

[90] Dyhouse, *Girls Growing up in Late Victorian and Edwardian England*, 135.
[91] Ibid. See also Paul Atkinson, 'Fitness, Feminism and Schooling', in Sara Delamont and Lorna Duffin (eds.), *The Nineteenth Century Woman: Her Cultural and Physical World* (London: Croom Helm, 1978), 107–117.
[92] Sara Burstall, 'Preface', in Catherine Chisolme, *The Medical Inspection of Girls in Secondary Schools* (London: Longmans, 1914), 8–9.
[93] Dyhouse, *Girls Growing up in Late Victorian and Edwardian England*, 136.
[94] Paul B. Rich, *Race and Empire in British Politics* (Cambridge University Press, 1990).
[95] McClintock, *Imperial Leather*, 507.

value women'.[96] Ironically, while women themselves may not have been valued, their reproductive capacities were increasingly regarded as a valuable asset with which to produce, and reproduce, a strong British race, empire, and army. But, if strong physiology was desirable, that which was tainted, or was regarded as being outside the accepted domestic sphere and role of a dutiful woman, could also be defined as a potential threat to the state. Women, or more specifically, women's bodies, would, 'bear the full burden of state regulation in order to protect the public interest, as defined by experts'.[97]

The 'eugenically inspired interest' noted above by Price, was founded in a new type of Victorian science which, from the end of the nineteenth century, began to influence the way in which women's physiology was surveilled and examined. The eugenics movement, founded by Francis Galton, applied Darwin's theory of evolution to humans. Attempts at classifying humans based on taxonomies of skin colour had been established by Carl von Linnaeus during the eighteenth century, but Victorian science took this a step further as Haller has shown in his study of anthropological concepts of racial inferiority during the Victorian era.[98] Darwin's theory that humans had evolved from apes played into racial stereotypes of the era, reinforcing notions of mental inferiority in those of coloured skin. Women were also regarded as less evolved than men, where the male 'brain is absolutely larger ... the formation of [the female] skull is said to be intermediate between the child and the man'.[99] As Steven Rose has argued, 'such nineteenth century differentiation between the sexes was crucial in providing an alleged biological basis for the superiority of the male'.[100]

This late Victorian idea that genetics predetermined one's intellect and character traits also gave rise to the notion that there were physical and bodily indicators of degeneracy, vice, and criminality which could be observed in both men and women.[101] This desire to explain humanity on a scientific, rational basis once again mirrored wider developments in the Victorian state, and became strongly connected to the idea of race. Darwin's *Origin of Species* of 1859, and his later *Descent of Man* of 1871, popularised the idea that humans were descended from apes, and many periodicals and satirists of the time used the ape-like protruding jaw as an indicator of lower or incomplete mental and physical development. Darwin's description of the 'less highly evolved female brain' reflected contemporary ideas of female

[96] Ryan (ed.), *Identity Politics in the Women's Movement*, 10.
[97] Roberts, 'Feminism and the State in Later Victorian England', 88.
[98] John S. Haller Jr, 'Concepts of Race Inferiority in Nineteenth-Century Anthropology', *Journal of the History of Medicine and Allied Sciences* 25, no. 1 (1970): 40–51.
[99] Charles Darwin, *The Descent of Man, and Selection in Relation to Sex* (London: John Murray, 1871), vol. 2, 317.
[100] Steven Rose, 'Darwin, Race and Gender', *EMBO Reports. Science and Society* 10, no. 4 (2009): 297–298.
[101] See on this subject, Angelique Richardson, *Love and Eugenics in the Late Nineteenth Century* (Oxford University Press, 2008).

frailty.[102] In his investigation into *London Labour and the London Poor* of 1862, Henry Mayhew described the poor of East London as so different to the wealthier classes of the West that 'it is as if we were in a new land, and among another race'.[103] The working classes and the Irish became particular victims of this racial stereotyping with periodicals such as *Punch* regularly publishing cartoons depicting them as apes or with ape-like features to suggest a less evolved brain, than their wealthier English counterparts.[104] Class, race, and gender were intrinsically linked within Victorian ideology. Working-class bodies were often viewed as fundamentally diseased and degenerative, something which contemporaries often attributed more to a component of lower social class (Mayhew's 'another race') than to the ill-effects of poverty and malnutrition. Whilst working-class women were rarely diagnosed with the symptoms of middle-class hysteria, other social and cultural norms still influenced how women, and wider society, saw themselves and their bodies. Indeed, working-class bodies 'were conceptualised and represented as quantitatively different from those of the elite classes'.[105]

British women, or at least those who veered away from the path of domesticity and motherhood, were also identified as having their own particular physiognomy. In his book *The Female Offender*, the Italian criminologist Cesare Lombroso included fervent descriptions of the physiognomies of criminal women, 'proving' that normal or non-deviant women, had different skull shapes from men but that the skulls of criminal women looked like ancient man – that is, savage and uncivilised.[106] Thinkers of the day believed that deviant or delinquent women could be recognised by more than just their phrenology – they could also be identified by large jaws, short arms and 'badly shaped heads' according to one doctor.[107] Another wrote of the link between physical attributes, deviance, and disorder, considering female degeneration as a regressive force and threat to evolution and moral progress.[108] Specialists purported to show that women guilty of infanticide had excess facial hair, while

---

[102] Charles Darwin, *The Descent of Man, and Selection in Relation to Sex* (London: John Murray, 1871).

[103] Henry Mayhew, *London Labour and London Poor* (London, 1862), iii, 243.

[104] See, e.g., L. P. Curtis, *Apes and Angels: The Irishman in Victorian Caricature* (Washington DC: Smithsonian Books, 1971).

[105] Price, *British Society 1680–1880*, 223.

[106] Cesare Lombroso and William Ferrero, *The Female Offender* (New York: D. Appleton & Company, 1895), English translation. The results of Lombroso's work are highly refutable since his anthropometric control group featured only fourteen women. Contemporary critic Frances Kellor repeated his measurements on a much larger control group in 1901 and consequently contested the notion of female criminality as biologically determined. See discussion in Lucia Zedner, *Women, Crime and Custody in Victorian England* (Oxford: Clarendon Press, 1991), 80–83.

[107] Lyttleton Forbes Winslow, *The Insanity of Passion and Crime* (London: Ouseley, 1912), 287.

[108] Henry Maudsley, *Body and Mind: An Inquiry into their Connection and Mutual Influence* (New York: D. Appleton and Company, 1871), or any of the other many publications by Maudsley.

female thieves had underdeveloped teeth. Criminologists claimed that criminal women in general had hair that turned grey faster than non-criminal women and they were ugly and unsightly as well.[109] Not only were Victorian notions of race, gender, and class fluid and interwoven, but such racial constructs perpetuated the Otherness of the female body.

Even criminality could be perceived as different for women. Lucia Zedner has argued that contemporary authorities perceived and defined crime according to the gender of the offender, and that during the nineteenth century they identified women as being fundamentally and ideologically moral. Indeed, there were hundreds of legal cases during the nineteenth century of (mostly middle class) women being judged kindly by the courts because of the widely accepted idea that women were prone to uncontrollable acts of insanity entirely due to their different biology.[110] Female criminality therefore not only broke the law but broke a Victorian idealised and cultural role of women as wives and mothers.[111] Within prisons 'a much higher level of surveillance over women patrolled every aspect of their demeanour and behaviour for every possible fault'.[112] Medical experts, such as Auguste Comte and Herbert Spencer, argued that mental degeneracy or crime was the result of genetics, and therefore out of the control of the individual woman. There was, therefore, less of a moral outrage at female offenders per se but rather more of a concern about how to protect women from the dangers of their inherent, unavoidable, biologically driven behaviours. This concern could be benevolent in intent, with attempts to apply male medical science of the day to prevention, but there could also be undertones of control and power, of ensuring that women maintained the proper behaviours and boundaries expected of them, and fed into the process of corporeal racialisation.

Fears for the declining health of the nation and the army as a result of poor mothering, coupled with anxiety over the eugenic implications of female crime led to 'a new impetus to control those women' or their offspring and their genetics would potentially taint society and the British race.'[113] Writers such as Benjamin Kidd and Karl Pearson were drawn directly into such discussions, using as justification for their behaviours the notion that, as Carol Dyhouse has put it, 'women were the guardians of racial progress'.[114] Precisely because 'of their crucial role at home [women] were also identified as potential internal enemies', or deviants, who could undermine the war effort by not fulfilling their patriotic duty as wives and mothers.'[115]

---

[109] Havelock Ellis, *The Criminal* (London: Walter Scott, 1890), 217.
[110] Ruth Harn, *Murders and Madness: Medicine, Law and Society in the Fin de Siecle* (Oxford University Press, 1989).
[111] Zedner, *Women, Crime and Custody in Victorian England*, 2.
[112] Ibid., 210.
[113] Ibid., 5–6.
[114] Dyhouse, *Girls Growing up in Late Victorian and Edwardian England*, 91.
[115] Abrams, *The Making of the Modern Woman*, 304.

This duty to be wives and mothers, the fundamental 'separate spheres' ideology, remained remarkably constant throughout this period. From the wandering womb of the Enlightenment to the diagnoses of hysteria of the nineteenth century and the perceived national duty to the Empire of the early twentieth century, the surveillance and control of women through their bodies can be understood to be, at its very essence, racial. 'Women were', as Koskela argues, 'claimed to be different just by virtue of being (biologically) women', and this idea continued to be driven by late Victorian ideas of eugenics, evolution, and colonial tensions.[116] This physical difference, this bodily Otherness, fed into the racialisation of women during the long nineteenth century. Victorian science was used 'as a circular proof seeking to justify what nearly everyone already accepted as true'.[117]

Understanding the racialisation of women in gender terms in this period is important. It is rare to find studies of women's rights that take into account rise of the information, or surveillance, state in Britain in this period. Conversely, accounts of the surveillance state and the welfare/warfare drivers do not usually mention women as more than a sideline, or as a note related to the growth in women's rights and the women's movement. Exploring these historical drivers as connected and related phenomenon allows for an understanding of surveillance and race that is more subtle but equally powerful. Both working-class women and those perceived as from a more respectable social class became what can be termed as physical 'information objects' during this period. Attempts to survey, monitor and control women's bodies were legitimised on the grounds of Victorian medical science, on the preservation and protection of the (white) British race, and in terms of protecting women from biologically driven behaviours which they could not control. The result was a complex mingling of race, gender, and class ideologies which played out amongst the broader political climate of imperial tensions, changing social norms, and challenges to the long-established male arenas of power.

It would be too simplistic to think of this purely in terms of the 'tyranny of the patriarchal state' however.[118] Throughout this period, women could also be surveilling each other, subjecting other women to monitoring and judgment. Until the twentieth century and the post-war liberties granted to women, women themselves were largely forced to operate within the confines of male dominated environs and established conventions. As Omi and Winant argue, 'the master category of race profoundly shaped gender oppression'.[119] However, for the most part, British notions of race, gender, and class were applied to white women; this experience was not analogous to that of women of colour, whether in Britain or as part of the Empire. Significantly, as Cannadine has explored in relation to the British Empire, Victorian

---

[116] Koskela, '"You Shouldn't Wear That Body"', 49.
[117] Haller Jr, 'Concepts of Race Inferiority in Nineteenth-Century Anthropology', 51.
[118] Virginia Woolf, *Three Guineas* (London: The Hogarth Press, 1938).
[119] Omi and Winant, *Racial Formation in the United States*, 108.

concepts of race could be just as much about maintaining 'traditional rulerships ... in a changing world' as it was the colour of someone's skin.[120] Such established hierarchies were of particular significance during this period as women began to demand more social and political power. Inwood and Yarborough have shown how the constructions of racialised identity can shape both the lives and identities of individuals, which ultimately have, as Nash has argued, 'material effects in terms of the unequal distribution of power and wealth'.[121] The politics of nineteenth-century feminism were therefore to some extent entwined with the racialisation of the female body. Within Britain, growing interest in the collection of information and surveillance, alongside the hierarchies of class and gender, contributed to a complex but highly significant racialisation of women during this period. Women's biology formed an intrinsic part of the male-dominated nineteenth-century rhetoric of control, moral superiority, progress, and race.

[120] K. O. Kupperman, *Settling with the Indians: The Meeting of English and Indian Cultures in America, 1580–1640* (New Jersey: Rowman and Littlefield, 1980), 2; Cannadine, *Ornamentalism*, discusses Kupperman quote on p. 124.

[121] Inwood and Yarbrough, 'Racialized Places, Racialized Bodies', 299–301; Catherine Nash, 'Cultural Geography: Anti-Racist Geographies', *Progress in Human Geography* 27, no. 5 (2003): 637–648, 639.

5

Linking Caste and Surveillance

How Digital Governance Has Legitimised Caste Discrimination in India

Amber Sinha and Shruti Trikanad

INTRODUCTION

The goals of independent India of achieving the constitutional promise of an egalitarian society have largely been led by an emphatic endorsement of the right to equality on one hand, and the implementation of positive discrimination measures, such as caste-based reservations in public employment and education, on the other. The idea of redistributive justice was a common theme often visited in the Constituent Assembly Debates.[1] India shares a long history of social and economic oppression with most other countries in the developing world. While the markers for such oppression are often race and socio-economic status, or both, in most parts of the world, in India, caste and tribal identity remain the most important vectors for discriminatory practices and structural inequities.[2]

The visual cues that accompany racial discrimination in most parts of the world are absent in caste and in some cases, even in tribe-based discrimination in India. As described by Narual, these markers of discrimination in India are 'like oxygen – it is both invisible and indispensable'.[3] While the absence of visual cues makes little or no difference to structural inequities and the ability of those with power to discriminate, it does manage to shift attention away due to a lack of appreciation for non-racial discrimination. In response to the UN Committee on the Elimination of Racial Discrimination's request that the government submit information on issues pertaining to Scheduled Castes and Scheduled Tribes, the Indian government stated that caste and race cannot be equated under 'descent' in Article 1 of the

---

[1] S. V. Narayanan, 'How Far Have We Deviated from the Identity of Our Constitution?' *The Wire*, November 26, 2019, https://thewire.in/caste/how-far-have-we-deviated-from-the-ideology-of-our-constitution.
[2] Smitha Narula, 'Equal by Law, Unequal by Caste: The "Untouchable" Condition in Critical Race Perspective', *Wisconsin International Law Journal* 26, no. 2 (2008).
[3] Narula, 'Equal by Law, Unequal by Caste'.

International Convention on the Elimination of All Forms of Racial Discrimination. Of note, 'discrimination based on "descent" includes discrimination against members of communities based on forms of social stratification, such as caste and analogous systems of inherited status' as per the Committee's interpretation of Article 1 in General Recommendation XXIX.[4]

Nevertheless, the oppression faced by these communities was attempted to be addressed by the Constitution of India, which provided for special treatment of those believed to suffer from exploitation or discrimination. India's caste system is one of the oldest, most resilient, and rigorously enforced systems of social hierarchy. It represents a very complex form of social and economic stratification and hierarchy which pervades all walks of life, is birth-ascribed, and rigid to the point of prohibiting any mobility.[5] Scheduled castes comprise 16.6 per cent of the Indian population, and include 1,206 castes that were considered untouchable.[6] On the other hand, scheduled tribes under the constitutional framework were created to include indigenous tribes characterised by what past and subsequent constitutional processes described as 'primitive traits, distinctive culture, geographical isolation, shyness of contact with the community at large, and backwardness'.[7] They consist of 701 tribes and constitute 8.6 per cent of India's population.[8] By prohibiting negative discrimination, and making these groups eligible for the benefits of positive discrimination, the makers of the constitution opened one of the most important debates about equality in India.

In this chapter, we will analyse the evolution of the Indian digital state over the last two decades, characterised by data-driven and 'digitalised' public decision-making, reliant on an indiscriminate collection of personal data about citizens to inform eligibility decisions regarding entitlements, benefits, and welfare. The surveillance-based reconfiguration of the Indian welfare state has discriminatory and exclusionary implications. We will focus on digital identity and e-governance as a case study. This initiative forcefully pushes for a state and private-sector driven agenda that argues for a prejudiced view of development and efficiency at the cost of the rights of marginalised groups. Relying on facially neutral and objective technological systems, these initiatives were intended as a panacea for India's varied problems of human-driven prejudices and corruption. Yet, their implementation has only amplified the discriminatory effects of public policy-making, as they rely on increased surveillance driven by collection of massive amounts of personal data,

---

[4] Human Rights Watch, 'Hidden Apartheid: Caste Discrimination against India's "Untouchables"', February 2007, www.hrw.org/report/2007/02/12/hidden-apartheid/caste-discrimination-against-indias-untouchables.

[5] A. L. Kroeber, 'Caste', in *Encyclopaedia of the Social Sciences* (New York: Macmillan, 1930), 254–257.

[6] Ibid.

[7] Additions and Deletions in Constitution (Scheduled Tribes) Order, 2002, https://archive.pib.gov.in/archive/releases98/lyr2002/rjun2002/08062002/r080620022.html.

[8] Census of India, 2011, www.censusindia.gov.in/2011census/PCA/presentation.pdf.

which informs public-sector and private-sector decision-making. These measures also run parallel to the Indian judiciary's attempts to reframe both privacy and equality rights in a way that may articulate a positive agenda for the state to protect its marginalised groups against both surveillance and discrimination. We will briefly narrate the successes and failures of these attempts to arrest the indiscriminate rise of digital identity's discriminatory effects.

HISTORY OF SURVEILLANCE ON THE BASIS OF PROTECTED GROUNDS IN INDIA

The disproportionate impact of group surveillance, and consequent discrimination on certain communities in India is most acutely exemplified by the Criminal Tribes Act 1871 (CTA) a colonial legislation targeted at certain castes or tribes. This legislation sought to notify and list 'criminal tribes', and establish a system of surveillance involving local government and village folk.[9] As a result of steps taken by British administration in India, the upheaval of the political and economic system in rural India resulted in several communities losing their means of livelihood, and resorting to thievery. The colonial focus on tribes was prompted by two ideas – first, the administration believed that the persons belonging to these groups took to crime because of their membership in a tribe that followed a hereditary occupation. Second, it was believed that crime was linked with particular styles that marked specific tribes, and with the worship of deities or performance of rituals. This legislation sought to simultaneously describe a demographic as *'addicted to the systematic commission of non-bailable offences'*,[10] and control their behaviour of 'habitual criminality' by imposing restrictions on their movements.[11] Further, the legislation also sought to exercise 'welfare governance' of these tribes by instituting methods of reforms and rehabilitation of the tribe, again through surveillance.

The local government, typically with the assistance of village headmen and landlords, reported to the governor-general any tribe that they suspect to be criminal.[12] If the governor-general was satisfied with the report, a notification was published, declaring the tribe to be a 'criminal tribe'. This notification could not be challenged in a court of law,[13] thereby sealing a tribe to a criminal fate without ever hearing a member. There were also cautionary principles to state the reasons for considering any group to be addicted to the systematic commission of non-bailable offences, along with the nature and circumstances of the offences in which the members of the tribe were said to have committed the crimes. However, this caution was reportedly more theoretical than actually being followed in practice anywhere.

[9] Preamble, CTA 1871.
[10] Section 2, CTA 1871.
[11] Sections 13–17, CTA 1971.
[12] Section 2, CTA 1871.
[13] Section 6, CTA 1871.

Even notwithstanding its treatment of criminal tribes, the Act was lacking in one crucial respect. It had no clear principles guiding the classification of criminal tribes. In operation, three important interrelated principles governed the classification – residence, profession, and contiguity: wandering tribes that did not have a fixed residence; groups that did not have professions or livelihoods; and, finally, blood relationships, allowing family members to be classified based on a kinship alone.

Following notification, the tribe could be relocated to a prescribed place of residence,[14] or placed in a 'reformatory settlement'.[15] It was widely known, however, that the reformatory settlements were not intended to achieve any reformation, but simply to compel the tribe, through mandatory registration and roll-call, to quarantine within their settlement. This had an effect beyond that of forcibly reshaping the existence of these tribes; it resulted in a social quarantine of the tribe members as any similarity or connection to the ways of these tribes were considered criminal. Local government was empowered with rule-making power for all aspects of their governance, including the nature of passes (to leave the settlement), conditions required for a pass, etc. Local authorities were also endowed with discretionary powers to enhance surveillance, or inspect the place of residence of a member. Any member that violated these rules was required to be punished, with rigorous imprisonment, fine, or whipping. The Act also included in its surveillance system local village headmen, watchmen, and landlords ('*zamindars*'), who had a duty to give information about the failure of any person to appear when required, or their absence from the settlement.[16] They were liable for punishment under the Indian Penal Code if they did not comply.[17] As a result, the settlements were heavily guarded, punishments for 'violators' were readily handed out, and the members were isolated within their settlements.

In 1949, the CTA was finally repealed, but quickly replaced by an equally draconian set of laws, the Habitual Offenders Act(s). These were a series of state-wide laws that followed a similar pattern of establishing a surveillance and restriction regime, akin to the one under the CTA, on 'habitual offenders'. The only major change it introduced was a moving away from the 'inherently born criminal' to a system where the person was convicted or imprisoned for offences a prescribed number of times; however, seeing as how stigmatised and surveilled these groups were, the change made little difference as members of notified tribes were often the first to be suspected for any crime by the police, and were even used as scapegoats for crimes they did not commit.[18]

---

[14] Sections 13, 14, CTA 1871.
[15] Section 18, CTA 1871.
[16] Section 21, CTA 1871.
[17] Section 22, CTA 1871.
[18] Susan Abraham, 'Steal or I'll Call You a Thief: Criminal Tribes of India', *Economic & Political Weekly* 34, no. 27 (1999): 1751–1753, 1751; Dilip D'Souza, 'De-Notified Tribes: Still "Criminal"?', *Economic & Political Weekly* 34, no. 51 (1999): 3576–3578, 3578.

Since colonial time, law enforcement agencies in India have had a practice of maintaining databases of 'history sheeters', individuals accused, but not necessarily convicted of a crime, and put on police surveillance lists. Mrinal Satish has shown that certain categories of persons continue to be under continual surveillance by the police.[19] These include 'criminal tribes', a racist epithet for classes of people considered genetically criminal and habituated to a life of crime. Aside from this, police in various states in India also maintain databases of individuals classified as '*goondas*' and 'bad characters.' These 'history sheets' translate into constant supervision or surveillance of individuals, and often leads to selective application of laws against them. The use of biometric and digitally conjoined databases, as we will discuss below, increases the risks of surveillance many times over.

RACIAL PREJUDICES IN POLICY-MAKING

The CTA is part of a long trend of criminalising features or attributes of persons, regardless of their own criminal behaviour. They share the idea that criminality was the domain of one section of the population, who could be identified and addressed preventively. In the early nineteenth century, the Western world held a popular notion of criminality moulded by the interaction of the administrative and scientific community; criminals had typical physiological features, such as flattened nose, scanty beard, and lopsided skull. Around the same time, a different theory of group criminality arose in France, quickly replacing the biological explanation, in which crime was seen as a social fact moulded by its environment.[20] The focus shifted to the living conditions of groups, and the factors that led them to crime. This created the 'dangerous class', a group of people who lived at the margins of society and moved around in search of livelihood. These classes came to be feared, and an active attempt was made to identify and name them. In 1824, the Vagrancy Act was enacted in England – to restrain vagabondage – targeting nomads and the wandering population.[21]

In India, this concept translated into a focus on castes, as the British viewed India as a collection of castes. Castes already have measurable traits, occupations, and common rituals and/or traditions, and were thus easy to identify and group.[22] In 1855, A. O. Hume wrote a sympathetic account of the criminal tribes of the Berias,

[19] Mrinal Satish, '"Bad Characters, History Sheeters, Budding Goondas and Rowdies": Police Surveillance Files and Intelligence Databases in India', *National Law School of India Review* 23, no. 1 (2011): 133.
[20] Adolphe-Jacques Quetelet and Andre Michel Guerry were pioneers in the field of scientific study of the health and functioning of society in France.
[21] Vagrants, or 'the idle disorderly persons', were considered most vulnerable to opportunities of crime, as they lacked a livelihood.
[22] Bernard S. Cohn, 'Notes on the History of the Study of Indian Society and Culture', in Milton Singer and Bernard S. Cohn (eds.), *Structure and Change in Indian Society* (Chicago, IL: Aldine, 1968), 15.

Sanorias, Nats, and Harburahs.[23] He considered their criminality a consequence of the hardship and intolerance they face, and particularly of the brutal attitude of the police. Though he meant for the report to reform the living conditions of these tribes, it was cited by the government of Punjab to claim extraordinary police powers for the surveillance of criminal tribes and castes. This was one of the foremost accounts of surveillance and administrative action directed towards criminal tribes in India.

The idea that criminality can be inherent, and evinced by physical features dates back to the early 1800s. The practice of using people's outward characteristics to infer inner character is called 'physiognomy', and while easily understood as a pseudoscience now, was widely accepted before, and even codified into law. Physiognomy fuelled scientific racism in the nineteenth and twentieth century, and was used as a tool to demonize certain communities.[24] Although this may seem like a concern of the past, what has endured is the idea that criminality (or *likelihood* of criminality) of a person can be inferred from features, race, or other similar proxies. Applications of this notion can be seen in artificial intelligence and machine learning (ML) models today.[25]

For instance, in 2016, Wu and Zhang published a paper titled 'Automated Inferences on Criminality using Face Images'[26] where they used machine learning techniques to predict (from random driver's licence photographs) the likelihood that a person is a convicted criminal, with a claimed 90 per cent accuracy. This paper even went so far as to specify that the inference is 'free of any biases of subjective judgments of human observers'.[27] They claimed that their motive in building this model was to examine whether ML has the potential of acquiring human-like social perception of faces; in being able to identify faces not just by biometric dimensions,[28] but also by socio-psychological features.[29] The researchers concluded that the model, by assessing varied facial features,[30] discovered that criminals have a higher degree of dissimilarity in appearance than the non-criminals,[31] proving that

---

[23] Sanjay Nigam, 'Disciplining and Policing the "Criminals by Birth", Part 1: The Making of a Colonial Stereotype: The Criminal Tribes and Castes of North India', *Indian Economic and Social History Review* 27, no. 2 (1990): 131–164, 150.
[24] Richard T. Gray, *About Face: German Physiognomic Thought from Lavaer to Auschwitz* (Detroit, MI: Wayne State University Press, 2004), 427.
[25] See Predictive Policing, Correctional Offender Management Profiling for Alternative Sanctions (COMPAS).
[26] Xiaolin Wu, Xi Zhang, 'Automated Inference on Criminality Using Face Images' (2016), https://arxiv.org/pdf/1611.04135v2.pdf.
[27] Ibid.
[28] Such as race, gender, age, facial expression, etc.
[29] Xiaolin Wu and Xi Zhang, 'Responses to Critiques on Machine Learning of Criminality Perceptions (Addendum of ArXiv:1611.04135)' (2016), https://arxiv.org/pdf/1611.04135.pdf.
[30] Such as distance between eyes, shape of mouth, etc.
[31] Wu and Zhang, 'Automated Inference'.

'being a criminal requires a host of abnormal (outlier) personal traits'.[32] This sounds astonishingly similar to the physiognomy claims of the nineteenth century.

In 2017, Michal Kosinski, a researcher affiliated with Stanford University, co-authored a paper that claimed that facial recognition technology along with deep neural networks could be used on profile pictures uploaded on social media to predict sexual orientation.[33] What Kosinski's paper actually showed was that algorithms could detect a pattern in the appearance of a small subset of out white gay and lesbian people on dating sites. The algorithm detected differences and similarities in facial structure, and tried to predict sexual orientation on the assumption that gay men's faces were more feminine than straight men, and lesbian women's faces were more masculine than straight women. According to the paper, this finding was based on the prenatal hormone theory of sexual orientation. This theory suggests that our sexuality is, in part, determined by hormone exposure in the womb. Kosinski's critics pointed out that factors such as less facial hair in the case of gay male subjects may as easily be a consequence of fashion trends and cultural norms as prenatal hormonal exposure. More importantly, critics felt the paper was dangerous and irresponsible because it could be used to support an authoritarian and brutal regime's efforts to identify and/or persecute people they believed to be homosexual. After the paper was published, Kosinski went on to claim that similar algorithms could help measure intelligence quotient, political orientation, and criminal inclinations of people from their facial images alone.

These researchers completely fail to account for the fact that who gets tagged 'criminal' or problematic by such ML algorithms is rarely unbiased.[34] Impressions formed by the police, and other members of the criminal justice system on what a 'criminal appearance' is – which is seemingly the entire purpose of the research experiment – play a big role in persons' convictions.[35] As a result, the disproportionate number of convictions of those that appear criminal will in turn reinforce the idea, through an 'unbiased' AI, that criminals often look like this. AI models often exhibit discriminatory tendencies largely because of biased data collection or data labelling methods.[36] If the data set used to train the model over-represents or

---

[32] Ibid.
[33] Yilun Wang, and Michal Kosinski, 'Deep Neural Networks Are More Accurate than Humans at Detecting Sexual Orientation from Facial 10 Images', *Journal of Personality and Social Psychology* 114, no. 2 (2018): 246–257.
[34] In a new preface to the paper responding to criticism, they admitted that taking a court conviction as the 'ground truth' was a serious oversight on their part. However, it still read as a statistical or empirical error they identified, and not a case of bias in convictions.
[35] Catherine Stinson, 'Algorithms Associating Appearance and Criminality Have a Dark Past', *Aeon*, May 15, 2020, https://aeon.co/ideas/algorithms-associating-appearance-and-criminality-have-a-dark-past.
[36] Solon Barocas and Andrew D. Selbst, 'Big Data's Disparate Impact', *California Law Review* 104, no. 3 (2016): 671–732: Prof. Frederik Zuiderveen, 'Discrimination, Artificial Intelligence, and Algorithmic Decision-Making', Council of Europe Borgesius, https://rm.coe.int/discrimination-artificial-intelligence-and-algorithmic-decision-making/1680925d73.

under-represents a certain community, then the resulting model will reproduce the same bias.[37] In this example, the data set may be skewed by disproportionate convictions caused by intense policing of particular communities, or inequality of access to legal representation.[38] For instance, the COMPAS (Correctional Offender Management Profiling for Alternative Sanctions) algorithm, used by judges in the United States to predict whether defendants should be detained or released on bail pending trial, was found to be biased against African-Americans.[39] This was linked with the historical racism, disproportionate surveillance, and other inequalities in police practices, and the criminal system that makes African Americans more likely to be arrested or incarcerated in the United States.[40] These arrests are then reflected in the training data used to make models that will suggest whether a defendant should be detained. The ML model, while associating certain facial features with criminality, is influenced by biased data to 'criminalise' certain features associated with already marginalised communities.[41] This is closely tied with surveillance, as surveillance data would directly feed into over- or under-representing marginalised communities. What is worth noting here is that the technological paradigms which have contributed historically to racism are also the ones central to digital identification systems.

THE DIGITAL REINVENTION OF THE INDIAN STATE

The Birth of Digital National Identity in India

The story of digitisation of public records in India goes back to the UPA-I government. In 2006, the Manmohan Singh-led union government launched the National e-Governance Project (NeGP). The project began with schemes to digitise different aspects of governance. To begin with, the filing, payment, and redressal mechanisms for taxes moved online. All corporate compliance gradually moved to an online portal. The applications, appointments, and tracking of passports were shifted

---

[37] Kristian Lum and William Isaac, 'To Predict and Serve?', *Significance*, 7 October 2016, https://doi.org/10.1111/j.1740-9713.2016.00960.x. As Lum and Isaac note, 'If police focus attention on certain ethnic groups and certain neighbourhoods, it is likely that police records will systematically over-represent those groups and neighbourhoods.'
[38] Stinson, 'Algorithms Associating Appearance and Criminality Have a Dark Past'.
[39] Julia Angwin et al., 'Machine Bias', *ProPublica*, 23 May 2016, www.propublica.org/article/machine-bias-risk-assessments-in-criminal-sentencing. See also Tim Brennan, William Dieterich, and Beate Ehret, 'Evaluating the Predictive Validity of the COMPAS Risk and Needs Assessment System', *Criminal Justice and Behavior* 36 (2009): 21–40.
[40] Nicol Turner Lee, Paul Resnick, and Genie Barton, 'Algorithmic Bias Detection and Mitigation: Best Practices and Policies to Reduce Consumer Harms', *Brookings*, 22 May 2019, www.brookings.edu/research/algorithmic-bias-detection-and-mitigation-best-practices-and-policies-to-reduce-consumer-harms/#footref-18.
[41] In this particular case it is facial features, but can be associated with name, family background, educational background, nationality, residence, etc. Any of these could act as proxies for discrimination of marginalised communities.

online. With time, the project began to include all aspects of governance. In 2014, when the Bharatiya Janata Party (BJP)-led National Democratic Alliance (NDA) government came to power, they quickly made 'Digital India' their flagship project, and adopted the NeGP plan under it. The project envisioned moving virtually all aspects of governance online, including the disbursal of benefits and subsidies.

Government departments and institutions in India have always maintained databases on the Indian population, but due a lack of technology, these databases do not 'talk to each other'. To overcome the limitations of hosting data in these 'separate silos', tech developers began to create a system which enables interaction across databases. The linchpin of this interaction has been the move towards e-governance, which began under the NeGP. The Unique Identity Project in India, Aadhaar, which has over 1 billion registrants[42] is an online, digital, and paperless identity system[43] which can act as a platform for a number of digital services, all of which produce enormous troves of data, precious to both the government and the private sector. Prior to the Aadhaar number, there were at least eighteen different documents that were recognised as acceptable proofs of identity.[44] The objective of the scheme has been for the Unique Identification Authority of India (UIDAI) to issue every resident in India a unique identification number (UID) based on an individual's biometrics, which can be authenticated and verified online. The system was conceptualised and implemented as a platform to facilitate identification, avoid fake identity issues, and facilitate delivery of government benefits based on the demographic and biometric data available to the Authority.[45] The Aadhar number is a twelve-digit randomly generated unique number issued linked to user data collected by the UIDAI, which includes thirteen points of biometric data: iris scans (both eyes), fingerprints (all ten fingers) and a picture of the face.

Justifications for the Digital Identity Initiative

Proposals for a national identification scheme first emerged out of a narrative to ensure a registry of citizens for national security purposes. The National Citizen

[42] 'Aadhaar Enrollment Crosses 1 Billion Mark: Ravi Shankar Prasad', NDTV, 4 April 2016, www.ndtv.com/india-news/aadhaar-enrollment-crosses-1-billion-mark-ravi-shankar-prasad-1338621.
[43] Jake Kendall, Stephen Deng, 'It's the Ecosystem, Stupid – Exploring the "Digital Poverty Stack", Part 1', Next Billion, 29 August 2016, http://nextbillion.net/nexthought-monday-its-the-ecosystem-stupid-exploring-the-digital-poverty-stack-part-1.
[44] These include passport; PAN card; ration/PDS photo card; voter id; driving licence; government photo id cards; NREGS job card; photo id issued by a recognised educational institution; arms licence; photo bank ATM card; photo credit card; pensioner photo card; freedom fighter photo card; kissan photo passbook; CGHS/ECHS photo card; address card having name and photo issued by department of posts and certificate of identify having photo issued by group a gazetted officer on letterhead; disability ID card/handicapped medical certificate issued by the respective State/Union Territories.
[45] 'Aadhaar Features, Eligibility', FAQ, UIDAI, last updated 24 January 2019, https://uidai.gov.in/contact-support/have-any-question/286-faqs/your-aadhaar/aadhaar-features,-eligibility.html.

Register, which has had a limited implementation, was enacted out of this idea.[46] However, by the time the Aadhaar project was conceptualised, the focus of the identification projects had shifted to identification rather than citizenship. Therefore, the Aadhaar project aims to enrol all residents as opposed to all citizens in India.

In its early days, the UIDAI project sought support from the idea that a unique identity was required to effectively provide services, benefits, and subsidies to eligible individuals. This was based on the assumption that the leakages in the welfare schemes arose due to a lack of single identification scheme.[47] Over the last few years, however, this assumption has been severely tested. Social welfare researchers have shown that the leakages in the benefits and subsidies systems in India such as the Public Distribution Systems for free and subsidised food rations, and the Liquefied Petroleum Gas (LPG) system for subsidies, do not arise through issues of identity. There are significant leakages that arise before the benefits reach the point-of-sale shops which cannot be addressed by a unique identification scheme, nor can corruption in point of sale be addressed by simply correctly identifying the beneficiaries. It is probable that only a small part of the problem of leakages is due to the lack of reliable identification programme.[48]

The other significant justification provided for a national digital identification scheme was that the inability to produce an identification document was one of the biggest barriers preventing the poor, particularly those disadvantaged by caste and tribal barriers, from accessing benefits and subsidies and participating in the formal economy. To address this issue, the UIDAI conceptualised an innovation called the introducer system, which would involve those without identity documents being able to furnish letters of introduction from prominent local citizens from both government and non-government sectors. This would ensure that those outside formal systems of enrolment would gradually come within it. However, Right to Information applications filed with the UIDAI have revealed that only a very small fraction of registrants has utilised the introducer systems (less than 0.08 per cent). This means that 99.9 per cent of registrants already had another identification number.[49]

A 'Cradle to Grave' Identity

When the Digital India programme was approved by the Cabinet of Ministers, the press release mentioned the 'cradle to grave' digital identity as one

---

[46] Deepa Ollapalli, 'India's National Identity and Its Impact on Security Policy under Modi', *Asan Forum* 8, no. 6 (2015): www.theasanforum.org/indias-national-identity-and-its-impact-on-security-policy-under-modi.

[47] Ibid.

[48] Reetika Khera, 'Impact of Aadhaar in Welfare Programmes', *Countercurrents*, October 2017, https://countercurrents.org/wp-content/uploads/2017/10/aadhar-welfare.pdf.

[49] Government of India, UIDAI-RTI reply (28 December 2016), www.thehinducentre.com/multimedia/archive/o3221/RTI___reply_introd_3221771a.pdf.

its visions.[50] The characteristics of this identity are mentioned as 'unique, lifelong, online and authenticable'. In order to provide welfare and other services effectively, the e-governance schemes would collect and store information through the lifecycle of an individual. The result, as we can see is building databases on individuals, which, when brought together, can provide a 360-degree profile of citizens.

The creation of a lifelong and unique profile involves several e-governance schemes which document different aspects of a citizen's interaction with the state. For instance, the Ministry of Health and Family Welfare is developing infrastructure to facilitate the sharing of health information through a National Health Portal and the establishment of a national database containing records of citizens from birth to death. Similarly, the ominously named health-care project, Mother and Child Tracking System, is a system for improving the delivery of health services to pregnant women and children up to five years of age through name-based tracking of documents after each and every hospital visit. There are several education-sector projects which seek to document different aspects of school life and records, and a combination of these databases could provide a comprehensive view of the educational history of an individual. The Employment Exchange project creates a database of potential employees to match against employer requirements. When eOffice is fully implemented, it will have the performance and attendance details of all the government employees. The tax databases for both direct and indirect taxes are already being maintained. At more local levels, projects such as e-District would be responsible for issuing certificates for income, domicile, caste, birth, and death, as well as issuing licences such as arms licences, ration cards, disbursing pensions, processing utility payments, and linking to other relevant government projects. They would also be responsible for the provision of marriage certificates, and will collect personal data on previous marital status, religion, along with personal details about witnesses to the marriage. Alongside, the Crime and Criminal Network and Tracking System is intended to connect all police stations across the country, and allow records of any individuals at a local police station to be made available nationally. Schemes such as the Pensioners Portal are already live, and they function as the platform for retired government employees to register and seek their pensions. These initiatives have very limited or no opt-out as they entail essential services. While op-out may technically be an option, due to the nature of services being provided, it is not a real option for many.

These projects were designed to formalise the process of governance and bring about significant efficiency gains. One would have expected that this formalisation would have been accompanied by the creation of policies to protect the

---

[50] Press Information Bureau, 'Digital India – A Programme to Transform India into Digital Empowered Society and Knowledge Economy', Government of India, Cabinet, 20 August 2014, http://web.archive.org/web/20150209100322/http://pib.nic.in/newsite/PrintRelease.aspx?relid=108926.

huge amounts of personal data being collected, how it is used, and who can access it. However, as this has not happened, massive swathes of data collected have been handled very poorly by the departments charged with it. In 2017, it was discovered that several government departments were publishing spreadsheets of citizens' data on their website, which was estimated to be in some cases, that of more than 100 million people.[51] The government, in response to a question in Parliament, said that up to 226 government websites had been publishing sensitive personal data.[52]

While legislation governing Aadhaar prohibits storing the details about religion, caste, race, ethnicity, language, records of entitlement, income, or medical history for the purpose of Aadhaar authentication, this information is currently collected by various government agencies. This information is supposed to be used strictly for the purpose for which it was collected, but investigative reporting found that instances of caste information have been shared publicly on several government portals.[53]

Information and data leaks have been occurring in India for a long time. But with the scale and design of e-governance projects which work under Digital India, any information being disclosed has the potential to be dangerous, and its impact is often irreversible. Young described the Aadhaar Number as the 'center of a bottleneck in an ecosystem'[54] where national identity numbers are perceived as the equivalent of IP addresses in a digital network. This risks vast datasets being used for commercial and government surveillance.

Digitalisation of Citizenship and Knowledge Structures

The evolution of the UIDAI project as central to India's state's governance framework – alongside the marginalisation of the transparency measures under the Right to Information Act and related measures – exhibits a particular narrative of knowledge and authority resting in the state through a one-way expectation of transparency. In just over a decade since its inception, the Aadhaar project has moved way past beyond its original objective of fixing leakages in the public distribution system (PDS) in India to its current avatar as the foundational technological architecture for a governance systems that is built around the identification and verification of

---

[51] Staff, Scroll, 'Government Website Leaked 1.3 Lakh Aadhaar Numbers, Linked Them with Caste, Religion: Researcher', *Scroll.in* (April 24, 2018), https://scroll.in/latest/876775/government-website-leaked-1-3-lakh-aadhaar-numbers-linked-them-with-caste-religion-researcher.

[52] Yunus Y. Lasania, 'YSRCP Alleges IT Grids Conspiring to Create Disturbances on Counting Day', *Mint* (April 30, 2019), www.livemint.com/elections/lok-sabha-elections/ysrcp-alleges-it-grids-conspiring-to-create-disturbances-on-counting-day-1556627917542.html.

[53] Lasania, 'IT Grids.'

[54] Kaliya Young, 'Key Differences between the U.S. Social Security System and India's Aadhaar System', *New America*, 5 August 2019, www.newamerica.org/fellows/reports/anthology-working-papers-new-americas-us-india-fellows/key-differences-between-the-us-social-security-system-and-indias-aadhaar-system-kaliya-young.

identities, 'a single cog linking a discrete set of giant wheels'.[55] This means that both its problems, described in some detail below, as well as its purported benefits, are fundamental in character, arising from its materiality which is digital. Maya Ganesh described Aadhaar as 'a public–private partnership and a government project, critical public infrastructure, a complex socio-technical system, a biometric database, a contested legal subject, and now, a flagrant security risk',[56] making it a sum of multiple material parts, whose character pervades the existing and intended state machinery.

As mentioned above, the Indian state (much like other nation-states) has always collected data about its citizens to facilitate its governance. The history of identification in post-colonial India initially commenced with the intention of establishing citizenship in the newly formed Republic in India, later evolving over time to facilitate inclusion through national ID cards, voter IDs, censuses, and national surveys. Soon after India's independence, the Indian Constituent Assembly Secretariat was tasked with creating an electoral roll in the absence of any system to document the influx of refugees. Notably, refugees were allowed to self-assert their identities by filing a declaration to reside permanently in that constituency. This evolution of identification in India has continued to its present, controversial attempt to distinguish between legal and illegal immigrants on the basis of religion.

The history of identification in India is very much the history of welfare surveillance and consequent discrimination. Rationing was introduced in India as a wartime measure during World War II. Between 1943 and 1945, ration cards were initially assigned as a welfare measure to heavy manual workers to entitle them to additional rations, but its push was also largely driven by fears of hoarding by residents that would hamper war efforts.[57] Allotment of a ration card relied on proof of a stable residential address, which automatically excluded a large section of the population, such as nomadic tribes or migrant workers, from its ambit. The practice of tethering food rations to proofs of residence continues to this day. This requirement, as well as the bureaucratic maze that had to be navigated to meet basic requirements, resulted in the ration card becoming a scarce commodity for the undocumented poor who most needed it to access their entitlements. In order to enable migrant workers and their families to access PDS entitlements from a Fair Price Shop anywhere in the country, the government initiated a scheme titled 'One Nation, One Ration Card,' that has been implemented across the country as of June

---

[55] Ashish Rajyadhaksha, 'In the Wake of Aadhaar: The Digital Ecosystem of Governance in India', Centre for Study of Culture & Society (May 2013), www.scribd.com/document/179127122/In-the-Wake-of-Aadhaar-The-Digital-Ecosystem-of-Governance-in-India.

[56] Maya Ganesh, 'Scenes from #DIGITALINDIA: Fintech, Aadhaar and Contesting Identities', Tactical Tech, https://ourdataourselves.tacticaltech.org/posts/50-fintech-aadhaar-and-contesting-identities.

[57] Tarangini Sriraman, 'Revisiting Welfare: Ration Card Narratives in India', *Economic & Political Weekly* 46, no. 38 (2011).

2022.[58] This new digital measure also promises to bring in its own brand of exclusions. During the Covid-19 pandemic, the welfare rations were denied to those migrant labourers who were unable to produce an Aadhaar card.[59]

In the aftermath of the Kargil war in 1998, a Kargil Review Committee was set up in India to recommend measures to 'safeguard national security against such armed intrusions'. In addition to its recommendations to introduce a comprehensive space and aerial-based surveillance system, it also pushed for ID cards to be issued in sensitive border areas.[60] The attack on Parliament in 2001 served as a further impetus to issue smart cards as identification documents, particularly at airports and to access PDS. In 2001, a Group of Ministers, in their report titled 'Reforming the National Security System', proposed a multipurpose national identity card (MNIC). A pilot project for MNIC was launched in 2003[61] as a means to address 'illegal' immigration and identify citizens and legal residents in India. The MNIC project envisioned the idea of a single national identity through a unique national identification number issued to every citizen and resident in the country. The MNIC faced various hurdles in execution such as non-availability of data-entry operators in regional languages, difficulty in capturing photographs and finger biometrics, as well as a weak document base,[62] in addition to claims by state governments that the problem of unlawful immigration was exaggerated, rendering the MNIC unnecessary.[63] Ultimately, it was observed that 'citizenship was a very complex and complicated issue', and the MNIC in its intended form was abandoned in 2009 after it could only establish the citizenship of less than half the residents who participated in the pilot project.[64]

The gamut of identification- and citizenship-related efforts are governed by the Citizenship Act, enacted in 1955 to lay down rules for the determination or acquisition of Indian citizenship. All persons living within the territory of India as on 26 November 1949 automatically became citizens when the relevant provisions of

---

[58] Sandip Das, 'India Completes One Nation One Ration Card Implementation', *Financial Express*, 22 June 2022, www.financialexpress.com/economy/india-completes-one-nation-one-ration-card-implementation/2568642/.

[59] Rakhi Ghosh, 'COVID-19: Odisha Workers Stranded Because They Don't Have Aadhaar', *The Wire*, 9 May 2020, https://thewire.in/labour/covid-19-odisha-workers-stranded-because-they-dont-have-aadhaar.

[60] 'Executive Summary of the Kargil Committee Report', Internet Archive, 2 October 2008, https://web.archive.org/web/20081002125842/http://rajyasabha.nic.in:80/25indi1.htm.

[61] 'Parliamentary Consultative Committee of MHA Discusses Multi-Purpose National Identity Card Project', Ministry of Home Affairs, 21 August 2003, https://archive.pib.gov.in/archive/releases98/lyr2003/raug2003/21082003/r2108200315.html.

[62] Sushant Singh, 'Once Upon a Time, a National ID Project Found: Complicated to Prove Citizenship', *Indian Express*, 9 February 2020, https://indianexpress.com/article/india/once-upon-a-time-a-national-id-project-found-complicated-to-prove-citizenship-6258291.

[63] Dipak Mishra, 'Bihar Govt Refuses to Implement ID-Card Plan', *Times of India*, 13 February 2003, https://timesofindia.indiatimes.com/city/patna/Bihar-govt-refuses-to-implement-ID-card-plan/articleshow/37306745.cms.

[64] Singh, 'Once Upon a Time, a National ID Project Found'.

the Constitution of India came into force. Citizenship can be acquired through birth, descent, registration, and naturalisation.[65] The Act has been amended multiple times, with almost every amendment narrowing the conditions under which citizenship could be claimed. A 2003 amendment of the Act introduced the definition of 'illegal immigrants', and mandated the preparation of a National Register of Citizens. A 2019 amendment of the Act provided illegal immigrants of Hindu, Sikh, Buddhist, Jain, Parsi, and Christian religious minorities, who had fled persecution from Pakistan, Bangladesh and Afghanistan before December 2014 with a path to citizenship (notably excluding Muslim refugees from these countries).[66] This was the first instance of the law governing Indian citizenship being based on an overt religious criterion.

During discussions around the 2019 amendment in Parliament, the government announced that it would be initiating a nationwide National Register of Citizens (NRC). The NRC is an official demographic record of all persons who qualify as 'legal' citizens of India under the Citizenship Act 1955.[67] At present, only Assam has maintained an updated database; however, the government declared last year that this register would be extended to the entire country. The final draft of the controversial NRC exercise in Assam has excluded the names of over 4 million people who claim to be bona fide citizens.[68]

The government has also stated in Parliament that it is preparing a National Population Register (NPR) which will enumerate 'usual residents'[69] and verify the citizenship status of each individual, as a first step towards the NRC.[70] While the Home Ministry has claimed that the NPR will not collect biometrics,[71] the Office of the Registrar General & Census Commissioner still includes collection of 'biometric particulars' as a stated objective of the Register. The NPR will have three data elements: (a) demographic information, (b) biometric information, and (c) Aadhaar Number. This activity intended for 2020 has been postponed to September 2022 – along with the 2021 Census – due to the Covid-19 pandemic. This is intended to be followed by the National Register of Indian Citizens (NRIC) exercise. The NRIC is

---

[65] Citizenship Act 1955.
[66] 'Parliament Passes the Citizenship (Amendment) Bill 2019', *Press Information Bureau*, 11 December 2019, https://pib.gov.in/PressReleseDetailm.aspx?PRID=1596059.
[67] Amit Ranjan, 'National Register of Citizen Update: History and Its Impact', *Asian Ethnicity* 22, no. 3 (2019): 447–463, www.tandfonline.com/doi/abs/10.1080/14631369.2019.1629274?journalCode=caet20.
[68] Ibid.
[69] A usual resident is defined for the purposes of NPR as a person who has resided in a local area for the past six months or more or a person who intends to reside in that area for the next six months or more.
[70] 'Rajya Sabha Unstarred Question No. 378', Ministry of Home Affairs (2014), www.mha.gov.in/MHA1/Par2017/pdfs/par2014-pdfs/rs-261114/378.pdf.
[71] 'No Documents or Biometric to Be Taken for NPR: Home Ministry', *Bloomberg*, 15 January 2020, www.bloombergquint.com/politics/no-documents-will-be-asked-or-biometric-taken-for-npr-home-ministry.

envisioned to be a more complex and granular set of databases relying on several large national databases such as 'EPIC (Electors Photo Identity Card), Census (2011 and 2021), last Socio-Economic (Caste) Census, BPL list, MNREGA, Aadhaar, PAN (income tax), GST (indirect tax), ration card, the telecom users list, banking, various benefit schemes'.[72]

DIGITAL IDENTIFICATION AND DISCRIMINATORY IMPACTS

The new forms of digital identification amplify the discriminatory implications of identity systems by classifying the population into 'desirable' and 'undesirable' groups. In times past, this was done by using pseudoscientific biometric studies that correlate physical measurements to group-based characteristics, such as intelligence and morality. Inspired by social Darwinist theories of racial inequality, European scientists rationalised racial inequalities through the fields of anthropometry (study of the measurements and proportions of the human body), craniology (study of the shape and size of the skulls of different human race), and phrenology (study of the shape and size of the cranium as a supposed indication of character and mental abilities). This was a disputed/controversial practice, because of the communities it demonised and the discrimination it encouraged. As we will show in this section, today, this group prejudice and stereotyping are reinforced through new biometric identification systems.[73]

Technological Discrimination

In the case of Aadhaar, the discriminatory implications of the identification technology manifest themselves most notably in the form of exclusions of demographics comprising manual labourers, a group dominated by underprivileged castes and tribes. The use of light-based biometric scanners with relatively high false-positive rates makes the technology inherently more biased against certain demographics.

The use of biometric authentication for access to important goods and services has undeniable risks. Residents who do not or are unable to obtain the Aadhaar ID cannot gain access to these services that they were previously entitled to. Even for ID holders, the Aadhaar programme created controversy by failing to authenticate those in need of social services, in several cases ultimately leading to the death of some Aadhaar holders. The 2016–17 Government of India Economic Survey estimated that the authentication failure rate for Aadhaar was as high as 49% for Jharkhand, 6% for Gujarat, 5% for Andhra Pradesh, and 37% for Rajasthan.[74] The eroding of

---

[72] C. P. Jeevan, 'Centre Holds the Aces: Frankenstein of NRIC Is Real', *National Herald*, 16 January 2020, www.nationalheraldindia.com/opinion/centre-holds-the-aces-frankenstein-of-nric-is-real.

[73] David Lyon, *Identifying Citizens: ID Cards as Surveillance* (Cambridge: Polity, 2009).

[74] 'Economic Survey 2016–17', *Government of India*, 173, www.thehinducentre.com/multimedia/archive/03193/Economic_Survey_20_3193543a.pdf.

biometric features such as fingerprints due to manual labour, the lack of reliable internet and mobile network technology, and the employment of workers unfamiliar with this technology etc., all work together to produce authentication failures, and consequently restrict access to essential goods and services, such as subsidies and rations. The Aadhaar system requires the interplay of multiple fragile technologies, working simultaneously: the Point-of-Service (PoS) machine, biometrics, internet connectivity, remote servers, and, in many cases, other elements such as local mobile networks.[75]

The State of Aadhaar report in 2019 found that those who did not have Aadhaar were not a random cross-section of the population, but rather, highly marginalised communities such as trans people and homeless people, who had a much lower enrolment level. About one-third (30%) of all homeless and about one-quarter (27%) of third-gender people did not have Aadhaar, despite over 80% of them trying to register, often with multiple attempts.[76] It also found that enrolment was almost always lower for groups commonly perceived as socio-economically less well off: some minority religions (Muslim, Christian) have lower enrolment levels than the national average; scheduled tribes have lower levels than Other Backward casts (OBC)[77] or intermediate castes.[78] A report released by the Right to Food campaign detailing deaths due to starvation for those who failed to obtain Aadhaar accounts was illuminating; they almost entirely comprised persons from the Dalits,[79] adivasi, OBC, or Muslim community.[80]

Over the last few years, UIDAI has indicated that it will incorporate facial recognition technology (FRT). UIDAI is running pilot projects to test the functionality of the FRT application program interface (API) for financial services.[81] Facial recognition technology is essentially a kind of biometric identification technology, much like fingerprints and iris scans. Using local feature analysis algorithms, the technology analyses photographs and video to measure metrics such as the shape of

---

[75] Jean Dreze, 'Dark Clouds over the PDS', *The Hindu*, 10 September 2016, www.thehindu.com/opinion/lead/Dark-clouds-over-the-PDS/article14631030.ece.

[76] Dalberg, 'State of Aadhaar: A People's Perspective' (2019), 15–18, https://stateofaadhaar.in/assets/download/SoA_2019_Report_web.pdf.

[77] 'Other Backward Class' is an official classification of the population of India by the government of India, along with 'General Class', 'Scheduled Castes and Scheduled Tribes', referring to castes that are educationally or socially disadvantaged.

[78] Dalberg, 'State of Aadhaar'.

[79] 'Dalit' is a name referring to people belonging to the most excluded and disadvantaged caste in India.

[80] 'In the Absence of Aadhaar, Starvation Deaths Continue in Jharkhand', *Sabrang India*, 21 November 2018, https://sabrangindia.in/tags/starvation-deaths; Rahul Bhatia, 'How India's Welfare Revolution Is Starving Citizen', *New Yorker*, 16 May 2018, www.newyorker.com/news/dispatch/how-indias-welfare-revolution-is-starving-citizens.

[81] Ashwin Manikandan and Saloni Shukla, 'Facial Recognition, Iris Scans May Be Used for Welfare Scheme Payouts', *Economic Times*, 26 August 2020, https://economictimes.indiatimes.com/corporate/facial-recognition-iris-scans-may-be-used-for-welfare-scheme-payouts/articleshow/77753699.cms.

chin, the distance between the eyes, and other distinctive facial characteristics to create a mathematical sequence, called a face template. This face template, much like the fingerprint biometric sequence, is the unique identifier of a person.

When used to identify unknown persons, FRT often intrudes on privacy because it is a covert, remote, and mass authentication technology. This means that it works without providing notice of its existence and use, requires no direct interaction with the subject, and its intended deployments are usually not targeted at suspects, but are instead designed to surveil everyone. Therefore, significant privacy and free-speech concerns exist with deployment of this technology for law enforcement purposes.

If facial recognition is used to capture images of persons attending a protest or at places deemed suspicious, it can be used to authenticate them against centralised databases such as Aadhaar (this is currently not permitted under the Aadhaar Act unless authorised in the interest of national security), and if this information is used to populate suspects' databases, it could have chilling effects on free speech and expression. Reportedly,[82] the Delhi police has used FRT to screen crowds of people who had attended a rally held by the prime minister using a photo dataset of 'history sheeters' for routine crime investigations, images of terror suspects, and a third category of 'miscreants.'

The problem is further exacerbated when the FRT being employed by the law enforcement agencies has the potential to confirm the bias of the police when it comes to dissent and criminal activities. This can be used to target communities which have historically been discriminated against and targeted by law enforcement, such as religious minorities, scheduled castes and scheduled tribes. These groups constitute approximately 39 per cent of India's population, but they constitute a much higher percentage of the prison population – 55 per cent of the the population detained in prison pending trial during the period of investigation. A high number of those detained pending trial and convicts from marginalised groups would inevitably lead to the facial recognition system technology having a disproportionate data set representing these communities; consequently, the technology may be biased from its very inception, leading to 'false positives' being generated.

Discrimination by Proxy

The emergence of India Stack – a set of APIs built on top of the Aadhaar system, to be deployed and managed by several agencies, including the National Payments Corporation of India – promises to provide a platform over which different private players can build their digital applications. An architecture like India Stack works as

---

[82] Jay Mazoomdar, 'Delhi Police film protests, run its images through face recognition software to screen crowd', *Indian Express* (December 28, 2019): https://indianexpress.com/article/india/police-film-protests-run-its-images-through-face-recognition-software-to-screen-crowd-6188246/.

an interface for financial transactions, enabling datafication of financial transactions by ingesting transaction data for further data analysis. However, this move towards a cashless economy with sharp nudges from the government could lead to a lack of financial support in case of technological failures. Lack of regulation in emerging data-driven sectors, such as financial technology, can enable predatory practices where the right to remotely deny financial services can be granted to private-sector companies.

In India, and the Global South, fintech is often portrayed as a force of inclusion and empowerment for the 'unbanked' poor majority.[83] Prominent business areas in the fintech sector in India include credit scoring, lending, payments, brokerage, and insurance.[84] One of the fast-emerging areas of opportunity is social credit scoring, due to the low penetration of financial services, and the emphasis on financial inclusion by the government.[85] With the increased use of information and communication technology, particularly through mobile phone penetration, everyday activities of people leave behind a much larger digital footprint, which can serve as behavioural data. This 'big data' phenomenon has also impacted financial institutions, and there is a greater push to move beyond traditional sources of data for credit scoring and underwriting, as well as use of big data technologies along with the conventional statistical techniques.[86] Big data proponents claim that it will give creditors a fuller picture of a consumer, and therefore give a more accurate prediction of the consumer's ability to repay. These practices involve analysis of numerous 'potential credit variables' in a manner which provides insights about an applicant's creditworthiness.

Credit scoring using alternate data in a regulatory vacuum also poses the risk of bad lending decisions, discriminatory results, and mission creep. Big data-enabled credit scoring works by collecting, identifying, and analysing data that can be used as proxies, as mentioned above, for the three key questions in any credit scoring model – (a) identity, (b) ability to repay, and (c) willingness to repay. With the advent of big data and greater digitization and datafication of information, new data sources such as telecom data, utilities data, retailers, and wholesale data and government data, are available.

Big data-enabled credit scoring poses the challenge of opaque algorithms using undisclosed and proprietary methodology which could be used to circumvent fair

---

[83] Aneel Karnani, 'Romanticizing the Poor', *Stanford Social Innovation Review* (2009), http://ssir.org/articles/entry/romanticizing_the_poor.

[84] Sindhu Kashyap, 'Already Touching over 46 Deals and $285.65 mn, Is Fintech the Name of the Game for 2016?' *YourStory*, 14 July 2016, https://yourstory.com/2016/07/fintech-startups-2016.

[85] Bala Srinivasa, 'The Parallel Universe of Indian Fintech?' *YourStory*, 5 August 2016, https://yourstory.com/2016/08/the-parallel-universe-of-indian-fintech.

[86] Billie Anderson and Michael Hardin, 'Credit Scoring in the Age of Big Data', *Encyclopedia of Business Analytics and Optimization* (2014), 549–557, www.semanticscholar.org/paper/Credit-Scoring-in-the-Age-of-Big-Data-Anderson-Hardin/f5562611e28df691b1846d9bf0025e09b2fd6c66#citing-papers.

lending regulations.[87] Even in jurisdictions which provide a right of access to citizens to check and verify their credit reports,[88] use of credit scoring using big data will prevent an examination of how loan eligibility was determined.[89] There is a lack of non-discrimination regulations in the credit scoring industry in India which prevent intentional discriminatory use of data or obligations to safeguard against unintentional disparate impacts of data-driven decision-making. Thus, there are no laws which prevent the firms from collecting data on religion, caste, etc. which can be used toward disparate treatment. Even in other jurisdictions, there is a call for fintech firms to be exempt from equal credit opportunity and fair credit regulations.[90] Instead of using discriminating factors such as religion and caste which could potentially be addressed by non-discrimination laws, firms might use proxies of such factors such as neighbourhood of residence and purchasing habits. Because big data scores use closed and proprietary algorithm-based technologies, it is impossible to analyse them for potential discriminatory impact. There are no regulations that may be used to address discrimination on the basis of the disparate impacts of data-driven decision-making in India.

In India, the government has rolled out the direct benefits transfer (DBT) scheme in various states where benefits and subsidies are transferred to the bank accounts seeded with the Aadhaar numbers of the individuals directly, in order to do away with the intermediaries involved in the flow of funds, thereby reducing leakages.[91] In the absence of regulations governing lending practices and credit reporting for small loans, lending companies could provide small loans to even those who may not have the capability to pay back loans, as long as they can deduct the DBT benefits reaching the borrower's bank account towards repayment of loans. The only way fintech firms can drive financial inclusion is by 'de-risking' those who otherwise be considered as risky borrowers.

The Struggle for Substantive Equality

As discussed in the introduction, the fulcrum for anti-discrimination laws in India are the constitutional provisions protecting equality. Article 15 of the Constitution

---

[87] 'Examining the Opportunities and Challenges with Financial Technology ("FinTech"): The Development of Online Marketplace Lending', Testimony by Gerron S. Levi before the Subcommittee on Financial Institutions & Consumer Credit House Committee on Financial Services, US House of Representatives (12 July 2016) https://web.archive.org/web/20181223074901/https://financialservices.house.gov/uploadedfiles/hhrg-114-ba15-wstate-glevi-20160712.pdf (archived).

[88] The Fair Credit Reporting Act requires credit bureaus to permit individuals to dispute negative information on their credit reports and to give their own side of the story on disputed information in reports generated for potential creditors, insurers, and employers. It also requires that consumers receive some account of why their credit reports might have led to a denial of credit.

[89] US Department of the Treasury, *Opportunities and Challenges in Online Marketplace Lending*, 10 May 2016, 20.

[90] 'Examining the Opportunities and Challenges with Financial Technology ("FinTech")'.

[91] 'Home', Direct Benefits Transfer, https://dbtbharat.gov.in.

prohibits the Indian state from discriminating on the grounds of religion, race, caste, sex, and place of birth in various day-to-day activities, including but not limited to employment opportunities. Article 14 of the Constitution of India guarantees equality before the law and equal protection of the laws to all persons in India, but allows affirmative action measures under some circumstances.

Article 15 also articulates the positive discrimination agenda of the Indian state by enabling special reservation for women and socially and educationally less-developed classes of citizens, including scheduled castes and scheduled tribes, in educational institutions. The socio-economic rights under Article 39 of the Constitution also urge the state to ensure that citizens, men and women equally, have the right to an adequate means of livelihood, right to shelter, food, education and work. The Constitution was guided by B. R. Ambedkar's vision that 'political democracy cannot succeed where there is not social and economic democracy', and the Indian constitutionalism must balance equality with liberty.

However, most identity-based legislations in India are primarily penal statutes, which sanction violation of anti-discriminatory duties imposed on public authorities. Further, barring a couple of exceptions, most existing laws and policies are focused only on single-axis discrimination and do not have any element of intersectionality. As more and more research suggests that discrimination is often aligned along multiple factors of identity, this remains problematic. In the absence of an all-encompassing anti-discrimination law that would adequately address the varied dimensions of inequality, the state's welfare agenda is still falling short.

Even within this agenda, the supposed role that private actors are meant to play in providing more opportunities to the unbanked ensures that the agenda is still being implemented by the same surveillance systems that have endangered racially underprivileged groups. Biometric technologies, reliance on digital surveillance to control the behaviour of targeted groups, and the use of sorting algorithms to classify groups into desirables and undesirables very much follow in the footsteps of the technological paradigms that have systematically led to the marginalisation of and discrimination against the groups that it now seeks to empower. As is clear from the account of systemic exclusions and discrimination resulting from the digital welfare system in India, the consequences of these systems, both when they fail due to flaws in design and even when they work as intended, are to amplify the existing socio-economic inequities.

6

Surveillance in South Africa

From Skin Branding to Digital Colonialism

Michael Kwet

INTRODUCTION

South Africa's long legacy of racism and colonial exploitation continues to echo throughout the post-apartheid era. For centuries, European conquerors marshaled surveillance as a means to control people of color. This began with the requirements for passes to track and control the movements, settlements, and labor of Africans. Over time, surveillance technologies evolved alongside complex shifts in power, culture, and the political economy.

This chapter explores the evolution of surveillance regimes in South Africa. The first surveillance system in South Africa used paper passes to police slave movements and enforce labor contracts. To make the system more robust, various white authorities marked the skin of workers and livestock with symbols registered in paper databases. At the beginning of the twentieth century, fingerprinting was introduced in some areas to simplify and improve the passes. Under apartheid, the National Party aimed to streamline a national, all-seeing surveillance system. It imported computers to impose a regime of fixed racial classification and keep detailed records about the African population. The legal apparatus of race-based surveillance was finally abolished during the transition to democracy. However, today a regime of big data, artificial intelligence, and centralized cloud computing has ushered in a new era of mass surveillance in South Africa.

South Africa's surveillance regimes were always devised in collaboration with foreign colonizers, imperialists, intellectuals, engineers, and profit-seeking capitalists. In each era of history, the United States increased its participation. During the period of settler conquest, the United States had a minor presence in Southern Africa. With the onset of the minerals revolution, however, US presence expanded, and American capitalists and engineers with business interests in the mines pushed for an improved pass system to police African workers. Under apartheid, American corporations supplied the computer technology essential to apartheid governance and business enterprise. Finally, during the post-apartheid era, Silicon Valley corporations, together with US surveillance agencies, began imposing surveillance capitalism on South Africa. A new form of domination, digital colonialism, has emerged, vesting the United States with unprecedented control over South African society. To counter the force of digital colonialism, efforts are taking hold to redesign the digital ecosystem as a socialist commons based on free and open source technology, knowledge sharing, internet decentralization, critical education, universal accessibility, communal ownership, and bottom-up democracy.

COLONIAL SURVEILLANCE: FROM SLAVERY TO MINING

European colonists began settling in Southern Africa in the seventeenth century. In 1652, Jan van Riebeeck established a refreshment station in what became the Cape Colony of the Dutch East India Company. While the station was initially an outpost for maritime trade routes connecting the Netherlands to the East Indies, the Dutch quickly established permanent settlements. They conquered the land, put the indigenous Khoikhoi to work, and imported slaves across Indian Ocean territories.

To manage indentured and slave labor, the Europeans eventually instituted *pass law* systems of surveillance. The first passes were introduced in 1760 at the Cape Colony to control the movement of slaves, and were extended to the Khoikhoi in 1797. While pass systems varied according to time and place, all passes met two fundamental criteria: (1) they were required for lawful movement into and out of a specified area; and (2) they must be produced when demanded by an authority; failure to do so constituted an offense.[1] This first pass law system was designed to restrict the migration of black agricultural labor within the Cape and prohibit movement across the frontier border.

At the turn of the century, the English wrestled control of the Cape from the Dutch. In reaction to the abolition of the slave trade in 1807 and growing support for emancipation, the Earl of Caledon countered black liberation with the infamous Hottentot Proclamation[2] – pass laws which restricted the free movement of African labor and set the basis for the racially segregated society that would eventually culminate in apartheid.[3]

Caledon's Code was designed to bind workers to their employers. The Code required the Khoikhoi to register a fixed place of residence and carry a pass when moving outside their homes. It also introduced compulsory registration of contracts through district authorities in order to prevent the desertion of African slaves and

---

[1] Ellison Kahn, "The Pass Laws," in Ellen Hellman and Leah Abrahams (eds.), *Handbook on Race Relations in South Africa* (Cape Town: Oxford University Press, 1949), 275.
[2] "Hottentot" was a derisive term for the Khoikhoi.
[3] Walter Sisulu, "The Extension of the Pass Laws," *Liberation* 17 (1956): 12–14, http://disa.ukzn .ac.za/sites/default/files/pdf_files/LiMar56.1729.455X.000.017.Mar1956.6.pdf.

keep Khoikhoi workers beyond their terms of contract. Movement was prohibited across the Cape border which, at least in theory, locked workers to the land.

With Ordinance 50 of 1828, the Caledon Code was repealed. The Khoikhoi received formal legal equality, and slavery was to be abolished five years later.[4] Despite these reforms, new laws adapted surveillance to white interests. Ordinance 49 mandated a pass for "Native foreigners" (Africans from outside the Colony) and ended the blanket prohibition against cross-border travel. Passes were issued by whites at the border to manage the flow of migrant labor coming into the Cape.[5] The final arrangement facilitated an economy mixing market allocation with forced servitude.[6]

As the nineteenth century progressed, several new developments took place. In the Cape, Governor Sir George Grey's Employment Act integrated the pass system into a labor bureau, which placed regulatory power over work contracts and labor flows into the hands of government officials. In the eastern province of Natal, each Indian immigrant was assigned a unique identity number and profiled by authorities in permanent documentary records. And in the Boer republics,[7] a registration regime rationalized commando raids used to capture African children for unofficial slavery.[8]

Overall, it was too difficult for white authorities to register and ensnare the majority of the black population, as the technologies available were too primitive. With a paper-and-pen system, for example, masters could merely name and describe a person's characteristics (such as height, age, and tribe) using written text. Pass-holders could forge copies or swap passes with relative ease. Without reliable authentication, there is no way to ensure that individuals really are who they say they are.

In the absence of advanced technology, whites resorted to barbarous techniques. To boost the reliability of surveillance, settlers resorted to "writing on the skin" of Africans and livestock. Using hot irons, needles, and Indian ink, they branded bodies with unique symbols also listed in paper registers. Marks on Africans or (allegedly)

---

[4] The Emancipation Act of 1833 abolished slavery throughout the British empire. In the Cape Colony, it went into full effect in 1838.

[5] Those without a pass could be sentenced to forced labor for up to a year, and contracts shortened terms for African labor to a one- to twelve-month period. Keith Breckenridge, "Power without Knowledge: Three Nineteenth Century Colonialisms in South Africa," *Journal of Natal and Zulu History* 26 (2005): 3–30.

[6] Doug Hindson, "Origins of Pass Controls in Agriculture and on the Mines," in *Pass Controls and the Urban Proletariat in South Africa* (Johannesburg: Ravan Press, 1987), 15–27.

[7] "Boers" refers to the first white settlers of Dutch and French Huguenot descent. The Boer republics were established in the nineteenth century by the Boers when they decided to move inland in reaction to the British takeover of the Cape Colony, which started at the end of the eighteenth century. Boers were farmers who wanted to retain a system of slavery; they would eventually self-identify as "Afrikaners."

[8] In this system, child "apprentices" called *inboekelings* were often stolen from their parents, who were sometimes murdered in the process. The trade in children was known "black ivory." In the far north district of Zoutpansberg, black ivory outstripped the trade in white (elephant) ivory – a primary commodity for export prior to the discovery of diamonds and gold. See Martin Meredith, *Diamonds, Gold and War: The Making of South Africa* (London: Simon & Schuster UK Ltd, 2007), 7–8; Breckenridge, "Power without Knowledge," 24–26.

stolen animals could then be checked against a paper register of symbols (similar to a phone book) distributed to local officials.[9]

The skin branding system strengthened identity verification. However, as Lance van Sittert notes, the creation of a special registration system was limited by thin communications infrastructure and administrative capacity. Colonists thus opted for "makeshift regional-scale registration systems within the penal system (for stock thieves and other convicts) and veterinary department (for livestock) at minimal cost to the public purse."[10]

Shamefully, flogging was also used for tracking. White colonists believed police failed to suppress black stock theft, so they took matters into their own hands. In the final third of the nineteenth century, they administered corporal punishment at an industrial scale.[11] "The cat to scratch a man's back raw" would punish alleged miscreants and administer "a brand mark to be left on them to denote that they are felons." Scarred flesh would "disgrace" the "Kafir" and show him "as long as he lives, something has gone wrong with him."[12] Africans would think twice before they stole from colonists.

SURVEILLANCE UNDER THE MINING MAGNATES

Simple surveillance technologies would persist for many years to come. However, the discovery of diamonds and gold concentrated populations into smaller areas and changed the nature and distribution of power. The rise of industrial capitalism, combined with the invention of fingerprinting, altered the surveillance landscape.

In 1871 diamonds were unearthed in the fields of Colesberg Kopje in Griqualand West while in 1886, vast seams of deep-level gold were discovered at a Transvaal farm on the Witwatersrand.[13] These fateful findings transformed the history of Southern Africa. A struggle for mineral-rich land soon culminated in the Anglo-Boer Wars (1880–1881; 1889–1902) between the British and the Afrikaner settlers. In 1902, the Treaty of Vereeniging ended the Second Boer War and paved the way for the establishment of the Union of South Africa in 1910. United in a racist pact, the

---

[9] The addition of wire fencing channeled "all human and animal traffic onto a few main roads," which made it easier to stop and check Africans for passes. Lance van Sittert, "Writing on Skin: The Entangled Embodied Histories of Black Labour and Livestock Registration in the Cape Colony, c.1860–1909," *Kronos* 40 (2014): 74–98, 96–97.

[10] From 1880–1910 (the only time period for which we have data), approximately 150,000 blacks were prosecuted for stock theft; two-thirds were convicted. Ibid., 81.

[11] Between 1893 and 1909, "stock thieves comprised half the more than 40,000 new prisoners incarcerated annually in the Colony's convict stations and one-fifth of them (some 4,000 men) were flogged each year as part of their sentence ... at an average of more than 18 lashes per man." Ibid., 83.

[12] Ibid., 82. The term "cat" refers to the "cat o' nine tails," a multitailed whip used for severe physical punishment. The term "kaffir" is a racist word for blacks in South Africa.

[13] Diamonds were first discovered in 1867 along the banks of the Orange River. For a history, see Meredith, *Diamonds, Gold and War*.

white settlers further dispossessed blacks of their land, entrenched the migratory labor system, and deepened the stranglehold of white minority power.

As "diamond fever" took hold in the 1870s, thousands of "diggers," mainly Southern Africans, flooded into Kimberley looking to strike it rich. Yet land claims quickly concentrated into the hands of whites and a few large mining companies established by the white settlers. Settlements clustered around the company lands, and migrant labor become the new norm.

White claim-holders were intent on exploiting black labor. Without labor regulations to prevent desertion, and facing losing battles against the mining magnates, small white claim-holders pinned their problems on the black population. In response, by 1872, they demanded sweeping labor regulations. The British acceded with Proclamation 14, which, Martin Meredith explains:

> laid down a new regime for labour contracts, linking it to a system of pass laws that became the main device for controlling black labour throughout southern Africa for decades to come. On arrival in Kimberley, black migrants – "servants" – were required to register at a depot and obtain a daily pass until they had secured employment. The labour contract they were given showed the name of the servant, his wages, his period of service and the name of his master. Once employed, the servant was required to carry a pass signed by his master.[14]

At the Kimberley mines, whites created the segregated housing arrangement foundational to South Africa's iconic migratory labor system. Initially, black laborers stayed in compounds with white diggers or housed themselves in tents or sheds. New laws eventually herded blacks into fenced and guarded barracks owned and controlled by the mining companies. The "closed compound system," as it came to be known, was based on a convict station built by Cecil Rhodes's De Beers mining company in 1885. At the station, black "convicts" were housed and fed by the company while they performed unpaid compulsory labor.

Mining companies implemented the panoptic surveillance model for black laborers as a mechanism of worker control.[15] Panopticons are arrangements which place surveillance authorities in a physical location which obscures the watcher. Those under the authority of the watcher(s) must assume they are being watched at any point in time, leading them to behave as if the authority is always watching them, thereby conforming to the expectations of the watchers.

---

[14] Ibid., 45. Punishments for violations included a £7 fine, three months' hard labor, or flogging. Masters were permitted to search the person, residence, or property of their servants without a warrant. The law was color-blind in theory, but singled out blacks in practice. Until the 1880s, a large proportion of African mineworkers did not register service contracts, and the pass system in place was poorly administered. See Hindson, 'Origins of Pass Controls', 21.

[15] Ibid., 157. See also, Jonathan Crush, "Scripting the Compound: Power and Space in the South African Mining Industry," *Environment and Planning D: Society and Space* 12, no. 3 (1993): 301–324.

Restricted by fences and barbed wire, the closed compound system provided a means to control diamond theft and the mobility of workers. It also tore apart the black family, keeping male workers away from their loved ones for long stretches of time. A regime of social control eventually encompassed all African living space. By the mid-1880s, "there was little discernible difference between the workplace, the compound, the location, and the jail in Kimberley; all were part and parcel of the same system of labor control."[16] A similar process unfolded in the Transvaal. On the gold mines, semiclosed compounds could close off premises to the outside world, but permitted workers to enter surrounding townships and slums – provided they secured passes.[17]

Deep-level digging was onerous and dangerous work and the mining magnates soon found themselves in need of more bodies. In 1889, the Witwatersrand Chamber of Mines was established to increase and regulate African labor and lower wages.[18] A variety of sources weighed in on the problem, including US elites. By 1895, at least half of the new gold mines were managed by Americans, and their engineers became "a 'new industrial intelligentsia' ... fitted to resolve [South Africa's] social conflicts."[19] The Americans wanted the pass laws strengthened for worker control. In a report compiled by the Witwatersrand Chamber of Mines, a leading American engineer, Sydney Jennings, stated:

> We have here a most excellent law, in my opinion – namely, the Pass Law – which, if properly carried out, and efficiently administered, will enable us to get complete control over our kaffir labourers ... We can get kaffirs here from other places on a contract for twelve months, but they work for only two weeks and then leave, and it is impossible to find them ... If every kaffir could be traced; if it could be told whether they have been registered before, or been in the service of a company, then we would have control over them.[20]

---

[16] William Worger, *South Africa's City of Diamonds: Mine Workers and Monopoly Capitalism in Kimberley, 1867–1895* (New Haven, CT: Yale University Press, 1987), 146.

[17] By 1910, "there were over fifty compounds on the Witwatersrand, housing 200,000 miners." Crush, "Scripting the Compound," 306. See 305–311 for pictures.

[18] For the sentiments of the Chamber, see The Witwatersrand Chamber of Mines, Johannesburg, S.A.R., *The Mining Industry: Evidence and Report of the Industrial Commission of Enquiry* (Johannesburg: Times Printing and Publishing Works, 1897).

[19] Shula Marks and Stanley Trapido, "Lord Milner and the South African State," *History Workshop* 8, no. 1 (1979): 61–62. The engineers harbored deeply racist views and had influence upon the "courts, schools, government, commissions, factories, and prisons." William Honnold, co-founder of the Anglo-American Corporation, held that the importation of "niggers" from the United States would "become a great nuisance by reason of the distorted American ideas of liberty and equality" that would "awake[n] a spirit of insubordination among the ordinary natives." Honnold preferred the importation of Chinese indentured servants to plug labor shortages on the mines. See John Higginson, "Privileging the Machines: American Engineers, Indentured Chinese and White Workers in South Africa's Deep-Level Gold Mines, 1902–1907," *International Review of Social History* 52, no. 1 (2007): 6–16.

[20] The Witwatersrand Chamber of Mines, *The Mining Industry*, 44; see also, Keith Breckenridge, *Biometric State: The Global Politics of Identification and Surveillance in South Africa, 1850 to the Present* (Cambridge University Press, 2014), 67–70.

To trace every African, however, was a daunting task. There were many thousands of Africans, with little more than a pass card issued by a company to keep tabs. Fingerprinting was introduced as a solution, thanks in large part to the work of Sir Francis Galton. The British cousin of Charles Darwin, Galton created the field of biometrics, comprised of two branches: the statistical science of measuring living animals and the technology of biological measurements used for identification. Galton's work would leave an indelible mark on the history of racism.

In 1850, Galton embarked on a two-year trip from Cape Town to present-day Namibia. He documented his travels in *Tropical South Africa*, a pseudo-anthropology hit that catapulted him into the elite ranks of the British intelligentsia. Galton wrote that the "Hottentots" were "greasy savages" that "clicked, and howled, and chattered, and behaved like baboons," "loved nothing," and were "made for slavery."[21] While in Southern Africa, Galton began forming notions of hereditary racial hierarchies that would inform his contributions to statistics, give rise to the pseudoscientific theory of race-based IQ, and influence the field of Social Darwinism.[22] Galton also coined the term "eugenics" – the selective breeding of humans to "improve" the human race. In 1873, he wrote that the "civilized world" would gain "immensely" if Africans were "out-bred" and "finally displaced" by Chinese migrants to the continent.[23]

Soon thereafter, Galton invented the modern fingerprint classification system. Understanding his technique could be used to track criminals and police the poor, he recommended fingerprinting illiterate subjects in the English colonies. The moment came in 1902 when, at the behest of Joseph Chamberlain, a self-described "imperialist," Sir Edward Henry was appointed as Transvaal Commissioner of Police. Henry introduced fingerprinting and a single, centralized register to verify African identities in the Transvaal. The Henry Classification fingerprinting system[24] – an improvement to Galton's scheme – aimed to kill two birds with one stone. It provided an alternative to written documentation for contract and signature by illiterate Africans, and it offered a fool-proof method of authentication.

Hundreds of thousands of Africans were soon registered with passes. However, due to resource constraints, only those convicted of a crime or accused of desertion

---

[21] Francis Galton, *The Narrative of an Explorer in Tropical South Africa* (London: J. Murray, 1853), 15, 21, 73.

[22] Stuart Ewen and Elizabeth Ewen, *Typecasting: On the Arts and Sciences of Human Inequality*, rev. ed. (New York: Seven Stories Press, 2006/2008), 291–308; Stephen Jay Gould, *The Mismeasure of Man*, revised and expanded (New York: W. W. Norton & Company, Inc., 1981/1996), 107–109; Breckenridge, *Biometric State*, 28–62.

[23] Francis Galton, "Africa for the Chinese," *The Times*, June 5, 1873, http://galton.org/letters/africa-for-chinese/AfricaForTheChinese.htm.

[24] The system, which became the global standard for fingerprinting, was designed by a team working for Sir Henry, including two Indian policemen, Azizule Haque and Hem Chandra Bose, whose contributions were erased from history. G. S. Sodhi and Jasjeet Kaur, "The Forgotten Indian Pioneers of Fingerprint Science," *Current Science* 88, no. 1 (2005).

were placed into Henry's fingerprint system. At the behest of the mines, Henry also issued a new law requiring police to detain Africans without passes so they could check their fingerprints. As Keith Breckenridge notes, this became a signature element of South African racism. Throughout the twentieth century, ten percent of African males (and, in increasing numbers, females) were imprisoned every year due to pass violations.[25]

During this time, fingerprinting failed to achieve universal coverage. Highly publicized resistance from Mahatma Gandhi and the Indian population of Natal soured white opinion of fingerprinting in the Cape, while the cost of widespread implementation remained prohibitive. It wasn't until the rise of apartheid that fingerprint biometrics would touch the lives of every African.

APARTHEID SURVEILLANCE

The previous sections detailed the extent to which many of the practices characteristic of the apartheid state had already been implemented during earlier periods. Before the apartheid regime was established in 1948, biometric technologies and pass laws were adapted to local conditions and unevenly applied throughout the South African landmass. The apartheid government introduced a more unified surveillance regime that covered the entire country. In some areas, statutes were too difficult or impossible to enforce. Yet throughout the territories, some form of a pass system was used for segregation, labor control, and punishment.

The apartheid government introduced a more unified surveillance regime that covered the entire country.[26] The National Party (NP) was elected to office by whites in 1948 on the platform of apartheid (meaning "apartness") – a legal system that institutionalized the separation of the races politically, economically, and socially for the benefit of white minority rule.[27] To administer the new racial order, the NP began constructing a totalitarian surveillance state. The project began by assigning fixed, unambiguous racial identities to each person. The Population

---

[25] Breckenridge deems "the automatic imprisonment" for pass violations "the distinguishing characteristic of the [twentieth century] South African state." See Breckenridge, *Biometric State*, 73, 76–77.

[26] For example, pass laws dated back to the slave era. The Glen Grey Act of 1894, the Mines and Works Act of 1911, and the Natives Land Act of 1913 segregated employment and the land, while mixed-race sexual relations were culturally and legally prohibited in various forms dating back to Dutch settlement. For a historical discussion, see William Beinart and Saul Dubow (eds.), *Segregation and Apartheid in Twentieth-Century South Africa* (London: Routledge, 1995).

[27] The apartheid concept was used by the National Party to lure white voters away from the liberal United Party. The NP received less votes than the liberal United Party, but took more seats in the House of Assembly, and were able to form a new government under the leadership of Daniel Malan. See H. J. Simons, "Concepts of Apartheid (Conclusion)," *Liberation* 36 (1959): 16–25.

Registration Act of 1950 sorted the public into three races: white, "coloured," and Native (later called Bantu and then "black").[28] In 1961, "Indian" became the fourth official race.[29] Tens of legislative acts were passed to segregate residential housing, marriage, sex, access to public facilities, schooling, and urban space.[30] The outcome entrenched racial identity deep into the psyche of the people: "For those who had little option but to live within the framework of these categories, the habit of reading the symptoms of race was naturalised widely" in everyday life.[31]

With complete categorization in place, the government added a second component, the passbooks. All Africans over the age of 16 received identity cards affixed to a "reference book," also called Bewysboek (by Afrikaners) or Dompas (by Africans, meaning "dumb pass"). Information in the Dompas included the personal history and movements of each carrier, official permissions, medical records, employer information, and tax receipts, while photographs and fingerprints were used to verify individuals against a central register. The new system consolidated disparate paper records into a "personal file" for each African.[32]

As the Population Registration Act was being implemented, the National Party passed the Bantu Authorities Act in 1951 to force all Africans into ten nominally independent "Bantustans" (what the NP called "homelands") that were overseen and administered by white authorities, each corresponding to an African ethnic group. The Bantustans were designated thirteen percent of the land, even though blacks comprised around 75 percent of the population. The Nationalists used vast collections of data to help them segregate the society. Comprehensive data was needed to stem the tide of African movements to the cities and enforce residential quotas. As a former prime minister, Jan Smuts, remarked, "you might as well try to sweep the ocean back with a broom. A "mania for measurement" thus pervaded the Department of Native Affairs, rooted in the impulse to "count and control." According to Deborah Posel, what makes apartheid distinct from the previous era is "a concerted bid to 'modernise' racial domination" through a state "sufficiently large, powerful,

---

[28] Deborah Posel, "Race as Common Sense: Racial Classification in Twentieth-Century South Africa," *African Studies Review*, 44, no. 2 (2001): 87–113; Roger Omond, *The Apartheid Handbook: A Guide to South Africa's Everyday Racial Policies* (Harmondsworth, Middlesex: Penguin, 1986), 24–25. Criteria in the 1951 census was based on physical appearance and social status ("common sense") rather than genealogy. Once the initial assessment was put into place, whites with black ancestors were in the clear. In 1962, the law was amended to redefine race according to parental status. See Omond, *The Apartheid Handbook*, 25.
[29] Karyn Pillay, "Perpetual Foreigners: Indian Identity in South Africa, 1948–1994," *Diaspora Studies* 10, no. 11 (2017): 45–63.
[30] Omond, *The Apartheid Handbook*.
[31] Deborah Posel, "What's in a Name? Racial Categorisations under Apartheid and their Afterlife," *Transformation* 47 (2001): 59–82, 74.
[32] Breckenridge, "Power without Knowledge," 85.

bureaucratically expert and knowledgeable to keep each race in its proper place economically, politically and socially."[33] Apartheid elites firmly believed in the power of data to manipulate the masses.[34]

In 1952, IBM South Africa imported the electronic tabulating punched card machines needed to process the census.[35] The population registration was successful; however, within months, it became apparent that the rest of the project was in peril. In Pretoria, paperwork ballooned out of control, while extensive backlogs formed for lost and duplicate Dompas and fingerprint registration.[36] The technology available could not handle the information overload, and the fantasy of God-like oversight and management of the apartheid order quickly collapsed.

Nevertheless, white elites marched forward with as much surveillance as they could handle. More generally, electronic data processing remained essential to the apartheid project. US tech corporations were the central suppliers of the computers needed for governance and business enterprise. In those days, computers were refrigerator-sized machines that cost hundreds of thousands of dollars. South Africa did not have a native computer industry, so it depended on imports. For every computer lost, hundreds of bookkeeping staff were required to conduct work by hand – staff that were not available on the market. Without computer automation, the administrative capacity of the state and industry would have suffered greatly, if not collapsed.[37]

During the apartheid era, American involvement reached new heights, extending from the military, air defense, and explosives to mining, business, and finance. A variety of US corporations profited handsomely and sought to keep the gravy train flowing.[38] Moreover, Washington aimed to pacify Southern African liberation movements as part of its Cold War strategy.[39] The US government and its

---

[33] Deborah Posel, "A Mania for Measurement: Statistics and Statecraft in the Transition to Apartheid," in Saul Dubow (ed.), *Science and society in Southern Africa* (New York: Manchester University Press, 2000), 116, 126, 131.

[34] In this regard, we can note that some of the techniques currently employed by big data and artificial intelligence systems were envisioned for National Party governance. For example, Posel remarks that the Department of Native Affairs "imagined the possibility of its own omniscience in the form of all-encompassing racially disaggregated and elaborately cross-referenced statistical data, which quantified the extent of a host of 'problems' confronting the state and the manner of their 'solutions.'" Ibid., 116.

[35] IBM also bid to service the reference book system imposed on Africans, but it lost the contract to British-based International Computers Limited.

[36] Keith Breckenridge, *Biometric State*, 147–160.

[37] NAMRIC/American Friends Service Committee (AMFC), *Automating Apartheid: U.S. Computer Exports to South Africa and the Arms Embargo* (Philadelphia, PA: Omega Press, 1982).

[38] Henry Jackson, *From the Congo to Soweto: U.S. Foreign Policy toward Africa since 1960* (New York: William Morrow and Company, 1982), 244–282. See also Richard Knight, *US Computers in South Africa* (New York: The Africa Fund, 1986).

[39] President Ronald Reagan placed the African National Congress on the government's terrorist list. Though records have not been "confirmed or denied," two weeks before his death, former

corporations thus had convergent interests in the shipment of computers to the apartheid regime.[40]

International grassroots pressure soon formed in response to horrific incidents like the 1955 Women's March in Pretoria and the 1960 Sharpeville Massacre, where police shot and killed sixty-nine protesters demonstrating against the passes. Calls for non-binding sanctions were made at the United Nations in 1962, but the United States and several allies rejected it. Soon thereafter, the United States implemented its own weak arms embargo that left the status quo intact. When more comprehensive bans were approved in 1977, behind the scenes, US corporations and their subsidiaries were "determined to undercut any sanctions action and ... made plans to camouflage their operations through subterfuges arranged with affiliates in other countries."[41] Sanctions were fraught with loopholes and exceptions; by the early 1980s, nearly three-quarters of all computers in South Africa were still provided by US firms.[42]

Around 1970, the National Party began initiating plans to improve civil registration through the "Book of Life" registry. The new Book of Life booklet – distinct from the passbooks – further centralized the population register by indexing all public documents and records to a single identity book with a unique number. By extending the book to all races, including whites, it further solidified state-mandated racial classifications. Coupled with the Bantu Homelands Citizenship Act of 1970 (allocating Africans to homelands), the Book of Life stripped native peoples of their

---

CIA spy, Donald Rickard, "admitted" to providing the intelligence that led to Nelson Mandela's August 1962 arrest. See Feliks Garcia, "Former CIA Agent Admits Involvement in Nelson Mandela's Arrest," *The Independent*, May 15, 2016, www.independent.co.uk/news/world/africa/nelson-mandela-cia-arrest-south-africa-a7030751.html.

[40] Hundreds of thousands of Africans were killed in the Angolan independence struggle alone, largely at the hands of the US-backed South African Defense Force, which imported US computers to bolster its military capacity. See Abayomi Azikiwe, "Henry Kissinger's War Crimes Should Not Be Forgotten," *Africa Insight* 32, no. 2 (2002): 59–64; Paul N. Edwards and Gabrielle Hecht, "History and Technopolitics of Identity: The Case of Apartheid South Africa," *Journal of Southern African Studies* 36, no. 3 (2010): 619–639; "Partners in Apartheid: U.S. Policy on South Africa," *Africa Today* 11 no. 3 (1964): 2–17. For details on computer sales to the military, see Gert Slob, *Computerizing Apartheid: Export of Computer Hardware to South Africa* (Amsterdam: Holland Committee on Southern Africa, 1990), 20–36; NAMRIC/AMFC, *Automating Apartheid*, 40–60.

[41] US Embassy, Pretoria, Cable to Secretary of State, October 13, 1978, as quoted in NAMRIC/AMFC, *Automating Apartheid*, 9.

[42] By the 1980s, IBM controlled about 40% of the estimated 4,500 computers in South Africa. Major US actors included: Control Data, Burroughs, Sperry Rand, IBM, Hewlett-Packard, NCR, Mohawk Data Sciences, and Computer Sciences Corporation. Additional brands included Intel, RCA, General Electric, 3M, Kodak, Motorola, and Apple. American computer manufacturers sold devices directly to South Africa or, when restricted by sanctions and popular pressure, through distributors. See NAMRIC/AMFC, *Automating Apartheid*, 6–7; Knight, *US Computers*, 8–9. For a summary of sanctions-busting under Reagan, see Hennie van Vuuren, *Apartheid, Guns and Money: A Tale of Profit* (Auckland Park, South Africa: Jacana Media (Pty) Ltd., 2017), 287–334.

South African citizenship.[43] The project aimed to bring the vision of grand apartheid to completion.[44]

IBM serviced the Book of Life contract, operating a special computer room in the basement of the thirty-story Civitas building in Pretoria. When questioned about its role, an IBM official brushed off the notion it was assisting apartheid. The official stated that IBM's technology is politically neutral, that IBM would never sell equipment used for repression, and that "the pass system could be done in many other ways besides computers."[45]

Local government policymakers planned a transition to electronic governance in accordance with US models. Foreshadowing cloud-based surveillance, one Pretoria bureaucrat said they were moving towards "total computerization of local government," following the lead of many US cities, by integrating information into "a large central computer with remote terminal links for planning agencies, engineers, administrators, educators and the police." Cities even planned to issue warnings based on "concentrations of crime" in "problem areas," much like today's predictive policing.[46]

In addition to the state, computerized surveillance was deployed internally by the private sector. In the 1980s, facing an outbreak of strikes and subversion, the Chamber of Mines created a centralized database which kept fingerprints and dossiers on each recruit for potential blacklisting.[47] IBM provided the guidance for the system, which computerized storage and access to employment and fingerprint records. Fingerprinting was coupled with an ID card and a unique employee number. With a shared industry database, a worker could be labeled "undesirable"[48] at one mine and blacklisted from the others. Centralization and networking were paramount: in 1988, various mining houses "agreed to move towards a system of one mineworker, one card" for tracking within and across mining compounds. TEBA recruiting corporation created a "wide area network" used to blacklist those designated undesirable, who had little awareness of the tech being used or the bargaining power to resist.[49]

Across the spectrum of society, panoptic capabilities frequently fell short of grandiose aspirations, largely due to a lack of technological sophistication and resources – a recurring theme dating back to the first passes. Nevertheless,

---

[43] Electronic Frontier Foundation (EFF), "EFF Amicus Brief IBM S. African Apartheid," (2014), 6–7, www.eff.org/document/eff-amicus-brief-ibm-ats-claim.
[44] Edwards and Hecht, "History and the Technopolitics," 625.
[45] As quoted in NAMRIC/AMFC, *Automating Apartheid*, 15.
[46] Ibid., 24.
[47] Crush notes that from 1908 to 1991, recruiting and services corporation TEBA amassed 10.5 million dossiers, with one official stating, "No record is ever destroyed." Jonathan Crush, "Power and Surveillance on the South Africa Gold Mines," *Journal of Southern African Studies* 18, no. 4 (1992): 825–844, 829.
[48] The "undesirable" category included, "'malicious damage', 'riotous behaviour', 'theft', 'forgery', falsifying records', illegal work stoppages', restricting production', intimidation', 'fighting', possession of or under the influence of alcohol', 'disorderly conduct', negligence', 'insubordination' and 'immoral behavior.'" Ibid., 837–838.
[49] Ibid., 839–840.

surveillance passes devastated the African population. According to government data, 637,584 Africans were arrested for not carrying official identity documents in the ten years prior to 1985. By contrast, two coloureds, zero Indians, and zero whites were arrested.[50] In practice, more than anything else, the Dompas provided a thin legal cover for mass incarceration and police brutality.[51]

To put a human face on this, consider the testimony of Elsie Gishi provided in a 2002 law suit against IBM New York. On December 26, 1976, police and military officers kicked in Gishi's door and shot her in the back, arm, and neck. One bullet remains lodged in her throat, and one in her left arm. The entire left side of her body is lame, and she can no longer lift her arm, bathe herself, or do other washing.[52] Racist savagery, sanctioned by pass violations, has left Ms. Gishi with permanent respiratory dysfunction and kidney problems. Other testimonies, such as that of Thandiwe Shezi, describe extreme torture and rape in the most grotesque ways imaginable.[53]

In 1994, Nelson Mandela was elected to president, and the savage pass laws were put to rest. The Dompas remains the most hated symbol of apartheid, a relic of a nightmare past. Yet today, mass surveillance has returned through a different, more insidious form: digital colonialism.

DIGITAL COLONIALISM: AMERICA'S TECH EMPIRE RETURNS

The prior eras of surveillance in South Africa were initiated through colonization – first by Dutch settlers in the early colonial period; then through British colonization of the Cape, mining, and industrialization; and, finally, by the Afrikaners under the apartheid state. In the early period, the United States appears to have had zero participation.[54] During the minerals revolution, American capitalists and engineers pushed for greater worker surveillance. Under apartheid, US corporations supplied the computers needed for population registers, records keeping, military combat, policing, and data processing. During each wave, surveillance tech was upgraded and US participation increased. In all previous eras, however, the United States merely supported South African elites aligned to its geopolitical interests and corporate profits.

---

[50] 17.12 million were arrested for violating pass laws between 1916 and 1981. In 1982, Parliament was told pass law arrests averaged one person every two and a half minutes. About 60% of Africans were convicted on their first appearance in court. See Omond, *The Apartheid Handbook*, 123–130.

[51] On this point, see Breckenridge, *Biometric State*. The true extent of the policing system is likely lost to history: the apartheid police services destroyed their records in 1992 during the transition to democracy. Edwards and Hecht, "History of Technopolitics," 634.

[52] Khulumani et al. v. Barclays National Bank et al., (2008), 7–8, https://www.asser.nl/upload/documents/DomCLIC/Docs/NLP/US/Khulumani_Complaint_24-10-2008.pdf.

[53] Ibid, 10–11.

[54] For a review of US relations in colonial South Africa, see Y. G.-M. Lulat, *United States Relations with South Africa: A Critical Overview from the Colonial Period to the Present* (New York: Peter Lang Publishing, Inc. 2008).

The current wave of US surveillance is imposed by Americans themselves on South African society through digital colonialism – the use of technology for political, economic, and social domination of another territory.[55] Led by Silicon Valley, US transnational corporations are actively colonizing the "digital land" of the global tech economy. As partners to domestic intelligence agencies, they also provide the American government with surveillance powers to bolster its geopolitical power.[56]

The proximate origins of this story date back several decades. As South Africans were celebrating the beginnings of electoral democracy, across the Atlantic, the digital revolution was advancing within the Global North. Tim Berners-Lee had invented the World Wide Web, and personal internet connectivity became commonplace among middle- and upper-class households in wealthy countries. Dreams of an internet ruled by the world's people – rather than governments and corporations – inspired many at the "electronic frontier" of internet connectivity.[57]

Arguably, the high-water mark of digital freedom came in the mid-2000s.[58] Personal computers and internet connectivity had dropped in price, Free and Open Source Software – commons-based software with no private owners – became entrenched in many parts of the digital ecosystem, and platforms like Wikipedia enabled greater public participation in the production of free, often high-quality information. Music became more accessible, in large part due to technologies like Napster, KaZaa, and bit torrent. Peer-to-peer networking was on the rise, and scholars were celebrating "commons-based peer production."[59] The use of the

---

[55] Michael Kwet, "Digital Colonialism: US Empire and the New Imperialism in the Global South," *Race & Class* 60, no. 4 (2019): 3–26; Michael Kwet, "Digital Colonialism: South Africa's Education Transformation in the Shadow of Silicon Valley," PhD Dissertation, Rhodes University (2019), https://papers.ssrn.com/sol3/papers.cfm?abstract_id=3496049 (see 25–27 for a partial overview of digital colonialism scholarship). Of course, neocolonial elites exploit the people living inside their own borders.

[56] See, among others, James Bamford, *The Shadow Factory: The NSA from 9/11 to the Eavesdropping on America* (New York: Anchor Books, 2009); Glenn Greenwald, *No Place to Hide: Edward Snowden, the NSA, and the U.S. Surveillance State* (New York: Metropolitan Books, 2013); Jennifer Stisa Granick, *American Spies: Modern Surveillance, Why You Should Care, and What to Do About It* (New York: Cambridge University Press, 2017).

[57] John Perry Barlow, "A Declaration of the Independence of Cyberspace," 1996, www.eff.org/cyberspace-independence. Barlow has been criticized for downplaying capitalism, corporate power, and the need for government regulation. In response, he said he has a "Marxist sense" that "there will be a global commons that includes all of humanity" not subservient to governments. Andy Greenberg, "It's Been 20 Years since this Man Declared Cyberspace Independence," *Wired*, February 8, 2016, www.wired.com/2016/02/its-been-20-years-since-this-man-declared-cyberspace-independence.

[58] See Yochai Benkler (with Eben Moglen), "Degrees of Freedom, Dimensions of Power," 2017, https://downloads.softwarefreedom.org/2017/conference/0-keynote.webm; Yochai Benkler, "Degrees of Freedom, Dimensions of Power," *Daedalus* 145, no. 1 (2016): 18–32.

[59] Yochai Benkler, *The Wealth of Networks: How Social Production Transforms Markets and Freedom* (New Haven, CT: Yale University Press, 2006).

internet for educational purposes was poised to challenge commercial interests that saw it as an untapped market for profit and exploitation.[60]

This configuration changed quickly, however, with the rise of centralized platforms, big data, and cloud computing. Google rapidly wiped out competition from the likes of Yahoo, Lycos, and AltaVista to become king of the search engine. Soon thereafter, it purchased DoubleClick and exploited its position as an intermediary to become an ad behemoth. Facebook overtook MySpace, centralized control of the social networking space, and a Google–Facebook duopoloy in internet advertising ensued. Microsoft retained hegemony over the desktop and laptop operating system, while Apple and Google took control of the smartphone market. Within a short amount of time, a handful of Silicon Valley corporations colonized the digital economy.

By 2021, GAFAM (Google/Alphabet, Apple, Facebook/Meta, Amazon, and Microsoft) had a combined market cap exceeding $7 trillion,[61] and most of the world's digital products and services outside of mainland China were privately owned and controlled by US transnational corporations. A partial list includes: search engines (Google); web browsers (Google Chrome); smartphone/tablet operating systems (Google Android, Apple iOS); maps (Google); chat apps (Meta's WhatsApp, Facebook Messenger, Snapchat); email (Google, Microsoft, Yahoo); desktop/laptop operating systems (Microsoft Windows, macOS); office software (Microsoft Office, Google Workspace); cloud infrastructure and services (Amazon, Microsoft, Google's); social networking platforms (Facebook, Twitter); transportation (Uber, Lyft); business networking (Microsoft's LinkedIn); streaming video (Google YouTube, Netflix, Hulu); online advertising (Google, Meta); and computer processors (Intel, AMD, Nvidia, Qualcomm, Broadcom).

China, by contrast, has gained a notable market share outside its borders across a few industries or products, such as 5G, CCTV cameras, commercial drones, safe and smart cities projects, and its TikTok social media service. A sub-imperial power, it also has substantial market share in minerals extraction from countries like the Democratic Republic of Congo, and its tech giants exploit labor in the Global South. Yet outside of US and Chinese borders, the digital economy remains dominated by US transnationals.

Commentators often portray the global digital economy as a battle between the United States and China, as if there is parity between the two, but this is not empirically accurate. Economist Sean Starrs profiled the world's top 2,000 publicly traded companies, as ranked by *Forbes Global 2000*, and organized them according to twenty-five sectors, showing the dominance of US transnationals. As of 2013, they

---

[60] Eben Moglen, "The Invisible Barbecue," *Columbia Law Review* 97, no. 4 (1997): 945–954.
[61] Ryan Vlastecila and Dina Bass, "Microsoft Rises to Join Apple in Exclusive $2 Trillion Club," Bloomberg, June 22, 2021, www.bloomberg.com/news/articles/2021-06-22/microsoft-rallies-to-join-apple-in-exclusive-2-trillion-club.

dominated in terms of profit shares in eighteen of the top twenty-five sectors.[62] By 2020, the gulf remained. For IT Software & Services, US profit share was 76 percent versus China's 10 percent; for Technology Hardware & Equipment, it was 63 percent for the US versus 6 percent for China; and for Electronics, it was 43 and 10 percent, respectively. Other countries, such as South Korea, Japan, and Taiwan, often fare better than China in these categories as well. The United States also dominates the domains of investment and intellectual property well beyond that of any other country, including China.[63]

The centralization of technological power into the hands of American Big Tech firms is derived from ownership and control of the core pillars of the digital ecosystem: software, hardware, and network connectivity. Software is the set of coded instructions that tell computers what to do. Hardware is the components which comprise the devices that run computer software. Network connectivity connects computers together through platforms, common standards, and protocols so they can communicate with each other. Information flowing through the internet is shaped by the power relations that structure the digital ecosystem.[64] Private owners are dominant, and they use their power to keep knowledge and information locked behind paywalls, forcefully extract data from the population, and force ads on consumers.

Other factors produce market concentration. With *network effects*, each additional node makes the network more valuable. Just as people do not want to have to use fifty different phone networks, people do not want to use fifty social networking or e-hailing apps. Eventually, users flock to one or a few networks, as we see with Facebook, Twitter, and TikTok.[65] Added to this, *economies of scale* make it expensive to create competitor products. A YouTube competitor, for example, would need to spend billions of dollars on server infrastructure, advanced computer engineers, expensive software that screens out copyrighted works, and a team of lawyers, among other expenses. Monopolistic practices such as *mergers and acquisitions* also fatten the pockets of tech giants. YouTube was acquired by Google, Instagram and

---

[62] Sean Starrs, "American Economic Power Hasn't Declined—It Globalized! Summoning the Data and Taking Globalization Seriously," *International Studies Quarterly* 57 no. 4 (2013): 817–830; Sean Starrs, "Can China Unmake the American Making of Global Capitalism?" *Socialist Register* (2018): 173–200.

[63] Sean Starrs, personal email, October 18, 2020. See also, Sean Starrs, *American Power Globalized: Rethinking National Power in the Age of Globalization* (New York: Oxford University Press, under review); Cecilia Rikap, *Capitalism, Power and Innovation: Intellectual Monopoly Capitalism Uncovered* (New York: Routledge, 2021).

[64] Eben Moglen, ""Die Gedanken Sind Frei": Free Software and the Struggle for Free Thought," *Wizards of OS 3*, June 10, 2004, http://moglen.law.columbia.edu/publications/berlin-keynote.html.

[65] Michael Kwet, "Fixing Social Media: Toward a Digital Democratic Commons," *Markets, Globalization & Development Review* 5, no. 1 (2021): 1–12, https://digitalcommons.uri.edu/mgdr/vol5/iss1/4; Michael Kwet, "Social Media Socialism: People's Tech and Decolonization for a Global Society in Crisis," *SSRN*, https://papers.ssrn.com/sol3/papers.cfm?abstract_id=3695356.

WhatsApp by Facebook, LinkedIn and Skype by Microsoft – the examples are extensive.[66] Additionally, there are tactics available to the wealthy corporations, such as the capacity to lobby government and international trade organizations for favorable policies,[67] the ability for rich investors to shape the content and objectives of tech startups, and government funding for technology development.[68]

Though it is not often stated by intellectuals, colonialism *is* the business model of digital capitalism. Today, most of the people using the products and services provided by GAFAM are outside US borders, and the majority of revenues from many Big Tech giants are now derived from foreign territories.[69]

Digital colonialism exists because transnational corporations own and control the global digital ecosystem, which confers the power to design it for profit and plunder across the "open" internet. American firms exploit their position as infrastructure owners to generate revenue by charging end-users for a product or service, or by imposing ads and monetizing surveillance. Digital colonialism is thus inherently anti-poor, as the billions living on less than $7.40 per day – the amount needed for basic nutrition and normal life expectancy – lack the disposable income to pay for products and must therefore be force-fed ads and/or spied on to generate revenue and a profit.

Digital colonialism also undermines environmental sustainability, in large part because it exacerbates inequality and fuels destructive economic growth. This, in turn, accelerates the ecological crisis, because it is not possible to keep growing economies without destroying the environment and with it, much of life on earth.[70] In the twenty-first century, the global society is tasked to implement a degrowth-based economy which redistributes income and wealth the world's poor and reduces the material consumption of the middle and upper classes. Tech development must intersect with socialist restructuring for global equality and green economy.[71]

---

[66] See, among others, Robert McChesney, *Digital Disconnect: How Capitalism Is Turning the Internet against Democracy* (New York: The New Press, 2013); Douglas Rushkoff, *Throwing Rocks at the Google Bus: How Growth Became the Enemy of Prosperity* (New York: Penguin Random House LLC, 2016); Paris Martineau and Lousie Matsakis, "Why It's Hard to Escape Amazon's Long Reach," *Wired*, December 23, 2018, www.Wired.Com/Story/Why-Hard-Escape-Amazons-Long-Reach; Kiran Stacey, James Fontanella-Khan, and Stefania Palma, "Big Tech Companies Snap Up Smaller Rivals at Record Pace," *Financial Times*, September 19, 2021, www.ft.com/content/e2e34de1-c21b-4963-91e3-12dff5c69ba4.

[67] Burcu Kilic and Renata Avila, "Opening Spaces for Digital Rights Activism: Multilateral Trade Negotiations," May 31, 2018, www.citizen.org/article/51451-2.

[68] Rushkoff, *Throwing Rocks*, 168–224.

[69] Michael Kwet, "A Digital Tech New Deal to Break Up Big Tech," *Al Jazeera*, October 26, 2020, www.aljazeera.com/opinions/2020/10/26/a-digital-tech-new-deal-to-break-up-big-tech.

[70] See, among others, Kate Raworth, *Doughnut Economics: Seven Ways to Think Like a 21st Century Economist* (White River Junction, VT: Chelsea Green Publishing, 2017); Vishwas Satgar, *The Climate Crisis: South African and Global Democratic Eco-Socialist Alternatives* (Johannesburg: Wits University Press, 2018); Jason Hickel, *Less Is More: How Degrowth Will Save the World* (London: Penguin Random House, 2020).

[71] Michael Kwet, "The Digital Tech Deal: A Socialist Framework for the Twenty-First Century," *Race & Class* 63, no. 3 (2022).

On the state side of digital colonialism, in the wake of 9/11, the National Security Agency (NSA) and its allies piggybacked off corporate surveillance to construct the largest global surveillance apparatus in human history. As a succession of US whistleblowers revealed, by tapping the commercial internet backbone and obtaining direct access to the data collected by tech giants, government spies have gained unprecedented access to the world's private communications. Law enforcement agencies are following suit by requesting data from tech firms for policing activities. Scholars refer to the twenty-first-century state-corporate surveillance society constructed by the United States as "surveillance capitalism."[72]

The US empire not only overpowers emerging markets with foreign-owned infrastructure and services designed for state-corporate control, but it also dominates the conceptualization of how the internet society should work. This compares directly with the colonial past. Let us consider each in turn.

THE MECHANICS OF DIGITAL COLONIALISM IN SOUTH AFRICA

Under classical colonialism, Europeans seized and settled other people's land across the world. They built infrastructure, such as railroads and sea ports, not for the surrounding community, but for economic, political, and military domination. The settlers constructed heavy machinery and exploited people of color to extract raw materials for manufacturing at the mother country. As we saw earlier, in places like South Africa, engineers were hired to produce the chemicals needed to exploit the minerals, while panoptic structures were erected to police workers. The metropolis would then export cheap manufactured goods back to the colonized areas, destroying any prospect for local development. Dispossessed of resources and opportunities, the victims of empire became perpetually dependent on the colonial masters, who presided over an unequal global division of labor and expanded market, diplomatic, and military domination for profit and plunder.[73]

Today, Eduardo Galeano's "open veins" of the Global South are the "digital veins" traversing the ocean floors, wiring up a tech ecosystem owned and controlled by a handful of mostly US-based corporations. The transoceanic cables are often fitted with strands of fiber owned or leased by the likes of Google and Facebook for

---

[72] The term "surveillance capitalism" is frequently misattributed to Shoshana Zuboff. It was introduced by a diverse collection of scholars in the July–August 2014 special issue of *Monthly Review*. See "Notes from the Editors: May 2016 (Volume 68, Number 1)," *Monthly Review*, May 1, 2016, https://monthlyreview.org/2016/05/01/mr-068-01-2016-05_0.

[73] Walter Rodney, *How Europe Underdeveloped Africa (Revised Edition)* (Washington DC: Howard University Press, 1972/1981); Samir Amin, *Unequal Development: An Essay on the Social Formations of Peripheral Capitalism* (Sussex, UK: The Harvester Press Limited, 1976); L. S. Stavrianos, *Global Rift: The Third World Comes of Age* (New York: William Morrow and Company, Inc., 1981); Eduardo Galeano, *Open Veins of Latin America: Five Centuries of the Pillage of a Continent* (New York: Monthly Review Press, 1973/1997).

the purpose of data extraction and monopolization. The cloud centers are the heavy machinery dominated by Amazon and Microsoft, proliferating like military bases for US empire, with Google, IBM, and Alibaba following behind. The engineers are the corporate armies of elite programmers numbering the hundreds of thousands, with generous salaries of R4 million (US$250,000) or more as compensation. Those employees, in turn, consume tons of material goods produced by workers in the Global South through a process of ecologically unequal exchange.

The exploited laborers are the people of color producing the minerals in the Congo and Chile, the armies of cheap labor annotating artificial intelligence data in China and Africa, the East Asian workers enduring PTSD to cleanse Big Social Media of graphic content, and the vast majority of people asked to specialize in nondigital goods and services. The centralized intermediaries and spy centers are the panopticons, intellectual property and private ownership of the means of computation is the "land" used to extract rent, and data is the raw material processed for artificial intelligence services.[74]

The United States is at the helm of advanced economic production, which it dominates through the ownership of knowledge and core infrastructure, backed by imperial trade policies at the World Trade Organization. The missionaries are the World Economic Forum elites preaching the "Fourth Industrial Revolution," the CEOs of Big Tech corporations, and the mainstream "critics" centered in the United States who dominate the "resistance" narrative, many of whom work for or take money from Big Foundations or corporations like Microsoft and Google, and integrate with a network of US–Eurocentric intellectuals drawn from elite Western universities. Added to this, state-corporate elites, startups, and universities in the Global South are replicating the Silicon Valley model of digital capitalism.

The results are just beginning to alarm South Africans: Netflix is eating into the local pay-television market and takes a large share of subscriber video-on-demand; Google and Facebook now dominate the advertising revenue and distribution network previously owned by local media; and Uber is undercutting the metered taxi industry while exploiting its own workers.[75] In the developed world, concerns about Big Tech tend to revolve around the lives of US and European citizens. Yet in

---

[74] Michael Kwet, "Digital Colonialism: The Evolution of American Empire," *ROAR Magazine*, March 3, 2021, https://roarmag.org/essays/digital-colonialism-the-evolution-of-american-empire.
[75] Ferial Haffajee, "Uber, Netflix, Love and Taxes," *Business Live*, May 13, 2018, www.businesslive.co.za/bt/opinion/2018-05-12-ferial-haffajee-uber-netflix-love-and-taxes; Anton Harber, "How Google and Facebook Are the Biggest Threat to South African News Media," *Financial Mail*, November 16, 2017, www.businesslive.co.za/fm/features/cover-story/2017-11-16-how-google-and-facebook-are-the-biggest-threat-to-south-african-news-media; Camilla Houeland, "What Is Uber Up to in Africa?", *Africa Is a Country*, April 9, 2018, https://africasacountry.com/2018/04/what-is-uber-up-to-in-africa; Edward Webster and Fikile Masikane, "'I Just Want to Survive': A Comparative Study of Food Courier Riders in Three African Cities," December 2021, www.wits.ac.za/media/wits-university/faculties-and-schools/commerce-law-and-management/research-entities/scis/documents/I_just_want_to_survive.pdf.

Africa, when taxi business is lost to a transnational colonizer like Uber, people burn each other to death – and it's scarcely (if ever) reported in the North.[76]

One of the central case examples of digital colonialism in South Africa is unfolding through the education system. In 2015, the South African government created a plan called "Operation Phakisa in Education" behind closed doors to fast-track computers into all 26,000 South African schools. Despite South Africa's 2007 Free and Open Source Software (FOSS) policy giving preference to the use of FOSS in the public sector – including schools – the government is opting to use Microsoft and Google Android products in classrooms. Most African children have little more than a feature phone or low-grade smartphone, and are therefore completely reliant upon the state to provide them with a laptop or tablet. By supplying Microsoft or Google devices, children's future software knowledge and preferences will be biased towards Big Tech products and their technology platforms. The country's future technology developers will also likely develop products that plug into Microsoft or Google ecosystems, reinforcing their dominance. Product placement in the schools also deepens dependence upon centralized cloud services and places children under the watchful eye of corporations and the state, as if surveillance and corporate control is normal.[77]

In the domain of carceral surveillance, outcomes are equally alarming. The Global North has developed "smart" surveillance for military and law enforcement applications that has found its way to South Africa. In 2011, IBM renewed its commitments to the surveillance-based policing for profit through a five-year contract with the City of Johannesburg to offer "smart" policing. The IBM project included plans for crime prevention, investigation, and a data center with predictive analytics,[78] and its surveillance tech is being used by the Johannesburg policing authorities in their surveillance "nerve center."[79] In the United States, predictive policing has been criticized for racial bias, as has the use of software to predict future

---

[76] See, e.g., Virgilatte Gwangwa, "Death in Taxi War," *IOL*, July 18, 2017, www.iol.co.za/pretoria-news/death-in-taxi-war-10346054.

[77] Michael Kwet, "Operation Phakisa Education: Why a Secret? Mass Surveillance, Inequality, and Race in South Africa's Emerging National e-Education System," *First Monday* 22, no. 12 (2017), http://firstmonday.org/ojs/index.php/fm/article/view/8054; Michael Kwet, "Big Brother Set to Watch Each Pupil," *Mail & Guardian*, December 8, 2017, https://mg.co.za/article/2017-12-08-00-big-brother-set-to-watch-each-pupil; Michael Kwet, "The Dangers of Paperless Classrooms," *Mail & Guardian*, October 9, 2015, https://mg.co.za/article/2015-10-07-the-dangers-of-paperless-classrooms.

[78] Michael Kwet, "Apartheid in the Shadows: The USA, IBM and South Africa's Digital Police State," *Counterpunch*, May 3, 2017, www.counterpunch.org/2017/05/03/apartheid-in-the-shadows-the-usa-ibm-and-south-africas-digital-police-state.

[79] Michael Kwet, "The City Surveillance State: Inside Johannesburg's Safe City Initiative," *South Africa Institute for International Affairs (SAIIA)*, March 2021, https://saiia.org.za/research/the-city-surveillance-state-inside-johannesburgs-safe-city-initiative.

criminals.[80] The contract for smart policing has ended, while details about IBM's previous and current role remains off-the-record.

While the South African government should be fully transparent about surveillance technologies and vendor contracts, the deeper issue is the conceptual *model* of digital policing. The North has set the frame, even when it is not providing the products directly. Major cities are now implementing facial recognition and other forms of video analytics for smart surveillance, drawing on US–European law, such as the American notion that there is usually no "reasonable expectation of privacy in public," and weak regulations like General Data Protection Regulation (GDPR), to justify it.[81]

The Council of Scientific and Industrial Research (CSIR) has played its own part through the creation of surveillance software called Cmore. The system brings data streams from CCTVs, drones, cellular towers, and other sources into one platform, Cmore, for total surveillance of an area. The project was developed to prevent rhino poaching but was subsequently appropriated for border patrol and piloted for the South African Police Service (SAPS). Information about Cmore has been published online – but in outlets tucked away from public view, with few details about police applications.[82]

South Africa is often called "the protest capital of the world." Blanket CCTV coverage of urban areas could undermine the civil rights and liberties of those attempting to change the society through protest and disruption. Much like their colonial predecessors, some citizens who are not happy with the SAPS are taking matters into their own hands. The first residential neighborhood in South Africa to receive fiber internet was primarily motivated to build smart surveillance video feeds. Located in Parkhurst, Johannesburg, the town's SafeParks leadership believes that smart surveillance will help prevent "outsiders" from causing trouble in their town. Residents hope to employ facial recognition and infrared cameras, while "algorithmic interpretation" is used for "unusual behavior detection," which ostensibly contrasts loitering, panhandling, and other "abnormal" movements against "typical movements of people in a neighborhood, walking their dogs and so on." Put another way, they will use video analytics to police and target poor blacks and other "outsiders."[83]

---

[80] Julia Angwin et al., "Machine Bias," *ProPublica*, May 23, 2016, www.propublica.org/article/machine-bias-risk-assessments-in-criminal-sentencing; Kristian Lum and William Isaac, To Predict and Serve? *Significance* 13, no. 5 (2016): 14–19, https://rss.onlinelibrary.wiley.com/doi/full/10.1111/j.1740-9713.2016.00960.x.

[81] One of South Africa's Protection of Personal Information Act regulators, Collen Weapond, has stated that mass CCTV surveillance networks sprawling across the country are justifiable under the law. See Weapond quoted in Michael Kwet, "Smart CCTV Networks Are Driving an AI-Powered Apartheid in South Africa," *VICE News/Motherboard*, www.vice.com/en_us/article/pa7nek/smart-cctv-networks-are-driving-an-ai-powered-apartheid-in-south-africa.

[82] Michael Kwet, "Cmore: South Africa's New Smart Policing Surveillance Engine," *Counterpunch*, January 27, 2017, www.counterpunch.org/2017/01/27/cmore-south-africas-new-smart-policing-surveillance-engine.

[83] Michael Kwet, "Apartheid in the Shadows"; VPRO, "Bringing Internet to Africa," https://youtu.be/qlTZetW1Sy8?t=1942.

The cameras became a topic of national conversation in 2019, when Parkhurst's fiber provider, Vumatcl, alongside private security industry heavyweight, Ricky Croock, formally announced Vumacam – a surveillance company that would "blanket Johannesburg" with a wide-area smart camera network. Most of Vumacam's advance components originate in the Global North: Denmark-based Milestone provides the video management software; Microsoft provides cloud computing services; while Israel-based BriefCam and iSentry, a product based on Australian military technology, provide video analytics.[84]

The Parkhurst initiative recalls the colonial forefathers of surveillance innovation. As we saw earlier, when written "dumb" passes failed to effectively police alleged African livestock thieves, colonists attempted to enhance the system by branding skin and distributing copies of registers that would expand surveillance coverage to surrounding areas. In today's world, wealth South Africans seek to upgrade "dumb" analogue cameras to smart ones that can identify behaviors (with video analytics), track down vehicles from license plate registers (using automatic number plate readers), enable archival searches of recorded footage, and network together cameras to cover vast terrains (so criminals cannot "escape the grid" of a small CCTV network). Telecoms companies like Vox are even developing "internet of things" animal trackers to prevent livestock theft.[85]

Smart surveillance is also being integrated into "safe" and "smart" city projects. The City of Johannesburg and the City of Cape Town are rapidly expanding their own camera networks in centralized metropolitan "nerve centers."[86] Microsoft is now offering an "internet of things"-enabled cop car solution for "zero tolerance" policing. Its technologies include automatic license plate reader, a facial recognition camera, and other solutions for storage and analytics on the Microsoft Azure cloud.[87]

TECH HEGEMONY: RESISTANCE MOVEMENTS AND MISSIONARY NARRATIVES

In South Africa, and broader parts of the Global South, resistance to the current wave of digital colonialism began almost alongside the spread of the internet. In the early 2000s, South African policymakers understood that the digital revolution was under way, and they commissioned a series of reports to assess the ideal software

---

[84] Michael Kwet, "Smart CCTV Networks." China's Hikvision provides "dumb" cameras, and there are some South African components, including Croock's Calabash Storage Systems. On Microsoft's role, see Highpeak Technology Services, "A safer Johannesburg, a smarter IT solution," *TechCentral*, December 9, 2019, https://techcentral.co.za/a-safer-johannesburg-a-smarter-it-solution-tarprom/180754.
[85] Personal interviews with Rudy Potgieter (Vox), November 28 and December 2, 2019.
[86] For an overview, see Kwet, "The City Surveillance State."
[87] Michael Kwet, "The Microsoft Police State: Mass Surveillance, Facial Recognition, and the Azure Cloud," *The Intercept*, July 14, 2020, https://theintercept.com/2020/07/14/microsoft-police-state-mass-surveillance-facial-recognition.

policy for the country. Working groups were formed, and several reports spanning hundreds of pages concluded that South Africa should adopt FOSS in the public sector in order to develop a commons-based tech ecosystem based on the sharing of knowledge and software code rather than proprietary ownership.[88]

In those days, Microsoft was the dominant colonizer, with products that were sold by the unit. The rise of cloud-based "free" (as in price) software products was only developing in the background. South African policy documents named Microsoft as the primary threat, and recommended that the government counter its power through the use of FOSS.[89]

In 2007, Archbishop Desmond Tutu declared, "There are those who will take the fruits of the human mind and lock them up, dishing them out to us in metered amounts for a fee that locks most of our people out. And there are laws that are reserved for business reasons and changed to rob society of its own rights." To counter this trend, Tutu endorsed FOSS and "Free and Open Resources for Education."

FOSS, also called Free Software, aims to provide users the liberty to control their own technology by granting them the freedom to use, study, modify, and share software. Through this process, the Free Software Movement aims to replace the proprietary enclosure of information and technology with a knowledge commons.[90]

At the CSIR, Nhlanhla Mabaso spearheaded the formation of the Meraka Institute, dedicated to Free and Open Source technology.[91] Meanwhile, Geraldine Fraser-Moleketi, then minister of Public Service and Administration, pushed for FOSS policy in government. By 2007, the South African Cabinet, backed by civil society organizations, passed a Free and Open Source Software Policy Preference, which stipulated that public institutions must give preference to FOSS.[92]

The policy was scarcely implemented, however. Big Tech corporations diversified their sources of power – especially through the centralization of services in the cloud – and continued their spread into the society. In 2016, the City of Johannesburg announced that Microsoft would train over 1 million adults in computer literacy – using Microsoft software. Universities entered into partnerships with Microsoft and other Big Tech firms like IBM and Cisco. Facebook opened its office without protest, while tech giants opened cloud centers in Johannesburg (Microsoft) and Cape Town (Microsoft, Amazon). US corporate colonization proceeded apace.

During the 2000s, mainstream conversations about tech politics were few and far between, but there was an egalitarian and socialist-oriented movement – represented

---

[88] For a comprehensive overview of this process, see Kwet, "Digital Colonialism: South Africa's Education Transformation."

[89] Ibid., 180–190.

[90] Richard Stallman, *Free Software, Free Society: Selected Essays of Richard M. Stallman*, 3rd ed. (Boston, MA: Free Software Foundation, 2002/2015); Christopher Tozzi, *For Fun and Profit: A History of the Free and Open Source Software Revolution* (Cambridge, MA: The MIT Press, 2017).

[91] "Meraka" is Sesotho for "open grazing land."

[92] Kwet, "Digital Colonialism: South Africa's Education Transformation," 180–81, 209–10.

by the best of the Free Software community – driving the human rights conversation and efforts to beat back digital colonialism. As technology became more widespread and more intellectuals entered the fray, the Free Software Movement was drowned out. Three dominant global narratives emerged, each with their own missionary character supporting colonial conquest.

First, ruling-class elites, especially in the United States, pushed "tech solutionist" notions that technology is the savior of society.[93]

Second, elites outside the United States pushed a neocolonial ideology called the "Fourth Industrial Revolution" (4IR), coined by World Economic Forum leader Klaus Schwab. According to the 4IR, humanity is stuck with big data, intellectual property, centralized clouds, the "internet of things," "smart" and "safe" cities littered with surveillance, automation, algorithmic decision-making, Big Tech corporations, and surveillance capitalism.[94]

Operating within the 4IR framework, South Africa has been trying to "catch up" with the North through assimilation into the Silicon Valley ecosystem. US tech giants are being embraced by the South African government, the private sector, and universities, and their products and services are spreading throughout the country. While South Africans cannot compete with Big Tech for core services like operating systems and office suites, where they do aspire to develop new technologies, they often seek to replicate Silicon Valley model of rent extraction through surveillance and proprietary ownership. Domestic corporations and local startups are emulating Silicon Valley with ambitions to strike it rich and, in some cases, get bought up by foreign transnationals.

Third, Western intellectuals concentrated inside the United States have formulated a faux resistance doctrine, sometimes called the "techlash," that claims it is critical of Big Tech. Techlash intellectuals focus on a narrow set of problems, such as algorithmic bias; facial recognition; unionizing tech workers (without challenging private property or digital colonialism); weak "privacy" laws (like Europe's General Data Protection Regulation); content moderation; public options ("public interest technology") in a mixed capitalist economy; and antitrust, a legal regulatory apparatus committed to "competitive capitalism" and oriented to profit, expansion, and growth. In this worldview, problems revolve around making Big Tech and digital capitalism nicer – much like the Sullivan Principles during apartheid[95] – instead of phasing out and ultimately abolishing Big Tech corporations, capitalism, and the

---

[93] Evgeny Morozov, *To Fix Everything, Click Here: The Folly of Technological Solutionism* (New York: PublicAffairs, 2014).
[94] Klaus Schwab, *The Fourth Industrial Revolution* (New York: Crown Business, 2016); Michael Kwet, "Break the Hold of Digital Colonialism," *Mail & Guardian*, June 29, 2018, https://mg.co.za/article/2018-06-29-00-break-the-hold-of-digital-colonialism.
[95] The Sullivan Principles were introduced by Reverend Leon Sullivan, a board member of General Motors, as a set of corporate social responsibility principles forming a "code of conduct" for transnational corporations operating in apartheid South Africa. See Elizabeth Schmidt, *Decoding Corporate Camouflage: U.S. Business Support for Apartheid* (Washington

neocolonial global divide driven by American empire. This "tech ethics" circuit is dominated by US–Eurocentric researchers working for or taking money from Big Tech corporations like Microsoft, Facebook, and Google;[96] academics at elite Western universities; prominent nongovernmental organizations; rich foundations and philanthropists; government institutions; and big corporate media outlets, who together form a network of connections and shared ideology. Universities in the Global South are starting to follow suit by taking money from Big Tech and rich donors.[97]

The dominant voices in the US-centered "techlash" have a framework problem: they fail to address that digital capitalism is an American empire project exacerbating global inequality while rapidly destroying the planet.[98] Digital colonialism is rarely mentioned, and when it is, it is almost always in the abstract, without mentioning the American empire, its connection to digital capitalism, the relationship of tech to unsustainable growth, and the need for fundamental changes to the global digital economy. Reading mainstream "tech left" literature, one would never know that South Africa and most other countries in the South are now digital colonies of the United States which are unable to escape unequal development and hyperexploitation without reparations and deep structural changes to the status quo.[99]

Despite these developments, a new wave of activism against tech corporations is bubbling. The first wave of resistance to Big Tech in the Global South called to ban the sales of corporate equipment to the apartheid regime. In the post-apartheid period (also deemed neo-apartheid), the Treatment Action Campaign successfully challenged Big Pharma's intellectual property regime. Today, a "People's Tech for People's Power" movement committed to a socialist tech economy is just beginning to challenge digital colonialism.[100] Indigenous Khoisan groups have challenged the construction of a new Amazon regional base in Cape Town,[101] taxi drivers are protesting against e-hailing companies like Uber and Estonia-based Bolt, and a

DC: The Institute for Policy Studies, 1980), http://kora.matrix.msu.edu/files/50/304/32-130-24F-84-Decoding%20Corporate%20Camouflage%20resized%200pt.pdf.
[96] Yarden Katz, *Artificial Whiteness: Politics and Ideology in Artificial Intelligence* (New York: Columbia University Press, 2020), 127–184; Kwet, "The Microsoft Police State."
[97] Michael Kwet, "Digital Colonialism and Infrastructure-as-Debt," *University of Bayreuth African Studies Online* (2022), https://papers.ssrn.com/sol3/papers.cfm?abstract_id=4004594.
[98] In this regard, the US-centered "tech left" is much like Louis Brandeis – the inspiration for their views on antitrust – who ignored the issue of racism, even though he was living during the Jim Crow era. For a review of Brandeis's treatment of race, see Christopher A. Bracey, "Louis Brandeis and the Race Question," *Alabama Law Review* 52, no. 3 (2001).
[99] Kwet, "The Digital Tech Deal."
[100] Michael Kwet, *People's Tech for People's Power: A Guide to Digital Self-Defense and Empowerment* (South Africa: Right2Know, 2020), www.r2k.org.za/wp-content/uploads/Peoples-Tech_August-2020.pdf.
[101] Alexandra Wexler, "Amazon Faces Headquarters Controversy – This Time in Africa," *Wall Street Journal*, September 23, 2021, www.wsj.com/articles/amazon-faces-headquarters-controversythis-time-in-africa-11632389400.

Friends of a Free Internet movement has just emerged.[102] It remains to be seen if a powerful new movement will emerge to liberate the country from digital colonialism and new forms of oppressive surveillance.

CONCLUSION

Surveillance has been central to colonial conquest in South Africa. Mass surveillance began with the introduction of passes and skin branding techniques to African slaves and the indigenous Khoikhoi during the age of colonial conquest. During the minerals revolution, the closed compound was invented to facilitate the panoptic surveillance of workers. Over time, technologies like fingerprinting, photography, and computers were added to the mix.

The apartheid government attempted to implement a strictly regimented racial order through the fixing of race coupled to centralized surveillance controls. It used computers to successfully register and impose fixed racial categories on the entire population. However, the ultimate fantasy – real-time planning by an all-seeing state – failed, due to the limitations of computers and human resources. Nevertheless, white elites in the public and private sector administered a dystopian surveillance state which brutalized and humiliated Africans for centuries. Colonial powers collaborated with local elites on projects of mass surveillance. The role of the United States intensified in each of these historical eras.

The apartheid pass law system was put to rest by the anti-apartheid movement, and South Africans enjoyed a period of time free from mass surveillance aided and abetted by the United States. This would not last. During the post-apartheid era, US corporations colonized the digital ecosystem and, through it, began imposing their own surveillance through the internet. Often working together, American tech transnationals and Western intelligence agencies are imposing surveillance capitalism on the world's people. By designing the digital ecosystem for centralized ownership and control, a new form of structural power, digital colonialism, is concentrating power into the hands of US elites. In response, a People's Tech liberation movement is starting to form, and may help overturn modern forces of digital colonialism and surveillance in South Africa and beyond.

---

[102] Markus Bell and Rosita Armytage, "What's Fueling South Africa's Violent Uber Wars," *Fast Company*, September 15, 2017, www.fastcompany.com/40467817/south-africas-violent-uber-wars-are-driven-by-a-deep-economic-anxiety.

7

Israel/Palestine, North America, and Surveillance

Yasmeen Abu-Laban and Abigail B. Bakan

In March 2017, the Israeli Knesset (Parliament) passed a law allowing for the denial of entry or residence to foreign nationals who support Boycott, Divestment and Sanctions (BDS) against the state of Israel or its settlements.[1] Proponents of BDS are part of a now global nonviolent movement of civil society (non-state) actors challenging the government of Israel's policies towards Palestinians. Reflecting that the movement also has supporters within Israel, less than three weeks later it was revealed that Israel's then Minister of Strategic Affairs, Gilad Erdan, also sought to expand his ministry's collection of information on activists who support BDS to include Israeli citizens as well as foreigners.[2] Governmental development of such a database on citizens was questionable both on grounds of extant Israeli law and the protection of privacy rights. However, this practice stands as a telling example of how the BDS movement has moved to the front line of Israel's contemporary surveillance efforts.

The BDS movement has become central to Israel's contemporary surveillance practices. State officials such as Erdan, now Israel's representative to the United Nations (UN), have generated a militarized discourse that incorrectly conflates a series of issues as equivalencies in such a way to advance legitimacy for heightened surveillance and repression. This discourse conflates nonviolence with violence, BDS activism with terrorism, and by extension, a war on BDS with a war on terrorism.[3] These false equivalencies also advance and construct certain racialized discourses

---

[1] Jonathan Lis, "Israel's Travel Ban: Knesset Bars Entry to Foreigners who Call for Boycott of Israel or Settlements," *Haaretz*, March 7, 2017, www.haaretz.com/israel-news/.premium-israel-bars-entry-to-foreigners-who-call-for-boycott-of-settlements-1.5445566.
[2] Barak Ravid, "Israeli Ministry Trying to Compile Database of Citizens who Support BDS," *Haaretz*, March 21, 2017, www.haaretz.com/israel-news/1.778516.
[3] Eliyahu Kamisher, "Erden at JPost Conference: Terror and BDS Share the Same Ideological Roots," *Jerusalem Post*, November 23, 2016, www.jpost.com/Arab-Israeli-Conflict/Erdan-at-Jpost-Conference-Terror-and-BDS-share-the-same-ideological-roots-473424.

wherein Muslim and Arab populations are treated as inherently threatening, and Israel is treated as an unproblemetized "Jewish state." Many Jewish citizens within and beyond Israel increasingly challenge the legitimacy of the Israeli state as a representative of their interests, and the assumed universality of these interests is itself contentious. The result of these rhetorical moves is that challenges to Israel's policies are read as antisemitism, here meaning anti-Jewish racism.

In this chapter, we elaborate on the origins and calls of the BDS movement and responses to this movement in Canada and the United States. Following the events of September 11, 2001 both these states were drawn into the US-led global war on terror, a war that former US President George W. Bush (2001–2009) memorably posited as having no end.[4] Although US President Barack Obama (2008–2016) rejected the language of a "war on terror," there have been continuities in relation to national security under Presidents Bush, Obama, and, more recently, Donald Trump and Joe Biden. These continuities have reaffirmed pre-existing alliances with the state of Israel and legitimized racialized surveillance practices directed at citizens and noncitizens perceived as Muslim and/or Arab.[5] In both Canada and the United States, the BDS movement and its activists have been the subject of governmental policy discussions, as well as the object of forms of surveillance. Such discussions and acts of surveillance have largely taken place in the absence of any broad or deep historical or contemporary conversation with or about Palestinians, their experiences, or their claims.[6] In the discussion that follows, we demonstrate that in the US and Canadian contexts, opposition to the BDS movement has tended to be framed as if it is opposition to antisemitism. As such, anti-Semitism has been erroneously conflated with criticism of the state of Israel's policies regarding Palestinians and Palestine. However, the rights of Palestinians demand attention and solidarity internationally. Palestinians are a stateless population, and include a minority within Israel who may hold Israeli citizenship, as well as those in the Occupied Palestinian Territories, and those in the diaspora.

In advancing this argument, this chapter takes a twofold approach. In the first part of the chapter, we consider the BDS movement and the responses to it in Canada and the United States since its launch in 2005, a time when various post 9/11 surveillance practices were also being solidified in both countries. In the second part of the chapter, we further explain these responses in relation to long-standing and still evident practices of surveillance and social sorting, as well as anti-Jewish,

---

[4] See Sunera Thobani, "White Wars: Western Feminism and the 'War on Terror'," *Feminist Theory* 8, no. 2 (2007): 169–185.
[5] Yasmeen Abu-Laban and Abigail B. Bakan, "The 'Israelization' of Social Sorting and the 'Palestinianization' of the Racial Contract: Reframing Israel/Palestine and the War on Terror," in Elia Zureik, David Lyon, and Yasmeen Abu-Laban (eds.), *Surveillance and Control in Israel/Palestine: Population, Territory and Power* (London and New York: Routledge, 2011), 276–294.
[6] Yasmeen Abu-Laban and Abigail B. Bakan, "The Racial Contract: Israel/Palestine and Canada," *Social Identities: Journal for the Study of Race, Nation and Culture* 14, no. 5 (2008): 637–660.

anti-Arab, and anti-Muslim racisms. We conclude by considering current changes in the US and Canadian political landscapes and implications for advancing consistent anti-racist movements and policies in the context of human rights.

POST 9/11 SURVEILLANCE AND THE BDS MOVEMENT

In reflecting on the relationship between race and surveillance in the context of Israel/Palestine, it is important to center on the now global BDS movement, which emerged in the post 9/11 period. This movement stems from a unified Palestinian call in 2005 for systematic boycott, divestment, and sanctions against the state of Israel, based on opposition to Israel's ongoing denial of the human rights of Palestinians in violation of international law. The BDS call came from within Palestine, as an appeal based on nonviolent action and education, and is addressed to all progressive forces internationally. When launched in 2005, the call was endorsed by over 170 civil society groups within Palestine. The demands of the Palestinian civil society call for BDS are in keeping with the UN support for universal human rights. Specifically, the BDS movement makes three demands, which call on Israel to comply with international law by:

1. Ending its occupation and colonization of all Arab lands and dismantling the wall [sometimes referred to as a separation barrier, this is a network of electronic walls and fences over 400 miles long snaking into Palestinian territory in the Israeli occupied West Bank];
2. Recognizing the fundamental rights of the Arab-Palestinian citizens of Israel to full equality; and
3. Respecting, protecting and promoting the rights of Palestinian refugees to return to their homes and properties as stipulated in UN resolution 194 of 1948 [a resolution which allows for the return of Palestinian refugees as well as compensation for loss or damage to property].[7]

As an Arab population that includes both Muslim and Christian adherents, Palestinians have been subject to extreme racism, repression, and surveillance within and beyond the state of Israel and the areas under its control.[8] Given these realities, advancing a unified call for Palestinian human rights addressed to the global community marked a major turning point. It served to focus attention on an oppressed population that is racialized both in the context of the conflict zone of Israel/Palestine as well as globally.[9]

In point of fact the demands of the BDS movement for ending colonization and occupation, and calling for equal treatment, and the right of return for refugees, are not, in themselves, radical or extreme; rather, they are consistent with the liberal

---

[7] Palestinian Civil Society, "Palestinian Civil Society Call for BDS," bdsmovement.net, 2005, https://bdsmovement.net/call.
[8] Abu-Laban and Bakan, "The Racial Contract."
[9] Ibid.

democratic human rights framework and other aspects of international law.[10] Israel, however, is a state which claims exceptionality amongst the world's states,[11] and this exceptionality has rendered it difficult to hold the country accountable to international law. For example, the UN General Assembly and the International Court of Justice have repeatedly passed resolutions calling for rectification of the issues signaled in the three demands of the BDS call.[12] Yet, Israel has not faced consequences or sanctions for its failure to adhere to these resolutions associated with the rights of Palestinians.[13]

The antiracist and human rights dimension of the BDS call has been complicated, however, as the indigenous land of Palestine has been occupied by a state claiming to represent another racialized group, the international Jewish community.[14] While Israel's violent 1948 foundation and evolution since then is in keeping with other settler-colonial state contexts,[15] Israel's claimed exceptionality as a "Jewish state" makes it distinct in comparison to liberal-democratic Western states, defining itself in singular terms that are ethnoreligious. It is notable that the discourse of Israeli state officials simultaneously claims to embrace "normal" Western values and democracy,[16] while also claiming a unique status as the only "Jewish" state in the world. The depiction of Israel as a "Jewish state" is in keeping with the tenets of a Zionist political project.

Zionism as a political project emerged in Europe in the late nineteenth century in the context of rising nationalism and virulent antisemitism. This political project came to hold that the only way European Jews would be safe was to have a separate, ethnically defined state, ultimately to be settled in historic Palestine. Today, the main political parties in Israel are unanimous in their adherence to the idea of Israel as a

---

[10] Ali Abunimah, *The Battle for Justice in Palestine* (Chicago, IL: Haymarket Books, 2014). Neve Gordon, *Israel's Occupation* (Berkley, CA: University of California Press, 2008); Jimmy Carter, *Palestine Peace Not Apartheid* (New York: Simon and Schuster, Inc., 2006).

[11] Abigail B. Bakan and Yasmeen Abu-Laban, "Palestinian Resistance and International Solidarity: The BDS Campaign," *Race and Class* 51, no. 1 (2009): 29–54.

[12] Abu-Laban and Bakan, "The Racial Contract"; Edward C. Corrigan, "Israel and Apartheid: A Framework for Legal Analysis," in Ghada Ageel (ed.), *Apartheid in Palestine: Hard Laws and Harder Experiences* (Edmonton: The University of Alberta Press, 2016), 213–245.

[13] Rafeef Ziadah, "Palestine Calling: Notes on the Boycott, Divestment, and Sanctions Movement," in Ghada Ageel (ed.), *Apartheid in Palestine: Hard Laws and Harder Experiences* (Edmonton: The University of Alberta Press, 2016), 91–106.

[14] Chandni Desai, "'The Land Is Talking to Me': An Interview with Jamal Juma on Meanings of Land, Decolonization, Resistance and Solidarity from Palestine." *Decolonization: Indigeneity, Education and Society* 6, no. 1 (2017): 120–129; Virginia Tilley, *The One-State Solution: A Breakthrough for Peace in the Israeli-Palestine Deadlock* (Ann Arbor, MI: University of Michigan Press, 2005); Abigail B. Bakan, "Race, Class and Colonialism: Reconsidering the 'Jewish Question'," in Abigail B. Bakan and Enakshi Dua (eds.), *Theorizing Anti-Racism: Linkages in Marxism and Critical Race Theories* (University of Toronto Press, 2014), 252–279.

[15] Patrick Wolfe, "Settler-Colonialism and the Elimination of the Native," *Journal of Genocide Research* 8, no. 4 (2006): 487–409.

[16] David Lloyd, "Settler Colonialism and the State of Exception: The Example of Israel/Palestine," *Settler Colonial Studies* 2, no. 1 (2012): 59–80.

Jewish state, but this political expression should not be equated with either Jewish identity or Judaism. The fact that it often is arises from a hegemonic, widespread misunderstanding that equates the actions of the state of Israel as standing in for Jewish interests and/or Jewish people internationally. In advancing Zionism as a political project and ideology, this form of Zionism claims that Jews, universally, can only live and prosper if removed from non-Jewish citizens within the borders of an ethnically defined Jewish state. However, Zionism should not be treated as identical to an ethnic identity, religion, or theology precisely because Jewish identity, beliefs, religious practices, and culture are diverse and varied. Such a diverse population is neither the same as, nor equivalent to, any singular political ideology, despite the fact that political Zionism insists on its claim to sole representation.[17] The BDS call challenges the Israeli state's violation of human rights, and serves to advocate for the rights of Palestinians in a manner that is consistent with human rights policies internationally. The call has been forwarded with a view to public education as well as action, effectively challenging the discourse of Israeli exceptionalism and seeking to ensure that Palestinian rights are both seen to be and respected as human rights.

The call for boycott, divestment, and sanctions against Israel has found considerable resonance among civil society groups internationally, including responses in the United States and Canada. As the BDS movement has gained support, those who ally with this movement in both the United States and Canada have faced a dramatic rise in repression, accompanied by surveillance and/or racialized targeting against organizations and individuals. In the post 9/11 period, supporters of the BDS movement have fallen under the general wave of enhanced legitimation of state surveillance and repression faced by those of Muslim or Arab descent. This kind of profiling is also seen to be a form of anti-Muslim racism,[18] anti-Arab racism,[19] and/or Islamophobia.[20] Palestinians have long been associated with the charge of "terrorism" in the Middle East. This is a false and negative racial stereotype without basis in fact, but one that has received heightened influence after the events of 9/11.[21]

---

[17] See Bakan, "Race, Class and Colonialism," 252–279; Judith Butler, *Parting Ways: Jewishness and the Critique of Zionism* (New York: Columbia University Press, 2012); Jonathan Boyarin and Daniel Boyarin (eds.), *Jews and Other Differences: The New Jewish Cultural Studies* (Minneapolis, MN: University of Minnesota Press, 1997); Jonathan Boyarin and Daniel Boyarin, *Powers of Diaspora: Two Essays on the Relevance of Jewish Culture* (Minneapolis, MN: University of Minnesota Press, 2002); Uri Davis, *Apartheid Israel: The Possibilities for the Struggle Within* (London and New York: Zed Books, 2003); John Rose, *The Myths of Zionism* (London: Pluto Press, 2004).

[18] Sherene Razack, *Casting Out: The Evictions of Muslims from Western Law and Politics* (University of Toronto Press, 2008).

[19] Steven Salaita, *Anti-Arab Racism in the USA: Where It Comes from and What It Means for Politics Today* (London: Pluto Press, 2006).

[20] Deepa Kumar, *Islamophobia and the Politics of Empire* (Chicago, IL: Haymarket Books, 2012).

[21] Abu-Laban and Bakan, "The Racial Contract," 637–660; Yasmeen Abu-Laban and Abigail B. Bakan, "After 9/11: Canada, the Israel/Palestine Conflict, and the Surveillance of Public Discourse," *Canadian Journal of Law and Society* 27, no. 3 (2012): 319–340.

Those standing in solidarity with the Palestinian call for BDS, including those of Jewish identity both within and outside of Israel, have also faced heightened surveillance and repression.[22] There are numerous examples of the growth of surveillance and repression directed towards those who advocate and support the call for boycott, divestment, and sanctions against Israel in the United States and Canada, including in universities where academic freedom is challenged and often compromised.[23] While the specifics of the numerous cases vary, there is generally a common claim that solidarity with Palestine and Palestinians, as indicated in the BDS call, is motivated not by antiracism and support for human rights, but by the opposite – a particular expression of racism and opposition to human rights, in the form of anti-Jewish racism, or antisemitism.

Significantly, discussions in party politics and policies targeting those who support the BDS movement have been advanced in both the United States and Canada in recent years. The advancement of federally legitimated state policy has given license to repression of freedom of expression, and enabled a climate of surveillance at the national, state, and municipal levels.[24] Notably, this climate of repression against the BDS movement has been advocated across the spectrum of political parties, in the United States spanning the administrations of Democratic President Barack Obama (2009–2017) and Republican President Donald Trump (2017–2021). Since the inauguration of Democratic President Joe Biden in 2021, we see a continuation of this anti-BDS approach. In Canada, there has been similar repression of the BDS movement spanning Conservative Prime Minister Stephen Harper (2006–2017) and Liberal Prime Minister Justin Trudeau (2015 to present).

In the United States, there have been several efforts to enact anti-BDS legislation. While many of these have not been successfully passed into law, the attempts to repress the movement have indicated the climate of legitimacy for increased scrutiny, suspicion, and surveillance. The US Supreme Court has held that political boycott is a right that is protected under the First Amendment of the Constitution.[25] Legislators have repeated the campaign of repression through issues of trade. In May

---

[22] Butler, *Parting Ways*.
[23] See Susan G. Drummond, *Unthinkable Thoughts: Academic Freedom and the One-State Model for Israel and Palestine* (Vancouver: UBC Press, 2013); Ashley Dawson and Bill V. Mullen (eds.), *Against Apartheid: The Case for Boycotting Israeli Universities* (Chicago, IL: Haymarket Books, 2015); Omar Barghouti, *Boycott, Divestment and Sanctions (BDS): The Global Struggle for Palestinian Rights* (Chicago, IL: Haymarket Books, 2011); Mazen Masri, "A Tale of Two Conferences: On Power, Identity and Academic Freedom," *Journal of Academic Freedom* 2 (2011): 1–28; Mary-Jo Nadeau and Alan Sears, "The Palestine Test: Countering the Silencing Campaign," *Studies in Political Economy* 85 (2010): 7–33; Jon Thompson, *No Debate: The Israel Lobby and Free Speech at Canadian Universities* (Toronto: James Lorimer and Co., 2011); Steven Salaita, *Uncivil Rights: Palestine and the Limits of Academic Freedom* (Chicago, IL: Haymarket Books, 2015).
[24] Ghada Ageel (ed.), *Apartheid in Palestine: Hard Laws and Harder Experiences* (Edmonton: University of Alberta Press, 2016).
[25] NAACP v. Claiborne Hardware Co., 458 US 886 (1982), at 911–912.

of 2015, then US President Obama signed into law a "fast track" authorization focused on enabling negotiators to address the controversial Trans-Pacific Partnership and other trade arrangements with Asian states and the European Union. The Trade Promotion Authority legislation, however, also included guidelines for negotiators to discourage foreign partners from supporting boycott, divestment, and sanctions against Israel. This is only one example. Another took place on January 1, 2017, when Republican Senator Marco Rubio introduced a bill, titled "Combating BDS Act of 2017," that would allow a state or local government to divest or prohibit investment with any entity that engages with commerce or investment related to "boycott, divestment, or sanctions activity targeting Israel."[26]

The apparent normalization of federal measures intended to punish domestic or international actors – from individuals, to organizations, to states – that participate in the BDS movement is indication of the impact of this civil society initiative. But it also reveals a legitimated climate of political repression. It challenges a movement committed to implementation of international law and human rights. Growing surveillance from both state and civil society actors, and attempted silencing of BDS supporters, have increased in relation to university campuses, labor unions, political parties, churches and other religious institutions, and some academic professional associations (such as the American Studies Association) across the United States.[27] A similar climate has advanced in Canada.[28]

One major target of repression against the BDS movement relates to a series of annual educational conferences on university campuses, originating at the University of Toronto in 2005, titled Israeli Apartheid Week (IAW). The designated week is devoted to education related to the BDS call. The application of the term apartheid (a word of Afrikaans origin, meaning "apartness") to states beyond South Africa, and referring to legalized racial separation, has been recognized in international law and a wide body of literature.[29] Challenges to the legitimacy of IAW in Canada, however, have repeatedly posited that the event propagates hate, based on the widespread but erroneous assumption that challenges to Israel's violation of Palestinian human rights is tantamount to antisemitism. In 2009, under the administration of Prime Minister Stephen Harper, then Minister of Citizenship and

---

[26] 115th Congress Senate Committee on Banking, Housing and Urban Affairs, "S.170 – Combating BDS Act of 2017." Sponsored by Senator Marco Rubio (R-FL). Introduced January 1, 2017, www.congress.gov/bill/115th-congress/senate-bill/170.

[27] Dawson and Mullen, *Against Apartheid*.

[28] Abu-Laban and Bakan, *After 9/11*, 319–340; James Cairns and Susan Ferguson, "Political Truths," in Ghada Ageel (ed.), *Apartheid in Palestine: Hard Laws and Harder Experiences* (Edmonton: The University of Alberta Press, 2016), 181–198.

[29] See, e.g., Abigail B. Bakan and Yasmeen Abu-Laban "Israel/Palestine, South Africa and the 'One-State Solution': The Case for an Apartheid Analysis." *Politikon: South African Journal of Political Studies* 37, no. 2–3 (2010): 331–351; United Nations Economic and Social Commission for Western Asia (ESCWA), "Israeli Practices towards Palestinian People and the Question of Apartheid," *Palestine and the Israeli Occupation*, Issue no. 1 (2017); Carter, *Palestine Peace Not Apartheid*.

Immigration Jason Kenney issued a public statement indicating that he was "deeply concerned" about Israeli Apartheid Week, and asked rhetorically whether IAW was "simply an effort to cloak hatred and intolerance in an outward appearance of 'intellectual inquiry'."[30] Notably, this approach has been continued under the Liberal administration of Prime Minister Justin Trudeau. On March 13, 2015, a few months prior to his election, Trudeau tweeted "The BDS movement, like Israeli Apartheid Week, has no place on Canadian campuses."[31] More significantly perhaps, in February 2016, the Canadian federal Parliament, with a majority Liberal government, passed a motion that called on the government to "condemn any and all attempts by Canadian organizations, groups or individuals to promote the BDS movement, both here at home and abroad," and states further that the movement "promotes the demonization and delegitimization of the State of Israel."[32]

With the highest levels of government in both the United States and Canada formally challenging the BDS movement, and actively advancing claims that supporters of this movement are motivated by racist hatred against Jewish people, a climate of increased surveillance and repression has been endorsed and legitimated. Taking place in the shadow of 9/11 and the attendant war on terror, it is relevant to consider the wider context of racialization processes and surveillance both historically and politically, particularly as it pertains to two key groupings who have uniquely come together to support BDS: American and Canadian Arabs and Jews.

SITUATING THE POST 9/11 MOMENT AND BDS HISTORICALLY

In light of the alliances forged in the BDS movement across lines of difference (religion, ethnicity, race, etc.) in both Canada and the United States, it is important to consider forms of repression and surveillance directed at this movement in relation to the long histories of surveillance and social sorting that have differentially impacted both those of Jewish and Arab origin. Also significant are the distinct colonial contexts in which these practices emerged. Indeed, although it may be tempting to paint the post-9/11 moment and attendant responses to BDS as unique, in point of fact both the United States and Canada are settler-colonial states where processes relating to surveillance and social sorting along lines of race, ethnicity, and

---

[30] Citizenship and Immigration Canada, "Minister Kenney Issues Statement on 'Israeli Apartheid Week'," Ottawa: Citizenship and Immigration Canada Press Release, March 3, 2009, www.marketwired.com/press-release/minister-kenney-issues-statement-on-israeli-apartheid-week-956590.html.

[31] Justin Trudeau, *Twitter Post*, March 13, 2015, 3:31 p.m., https://twitter.com/justintrudeau/status/576465632884981760?lang=en.

[32] House of Commons, Canada, "Vote no. 14: 42nd Parliament, 1st Session, Sitting no. 22," sponsor, Tony Clement, February 22, 2016; Patrick Martin, "Parliament Votes to Reject Israel Boycott Campaign," *The Globe and Mail*, February 23, 2016, www.theglobeandmail.com/news/world/parliament-votes-to-reject-campaign-to-boycott-israel/article28863810.

religion were foundational, and operated with the similar logic of what Wolfe terms the "elimination" of the native.[33]

For example, in both countries Indigenous peoples have been the objects of forms of surveillance aimed at entrenching colonial rule. As a consequence of such practices, in both Canada and the United States, Indigenous peoples have endured similar histories of oppression, land expropriation, gender-based violence, and non-recognition of treaties that serve to compromise their collective rights to self-determination and to create conditions of persistent disadvantage.[34] Both countries also, significantly, have histories of slavery and anti-Black racism, although in Canada this history is less readily acknowledged.[35]

Also, in both Canada and the United States, preference was historically given to white British-origin Protestant populations for entry and potential citizenship. This began to change somewhat by the late nineteenth century with the arrival of Jewish and other immigrants from eastern and southern Europe to both countries. For much of the respective histories of Canada and the United States, however, both Jews and Arabs were seen as groupings whose "whiteness" was suspect, and conditional, and whose presence at the borders was therefore to be controlled.[36] These efforts were aided by legislation such as the Canadian 1908 Continuous Passage Act, which denied entry to those who could not reach Canada by one continuous journey from their country of origin, effectively limiting the number of Arabs.[37] Similarly, in the United States, the 1924 National Origins Act established a system of quotas that effectively limited the number of southern and eastern Europeans admitted to the United States, affecting Jewish migration particularly.

Exclusionary policy responses reached heightened proportions in 1939 when the ship *MS St. Louis*, transporting more than 900 Jewish passengers fleeing Nazi persecution, was denied entry into both Canada and the United States. Those passengers were turned back to Europe, and for many this meant being condemned

---

[33] Wolfe, "Settler Colonialism and Elimination of the Native," 487–409.

[34] Keith D. Smith, *Liberalism, Surveillance and Resistance: Indigenous Communities in Western Canada: 1877-1924* (Athabasca University Press, 2009); Craig Proulx, "Colonizing Surveillance: Canada Constructs an Indigenous Terror Threat," *Anthropologica* 56, no. 1 (2014): 83–100; United Nations General Assembly, Human Rights Council, *Report of the Special Rapporteur on the Rights of Indigenous Peoples, James Anaya: The Situation of Indigenous Peoples in the United States of America*, 2012; United Nations General Assembly, Human Rights Council, *Report of the Special Rapporteur on the Rights of Indigenous Peoples, James Anaya: The Situation of Indigenous Peoples in the United States of America*, 2014.

[35] Afua Cooper, *The Hanging of Angélique: The Untold Story of Canadian Slavery and the Burning of Old Montreal* (Toronto: Harper Collins, 2006); Katherine McKittrick, *Demonic Grounds: Black Women and the Cartographies of Struggle* (Minneapolis, MN: University of Minnesota Press, 2006); Katherine McKittrick and Clyde Woods (eds.), *Black Geographies and the Politics of Place* (Toronto: Between the Lines, 2007).

[36] Abu-Laban and Bakan, *The Racial Contract*, 637–660.

[37] Jenna Hennebry and Zainab Amery, "'Arab' Migration to Canada: Far from Monolithic," in Bessma Momani and Jenna Hennebry (eds.), *Targeted Transnationals: The State, the Media and Arab Canadians* (Vancouver: University of British Columbia Press, 2013), 15–31.

to the death camps. Such an outcome was in keeping with the view of one high-ranking Canadian official who infamously responded that "none is too many" when asked about Canada's possible intake of Jewish refugees.[38] The presence of Jews in major social institutions, such as universities, was also variously regulated through the use of quotas in both the United States and Canada from the 1920s through the 1950s and speaks to the widespread nature of antisemitism in both countries.[39]

In both Canada and the United States, early waves of immigrants of Arab origin, from the late nineteenth century through the end of World War I, were largely from present day Syria and Lebanon, and were predominantly Christian. After World War II, however, source countries diversified, and there were more Muslims who immigrated to both Canada and the United States.[40] It is evident that the experience in North America of those who are, or are perceived to be, Muslim and/or Arab changed dramatically after September 11, 2001. This was because of the combination of the global war on terror involving both Canada and the United States, a deepening of surveillance practices augmented by fear and new technological possibilities, as well as by racialized security and surveillance practices.[41] This focus on Muslims as a threat feeds on long-standing forms of Islamophobia (anti-Muslim racism) as well as discourses on terrorism which have historically been applied to those who resist colonial subjugation – with Palestinians being a key grouping associated with terrorism since the late 1960s.[42]

However, in the context of settler colonial states which typically are demographically diverse and engage in "divide and conquer" strategies along lines of Indigeneity, race, ethnicity, class and gender, it is evident that security and surveillance have never been neutral. For instance, as demonstrated in the growing literature on surveillance and security, at least since the founding of the modern state in 1867, Canada has frequently engaged in security intelligence. This has often occurred with questionable aims, directed at its own citizens, typically also involving the policing of difference, especially by way of immigration status, race, ethnicity, and/

---

[38] Irving Abella and Harold Troper, *None Is Too Many: Canada and the Jews of Europe 1933–1948* (University of Toronto Press, 2012).

[39] Jerome Karabel, *The Chosen: The Hidden History of Admission and Exclusion at Harvard, Yale and Princeton* (Boston, MA: Houghton Mifflin, 2005); Abella and Troper, *None Is Too Many*, 51.

[40] Hennebry and Amery, "'Arab' Migration to Canada," 16; Jen'nan Ghazal Read, "Discrimination and Identity in a Post 9/11 Era: A Comparison of Muslim and Christian Arab Americans," in Amaney Jamal and Nadine Naber (eds.), *Race and Arab Americans Before and After 9/11: From Invisible Citizens to Visible Subjects* (Syracuse University Press, 2008), 307.

[41] Yasmeen Abu-Laban, "The Politics of Surveillance: Civil Liberties, Human Rights and Ethics," in Kirstie Ball, Kevin D. Haggerty, and David Lyon (eds.), *Routledge Handbook of Surveillance Studies* (London and New York: Routledge, 2012), 420–427; Yasmeen Abu-Laban, "Gendering Surveillance Studies: The Empirical and Normative Promise of Feminist Methodology," *Surveillance and Society* 13, no. 1 (2015): 44–56.

[42] Abu-Laban and Bakan, "The 'Israelization' of Social Sorting."

or religion.[43] For example, after the Russian Revolution, Canadian state security and surveillance practices focused on "dangerous foreigners" for their perceived radical left or communist activities associated with the Winnipeg General Strike of May and June 1919, and explicitly blamed Austrians, Galicians, and Jews.[44] Indeed, the response of the Canadian state to this major political strike was to arrest and deport those workers without citizenship, an action that linked antipathy towards immigrants with antipathy towards working-class activists.

Such similar practices are also in evidenced in the United States in what is sometimes referred to as the first "Red Scare" (as distinct from the second "Red Scare" targeting perceived communist sympathizers over the period 1947–1956 and associated with Senator Joseph McCarthy). Specifically, the first of these scares involved the arrests of thousands of noncitizens for their perceived radical left or communist political associations, at the time of the Palmer Raids in late 1919 and early 1920, led by Attorney General Alexander Mitchell Palmer. As in Canada, these raids were fueled by anti-immigrant and anti-Jewish sentiments as well as anti-working-class sentiments.[45] As David Cole traces, in the 1940s and 1950s the first "Red Scare" evolved into the extended targeting of American citizens in the McCarthy era.[46] In the context of the McCarthy era, it is striking that one of the most covered trials of the period involved second-generation Jewish Americans Ethel and Julius Rosenberg. They were famously accused and convicted of espionage on grounds of participating in a Soviet spy ring. Ultimately, they were executed in 1953, in a context of widespread antisemitism. As one analyst observes, "while their guilt is today assumed by many, little is said any longer about the trial itself, which rivals the case of Dreyfus in France, or the Doctors' Trial in the Soviet Union, for the under-current of antisemitism that tainted the constitutional process."[47] Further, this trial was one that left a heavy and divisive mark on second-generation Jewish Americans, especially from New York, as the Rosenbergs hailed from the Lower East Side, and it "hastened and legitimated the purge of the Jewish left from the organized Jewish community."[48] Moreover, fearing any association with communism, many Jewish organizations shared information and files on purported communists with the House Un-American Activities Committee.[49]

[43] Reg Whitaker, Gregory S. Kealey, and Andrew Parnaby, *Secret Service: Political Policing in Canada from the Fenians to Fortress America* (University of Toronto Press, 2012), 521–544.
[44] Gerald Tulchinsky, *Canada's Jews: A Peoples Journey* (University of Toronto Press, 2008), 187.
[45] Karen Brodkin, *How the Jews Became White Folks and What that Says about Race in America* (New Brunswick, NJ: Rutgers University Press, 1998), 27.
[46] David Cole, "Their Liberties, Our Security: Democracy and Double Standards," *Boston Review* (December/January 2002/2003), 304, https://scholarship.law.georgetown.edu/facpub/924/.
[47] Bruce Afran, "The American Republic vs. Julius and Ethel Rosenberg," in Bruce Afran and Robert A. Garber (eds.), *Jews on Trial* (Jersey City, NJ: Ktav Publishing House, 2005), 163.
[48] Deborah Dash Moore, "Reconsidering the Rosenbergs: Symbol and Substance in Second Generation Jewish Consciousness," *Journal of American Ethnic History* 8, no. 1 (1988): 26.
[49] Ibid.

This included the Anti-Defamation League of B'nai Brith (now Anti-Defamation League/ADL) which had formed in 1913.[50]

Compared to the immigration and organizing history of Jewish Americans and Jewish Canadians, the immigration of Arabs to North America came later. National organizing among this community in the United States and Canada emerged mainly after the 1967 Arab–Israeli war. This organizing was largely in response to what was perceived to be negative, stereotyped, and inaccurate media reporting on Arabs in the North American media.[51] The decade of the 1960s was a galvanizing moment for many of the progressive ("new") social movements in both countries. In the case of Canada, Arab Canadians came to work primarily in the context of the opportunities and funding structures provided by the country's 1971 national policy of multiculturalism and antiracist initiatives.[52] This process has become more complicated as funding and support for multiculturalism declined over the 2000s, and elected officials became hostile to claims.[53]

In the case of the United States, organizing of Arab Americans has taken place without the same kind of federal state support. In covering the rise of the Arab American left from the 1960s to the 1980s, Pennock traces the formation, strategies, and actions of key Arab American organizations, showing how these linked with other movements and organizations committed to workers' rights, as well as to anti-imperialist and antiracist struggles.[54] However, Arab American organizing was viewed with suspicion by some organizations committed to a pro-Israel position and the Zionist political project. This feature was also evident in Canada, since the Zionist political project created a divide between many Arabs and Jews dating back to the 1940s.[55] Additionally, Arab organizing was viewed with suspicion by the American state, which under then President Richard Nixon launched "Operation Boulder" in 1972, profiling Arab-origin travelers to the United States, and surveilling activities of Arab Americans particularly in relation to Palestine solidarity.[56]

The case of Arab-origin civil rights lawyer and co-founder of the American Arab Anti-Discrimination Committee Abdeen Jabara is especially significant in this context. Jabara launched a court case against the Federal Bureau of Investigation

---

[50] Ibid.
[51] Yasmeen Abu-Laban, "On the Borderlines of Human and Citizen: The Liminal State of Arab Canadians," in Bessma Momani and Jenna Hennebry (eds.), *Targeted Transnationals: The State, the Media and Arab Canadian* (Vancouver: University of British Columbia Press), 68–85.
[52] Abu-Laban, "On the Borderlines of Human and Citizen," 68–85.
[53] Ibid.
[54] Pamela E. Pennock, *The Rise of the Arab American Left: Activists, Allies and Their Fight against Imperialism and Racism, 1960s–1980s* (Chapel Hill, NC: University of North Carolina Press, 2017).
[55] Abu-Laban, "On the Borderlines of Human and Citizen," 68–85; Dan Freeman-Maloy, "AIPAC North: 'Israel Advocacy' in Canada," *ZNet*, June 26, 2006, https://zcomm.org/znetarticle/aipac-north-by-dan-freeman-maloy-1.
[56] Pennock, *The Rise of the Arab American Left*.

in 1972, which ultimately led the United States National Security Association (NSA) to admit it had been illegally spying on Jabara since 1967. The focus of the NSA surveillance was Jabara's legal defense of Arab Americans.[57] Although Jabara's files were destroyed and he was fully exonerated from any criminal wrong doing, this case remains notable for three reasons. First, it underscores the racialized nature of surveillance in relation to Arab Americans. Second, the case suggests that lawyers can be surveilled simply for defending certain clients.[58] Third, this was the first time that the NSA admitted to spying on an American citizen, long before the 2013 revelations of Edward Snowden which revealed the security organization's mass surveillance program implicating American citizens and others.

CONCLUSION

Given the history summarized here, it is helpful to return to where this argument began, specifically the surveillance of those in the United States and Canada who support the BDS movement. This chapter has traced the 2005 rise of the BDS movement, directed at challenging the treatment of Palestinians by the state of Israel. The BDS movement is one that, significantly, has attracted support across diverse populations, and across divides based on religion, ethnicity, and race. Support has been expressed from Indigenous and Black movements in both the United States and Canada who identify with the movement for Palestinian rights.[59] Indeed, the movement was originally inspired by the boycott, divestment and sanctions movement that was part of a successful challenge to apartheid South Africa, and many supporters have drawn on these experiences internationally.[60] It has also brought progressive Jewish and Arab Palestinian supporters of Palestinian human rights in both the United States and Canada together in common cause.

As this chapter has noted, currently there is an established pattern of surveillance of the BDS movement and its proponents in both Canada and the United States. While those who are (or are perceived to be) Arab and/or Muslim have also been the objects of increased surveillance since September 11, 2001, the targeting of BDS activists cuts across lines of religion, race, and ethnicity. In also targeting Jewish

---

[57] Traci Yoder, *Breach of Privilege: Spying on Lawyers in the United States*, National Lawyers Guild Report (April 2014), 3.
[58] Ibid.
[59] Angela Y. Davis, *Freedom Is a Constant Struggle: Ferguson, Palestine and the Foundations of a Movement* (Chicago, IL: Haymarket Books, 2016); Ziadah, "Palestine Calling," 91–106; David Roediger, *Class, Race and Marxism* (London and New York: Verso, 2017); Bassem Masri, "The Fascinating Story of How the Ferguson-Palestine Solidarity Movement Came Together," *AlterNet*, February 8, 2015, www.alternet.org/2015/02/frontline-ferguson-protester-and-palestinian-american-bassem-masri-how-ferguson2palestine; Kristian Davis Bailey, "Dream Defenders, Black Lives Matter and Ferguson Leaders Take Historic Trip to Palestine," *Ebony*, January 9, 2015, www.ebony.com/news/dream-defenders-black-lives-matter-ferguson-reps-take-historic-trip-to-palestine.
[60] Barghouti, *Boycott, Divestment and Sanctions (BDS)*.

Americans and Jewish Canadians it harkens back to historic practices targeting North American Jews for their purported left sympathies. Given the lengthy history of surveillance and repression and the "divide and conquer" strategies inherent in settler colonial states, it is perhaps not surprising that the BDS movement is perceived as a threat to the status quo.

The BDS movement, however, is committed to human rights based in international law, and is nonviolent and focused on education in its approach and political strategy. As such, BDS expresses forms of solidarity and consistent anti-racism that reveal the gross inequality and violence in the policies and practices of the Israeli state since its foundation in 1948. The tragic regularity of the claim, forwarded in both the United States and Canada, that the movement is anti-Semitic – that it is based on anti-Jewish racism and hate – is not only a false cover to legitimate extreme surveillance and repression, but also serves to trivialize real histories and present realities of antisemitism in both countries. This consistency should not, however, serve to blur the changes that have taken place in governmental administrations over time. Indeed, the extreme and overt legitimization of far-right, pro-Nazi organizations in the United States under former US President Donald Trump did not lead to similar official endorsement in the administration of Canadian Prime Minister Justin Trudeau, or more recently President Joe Biden. While such forces exist in both countries, our argument here is not to suggest that political orientations are always identical across the US–Canada border. Instead, we emphasize that despite variations, the misplaced dominant perspective that support for Palestine and Palestinians, and the BDS movement in particular, is grounded in anti-Semitism is notable. To its credit, the global BDS movement, and its supporters in both the United States and Canada, have consistently challenged such charges, and have in fact been at the forefront of solidarity actions supported by Palestinian, Jewish, and other anti-racist advocates. Despite the challenges, the placement of the BDS movement in the context of wider anti-racist and anti-colonial struggles points to a future where human rights will be more than a slogan or UN policy, but a reality.

8

Colonialism's Uneasy Legacy

Topologies of Race and Surveillance in São Paulo

Claudio Altenhain, Ricardo Urquizas Campello, Alcides Eduardo dos Reis Peron, and Leandro Siqueira

INTRODUCTION

Roaming around in São Paulo can be quite a stimulating experience: The city's bustling rhythm, its effervescent cultural life, and its ethnic heterogeneity leave little room for doubt as to why Brazil's largest city is generally considered South America's most vibrant and cosmopolitan metropolis. Meanwhile, the city's "tough concrete poetry"[1] also bespeaks a configuration in which human bodies are dwarfed and citizens are constantly reminded of their respective place – a proverbial "city of walls"[2] in which the utopia of a universally accessible and politically empowering public space has long since been thwarted by a maze of privatized streets, fortified urban enclaves, and an omnipresent array of surveillance devices. Despite the local elites' attempts to depict São Paulo as a place which is defined by both its tolerance and its diversity,[3] the city's very material configuration thus indicates an urbanistic model which segments and separates more than it joins and unites. Rather than the clichéd melting pot, São Paulo resembles a kaleidoscope in which social class and ethnic affiliation assign each citizen a precise spatial coordinate in a cityscape defined by a mesh of internal frontiers – some brutally physical, others more subtle and ethereal – and the corresponding characteristic of an almost suffocating impermeability.

Taking this observation of a firmly segregated and, therefore, profoundly undemocratic urban space as a phenomenological point of departure, the present chapter

---

[1] According to singer-songwriter Caetano Veloso in his 1978 *Sampa*, a famous hymn to the city's gruff and brittle charm.
[2] Teresa P. R. Caldeira, *City of Walls: Crime, Segregation, and Citizenship in São Paulo* (Berkeley, CA: University of California Press, 2001).
[3] Thus, in an anglophone marketing clip launched by the municipal government in an effort to attract foreign direct investments, the voiceover claims that "multicultural and friendly, São Paulo welcomes and embraces" while the video shows *Paulistanas* and *Paulistanos* of Japanese, Italian, and Lebanese descent. See www.youtube.com/watch?v=k4BjhNw-GIU&t=46s.

sets out to situate São Paulo's contemporary urban form within a (post)colonial *longue durée* characterized by the persistent sociospatial marginalization as well as the violent exploitation of Black subjects; challenging Brazil's founding myth of a postracial society, indeed the argument to be made holds that the *fazenda* – namely, the colonial sugar plantation – and its segregation of human bodies according to their skin color keeps haunting the daily reality of South America's largest metropolis up to the present day. While, to be sure, slavery has been officially abolished over 130 years ago, the point to be made is that the race-specific system of social domination it encapsulates keeps impregnating both the configuration of the city's built environment and the moral typology distinguishing trustworthy "good citizens" from dangerous "outlaws" and "bandits." Culminating in an increasingly sophisticated technoscape of urban surveillance and control while steadily negating its markedly racialized implications, the concomitant asynchrony of a hypermodern surveillance apparatus on the one hand and the persistent effects of colonialism and slavery on the other shall thus be scrutinized as a peculiarly Brazilian regime of marking bodies, dividing up spaces, and distinguishing beneficial circulations from illicit transgressions.

The concomitant effects of spatial marginalization are to be borne unequally by different segments of the urban population. Indeed, with Brazil's history deeply enmeshed in the violent exploitation of African slaves it is no wonder that São Paulo's dark-skinned citizens remain amongst the city's most disadvantaged groups in all kinds of social contexts. According to activist-scholar Jaime Alves, this state of affairs is anything but arbitrary inasmuch as São Paulo has to be understood as an eminently "anti-Black city":[4] falling victim to a racist necropolitics enacted by the police forces and a whole range of nominally democratic public institutions, the abused bodies of São Paulo's Black population would serve as an indispensable substrate for the city's white "civil society" to thrive and prosper. In this configuration, the Black subject would necessarily upset hegemonic definitions of public order and, therefore, constantly run the risk of falling victim to a public–private politics of punitive intervention.[5]

---

[4] Jaime Amparo Alves, *The Anti-Black City: Police Terror and Black Urban Life in Brazil* (Minneapolis and London: University of Minneapolis Press, 2018).

[5] Ibid., 3; Christen A. Smith, "Strange Fruit: Brazil, Necropolitics, and the Transnational Resonance of Torture and Death," *Souls* 15, no. 3 (2013): 177–198. In the present chapter, we have chosen to capitalize the denominations "Black" and "Indigenous" in order to augment the visibility of Brazil's two main non-white ethnic constituencies – in spite and fully conscious of the country's idiosyncratic tradition of ascribing ethnic identities which will be broached in what follows. The only exception to be made is where "black" refers to the official census category *preto* (i.e., of Afro-Brazilian origin) as opposed to *pardo* ("brown" – i.e., of mixed black, white, and/or Indigenous origin); in this sense, both *pretos* and *pardos* are understood as Black inasmuch as both groups represent main objects of the practices of racialized surveillance and punishment which shall be discussed throughout what follows. Our usage of "Black" thus rather corresponds to the term *negro* as both a function of the Brazilian police state – in which, according to Alves, race is ultimately an effect of an institutionalized necropolitical

Meanwhile, a main difficulty in analyzing the "Brazilian apartheid"[6] and its manifestations in urban space consists in the fact that, paradoxically enough, race remains a somewhat ephemeral category in both public and academic discourse. Encapsulated in the highly influential trope of a "racial democracy," common knowledge holds that, due to the historically widespread practice of miscegenation, the original trinity of an African, an Amerindian, and a European "race" would have given way to a chromatic continuum in which clear-cut definitions of "Black" and "white" become largely obsolete – resulting in a steady "hyperconsciousness of race and its negation."[7] Although demographic indicators evince a persistent discrimination against dark-skinned citizens in most spheres of public life, and the violent heritage of colonialism and slavery is immediately apparent for those who dare to face it, everyday culture and its institutional embedding provide a whole array of devices fit to relativize or completely ignore it.

It is against this backdrop of a negated-yet-manifest racism impregnating and organizing social relations in contemporary Brazil that the present chapter reexamines two paradigmatic settings – the *condomínio fechado*[8] and the prison – as nodal points in an urban topology of racialization: a spatial as well as institutional configuration in and through which bodies are constantly "put into their place" according to their skin color.

While, to be sure, *condomínio* and prison represent but two of multiple locales which would deserve closer attention in this context, we selected them for several reasons. First and foremost, as shall be argued in what follows, both settings have evolved from an eminently colonial logic of sorting bodies and dividing up space – namely, the racialized juxtaposition of *casa-grande* (the landowner's "big house") and *senzala* (the slaves' quarters), characteristic of Brazil's early colonization marked by a quasi-absent colonial state and a thriving sugarcane economy.

Second, it is hard to ignore that, topologically speaking, prison and *condomínio* represent virtual mirror images of each other, the objective of the former consisting in assuring a scheme of confinement while the purpose of the latter is to maintain a regime of exclusion. Both *condomínios* and prisons have been mushrooming all over

---

calculus – *and* an ethnic autodenomination which is characterized by its relative independence from a person's specific ancestry. Originating during the early years of colonization as an umbrella term for the African slaves working on the sugar plantations, the expression has thus been appropriated and resignified by the subjects in question, effectively conflating a plurality of marginalized racial identities and the corresponding political struggles. It is in this sense that *negro* – rather than *preto* and *pardo* – constitutes the semantic pivot of both a whole array of discriminatory state practices and of emancipatory politics aiming at the constitution of a racially just society.

[6] João H. Costa Vargas, "Apartheid brasileiro: raça e segregação residencial no Rio de Janeiro," *Revista de Antropologia* 48, no. 1 (2005): 75–131.
[7] João H. Costa Vargas, "Hyperconsciousness of Race and Its Negation: The Dialectic of White Supremacy in Brazil," *Identities: Global Studies in Culture and Power* 11, no. 4 (2004): 443–470.
[8] Literally, a closed condominium (i.e., a gated community).

São Paulo throughout the past few decades, thus representing an increasingly common "place of residence" for a growing share of the state's population.

Finally, prisons and *condomínios* both represent prominent sales markets for information and communications technology (ICT)-driven security "solutions" – i.e., for an industry which has been steadily expanding and refining its products and services in the recent past. As a noteworthy side effect, what can be observed is a gradual "deterritorialization" of both the *condomínio* and the prison – that is, their interlinkage with an array of devices, infrastructures, and technologies enabling their partial transposition into open space. As shall be argued in what follows, the concomitant subjection of public urban space to a regime of digitally enforced surveillance and control is likely to further reinforce the entrenched logic of a racially differentiated government – that is, to perpetuate a markedly (neo)colonialist "moral economy of safe circulations"[9] by deploying the high-tech gadgetry of the twenty-first century.

Indeed, the patent asynchrony of a fetishistic, technology-driven type of "modernization" on the one hand, and the persistence of a social formation still bearing the visible mark of colonialism and slavery on the other, will be taken up repeatedly throughout this chapter, not least because it so aptly characterizes contemporary São Paulo. Aggressively reshaping the urban fabric in the stereotypical image of a global city, local elites have erected simulacra of Western business districts, replete with shiny skyscrapers and Starbucks franchises; at the same time, hundreds of thousands of families are still living in *favelas*, often without regular access to the most basic infrastructures and threatened by eviction at any moment.

It is in view of these violent contrasts – which, as suggested above, entail a markedly racialized edge – that Fix and Arantes[10] have coined the polemic term, a "platypus-metropolis" (*metrópole-ornitorrinco*): neither modern nor archaic, neither first nor third world, neither fully central nor truly marginal, São Paulo as the paradigmatic case of a "peripheral global city" would amalgamate modes of production, forms of subsistence, and ways of life which are not only profoundly heterogeneous, but indeed belong to incommensurate scales and temporalities altogether. Describing a scenario of customized access for the few and wholesale exclusion for the many, the "platypus" model thus captures how the city's ruling classes are largely indifferent about the population's general welfare, and have embraced the perpetual "administration of the exception" – that is, the fortification of the city's prime areas and the aggressive policing of its social margins – as the most obvious "solution" to a problem which vastly exceeds the narrow domain of public safety.[11]

---

[9] Allen Feldman, "Securocratic Wars of Public Safety: Globalized Policing as Scopic Regime," *Interventions* 6, no. 3 (2004): 330–350.

[10] Mariana Fix and Pedro Arantes, "São Paulo: Metrópole-Ornitorrinco," *Correio da Cidadania* 383 (2004) online.

[11] Fix and Arantes adopt the metaphor of the *ornitorrinco* from sociologist Francisco de Oliveira who, since the early 1970s, has been devising a critique of developmentalism – both as an

TOPOLOGIES OF RACE IN URBAN BRAZIL: A VERY BRIEF GENEALOGY

Before examining the technologies governing race, we will briefly review the process of spatializing race – which, *nota bene*, is intimately bound up with the corresponding process of racializing space in São Paulo.

The perspective adopted in this synopsis is inspired by Mbembe's[12] conceptualization of race as a technology of government, deployed to organize and administer multiplicities in space according to a logic of enclosure. Focusing on the seventeenth century's European colonies which would later become the Southern United States, Mbembe relates the advent of the modern "Black Man" to the emergence of plantation slavery, which facilitated both an unprecedented accumulation of wealth and the effective integration of colonial territories into the commercial circuits of metropolitan capitalism. It was the brutal arrangement of plantation-space by means of which the "Black Man" was deprived of his liberty, subjected to a routine of perpetual surveillance, and forced into a regime of grueling labor sanctioned through the virtually unlimited deployment of physical violence on behalf of his white masters. Against this backdrop, it is only consequent that Mbembe considers the colonial plantations as "factories par excellence of race and racism."[3]

Relocating the focus of analysis further south, the classical essays of Brazilian sociologist, anthropologist, historian, and congressman Gilberto Freyre provide insights into another process of spatializing race taking off in the sixteenth century; a process which, apart from confining and distributing population groups in(to) enclosed physical spaces, would leave a lasting imprint on the sociopolitical formation of a whole new country. Emerging from a Portuguese colony of quasi-continental dimensions, in Freyre's depiction, the estate-based society of the Brazilian Empire (1822–1889) developed out of the specific configuration of the sugar cane plantation – the *fazenda* – and its peculiar mode of spatializing race; namely, the *casa-grande* (the tropical mansion where the *senhor das terras* – namely, the landowner – and his family would reside) connected to the *senzala* (the makeshift cottage where the slaves were accommodated). This paradoxical amalgamation would end up representing "an entire economic, social, and political system."[4] Both sides of the equation – which, in fact, would have to be understood

---

economic theory and as a political ideology – by pointing out how the supposedly "underdeveloped" and/or not entirely "modern" sectors of Brazilian society were in fact integral and fully functional to a politico-economic model whose very foundations consisted – and continue to consist – in the perpetual reproduction of profound social inequalities. See Francisco de Oliveira, *Crítica à razão dualista/O ornitorrinco* (São Paulo: Boitempo, 2003), 121ff.

[12] Achille Mbembe, *Critique of Black Reason* (Durham, NC: Duke University Press, 2017).
[13] Ibid., 36.
[14] Gilberto Freyre, *The Masters and the Slaves: A Study in the Development of Brazilian Civilization* (Berkeley, CA: University of California Press, 1986), xxxiii.

as a "process of balancing antagonisms"[15] – were held together by the integrating forces of familial patriarchalism; a defining feature of the nascent society inasmuch as Brazil's effective colonization – that is, the settlement, cultivation, and political administration of the colony's hinterland – had been largely delegated to private initiative by the Portuguese Crown.

Since the very beginning of colonization, populations were distributed across space according to their racial identity. White *senhores* and their families would live in the *casa-grande*, Black slaves had to remain in the *senzala*, and the Indigenous – considered physically unfit for working in the plantations and, therefore, economically less profitable than the Black workforce[16] – were quickly decimated or escaped. As compared to the other European empires' colonial projects, Freyre insists that the Portuguese colonization of Brazil would have been unique due to the relative proximity it permitted between African slaves, Indigenous Americans, and European settlers, giving rise to an unparalleled degree of miscegenation. Brazilian society would therefore accommodate a multitude of *mestiços* (descendants from two or more different races): *cafuzos* (Indigenous and Black), *mulatos* (Black and white), *mamelucos* or *caboclos* (white and Indigenous), *juçaras* (Black, white, and Indigenous), etc.

Subverting clear-cut phenotypical differentiations between *brancos* (whites) and *negros* (Blacks) as defined by the slavocratic order, Freyre affirms that *mestiços* enjoyed a relative liberty to circulate freely in both *casa-grande* and *senzala*. Confounding the racialized topology of the colonial *fazenda*, the *mestiço*'s intermediate position would eventually be resolved by the *senhor*'s sovereign prerogative. Especially if the subject in question was the *senhor*'s illegitimate child, chances were that (s)he would grow up in the *casa-grande*. Likewise, the *senhor* was able to allow some *negros* to live under his roof – these slaves would then constitute a quasi-feudal entourage, more often than not assigned to take care of the *senhor*'s progeny. Not least, the *senhor* could appoint some of his slaves to carry out domestic tasks and/or to cater to his sexual desires; therefore, despite the fact that the system of *casa-grande* and *senzala* supposedly constituted a clearly demarcated segregational grid keeping both *brancos* and *negros* in their respective places, the *senhor*'s sovereign will could always override the established spatioracial order.[17]

---

[15] Ibid., 79.
[16] Stuart B. Schwartz, "A Commonwealth within Itself: The Early Brazilian Sugar Industry, 1550–1670," in Stuart B. Schwartz (ed.), *Tropical Babylons: Sugar and the Making of the Atlantic World, 1450–1680* (Chapel Hill, NC and London: University of North Carolina Press, 2004), 158–200, 188f.
[17] Amongst the authors investigating how Brazil's historical miscegenation entailed the emergence of specific discriminatory practices, Nogueira distinguishes the Brazilian prejudice against *negros* and *mestiços* from the "one-drop rule" racism characteristic of the United States: while the latter would define an individual's racial identity by referring to their ancestry

The Portuguese Crown's relocation to Rio de Janeiro in 1808 – the court had had to flee from Napoleon's advancing troops – accelerated Brazil's urbanization. Meanwhile, the racialization of space underwent a reconfiguration as a new urban lifestyle began to take hold. Again, it was Freyre who, in *Sobrados e Mucambos* ("The Mansions and the Shanties"), described the corresponding transformations most vividly. In the city, the *senhor* of the *casa-grande* would come to inhabit a mansion – the *sobrado* – a structure characterized by a series of extensions where the domestic slaves were accommodated. Once these annexes were refurbished for other purposes – a process which gained momentum after the abolition of slavery in 1888 – former slaves would end up dwelling in "settlements [that] grew up near the city mansions and country places, filled with shanties and shacks. They began to spread over the poorest areas of the cities."[18] Generally speaking the process of urbanization had a deteriorating impact upon the living conditions of liberated slaves since, without regular employment, they were unable to afford even the most basic goods, including alimentation.

Meanwhile, the abolition of slavery soon had *negros* and *mestiços* experiencing contemporary liberalism's elective affinity with the ideology of biological determinism. Having escaped the *senzalas*, they soon turned into the objects of scientifically legitimized racism. Perhaps most prominently, forensic doctor Raimundo Nina Rodrigues challenged the legal equality embraced by the recently founded Republic, and instead argued for the adoption of separate penal codes, well in line with his belief in race-specific inclinations to crime.[19] Indeed, the corresponding theory of social degeneration did not only postulate the biological inferiority of *indígenas, negros*, and *mulatos*, but also branded them with the stigma of abnormality, immorality, and delinquency. It was in this ideological context that the "liberated" *negro* emerged as the personification of an omnipresent criminal threat. In the rapidly expanding urban agglomerations of São Paulo, Rio de Janeiro, and Minas Gerais, dark-skinned Brazilians, unable to obtain formal employment in a highly competitive labor market, rapidly found themselves labeled as *vadios*

and largely ignore phenotypical markers of Black- or whiteness, in Brazil physical appearances would be of utmost importance, including details such as gestures and bodily conduct. This "racism of marks" would most palpably manifest itself in a perennial "colorism," i.e., a discriminatory practice in which brighter-skinned *mestiços* may even pass as whites while those with darker complexions and Afro-Brazilians are constantly among the most stigmatized parts of the population. See Oracy Nogueira, "Preconceito racial de marca e preconceito racial de origem: Sugestão de um quadro de referência para a interpretação do material sobre relações raciais no Brasil," *Tempo Social* 19, no. 1 (2006): 287–308.

[18] Gilberto Freyre, *The Mansions and the Shanties: The Making of Modern Brazil* (New York: Knopf, 1963), 108.

[19] Marcos César Alvarez, "A Criminologia no Brasil ou Como Tratar Desigualmente os Desiguais," *DADOS - Revista de Ciências Sociais* 45, no. 4 (2002): 677–704; Lilia Moritz Schwarcz, "Nina Rodrigues: um radical do pessimismo," in André Botelho and Lilia Moritz Schwarcz (eds.), *Um enigma chamado Brasil: 29 intérpretes e um país* (São Paulo: Companhia das Letras, 2009), 90–103.

(vagrants), *malandros* (tricksters), or *bandidos* (outlaws).[20] These widespread racialized prejudices complicated the integration of *negros* and *mestiços* into an emergent wage labor economy.[21]

Florestan Fernandes, another classic exponent of Brazilian social thought, examined the contradictory integration of the recently liberated *negros* into Brazil's emerging class society. The object of his analysis, conducted in the 1960s, was the Black population of São Paulo – a city which, due to its lucrative coffee business, had become the country's most vibrant economic hub in the late nineteenth century. In this first truly bourgeois Brazilian city, landowner families from the state's interior began to settle in large residencies and palazzos, all the while ever-increasing numbers of white European immigrants – mostly working-class – and black and *mestiço* domestic migrants arrived in São Paulo trying to make a living. Fernandes set out to analyze the economic activities of the various population groups settling in Brazil's coffee capital. The landowners' main pursuit consisted in supervising agricultural production at their plantations situated in prosperous regions upstate. Within the city limits, their occupational profile was centered around the commercial, banking, and speculative sectors which had emerged due to the coffee business. Meanwhile, crafts and retail trade were virtually monopolized by the city's white population, especially by the Europeans who had come to Brazil in order to make a fortune. Even among the occupations considered as degrading, such as bootblacks, fishmongers, or newspapermen, Italian immigrants were more common than former slaves.

In this diagram of economic activities defining São Paulo's new competitive society, *negros* and *mestiços* – unless they migrated to the hinterland in order to subsist from what they were able to cultivate – were forced into the most marginal and transitory sectors of capitalist production. Without the professional instruction necessary to qualify as skilled labor, they would do odd jobs and spend their free time in bars and taverns (Black females tended to be slightly better off as they were able to find employment as domestic servants or to earn some money as laundresses, ironers, or sewers). Against this backdrop of *negros*' and *mestiços*' paradoxical (dis)integration into the postabolition class society, it becomes evident that the processes of racialization – and the corresponding organization of social space – were not historically limited to the definition and distribution of population groups within the stratified agricultural spaces of colonial and imperial Brazil. With the introduction of wage labor, they also came to identify and associate ethnic groups to

---

[20] Andrej Koerner, "Punição, disciplina e pensamento penal no Brasil do século XIX," *Lua Nova* 68 (2006): 205–242, 218ff.; Alessandra Teixeira, Fernando Afonso Salla, and Maria Gabriela da Silva Martins da Cunha Marinho, "Vadiagem e prisões correcionais em São Paulo: Mecanismos de controle no firmamento da República," *Estudos Históricos* 29, no. 58 (2016): 381–400.

[21] Raquel Rolnik, *A cidade e a lei: legislação, política urbana e territórios na cidade de São Paulo* (São Paulo: Studio Nobel, 1997), 69ff.

social classes. In the course of this fundamental socioeconomic transformation, *negros* and *mestiços* found themselves at the very bottom of society, exposed to poverty and misery.

Fernandes's analyses were the first to examine the relation between race and class, diagnosing a state of social anomy among *negros* and *mestiços* and highlighting the continuity of slavocratic structures in postabolition Brazil. Revisiting the accounts of both Freyre and Fernandes thus enables a better understanding of how, against the background of increasing urbanization and an economy based on wage labor, processes of racialization became both more complex and more problematic than they used to be before.

It is apparent that, once the precarious unity of *casa-grande* and *senzala* – characterized by the *senhor*'s sovereign power over both slaves and territory – was split apart, processes of racialization quickly affected other settings and contexts where they would identify, distribute, and spatially confine different ethnic groups. According to Jessé Souza,[22] an institutionalized framework able to equilibrate and pacify slavocracy's inherent antagonisms gave way to a scenario defined by the proliferation of social conflict. It is in this context that the prison as a disciplinary apparatus was effectively incorporated as a punitive technology geared to domesticating social conflicts, suppressing acts of resistance, and drilling liberated slaves so as to make them fit for wage labor. Complemented by the construction of asylums and penitentiaries for adolescents, vagrants, and "invalids," the prison thus materialized as an institution whose main purpose would consist in absorbing the now-superfluous *negros* and *mestiços* in order to transform and exploit them within the new regime of industrial production and "free" labor.[23] The modernization of the Brazilian prison system – substantially promoted by the state of São Paulo – was thus intrinsically geared towards rendering docile and disciplining the former slaves' bodies.[24]

The combined forces of social marginalization, racial stigmatization, and the state's policy of penal internment thus came to constitute a politico-economic regime suitable for confining former slaves and their descendants to a subaltern class position. While space remained a vital category of social stratification – as could be witnessed by the moral denigration of predominantly Black urban neighborhoods in the decades following abolition[25] – the wage labor society and the emerging class order entailed adversities of a whole different order, as it deprived *negros* and *mestiços* of their means of subsistence, exposing them to the steady threat of hunger and homelessness.

---

[22] Jessé Souza, *A elite do atraso: da escravidão à Lava Jato* (Rio de Janeiro: Leya, 2017).
[23] Fernando Salla, *As prisões em São Paulo: 1822–1940* (São Paulo: Annablume, 2006).
[24] Ibid.; Teixeira, Salla, and Marinho, "Vadiagem e prisões correcionais."
[25] Rolnik, *A cidade e a lei*, 67ff.

Taking up Florestan Fernandes' pioneering analyses, it is Souza et al.[26] who identify the striking continuities between the "wretched race" of the nineteenth century and the "wretched class" of the twenty-first century. In a critical examination of Brazilian society under the center-left presidency of Luiz Inácio Lula da Silva (2003–2010), they highlight the racialized dimension of a social stratum commonly known as the *ralé* (literally: scum, riffraff). Composed of individuals unprepared and unqualified for the rising cognitive demands of a postindustrial economy, the *ralé* – amounting to as much as a third of the country's overall population – would be predominantly dark-skinned, bearing witness to the continuing marginalization of *afrodescendentes* – that is, the heirs of former African slaves. Thus excluded from finding regular employment in São Paulo's thriving service sector, the members of the *ralé* would be forced into the leftover niches of physical labor and/or the city's vast informal economy, be it as domestic servants, cleaners, prostitutes, street vendors, security guards, or porters. Reduced to a state of mere corporeality and scratching along earning paltry wages, the *ralé* would find itself ignored and invisibilized unless it would surface as a stain in the city's glitzy upper-class districts and/or as a supposed threat to public order in the guise of the proverbial *bandido*.[27]

Indeed, Souza et al. observe that, if the steady deprivations and the constitutive self-denial characteristic of the "honest" life turn any perspective of future improvement into a vain hope, the *ralé* may well fall back on illegal activities, such as providing muscle for organized crime or dealing drugs."[28] Between the bone-grinding *dignidade* ("dignity") of miserably paid odd jobs and the immoral and risky path of criminal *delinquência* ("delinquency"), the *ralé* has no plausible third option. Meanwhile, largely independent of the specific "career" they end up pursuing, its members remain stigmatized as constituents of an aesthetically disturbing and morally dubious "dangerous class" and, therefore, represent a preferred target of the Brazilian police state and its affiliated white "civil society." While the politico-economic significance of race has changed considerably since slavery was abolished in 1888, the *ralé* thus represents a contemporary revenant of Brazil's enslaved population not only due to its hopelessly subaltern social position, but also insofar as it triggers a securitarian reflex whose main purpose consists in putting Black bodies in their respective place – a postulate which shall be empirically corroborated throughout what follows.

---

[26] Jessé Souza et al., *A ralé brasileira: quem é e como vive* (Belo Horizonte: Editora UFMG, 2009).
[27] Michel Misse, "Crime, sujeito e sujeição criminal: aspectos de uma contribuição analítica sobre a categoria 'bandido'," *Lua Nova* 79 (2010): 15–38.
[28] Souza et al., *A ralé brasileira*, 241ff.

EVERYTHING IN ITS RIGHT PLACE: GOVERNING CIRCULATIONS IN THE *CONDOMÍNIO FECHADO*

> The apartment's total size is 500 square meters. Located in São Paulo's exclusive Jardim Europa neighborhood, it occupies the 14th floor of the Viva Real – a high-end condominium equipped with two swimming pools, a private spa, a gym, and a tennis court.
>
> Furnished with elegant timber flooring, the spacious living room merges with the home theater equipped with the latest entertainment electronics. Passing through the majestic gallery, two junior suites can be accessed. Further down the hallway the master suite offers a deluxe double bed and two separate bathrooms, the larger one featuring a Jacuzzi.
>
> The service area is equipped with a separate entry and comprises a professional kitchen, a pantry, and a laundry room. There is also a waiting room for the chauffeur, as well as two bedrooms and one small bathroom for the domestic servants.
>
> The Viva Real was completed in 2012. Offering top-notch luxury in one of São Paulo's most prestigious areas, apartments sell at around R$ 20 million.

Phenotypically speaking, São Paulo's contemporary cityscape hardly bears any resemblance to the days when plantation owners and coffee barons ran the local economy. Perhaps most iconically, the downtown *Avenida Paulista*, once lined with the palatial domiciles of the city's high society, has since the 1960s been transformed into a bustling commercial district crammed with futuristic skyscrapers providing office space for stock-listed companies both national and international. Characteristically enough, the avenue's last remaining *sobrado* – the *Residência Joaquim Franco de Melo*, a thirty-five-room mansion built in 1905 – has been lying vacant for decades and is now visibly decaying, appearing strangely out of place and time in a sea of glitzy high-rises. A crumbling ruin in the midst of what is one of São Paulo's most prosperous and economically dynamic areas, the *Residência* stands metonymically for the striking lack of historical consciousness characterizing both the high-modern "city that cannot stop"[29] and the ensuing era defined by economic crisis, sweeping privatization, and Brazil's contradictory integration into a globalized financial economy.[30]

---

[29] *São Paulo não pode parar* ("São Paulo cannot stop") became a popular slogan in the mid-twentieth century, condensing the local pride of the city's staggering growth rates both economically and demographically.

[30] Teresa P. R. Caldeira, "From Modernism to Neoliberalism in São Paulo: Reconfiguring the City and Its Citizens," in Andreas Huyssen (ed.), *Other Cities, Other Worlds: Urban Imaginaries in a Globalizing Age* (Durham, NC and London: Duke University Press, 2008), 51–77.

In the meantime, São Paulo's economic elite has largely resorted to a new residential model which quickly became attractive for broader strata of the urban population and, by consequence, is now defining major parts of the city's central and some of its peripheral areas – namely, the *condomínio fechado* ("closed condominium").[31] It essentially designates any development combining freehold properties – typically individual apartments in a residential high-rise – with a series of security measures (fencing, a doorman, CCTV cameras ...) and "exclusive" facilities (a pool, a gym, a playground ...). More than an ultimately private manifestation of individual lifestyle choices, it is fair to say that the *condomínio* has had a lasting impact not only upon the way in which urban space and social relations are materially configured but, indeed, of how they have come to be imagined, feared, and desired. The *condomínio* has, in a word, turned into a diagram[32] by means of which subjectivities are shaped, social imaginaries are produced, and a specifically Brazilian version of civilizational discontent is perpetually enacted.[33]

In the given context the most crucial aspect of the *condomínio* might consist in its peculiar configuration of hermeticity and permeability. Despite its frequently imposing and, at times, even fortress-like architectural features, the *condomínio* maintains

---

[31] In the present chapter, the terms *condomínio* and *condomínio fechado* are being used interchangeably. While the additional *fechado* seems to suggest otherwise, in fact in contemporary São Paulo there is virtually no *condomínio* without at least the most basic security infrastructures comprising walls, surveillance systems, and some kind of access control. Likewise, the present chapter concentrates on "vertical" *condomínios* consisting of one or several apartment towers as opposed to their homonymous "horizontal" version which is more widespread in São Paulo's sub- and peri-urban areas and which closely resembles the Anglo-American concept of a "gated community." Finally, the focus rests on "professional" developments, i.e., real estate projects which are planned, built, and sold by specialized companies. This specification is vital because at least the "horizontal" *condomínio* has long since made its way into the "Black" space of the urban peripheries and *favelas*, where it is being replicated in a makeshift way by the local population both in order to protect a community from criminal invaders and to restrain violent and abusive police activities. See Moises Kopper and Matthew A. Richmond, "Walling the Peripheries: Porous Condominiums at Brazil's Urban Margins," unpublished manuscript (2020); João H. Costa Vargas, "Apartheid brasileiro: raça e segregação residencial no Rio de Janeiro," *Revista de Antropologia* 48, no. 1 (2005): 75–131.

[32] In the sense of Thomas Osborne and Nikolas Rose, who introduce the notion of the diagram as an attempt to "capture the different ways in which government has been territorialised in an urban form." By consequence, the city – and the infrastructures which constitute it – would have to be understood as a "way of diagramming human existence, human conduct, human subjectivity, human life itself – diagramming it in the name of government." Thomas Osborne and Nikolas Rose, "Governing Cities: Notes on the Spatialisation of Virtue," *Environment and Planning D: Society and Space* 17, no. 6 (1999): 737–760 at 737. In a similar vein, Michel Foucault affirms that "the Panopticon ... is the diagram of a mechanism of power reduced to its ideal form; its functioning, abstracted from any obstacle, resistance or friction, must be represented as a pure architectural and optical system: it is in fact a figure of political technology that may and must be detached from any specific use." Michel Foucault, *Discipline and Punish: The Birth of the Prison* (New York: Vintage Books, 1995), 205.

[33] Christian Ingo Lenz Dunker, *Mal-estar, sofrimento e sintoma: uma psicopatologia do Brasil entre muros* (São Paulo: Boitempo, 2015).

a whole series of vital relations with its urban environment – including both its necessary connection to urban infrastructure networks and the multitude of nannies, cleaners, gardeners, janitors, and concierges circulating on its premises, enabling the "carefree" upper-middle-class way of life which, more often than not, represents the unique selling point of residential property in a *condomínio*.[34] The *condomínio* may thus justifiably be considered a schizophrenic arrangement inasmuch as its quasi-martial securitarian aesthetics is constantly belied by the necessary influx of working-class citizens – a condition which, rather than a state of hermetic seclusion, would announce a relationship of co-fragility with the *condomínio*'s urban environment both material and social.[35]

Meanwhile, as James Holston points out in his study of "insurgent" practices of citizenship in São Paulo's urban space, the Brazilian *condomínio* might be unique due to one specific architectural characteristic – to wit, the physical separation of two discrete circuits, one for the residents and another for domestic employees. The widespread use of two particular elevators – one designated *social* ("social"), the other *serviço* ("service") – conspicuously illustrates how the *condomínio* resembles a huge sorting machine for human bodies, bringing them together when deemed necessary for the residents' comfort and keeping them neatly apart from each other for the rest of the time.[36]

While historical accuracy advises against precipitously identifying the *condomínio*'s regime of segregated circulations with the racialized space of the *casa-grande* as described by Gilberto Freyre – after all, dark-skinned Brazilians can and do acquire properties in *condomínios* while white citizens may well work on its premises as doormen, gardeners, or cleaners – it is no overstatement to describe the *condomínio* as an ideal-typical incarnation of "white space"[37] inasmuch as its main promise consists in reinstating a mode of sociality in which everybody – that is, literally, every *body* – remains in her or his proper place. Functioning as a "new form of [symbolically mediated] racism,"[38] the "white space" of the *condomínio* would thus essentially consist in the hegemony of an aesthetic *doxa* according to which the Black body has to provide some kind of credible authorization and/or adopt an inconspicuous, deferential kind of habitus if it is to circulate freely in a setting which traditionally has been a paragon of white privilege.[39] Indeed, as an ideal-typical instantiation of a "domesticated" type of social as well as racial diversity, the *condomínio* forms part of a whole archipelago of mass private properties

---

[34] Caldeira, *City of Walls*, 256ff.
[35] Francisco Klauser, "Splintering Spheres of Security: Peter Sloterdijk and the Contemporary Fortress City," *Environment and Planning D: Society and Space* 28, no. 2 (2010): 326–340.
[36] James Holston, *Insurgent Citizenship: Disjunctions of Democracy and Modernity in Brazil* (Princeton University Press, 2009), 275ff.
[37] Elijah Anderson, "The White Space," *Sociology of Race and Ethnicity* 1, no. 1 (2015): 10–21.
[38] Ibid., 20.
[39] Souza et al., *A ralé brasileira*, 371f.

comprising airports, high-end office buildings, and upscale shopping malls in which, until very recently, the presence of dark-skinned persons was largely restricted to the performance of menial tasks such as cleaning, maintenance, and access control.

It is therefore fair to say that the *condomínio*'s main proposition consists in suspending the unresolved conflicts which have been defining Brazilian society since the days of colonization and, in fact, enacting an idealized version of pacified sociality providing a temporary relief from the democratic impositions characterizing the public sphere.[40] Pondering the inescapably precarious nature of such an "isolationist" endeavor, Ingo Lenz Dunker emphasizes the importance of the *síndico*[41] as a key figure in the *condomínio*'s symbolic order. Taking care of the property's smooth operation in infrastructural as well as in social and legal terms, the good *síndico* is the pivot on which ultimately depends the realization of the *condomínio*'s core promise – that is, of living a happy and fulfilled life in the midst of – yet neatly separated from – a brutally unequal society. The *síndico*'s main function would therefore consist in looking after the inevitable "soft" factors in a configuration which, from a mere lifestyle option for a small social elite, would long since have turned into an "obscene obligation of happiness"[42] drawing in an ever-increasing share of São Paulo's general population.[43]

[40] The inherently regressive trait of such halcyon fantasies became manifest in a paradigmatic way when, in 2018, a white adolescent from the northern city of Belém decided to celebrate her fifteenth birthday with a historical reenactment of imperial Brazil: photos on her Instagram channel showed the young woman wearing a sumptuous white dress with golden embroidery, being served her breakfast by two dark-skinned "slaves." After a public outcry the adolescent affirmed that "it was never our aim to depict slavery as something good in our history. Our only intention was to reenact the age of the Empire which, unfortunately, included slavery." See www.feedclub.com.br/sem-nocao-familia-usa-escravidao-como-tema-para-festa-de-15-anos. Our translation.
[41] Ingo Lenz Dunker, "A Lógica do Condomínio ou: o Síndico e seus Descontentes," *Revista Leitura Flutuante* 1 (2009). Literally translating into "receiver" or "landlord," the *síndico* is the person in charge of the *condomínio*'s administration, including the premises' security, cleanliness, and legal supervision. The *síndico* may either be a resident elected by his neighbors or a professional appointed by a real estate agency.
[42] Ibid., our translation.
[43] In 2014, in the city of São Paulo 37% of the population lived in a *condomínio*, indicating an increasing market differentiation: once only affordable for the very wealthy, the *condomínio* has become the predominant type of residence in São Paulo's central neighborhoods – mostly as the collateral effect of urban densification and a booming real estate market. By consequence, owning property in a *condomínio* has become widespread well below the city's upper middle class, a phenomenon corresponding to the emergence of more humble developments dispensing with most of the luxury facilities characterizing the upper end of the market and focusing on the "basic package" of access control and some modest amenities. Nonetheless, even in the most basic *condomínios* remnants of the historically established "differentiated" regime can usually be discerned, most noticeably by the persistence of two separate elevators and an annex-like "service area" reminding of the servant's quarters which remain an altogether common feature in high-end developments. It can thus be affirmed that, in spite of the *condomínio*'s gradual popularization, its spatial configuration reproduces a pattern which is profoundly

As if anticipating Lauren Berlant's remarks on "cruel optimism" – understood as "the affective attachment to what we call 'the good life', which is for so many a bad life that wears out the subjects who nonetheless, and at the same time, find their conditions of possibility within it"[44] – Dunker's definition of the *condomínio* logic as an ubiquitous "administration of discontent" thus accentuates the (aspiring) middle-class subject's toxic identification with a commodified form of sociality which is never quite able to deliver the gratifications it has been sold with. Rather than suspending the inherent contradictions of a society which constitutively denies its lasting heritage of colonialism and slavery, the *condomínio* would effectively reproduce them in the guise of numerous minor nuisances – noisy neighbors, sluggish employees, defective facilities – and, most palpably, a steady concern about the premises' security, entailing a hermeneutics of suspicion contaminating social interactions between residents, employees, and external contractors such as builders, delivery boys, or private tutors.

It is therefore hardly surprising that the *condomínio* has turned into a veritable node of securitarian discourses, knowledges, and practices, giving rise to a host of pertinent manuals and booklets[45] and fostering the emergence of a whole "technosphere" of security devices catering to the specific necessities of Brazil's urban middle class.[46] Indeed, it is fair to say that the country's real estate sector and the security industry have entered a quasi-symbiotic relationship, as could be witnessed when Selma Migliori, president of Brazil's electronic security industry association, received the 2020 *Top Condomínios* award for her commitment to deepening the two sectors' partnership while fostering technological innovation.[47] As a consequence, the "intelligent" *condomínio* saturated with cameras and sensors and fully embedded into a multiplicity of electronic information circuits is now being advertised as the epitome of "modern" urban life, promising to guarantee unprecedented levels of comfort and security while significantly reducing personnel costs.

Taking up the aforementioned notion of the urban "platypus" as a metaphor condensing the asynchronies and contradictions characterizing contemporary São Paulo, it can thus be affirmed that the *condomínio fechado* constitutes a focal point of technological innovation while simultaneously representing an ill-concealed

elitist. See Edison Veiga and Fábio Rossini, "210 mil pessoas trocam casa por prédio em 5 anos e 1/3 de SP vive em condomínio," *O Estado de São Paulo*, July 27, 2014, https://sao-paulo.estadao.com.br/noticias/geral,210-mil-pessoas-trocam-casa-por-predio-em-5-anos-e-13-de-sp-vive-em-condominio,1534756.

[44] Lauren Berlant, *Cruel Optimism* (Durham, NC and London: Duke University Press, 2011), 27.
[45] AABIC, "Dicas de segurança em condomínios" (São Paulo: AABIC, 2009); Polícia Militar do Estado de São Paulo, "Segurança em Condomínios" (São Paulo: Polícia Militar do Estado de São Paulo, n.d.); Sindicond, "Segurança em Condomínios" (São Paulo: Sindicond, n.d.).
[46] Lucas Melgaço, "Securização urbana: da psicoesfera do medo à tecnoesfera da segurança," PhD Thesis, Universidade de São Paulo (2010).
[47] "Selma Migliori recebe Prêmio Top Condomínios," ABESE, https://abese.org.br/selma-migliori-recebe-premio-top-condominios.

remnant of Brazil's colonial past and its markedly racist underpinnings; indeed, as an elaborate arrangement of spaces, circulations, and (in)visibilities the *condomínio* may itself be considered an "agentic" configuration as it assigns every body to her or his place, thereby stabilizing a system of race- and class-based domination by abetting its aesthetic normalization. Each and any technological "upgrade" presented and merchandised by the economic alliance of the real estate and the electronic security industry will therefore have to be analyzed concerning its potential function in perpetuating a historically deep-rooted model of unequal citizenship – also, and especially, if the devices and "solutions" in question are being depicted as politically neutral.[48]

Having thus outlined the *condomínio fechado* as an ideal-typical "white space" of contemporary São Paulo (and, regional variations of skin color aside, of any other major Brazilian city), the following section is going to introduce the prison as the materialization of a hyperpunitive (anti-)"Black space" and, in fact, the *condomínio*'s antithetical equivalent: containing an ever-increasing amount of dark-skinned bodies, inhibiting their free movement and physically stigmatizing them, São Paulo's prison archipelago plays a hidden-yet-eminent role in reproducing the preconditions of racialized domination.

TORTUROUS ASYNCHRONIES: SUBJUGATING BLACK BODIES IN SÃO PAULO'S PRISON ARCHIPELAGO

The structure consists of two quadrilateral blocks of similar dimensions, which together occupy 27,000 square meters of built-up area. To the left, an alley passes through four external concourses intersecting with the cell blocks arranged side by side. Following the blueprint of the "compact" or "synthetic" unit – a reduced and readjusted version of the widespread "fishbone pattern" – every block is cut through by a central longitudinal axis, where the main internal circulations occur.

Interspersed with security gates and cluttered with hydraulic pipes and electric wires, the axis is lined with steel doors which separate it from the hallways and the ambulatory. There are eight hallways in each unit, four to each side, parallel to each other and perpendicular to the main axis. Every hallway contains a courtyard facing eight cells of approximately 16 square meters each.

The whole structure is built on ground level, except for the concourses in front of the hallways accessing the high-security wing and the isolation cells on the first floor. The complex's outer perimeter is surrounded by a rectangular wall comprising six surveillance towers – one at each corner and two bisecting the rectangle's long sides – constituting the facility's outer membrane.

---

[48] Ruha Benjamin, *Race after Technology: Abolitionist Tools for the New Jim Code* (Medford, MA: Polity, 2019).

Located at the shores of the Tietê river in São Paulo's eastern zone, the Chácara Belém prison complex comprises two *Centros de Detenção Provisória* (provisional detention centers, CDPs) and two *Alas de Progressão Penitenciária* (penitentiary progression wings, APPs). In São Paulo's penal system, the CDPs are reserved for prisoners awaiting trial – the so-called *provisórios*. Because they were mainly planned for detainees serving short-term custody, they are smaller and less elaborate than regular prison units. In turn, the APPs are specific wards accommodating convicts kept in semi-open detention, which entails the possibility of working outside prison. Thus serving distinct purposes, the prison's interior consists of discrete sectors and subsectors, annexes, and extensions – both planned and improvised – whose daily grind is characterized by the asphyxia of its sealed compartments and the agony caused by its overcrowding. Each ward holds dozens or even hundreds of men awaiting a reply, be it from a lawyer, a doctor, or their kin.

Chácara Belém's inmates are mostly dark-skinned – a striking difference to São Paulo state's general population, which is predominantly white. In fact, the prison's conspicuous overrepresentation of Black bodies may well be considered paradigmatic. In 2015, a government survey revealed that, of all Brazilian states, São Paulo exhibited the highest incarceration rate of black (*preto*) and brown (*pardo*) persons. Indeed, for every 100,000 Black citizens 595 were imprisoned, twice as high as the incarceration rate among white *paulistas*.[49] Today, out of São Paulo's 230,000 prisoners, almost 59 percent are black or brown,[50] while the share of *pretos* and *pardos* amongst the state's general population is about 35 percent.

The skewed racial composition of São Paulo's prison population does not least arise from the notably biased approach characterizing the state's security authorities; the police forces' racially discriminatory practices are notorious and have been demonstrated by various researchers.[51] In 2010, in the city of São Paulo, Black persons were twice as likely to be arrested by the police forces as white citizens. In São Paulo state, between 2008 and 2012 out of 100,000 white persons 14 were arrested while out of 100,000 black and brown persons 35 were arrested.[52] The racial bias of São Paulo's police agencies and, more generally, race- and class-specific processes of

---

[49] Secretaria-Geral da Presidência da República, "Mapa do encarceramento: os jovens do Brasil" (Brasília: Secretaria Nacional de Juventude, 2015).
[50] Departamento Penitenciário Nacional, "Levantamento Nacional de Informações Penitenciárias" (2020), https://app.powerbi.com/view?r=eyJrIjoiMmU4ODAwNTAtY2IyMS00 OWJiLWE3ZTgtZGNjY2ZhNTYzZDliIiwidCI6ImViMDkwNDIwLTQoNGMtNDNmNyo5 MWYyLTRiOGRhNmJmZThlMSJ9.
[51] Geová da Silva Barros, "Filtragem racial: a cor na seleção do suspeito," *Revista Brasileira de Segurança Pública* 3, no. 1 (2008), 134–155; Jacqueline Sinhoretto, Giane Silvestre, and Maria Carolina Schlittler, "Desigualdade Racial e Segurança Pública em São Paulo: Letalidade policial e prisões em flagrante," Research Report (Universidade Federal de São Carlos, 2014); Maria Carolina Schlittler, "Matar muito, prender mal: A produção da desigualdade racial como efeito do policiamento ostensivo militarizado em SP," PhD Thesis, Universidade Federal de São Carlos.
[52] Schlittler, "Matar muito, prender mal," 294.

criminalization thus end up constituting the state's prison archipelago as a predominantly Black space.

To be fair, describing São Paulo's prison system exclusively in terms of its racializing functions would be a rather partial approach – after all, it would ignore the tens of thousands of white inmates distributed across the state's penitentiaries. This caution notwithstanding, the combination of ethnographic observation and the state's official statistics corroborates the disproportionate predominance of dark-skinned persons awaiting trial or serving sentences behind bars. As in a photographic negative of what has been observed concerning the *condomínio fechado*, it can thus be affirmed that the prison complements São Paulo's upper-middle-class enclaves in a contemporary incarnation of the binary social model introduced by the colonial topology of *casa-grande* and *senzala*. In this sense, the operating principle of São Paulo's penal institutions exhibits some of the core functionalities attributed to the state's public security policies by critical scholars – that is, the administration and reproduction of the ethnoracial hierarchy which defines Brazilian society, also and especially in its largest metropolis.

Once absorbed into the entrails of São Paulo's prison system, detainees are subjected to multiple forms of punitive control, characterized by a seemingly asynchronous articulation of the old and perennial spaces of carceral confinement on the one hand and the implementation of new, ICT-driven devices of remote surveillance on the other. In Chácara Belém's APPs, right next to the main security gate, a desktop computer has been installed by means of which hundreds of mobile transmitters can be located via GPS, thus controlling the movements of detainees working outside the prison's walls. Inmates wait in line in front of the lattice door separating the cell ward from the administrative sector. Their ankle monitors stick out from under their threadbare uniform trousers. At the prison's main entrance, access control measures include an array of walk-through metal detectors, x-ray screening devices, and CCTV cameras. A side room contains the body scanners deployed to frisk arriving visitors.

The curious simultaneity of a crude carceral mechanics and the highly sophisticated paraphernalia of a digital age is hardly surprising given the security industry's rapid innovation cycles; indeed, high-tech penitentiaries have been a recurrent topic of both sociological and criminological research for decades.[53] In Brazil, technology companies in the field of penal surveillance and prison security have been prospering as of recently, notably since so-called criminal factions began to organize prison riots in the early 2000s.[54] Likewise, partnerships between

---

[53] Nils Christie, *Crime Control as Industry: Towards Gulags, Western Style* (London and New York: Routledge, 2000); Loïc Wacquant, *Prisons of Poverty* (Minneapolis, MN: University of Minnesota Press, 2000); Gilles Chantraine, "La Prison post-disciplinaire," *Déviance et Société* 30, no. 3 (2006): 273–288.

[54] Ricardo Urquizas Campello, "Faces e interfaces de um dispositivo tecnopenal: o monitoramento eletrônico de presos e presas no Brasil," PhD Thesis, Universidade de São Paulo (2019), 140ff.

the state and private companies have become widespread throughout the country's penitentiary archipelago, with São Paulo being the national spearhead of an emerging public–private penal economy. Meanwhile, what stands out against the backdrop of its much-vaunted tech-propelled "modernization" is the fact that the state's prison system is so conspicuously defined by a multiplicity of overtly abusive practices employed against both prisoners and their family members[55] – a finding which does not contradict, but is in fact part and parcel of this contradictory process of carceral "reform."[56]

Throughout the past decade social movements, researchers, and human rights agencies have repeatedly denounced the degrading conditions which characterize São Paulo's prison system:[57] overcrowded cells, deteriorated facilities, deficient medical assistance, spoiled alimentation, an insufficient water supply, and physical aggressions on behalf of the prison staff are experiences which are commonplace in detainees' daily life. Likewise, the state's penitentiaries are defined by recurrent cases of torture, both physical and psychological. The periodic episodes of beatings, drownings, electrical shocks, and other incidences of violent abuse described by prisoners "prolongate and individualize a form of violence defined by its continuity and its diffusivity, entrenched in the ordinary and quotidian functioning of the different agencies which compose the criminal justice system."[58]

The articulations between these forms of institutionalized violence and the implementation of "innovative" surveillance technologies would be curious were they not so dramatic. At Chácara Belém's APPs, monitored prisoners suffer from sore ankles, caused by the constant attrition between the tag's strap and the skin. Some have suffered burns caused by the device's heating-up when being recharged. Besides, inmates report being beaten and locked up in isolation cells if they are found guilty of having violated their stipulated motion profile – a sanction which may affect even those prisoners making painstaking efforts to play by the rules, due to the system's susceptibility to errors and malfunctions.[59] Visitors – almost exclusively dark-skinned females – have to queue the whole night, between eight and twelve hours, before passing through the security check in the stuffy reception room at some point in the morning. The body scanners were purchased after years of political pressure by social

[55] Rafael Godoi, "Fluxos em cadeia: as prisões em São Paulo na virada dos tempos," PhD Thesis, Universidade de São Paulo (2015); Rafael Godoi, "Tortura difusa e continuada," Fábio Mallart and Rafael Godoi (eds.), BR 111: A rota das prisões brasileiras (São Paulo: Veneta, 2018), 117–126; Salla, As prisões em São Paulo.
[56] Campello, "Faces e interfaces."
[57] Instituto Terra, Trabalho e Cidadania, "Tecer Justiça: Presas e presos provisórios da cidade de São Paulo" (São Paulo: ITTC, 2012); Pastoral Carcerária Nacional, "Tortura em tempos de encarceramento em massa no Brasil," Research Report (São Paulo: Pastoral Carcerária Nacional, 2016); Godoi, "Fluxos em cadeia"; Godoi, "Tortura difusa e continuada"; Fábio Mallart, "Findas linhas: circulações e confinamentos pelos subterrâneos de São Paulo," PhD Thesis, Universidade de São Paulo (2019).
[58] Godoi, "Fluxos em cadeia," 118.
[59] Campello, "Faces e interfaces," 40ff.

movements and human rights agencies demanding the abolition of so-called *revistas vexatórias* – that is, humiliating frisk- and strip-searches. Meanwhile, even five years after the equipment's installation, recent investigations have confirmed that *revistas vexatórias* are still common practice in most of São Paulo's prisons.[60]

Against this backdrop it can be affirmed that the punitive technologies deployed by the state of São Paulo are qualified and mediated by a mesh of superimposed practices articulating imprisonment, surveillance, and multiple forms of humiliation and physical violence. Given the odd synergy of the manifestly asynchronous punitive practices and rationales which have been discussed so far, it is highly suggestive to reiterate the metaphor of the platypus – an altogether improbable creature conflating precarity and development, the supposed backwardness typifying the (post)colonial periphery with the slick technological modernity characterizing the capitalist center. In this sense, rather than denouncing its internal incoherences and clinging to a positivistic agenda of sweeping institutional "modernization," a more promising critique would consist in conceiving of São Paulo's prison system as a *punitive platypus* – a fragmented entity betwixt and between, integrating both the modernizing promise of technoscientific penal surveillance and the archaic practice of brute physical torture.

As pointed out earlier, the main targets of this vast and heterogeneous repertoire of punishment and control are Black bodies. In a historical perspective, the conjunction of "innovative" surveillance technologies and seemingly archaic forms of violence and torture as a means to penalize and subjugate the nonwhite population is integral to the very genesis of Brazil's penal system as an institutional entity both complementary to and intertwined with the political economy of slavery. In his analysis of nineteenth-century Brazil's penitentiary politics, Andrei Koerner discusses the importation of European prison models – notably the panopticon – and their coexistence with and adaptation to local modes of punishment[61] – especially the whip and the death penalty, which would only be administered to insubordinate slaves. Over the course of the century, public torture and forced labor were progressively substituted by sentences to be served within the recently built penitentiaries inspired by the latest European concepts.

One of the most iconic examples of Brazil's nineteenth-century prisons consisted in Rio de Janeiro's *Casa de Correção da Corte*, conceived along the lines of the famous Benthamian prototype and adapted according to the necessities of a slavocratic society – that is, the violent subjection of commodified Black bodies. Falling short of, while simultaneously transcending, the ideal image of a "modern" penal institution, the *Casa de Correção* eventually emerged as a paradoxical space of occult chastisements,

---

[60] "#Mulheresemprisão: Revista Vexatória e Audiências de Custódia," Instituto Terra, Trabalho e Cidadania, http://ittc.org.br/revista-vexatoria-audiencias-de-custodia.

[61] Andrei Koerner, "O impossível 'panóptico tropical-escravista': práticas prisionais, política e sociedade no Brasil do século XIX," *Revista Brasileira de Ciências Criminais* 35 (2001).

Colonialism's Uneasy Legacy

or an "impossible tropical-slavocratic panopticon" – that is, a carceral institution defined by its strategic opacity, and within which torture was commonplace.[62]

At present, the various layers of punitive technologies inflicted upon Black bodies is further complexified by the vast array of devices available on the thriving markets of punishment and prison security. An updated version of the slavocratic *senzala* is thus being established within the confines of São Paulo's penitentiary units, contrived and equipped by a booming penal industry. Echoing Mbembe's remarks on the performative qualities of plantation-space, Brazil's proliferating prison archipelago – and, more recently, its multiple technosecuritarian extensions – plays a vital part in normalizing a topology of punitive segregation while effectively reproducing a historically established system of racialized domination.

JUST-IN-TIME SEGREGATION? TOWARDS THE SECUROCRATIC MODULATION OF SÃO PAULO'S OPEN SPACES

Having established the *condomínio fechado* and the prison as two paradigmatic instantiations of contemporary São Paulo's racialized topology, the chapter's closing section broadens the perspective by taking into account more recent tendencies pointing towards a relative spatial dispersion of surveillance and control; that is, their successive deterritorialization as both a response to intensifying mobilities – spatial as well as social – on the one hand and the result of an increasingly ubiquitous presence of networked ICT on the other. The governmental desire behind these emerging public–private infrastructures of real-time securitarian administration would consist in a digitally enhanced micromanagement of circulations and encounters, thus reconciling the economic ideal of unrestrained permeability with the entrenched pattern of (neo)colonial domination which keeps defining Brazilian society. Taking up Jefferson's[63] and Scannell's[64] critique of the United States' "carceral city" and its racialized code/space,[65] this last section's purpose thus consists in briefly highlighting similar phenomena taking hold in the city of São Paulo, albeit with an irreducibly "local" twist which requires a certain degree of contextualization.

Throughout the twenty-first century's first decade, during the Workers' Party presidencies of Luiz Inácio Lula da Silva and, in part, of Dilma Rousseff, Brazil experienced sustained economic growth rates which enabled a considerable redistribution of wealth and, indeed, a historically unparalleled degree of upward social

---

[62] Ibid.
[63] Brian Jefferson, *Digitize and Punish: Racial Criminalization in the Digital Age* (Minneapolis, MN: University of Minnesota Press, 2020).
[64] R. Joshua Scannell, "Electric Light: Automating the Carceral State During the Quantification of Everything," PhD thesis, The City University of New York (2018).
[65] Rob Kitchin and Martin Dodge, *Code/Space: Software and Everyday Life* (Cambridge and London: MIT Press, 2011).

mobility. The advancement of previously subaltern population groups has been analyzed in terms of an emerging "new middle class"[66] or of working-class "fighters" claiming their right to belong and consume.[67] Likewise, income-generating policies for the very poor and affirmative action programs conceived to augment the share of Black, Indigenous, and socially disadvantaged university students played a vital part in transforming Brazil's social panorama – not forgetting the government's efforts to tackle exploitative working conditions which resulted in significant improvements for the country's myriad domestic servants.

On a more quotidian level, working-class (that is, predominantly dark-skinned) Brazilians became more visible in settings formerly restricted to the (mostly white) urban middle class such as airports or shopping malls. In fact, James Holston's analysis of São Paulo's public space as an arena in which the terms and conditions of citizenship are perpetually contended and renegotiated describes this constellation as a historical turning point. Certain privileges which, for decades on end, had been enjoyed by but a small minority of the city's population would turn into objects of public contestation – on the level of institutionalized politics but also, and even more significantly, in the sphere of everyday practices.[68]

Meanwhile, throughout the past two decades, the government of São Paulo has been making sustained efforts to augment the efficiency of both the police forces and the state's penal system, notably by introducing a whole series of ICT-driven tools and devices.[69] As the first federal unit to implement electronic monitoring of prisoners, computerized data banks of criminal offenses, and digital heatmaps to streamline the deployment of police patrols, the state quickly gained the reputation of an early adopter and turned into an emblematic case of an emphatically technological "modernization" in all spheres of public security. Simultaneously, São Paulo's urban space has been swamped by a multitude of CCTV cameras, sensors, and tracking devices, mostly deployed by the private sector – either by individuals seeking to protect themselves and their property from robberies and assaults or by private security companies offering an increasingly sophisticated range of products and services. As a palpable result, São Paulo has turned into Brazil's most densely

---

[66] Marcelo Neri, A nova classe média: O lado brilhante da base da pirâmide (São Paulo: Saraiva, 2011).
[67] Jessé Souza et al., Os batalhadores brasileiros: nova classe média ou nova classe trabalhadora? (Belo Horizonte: Editora UFMG, 2012).
[68] Holston, Insurgent Citizenship.
[69] Rogério Cabral Camargo, "Governança tecnológica: A evolução do gerenciamento de serviços de tecnologia da informação e comunicação no CPD da PMESP," www.policiamilitar.sp.gov.br/unidades/caes/artigos/Artigos%20pdf/Rog%C3%A9rio%20Cabral%20Camargo.pdf; Governo do Estado de São Paulo, "Modernização da Polícia paulista se consolida com treinamento, equipamentos e tecnologia de ponta" (2001), formerly available via www.saopaulo.sp.gov.br/ultimas-noticias/modernizacao-da-policia-paulista-se-consolida-com-treinamento-equipamentos-e-tecnologia-de-ponta/.

surveilled city, with a total of over 1.5 million CCTV devices impregnating its urban fabric.[70]

Since 2014, both the state and the municipality of São Paulo have been making considerable efforts to implement "intelligent" surveillance schemes which would connect both public and private cameras to a range of command-and-control centers, thus generating synergy effects allegedly helping the police forces to prevent, repress, and investigate street crime. The state's program – a modified version of Microsoft's Domain Awareness System (a.k.a. Microsoft Aware), first deployed by the New York Police Department – became known under the name of *Detecta*, while the municipality's solution – an online platform developed by a cluster of local tech companies – was dubbed *City Câmeras*.[71] *Detecta* was introduced with the promise that it would include analytic tools enabling an automatic identification of "suspicious" behaviors, thus facilitating a quasi-preemptive mode of police intervention;[72] however, these early claims of a virtually panoptic and largely automated law enforcement were soon debunked by a public inquiry pointing out the system's multiple shortcomings (Tribunal de Contas do Estado de São Paulo 2016).[73] Somewhat less ambitious in terms of "smart" analytic capabilities, the *City Câmeras* project was announced with the goal to swiftly integrate 10,000 cameras and store their footage for seven days, providing the police forces with an encompassing visual archive to be used for investigative purposes. Meanwhile, three years after the program's initial presentation the total number of cameras tapped kept hovering around 3,000, indicating a certain reluctancy to adhere on behalf of the scheme's main target group – that is, essentially, *condomínios fechados* and their respective *síndicos*.[74]

Their somewhat questionable success notwithstanding, it is apparent that both schemes, adopted and conceived by the public authorities, have stimulated a whole range of minor projects unfolding at the neighborhood level, mostly in accordance with Brazil's eminently privatist tradition of governing public security. Embracing a configuration in which neighborhood associations join forces with both private security companies and the responsible police precinct's liaison officers, the underlying ideal would consist in a public–private "co-production" of secure urban spaces, notably facilitated by a participatory network of digital surveillance and control devices. Suggesting the notion of "security perimeters," Peron and Alvarez identify

[70] Janaína Lepri, "São Paulo é a cidade com o maior número de câmeras do Brasil," G1, October 22, 2013, http://g1.globo.com/jornal-da-globo/noticia/2013/10/sao-paulo-e-cidade-com-o-maior-numero-de-cameras-do-brasil.html.
[71] See www.citycameras.prefeitura.sp.gov.br.
[72] See www.youtube.com/watch?v=KcUH7_-usTs.
[73] Tribunal de Contas do Estado de São Paulo, "Relatório de Fiscalização de Natureza Operacional: Solução de Consciência Situacional - DAS Detecta," Official Report (São Paulo: Tribunal de Contas do Estado de São Paulo, 2016).
[74] Thiago Amâncio, "Plano de Doria para interligar 10 mil câmeras de segurança em SP empaca," *Folha de São Paulo*, November 19, 2019, www1.folha.uol.com.br/cotidiano/2019/11/plano-de-doria-para-interligar-10-mil-cameras-de-seguranca-em-sp-empaca.shtml.

various instantiations of such "assembled" surveillance apparatuses, notably in and around certain upper-middle-class residential neighborhoods, university campuses, shopping malls, hospitals, or on extraordinary occasions such as sporting events or São Paulo's annual street carnival.[75]

While the perimeters' sociotechnical setup varies with their specific function – for instance, whether their purpose is temporary or permanent, more preventative or investigative, focused on individualizing surveillance or "dividualizing" control[76] – it is conspicuous that the settings in which they emerge are usually rather affluent and, by implication, racially segregated – that is, they have traditionally been dominated by whites. Keeping in mind Holston's[77] argument concerning the heavily contested character of São Paulo's public space and, even more importantly, the finding that the emergence of a "new middle class" has disproportionately benefited dark-skinned citizens,[78] indeed it is eminently reasonable to analyze the city's emerging "security perimeters" in terms of their racializing implications – even if, for the historical reasons provided above, more often than not race and class do overlap in ways which are tricky to disentangle.

In this sense, an event which may well be considered paradigmatic – and, therefore, serve as an epistemic prism through which the racializing effects of São Paulo's "security perimeters" become visible – consists in the so-called *rolezinhos* ("little strolls") which occurred in late 2013 and early 2014. Organizing themselves via social media, large groups of predominantly dark-skinned adolescents from São Paulo's poor peripheral neighborhoods would meet in the city's shopping malls, take snapshots with some local YouTube starlets, and flirt with their coevals. Starting off at Shopping Metrô Itaquera, a major mall in São Paulo's working-class eastern district, the *rolezinhos* quickly spread to other neighborhoods, causing a moral panic stirred by sensationalist media reports depicting the flash mobs as hotbeds of vice and criminal activities. Shopping malls such as the elite *JK Iguatemi* were quick to issue special decrees prohibiting crowds of young people on their premises, and São Paulo's *Polícia Militar* readily supported the malls' private security services, going as far as deploying tear gas and rubber bullets to disperse the gatherings on at least one occasion[79] – a circumstance which, ironically enough, reverberates with the tacit complicity of private elites and public authorities Koerner identifies when describing colonial Brazil's regime of punishing fugitive and/or unruly slaves: "concerning punitive state practices, in the slavocratic cities there was a collaboration between

---

[75] Alcides Eduardo dos Reis Peron and Marcos César Alvarez, "Governing the City: The Detecta Surveillance System in São Paulo and the Role of Private Vigilantism in the Public Security," *Sciences et Actions Sociales* 12 (2019).
[76] Gilles Deleuze, "Postscript on the Societies of Control," *October* 59 (1992): 3–7.
[77] Holston, *Insurgent Citizenship*.
[78] Neri, *A nova classe média*.
[79] Bruno Ribeiro and Marina Azevedo, "PM usa bala de borracha e gás lacrimogêneo em 'rolezinho'," *O Estado de São Paulo*, January 11, 2014, https://sao-paulo.estadao.com.br/noticias/geral,pm-usa-bala-de-borracha-e-gas-lacrimogeneo-em-rolezinho,1117420.

public authorities and the slaves' *senhores* in order to punish, deter, control the slaves' circulation and their activities in the streets."[80]

Although the phenomenon subsided after a few weeks, the *rolezinhos* remain a highly significant event due to their exemplary condensation of the *condomínio* logic and the specters of (post)coloniality which keep haunting it. Although the adolescents did not engage in any criminal activity whatsoever, their race and class background would turn them into targets not only for the malls' security contractors, but indeed for São Paulo's state police who thus helped to enforce an eminently privatist version of public order. Symptomatic of a "white" aesthetic *doxa*, whereas the physical presence of dark-skinned (and, therefore, visibly lower-class) bodies in and by itself would most likely not have caused any comparable degree of discomfort, the proper scandal consisted in the fact that the adolescents publicly affirmed their cultural identity – that is, by collectively chanting the "vulgar" lyrics of their favorite *funk* MCs – while expressing their desire to participate in the sphere of materialistic self-fulfillment and conspicuous consumption. Irrespective of their manifest motivations, the *rolezinhos* thus constituted a thoroughly political incident inasmuch as their transgressive momentum starkly revealed both the internal demarcation lines dividing Brazilian society into a mosaic of "differentiated citizenships"[81] and the executive's violent complicity with the country's social elite when it comes to maintaining the heavily discriminatory status quo.[82]

While the case of the *rolezinhos* arguably represents the most emblematic incident of a public–private, surveillant-penal apparatus being triggered by Black bodies "out of place," it is by far not its only manifestation; to the contrary, with the growing amount of "security perimeters" scattering the city's affluent neighborhoods, its exclusionary implications are likely to prevail in a whole variety of urban settings. As insinuated above, this tendency does *not* entail an overall recrudescence of segregationist tendencies; to the contrary, at least in part it has to be understood as a *post hoc* reaction to a state of intensified urban mobilities which threatens to profane the formerly inviolable sanctuaries of São Paulo's white upper-middle class. Against this backdrop, it is a telling coincidence that the prestigious University of São Paulo (USP) implemented its own CCTV surveillance network, complete with a command-and-control center and linked up to the state's *Detecta* system, in the very

---

[80] Koerner, "O impossível 'panóptico tropical-escravista'," our translation. For footage of a *rolezinho* and its repression by the *Polícia Militar*, see www.youtube.com/watch?v=6yoytvTKrBg&t=37s.

[81] Holston, *Insurgent Citizenship*.

[82] Teresa P. R. Caldeira, "Qual a novidade dos rolezinhos? Espaço público, desigualdade e mudança em São Paulo," *Novos Estudos* 98 (2014): 13–20; Rosana Pinheiro-Machado and Lucia Mury Scalco, "Rolezinhos: Marcas, consumo e segregação no Brasil," *Revista Estudos Culturais* 1, no. 1 (2014); Darlene Fróes da Silva and José Carlos Gomes da Silva, "'Rolezinhos': sociabilidades juvenis, discriminações e segregação urbana," *Revista Pensata* 3, no. 2 (2014): 17–35; João H. Costa Vargas, "Black Disidentification: The 2013 Protests, Rolezinhos, and Racial Antagonism in Post-Lula Brazil," *Critical Sociology* 42, no. 4–5 (2014): 551–565.

same year in which it finally had to give up its decades-long resistance against the adoption of affirmative action policies, thus significantly increasing the number of nonwhite students frequenting its main campus.[83] Indeed, during an ethnographic excursion to the system's control room, we were able to verify that dark-skinned persons were clearly among the main targets of observation, thus revealing the surveillance workers' culturally entrenched *olhar maldoso* (roughly: "cunning gaze") attributing malicious intents to certain phenotypical and/or habitual markers – that is, their adherence to an eminently racialized typology of suspicion.[84]

A similar configuration can be observed in the elite neighborhood of Higienópolis where, symptomatically enough, local residents had mobilized in order to prevent the construction of a subway station which, supposedly, would have facilitated the influx of *gente diferenciada* (literally: "special" or "distinct people," i.e., those which would not fit into the neighborhood's social and racial profile).[85] Distressed by the presence of homeless persons camping on the region's pavements – situated in São Paulo's central region, Higienópolis is within walking distance from the city's most infamous skid row – residents expressed their anger on social media, demanding a "cleanup" of the neighborhood in a Facebook group aptly called *Me devolva Higienópolis!* ("Give me Higienópolis back!").[86] Likening homeless people to trash and filth which would have to be removed from the region's streets by all means necessary, many comments were in fact epitomizing Mary Douglas' classic definition of dirt as "matter out of place"[87] – a detail which turns all the more significant given the neighborhood's distinctive name and the racialized implications of Brazil's "hygienist" urbanism.[88]

---

[83] Ricardo Alexino Ferreira, "O sistema de cotas étnico-raciais adotado pela USP," *Jornal da USP*, January 5, 2018, https://jornal.usp.br/artigos/o-sistema-de-cotas-etno-raciais-adotado-pela-usp; Erika Yamamoto, "USP inaugura Centro de Monitoramento Eletrônico," *Jornal da USP*, January 10, 2018, https://jornal.usp.br/?p=141419.

[84] Bruno Cardoso, *Todos os olhos: Videovigilâncias, voyeurismos e (re)produção imagética* (Rio de Janeiro: Editora UFRJ, 2014), 214ff.

[85] James Cimino, "Moradores de Higienópolis, em SP, se mobilizam contra estação de metrô," *Folha de São Paulo*, August 13, 2010, www1.folha.uol.com.br/cotidiano/2010/08/782354-moradores-de-higienopolis-em-sp-se-mobilizam-contra-estacao-de-metro.shtml.

[86] Revista Fórum, "Moradores do Higienópolis querem 'limpeza' de população de rua," *Revista Fórum*, January 12, 2019, https://revistaforum.com.br/direitos/moradores-do-higienopolis-querem-limpeza-de-populacao-de-rua.

[87] Mary Douglas, *Purity and Danger: An Analysis of the Concepts of Pollution and Taboo* (London and New York: Routledge, 2001).

[88] Jeff Garmany and Matthew A. Richmond, "Hygienisation, Gentrification, and Urban Displacement in Brazil," *Antipode* 52, no. 1 (2019): 124–144. As a matter of fact, out of São Paulo's estimated total of 25,000 homeless citizens almost 70% are *pardos* or *pretos* – i.e., a share almost twice as high as amongst the city's general population. See Prefeitura Municipal de São Paulo, "Pesquisa censitária da população em situação de rua, caracterização socioeconômica da população em situação de rua e relatório temático de identificação das necessidades desta população na cidade de São Paulo," Official Report (São Paulo: Prefeitura Municipal de São Paulo, 2019).

In 2013, a local businessman-cum-politician came up with a "panic button" smartphone app geared to connect residents, *síndicos*, and beat cops patrolling the area so as to facilitate information flow and minimize response times in case of emergencies.[89] Infamously comprising the categories *andarilho* ("drifter") and *pedinte* ("beggar") – conducts which are both perfectly legal – the app caused a certain degree of controversy and was eventually abandoned; nonetheless, its functional principle perfectly encapsulates a securitarian desire which envisions the neighborhood as some kind of extended private property and, consequently, solicits the police to enforce an aesthetics of social homogeneity which inevitably excludes those unable or unwilling to conform to a highly moralized code of "normal" conduct.

Meanwhile, CCTV footage of robberies and assaults, as well as pictures of "suspicious" persons or mugshots of caught offenders, keep circulating on social media, thus feeding back into – and retroactively justifying – the isolationist attitudes and fearful affects which fuel the demand for ever more secure urban enclaves, whether built of steel and concrete or made of sensors and code in the first place. As Comaroff and Comaroff have aptly pointed out, this seemingly anachronous politics of spectacle demands more fine-grained attention, as it entails a very specific kind of productivity which a unilateral focus upon the "capillary" effects of surveillance technologies is likely to miss – namely, a choreography of transgression and revenge in which the terms and conditions of sovereign power are constantly performed and enacted.[90]

While a more detailed analysis of the corresponding visual economies and their twisted relation to a popular imaginary of sovereignty and statehood would go beyond this chapter's scope, it can be affirmed that they echo an eminently colonial politics of punitive spectacle, performing the sovereign's sanctity by publicly inscribing itself into the slave's humiliated body – a prerogative which, notably, would be split up and divided between the institutions of the state (the Portuguese colonial administration and, later, the Brazilian Empire) on the one hand and the quasi-autocratic rule of the private *senhores* on the other.[91] It is in this sense that the widespread "recycling" of crime-related CCTV footage and police mugshots on both social media and television entails a thoroughly productive dimension as it sustains a peculiar iconography of criminal threat and sovereign retaliation – a phenomenon which, more often than not, participates in the spectacular

---

[89] André Caramante, "Moradores de Higienópolis começam a testar 'botão de pânico'," *Folha de São Paulo*, October 3, 2013, https://m.folha.uol.com.br/cotidiano/2013/10/1351012-higienopolis-comeca-a-testar-botao-de-panico.shtml.

[90] Jean Comaroff and John L. Comaroff, "Criminal Obsessions, after Foucault: Postcoloniality, Policing, and the Metaphysics of Disorder," *Critical Inquiry* 30, no. 4 (2004): 800–824.

[91] Marcelo Ferraro, "As práticas de controle e punição na sociedade escrava cafeicultora do Brasil oitocentista: uma análise à luz do pensamento de Michel Foucault," *Epígrafe* 0 (2013): 7–42; Koerner, "Punição, disciplina e pensamento penal," 224f.; Vilson Pereira dos Santos, "Técnicas da tortura: punições e castigos de escravos no Brasil escravista," *Enciclopédia Biosfera* 9, no. 16 (2013): 2393–2408.

(re)production of racialized bodies and their symbolic classification according to a historically entrenched typology of social positions and moral conducts.[92]

As a concluding observation, it can thus be affirmed that the various types of racialized space – and the multiple apparatuses of surveillance and control which constitute and stabilize them – examined in the present chapter inevitably bear the mark of colonialism's primordial violence, notably the genocide of the Indigenous populations and almost four centuries of Black slavery. While, to be sure, São Paulo's (and Brazil's) political economy has undergone a series of profound transformations since the early days of plantation capitalism, the topology of *casa-grande* and *senzala* still constitutes a remarkably fertile model when it comes to examining the spatialization of race as it empirically occurs in some of the city's most paradigmatic settings – not only in how they sort and distribute human bodies according to their racial identity, but also in how they epitomize a colonial model of distributed sovereignty, now reappearing under the slick façade of the ICT-driven public–private partnership.

Meanwhile, whereas the colonial *fazenda* did constitute an overtly and admittedly segregationist configuration in which skin color and the *senhor*'s caprice would effectively determine the spaces a specific subject was (not) entitled to access, what can be observed at present is the increasing dissemination of digitally enhanced surveillance as "a perfect technology of non-racist racism"[93] – that is, the proliferation of certain infrastructures and devices whose common effect consists in normalizing and, by consequence, invisibilizing a historically entrenched pattern of racialized domination. It is not least in this sense that the widespread faith in an emphatically "technical" surveillance and its aura of disinterested objectivity dovetail perfectly well with the "hyperconsciousness of race and its negation" as mentioned in the chapter's introduction. Although rhizomatic and far from panoptic, contemporary São Paulo's "surveillant assemblage"[94] and the regimes of (in)visibility[95] it sustains seem to reaffirm and stabilize a specific distribution of racialized

---

[92] Alves, *The Anti-Black City*; Erika Robb Larkins, *The Spectacular Favela: Violence in Modern Brazil* (Oakland, CA: University of California Press, 2015); Vargas, "Hyperconsciousness of Race."

[93] John Fiske, "Surveilling the City: Whiteness, the Black Man and Democratic Totalitarianism," *Theory, Culture & Society* 15, no. 2 (1998): 67–88, 71.

[94] Kevin D. Haggerty and Richard V. Ericson, "The Surveillant Assemblage," *British Journal of Sociology* 51, no. 4 (2000): 605–622.

[95] Hempel et al. define regimes of visibility as "social and technical arrangements whose purpose is to create or stabilize order, avert danger, and rectify deviations and which in turn also establish a configuration of observing and being observed, of revealing and concealing. ... They define the problems to which they are supposed to be a solution; they demarcate public and private spheres and thus generate differentiated zones of transparency and opacity." See Leon Hempel, Susanne Krasmann, and Ulrich Bröckling, "Sichtbarkeitsregime: Eine Einleitung," in Leon Hempel, Susanne Krasmann, and Ulrich Bröckling (eds.), *Sichtbarkeitsregime: Überwachung, Sicherheit und Privatheit im 21. Jahrhundert* (Wiesbaden: VS Verlag für Sozialwissenschaften, 2010), 7–24, 8f., our translation.

bodies in urban space rather than challenging it[96] – an economy of visuality and power which, noticeably, contaminates even attempts at popular counterveillance, such as the visual documentation of police violence in lower-class neighborhoods and *favelas*.[97]

In this sense, the endeavor of an anti-racist "Black urbanism"[98] – essentially understood as a political device suitable to "transform the objectifying and alienating spatial arrangements that racialized encounters produce in urban life"[99] so as to retrieve the "existence of undocumented worlds of limited visibility ... or posit radically different ways of being in the city"[100] – would not merely consist in challenging São Paulo's racialized topologies and the ways in which they arrange bodies across space, but also in disrupting the aesthetic regimes which constantly camouflage and normalize them; it would, indeed, have to entail altogether different modes of seeing and perceiving the urban environment which would – for instance – be capable of dismantling or at least unsettling a historically deep-rooted mode of deducing an individual's moral character from its phenotypical appearance. Meanwhile, whereas it is virtually impossible to accurately assess the cumulative impact of São Paulo's increasingly many-eyed securityscape, the cases discussed throughout the present chapter all point towards a rather discomforting conclusion – namely, that the sweeping implementation of digital surveillance technologies has promoted rather than impeded an emphatically asynchronous mode of social organization in which the remnants of colonialism and slavery have repeatedly turned out perfectly compatible with consecutive stages of institutional "modernization."

---

[96] This pessimistic outlook is corroborated by the finding that, between March and October of 2019, amongst the 151 persons who found themselves imprisoned after being identified by facial recognition CCTV cameras in the Brazilian states of Bahia, Rio de Janeiro, Santa Catarina, and Paraíba, available data suggest that Black citizens were grossly overrepresented. See Pablo Nunes, "Novas ferramentas, velhas práticas: reconhecimento facial e policiamento no Brasil," in Rede de Observatórios da Segurança (ed.), *Retratos da Violência: Cinco meses de monitoramento, análises e descobertas. Junho a outubro – 2019* (Rio de Janeiro: Centro de Estudos de Segurança e Cidadania, 2019), 67–70.
[97] Joseph Brandim Howson, "The Visuality of Professionalised Sousveillance," *Surveillance & Society* 18, no. 2 (2020): 276–279.
[98] AbdouMaliq Simone, *City Life from Jakarta to Dakar: Movements at the Crossroads* (New York: Routledge, 2010), 263ff.
[99] Ibid., 290.
[100] Ibid., 285.

9

China's Surveillance and Repression in Xinjiang

Myunghee Lee and Emir Yazici[*]

INTRODUCTION

The Xinjiang Uyghur Autonomous Region has received global attention since 2017 due to China's massive crackdown on Uyghurs and other ethnic minorities in the region. Since 2017–2018, the Chinese Communist Party (CCP)'s crackdown on Uyghur and other Muslim minorities in Xinjiang has become unprecedented in its scope and intensity. Reports on the CCP's highly repressive strategies in that region led to a formal expression of concern by the United Nations Committee on the Elimination of Racial Discrimination in August 2018[1] and several legislative hearings in the United States.[2] In 2020, the United States imposed sanctions on three officials, including Chen Quanguo, who are in charge of the Xinjiang's recent development and a major economic and paramilitary organization, the Xinjiang Production and Construction Corps (known as *bingtuan*), accusing it of "facilitating widespread abuses against Uighur Muslims."[3] On January 19, 2021, Mike Pompeo, US Secretary of State, officially asserted that a "genocide is

---

[*] The authors of this chapter do not necessarily endorse any of the cited authors' political stances, religious orientations, or personal beliefs.
[1] "Committee on the Elimination of Racial Discrimination Reviews the Report of China," *United Nations Human Rights – Office of the High Commissioner*, August 13, 2018, www.ohchr.org/en/NewsEvents/Pages/DisplayNews.aspx?NewsID=23452&LangID=E.
[2] "Surveillance, Suppression, and Mass Detention: Xinjiang's Human Rights Crisis," *Congressional-Executive Commission on China*, July 26, 2018, www.cecc.gov/events/hearings/surveillance-suppression-and-mass-detention-xinjiang's-human-rights-crisis; Sheena Greitens, Myunghee Lee, and Emir Yazici, "Counterterrorism and Preventive Repression: China's Changing Strategy in Xinjiang," *International Security* 44, no. 3 (2020): 9–47.
[3] "US Imposes Sanctions on Chinese 'State-within-a-state' Linked to Xinjiang Abuses," *The Guardian*, July 31, 2020, www.theguardian.com/world/2020/jul/31/us-sanctions-china-xinjiang-uighurs.

ongoing" and "we are witnessing the systematic attempt to destroy Uyghurs by the Chinese party-state."[4]

Reports suggest that over a million Uyghur and other Muslim minorities in Xinjiang have been forcefully detained in recently constructed camps.[5] In the camps, they are subjected to political indoctrination. Apart from these detention camps, the Muslim population in the region are subject to surveillance and control. The CCP has utilized both manpower and high technology tools to control and reengineer Uyghur communities. The number of police officers has increased dramatically since 2016, while Han civil servants have visited rural Uyghur communities to monitor villagers' daily lives. Moreover, the CCP has introduced advanced technological tools and biometric data for a more comprehensive and effective surveillance network in Xinjiang. Advanced surveillance technologies include smart phone applications to track citizens' communication, surveillance of vehicles, CCTV cameras, facial-recognition technology, and emotion recognition technology. The CCP is implementing unprecedented societal control policies in Xinjiang.

This chapter will proceed as follows. First, we will review China's history of ethnic minority policies in the Xinjiang region. Second, we will briefly discuss the policy shift from a selective and reactive repression to collective and preventive one since 2017–2018 and provide explanations for why the CCP has changed its Uyghur policy.

---

[4] Jennifer Hansler, Zamira Rahim, and Ben Westcott, "US Accuses China of 'Genocide' of Uyghurs and Minority Groups in Xinjiang," *CNN*, January 20, 2021, www.cnn.com/2021/01/19/us/us-xinjiang-china-genocide-intl/index.html. The attribution of genocide to CCP abuses in Xinjiang is widespread, but contested. For critical takes, see Jeffrey D. Sachs and William Schabas, "The Xinjiang Genocide Allegations Are Unjustified," Project Syndicate, April 20, 2021, www.project-syndicate.org/commentary/biden-should-withdraw-unjustified-xinjiang-genocide-allegation-by-jeffrey-d-sachs-and-william-schabas-2021-04; John Power, "Australian Parliament Refuses to label China's Xinjiang Actions as Genocide," *South China Morning Post*, March 15, 2021, www.scmp.com/week-asia/politics/article/3125501/australian-parliament-refuses-label-chinas-xinjiang-actions; The Economist, "'Genocide' Is the Wrong Word for the Horrors of Xinjiang," February 13, 2021, www.economist.com/leaders/2021/02/13/genocide-is-the-wrong-word-for-the-horrors-of-xinjiang. In its investigation, Human Rights Watch deemed CCP abuses "crimes against humanity" but "has not documented the existence of the necessary genocidal intent at this time." See Human Rights Watch, "'Break Their Lineage, Break Their Roots': China's Crimes against Humanity Targeting Uyghurs and Other Turkic Muslims," April 19, 2021, www.hrw.org/news/2021/04/19/china-crimes-against-humanity-xinjiang. Amnesty International balked at the term, opting to label CCP abuses "crimes against humanity" while citing sources that both deny and affirm the genocide label. See Amnesty International, "'Like We Were Enemies in War': China's Mass Internment, Torture and Persecution of Muslims in Xinjiang" (2021), 142, www.xinjiang.amnesty.org/wp-content/uploads/2021/06/ASA_17_4137-2021_Full_report_ENG.pdf.

[5] Bethany Allen-Ebrahimian, "Exposed: China's Operating Manuals for Mass Internment and Arrest by Algorithm," *International Consortium of Investigative Journalists*, November 24, 2019; Patrick deHahn, "More Than 1 Million Muslims Are Detained in China: But How Did We Get that Number?" *Quartz*, July 4, 2019, https://qz.com/1599393/how-researchers-estimate-1-million-uyghurs-are-detained-in-xinjiang/; Jessica Batke, "Where Did the One Million Figure for Detentions in Xinjiang's Camps Come From?" *China File*, January 8, 2019, www.chinafile.com/reporting-opinion/features/where-did-one-million-figure-detentions-xinjiangs-camps-come.

Third, we will discuss the policy change in detail. In particular, we will first examine the mass detention camps and more conventional societal control and surveillance strategies, and then we will focus on the installation of a high-tech surveillance system in Xinjiang. We conclude this chapter by emphasizing that the intensification of the surveillance network in Xinjiang is an extension of the overall shift in CCP's strategy in the region and presenting our policy recommendations for the international community.

THE PRC'S ETHNIC MINORITY POLICY IN XINJIANG: FROM THE 1950S TO THE 2000S

The Xinjiang Uyghur Autonomous Region is located at the northwest side of the People's Republic of China (PRC) and borders Mongolia, Russia, Kazakhstan, Kyrgyzstan, Tajikistan, and Afghanistan. The region spans over 1,664,900 square kilometers. It was not until the eighteenth century that the region was integrated into a political unit.[6] Before then, it was ruled by local oasis rulers and warring empires.[7] In the 1750s, the Qing Dynasty – the last imperial dynasty of China – conquered Xinjiang and began ruling the region. After the collapse of the Qing, Guomindang (or Kuomintang) reigned over the region for a while. Then, from 1949, The Chinese Communist Party (CCP) incorporated Xinjiang into the PRC. The majority population of the region is Uyghur, but there are other ethnic groups, such as Kazakhs, Kyrgyz, Hui, and Mongols. Due to the policy that encouraged Han (the dominant ethnic group of China) migration to the region, the Han population keeps growing. In this section, we will review a history of the CCP's Xinjiang ethnic policies and discuss how they have impacted Uyghurs' culture, religion, language, and lives. We will also discuss a brief history of Uyghur dissent in the early 2000s.

PRC's Early Control and the Implementation of Socialism in Xinjiang

When the People's Liberation Army (PLA) entered Xinjiang in September and October of 1949, the CCP's experiences with non-Han peoples in Xinjiang were very limited.[8] In the following years, from 1949 to 1958, the party began implementing state-led socialist land reforms and purging many Turkic leaders of the pre-PRC era. The CCP also had developed an ethnic minority system based on two key concepts:

---

[6] James A. Millward, *Eurasian Crossroads: A History of Xinjiang*. (Columbia University Press, 2007); Eric T. Schluessel, "History, Identity, and Mother-Tongue Education in Xinjiang," *Central Asian Survey* 28, no. 4 (2009): 383–402; Sean R. Roberts, "The Roots of Cultural Genocide in Xinjiang: China's Imperial Past Hangs Over the Uyghurs," *Foreign Affairs*, February 10, 2021, www.foreignaffairs.com/articles/china/2021-02-10/roots-cultural-genocide-xinjiang.

[7] Millward, *Eurasian Crossroads*, 4.

[8] Ibid., 237.

minzu (nationality) and *zizhi* (autonomy) and had implemented Han migration and settlement policies in the region.

Establishment of Ethnic Policies
At first, the PRC borrowed the Soviet Union's concept of "nationality" (*minzu*) to refer to ethnic groups in China and identified fifty-five "national minorities" in China.[9] However, its ethnic minority policies are quite different from the Soviet model. Chinese leaders introduced "a system of theoretical self-rule or autonomy (*zizhi*)" to non-Han regions. Xinjiang is one of those five autonomous regions, with its official name of the Xinjiang Uyghur Autonomous Region (XUAR).[10] According to Millward, the theory behind the *zizhi* system reflects the PRC's effort to disconnect its ethnic minority policy from Guomindang's assimilationism while discouraging separatism in the frontier regions.[11] Clarke also claims that the CCP's policies in the region in the early period (1949–1976) were aimed at "internally consolidating and accelerating the region's integration with China and isolating it from Soviet influence."[12] Although the system intended to grant autonomous status to non-Han peoples – meaning that various recognized "nationalities" serve in offices as representatives – the actual practice of granting autonomy and the non-Han representation has not been well-implemented in Xinjiang. Non-Hans have held fewer government offices proportional to their population than have Han cadres in Xinjiang.[13]

Han Migration and Settlement
From the early 1950s, the CCP deployed 103,000 demobilized soldiers to Xinjiang. These men engaged in agriculture, stock-raising, civil engineering, industry, and mining. From 1952 to 1954, the CCP organized the Production-Construction Corps (*Shengchan jianshe bingtuan*, often referred to as *bingtuan*) and soon it became the main organization that promoted Han migration to Xinjiang. In fact, according to Millward, "most of the Han migrants to Xinjiang in the 1950s–70s were resettled and put to work by the *bingtuan*."[14] Rather than being supervised by local governments in Xinjiang, the quasi-military organization was under more direct supervision of the party and Beijing. Seymour's view is that, in addition to playing a significant role in the region's economy, the organization helped the CCP's efforts to Sinicize Uyghurs.[15]

---

[9] Ibid., 244.
[10] The other four autonomous regions are Guangxi, Inner Mongolia, Ningxia, and Tibet (Xizang).
[11] Millward, *Eurasian Crossroads*, 243.
[12] Michael E. Clarke, *Xinjiang and China's Rise in Central Asia: A History* (New York: Routledge, 2011), 12.
[13] Millward, *Eurasian Crossroads*, 347.
[14] Ibid., 253.
[15] James D. Seymour, "Xinjiang's Production and Construction Corps, and the Sinification of Eastern Turkestan," *Inner Asia* 2, no. 2 (2000): 171–193.

Xinjiang during the Cultural Revolution (1966–1976)

During the Cultural Revolution, Xinjiang experienced political and social turbulence. Most factional conflicts and political struggles in the region among the Han population happened around the *bingtuan*.[16] However, the campaign also brought about more aggressive chauvinistic assaults on non-Han cadres and non-Han culture.[17] During the campaign, under the guise of "class struggle," Xinjiang's non-Han cadres were accused as "revisionists" and purged. Millward points out that the number of non-Han government officials dropped, from 111,500 in 1962 to 80,000 in 1975.[18] As a result, the foundational idea of the "autonomous region" (*zizhiqu*) system was not reflected in the region's existing politics, and the non-Han representation was further reduced during the Cultural Revolution. Furthermore, Uyghur cultural and religious practices were tightly restricted. Qur'ans were burned and mosques were closed, while non-Han intellectuals and religious leaders were attacked and humiliated. Non-Han customs were also banned. In short, the campaign aimed to forcefully assimilate non-Han persons into the nationally dominant Han culture.

Xinjiang during the Reform Era (1978–1980s)

During the reform era under Deng Xiaoping, Beijing started to criticize the minority policies of the Cultural Revolution, which eroded the *zizhi* system in autonomous regions and attacked ethnic minorities' cultural and religious practices.[19] Aggressive assimilation policies during the Cultural Revolution were criticized within the CCP and many Uyghur cadres purged during the Cultural Revolution were reinstated.[20] Deng Xiaoping endeavored to restore the local autonomy system. The National People's Congress passed a law that reinforced the local autonomy provisions, which had already been enshrined in the constitution, in 1984.[21] Non-Han cadre appointments and training were encouraged. Non-Han cultural practices and non-Han language publishing were repromoted. Although the "ultimate control" by Han officials remained, non-Han representation in government organs was improved and non-Han cultural practices that had been strictly restricted were restored.[22]

---

[16] Ibid.; Millward, *Eurasian Crossroads*.
[17] Donald H. McMillen, "China, Xinjiang and Central Asia: 'Glocality' in the Year 2008," in Colin Mackerras and Michael Clarke (eds.), *China, Xinjiang and Central Asia* (New York: Routledge, 2009), 1–20.
[18] Millward, Eurasian Crossroads, 272.
[19] Clarke, Xinjiang and China's Rise in Central Asia, 73.
[20] Ibid., 74.
[21] Millward, Eurasian Crossroads, 278.
[22] Ibid., 279.

Xinjiang from the 1990s to the 2000s

Economic Development and the Han Settlement in Xinjiang

Deng Xiaoping's economic development plan was a two-stage one: "first on the coast and then in the interior."[23] China's initial focus on the coastal regions was evident with a series of five-year development plans. As a result, the eastern coastal area has achieved tremendous economic development. China, then, needed to address the regional inequalities. In the 1990s, the PRC leaders promoted many policies and programs to develop western regions. This set of programs are known as the Great Development of the West. In particular, the Eighth Five-Year Plan (1991–1995) stated that the coastal areas and cities need to select an interior underdeveloped area as an "economic partner."[24] In 1992, Deng promised that the economic benefits of his Reform and Opening-Up policy (*Gaige Kaifang*) would be extended to the non-Han areas.[25] Accordingly, Xinjiang has experienced economic and social changes under the state-driven economic development.

First and foremost, the party's western drive facilitated Han migration to Xinjiang.[26] In the past, the Han resettlements were mostly coordinated by the center with the *bingtuan*. In the 1990s, although there were official encouragements of Han migration, no state-sponsored, large-scale planned programs took place.[27] Rather, the western development campaign incentivized Hans to go to Xinjiang for economic reasons. The Han population in Xinjiang has steadily increased. In 1947, Uyghurs comprised an estimated 75% of the population in Xinjiang and the Han just 5%. By 2000, Uyghurs declined to 45% of the population and the Han increased to 43%.[28]

With the increased Han population, tensions between minority ethnic groups and Han have intensified.[29] Yee revealed that only 43% of Uyghurs strongly believe Xinjiang has been part of China since ancient times while 72% of Han do. Moreover, 40% of Uyghurs believe that their living standards have improved at a much slower rate than those of Hans, a sentiment which indicates rising tensions between the two ethnicities.[30]

---

[23] Hongyi Harry Lai, "China's Western Development Program: Its Rationale, Implementation, and Prospects," *Modern China* 28, no. 4 (2002): 433.
[24] Ibid., 435. Clarke, Xinjiang and China's Rise in Central Asia, 114.
[25] Millward, Eurasian Crossroads, 290.
[26] Agnieszka Joniak-Lüthi, "Han Migration to Xinjiang Uyghur Autonomous Region: Between State Schemes and Migrants' Strategies," *Zeitschrift für Ethnologie* 138, no. 2 (2013): 155–174; Nicolas Becquelin, "Xinjiang in the Nineties," *China Journal* 44 (2000): 65–90; Isabelle Côté, "Political Mobilization of a Regional Minority: Han Chinese Settlers in Xinjiang," *Ethnic and Racial Studies* 34, no. 11 (2011): 1855–1873.
[27] Millward, Eurasian Crossroads, 309.
[28] Ibid., 306
[29] Côté, "Political Mobilization of a Regional Minority."
[30] Herbert S. Yee, "Ethnic Relations in Xinjiang: A Survey of Uygur–Han Relations in Urumqi," *Journal of Contemporary China* 12, no. 36 (2003): 431–452; Millward, Eurasian Crossroads, 351.

Domestic Unrest and Repression

In the 1990s and the 2000s, foreign journalists were given unprecedented access to the region, and there was an uptick in reports on Uyghur separatist activities. Also, from the 1990s, religious practices that had been liberalized during the 1980s were restricted again. Many privately run Islamic schools were closed, while cadres' and party members' participation in religious activities was strongly discouraged. This furthered grievances among Uyghurs, leading them to participate in protests.

From the 1990s, there had been protests and violent activities carried out by Uyghurs. In 1990, 200 demonstrators surrounded a Baren County compound where government and security offices were located and shouted Islamic slogans. The police responded by cracking down on the protest. Soon, the confrontation escalated and resulted in, according to a Chinese source, 16 rebel deaths in fighting, 124 arrests, 40 convictions, and 3 executions.[31] Another street demonstration took place in 1995 in Ili Prefecture near the Sino-Kazakh border. At first, about 50,000 Uyghurs and Kazaks held antigovernment rallies. In two days, the number of rally participants rose to 100,000, demanding the end of Chinese rule in Xinjiang.[32] The Ghulja uprising in 1997 is considered to be one of the largest mobilizations in the region. Violence escalated quickly and the state repression was harsh, making over 1,000 arrests.[33] Bombing attempts were also made by a small Uyghur group, targeting civilians in a bus station in Kucha in 1991 and in Urumchi in 1992.[34]

These dissident activities were harshly repressed. In 1996, the CCP announced the first 'Strike Hard' campaign against separatist activities. Under the campaign, it is claimed that from 1,700 to several thousand suspected terrorists, separatists, and criminals were arrested.[35] In 1997, three bombs exploded on Urumchi public buses, killing nine and injuring twenty-eight people, which led to the ruthless regionwide crackdown, during which hundreds of arrests were made. Also, according to human rights organizations, religious organizations and religious schools were severely targeted during the campaign.

9/11 and Assimilation Policies

In the early 2000s, the CCP raised concerns about the possible connection between "an East Turkistan organization" and al-Qaeda.[36] On November 29, 2001, after the

---

[31] Millward, Eurasian Crossroads, 327.
[32] Clarke, Xinjiang and China's Rise in Central Asia, 115.
[33] Brent Hierman, "The Pacification of Xinjiang: Uighur Protest and the Chinese State, 1988–2002," Problems of Post-Communism 54, no. 3 (2007): 48–62; Millward, Eurasian Crossroads, 331; Joanne Smith Finley, "'No Rights Without Duties': Minzu Pingdeng [Nationality Equality] in Xinjiang since the 1997 Ghulja Disturbances," Inner Asia 13, no. 1 (2011): 73–96.
[34] Millward, Eurasian Crossroads, 328.
[35] Ibid., 331; Hierman, "The Pacification of Xinjiang," 48–49; Joshua Tschantret, "Repression, Opportunity, and Innovation: The Evolution of Terrorism in Xinjiang, China," Terrorism and Political Violence 30, no. 4 (2018): 569–588.
[36] Millward, Eurasian Crossroads, 323 and 340.

September 11th attacks, the CCP released a document, claiming that there was a Uyghur terrorist network which had ties with international terrorist organizations and started to use the "Global War on Terror" rhetoric in Xinjiang.[37] While not as extreme as the chauvinistic assaults on Uyghur culture during the Cultural Revolution, the CCP's approach to Uyghur culture in this period was more assimilationist than the reform era. Religious activities were further restricted. The number of Hans in township-level cadres was increased, and a multilingual education system was introduced to increase levels of Chinese fluency.

Summary

In short, China borrowed the term, "nationality" (*minzu*) from the Soviet Union and designed an autonomy (*zizhi*) system. Theoretically, the *zizhi* system was intended to increase minority group representation in local governments. In practice, however, the number of Hans in government offices has increased in Xinjiang while the number of non-Hans has decreased.

Uyghurs in Xinjiang were victims of chauvinistic attacks on their culture during the Cultural Revolution. During the reform era in the 1980s, Uyghurs experienced a slightly liberalized political and social atmosphere, enjoying less restrictions on their religious and cultural practices. However, in the 1990s and 2000s, the situation got worse and many Uyghur religious and cultural activities were either banned or regulated. These policy changes were attributable to the broad political, social, and economic transformations of China and the CCP's concerns about pacifying domestic unrest in Xinjiang.

XINJIANG IN RECENT YEARS: THE CCP'S CHANGING STRATEGY IN THE REGION

Targeted and selective detention and reeducation campaigns have been used in Xinjiang since 2013–2014. However, the most dramatic change in the CCP's strategy in Xinjiang took place in 2017–2018 when the scope and intensity of the repression on Turkic Muslims started to increase. Indiscriminate collective detentions have replaced selective repression along with a shift from assimilative education policies to intensive ideological reeducation campaigns.[38] The most controversial component of this shift is the detention camps (called "reeducation camps" by the CCP) in which as many as a million Uyghurs and other Muslims have been detained for intense and involuntary education.[39] The content of "reeducation" aims to achieve

---

[37] Sean R. Roberts, "The Biopolitics of China's 'War on Terror' and the Exclusion of the Uyghurs," *Critical Asian Studies* 50, no. 2 (2018): 232–258.
[38] Greitens, Lee, and Yazici, "Counterterrorism and Preventive Repression."
[39] Adrian Zenz, "'Thoroughly Reforming Them towards a Healthy Heart Attitude': China's Political Re-education Campaign in Xinjiang," *Central Asian Survey* 38, no. 1 (2019): 102–128.

national unity and fight the "three evils" (terrorism, separatism, extremism) preventively by obliterating the ethnic and religious identities of the minority groups.[40] Furthermore, the CCP has tightened the scrutiny for Uyghurs abroad and increased diplomatic pressure on the countries, where the Uyghur diasporas is active (e.g. Turkey), to return Uyghurs that escaped the repression in China. In sum, there is an overall shift from selective to collective repression, including indiscriminate detention, intense ideological reeducation, and pressure on Uyghurs' transborder networks. Several alternative explanations of this overall change in the CCP's strategy in Xinjiang help us better understand the surveillance trends in the region that we will discuss in the following two sections. Let us examine the contributions of each in turn. One explanation of the shift in the CCP's strategy can be the "dissent-repression cycle."[41] Increased contention among Uyghurs since around 2009 might have caused the increase in the level and scope of repression.[42] In fact, the coercive capacity and police presence in the region has increased since 2009 and the CCP was confident about its capacity to prevent domestic violence in the region by 2015–2016.[43] However, the shift that we described above occurred in early 2017. Also, if domestic unrest was the only reason for increased repression, then we should have observed a similar shift in the CCP's repressive strategy in Tibet, which experienced domestic unrests in 2008–2009 too. Moreover, the dissent–repression cycle does not account for the pressure on the Uyghur diaspora and foreign governments.

An alternative explanation of the increased repression is the increase in ethnic Han nationalism and assimilative minority policy of the CCP, especially after the domestic unrest and mobilization in both Xinjiang and Tibet since 2008–2009.[44] Assimilative minority policies explain the intense ideological reeducation campaign aiming to destroy non-Han Chinese identities. However, the shift towards a more assimilative minority policy dates back to 2009, whereas the reeducation camps and indiscriminate collective detentions have significantly increased since 2017. Moreover, there must be another reason that the Turkic Muslims (Uyghurs along

[40] The transcript of an interview with XUAR Governor Shohrat Zakir, "Full Transcript: Interview with Xinjiang Government Chief on Counterterrorism, Vocational Education, and Training in Xinjiang," *Xinhua*, October 16, 2018, www.xinhuanet.com/english/2018-10/16/c_137535821.htm.
[41] Christian Davenport, "State Repression and Political Order," *Annual Review of Political Science* 10 (2007): 1–23.
[42] Ben Hillman and Gray Tuttle (eds.), *Ethnic Conflict and Protest in Tibet and Xinjiang: Unrest in China's West* (New York: Columbia University Press 2016).
[43] Yao Tong, and Sui Yunyan, "Xinjiang fankong biaozhang ji dong'yuan bushu hui'yi zhokai Zhang Chunxian, Meng Jianzhu chuxi bing jianghua" [Zhang Chunxian and Meng Jianzhu speak at the XUAR counterterrorism meeting], *CPC News* (2015), http://cpc.people.com.cn/n1/2015/1213/c64094-27922213.html.
[44] James Leibold, "Xinjiang Work Forum Marks New Policy of 'Ethnic Mingling'," *China Brief* 14, no. 12 (2014): 3–6, https://jamestown.org/program/xinjiang-work-forum-marks-new-policy-of-ethnic-mingling.

with Kazakhs and Krygz) are particularly targeted by the CCP while the assimilative minority policy would be expected to affect all minorities in China in the same way. A third explanation focuses on the individual role of Xinjiang Party Secretary Chen Quanguo, who was appointed in 2016 after serving as the party secretary in Tibet since mid-2011.[45] Chen was known for his similar repressive strategies in Tibet and his personal governance style has been considered as one of the reasons for policy changes in Xinjiang. However, the scale and intensity of repression and reeducation in Xinjiang is still different than Chen's term in Tibet. More importantly, such a major policy change is likely to be a product of central decision-making processes within CCP rather than Chen's personal leadership.

The last noteworthy explanation proposes a changing perception by the CCP of the threat of transnational terrorism. Greitens, Lee, and Yazici argue that the CCP started to perceive a more dangerous relationship between the Uyghurs and the militant Islamic groups in the Middle East and Southeast Asia between 2014 and 2016.[46] Even though the fear of an alignment between radical Islamic groups and Uyghurs is not new, the perception of this threat has heightened, especially in light of the participation of a small number of Uyghurs in militant groups in Syrian civil war and several other organizations in Southeast Asia. Accordingly, the CCP considers the detention camps and intense ideological reeducation a preventive measure to fight the Islamist terrorist network. Unlike the domestic-level factors mentioned above, this security-oriented perspective explains both the timing of the increased repression in Xinjiang and why the Muslims (particularly Uyghurs) have been targeted by the CCP. All of these complementary explanations of the shift in the CCP's repressive strategies in Xinjiang (increased contention, rising ethnic nationalism and assimilative minority policies, regional leadership, and changing terrorism threat perception) help us contextualize the surveillance practices in the region.

MASS DETENTION AND INDOCTRINATION (SINCE 2017)

As discussed, since 2017, the Chinese government's repressive strategy in Xinjiang has changed.[47] There are four possible explanations about the policy change and we briefly reviewed each of them. In the following sections, we will review the new development in Xinjiang in detail.

The CCP has been emphasizing a struggle against the "three evil forces" of terrorism, separatism, and extremism in Xinjiang since 1990s. Under this slogan,

---

[45] Adrian Zenz, and James Leibold, "Chen Quanguo: The Strongman behind Beijing's Securitization Strategy in Tibet and Xinjiang," *China Brief* 17, no. 12 (2017): 16–24, https://jamestown.org/program/chen-quanguo-the-strongman-behind-beijings-securitization-strategy-in-tibet-and-xinjiang.

[46] Greitens, Lee, and Yazici, "Counterterrorism and Preventive Repression."

[47] The CCP's dramatic policy change in Xinjiang that we could observe started in 2017.

the level of repression escalated from time to time. The "Strike Hard" campaigns in the 1990s increased the level of repression in the region.[48] Also, after the domestic unrest in the capital of the Xinjiang Uyghur Autonomous Region, Urumqi, in 2009, often called the "7.5 incident," the region entered into a more repressive phase based on the aggressive embedding of security forces and party members in local Uyghur communities.[49]

Xi Jinping also stressed a new strategic plan for Xinjiang in the Politburo meeting in 2013, and the local government launched the "Strike Hard against Violent Terrorist Activity" campaign in 2014. Under the campaign, about 1 percent of Uyghur populations went through "re-education" or "transformation through education."[50] However, the CCP's approach in the region since 2017 differs significantly from the previous repressive strategies in its scope and intensity. According to Greitens, Lee, and Yazici, the CCP's internal security strategy is characterized by three features: "escalated use of collective detention, intensive ideological re-education, and the application of the intensified coercion to the Uyghur diaspora."[51]

The Chinese government has detained as many as a million or more Uyghurs and other ethnic minorities in Xinjiang since 2017. Most Uyghurs detained do not have formal criminal charges. Additionally, apart from the extrajudicial detention camps, the Chinese government has implemented aggressive indoctrination and assimilation policies coupled with the increased societal surveillance and control. In the remainder of this section, we will review this new development. We will focus on the detention camps and address who will be detained, the purpose of the camps, and what happens to Uyghurs in the camps and when they are released. This section will also examine the application of other indoctrination and societal control policies. Later, we will discuss the installation of high-tech surveillance systems in Xinjiang.

Mass Detention Camps

Testimonies of former detainees, internal Chinese government documents, and other evidence suggest that since April 2017 to the time of writing (late 2022), over 1 million Uyghurs and other ethnic minorities including Kazakhs and Uzbeks have been detained.[52] Most people in the camps have not been charged with crimes or

---

[48] See above, "Xinjiang from the 1990s to the 2000s."
[49] The "7.5 incident" refers to a series of protests and violent riots that broke out on July 5, 2009 in Urumqi.
[50] James Leibold, "The Spectre of Insecurity: The CCP's Mass Internment Strategy in Xinjiang," *China Leadership Monitor* 59 (2019), www.prcleader.org/leibold.
[51] Greitens, Lee, and Yazici, "Counterterrorism and Preventive Repression," 15.
[52] Elian Peltier, Claire Moses, and Edward Wong, "'I Have Told Everything,' says Whistle-Blower in China Crackdown," *New York Times*, December 7, 2019, www.nytimes.com/2019/12/07/world/europe/uighur-whistleblower.html; "Testimony of Deputy Assistant Secretary Scott Busby Senate Foreign Relations Committee Subcommittee on East Asia," *The Pacific, and*

gone through legal processes before their detentions. Chinese government claims that these camps are vocational training internment centers, aimed at providing jobs training to less skilled Uyghurs as a part of the country's Poverty Alleviation Program.[53] However, the extensive body evidence documenting militarized repression in Xinjiang, Uyghur testimonies speaking to the involuntary and repressive nature of the camps, the Sinicizing contents of the "reeducation" campaign, and inconsistent statements by the Chinese government make it impossible to take the CCP's claim at face value.

Who Will Be Detained?
The CCP has not revealed a clear standard about their selection of detainees for "reeducation" in Xinjiang. As a result, the minority population lives in constant fear of detention.[54] According to Greer, Uyghurs and Kazakhs have identified several phenomena that attract the attention of security agents including speaking the native language in schools, engaging in religious activities, and connections to Uyghur diasporas or foreigners.[55]

The list illuminates the main aim of the new security strategy. First, it targets locals who engage in activities that have to do with Uyghur ethnic identity. Performing traditional funerals, wearing shirts with Arabic letters, or speaking the native language in schools or in government work groups increase the risk of detention. Second, it aims to crack down on activities related to religious piety. Ethnic minorities practicing religious activities like attending mosques, abstaining from alcohol, praying, or fasting are highly likely to be targeted. Finally, the new strategy attempts to harass the Uyghur diaspora network and limit the ethnic minority group's connections with foreigners. Having traveled abroad, knowing

International Cybersecurity Policy, December 4, 2018, www.foreign.senate.gov/imo/media/doc/120418_Busby_Testimony.pdf; Austin Ramzy and Chris Buckley, "'Absolutely No Mercy': Leaked Files Expose How China Organized Mass Detentions of Muslims," *New York Times,* November 16, 2019, www.nytimes.com/interactive/2019/11/16/world/asia/china-xinjiang-documents.html; deHahn, "More than 1 Million Muslims Are Detained in China"; Ivan Watson and Ben Westcott, "Watched, Judged, Detained: Leaked Chinese Government Records Reveal Detailed Surveillance Reports on Uyghur Families and Beijing's Justification for Mass Detentions," CNN, February, 2020, www.cnn.com/interactive/2020/02/asia/xinjiang-china-karakax-document-intl-hnk/.

[53] Adrian Zenz, "Beyond the Camps: Beijing's Long-Term Scheme of Coercive Labor, Poverty Alleviation and Social Control in Xinjiang," *Journal of Political Risk* 7, no. 12 (2019), www.jpolrisk.com/beyond-the-camps-beijings-long-term-scheme-of-coercive-labor-poverty-alleviation-and-social-control-in-xinjiang.

[54] Tanner Greer, "48 Ways to Get Sent to a Chinese Concentration Camp: Something Terrible Is Happening in Xinjiang," *Foreign Policy,* September 13, 2018, https://foreignpolicy.com/2018/09/13/48-ways-to-get-sent-to-a-chinese-concentration-camp/; Sarah A. Topol, "Her Uighur Parents Were Model Chinese Citizens. It Didn't Matter," *New York Times Magazine,* January 29, 2020, www.nytimes.com/2020/01/29/magazine/uyghur-muslims-china.html.

[55] Greer, "48 Ways to Get Sent to a Chinese Concentration Camp: Something"; Watson and Westcott, "Watched, Judged, Detained."

someone who traveled, or contacting people aboard via Skype or WeChat are deemed "risky activities" that can attract the security forces' attention. Overall, CCP target selection illustrates that the Chinese government's Xinjiang strategy has changed from more "selective repression" to "collective repression," targeting the entire ethnic minority population.[56]

What Happens in the Camps?

The Chinese government initially denied the existence of such camps, but after reports and the leaked internal Chinese documents on detention camps materialized, they switched their position from denial and claimed that the detention facilities are "Vocational Skills Education Training Centers" (*Zhiye jineng jiaoyu peixun zhongxin*), aiming at providing job training for Uyghurs.[57] However, the claim is not plausible in light of revelations that exposed the highly repressive nature of the camps.

For starters, evidence suggests that these centers are used to indoctrinate the detainees with CCP propaganda designed for alignment with the CCP ideology.[58] Testimonies from long-term detainees confirm these claims.[59] According to Zenz, Xinjiang government or education institution websites describe that these "Vocational Skills Education Training Centers" wash clean the brains of people allegedly bewitched by the extreme religious ideologies of the "three forces of terrorism, separatism, and extremism."[60] Moreover, evidence shows that these trainees are detained involuntarily, as most detainees did not go through legal procedures and do not have formal charges or previous criminal histories.[61] Finally, these centers are heavily guarded by "very large" security forces to prevent detainees' escapes (*fang tuopao*).[62] Thus, the available evidence strongly suggests

---

[56] Greitens, Lee, and Yazici, "Counterterrorism and Preventive Repression."
[57] Ramzy and Buckley, "'Absolutely No Mercy'"; Adrian Zenz, "Brainwashing, Police Guards and Coercive Internment: Evidence from Chinese Government Documents about the Nature and Extent of Xinjiang's 'Vocational Training Internment Camps'," *Journal of Political Risk* 7, no. 7 (2019), www.jpolrisk.com/brainwashing-police-guards-and-coercive-internment-evidence-from-chinese-government-documents-about-the-nature-and-extent-of-xinjiangs-vocational-training-internment-camps; Zenz, "Beyond the Camps."
[58] Zenz, "Brainwashing, Police Guards and Coercive Internment."
[59] Matthew Hill, David Campanale, and Joel Gunter, "'Their Goal Is to Destroy Everyone': Uighur Camp Detainees Allege Systematic Rape," *BBC News*, February 2, 2021, www.bbc.com/news/world-asia-china-55794071; "Trapped in the System: Experiences of Uyghur Detention in Post-2015 Xinjiang," *Radio Free Asia*, In-Depth Interviews from November 2019 to May 2020, www.rfa.org/about/releases/trapped-in-the-system-experiences-of-uyghur-detention-in-post-2015-xinjiang-02022021061642.html/experiences_of_uyghur_detention_in_post-2015_xinjiang.pdf.
[60] Zenz, "Brainwashing."
[61] Ibid; Hill, Campanale, and Gunter, "'Their Goal Is to Destroy Everyone'"; Topol, "Her Uighur Parents Were Model Chinese Citizens."
[62] Zenz, "Brainwashing."

Vocational Skills Education Training Centers are involuntary detention camps, aiming at "reeducating" the Muslim population and altering their thinking.

What Happens after the Camps?
In and outside of the extrajudicial detention camps ("Vocational Training Centers"), Uyghurs and other ethnic minorities are forced to perform factory labor.[63] According to Zenz, there are at least three flow schemes to place Uyghurs and other ethnic minorities into factory work.[64] In the first flow, released trainees from the detention camps are relocated into camp factories or local satellite factories. The second flow places rural surplus laborers into centralized training and employment. The third flow places village women into full-time factory work.

All three types of forced labor reengineer Uyghur and ethnic minority communities. By relocating family members and requiring adults in families to work full-time, family interaction is significantly reduced. Children are "put into full-time (at least full day-time) education and training settings," which significantly reduces "intergenerational cultural, linguistic, and religious transmission."[65] According to a BBC report, Xinjiang's total number of children enrolled in kindergartens increased by more than half a million in one year, 2017, with more than 90 percent of that increase made up of Uyghur and other ethnic minority children.[66]

These children are subject to political indoctrination and cultural assimilation at schools.[67] State media portrays school education as "a key component of President Xi Jinping's campaign to wipe out extremist violence in Xinjiang."[68] Based on the leaked internal Chinese documents, the *New York Times* reports that Uyghur teachers have been replaced with teachers from across China, mainly Han Chinese.[69] Teachers are told to ensure that children learn to "love the party, love the motherland, and love the people."[70] Schools are tightly guarded and children in

---

[63] "Against Their Will: The Situation in Xinjiang – Forced Labor in Xinjiang," US *Department of Labor* (2021), www.dol.gov/agencies/ilab/against-their-will-the-situation-in-xinjiang; Amy K. Lehr, "Addressing Forced Labor in the Xinjiang Uyghur Autonomous Region: Collective Action to Develop New Sourcing Opportunities," *Center For Strategic and International Studies* (CSIS), February 3, 2021, www.csis.org/analysis/addressing-forced-labor-xinjiang-uyghur-autonomous-region.
[64] Zenz, "Beyond the Camps."
[65] Ibid.
[66] John Sudworth, "China Muslims: Xinjiang Schools Used to Separate Children from Families," *BBC News*, July 4, 2019, www.bbc.com/news/world-asia-china-48825090.
[67] Amy Qin, "In China's Crackdown on Muslims, Children Have Not Been Spared," December 28, 2019 (updated October 15, 2020), www.nytimes.com/2019/12/28/world/asia/china-xinjiang-children-boarding-schools.html.
[68] Ibid.
[69] Ibid; Ramzy and Buckley, "'Absolutely No Mercy'."
[70] Qin, "In China's Crackdown."

boarding schools are not allowed to freely visit with family, resulting in separating children from cultural, linguistic, and religious influences from their families.[71]

Societal Control and Assimilation Policies

Apart from the internment camps, the Chinese government has implemented assertive assimilation policies designed to eliminate Uyghurs' cultural, linguistic, and religious characteristics. Mosques have been destroyed for "safety concerns."[72] According to a report, since 2017, approximately 16,000 mosques in Xinjiang have been destroyed or damaged due to government policies.[73] Certain names such as Mohammed and Medina are banned for newborn babies.[74] The Xinjiang local government launched a campaign against halal food (such as meats) consistent with the Islamic faith, which makes it hard to find in Urumqi.[75]

Rural Uyghur and Turkic Muslim families have been visited by Han "relatives" who monitor and document ethnic minorities' daily lives and instruct them in the CCP's political ideology.[76] Since 2016, over 1 million civil servants have visited assigned Uyghur and other ethnic minority families. While spending a series of weeks with designated families, these civil servants monitor whether the family is religious, whether they adhere to their traditional lifestyles, and whether they speak Mandarin. These visitors also ask questions such as whether the host family has relatives living in "sensitive regions," or whether the family knows someone who lives abroad. Overall, according to Byler, these relatives "assess whether or not they should be sent into the mass reeducation camp system."[77] All the collected information would be documented and reported to the authorities.

Based on government statistics, state documents, and interviews with thirty ex-detainees, Associated Press claims the Chinese government have taken draconian

---

[71] Ibid.
[72] The Chinese government claims that buildings are unsafe for worshippers and demolishes mosques. This claim is not very convincing, given the government's recent crackdown on religious activities in Xinjiang. Lindsay Maizland, "China's Repression of Uighurs in Xinjiang," *Council on Foreign Relations*, June 30, 2020, www.cfr.org/backgrounder/chinas-repression-uighurs-xinjiang; Helen Davidson, "Thousands of Xinjiang Mosques Destroyed or Damaged, Report Finds," *The Guardian*, September 25, 2020, www.theguardian.com/world/2020/sep/25/thousands-of-xinjiang-mosques-destroyed-damaged-china-report-finds.
[73] Nathan Ruser et al., "Cultural Erasure: Tracing the Destruction of Uyghur and Islamic Spaces in Xinjiang," *Australian Strategic Policy Institute*, September 24, 2020, www.aspi.org.au/report/cultural-erasure.
[74] Maizland, "China's Repression of Uighurs in Xinjiang."
[75] Ibid.
[76] Darren Byler, "China's Nightmare Homestay: In Xinjiang, Unwanted Chinese Guests Monitor Uyghur Homes 24/7," *Foreign Policy*, October 26, 2018, https://foreignpolicy.com/2018/10/26/china-nightmare-homestay-xinjiang-uighur-monitor. Darren Byler, "Violent Paternalism: In the Banality of Uyghur Unfreedom," *Asia-Pacific Journal* 16, no. 24 (2018): 1–15.
[77] Byler, *Foreign Policy*.

measures of using intrauterine devices, abortion, and sterilization to control Uyghur and other Turkic Muslim's birth rates.[78] According to the report (2020), the government regularly conducts pregnancy checks of Uyghur women and "forces intrauterine devices, sterilization, and even abortion on hundreds of thousands."[79]

Policing

A plethora of evidence also demonstrates that Xinjiang has become a police state. After Chen Quanguo became the Party Secretary of the Xinjiang Uyghur Autonomous Region, the region experienced a drastic increase in the police presence.[80] According to Zenz and Leibold, between August 2016 and July 2017, Xinjiang had made 90,866 security-related job advertisements.[81] Because of the quota system (*bianzhi*) that assigns civil and public service recruitment quotas, the expansion of the formal police force is restricted.[82] To bypass these restrictions, in recent years, informal assistant police staff (*xiejing* or *fujing*) recruitment has increased to boost community policing capabilities. Zenz and Leibold estimate a total police stock figure of 112,886 in 2017 based on "a 75% recruitment rate estimate for all policing-related advertisements between 2008 and August 2017, as well as an annual attrition rate of 3% owing to retirement, death and other causes."[83] The per capita count is 478 in Xinjiang. This number is 2.3 times the estimated national per capita figure and 17 percent higher than that of Hong Kong.

---

[78] "China Cuts Uighur Births with IUDs, Abortion, Sterilization," *Associated Press*, June 28, 2020, https://apnews.com/269b3de1af34e17c1941a514f78d764c; Adrian Zenz, *Mandatory Birth Control: The CCP's Campaign to Suppress Uyghur Birthrates in Xinjiang* (Washington DC: The Jamestown Foundation, 2020), updated March 17, 2021, https://jamestown.org/wp-content/uploads/2020/06/Zenz-Internment-Sterilizations-and-IUDs-REVISED-March-17-2021.pdf? x80839; "Xinjiang Weiwu'er zizhiqu Kelamayi shi Dushanziqu weisheng hehehuohuohu jihuashengyu weiyuanhui bumen danwei nian bumen yusuan gongkai" [Publicizing 2019 budget of the Xinjiang Uyghur Autonomous Region Karamay City Dushanzi District's Committee on Hygiene and Family Planning], https://web.archive.org/web/20200515141652/http://www.dsz.gov.cn/uploads/cms/attachments/202003/579971d0a66491dc1d91088ea6436844.pdf.

[79] See also Zenz, *Mandatory Birth Control*; for criticisms of his approach, see Fangfei Lin, "Dui Zhengguo'en guanyu Xinjiang renkou wenti miulunde shishi huiji: jiyu Xinjiang gezu renmin shengyu yiyuande diaocha yanjiu baogao" [Critique and Fact Check on Zenz's False Claim of the Xinjiang Population Issue: Based on the Study Report on the Xinjiang Every Ethnic Group's Fertility Preference], Xinjiang University, September 14, 2020, https://archive.is/ZaWta.

[80] Adrian Zenz and James Leibold, "Xinjiang's Rapidly Evolving Security State," *China Brief* 17, no. 4 (2017), https://jamestown.org/program/xinjiangs-rapidly-evolving-security-state; Adrian Zenz, and James Leibold, "Securitizing Xinjiang: Police Recruitment, Informal Policing and Ethnic Minority Co-optation," *China Quarterly* 242 (2020): 234–348.

[81] Zenz and Leibold, "Xinjiang's Rapidly Evolving Security State."

[82] Zenz and Leibold, "Securitizing Xinjiang."

[83] Ibid.

Chen also introduced a grid-management system in which cities and villages in Xinjiang were divided into squares of about 500 people.[84] Each square is managed by a police station that monitors residents' activities regularly, and some cities have police checkpoints every 100 yards. High-tech surveillance systems have been installed to monitor inhabitants and pedestrians, which will be discussed in the next section.

TECHNOLOGICAL INNOVATION FOR MORE EFFECTIVE SURVEILLANCE

The CCP has been combining conventional surveillance methods discussed in the previous section with advanced technological tools and biometric data for a more comprehensive surveillance apparatus in Xinjiang. The scope and sophistication of surveillance is potentially unprecedented in human history. Advanced surveillance technologies include smart phone applications to track citizens' communication, automatic license plate readers to track vehicles, CCTV cameras, and video analytics that perform facial recognition, emotion recognition, and the automated detection of Uyghur minorities. In addition to these technological tools to surveil behaviors, communication, and movement of citizens, the CCP also collects biometric data (e.g. DNA, blood, and voice samples) from the majority of the Uyghur population.[85] While this multilayered system is allegedly designed to detect criminal and terrorist activities, as well as to determine which Uyghurs are potentially "dangerous" and need to be "transformed" in the detention camps, the pervasive surveillance system in Xinjiang also serves some other purposes, including social control, cultural assimilation, and economic gains.[86] Below, we briefly review the advanced technological tools of surveillance used by CCP in Xinjiang along with their limitations, problematic aspects, and international implications.

High-Tech Surveillance in Xinjiang

How Is the Surveillance Carried Out?
The CCP integrated the grid management system with sophisticated surveillance technology by installing thousands of CCTV cameras throughout the region in 2014,

---

[84] Maizland, "China's Repression of Uighurs in Xinjiang"; "China Has Turned Xinjiang into a Police State Like No Other," *The Economist*, May 31, 2018, www.economist.com/briefing/2018/05/31/china-has-turned-xinjiang-into-a-police-state-like-no-other.

[85] William Drexel, "Kashgar Coerced: Forced Reconstruction, Exploitation, and Surveillance in the Cradle of Uyghur Culture," Uyghur Human Rights Project (2020), https://uhrp.org/sites/default/files/UHRP-Kashgar-Coerced-Report-06_03_20%20Final.pdf; Emile Dirks, and James Leibold, "Genomic Surveillance: Inside China's DNA Dragnet," *Australian Strategic Policy Institute* (2020), www.aspi.org.au/report/genomic-surveillance.

[86] Darren Byler, "The Global Implications of 'Re-education' Technologies in Northwest China," *Center for Global Policy*, June 8, 2020, https://cgpolicy.org/articles/the-global-implications-of-re-education-technologies-in-northwest-china; James Leibold, "Planting the Seed: Ethnic Policy in Xi Jinping's New Era of Cultural Nationalism," *China Brief* 19, no. 22 (2019): 9–14.

using facial-recognition technology in Ürümqi and iris-recognition technology in Kashgar in 2016.[87] More recently, the CCP installed an emotion-recognition system which "identifies signs of aggressiveness and nervousness as well as stress levels and a person's potential to attack others" to prevent criminal and terrorist activities.[88] Taken together, these systems attempt to monitor each and every behavior of the Uyghurs in public. The CCP also requires drivers to install Beidou (China's version of the Global Positioning System) to track their vehicles.[89] Dove drones with high-definition cameras and satellite connections complement the Beidou system for full-time surveillance of the citizens without their consent and regardless of their criminal backgrounds.[90] Surveillance of the communication and online activities of citizens is not new in China. The Golden Shield and Great Firewall projects have been used to monitor and constrain the online activities of the citizens since the 1990s.[91] However, since the 2009 Ürümqi riots, the extent and level of online surveillance in Xinjiang is unmatched elsewhere in China.[92] Smartphone data-extraction intensified in 2017–2018,[93] although the most recent evidence shows that the CCP has started to hack and track Uyghurs' smartphones extensively as early as 2013.[94] The extensive data collected through sophisticated technological tools are combined in the "Integrated Joint Operations Platform" (IJOP), which serves as a hub of surveillance.

Why Is the CCP Using Mass Surveillance?

The CCP's stated objective is to prevent crime and terror-related activities.[95] Yet a combination of traditional and technological surveillance has clearly enabled a

[87] Zenz and Leibold. "Xinjiang's Rapidly Evolving Security State"; Leibold, "Planting the Seed"; Sheena Chestnut Greitens, "Domestic Security in China under Xi Jinping," *China Leadership Monitor* 59, no. 1 (2019), www.prcleader.org/greitens; Isobel Cockerel, "Inside China's Massive Surveillance Operation," *Wired*, May 9, 2019, www.wired.com/story/inside-chinas-massive-surveillance-operation.
[88] Sue Lin-Wong and Qianer Liu, "Emotion Recognition Is China's New Surveillance Craze," *Financial Times*, November 1, 2019, www.ft.com/content/68155560-fbd1-11e9-a354-36acbbbod9b6.
[89] Edward Wong, "Western China Region Aims to Track People by Requiring Car Navigation," *New York Times*, February 24, 2017, www.nytimes.com/2017/02/24/world/asia/china-xinjiang-gps-vehicles.html.
[90] Stephen Chen, "China Takes Surveillance to New Heights with Flock of Robotic Doves, but Do They Come in Peace?" *South China Morning Post*, June 24, 2018, www.scmp.com/news/china/society/article/2152027/china-takes-surveillance-new-heights-flock-robotic-doves-do-they.
[91] Xinmei Shen, "The Story of China's Great Firewall: The World's Most Sophisticated Censorship System," *South China Morning Post*, November 7, 2019, www.scmp.com/abacus/who-what/what/article/3089836/story-chinas-great-firewall-worlds-most-sophisticated.
[92] Leibold, "Planting the Seed."
[93] Greitens, "Domestic Security in China under Xi Jinping."
[94] Paul Mozur and Nicole Perlroth, "China's Software Stalked Uighurs Earlier and More Widely, Researchers Learn," *New York Times*, July 1, 2020, www.nytimes.com/2020/07/01/technology/china-uighurs-hackers-malware-hackers-smartphones.html.
[95] Maya Wang, "China's Algorithms of Repression," *Human Rights Watch*, May 1, 2019, www.hrw.org/report/2019/05/02/chinas-algorithms-repression/reverse-engineering-xinjiang-police-mass;

significant increase in the state's capacity to prevent "antistate" activities at the local level.[96] Moreover, the surveillance goes beyond Xinjiang and tracks the interaction between Uyghurs in Xinjiang, diaspora Uyghurs, and Turkic Muslims in other countries.[97] While this can be interpreted as a signal of CCP's concern regarding the transborder network of Uyghurs,[98] the surveillance system in Xinjiang is also designed to detect and report the peaceful acts of Uyghurs, including their religious and cultural rituals which are viewed with disdain by the government. Even trivial everyday behaviors, such as using popular apps (e.g. WhatsApp) or not socializing with neighbors, are enough to raise a red flag for the authorities.[99] With such comprehensive surveillance in place, Uyghurs face intense pressure to change their ways or potentially lose any real semblance of their identity. In addition to security and social control policies, the surveillance network in Xinjiang also form part of the economic policies of the CCP as Chinese companies have been exporting surveillance technologies to other countries.[100] Much like Microsoft's Domain Awareness System for the surveillance of New York City,[101] Xinjiang doubles as a lab to try out new projects and showcase for the global surveillance technology market.[102] Considering the slowdown in the economic growth of China, the opportunity to dominate this profitable sector is definitely an appealing aspect of the surveillance policies of the CCP.

Limitations and Problems

Despite the massive investments by the public and private sectors, the surveillance network in Xinjiang (and rest of China) is not fully effective and has several limitations. Leibold points out that the complex bureaucracy network of the CCP

"Xinjiang juxing fankong weiwen shishi dahui: Wang Ning, Chen Quanguo jianghua" [Xinjiang holds a counterterrorism and stability meeting: Wang Ning, Chen Quanquo speak], *Tianshanwang*, February 28, 2017, www.guancha.cn/local/2017_02_28_396305.shtml.

[96] Zenz and Leibold. "Xinjiang's Rapidly Evolving Security State."
[97] "China's Algorithms of Repression," *Human Rights Watch*.
[98] Greitens, Lee, and Yazici, "Counterterrorism and Preventive Repression."
[99] "China's Algorithms of Repression," *Human Rights Watch*.
[100] Sheena Chestnut Greitens, "Dealing with Demand for China's Global Surveillance Exports," *Brookings Global China Project*, April, 2020, 2, www.brookings.edu/research/dealing-with-demand-for-chinas-global-surveillance-exports/; Alina Polyakova and Chris Meserole, "Exporting Digital Authoritarianism: The Russian and Chinese Models," *Democracy & Disorder*, Brookings, 2019, www.brookings.edu/research/exporting-digital-authoritarianism; Jonathan E. Hillman and Maesea McCalpin, "Watching Huawei's "Safe Cities"," *CSIS Briefs*, November 4, 2019, www.csis.org/analysis/watching-huaweis-safe-cities; Linette Lopez, "China's Next Gambit to Save Its Economy Will Export Dystopia," *Business Insider*, December 15, 2019, www.businessinsider.com/china-economic-boost-surveillance-technology-uighurs-xinjiang-2019-12.
[101] Michael Kwet, "The Rise of Smart Camera Networks, and Why We Should Ban Them," *The Intercept*, January 27, 2020, https://theintercept.com/2020/01/27/surveillance-cctv-smart-camera-networks.
[102] Lopez, "China's Next Gambit"; Polyakova and Meserole, "Exporting Digital Authoritarianism."

makes it difficult to coordinate each agent's role and mission in the surveillance process.[103] Moreover, some of the surveillance systems rely on predictive AI models, which are particularly challenging and costly to develop in the multilingual and multicultural societies like Xinjiang.[104] Even if further investments and bureaucratic reforms can mitigate these problems to some extent, the cybersecurity capacity of China is not competent enough to protect the digital infrastructure of the surveillance system.[105] Hence both technical and bureaucratic difficulties limit the effectiveness of surveillance. The surveillance system is also likely to engender some unintended consequences for the CCP, such as the use of surveillance data by competing actors within the CCP and increased sense of insecurity among Uyghurs.[106]

Biometric Data Collection in Xinjiang

The surveillance of the behaviors, movements, and communication of Uyghurs has been complemented by mass and compulsory collection of biometric data, including facial imagery, fingerprints, iris scans, DNA samples, blood samples, and voice samples.[107] Since 2016, the government collected biometric data from around 23 million residents in Xinjiang.[108] This information is added to other data about each citizen.[109] The CCP officially claims it collects biometric data to protect public health, under a program called "Physicals for All."[110] However, most of the

[103] Leibold, "Planting the Seed," 7.
[104] Ibid., 7.
[105] Pieter Velghe, "'Reading China': The Internet of Things, Surveillance, and Social Management in the PRC," *China Perspectives* 1 (2019): 85–89; Jon R. Lindsay, "The Impact of China on Cyber Security: Fiction and Friction," *International Security* 39, no. 3 (2015): 7–47.
[106] James Leibold and Adrian Zenz, "Beijing's Eyes and Ears Grow Sharper in Xinjiang: The 27-7 Patrols of China's 'Convenience Police'," *Foreign Affairs*, December 23, 2016, www.foreignaffairs.com/articles/china/2016-12-23/beijings-eyes-and-ears-grow-sharper-xinjiang; Zenz, and Leibold. "Xinjiang's Rapidly Evolving Security State."
[107] The CCP also collects biometric data outside of Xinjiang; however, the extent, level, and purpose of its application are different outside the region (see Jessica Batke and Mareike Ohlberg, "China's Biosecurity State in Xinjiang Is Powered by Western Tech," *Foreign Policy*, February 19, 2020, https://foreignpolicy.com/2020/02/19/china-xinjiang-surveillance-biosecurity-state-dna-western-tech; and Dirks, and Leibold, "Genomic Surveillance"). "China: Minority Region Collects DNA from Millions," *Human Rights Watch*, December 13, 2017, www.hrw.org/news/2017/12/13/china-minority-region-collects-dna-millions; Byler, "The Global Implications of 'Re-education' Technologies in Northwest China"; Cockerel, "Inside China's Massive Surveillance Operation."
[108] Dirks and Leibold, "Genomic Surveillance," 4.
[109] "China: Minority Region Collects DNA from Millions," *Human Rights Watch*; Dirks and Leibold, "Genomic Surveillance."
[110] Mercy A. Kuo, "Uyghur Biodata Collection in China," *The Diplomat*, December 28, 2017, https://thediplomat.com/2017/12/uyghur-biodata-collection-in-china/; Sui-Lee Wee, "China Uses DNA to Track Its People, With the Help of American Expertise," *New York Times*,

biometric data collection is compulsory, involuntary, and opaque. Therefore, as Dirks and Leibold point out, "the mass and compulsory collection of DNA from people outside criminal investigations violates Chinese domestic law and international norms governing the collection, use and storage of human genetic data."[111]

Future of the Surveillance Technology in Xinjiang and International Implications

At the time of writing, the Chinese government continues to improve and expand its surveillance projects throughout China. One of its most ambitious projects, called *Sharp Eyes*, "aims to reach 100% coverage of all of China's public areas and key industries by 2020, relying not only on CCTV but also on cameras installed inside smart devices in people's homes, such as smart TVs."[112] Another project, called the *Social Credit System*, is designed as a reward and punishment system based on the activities and digital footprints of citizens and companies. The system has three components: (1) estimating financial credit scores to be used to assess one's eligibility for getting loans, (2) creating industry blacklists for those violate laws and regulations, and (3) educating both companies and citizens on the values of honesty and integrity.[113] However, most of the projects that have widespread media coverage in the West are local and experimental at best and it is not clear when they will be used at the national level.[114] Also, despite the portrayal of the social credit system as a mandatory system that determines citizens' place in the society based on a single score, the system is neither mandatory (yet) nor based on a single citizen score.[115] The most troubling aspect of the current system from the human rights perspective is the unclear standards for putting companies and people on blacklists which causes exclusion from certain public and private services.[116] Thus, while this project has been misconstrued by the Western press[117] – it is *not* a generic, single-number

---

February 21, 2019, www.nytimes.com/2019/02/21/business/china-xinjiang-uighur-dna-thermo-fisher.html.

[111] Dirks and Leibold, "Genomic Surveillance," 5.

[112] Velghe, "'Reading China'," 86.

[113] Jeremy Daum, "China through a Glass, Darkly," *China Law and Translate*, December 24, 2017, www.chinalawtranslate.com/en/china-social-credit-score.

[114] Louise Matsakis, "How the West Got China's Social Credit System Wrong," *Wired*, July 29, 2019, www.wired.com/story/china-social-credit-score-system.

[115] Daum, "China through a Glass, Darkly."

[116] Jamie Horsley, "China's Orwellian Social Credit Score Isn't Real," *Foreign Policy*, November 2018, https://foreignpolicy.com/2018/11/16/chinas-orwellian-social-credit-score-isnt-real; Matsakis, "How the West Got China's Social Credit System Wrong." Even though the CCP may attempt to incorporate the everyday behaviors (particularly the religious and cultural practices) of the members of the minorities into a single citizen score and impose punishments based on this score, it is unclear what would be the benefit of this for the CCP given the availability of other tools to address such political and security concerns (Horsley).

[117] Mara Hvistendahl, "Inside China's Vast New Experiment in Social Ranking," *Wired*, December 14, 2017, www.wired.com/story/age-of-social-credit.

ranking system to reward and punish general behavior (akin to the Black Mirror episode, Nosedive)[118] – it remains the case that "reward and punishment" social credit systems can threaten civil rights and liberties.[119] It is not clear how fast the CCP will be able to complete these projects. Nevertheless, the future of both the existing and new surveillance projects in Xinjiang is highly contingent upon the export of their technologies to other countries, involvement of Western companies in the development of surveillance technology, and reactions of the international community. Without foreign support, domestic surveillance projects can be significantly weakened.

Several Chinese companies, including Huawei, Hikvision, Dahua, and CEIEC (China National Electronics Import and Export Corporation), have exported surveillance technology (and other forms of security technology) to at least eighty countries between 2008 and 2020.[120] This strategic industry influences China's interaction with other states as well. States who import Chinese surveillance technology, such as Saudi Arabia, have expressed their support for the CCP's repressive policies in Xinjiang.[121] Hence it is important for democratic states to mobilize the international community to reduce the demand for authoritarian surveillance technology, which would affect the level and intensity for surveillance in Xinjiang. Yet, such an effort would be effective only if the democratic states clean up their own invasive surveillance systems, which have been used to repress the minority groups in these countries too (such as the use of high-tech surveillance against Muslims and black Americans in the United States).[122] Therefore, democratic states should first eliminate their own problematic surveillance system (such as CCTV cameras) and lead by example, if they are to mobilize the international community.

In line with decreasing the demand by other governments, another responsibility of democratic states to prevent the involvement of Western tech companies in developing Chinese surveillance technology. Several US companies have been providing technical and financial assistance to Chinese tech companies involved in the surveillance and biometric data collection projects in Xinjiang.[123] Some of

---

[118] Horsley, "China's Orwellian Social Credit Score Isn't Real."
[119] As Daum ("China through a Glass, Darkly") and Matsakis ("How the West Got China's Social Credit System Wrong") underline, exaggerated and inaccurate portrayals of the Chinese social credit system are problematic as they make invasive Western surveillance systems look more acceptable.
[120] Greitens, "Dealing with Demand for China's Global Surveillance Exports," 2; Polyakova and Meserole, "Exporting Digital Authoritarianism."
[121] Kelly A. Hammond, "Reconfiguring Geopolitics in the Era of the Surveillance State: The Uyghurs, the Chinese Party-State, and the Reshaping of Middle East Politics," *Hoover Institution*, June 27, 2019, www.hoover.org/research/reconfiguring-geopolitics-era-surveillance-state-uyghurs-chinese-party-state-and-reshaping.
[122] Kwet, "The Rise of Smart Camera Networks, and Why We Should Ban Them."
[123] "China's Algorithms of Repression," *Human Rights Watch*; Kayden McKenzie, "Lessons from Xinjiang: The Dangers of U.S. Investment in Chinese Surveillance Technology," *New*

these Chinese tech companies even sought funding from the World Bank.[124] The US Department of Commerce has been imposing sanctions on Chinese companies since 2019; but the effectiveness of these policies is again related to what extent democratic states limit their own invasive surveillance systems in their own countries. It is difficult and ethically problematic to ban the activities of Western tech companies in China while the same companies produce similar technologies for their own governments. After the elimination of similar technologies in their own countries, all democratic states should impose stronger and more comprehensive sanctions on all firms involved in surveillance in Xinjiang.[125] Otherwise, involvement of Western companies will lend legitimacy and help CCP further improve their surveillance technology.

Preventing the involvement of the Western companies and resisting use and spread of digital authoritarianism are especially important in the context of the current global health crisis. The surveillance methods that have been used in Xinjiang are now used in the rest of the country as a part of public health measures in response to the pandemic.[126] However, the Chinese government is planning to make the pervasive surveillance permanent even after the pandemic.[127] In the absence of global regulations and standards, it is likely that Chinese surveillance technology, which lacks transparency and respect for civil liberties, will be more appealing for the other countries in the midst of pandemic. As Greitens and Gewirtz argue, democratic countries should regulate the standards of surveillance technology for public health and promote successful democratic alternatives (such as South Korea and Taiwan) in the fight against pandemic to discourage countries from importing the Chinese model.[128]

In short, even though most of the surveillance technologies have been extensively used in Xinjiang and Tibet initially, involuntary and indiscriminate surveillance is now used in the entire country. It is likely that the CCP will continue developing

---

Perspectives in Foreign Policy Issue, Issue 18 (2019): 47–51, www.csis.org/lessons-xinjiang-dangers-us-investment-chinese-surveillance-technology; Batke and Ohlberg, "China's Biosecurity State in Xinjiang Is Powered by Western Tech"; Charles Rollet, "In China's Far West, Companies Cash In on Surveillance Program that Targets Muslims," *Foreign Policy*, June 13, 2018, https://foreignpolicy.com/2018/06/13/in-chinas-far-west-companies-cash-in-on-surveillance-program-that-targets-muslims.

[124] Allen-Ebrahimian, "Exposed."
[125] Byler, "The Global Implications of 'Re-education' Technologies in Northwest China."
[126] Alexandra Ma, "How the Coronavirus Outbreak Could Help Fuel China's Dystopian Surveillance System," *Business Insider*, March 7, 2020, www.businessinsider.com/coronavirus-china-surveillance-police-state-xinjiang-2020-2.
[127] Ibid.; Liza Lin, "China's Plan to Make Permanent Health Tracking on Smartphones Stirs Concern," *Wall Street Journal*, May 25, 2020, www.wsj.com/articles/chinas-plan-to-make-permanent-health-tracking-on-smartphones-stirs-concern-11590422497#:~:text=Liza%20Lin,-Biography&text=China%20created%20a%20smartphone%20tool,said%20to%20be%20an%20afterthoughtLin.
[128] Sheena Chestnut Greitens and Julian Gewirtz, "China's Troubling Vision for the Future of Public Health," *Foreign Affairs*, July 10, 2020, www.foreignaffairs.com/articles/china/2020-07-10/chinas-troubling-vision-future-public-health.

high-tech mass surveillance due to increasing international demand for the Chinese surveillance products. Democratic states have a responsibility to (1) eliminate their own invasive surveillance technology to lead by example, (2) prevent their companies from collaborating with the Chinese tech companies involved in surveillance in Xinjiang, (3) prevent China from shaping the global standards and regulations regarding surveillance technology, and (4) promote the democratic alternatives to Chinese digital authoritarianism.

CONCLUSION

Uyghurs and the other Muslim minorities in Xinjiang have been experiencing various forms and levels of repression for decades. However, both the scale and level of the repression has significantly increased since 2017. The unparalleled surveillance network in Xinjiang today, which constitutes the biggest open-air prison of the world, can be best understood as an extension of the shift in the CCP's changing strategy in Xinjiang. Today, the CCP uses indiscriminate collective detention, intense ideological reeducation, and a combination of both traditional and high-tech surveillance as a part of their new domestic security strategy in Xinjiang. Both domestic and international factors can explain this shift in the CCP's regional strategy, which impacts their surveillance policy. However, the surveillance network in Xinjiang (especially the high-tech surveillance methods) has been used widely throughout China and exported to other countries already. The demand for surveillance technologies due to pandemic-related public health concerns in particular will encourage China to develop, test, and export more surveillance products.

Besides the moral responsibility to take action in respect of crimes against humanity in Xinjiang, the spread of Chinese surveillance technology ("digital authoritarianism") to other countries makes this issue a strategic concern for democratic members of the international community. They should first clean up their own invasive surveillance practices and present democratic alternatives to reduce the demand for unchecked and intrusive surveillance technology around the world

10

Asian Americans as "the Perpetual Foreigner" under Scrutiny

Frank H. Wu

"Go back to China! Go back to your fucking country."
"I was born in this country!"

    – Exchange between a random stranger, not of Asian background, in New York City c.2016 and an editor at the *New York Times*, of Asian descent[1]

"You're American-born, but you're Chinese at heart."

    – FBI counterintelligence agent quoted as saying "she believes the generalizations are justified" about Chinese American disloyalty[2]

"If it was the French government that was attempting to steal U.S. technology in a massive, decade-long campaign, we'd look for French people. But it's not. It's the Chinese government."

    – Federal prosecutor denying racial profiling was being used in investigations[3]

INTRODUCTION: AN "ALL OF SOCIETY" THREAT

Asian Americans play a prominent role in the state surveillance story, because Asian Americans play an ambiguous role in both international relations and domestic

---

[1] Michael Luo, "An Open Letter to the Woman Who Told My Family to Go Back to China," *New York Times*, October 11, 2016, www.nytimes.com/2016/10/10/nyregion/to-the-woman-who-told-my-family-to-go-back-to-china.html.
[2] Peter Waldman, "Mistrust and the Hunt for Spies Among Chinese Americans," *Businessweek*, December 10, 2019, www.bloomberg.com/news/features/2019-12-10/the-u-s-government-s-mistrust-of-chinese-americans.
[3] Geoff Brumfiel, "U.S. Response to China's Talent Plan is Described as Heavy-Handed," *NPR*, February 13, 2020, www.npr.org/2020/02/13/805537113/u-s-response-to-chinas-talent-plan-described-as-heavy-handed.

race relations.[4] Although people of Asian descent have been arriving in the Americas since before the Civil War – Asian soldiers fighting on both sides of the internecine conflict – Asian immigrants and their American-born descendants, whatever their formal status and however assimilated, have been portrayed as "sojourners" only temporarily resident in the United States and likely to return to a homeland to which they have remained stealthily loyal.[5] The persistent theme has been that Asians are inassimilable into American society, whether by biology, culture, or their own collective choices. The assumption that it is contradictory to be both Asian and American has been used, explicitly and implicitly, to justify discrimination against Asian Americans. With conflict between the United States and China increasingly a dominant theme of public discourse, Asian Americans,

---

[4] "Asian American" is a contemporary term, introduced by scholar Yuji Ichioka c.1968. It reflects both pan-Asian identity and American identity, neither of which would be appropriate in Asia proper. In addition to the mistaken identity of Asian foreign nationals with Asian Americans, there is the mistaken identity of "you all look alike." In hate crimes against Asian Americans, for example, it is common for Asian Americans of different ethnic backgrounds to be confused for one another. For general histories of Asian Americans, see Erika Lee, *The Making of Asian American: A History* (New York: Simon & Schuster, 2016); Gary Okihiro, *American History Unbound: Asians and Pacific Islanders*. (Berkeley, CA: University of California Press, 2015). The role of race in foreign relations is a developing area of study. Thomas Borstelmann, *The Cold War and the Color Line: American Race Relations in the Global Arena*, rev. ed. (Cambridge, MA: Harvard University Press, 2003); Mary L. Dudziak, *Cold War Civil Rights: Race and the Image of American Democracy* (Princeton University Press, 2011); Michael Krenn, *The Impact of Race on U.S. Foreign Policy: A Reader* (Abingdon, UK: Routledge, 1999); Tony Smith, *Foreign Attachments: The Power of Ethnic Groups in the Making of American Foreign Policy* (Cambridge, MA: Harvard University Press). For Asian Americans in particular, see Cindy I-Fen Cheng, *Citizens of Asian America: Democracy and Race During the Cold War* (New York University Press, 2014); Peter H. Koehn and Xiao-huang Yin, *The Expanding Role of Chinese Americans in U.S.–China Relations: Transnational Networks and Trans-Pacific Interactions* (Armonk, NY: M. E. Sharpe 2002); Paul Y. Watanabe, "Asian American Activism and U.S. Foreign Policy," in Evelyn Hu-DeHart (ed.), *Across the Pacific: Asian Americans and Globalization* (Philadelphia, PA: Temple University Press, 1999); Myron Weiner, "Asian-Americans and American Foreign Policy," *Revue Europenne des Migrations Internationales* 5, no. 1 (1989): 97–111.

Asian Americans have been excluded, even from classic histories of immigration such as by John Higham. That prompted Ronald Takaki, *Strangers from a Different Shore: A History of Asian Americans*, rev. ed. (New York: Little Brown, 1998). Asian Americans also were absent from discussions of civil rights. Frank H. Wu, *Yellow: Race in America Beyond Black and White* (New York: Basic Books, 2001).

[5] The "perpetual foreigner" syndrome has become a recognized theme. See, e.g., Stacey J. Lee, Nga-Wing Anjela Wong, and Alvin N. Alvarez, "The Model Minority and the Perpetual Foreigner: Stereotypes of Asian American," in Nita Tewari and Alvin N. Alvarez (eds.), *Asian American Psychology: Current Perspectives* (New York: Psychology Press, 2008); Jennifer C. Ng, Sharon S. Lee, and Yoon K. Pak, "Contesting the Model Minority and the Perpetual Foreigner," *Review of Research in Education* 31, no. 1 (2007): 95–130. Among the earliest discussions is Neil Gotanda, "Other Non–Whites" in American Legal History: A Review of Justice at War," *Columbia Law Review* 85, no. 5 (1985): 1186–1192. See also Mia Tuan, *Forever Foreigners or Honorary Whites?* (New Brunswick, NJ: Rutgers University Press, 1999).

visible as such, have ended up overrepresented in the prosecution of espionage and associated crimes.

On February 13, 2018, prior to the Covid-19 global pandemic upending everything, FBI Director Christopher Wray was candid in this regard. He testified to Congress about an allegedly pervasive Chinese threat in the gathering of data:

> I think in this setting I would just say that the use of nontraditional collectors, especially in the academic setting, whether it's professors, scientists, students, we see in almost every field office that the FBI has around the country. It's not just in major cities. It's in small ones as well. It's across basically every discipline. And I think the level of naïveté on the part of the academic sector about this creates its own issues. They're exploiting the very open research and development environment that we have, which we all revere, but they're taking advantage of it. So one of the things we're trying to do is view the China threat as not just a whole-of-government threat but a whole-of-society threat on their end, and I think it's going to take a whole-of-society response by us. So it's not just the intelligence community, but it's raising awareness within our academic sector, within our private sector, as part of the defense.[6]

In Wray's formulation, there is a Chinese "whole of society" and an "us" that is a "whole of society." It is not apparent where Chinese Americans are supposed to be placed between these two stark opposites.[7] Ignoring criticism from civil rights groups for not distinguishing between foreign nationals and Asian Americans, Wray appeared on television to add, "To be clear, we do not open investigations based on race, or ethnicity, or national origin … But when we open investigations into economic espionage, time and time again, they keep leading back to China."[8] He repeated the sentiment again at the prestigious Aspen Institute that summer.[9]

---

[6] Hearing on Worldwide Threats, Before the Senate Select Committee on Intelligence, 115th Cong. 2nd session (February 13, 2018), www.intelligence.senate.gov/hearings/open-hearing-worldwide-threats-hearing-1#.

[7] Many Chinese Americans, in particular from immigration waves prior to normalization of relations between the United States and China, were from Taiwan, Hong Kong, and elsewhere, not the People's Republic of China. See Frank H. Wu, "The New Chinese Diaspora: Embracing the Model Minority and Perpetual Foreigner?," *Chinese Historical Society of America History and Perspectives*, Special Issue (2018): 99–106. See also Helen Zia, *Last Boat Out of Shanghai* (New York: Ballantine, 2020).

[8] Kimberly Yam, "FBI Director Defends Remarks that Chinese People in U.S. Pose Threats." *HuffPost*, last modified March 23, 2018, www.huffingtonpost.com/entry/fbi-christopher-wray-chinese-immigrants_us_5ab3d47fe4b008c9e5f51975.

[9] Christopher Wray, "A Chat with the Director of the FBI," July 18, 2018, The Aspen Institute, Aspen, CO, Video, 57:55, www.youtube.com/watch?v=NoFqNFxBECU. Wray later began using a disclaimer, which was repeated on the FBI website: "To be clear, the adversary is not the Chinese people or people of Chinese descent or heritage. The threat comes from the programs and policies pursued by an authoritarian government." FBI, "What We Investigate: The China Threat," www.fbi.gov/investigate/counterintelligence/the-china-threat.

In the ensuing months, Sino-American relations deteriorated further.[10] President Donald Trump opined to a gathering of his supporters that "almost every student that comes over" to the United States from China "is a spy."[11] China is said to rely on its numbers in the metaphor of "grains of sand": each individual, albeit an ordinary

---

[10] Leading "China hands" marked the end of "constructive engagement" with a call for "constructive vigilance." Larry Diamond and Orville Schell, *China's Influence & American Interests: Promoting Constructive Vigilance* (Palo Alto, CA: Hoover Institution Press, 2018). Other experts discussed the possibility of a new Cold War or an actual shooting war. Bob Davis and Lingling Wei, *Superpower Showdown: How the Battle between Trump and Xi Threatens a New Cold War* (New York: Harper Business, 2020); Graham Allison, *Destined for War: Can America and China Escape Thucydides's Trap?* (New York: Mariner, 2018). See also Peter Navarro, *The Coming China Wars*, rev. ed. (Upper Saddle River, NJ: FT Press, 2008); Peter Navarro and Greg Autry, *Death by China: Confronting the Dragon – A Global Call to Action* (London: Pearson FT Press, 2011). The threat from China has become a popular subject, with dozens of titles appearing from academic to ideological. Among the most useful are Rush Doshi, *The Long Game: China's Grand Strategy to Displace American Order* (New York: Oxford University Press, 2021); Martin Jacques, *When China Rules the World: The Rise of the Middle Kingdom and the End of the Western* World, rev. ed. (New York: Penguin, 2012); Peter Martin, *China's Civilian Army: The Making of Wolf Warrior Diplomacy* (New York: Oxford University Press, 2021); Kishore Mahbubani, *Has China Won? The Chinese Challenge to American Primacy* (New York: Public Affairs, 2020). See also Dan Blumenthal, *The China Nightmare: The Grand Ambitions of a Decaying State* (Washington DC: AEI, 2020); Clive Hamilton and Mareike Ohlberg, *Hidden Hand: Exposing How the Chinese Communist Party Is Reshaping the World* (London: Oneworld Publications, 2020); Brian T. Kennedy, *Communist China's War Inside America* (New York: Encounter, 2020); Gordon G. Chang, *The Great U.S.–China Tech War* (New York: Encounter, 2021); Michael Pillsbury, *The Hundred-Year Marathon: China's Secret Strategy to Replace America as the Global Superpower* (New York: Henry Holt and Co., 2015); Josh Rogin, *Chaos Under Heaven: Trump, Xi, and the Battle for the Twenty-First Century* (New York: Mariner, 2021); Robert Spalding, *Stealth War: How China Took Over while America's Elite Slept* (New York: Portfolio, 2019); Michael Schuman, *Superpower Interrupted: The Chinese History of the World* (New York: Public Affairs, 2020); Jim Sciutto, *The Shadow War: Inside Russia's and China's Secret Operations to Defeat America* (New York: Harper, 2019). Those who formerly warned about Japan, Incorporated, have adapted their arguments to China. Clyde Prestowitz, *The World Turned Upside Down: America, China, and the Struggle for Global Leadership* (New Haven, CT: Yale University Press, 2021); compare Clyde V. Prestowitz, *Trading Places: How We Are Giving Our Future to Japan & How to Reclaim It* (New York: Basic, 2019).
  For background on espionage conducted against the United States, see Michael J. Sulick, *Spying in America: Espionage from the Revolutionary War to the Dawn of the Cold War* (Washington DC: Georgetown University Press, 2013); Michael J. Sulick, *American Spies: Espionage against the United States from the Cold War to the Present* (Washington DC: Georgetown University Press, 2021).
  A comprehensive survey is Center for Strategic & International Studies, "Survey of Chinese Espionage in the United States Since 2000," www.csis.org/programs/technology-policy-program/survey-chinese-linked-espionage-united-states-2000. See also Alexander Holt, "A Brief History of US–China Espionage Entanglements," *MIT Technology Review*, September 3, 2020, www.technologyreview.com/2020/09/03/1007609/trade-secrets-china-us-espionage-timeline/.

[11] Annie Karni, "Trump Rants behind Closed Doors with CEOs," *Politico*, August 8, 2018, www.politico.com/story/2018/08/08/trump-executive-dinner-bedminster-china-766609.

person without training, brings back a single grain of sand, from which the government can piece together a picture of the beach.[12]

In this chapter, three contemporary cases centering on Asian Americans are explained, against the background of exclusion, expulsion, and imprisonment. These incidents reveal that Asian Americans, despite being celebrated as "the model minority" for academic attainment and entrepreneurial success, are vulnerable to racial profiling as secret agents sent by Beijing or Tokyo, infiltrating universities and civic institutions.[13] Officials draw conclusions about Asian Americans on the basis of their race, ethnicity, or national origin, about their propensity to engage in wrongdoing or interpret their actions differently than they would if individuals of other lineage displayed identical behavior. As described in detail below, Wen Ho Lee, Sherry Chen, and Xiaoxing Xi, all ethnic Chinese who naturalized to become citizens of the United States, exemplify the experience of Asian Americans. Accused of being spies, Asian Americans as a community are placed under scrutiny. Lee, Chen, and Xi all were victims. They have fought back.

HISTORY: FROM EXCLUSION TO INTERNMENT

The position of Asian Americans is still framed by their early rejection that followed upon exploitative recruitment by agents who made lavish promises about their financial prospects in the new world.[14] Once they finished their work, they were formally excluded. Chinese laborers, the most famous of whom were the more than 10,000 men in strict crews who built the western half of the transcontinental railroad, were viewed as a racial group to be an economic enemy.[15] The Golden

---

[12] The "grains of sand" thesis came to public attention with the Wen Ho Lee case. See Vernon Loeb and Walter Pincus, "China Prefers the Sand to the Moles," *Washington Post*, December 12, 1999: A2. The "grains of sand" concept has persisted, but it has been discredited by counterintelligence analysts. Peter Mattis and Matthew Brazil, *Chinese Communist Espionage: An Intelligence Primer* (Annapolis, MD: Naval Institute Press, 2019). See also Mike German, *Disrupt, Discredit, and Divide: How the New FBI Damages Democracy* (New York: New Press, 2019).

[13] The "model minority myth" is the other dominant theme in Asian American experiences. Madeline Y. Hsu, *The Good Immigrants: How the Yellow Peril Became the Minority* (New York: Oxford University Press, 2015); Ellen D. Wu, *The Color of Success: Asian Americans and the Origins of the Model Minority* (Princeton University Press, 2015). See also Rosalind S. Chou and Joe R. Feagin, *The Myth of the Model Minority: Asian Americans Facing Racism* (Boulder, CO: Paradigm Publishers, 2008).

[14] Iris Chang. *The Chinese in America: A Narrative History.* (New York, 2004: Penguin), 53–64.

[15] The leading works that include the Chinese contribution are by Gordon Chang and the Stanford Railroad Workers Project. A mass market publication, Gordon H. Chang, *Ghosts of Gold Mountain: The Epic Story of the Chinese Who Built the Transcontinental Railroad* (New York: Houghton Mifflin, 2019); more academic background is compiled in Gordon H. Chang and Shelley Fisher Fishkin, *The Chinese and the Iron Road: Building the Transcontinental Railroad* (Palo Alto, CA: Stanford University Press, 2019). Other leading accounts omit the Chinese for the most part. See, e.g., Stephen E. Ambrose, *Nothing Like It in the World: The Men Who Built the Transcontinental Railroad, 1863–1869* (New York: Simon & Schuster,

Spike was driven at Promontory Point, Utah in 1869, realizing the "Manifest Destiny" of bringing together the continent, at a ceremony from which almost all the Chinese workers were absent and after which they were no longer welcomed. They soon thereafter were targeted according to their race, as ethnicity would have been defined at the time, not their citizenship; their adversaries themselves often were white foreign nationals, such as the Irish who were coming throughout the same time period, most famous among them Denis Kearney, of County Cork.[16] Save for the Alien and Sedition Acts of 1798, which were limited in scope, the Chinese Exclusion Act of 1882 was the original federal regulation of the borders.[17] The act by its own terms relied on an ethnic category: Chinese, but not Irish or any other, laborers were to be kept out. As Representative Henry Naphen declared, "In other cases, we admit the people and exclude the individual. In the Chinese case, we admit the individuals and exclude the people."[18] That discrepancy generated the rhetorical question of Justice David Josiah Brewer's dissent in the *Fong Yue Ting* case, considering the amended version of the Exclusion Act and the constitutionality of deportation: "It is true this statute is directed only against the obnoxious Chinese, but, if the power exists, who shall say it will not be exercised tomorrow against other classes and other people?"[19]

Beyond the law, the Chinese were driven out forcibly.[20] Numerous frontier towns of the West had Chinese quarters. In rough territories, majority Chinese settlements flourished briefly. In places such as Rock Springs, Wyoming in 1885, and Los Angeles in 1871, white mobs instigated lynching, looting, and violence to expel their Asians in totality, killing at least twenty-eight in the former and seventeen in the latter. The perpetrators were not brought to justice.

Even if Chinese had migrated legally – and at the time, "illegal immigrant" did not carry its modern connotations – they were not allowed to naturalize. Under the governing statute, persons who pursued citizenship had to demonstrate that they were "free white persons" (or of "African nativity or descent"). In a pair of cases

---

2001), 150–153, 243. See also Alexander Saxton, *The Indispensable Enemy: Labor and the Anti-Chinese Movement in California* (Berkeley, CA: University of California Press, 1975).

[16] Timothy J. Meagher, *The Columbia Guide to Irish American History* (New York: Columbia University Press, 2005), 272–273.

[17] Hiroshi Motomura, *Americans in Waiting: The Lost Story of Immigration and Citizenship* (New York: Oxford University Press, 2007); Lucy Salyer, *Laws Harsh as Tigers: Chinese Immigrants and the Shaping of Modern Immigration Law* (Chapel Hill, NC: University of North Carolina Press, 1995); Bill Ong Hing *Making and Remaking Asian America through Immigration Policy, 1850–1990* (Palo Alto, CA: Stanford University Press, 1994). A useful reference work is Martin B. Gold, *Forbidden Citizens: Chinese Exclusion and the U.S. Congress, A Legislative History* (Alexandria, VA: TheCapitol.net, 2012).

[18] 35 Congressional Record 3695 (1902).

[19] *Fong Yue Ting v. United States*, 149 US 698, 743 (1893) (Brewer, J., dissenting).

[20] Beth Lew-Williams, *The Chinese Must Go: Violence, Exclusion, and the Making of the Alien in America* (Cambridge, MA: Harvard University Press, 2018); Jean Pfaelzer, *Driven Out: The Forgotten War against Chinese Americans* (Berkeley, CA: University of California Press, 2008).

decided in 1922 and 1923, the Supreme Court ruled that a Japanese and a South Asian were not, respectively, literally white nor scientifically Caucasian, and, that being so, could be refused equality under federal law.[21] As the Chinese Exclusion Act was expanded into an Asiatic Barred Zone, the first generation, the Asian immigrants, acquired the designation of "aliens ineligible to citizenship." The federal government opposed the recognition of birthright citizenship for the second generation, the few Chinese born on American soil (numbers being constrained due to the gender ratio of as many as one hundred Chinese men to one Chinese woman, thanks to exclusion and the blanket characterization of Chinese females as "lewd," meaning prostitutes).[22] Their briefs presented the argument that American citizenship would be degraded if it encompassed the Chinese. The argument was presented through a rhetorical question:

> Are Chinese children born in this country to share with the descendants of the patriots of the American Revolution the exalted qualification of being eligible to the Presidency of the nation, conferred by the Constitution in recognition of the importance dignity of citizenship by birth? If so, then verily there has been a most degenerate departure from the patriotic ideals of our forefathers; and surely in that case American citizenship is not worth having.[23]

The Supreme Court, however, held that the Fourteenth Amendment guaranteed the status.[24]

Even the scholarly studies of Chinese Americans that were generally friendly promoted the so-called "sojourner" thesis. In *Bitter Strength*, Gunther Barth suggested that Chinese immigrants were dissimilar from European peers, because they lacked the desire to join the democratic experiment.[25] By this standard, Chinese brought upon themselves abuse. Beyond the group, rather than individual, assessment of Chinese, this explanation is dubious. It is counterfactual, at least as to many of the persons, such as those who litigated the Supreme Court cases in an effort to establish themselves as stakeholders. Those campaigns were organized by community associations, who retained renowned (white) attorneys, contrary to the stereotype of submissive Asians. While some Chinese (and other Asians) did not persevere,

---

[21] The *Ozawa* and *Thind* cases are reproduced and analyzed in Ian Haney Lopez, *White by Law: The Legal Construction of Race* (New York University Press, 1996).

[22] *Chy Lung v. Freeman*, 92 US 275 (1876).

[23] The Brief on Behalf of Appellant, the government, is reproduced in full in Philip B. Kurland and Gerhard Casper, *Landmark Briefs of the Supreme Court of the United States: Constitutional Law*, vol. 14 (Arlington, VA: University Publications of America, 1975). The quoted passage, p. 34 of the brief itself, appears at p. 37. The document also is available at http://libraryweb.uchastings.edu/library/research/special-collections/wong-kim-ark/case.htm.

[24] *United States v. Wong Kim Ark*, 169 US 649 (1898).

[25] Gunter Barth, *Bitter Strength: A History of the Chinese in the United States, 1850-1870* (Cambridge, MA: Harvard University Press 1964). The concept was introduced more sympathetically in Paul C. P. Siu, *The Chinese Laundryman: A Study of Social Isolation*, ed. John Kuo Wei Tchen (New York University Press, 1988).

it is likewise true that many Europeans preferred "return migration."[26] Like Asians, Europeans who perceived of themselves as expatriates or exiles participated in "homeland" politics including global movements such as communism and anarchism. Perhaps the most troubling aspect of the identification of Asians as transient is the reversal of cause and effect. Instead of the proposition that Asians encountered prejudice because they probably would leave in any event, it may be that they departed due to the bias. They had a credible fear of being ejected.

Once official control of the Chinese population became the norm. Constant surveillance became an integral tactic. The Exclusion Act was expanded to the policing of Chinese whose status was defined by their race. In San Francisco, the most Chinese city within America, they were confined to a hypersegregated Chinatown with the risk of assault if they strayed beyond its boundaries.[27] Even those Chinese who were permitted to remain were required to carry papers at all times. Under the Geary Act, failure to show a resident permit was punishable by deportation or hard labor, the procedures were summary in nature without the protections of criminal due process, and Chinese testimony was inadmissible without Caucasian corroboration.[28] Cross-examination by an immigration officer

---

[26] Mark Wyman. *Round-Trip to America: The Immigrants Return to Europe, 1880–1930* (Ithaca, NY: Cornell University Press, 1993). See also Charlotte Brooks, *American Exodus: Second-Generation Chinese Americans in China, 1901–1949* (Berkeley, CA: University of California Press, 2019). A diaspora framing rather than immigrant framing is increasingly common. A synthesis is Wang Gungwu, *The Chinese Overseas: From Earthbound China to the Quest for Autonomy*, rev. ed. (Cambridge, MA: Harvard University Press, 2002). See Hong Liu (ed.), *The Chinese Overseas*, vols. 1–4 (London: Routledge, 2006); Lynn Pan (ed.), *The Encyclopedia of the Chinese Overseas* (Cambridge, MA: Harvard University Press, 1999); Chee-Beng Tan (ed.), *Routledge Handbook of the Chinese Diaspora* (London: Routledge, 2018); Ling-Chi Wang, *The Chinese Diaspora: Selected Essays*, vols. 1 and 2 (Singapore: Marshall Cavendish, 1998); Min Zhou (ed.), *Contemporary Chinese Diaspora* (Basingstoke, UK: Palgrave, 2017). See also Shelly Chan, *Diaspora's Homeland: Modern China in the Age of Global Migration* (Durham, NC: Duke University Press); Laurence J. C. Ma, *The Chinese Diaspora: Space, Place, Mobility, and Identity* (Lanham, MD: Rowman & Littlefield, 2002); Elizabeth Sinn (ed.), *The Last Century of the Chinese Overseas* (Hong Kong University Press, 1998). Multiple studies analyze the contemporary flow of transnational persons from China to the United States. See Vanessa L. Fong, *Paradise Redefined: Transnational Chinese Students and the Quest for Flexible Citizenship in the Developed World* (Palo Alto, CA: Stanford University Press, 2011); Robert Guest, *Borderless Economics: Chinese Sea Turtles, Indian Fridges, and the New Fruits of Global Capitalism* (New York: St. Martin's Press/Griffin, 2013); AnnaLee Saxenian, *The New Argonauts: Regional Advantage in a Global Economy* (Cambridge, MA: Harvard University Press, 2007). See also "Plight of the Sea Turtles," *Economist*, July 6, 2013, www.economist.com/china/2013/07/06/plight-of-the-sea-turtles. A self-published book considers specifically whether Chinese diaspora will act as agents of Beijing. Olivier Brault, *The Chinese Diaspora: China's Instrument of Power?* (Maxwell Air Force Base, AL: BiblioScholar, 2012).

[27] Charlotte Brooks. *Alien Neighbors, Foreign Friends: Asian Americans, Housing, and the Transformation of Urban California* (University of Chicago Press, 2009), 11.

[28] Geary Act of 1892, Public Law 52-60. The Act was upheld by the United States Supreme Court in *Fong Yue Ting v. United States*, 149 US 698 (1893).

became a Chinese American ritual.[29] They sought to catch specifically the Chinese cheats who were evading the racial mandate to stay out when they otherwise were lax about who was coming and going.

Photography, still a new technology, was crucial to policing the border. The images of Chinese at Angel Island, a detention center emphatically not the equivalent of Ellis Island to its east, were a means of enforcing exclusion.[30]

Asians in general were monitored in many other respects. They lived under restrictions on intermarriage, land ownership, and professional licensure.[31] These all made conspicuous racial distinctions, albeit when "separate but equal" was the Constitutional doctrine and in advance of enactment of civil rights legislation; African Americans, despite emancipation, were oppressed in virtually every aspect of public life. In *Plessy v. Ferguson*, which upheld Jim Crow Black Codes, the lone dissenter was Justice John Marshall Harlan, provoked in part by his anathema for the Chinese: he remarked in *dicta* that it was illogical to discriminate against African Americans but not Asians in railroad accommodations because Asians could be banned outright – and he was convinced, properly so – by the body politic.[32] But the Supreme Court had protected Asians against racially disparate application of neutral ordinances, in a landmark case about Chinese laundries in San Francisco, which had been denied permits, in comparison to white-owned rivals.[33]

After World War II, when Chinese Americans enjoyed more favor due to China and the United States having been allies, surveillance did not abate. Chinese Americans were caught up in the "confession" program.[34] Combating communism, law enforcement officials proposed to trade information from Chinese Americans

---

[29] Estelle L. Lau, *Paper Families: Identity, Immigration Administration, and Chinese Exclusion* (Durham, NC: Duke University Press, 2006); Erika Lee, *At America's Gates: Chinese Immigration During the Exclusion Era, 1882–1943* (Chapel Hill, NC: University of North Carolina Press 2003).

[30] Anna Pegler-Gordon, *In Sight of America: Photography and the Development of U.S. Immigration Policy* (Berkeley, CA: University of California Press, 2009).

[31] Regarding antimiscegenation, see Hrishi Karthikeyan and Gabriel J. Chin, "Preserving Racial Identity: Population Patterns and the Application of Anti-Miscegenation Statutes to Asian Americans, 1910–1950," *Asian American Law Journal* 9 (2002): 1–40. Regarding Alien Land Laws, see Keith Aoki, "No Right to Own? The Early Twentieth-Century 'Alien Land Laws' as a Prelude to Internment," *Boston College Third World Law Journal* 19, no. 1 (1998): 37–72.

Regarding professional licensure, see *Takahashi v. Fish & Game Commission*, 334 US 410 (1948).

[32] *Plessy v. Ferguson*, 163 US 537, 561 (1896) (Harlan, J., dissenting). The comparison of Justice Harlan's opinion in *Plessy* with his opinions in cases involving Chinese, and the analysis of the editing of Harlan's dissent, should be credited to Jack Chin. Gabriel J. Chin, "The Plessy Myth: Justice Harlan and the Chinese Cases," *Iowa Law Review* 82 no. 1 (1996): 151–182.

[33] *Yick Wo v. Hopkins*, 118 US 356 (1886).

[34] Mae M. Ngai, *Impossible Subjects: Illegal Aliens and the Making of Modern America* (Princeton University Press, 2004), 218–222; Him Mark Lai. 1993. "Unfinished Business: The Confession Program," in Robert A. Fung, *The Repeal and its Legacy: Proceedings of the Conference on the 50th Anniversary of the Repeal of the Exclusion Acts* (Chinese Historical Society of America and San Francisco State University, 1994), 47–56.

for adjustment of their citizenship status. Their methods had unintended consequences, along the lines of a self-fulfilling prophecy, producing the problem they anticipated. The prime example is the persecution of Tsien Hsue-Shen, a Chinese immigrant and United States Army officer who was a key participant in the Manhattan Project which developed atomic weapons during World War II. The unfounded allegation he was a Chinese communist culminated in his arrest and detention for five years.[35] He eventually was deported, in exchange for American POWs from the Korean War, whereupon he became the mastermind behind the Chinese counterparts in nuclear missiles. He came to be celebrated as the "father of Chinese rocketry." In his obituary, a former Naval Secretary said, "it was the stupidest thing this country ever did ... he was no more a Communist than I was, and we forced him to go."[36]

Japanese Americans fared barely any better.[37] They came shortly after the Chinese. Their striving to set themselves apart from the Chinese proved futile. They, too, were excluded, almost one generation before World War II.[38] The misfortune that befell Japanese Americans foreshadows all the more clearly the current persecution of Asian Americans. It set the pattern that Asians would be mistrusted as treacherous, because of their identity. They were, by a racial reckoning, naturally on the side of the enemy, because they shared the bloodline of the enemy. That would render them not even traitors in a technical sense, as they had not been real Americans in the first place.

In the wake of the Japanese sneak attack on military installations at Pearl Harbor, Hawaii, on December 7, 1941, President Franklin Delano Roosevelt ordered, with Congressional ratification, the mass imprisonment of Japanese Americans.[39] The

---

[35] Iris Chang, *Thread of the Silkworm* (New York: Basic Books, 1993). Another case is described in David Armstrong, Annie Waldman, and Daniel Golden, "The Trump Administration Drove Him Back to China, Where He Invented a Fast Coronavirus Test," *Pro Publica*, March 18, 2020, www.propublica.org/article/the-trump-administration-drove-him-back-to-china-where-he-invented-a-fast-coronavirus-test.

[36] Claire Noland, "Qian Zeusen Dies at 98; Rocket Scientist Helped Establish Jet Propulsion Laboratory," *Los Angeles Times*, September 16, 2014, www.latimes.com/nation/la-me-qian-xuesen1-2009nov01-story.html.

[37] Yuji Ichioka, *The Issei: The World of the First Generation Japanese Immigrants* (New York: Free Press, 1990). An early reference work is Frank F. Chuman, *The Bamboo People: The Law and Japanese-Americans* (Del Mar, CA: Publisher's Inc. 1976).

[38] Roger Daniels, *The Politics of Prejudice: The Anti-Japanese Movement in California and the Struggle of Japanese Exclusion* (New York City: Atheneum, 1962); Lon Kurashige. *Two Faces of Exclusion: The Untold History of Anti-Asian Racism in the United States* (Chapel Hill, NC: University of North Carolina Press, 2016); Michi Nishiura Weglyn, *Years of Infamy: The Untold Story of America's Concentration Camps*, updated ed. (Seattle, WA: University of Washington, 1996).

[39] See generally Roger Daniels, *Prisoners without Trial: Japanese Americans in World War II*, rev. ed. (New York: Hill & Wang, 2004); Roger Daniels, *Concentration Camps: North America Japanese in the United States and Canada During World War II* (Malabar, FL: Krieger Pub. Co., 1981); Greg Robinson, *A Tragedy of Democracy: Japanese Confinement in North America* (New York: Columbia University Press, 2009); Eric Y. Yamamoto et al., *Race, Rights &*

"Day of Infamy" ended American neutrality, ushering it into a two-front conflict against the Axis Powers of Imperial Japan across the Pacific, and Nazi Germany and Fascist Italy across the Atlantic. The calls for incarceration were immediate. Rumors spread, wholly false, that the Japanese pilots bombing the American ships had been guided by Japanese Americans who had grown crops to point the way, and so on.[40] Lieutenant General John L. DeWitt, commander of the Western Defense, stated bluntly, "In the war in which we are now engaged racial affinities are not severed by migration. The Japanese race is an enemy race and while many second and third generation Japanese born on United States soil, possessed of United States citizenship have become 'Americanized' the racial strains are undiluted . . . ."[41] Apparent assimilation was ridiculed by the mayor of Los Angeles as a trick, akin to the Japanese diplomats negotiating, even as their navy was sailing. The idea was floated by Congressman John Dingell of a "reprisal reserve," also taken up by popular columnist Westbrook Pegler as a place to hold hostage Japanese Americans, alongside Germans and Italians who were "subversive," to be executed at a 100 to 1 ratio if American prisoners of war were killed.[42]

The internment was ostensibly justified by military necessity. The argument is belied by the hostility toward Japanese Americans, which was rampant before the American entry into World War II. The hatred was well attested to, brazen rather than covert; the label is a product of neither hindsight nor interpretation. Japanese Americans had achieved surprising success in agriculture, inciting white farmers to complain they could not match Japanese Americans who toiled too hard, employed foreign techniques, and were willing to plant acreage that others deemed too difficult. Mainstream politicians ran for office on the platform of rooting out Japanese Americans.[43] Organizations such as the Native Sons of the Golden West were as averse to Japanese Americans as they had been to Chinese Americans, and Japanese Americans, with intact families, were even more dangerous because of the growing *nisei* (second generation) possessed of birthright citizenship. The Native Sons, for example, filed suit to have even Japanese Americans who were bona fide citizens stricken from voter rolls in San Francisco.[44]

Reparation: Law and the Japanese American Internment, 2nd ed. (New York: Aspen Publishers, 2013). Regarding the war years in general, see David M. Kennedy, *The American People in World War II* (New York: Oxford University Press, 2003).

[40] Daniels, *Concentration Camps*, 33.
[41] Ibid., 61; see also Commission on Wartime Relocation and Internment of Civilians (CWRIC), *Personal Justice Denied: Report of the Commission on Wartime Relocation and Internment of Civilians* (Washington DC: Civil Liberties Public Education Fund, 1997), 65–66.
[42] Daniels, *Concentration Camps*, 27–28, 33.
[43] Daniels *The Politics of Prejudice*. Even Earl Warren, then Attorney General of California, endorsed the internment. Robinson, *A Tragedy of Democracy*, 81.
[44] *Regan v. King*, 134 F.2d 413 (9th Cir. 1943).

Archival research has confirmed that government officials were aware at the time, based on surveillance preceding Pearl Harbor, that Japanese Americans in the aggregate did not constitute a significant threat of "fifth column" exploits.[45] An amateur agent sent into the field by the White House had reported back to that effect, as had a professional counterintelligence officer who published an anonymous magazine article to highlight his findings (the exceptions, they maintained, were *kibei*, Japanese Americans who as children had been sent to Japan for education).[46] Department of Justice lawyers made midnight hour edits to their legal briefs to avoid alerting Supreme Court Justices to their own misgivings about the allegations that had been made by General DeWitt. Consistent with his evocation of a racial war, he had summed up, "a Jap's a Jap, and that's all there is to it."[47] He had added that it was impossible in practical terms to separate the "sheep" from the "goats," oriental psychology being inscrutable to occidental analysis.[48] His Final Report stated, "It was impossible to establish the identity of the loyal and the disloyal with any degree of safety. It was not that there was insufficient time in which to make such a determination . . . ."[49] Interrogation would be futile.

Hence approximately 120,000 individuals, two-thirds of them native-born US citizens, men, women, children, and the elderly alike – including veterans of the US Army who had fought in what had been called "the Great War" (World War I) – were sent to assembly centers, and then "internment" camps, without individual charges. The violation of civil rights extended beyond violation of equal protection to deprivation of due process. Japanese American citizens were renamed "non-aliens." The Japanese Americans who at the outset were apprehended had been under ongoing surveillance, because they were leaders, reputed to have contact with Japanese nationals, served as martial arts instructors, had language skills, and so on. Their names had been placed on a watchlist. (Alaskan natives in the same manner were rounded up, and a handful of German and Italian foreign nationals as well.) They were told that they were in protective custody though the soldiers pointed the guns at them. The canard was circulated that they, outrageously, were being coddled while everyone else was enduring wartime deprivation, prompting First

---

[45] Peter Irons, *Justice at War: The Story of the Japanese-American Internment Cases* (Berkeley, CA: University of California Press 1983).
[46] CWRIC, *Personal Justice Denied*, 51–60. The amateur operative was Curtis B. Munson. His work is described in Weglyn, *Years of Infamy*, 34–46. His full report is available at www.michiweglyn.com/wp-content/uploads/2010/06/Munson-Report.pdf. Kenneth D. Ringle, who attained the rank of rear admiral, wrote the anonymous report. An Intelligence Officer, "The Japanese in America: The Problem and the Solution," *Harper's Magazine*, October 1942, 489–497. His full report is available at www.history.navy.mil/research/library/online-reading-room/title-list-alphabetically/r/ringle-report-on-japanese-internment.html.
[47] Irons, *Justice at War*, 193.
[48] John L. DeWitt, *Final Report: Japanese Evacuation from the West Coast, 1942* (Washington DC: US Gov't Printing. Office, 1943), 9.
[49] Ibid.

Lady Eleanor Roosevelt to visit an internment camp, and, based on her own observation, to make rebuttals in speeches and magazine articles.[50]

In a trilogy of cases, the Supreme Court upheld the internment without directly addressing its crux, the constitutionality of the indefinite detention.[51] In the most cited of the decisions, test litigation initiated by Fred Korematsu, Justice Hugo Black, writing for the majority, asserted, "Korematsu was not excluded from the Military Area because of hostility to him or his race. He was excluded because we are at war with the Japanese Empire . . . ."[52] The reasoning is self-contradictory. Only race related him as an individual to the Japanese Empire. Without referencing race as a nexus, it would be impossible to affiliate Korematsu or any other Japanese American for that matter to the Japanese Empire.

A less familiar companion case, concerning Mitsuye Endo, was decided simultaneously and as officials were preparing to close the internment camps anyway.[53] There, the government conceding that the petitioner for *habeas corpus* was in fact a loyal citizen, the justices said there was no justification for continuing to hold captive persons who, it was stipulated, had done no wrong.

The internment camps themselves were sites of comprehensive surveillance.[54] The Japanese Americans became the subjects of a massive sociological study. The inquiry itself, which produced two volumes on the effects of the internment, itself was controversial for data collection ethics.[55] "Troublemakers" were segregated out to the Tule Lake facility. Its security measures encompassed the widespread use of informants.[56] Japanese Americans also were extensively photographed, in an effort to

---

[50] Timothy Turner, "First Lady Here to Visit Hospitals," *Los Angeles Times*, April 27, 1943, 1. See also Eleanor Roosevelt, "A Challenge to American Sportsmanship," *Collier's*, October 16, 1943, 21, 71. Her manuscript on the subject is reprinted in Jeffrey Burton et al., *Confinement and Ethnicity: An Overview of World War II Japanese American Relocation Sites* (Seattle: University of Washington Press, 2002), 19–24, www.digitalhistory.uh.edu/active_learning/explorations/jap anese_internment/confinement_ethnicity_nps_sm.pdf.

[51] The cases were *Hirabayashi v. United States*, 320 US 81 (1943); *Yasui v. United States*, 320 US 115 (1943); and *Korematsu v. United States*, 323 US 215 (1944). A useful resource is Peter Irons, *Justice Delayed: The Record of the Japanese American Internment Cases* (Middletown, CT: Wesleyan University Press, 1989).

[52] *Korematsu*, 323 US 223.

[53] *Ex parte Endo*, 323 US 283 (1944).

[54] John Tateishi, *And Justice for All: An Oral History of the Japanese Detention Camps* (New York: Random House, 1984). See also Richard Drinnon, *Keeper of Concentration Camps: Dillon S. Myer and American Racism* (Berkeley, CA: University of California Press, 1989).

[55] Dorothy S. Thomas and Richard Nishimoto, *The Spoilage* (Berkeley: University of California Press, 1969 [1946]); Dorothy S. Thomas, *The Salvage* (Berkeley: University of California Press, 1952). For criticism, Lane Ryo Hirabayashi, *The Politics of Fieldwork: Research in an American Concentration Camp* (Tucson: University of Arizona Press, 1999) Yuji Ichioka (ed.), *Views from Within: The Japanese American Evacuation and Resettlement Study* (Los Angeles, CA: UCLA Asian American Studies Center, 1989).

[56] Japanese American informants were called "inu," or "dog," Brian Masaru Hayashi, "Informants/'inu'," *Densho Encyclopedia*, http://encyclopedia.densho.org/Informants_/_%22inu%22.

present them as smiling and happy, as if headed to a summer camp rather than a prison camp.[57] But the public works artists who were responsible were solicitous toward them, and, consequently, they were hampered by what they could depict; for example, no gun towers, and Dorothea Lange's images of families and children pledging allegiance ended up being impounded and kept out of view for decades.[58]

Eventually the War Relocation Authority administered to Japanese Americans a loyalty questionnaire.[59] They had to answer whether they were willing to serve on combat duty wherever ordered and if they would forswear allegiance to the emperor of Japan and swear unqualified allegiance to the United States. As Japanese Americans were resettled, granted clearance, or upon closure of the internment camps, they had to commit themselves to shunning one another.[60] Their dispersal was planned to prevent formation of community. In the normalcy of peacetime, the ostracism of Japanese Americans did not relent. Some denied the existence of the internment camps or that they had entailed coercion.[61] Others wished to prohibit Japanese Americans from coming home, or declined to restore properties held for safekeeping.[62]

Both the Chinese and the Japanese, even if native born United States citizens, confronted the notion they were invaders. The Supreme Court said of the Chinese, upholding their exclusion:

> To preserve its independence, and give security against foreign aggression and encroachment, is the highest duty of every nation, and to attain these ends nearly all other considerations are to be subordinated. It matters not in what form such aggression and encroachment come, whether from the foreign nation acting in its

---

[57] Jasmine Alinder, *Moving Images: Photography and the Japanese American Incarceration* (Chicago, IL: University of Illinois, 2009), 12–19.

[58] Numerous volumes have been published, detailing censorship. See Richard Calhan and Michael Williams, *Un-American: The Incarceration of Japanese Americans During World War II* (Chicago, IL: CityFiles Press, 2016); Linda Gordon and Gary Y. Okihiro, *Impounded: Dorothea Lange and the Censored Images of Japanese American Internment* (New York: W. W. Norton & Co., 2008); Gerald Robinson, *Elusive Truth: Four Photographers at Manzanar* (Nevada City, CA: Carl Mautz Publications, 2002); Peter Wright, *Manzanar* (New York: Times Books, 1988).

[59] Cherstin Lyon, "Questions 27 and 28," *Densho Encyclopedia*, https://encyclopedia.densho.org/Questions%2027%20and%2028.

[60] Lane Ryo Hirabayashi, Hikaru Iwasaki (photographer), Kenichiro Shimada (contributor), *Japanese American Resettlement Through the Lens: Hikaru Carl Iwasaki and the WRA's Photographic Section, 1943–1945* (Boulder, CO: University of Colorado Press, 2009), 2–7.

[61] Myrna Oliver, "Lillian Baker; Denied Japanese Incarceration," *Los Angeles Times*, October 29, 1996; Michelle Malkin, *In Defense of Internment: The Case for 'Racial Profiling' in World War II and the War on Terror* (Washington DC: Regnery Press, 2004).

[62] See generally Brian Komei Dempster, *Making Home from War: Stories of Japanese American Exile and Resettlement* (Berkeley, CA: Heyday Books, 2010); Greg Robinson, *After Camp: Portraits in Midcentury Japanese American Life and Politics* (Berkeley, CA: University of California Press, 2012). Regarding terrorist acts against returnees, see Brian Niiya, "Terrorist Incidents against West Coast Returnees," *Densho Encyclopedia*, http://encyclopedia.densho.org/Terrorist_incidents_against_West_Coast_returnees.

national character, or from vast hordes of its people crowding in upon us ... The existence of war would render the necessity of the proceeding only more obvious and pressing. The same necessity, in a less pressing degree, may arise when war does not exist, and the same authority which adjudges the necessity in one case must also determine it in the other.[63]

Justice Black said of the need to lock up Japanese Americans: "the properly constituted military authorities feared an invasion of our West Coast and felt constrained to take proper security measures."[64] The recurring skepticism that Asian Americans are real Americans has been purportedly legitimated by a pseudoscientific rationale. From the beginning of the twentieth century to the end, authors who appointed themselves as champions of the white race have warned others about the Yellow Peril; they also were enthusiastic about eugenics, and their philosophy was admired by Adolf Hitler. Lothrop Stoddard, Madison Grant, and others predicted race war in titles such as *The Rising Tide of Color: The Threat Against White World-Supremacy* and *The Passing of the Great Race: Or, the Racial Basis of European History*.[65] Their thesis was that Asia possessed such sizable populations they would overwhelm America in an invasion, making Asian immigrants to America a manifestation of that menace. They urged that public officials pay attention to Asian Americans.

That treatment would not be positive, but oriented toward containing the threat. Asian Americans themselves are enlisted to police the community. In the internment camps, Japanese Americans were called upon to patrol among themselves. Law enforcement operations aimed at Asian American suspects use Asian American officers.[66] In ordinary social settings, Asian Americans meet the "perpetual foreigner" syndrome in the repeated question of "where are you *really* from," even if they have answered where they are from as they define themselves.[67] Their neighbors and co-workers yearn to know about an individual's racial genealogy, rejecting that person's self-identity. As late as 2021, even those selected to represent the United States in its diplomatic corps may have their careers adversely affected by decisions

---

[63] *The Chinese Exclusion Case*, 130 US 581, 606 (1889).
[64] *Korematsu*, 323 US 223.
[65] Lothrop Stoddard, *The Rising Tide of Color against White World Supremacy* (New York: Charles Scribner's & Sons, 1922); Madison Grant, *The Passing of the Great Race*, rev. ed. (New York: Charles Scribner's & Sons, 1918).
[66] Federal agent Alton Wong, for example, "of Chinese ancestry," rang the doorbell while "the other federal officers remained nearby out of sight" in a drug raid, in *Wong Sun v. United States*, 371 US 471 (1963).
[67] Donald Trump, for example, displayed this curiosity as to Korean Americans both as a candidate and as president. Asma Khalid, "South Korea? Trump's 'Where Are You From' Moment," *National Public Radio*, October 15, 2015, www.npr.org/sections/itsallpolitics/2015/10/15/448718726/south-korea-trumps-where-are-you-from-moment; Vivian Salama. "Trumps History of Breaking Decorum with Remarks on Race, Ethnicity," *NBC News*, January 12, 2018, www.nbcnews.com/news/us-news/trump-s-history-breaking-decorum-remarks-race-ethnicity-n837181.

to preclude their service in certain posts due to doubts about their loyalty.[68] Before he was elected to the Congress, Andy Kim, a native born US citizen of Korean immigrant parents, was spontaneously informed he could not work on anything related to Korea, without his having expressed any interest in doing so.[69] During the Covid-19 global pandemic, a spate of hate crimes affected Asian Americans, who were blamed for the disease on a group basis, irrespective of ancestry or citizenship.[70] The severity of the attacks, which included mass murder, prompted passage of historic federal legislation.[71]

CONTEMPORARY CASES: DOUBLE STANDARDS AND DROPPED CHARGES

During peacetime, surveillance of Asian Americans continued. In pre-9/11 innocence, the *New York Times* broke the news of what was alleged to be the worst breach of national security perpetrated to date.[72] A physicist named Wen Ho Lee, who had come from Taiwan, naturalizing as a citizen, was said to have transmitted the "crown jewels" of the nuclear arsenal to China, the plans for the W-88 warhead, the most sophisticated in the arsenal.[73] At the time, China had not begun its ascent as a global superpower; it had yet to be admitted to the World Trade Organization. Taiwan, controlled by the Kuomintang, was the enemy of mainland China, the People's Republic of China controlled by the Communist Party. President Bill Clinton was beset by claims of "Chinese influence" related to his 1996 re-election

[68] Lydia DePillis, "At the State Department, Diversity Can Count against You," *Washington Post*, September 24, 2013, www.washingtonpost.com/news/wonk/wp/2013/09/24/at-the-state-department-diversity-can-count-against-you. See also Nicole Gaouette, "Asian American Diplomats Say Discrimination Holds Them Back as US Competes with China," CNN, May 7, 2021, www.cnn.com/2021/05/07/politics/state-diversity-aapi-china/index.html.
[69] Ari Shapiro, "Congressman Andy Kim on the Discrimination He Says He Faced in the State Department," *National Public Radio*, March 23, 2021, www.npr.org/2021/03/23/980462569/congressman-andy-kim-on-the-discrimination-he-says-he-faced-in-the-state-departm.
[70] Ibid.
[71] Covid-19 Hate Crimes Act, Pub. Law. 117-13 (2021). Expert testimony about anti-Asian attacks was considered. Erika Lee, "Discrimination and Violence Against Asian Americans," Testimony to the United States House of Representatives Committee on the Judiciary, Subcommittee on Civil and Constitutional Rights, March 18, 2021, https://docs.house.gov/meetings/JU/JU10/20210318/111343/HHRG-117-JU10-Wstate-LeeE-20210318-U23.pdf.
[72] The original article breaking the story was a lengthy lead article, James Risen and James Gerth, "Breach at Los Alamos: A Special Report: China Stole Nuclear Secrets for Bombs, U.S. Aides Say," *New York Times*, March 6, 1999, A1. For an analysis of *The Times*'s role in the case, see Robert Scheer "No Defense: How the New York Times Convicted Wen Ho Lee," *The Nation*, October 5, 2000, 11–12.
[73] Wen Ho Lee, with Helen Zia, *My Country Versus Me: The First-Hand Account by the Los Alamos Scientist Who Was Falsely Accused of Being a Spy* (New York: Hachette Books, 2003). For a legal analysis of the internment and Wen Ho Lee, see Thomas W. Joo, "Presumed Disloyal: Executive Power, Judicial Deference, and the Construction of Race Before and After September 11," *Columbia Human Rights Law Review* 34, no. 1 (2002): 1–47.

bid.[74] His political opponents suggested in the Congressional "Cox" Report that campaign contributions were illicit, and they demanded that the government become tough on China.[75]

Lee was an improbable candidate for such serious malfeasance but for his race. He had spent his career at the Los Alamos National Laboratory in New Mexico. He belonged to X Division, which was responsible for designing bombs. His wife, who sometimes served as hostess for visiting Chinese nationals, routinely passed along information to both the FBI and CIA. Observers noted that Lee attended professional conferences, exchanging information. They mentioned in internal reports that he may have been "naive" about the "ruthlessness" of those with whom he interacted. Bowing to guests, handing out business cards, and being thanked in the Mandarin language were all taken as hints of his misdoing. Investigators hypothesized he may have been helping not China but Taiwan, or possibly Australia or Switzerland, before guessing he might be looking to improve his own employment opportunities. Anonymous sources speculated that Lee carried out treason for purposes only he was privy to. The case against him was built through eventual around-the-clock surveillance. The *Times* reported: "Agents conducted 1,000 interviews over nine months, scouring the globe for evidence that Dr. Lee had leaked his secrets. The Federal Bureau of Investigation carried out its largest computer forensic investigation ever. Investigators traced years of Dr. Lee's telephone calls."[76]

The relentless press, relying on leaks, stressed how detrimental the information from Lee could be, in the proverbial wrong hands. Once arrested, he was placed into solitary confinement, chained even during his exercise period, for the better part of a year. Then, suddenly, the claims collapsed. Lee acquiesced to a single felony count of mishandling classified data. In a post-mortem that took to task its own staff, the *Times* summarized: "After a meandering five-year investigation, Dr. Lee was incarcerated and interrogated, shackled and polygraphed, and all but threatened with execution by a federal agent for not admitting spying. But prosecutors were never able to connect him to espionage."[77]

---

[74] Frank H. Wu and Francey Lim Youngberg, "People from China Crossing the River: Asian American Political Empowerment and Foreign Influence," in Gordon H. Chang (ed.), *Asian Americans and Politics: Perspectives, Experiences, Prospects* (Palo Alto, CA: Stanford University Press, 2002), 311–354; see also Michael Chang, *Racial Politics in an Era of Transnational Citizenship* (New York: Lexington Books, 2004).

[75] The official "Cox Report" was the most influential source for claims that China presented a national security threat to the United States. Select Committee on US National Security and Military/Commercial Concerns with the People's Republic of China, 105th Congress, 2nd Session, Report 105-851, *U.S. National Security and Military/Commercial Concerns with the People's Republic of China* (Washington DC: US Government Printing Office, 1999).

[76] Matthew Purdy and James Sterngold, "The Prosecution Unravels: The Case of Wen Ho Lee," *New York Times*, February 5, 2001, A1. See also James Lilley, "Undoing the Damage of the Wen Ho Lee Case," *New York Times*, September 12, 2000, A27.

[77] Matthew Purdy, "The Making of a Suspect: The Case of Wen Ho Lee," *New York Times*, February 4, 2001, A1.

The lead investigator overseeing leaks from Los Alamos, defending his own competence, stated that Lee had become the primary suspect, to the exclusion of other leads, because of his ethnicity.[78] The prosecution had been "built on thin air."[79] Prosecutor Randy Bellows investigated the prosecution. He concluded Lee had not been a high priority national security threat; the FBI failed to supervise the investigation; and, finally, for three years they "investigated the wrong crime."[80]

Lee's is a rare case with a direct comparator that proceeded in parallel. CIA Director John Deutch had pled guilty to a single misdemeanor count to settle charges.[81] The juxtaposition of the two cases highlighted the discrepancy. As commentators noted, while prosecutors "threw the book" at Lee, the more sensitive files were the ones put in jeopardy by Deutch. Besides that, the difference between Lee and Deutch is racial; Deutch was white. On his last day in office, President Clinton pardoned Deutch.[82]

History repeated itself soon enough with Sherry Chen and Xiaoxing Xi. Each of them fell under suspicion. Each of them was charged with federal felonies. Each of them was exonerated in full. They had their lives ruined for no reason. They have not been given any account of why.

A naturalized citizen from China, Chen was an award-winning hydrologist.[83] Employed by the National Weather Service, her life's work was writing an innovative computer program to predict floods. In May 2012, she visited China to pay respects to her elderly parents. While there, she chatted with an acquaintance from college, a Chinese official in a similar line of work now, at the behest of a nephew whose father-in-law had some sort of business dispute with the man. When she returned to the American Midwest, a colleague reported her, erroneously and in a *non sequitur*, as being "a US citizen, but a Chinese national" trying to send information illicitly.[84]

---

[78] Vernon Loeb, "U.S. Accused of Using Race to Target China Spy Suspect," *Los Angeles Times*, August 17, 1999, 17.
[79] The declaration is reproduced at 146 *Congressional Record* H9880 (October 12, 1999).
[80] United States Department of Justice, *Final Report of the Attorney General's Review Team on the Handling of the Los Alamos National Security Laboratory Investigation* (Washington DC: United States Department of Justice, 2000), www.fas.org/irp/ops/ci/bellow/index.html.
[81] Robert Scheer, "Was Lee Indicted, and Not Deutch?" *Los Angeles Times*, February 8, 2000, www.latimes.com/archives/la-xpm-2000-feb-08-me-62172-story.html.
[82] Marc Lacey, "Clinton Issues Pardons, Clearing Deutch and McDougal, but not Milken or Hubbell," *New York Times*, January 21, 2001, www.nytimes.com/2001/01/21/politics/clinton-issues-pardons-clearing-deutch-and-mcdougal-but-not-milken.html.
[83] See Nicole Perlroth. "Cleared of Spying for China, She Still Doesn't Have Her Job Back," *New York Times*, May 17, 2018, B3; Nicole Perlroth, "Chinese-American Cleared of Spying Charges Now Faces Firing," *New York Times*, September 15, 2015, B3; Nicole Perlroth, 2015. "Accused of Spying for China, Until She Wasn't," *New York Times*, May 9, 2015, B1.
[84] Initial Decision in *Xiafen Chen v. Department of Commerce*, Docket Number Ch-0752-17-0028-I-1, April 23, 2018 (US Merit Systems Protection Board Central Regional Office). The full text of the opinion by Chief Administrative Judge Michele Szary Schroeder is available at www.sherrychendefensefund.org/uploads/9/9/2/8/99280080/chen_v_dept_of_commerce-ch-0752-17-0028-i-1-_initial_decision.pdf.

The Chinese official had asked Chen a few questions. She answered with a modicum of research. As a judge would find, "All of the items and information requested by Ms. Chen was public information." She made no attempt at subterfuge insofar as she told her superiors about the query. In an email to the foreign bureaucrat, she refused to provide any data that was secure: after referring her correspondent to public websites, she abstained from supplying anything not available by those means, stating:

> However, this database is only for government users and nongovernment users are not able to directly download any data from this site. I contacted some people I worked with at the COE regarding public information sources such as the total dam capacity, policies, procedures and guidelines for dam permit, regulation, financial aids etc. I was told that the Water Management Divisions at the Corps of Engineer (COE) could answer dam related questions.

Placed under surveillance, then interrogated without legal counsel, Chen was accused of divulging the details of American dams to Chinese officials. On the eve of her federal criminal trial, the prosecutors dropped all charges. Yet on the same meritless suspicions, her bosses terminated her from employment.

Another naturalized citizen from China, Xi was chair of the Physics Department of Temple University.[85] In May 2015, federal agents stormed his house in Philadelphia, guns drawn, to arrest him. He was charged not with espionage but with violating a nondisclosure agreement by disseminating the blueprints for equipment called a "pocket heater."

As in the Chen case, the government then dropped all charges against Xi. Multiple experts submitted sworn affidavits to help him. The government had mixed up the science. Xi had been discussing schematics for an altogether different device, one of his own invention. The blunder should have been obvious, but it was obscured by bias. As Xi's lawyer commented, "It's like comparing a microwave to a toaster ... They're completely different technologies but, well, they both warm food."[86]

Numerous other cases are on the court dockets. Chen and Xi form part of a pattern. Their plights are not isolated instances. Another example that garnered media coverage involved researchers at the Eli Lily pharmaceutical firm in the same time period.[87] They too were prosecuted, with charges dropped.

---

[85] Matt Apuzzo, "U.S. Drops Charges that Professor Shared Technology with China," *New York Times*, September 11, 2015, A1.
[86] Matt Apuzzo, "Former Espionage Suspect Sues, Accusing F.B.I. of Falsifying Evidence," *New York Times*, May 10, 2017, A11.
[87] Jeff Swiatek and Kristine Guerra, "Feds Dismiss Charges against former Eli Lilly Scientists Accused of Stealing Trade Secrets," *Indianapolis Star*, December 5, 2014, www.indystar.com/story/news/crime/2014/12/05/feds-dismiss-charges-former-eli-lilly-scientists-accused-stealing-trade-secrets/19959235.

A statistical study has confirmed that Asian Americans (or people with Asian surnames, used as the best proxy) were likely to be significantly overrepresented in the pool of defendants, with as many as a quarter of them turning out to be false positives.[88]

Other cases exhibit prosecutorial overreach. Climate change scientist Chunzai Wang, another naturalized citizen of Chinese descent, was charged with moonlighting – that is, undertaking extra employment.[89] While on the federal payroll, he had been a visiting scholar at Ocean University during his vacation periods, supervising academic projects in his field, earning US$700 per year for each of three years. Forced to accept a plea bargain in February 2018, he stood before a federal judge who imposed the sentence of time served, one night in jail, and invited to come back to the United States to visit family when he wished. The Honorable Cecilia Altonaga, based in Miami, said to him:

> My only regret ... is that I have to adjudicate Mr. Wang ... given the nature of Mr. Wang's contributions to an area that is at the forefront of our daily review of news, climate change, given the nature of the research he conducts and – and the information he supplies and how valuable it is to all of us, certainly he made certain mistakes here, but it's regrettable that it could not have been taken care of, I think, by some type of pretrial diversion so that he would not be an adjudicated felon.[90]

Among the cases showing the range of surveillance toward Asian Americans was one centered not on a Chinese American but a white American married to a Chinese American, who had visited his in-laws in China.[91] Like the Chinese Americans implicated falsely, with the same intensity of investigation even after espionage was no longer a contention, Keith Gartenlaub was suspected of violating the law for the sake of the Chinese. A data compromise in an aviation project had been uncovered. Gartenlaub ultimately was indicted, not for any charge remotely connected to espionage, but emanating from forensic examination of his computer disk drives,

---

[88] Andrew Kim, *Prosecuting Chinese "Spies": An Empirical Analysis of the Economic Espionage Act* (New York: Committee of 100, 2017). The full text is available at https://committee100.org/wp-content/uploads/2017/05/2017-Kim-White-Paper-online.pdf. See also Alex Nowrasteh, "How Much of a Threat Is Espionage from Chinese Immigrants?," *National Interest*, February 20, 2021, www.cato.org/commentary/how-much-threat-espionage-chinese-immigrants.
[89] John Pomfret, "America's New – and Senseless – Red Scare," *Washington Post*, March 8, 2018.
[90] Transcript of Change of Plea Hearing, *United States of America v. Chunzai Wang*, Case N. 17-CR-20449-CMA, February 20, 2018: 20-21 (S.D. Fla.). The text is available at www.committee100.org/wp-content/uploads/2018/03/USA-v-CHUNZAI-WANG-02-20-18-Original-Transcript.pdf.
[91] Ellen Nakashima, "How a Federal Spy Case Turned into a Child Porn Prosecution," *Washington Post*, April 5, 2016. See also Jeff Stein, "How a Chinese Spy Case Turned into One Man's Child Porn Nightmare," *Newsweek*, May 24, 2016, www.newsweek.com/2016/06/03/fbi-keith-gartenlaub-chinese-spy-porn-462830.html.

for possession of child pornography. The investigation took twenty-one months, and all his files were examined. Although the evidence substantiated his avowal, he had not accessed any of the images at issue, he was convicted by an Orange County federal jury in December 2015.

These cases are not coincidence but an outcome of selective surveillance, applying techniques that incorporate racial stereotyping at worst or are influenced by implicit bias at best. FBI Director Wray is not a renegade official. The federal government had a "kindred spirit" counterintelligence program.[92] Its training materials for its agents featured Asian antagonists.[93] Upon protest, the Justice Department pledged reform.[94] It disavowed racial profiling, adopting procedures for central review of criminal indictments. Echoing Justice Black's explanation for the internment, the assistant director of the Office of the National Manager for Counterintelligence stated:

> [C]ounterintelligence concern with respect to China is not driven by race or ethnicity of the students that are in the United States. Our counterintelligence concern is driven by the fact that China has a publicly stated policy goal of acquiring sensitive information and technology around the world, to include here in the United States, and that they seek [to] access and recruit global experts regardless of their nationality to meet their science and technology aims.[95]

The implicit claim is that even if the selective targeting is racial, it also is rational.[96] As one of the lead federal prosecutors explained, "The bottom line is that this is an effort by a rival nation state to steal U.S. technology. And that rival nation is made up almost exclusively of Han Chinese. And so, unfortunately, a lot of our targets are going to be Han Chinese. If it were the French government targeting U.S. technology, we'd be looking for Frenchmen."[97] By that logic, if a

---

[92] Walter Pincus, 1999. "U.S. Cracking Down on Chinese Designs on Nuclear Data," *Washington Post*, February 17, 1999, A7.

[93] A clip from the video was shown by Bill Whitaker, "Collateral Damage," *60 Minutes*, CBS, May 16, 2015. Video is available here www.cbsnews.com/video/collateral-damage/; a transcript, here www.cbsnews.com/news/collateral-damage-60-minutes-bill-whitaker.

[94] Matt Apuzzo, "After Missteps, U.S. Tightens Rules for Espionage Cases," *New York Times*, April 26, 2016, A1. The rules are contained in the United States Department of Justice, *United States Attorneys' Manual* (Washington DC: US Department of Justice, 1997; revised on an ongoing basis), www.justice.gov/usam/usam-9-90000-national-security.

[95] Elizabeth Redden, "Did Trump Call Most Chinese Students Spies?," *Inside Higher Ed*, August 9, 2018, www.insidehighered.com/news/2018/08/09/politico-reports-trump-called-most-chinese-students-us-spies.

[96] For a discussion of Bayesian statistics and racial discrimination, see Jody David Armour, *Negrophobia and Reasonable Racism: The Hidden Cost of Being Black in America* (New York University Press, 2000).

[97] See Jeffrey Mervis, "U.S. Prosecutor Leading China Probe Explains Effort That Led to Charges Against Harvard Chemist," *Science*, February 3, 2020, www.science.org/news/2020/02/us-prosecutor-leading-china-probe-explains-effort-led-charges-against-harvard-chemist. The

street gang were made up of members of a certain background and attempted to enlist others from the same segregated neighborhood, investigation of persons solely based on the common characteristic would be proper. The common fallacy in such circumstances is of "illicit conversion," which is switching the subject and the predicate of a proposition: such a claim would be rendered as "all of the wrongdoers are of background X, therefore all individuals of background X are wrongdoers," the incorrectness of which is apparent with the example of "all men are humans, therefore all humans are men." The scale of China distorts comprehension.[98] Prior to its role as the alleged origin of a deadly virus, many in the West likely had not heard of the city of Wuhan. In Chinese rankings, it is not among the most important urban areas. It has more than 11 million inhabitants, though, a population exceeding New York City, the most sizable American metropolis. The province of Guangdong is more than 100 million strong, compared with Germany at 80 million and France at 70 million. The same scale extends to visitors overseas. China sends 350,000 or more students to the United States per annum.[99] If 350 were spies running around up to no good, that would be a major problem. Yet 350 such malefactors would constitute one-tenth of 1 percent of the number of Chinese students, and one-hundredth of the number of individuals of Chinese descent in the nation. Even at 3,500 offenders, an order of magnitude greater (and much more than any credible estimate), they are scarcely representative of the total population. The generalization extrapolates from the individual wrongdoers to the group of Chinese, crossing the line from foreigners to citizens. It is possible for some to be guilty and others to be innocent, since of course they are different individuals. Moreover, Chinese foreign nationals and Chinese Americans belong to legally distinct categories who appropriately ought to be accorded different

---

same prosecutor indicated letters to universities about their professors were deliberately designed for the "in terrorem effect ... And that's good, because you want a little bit of ear out there to sensitive people to the magnitude of the problem." As another federal prosecutor alleged, China has appealed to "patriotic overseas Chinese," based on "hundreds of documents he said he has read," which in turn justified the American reaction. Teresa Watanabe, "Leading Chinese American Scholars Decry Racial Profiling from Trump's Hard-Line Policies Against China," *Los Angeles Times*, September 29, 2019, www.latimes.com/califor nia/story/2019-09-28/leading-chinese-american-scholars-decry-fallout-on-them-of-trumps-hard line-policies-against-china. The prosecutor later entered private practice as a criminal defense specialist, representing, among others, Sherry Chen.

[98] The classic fear of Yellow Peril, a term coined in German by Kaiser Wilhelm II, sprang from the sheer numbers of Chinese people. See John Kuo Wei Tchen and Dylan Yeats, *Yellow Peril!: An Archive of Anti-Asian Fear* (New York: Verso, 2014). See also Michael Keevak, *Becoming Yellow: A Short History of Racial Thinking* (Princeton University Press, 2011).

[99] See, e.g., Institute of International Education, "Number of International Students in the United States Hits All-Time High," November 18, 2019, www.iie.org/Why-IIE/ Announcements/2019/11/Number-of-International-Students-in-the-United-States-Hits-All-Time-High.

status as any other foreign nationals compared to US citizens would be. To the extent a generalization is to be relied upon, the one available study indicates that native-born Americans who are ethnically Chinese are less likely, not more likely, to be spies.[100]

In late 2018, the Justice Department announced it would ramp up enforcement efforts through "the China Initiative" even though collaborative research, including participation in talent recruitment programs, had been encouraged until shortly prior.[101] Trump administration officials such as Secretary of State Mike Pompeo were alarmed by the prospect that Chinese operatives were even, according to him, insinuating themselves into PTA meetings.[102] Contact with China essentially became criminalized.[103] Participation in Chinese talent recruitment programs, once

---

[100] Nowrasteh, "How Much of a Threat Is Espionage from Chinese Immigrants?"

[101] The announcement of the China Initiative was November 1, 2018, at the Department of Justice. Attorney General Jeff Sessions personally delivered remarks. They are memorialized as Jeff Sessions, Speech, "Attorney General Jeff Sessions Announces New Initiative to Combat Chinese Economic Espionage," Washington DC, November 1, 2018, www.justice.gov/opa/speech/attorney-general-jeff-sessions-announces-new-initiative-combat-chinese-economic-espionage. See also US Department of Justice, "Attorney General Jeff Sessions's China Initiative Fact Sheet," November 1, 2018, www.justice.gov/opa/speech/file/1107256/download. Initial media reports were laudatory. Ellen Nakashima, "With New Indictment, U.S. Launches Aggressive Campaign to Thwart China's Economic Attacks," *Washington Post*, November 1, 2018, www.washingtonpost.com/world/national-security/with-new-indictments-us-launches-aggressive-campaign-to-thwart-chinas-economic-attacks/2018/11/01/70dc5572-dd78-11e8-b732-3c72cbf131f2_story.html.

[102] Deirdre Shesgreen, "'Painted as Spies': Chinese Students, Scientists Say Trump Administration Has Made Life Hostile amid Battle against Covid-19," *USA Today*, August 23, 2020, www.usatoday.com/story/news/world/2020/08/23/donald-trump-china-coronavirus-scientists-grad-students/5525846002. There is widespread concern about the Chinese Communist Party engaging in "United Front" activities within the United States. See Bethany Allen-Ebrahimian, "The Chinese Communist Party Is Setting Up Cells at Universities Across America," *Foreign Policy*, April 18, 2018, https://foreignpolicy.com/2018/04/18/the-chinese-communist-party-is-setting-up-cells-at-universities-across-america-china-students-beijing-surveillance; Bethany Allen-Ebrahimian, "China Built an Army of Influence Agents in the U.S.," *Daily Beast*, July 18, 2018, www.thedailybeast.com/how-china-built-an-army-of-influence-agents-in-the-us. See also Alexander Bowe, "China's Overseas United Front Work: Background and Implications for the United States," U.S.–China Economic Security Review Commission Staff Research Report (Washington DC: US–China Economic and Security Review Commission, August 24, 2018), www.uscc.gov/sites/default/files/Research/China%27s%20Overseas%20United%20Front%20Work%20-%20Background%20and%20Implications%20for%20US_final_0.pdf. See also Anastasya Lloyd-Damnjanovic, *A Preliminary Study of PRC Political Influence and Interference Activities in American Higher Education* (Washington DC: Woodrow Wilson Center, 2018), www.wilsoncenter.org/sites/default/files/prc_political_influence_full_report.pdf. For historical background, see Anne-Marie Brady, *Making the Foreign Serve China: Managing Foreigners in the People's Republic* (Lanham, MD: Rowman & Littlefield, 2003).

[103] Margaret K. Lewis, "Criminalizing China," *Journal of Criminal Law and Criminology* 111, no. 1 (2020): 145–225. See also Margaret K. Lewis, "Time to End the U.S. Justice Department's China Initiative," *Foreign Policy*, July 22, 2021, https://foreignpolicy.com/2021/07/22/china-initiative-espionage-mistrial-hu.

lauded, became a mark of corruption.[104] By 2020, more than a thousand investigations were underway.[105]

AFTERMATH: REGRETS, APOLOGIES, A GROSS MISCARRIAGE OF JUSTICE, AND THE REVELATION OF RACIAL PROFILING

Thus, Asian Americans have attracted law enforcement activity. The interest in Asian Americans is more than abstract possibility. They have been prosecuted though innocent, "collateral damage" in trade war and escalating conflict between the United States and China.[106] They have fallen under suspicion because of the color of their skin, the texture of their hair, and the shape of their eyes. Or their travel to and dealings with China have been considered clues and signs of perfidy and villainy. The media has been similarly skeptical about Asian Americans. When the late California State Treasurer Matt Fong, a native-born Chinese American and Air Force Academy graduate, ran for the United States Senate in 1998, securing the Republican nomination, journalists asked the US military veteran, a political conservative, which side he would fight on if war broke out with China.[107] Among the hardliners in the Trump administration, lawyer Nathan Charles pressed for prosecution of China Initiative cases under the Espionage Act of 1917, arguing the professors were nothing less than agents of Beijing: "It's the Chinese Communist Party that has set the research goals and priorities of the universities. The goal is to advance the interests of the Chinese Communist Party. Period." (Press accounts indicate he was overruled.)[108]

[104] Lewis, "Criminalizing China." See also Lewis, "Time to End the U.S. Justice Department's China Initiative." A Senate report on Chinese talent recruitment programs summarized the prevailing opinion: "This report exposes how American taxpayer funded research has contributed to China's global rise over the last 20 years. During that time, China openly recruited U.S.-based researchers, scientists, and experts in the public and private sector to provide China with knowledge and intellectual capital in exchange for monetary gain and other benefits. At the same time, the federal government's grant-making agencies did little to prevent this from happening, nor did the FBI and other federal agencies develop a coordinated response to mitigate the threat. These failures continue to undermine the integrity of the American research enterprise and endanger our national security." Staff Report, Permanent Subcommittee on Investigations, Committee on Homeland Security and Governmental Affairs, "Threats to the U.S. Research Enterprise: China's Talent Recruitment Plans," November 19, 2019, www.hsgac.senate.gov/imo/media/doc/2019-11-18%20PSI%20Staff%20Report%20-%20China's%20Talent%20Recruitment%20Plans%20Updated2.pdf.
[105] Catherine Matacic, "U.S. Attorneys Warn of Upcoming 'Spike' in Prosecutions Related to China Ties," *Science*, February 7, 2020, www.science.org/content/article/us-attorneys-warn-upcoming-spike-prosecutions-related-china-ties.
[106] Bill Whitaker, "U.S. Fight against Chinese Espionage Ensnares Innocent Americans," *60 Minutes*, May 15, 2016, www.cbsnews.com/news/us-fight-against-china-espionage-ensnares-innocent-americans-60-minutes-bill-whitaker.
[107] Howard Chua-Eoan, "Profiles in Outrage: America Is Home, but Asian Americans Feel Treated as Outsiders with Unproven Loyalties," *TIME* magazine, September 17, 2000, 40.
[108] Sheridan Prasso, "China Initiative Set Out to Catch Spies. It Didn't Find Many," *Bloomberg Business Week*, December 14, 2021, www.bloomberg.com/news/features/2021-12-14/doj-china-initiative-to-catch-spies-prompts-fbi-misconduct-racism-claims.

Americans of other ancestries have by and large escaped this form of antipathy. Talent recruitment programs, including those based on ethnic affinity, are not uncommon. Ireland, for example, has a diaspora office, headed by a minister of state for diaspora affairs, charged with enticing Irish Americans, among others, as entrepreneurs to invest in their putative homeland, or even to repatriate with their human capital.[109] Sinn Fein courts Irish Americans without subterfuge.[110] Irish American participation in "homeland politics" has been commended as a model.[111] Irish Americans have been blamed for their part in "the Troubles."[112] There has not been, however, the same categorical distrust of Irish Americans as of Asian Americans, or in particular Chinese Americans. An Irish American can visit her Irish cousins without incurring doubts about her loyalty. She also can do business in China without worrying that her endeavors will subvert her citizenship. For whites, guilt is attributed to an individual rather than imputed to a racial group. There are multiple cases of undisputed guilt. Aldrich Ames, a CIA agent convicted of spying for the Soviet Union in 1994, and Robert Hanssen, an FBI agent who pled guilty in 2001, did not inspire leeriness of all white men (though the latter's conservative Catholicism was mentioned by critics in passing); nor did even John Anthony Walker, a career US naval specialist/Soviet spy whose co-conspirators included his son. Their betrayals were systematic and long term. They were "moles" from the pages of cloak-and-dagger thrillers.[113]

The only other demographic groups with analogous problems are American Jews, and, following the attacks of 9/11, American Muslims.[114] The former often have been condemned for "dual loyalty," the latter suspected openly of being terrorists or

[109] An official policy statement is Department of Foreign Affairs and Trade, 2015. *Global Irish: Ireland's Diaspora Policy*, www.dfa.ie/media/globalirish/global-irish-irelands-diaspora-policy .pdf. Its official website for "global Irish" is at www.dfa.ie/global-irish. See also Sarah Taylor, "Between Two Worlds: After a Long Tradition of Leaving Ireland for Brighter Opportunities, Many Expatriates – Drawn by a Dramatic Economic Turnaround – Have Returned from Washington and Around the World," *The Washington Post*, February 3, 2002.
[110] Liam Stack, "New Sinn Fein Leader Has a Familiar Task: Wooing Irish-Americans," *New York Times*, March 17, 2018, www.nytimes.com/2018/03/17/world/europe/sinn-fein-ireland-mcdonald .html.
[111] Simon Carswell, "What Irish America Could Teach the World about Putting the Diaspora to Work," *Irish Times*, May 14, 2013.
[112] Regarding Irish American involvement in "homeland politics," see David Brundage, *Irish Nationalists in America: The Politics of Exile, 1798–1998* (New York City: Oxford University Press, 2016), 189–217; Meagher, *The Columbia Guide to Irish American History*, 198–213; Adrian Guelke, "The United States, Irish Americans, and the Northern Ireland Peace Process," *International Affairs* 72, no. 3 (1996): 521–536.
[113] Regarding Ames, Tim Weiner, "Why I Spied," *New York Times Sunday Magazine*, July 31, 1994, 16. Regarding Hanssen, Carol Morello and William Claiborne, "'A Question of Why?,'" *Washington Post*, February 25, 2001. Regarding the Walkers, Martin Weil, "John A. Walker Jr., Who Led Family Spy Ring, Dies at 77," *Washington Post*, August 30, 2014.
[114] An express comparison of American Jews and Chinese Americans is Peter Beinart, "A New Cold War Threatens Chinese Americans," *Jewish Currents*, April 30, 2020, https:// jewishcurrents.org/a-new-cold-war-threatens-chinese-americans.

aiding and abetting terrorists. Among American Jewry, the Jonathan Pollard case caused divisions.[115] After he was convicted of being an agent for Israel, an American ally, some urged more denunciation of him, others less.

The complication for Asian Americans is that China may be adopting an ethnonationalist worldview.[116] There are Chinese "sea turtles" who are transnational as they shuttle back and forth and "parachute kids" sent by Chinese elite and middle-class. The Chinese government apparently has sought to recruit persons of Chinese ethnicity for its undercover work.[117] Some among the Chinese diaspora have transgressed.[118]

---

[115] Stephanie Butnick, "Pollard's Potential Release Divides U.S. Jews," *Tablet*, April 4, 2014, www.tabletmag.com/scroll/168646/pollards-potential-release-divides-u-s-jews; Mark Landler, "Talk of Freeing a Spy for Israel Stirs Old Unease for U.S. Jews," *New York Times*, April 4, 2014, A1. See generally Dov Waxman, *Trouble in the Tribe: The American Jewish Conflict Over Israel* (Princeton University Press, 2016). The subject of "dual loyalty" is analyzed in Mona Harrington, "Loyalties: Dual and Divided," in Stephan Thernstrom (ed.), *Harvard Encyclopedia of American Ethnic Groups* (Cambridge, MA: The Belknap Press, 1980), 676–686. An author critical of diaspora identity is Samuel Huntington. Samuel P. Huntington, *Who Are We? The Challenges to America's National Identity* (New York: Simon & Schuster, 2005); see also Samuel P. Huntington, *The Clash of Civilizations and the Remaking of World Order* (New York: Simon & Schuster, 1996).

[116] Harry Kresja and Anthony Cho, "Is Beijing Adopting an Ethnonationalist Foreign Policy," *Foreign Affairs*, October 23, 2017, www.foreignaffairs.com/articles/asia/2017-10-23/beijing-adopting-ethnonationalist-foreign-policy. See generally Hong Liu, "New Migrants and the Revival of Overseas Chinese Nationalism," *Journal of Contemporary China*, 14, no. 43 (2005): 291–316. See also Kevin Joseph Carrico, *The Great Han: Race, Nationalism, and Tradition in China Today* (Berkeley, CA: University of California Press, 2017); Bill Hayton, *The Invention of China* (New Haven, CT: Yale University Press, 2020); Jonas Parello-Plesner and Mathieu Duchatel, *China's Strong Arm: Protecting Citizens and Assets Abroad* (New York: Routledge, 2015).

[117] The common perception is that Chinese intelligence sought to recruit Chinese Americans, but it has expanded its efforts beyond ethnic affinities. Jeff Stein, "Why the CIA is Increasingly Worried about China's Moles," *Newsweek*, March 31, 2017, www.newsweek.com/cia-chinese-moles-beijing-spies-577442.

[118] Yudhijit Bhattacharjee, "The Spy Who Was Innocent," *New Yorker*, September 18, 2015, www.newyorker.com/news/news-desk/the-spy-who-was-innocent; Yudhijit Bhattacharjee, "A New Kind of Spy," *New Yorker*, May 5, 2014, www.newyorker.com/magazine/2014/05/05/a-new-kind-of-spy. Systematic Chinese efforts to gain military intelligence and trade secrets are being documented. An especially detailed, thoughtful account of a case is Mara Hvistendahl, *The Scientist and the Spy: A True Story of China, the FBI, and Industrial Espionage* (New York: Riverhead, 2020). Mattis and Brazil, note 12 above, is an invaluable resource. See also William C. Hannas, James Mulvenon, and Anna B. Puglisi, *Chinese Industrial Espionage: Technology Acquisition and Military Modernisation* (New York: Routledge, 2013); David Wise, *Tiger Trap: America's Secret Spy War with China* (New York: Houghton Mifflin, 2011). See also Roger Faligot, *Chinese Spies: From Chairman Mao to Xi Jinping* (London: Hurst, 2019); William C. Hannas and Didi Kirsten Tatlow (eds.), *China's Quest for Foreign Technology* (New York: Routledge, 2020); Jon R. Lindsay, Tai Ming Cheung, and Derek S. Reveron (eds.), *China and Cybersecurity: Espionage, Strategy, and Politics in the Digital Domain* (New York: Oxford University Press, 2015); Dennis F. Poindexter, *The Chinese Information War: Espionage, Cyberwar, Communications Control, and Related Threats to United States Interests*, 2nd ed. (Jefferson, NC: McFarland, 2018). The procurement of government data and intellectual property, including by devious means, is described as a strategy for challenging the United

In 2016, for example, Chinese national Su Bin, a Canadian resident, pled guilty to cyberhacking.[119] Chinese state media then praised him as a hero.

Asian Americans confound a black and white racial paradigm, as they do the metaphorically black and white judgment of these scenarios. Asian Americans have yearned for their citizenship. During the Exclusion era, Chinese immigrants gained access as "paper sons."[120] Thanks to the San Francisco 1906 earthquake, which destroyed records, they could profess to be descendants of men already present prior to that time, enabling them to enter. Then, notwithstanding the internment, Japanese Americans sacrificed life and limb as members of the United States military. The 442nd Battalion and 100th Regimental Combat Team, all Japanese American (with white officers), were the most highly decorated units in history for their size and length of service, being assigned suicide missions throughout Europe.[121] Japanese Americans also contributed by volunteering for the Military Intelligence Service working directly against Japan.[122] The Japanese American Citizens League Creed proclaimed:

> I am proud that I am an American citizen of Japanese ancestry, for my very background makes me appreciate more fully the wonderful advantages of this Nation. I believe in her institutions, ideals, and traditions; I glory in her heritage; I boast of her history; I trust in her future. She has granted me liberties and opportunities such as no individual enjoys in this world today ... Although some individuals may discriminate against me, I shall never become bitter or lose faith, for I know that such persons are not representative of the majority of the American people ... I am firm in my belief that American sportsmanship and attitude of fair play will judge citizenship and patriotism on the basis of action and achievement, and not on the basis of physical characteristics ... Because I believe in America and I trust she believes in me, and because I have received innumerable benefits from

States. Bill Gertz, *Deceiving the Sky: Inside Communist China's Drive for Global Supremacy* (New York: Encounter Books, 2019).

There are antecedents here as well. A work that is contrarian about Japanese American assimilation prior to World War II, arguing Japanese Americans on the whole favored Japan, is Brian Masaru Hayashi, *For the Sake of Our Japanese Brethren: Assimilation, Nationalism, and Protestantism among the Japanese of Los Angeles, 1895–1942* (Palo Alto, CA: Stanford University Press, 1995).

[119] Stuart Leavenworth, "Chinese Hacker Who Tried to Steal US Military Data 'Deserves Respect' – State Media," *The Guardian*, March 25, 2016, www.theguardian.com/world/2016/mar/25/chinese-hacker-who-tried-to-steal-us-military-data-deserves-respect-says-state-media.

[120] Lau, *Paper Families*; Lee, *America's Gates*; Tung Chin, *Paper Son: One Man's Story* (Philadelphia: Temple University Press, 2000).

[121] Robert Asahina, *Just Americans: How Japanese Americans Won a War at Home and Abroad* (New York: Gotham Books, 2006); Chris Komai, *Proud to Serve: Japanese American World War II Veterans* (Los Angeles: Rafu Shimpo, 2012); Bill Yenne, *Rising Sons: The Japanese American GIs Who Fought for the United States in World War II* (New York: Thomas Dunne, 2007).

[122] Stanley L. Falk and Warren M. Tsuneishi, *American Patriots: MIS in the War Against Japan* (Washington DC: Japanese American Veterans Association, 1995).

her, I pledge myself to do honor to her at all times and in all places; to support her constitution; to obey her laws; to respect her flag; to defend her against all enemies, foreign or domestic; to actively assume my duties and obligations as a citizen, cheerfully and without any reservations whatsoever, in the hope that I may become a better American in a greater America.[123]

President Harry S Truman welcomed the returning soldiers to the White House. In a ceremony, he congratulated the veterans: "You fought not only the enemy, but you fought prejudice – and you have won."[124]

The nation, to the extent a sovereignty is capable of it, is sorry for its policies toward Asian Americans. In 2011 and 2012, the Senate and the House issued statements of regret (technically not apologies) for the Chinese Exclusion Act.[125] Congresswoman Judy Chu, who happened to be Asian American and who represented the Southern California bedroom community of Monterey Park, which became majority Asian American starting in the 1980s, was the lead sponsor. In 1988, Congress approved the Civil Liberties Act to pay redress to Japanese Americans who had been interned, in sums calculated to be pennies to the dollar for the direct financial losses.[126] Presidents of both parties from Gerald Ford to Barack Obama have repudiated the internment; the Solicitor General "confessed" error; and a blue-ribbon commission resolved that the internment was the result of racial prejudice, wartime panic, and lack of political leadership.[127] Finally, while upholding the "travel ban" against persons from predominantly Muslim nations, the Supreme Court expressly overruled the *Korematsu* decision.[128]

Closing out the Wen Ho Lee case in September 2000, Judge Parker delivered a peroration which from a federal jurist is unheard of:[129]

---

[123] Mike Masaoka and Bill Hosokawa, *They Call Me Moses Masaoka* (New York: William Morrow, 1987), 49–51.

[124] Harry S Truman: "Remarks upon Presenting a Citation to a Nisei Regiment," July 15, 1946, Gerhard Peters and John T. Woolley, The American Presidency Project, www.presidency.ucsb.edu/documents/remarks-upon-presenting-citation-nisei-regiment.

[125] US Congress, Senate, *A resolution expressing the regret of the Senate for the passage of discriminatory laws against the Chinese in America, including the Chinese Exclusion Act*, S. Res. 201, 112th Cong., 1st session, introduced May 26, 2011. US Congress, House, *Expressing the regret of the House of Representatives for the passage of laws that adversely affected the Chinese in the United States, including the Chinese Exclusion Act*, H. Res. 683, 112th Cong., 2nd session, introduced June 8, 2012.

[126] Civil Liberties Act of 1988, 50a U.S.C. sec. 1989b et seq. (1988).

[127] CWRIC, *Personal Justice Denied*. Regarding confession of error, Neal K. Katyal, "The Solicitor General and Confession of Error," *Fordham Law Review* 81, no. 6: 3027–3037. An official statement by Acting Solicitor General Katyal is available at www.justice.gov/archives/opa/blog/confession-error-solicitor-generals-mistakes-during-japanese-american-internment-cases.

[128] *Trump v. Hawaii*, 138 S. Ct. 2392, 2423 (2018).

[129] "Statement by Judge in Los Alamos Case, With Apology for Abuse of Power," *New York Times*, September 14, 2000, A25.

I find it most perplexing, although appropriate, that the executive branch today has suddenly agreed to your release without any significant conditions or restrictions whatsoever on your activities. I note that this has occurred shortly before the executive branch was to have produced, for my review in camera, a large volume of information that I previously ordered it to produce.

From the beginning, the focus of this case was on your motive or intent in taking the information from the secure computers and eventually downloading it on to tapes. There was never really any dispute about your having done that, only about why you did it.

What I believe remains unanswered is the question: What was the government's motive in insisting on your being jailed pretrial under extraordinarily onerous conditions of confinement until today, when the executive branch agrees that you may be set free essentially unrestricted? This makes no sense to me.

A corollary question I guess is: Why were you charged with the many Atomic Energy Act counts for which the penalty is life imprisonment, all of which the executive branch has now moved to dismiss and which I just dismissed? ...

Dr. Lee, you're a citizen of the United States and so am I, but there is a difference between us. You had to study the Constitution of the United States to become a citizen. Most of us are citizens by reason of the simple serendipitous fact of our birth here ...

I am sad for you and your family because of the way in which you were kept in custody while you were presumed under the law to be innocent of the charges the executive branch brought against you.

I am sad that I was induced in December to order your detention, since by the terms of the plea agreement that frees you today without conditions, it becomes clear that the executive branch now concedes, or should concede, that it was not necessary to confine you last December or at any time before your trial.

I am sad because the resolution of this case drug on unnecessarily long ...

I want everyone to know that I agree, based on the information that so far has been made available to me, that you, Dr. Lee, faced some risk of conviction by a jury if you were to have proceeded to trial. Because of that, I decided to accept the agreement you made with the United States executive branch under Rule 11(e)(1)(C) of the Federal Rules of Criminal Procedure.

Further, I feel that the 278 days of confinement for your offense is not unjust; however, I believe you were terribly wronged by being held in custody pretrial in the Santa Fe County Detention Center under demeaning, unnecessarily punitive conditions. I am truly sorry that I was led by our executive branch of government to order your detention last December.

Dr. Lee, I tell you with great sadness that I feel I was led astray last December by the executive branch of our government through its Department of Justice, by its

Federal Bureau of Investigation and by its United States attorney for the district of New Mexico, who held the office at that time ...

It is only the top decision makers in the executive branch, especially the Department of Justice and the Department of Energy and locally, during December, who have caused embarrassment by the way this case began and was handled. They did not embarrass me alone. They have embarrassed our entire nation and each of us who is a citizen of it.

I might say that I am also sad and troubled because I do not know the real reasons why the executive branch has done all of this. We will not learn why because the plea agreement shields the executive branch from disclosing a lot of information that it was under order to produce that might have supplied the answer.

Although, as I indicated, I have no authority to speak on behalf of the executive branch, the president, the vice president, the attorney general, or the secretary of the Department of Energy, as a member of the third branch of the United States Government, the judiciary, the United States courts, I sincerely apologize to you, Dr. Lee, for the unfair manner you were held in custody by the executive branch.

A generation later, Sherry Chen prevailed before the Merit Systems Protection Board.[130] Civil servants win only approximately 2 percent of cases before that appellate body.[131] In April 2018, the administrative law judge presiding over the case, in a ruling which ran to more than 130 pages, ruled that Chen was entitled to restoration of her employment after suffering a "gross miscarriage of justice."[132] Meanwhile, Xiaoxing Xi filed suit against the federal government for falsifying evidence.[133] His case was eventually dismissed.

As this volume was headed to press and as the Covid-19 global pandemic wound down, the proverbial "smoking gun" finally emerged. The United States Commerce Department, which employed both Sherry Chen and Chunzai Wang, was discovered to have had a unit which expressly targeted Asian Americans and those of Middle Eastern descent, without other reasonable bases.[134] According to two-dozen whistleblowers who testified in a Senate investigation, "agents would covertly search

---

[130] Chen v. Department of Commerce, Docket Number CH-0752-17-0028-I-1, US Merit Systems Board, April 23, 2018 (Schroeder, C.J.), www.sherrychendefensefund.org/uploads/9/9/2/8/99280080/chen_v_dept_of_commerce-ch-0752-17-0028-i-1-_initial_decision.pdf.

[131] Statistics for the body are published in its annual report. See US Merit Systems Protection Board, *Annual Report for FY 2017* (Washington DC: US Merit Systems Protection Board, 2018), 13–26. This official document is available at https://web.archive.org/web/20180124035413/.

[132] Chen v. Department of Commerce.

[133] Apuzzo, "Former Espionage Suspect Sues, Accusing F.B.I. of Falsifying Evidence."

[134] See Catie Edmondson, "'Rogue' U.S. Agency Used Racial Profiling to Investigate Commerce Dept. Employees, Report Says," *New York Times*, July 16, 2021, www.nytimes.com/2021/07/16/us/politics/commerce-department-senate-report.html. See also Shawn Boburg, "Commerce Department Security Unit Evolved Into Counterintelligence-Like Operation, Washington Post Examination Found," *Washington Post*, May 24, 2021, www.washingtonpost.com/investigations/2021/05/24/commerce-department-monitoring-itms.

employee's offices wearing face masks and gloves, sometimes picking locks to gain entry."[135] Ethnic surnames were sufficient to trigger suspicion. The official report concluded that the Investigations and Threat Management Service was "a rogue, unaccountable police force without a clear mission" but which nonetheless had opened thousands of cases.[136] Sherry Chen and Chunzai Wang were specifically cited among them. Hundreds of professors declared "I am Gang Chen" to side with their MIT colleague who was accused.[137] The first trial of the "China Initiative," brought against Anming Hu, ended in a hung jury subsequent to cross-examination of government witnesses which left the impression of perjury may have been committed.[138] Shortly thereafter, the government voluntarily dropped a half dozen other prosecutions, one against a medical researcher and five others accused of concealing their relationship to the Chinese military.[139] Finally, the judge in the Hu case dismissed the case, explaining in his opinion that the government had a theory of the case that was not legally sufficient to make out a crime and in any event would not be able to carry its burden of proof.[140]

[135] Edmondson, "'Rogue' U.S. Agency Used Racial Profiling to Investigate Commerce Dept. Employees, Report Says."
[136] US Senate Committee on Commerce, Science & Transportation, "Abuse and Misconduct at the Commerce Department," July 2021, www.commerce.senate.gov/services/files/3893917C-A6CE-4D6C-AA9D-781401322BF3.
[137] See Ellen Barry, "A Scientist Is Arrested, and Academics Push Back," *New York Times*, January 26, 2021, www.nytimes.com/2021/01/26/us/mit-scientist-charges.html. The petition was published as "Why Have We, a Group of MIT Faculty, Signed the Letter in Support of Gang Chen?," *MIT Faculty Newsletter* 23, no. 3 (2021), https://fnl.mit.edu/january-february-2021/why-have-we-a-group-of-mit-faculty-signed-the-letter-in-support-of-gang-chen. This is an allusion to the famous line, "I am Spartacus." The institutional response of MIT is very different than other institutions. Karin Fischer, "When a Scholar Is Accused of Being a Spy: How Investigations Play Out at Different Universities Reveals a Lot about Higher Education," *Chronicle of Higher Education*, Oct. 27, 2021, www.chronicle.com/article/when-a-scholar-is-accused-of-being-a-spy.
[138] See Jamie Satterfield, "Trial Reveals Federal Agents Falsely Accused a UT Professor Born in China of Spying," *Knoxville News*, June 13, 2021, www.knoxnews.com/story/news/crime/2021/06/14/federal-agents-falsely-accused-university-of-tennessee-professor-spying-china/7649378002. See also Karen Hao and Eileen Guo, "The FBI Accused Him of Spying for China. It Ruined His Life," *MIT Technology Review*, June 27, 2021, www.technologyreview.com/2021/06/27/1027350/anming-hu-china-initiative-research-espionage-spying; Mara Hvistendahl, "'Ridiculous Case': Juror Criticizes DOJ for Charging Scientists with Hiding Ties to China," *The Intercept*, June 23, 2021, https://theintercept.com/2021/06/23/anming-hu-trial-fbi-china.
[139] Regarding the researcher, see Vince Grzegorek, "Feds Drop Charges against Former Cleveland Clinic Researcher They Alleged Was Part of China's 'Thousand Talents Program'," *Cleve Scene*, July 19, 2021, www.clevescene.com/scene-and-heard/archives/2021/07/19/feds-drop-charges-against-former-cleveland-clinic-researcher-they-alleged-was-part-of-chinas-thousand-talents-program. Regarding the five, see Ellen Nakashuma and David Nakamura, "U.S. Drops Cases Against Five Researchers Accused of Hiding Ties to Chinese Military," *Washington Post*, July 23, 2021, www.washingtonpost.com/national-security/us-drops-cases-against-five-researchers-accused-of-hiding-ties-to-chinese-military/2021/07/23/54a8b268-ec04-11eb-8950-d73b3e93ff7f_story.html.
[140] *United States v. Hu*, Memorandum Opinion and Order, Case No. 3:20-CR-21-TAV-DCP-1 (Sept. 9, 2021 E.D. Tenn.), https://storage.courtlistener.com/recap/gov.uscourts.tned.93460/gov.uscourts.tned.93460.141.0.pdf.

Under the China Initiative, two individuals who were not of Chinese descent were guilty. Republican fundraiser Elliot Broidy pled guilty to serving as a foreign agent for the People's Republic of China.[141] President Trump pardoned him with seventy-two others on the last day of the administration.[142] Harvard professor Charles Leiber was convicted on all counts.[143] The case was only the second to proceed to trial, after Anming Hu.

The Gang Chen case was voluntarily dropped because prosecutors said they would not be able to meet the burden of proof.[144] Multiple reports by then had been released documenting the absence of actual espionage charges in these supposed "espionage" cases, the high rates of dismissals and acquittals, the ethnic patterns of the cases, and the fear among academics – which varied, understandably, by race.[145] *MIT Technology Review* prepared a painstaking study of all publicized

[141] United States Department of Justice, "Elliot Broidy Pleads Guilty for Back-Channel Lobbying Campaign to Drop 1MDB Investigation and Remove a Chinese Foreign National," October 20, 2020, www.justice.gov/opa/pr/elliott-broidy-pleads-guilty-back-channel-lobbying-campaign-drop-1mdb-investigation-and.

[142] United States White House, "Statement from the Press Secretary Regarding Executive Grants of Clemency," January 20, 2021, https://trumpwhitehouse.archives.gov/briefings-statements/statement-press-secretary-regarding-executive-grants-clemency-012021/. See Beth Reinhard et al., "The Cottage Industry Behind Trump's Pardons: How the Rich and Well-Connected Got Ahead at the Expense of Others," *Washington Post*, February 5, 2021, www.washingtonpost.com/politics/trump-pardons-lobbying/2021/02/05/896f0b52-624b-11eb-9430-e7c77b5b0297_story.html; Louis Keene, "Why Did These Rabbis Seek a Pardon for Elliot Broidy?," *The Forward*, January 27, 2021, https://forward.com/news/463064/why-did-these-rabbis-seek-a-pardon-for-elliot-broidy/.

[143] United States Department of Justice, "Harvard Professor Convicted of Making False Statements and Tax Offenses," December 21, 2021, www.justice.gov/usao-ma/pr/harvard-university-professor-convicted-making-false-statements-and-tax-offenses.

[144] Eric Tucker, "US Drops Case Against MIT Professor Accused of Ties to China," *Washington Post*, January 20, 2022, www.washingtonpost.com/politics/us-drops-case-against-mit-professor-accused-of-ties-to-china/2022/01/20/0f746944-7a02-11ec-9dce-7313579de434_story.html. Gang Chen was profiled sympathetically. Ellen Barry, "'In the End, You're Treated Like a Spy,' Says MIT Scientist," *New York Times*, January 24, 2022, at www.nytimes.com/2022/01/24/science/gang-chen-mit-china.html.

[145] Andrew Chongseh Kim and Committee of 100, "Racial Disparities in Economic Espionage Act Prosecutions: A Window into the New Red Scare," September 21, 2021, www.committee100.org/wp-content/uploads/2021/09/Whitepaper-Final-9.21-UPDATE-compressed.pdf; Jenny J. Lee, Xiaojie Li and the Staff at Committee of 100, "Racial Profiling among Scientists of Chinese Descent and Consequences for the U.S. Scientific Community," October 28, 2021, www.committee100.org/wp-content/uploads/2021/10/C100-Lee-Li-White-Paper-FINAL-FINAL-10.28.pdf. See Jeffrey Mervis, "China Initiative Spawns Distrust – and Activism," *Science*, November 5, 2021, www.committee100.org/wp-content/uploads/2021/11/science.acx9540.pdf. For media reports, see, e.g., Aruna Viswanatha and Sha Hua, "The U.S. Pursued Professors Working with China. Cases Are Faltering," *Wall Street Journal*, December 20, 2021, www.wsj.com/articles/criminal-charges-professors-china-mit-faltering-11640016143?st=goknnhyhw folaop&reflink=article_copyURL_share; Amy Qin, "As U.S. Hunts for Chinese Spies, University Scientists Warn of Backlash," *The New York Times*, November 28, 2021, www.nytimes.com/2021/11/28/world/asia/china-university-spies.html; Karin Fischer, "Has the Hunt for Chinese Spies Become a Witch Hunt? University Scientists Work in 'an Atmosphere of Fear'," *Chronicle of Higher Education*, August 11, 2021, www.chronicle.com/article/has-the-hunt-for-chinese-spies-become-a-witch-hunt.

cases that had been brought under the rubric of the China Initiative.[146] While they were researching it, the Department of Justice altered its website by eliminating references to its failures.

Following these developments, even those who had personally participated in prosecutions expressed doubts about the approach. In an investigative report by the *Washington Post*, three former federal prosecutors admitted the problems of the China Initiative and recommended reform. John Hemann, credited with successful prosecution of an early indictment in a China-related case (prior to formal commencement of the China Initiative), said the pressure to "show statistics ... has caused a program focused on the Chinese government to morph into a people-of-Chinese-descent initiative." Andrew Lelling, who initiated the case against Gang Chen, said "If I were in the department today ... I'd tell the field, 'Okay, slow down on new cases. Let's set the bar higher now.'" John Demers, who oversaw much of the work, said in cases involving only alleged grant fraud, the government should consider a system for self-disclosure by offering immunity from criminal prosecution.[147]

In early 2022, the White House Office of Science and Technology Policy issued a memorandum calling for clarity in disclosure rules for researchers.[148] In a speech delivered at George Mason University on February 23, 2022, Attorney General Matt Olsen announced the formal end of "the China Initiative."[149]

---

[146] Eileen Guo, Jess Aloe, and Karen Hao, "The US Crackdown on Chinese Economic Espionage Is a Mess. We Have the Data to Show It," *MIT Technology Review*, December 2, 2021, www.technologyreview.com/2021/12/02/1040656/china-initative-us-justice-department/. A companion article explains the methodology. Eileen Guo, Jess Aloe, and Karen Hao, "We Built a Database to Understand the China Initiative. Then the Government Changed Its Records," *MIT Technology Review*, December 2, 2021, www.technologyreview.com/2021/12/02/1039397/china-initiative-database-doj/.

[147] Ellen Nakashima and David Nakamura, "China Initiative Aims to Stop Economic Espionage. Is Targeting Academics Over Grant Fraud 'Overkill?'," *Washington Post*, September 15, 2021, www.washingtonpost.com/national-security/china-initiative-questions-dismissals/2021/09/15/530ef936-f482-11eb-9738-8395ec2a44e7_story.html.

[148] National Science and Technology Council, "Guidance for Implementing National Security Presidential Memorandum 33 on National Security Strategy for United States Government-Supported Research and Development," January 2022, www.whitehouse.gov/wp-content/uploads/2022/01/010422-NSPM-33-Implementation-Guidance.pdf?utm_medium=email&utm_source=FYI&dm_i=1ZJN,7OKSB,E29O1F,VB5UF,1.

[149] US Department of Justice Ends Controversial Probe of Researchers' China Ties," *Chronicle of Higher Education*, February 23, 2022, www.chronicle.com/article/u-s-department-of-justice-ends-controversial-probe-of-researchers-china-ties; the full text of his remarks is available as Matthew Olsen, "Remarks on Countering Nation-State Threats," February 23, 2022, www.justice.gov/opa/speech/assistant-attorney-general-matthew-olsen-delivers-remarks-countering-nation-state-threats.

11

The Great White Father and His Little Red Children

Surveillance and Race in Native America

Anton Treuer

Surveillance has always been at the heart of America's ongoing effort to subordinate and control the first people of the land. Contrary to the mythology about scattered bands of roaming nomads in the forest, America was at least as densely populated as Europe at the time of first contact with Europeans. Charles Mann and others have successfully narrowed the population estimate of North America to somewhere around 90 million people at the time of Columbus's arrival in the Caribbean.[1] The capital city of the Aztec Empire, Tenochtitlan, was three times larger than the largest city in all of Europe, which was London. Getting the land out of native hands was no small task, and a lot of blood and treasure was expended on the effort then. America's native nations still control substantial land and resources; and much blood and treasure are still spent today in a changed but obviously ongoing effort to take what's left. This chapter explores how surveillance was used to subjugate and colonize the Indigenous populations of North America.

While race is clearly a social construct, its construction is at the heart of America's rise. From the first permanent English colony at Jamestown to the present, surveilling race is the story of America.[2] The first English settlers were small in number compared to the millions of Indigenous inhabitants of North America. To get a foothold, they first began to study, surveil, and develop intelligence on the stewards of the land. It soon became clear that native America was as complex and as divided as the populations of Europe. The Powhatan were not one tribe, but many tribes, united in a loose confederacy, each with its own territory, language, and history. As English surveillance grew, so too did the taking. John Smith, who was in charge of security for the new colony, led foraging parties from Jamestown – not diplomatic

---

[1] Charles Mann, *1491: New Revelations of the Americas before Columbus* (New York: Knopf, 2005).
[2] Anton Treuer, *Everything You Wanted to Know about Indians but Were Afraid to Ask* (New York: Levine Querido, 2021), 57–58.

peace initiatives. The European newcomers were not self-sufficient. Their crops were not well-suited to the climate of the land. It took decades for them to adapt and adopt Indigenous agricultural practices and farm Indigenous foods – corn, beans, and squash. To address European settler food scarcity, they scouted Indigenous food supplies and crops. John Smith's surveillance identified the locations of abundant tribal food production, and his raids on tribal communities ignited a series of conflicts with the tribes. Smith and other English settlers were opportunistic, and successful because of their intelligence-gathering about native food production and about native people. Soon the British were using the tried-and-true tactics of division and conquest that had worked so well in colonial efforts elsewhere in the world. They surveilled tribe after tribe, drew maps around the various territories, and sought "peace and friendship treaties," trying to get tribes to agree to define their territories so the British could divide and conquer. This strategy was successfully employed by the British – and more specifically the English – previously when they sought to conquer and colonize the Irish, the Scottish, and others.

After the American Revolution, Britain's former subjects used the same approach to native peoples under governance by the United States. Revolutionary War veterans were not paid in coin or currency. They were paid in Indian land grants, even though the fledgling American government had yet to acquire the land from the Indians. The conquest of tribes was America's purpose, and its bureaucratic organization developed to deal with Indians (the Office of Indian Affairs) was housed in the Department of War. Surveillance was the means by which those wars were won. America could not possibly fight all tribes at once. They surveilled, divided, and conquered them one at a time.[3]

There was a predictable pattern to the assertion of American dominance and expansion: Tribes were surveilled. American agents then approached the surveilled tribes in an effort (often not well-understood by natives) to draw neat lines around their territories through peace and friendship treaties. Often those lines were disputed between tribes and through surveillance, the American government knew and exploited this information. For example, the US government tried to broker a peace treaty between the Ojibwe and Dakota at Prairie du Chien in 1825 and the US government eventually surveyed a dividing line between their respective territories years later. But members of both tribes pulled up the survey stakes because they were so upset about demarcations and they continued to fight one another for decades after the treaty. While this was happening, and escalating after the peace and friendship treaties, white settlers streamed into native lands to squat on lands the US government had just agreed belonged exclusively to whatever tribe had just signed the peace and friendship treaty. This was again done with the knowledge of the US government, which wanted to provoke incidents which would provide

[3] Anton Treuer, *The Indian Wars: Battles, Bloodshed, and the Fight for Freedom on the American Frontier* (Washington DC: National Geographic, 2017).

pretext and justification for war and the displacement of Indigenous peoples. The incidents usually came in the form of some settlers shooting at Indians to chase them off the farm they had built on land that still belonged to the tribe. The pattern was repeated across New York, Pennsylvania, Ohio, the western Great Lakes, and beyond. The Indians often retaliated, providing the cause the government needed to bring in the US army to protect white citizens. The Black Hawk War is a great example.[4] The Sac and Fox has signed a peace and friendship treaty with the US government. In 1832, Black Hawk led a group of tribal members to their seasonal corn fields to plant. There were 1,500 people in the Sac and Fox contingent. Most were children, elders, and women, rather than warriors. White settlers had already flooded into the Sac and Fox lands. They sent a militia to confront the Sac and Fox. Without seeking a parlay or even trying to ascertain the intentions of the Dac and Fox, they simply opened fire. The Sac and Fox quickly sought to protect their children and elders, returning fire. The ensuing conflict brought thousands of US soldiers to Iowa, Illinois, and Wisconsin to pursue the Sac and Fox. Abraham Lincoln was a captain in the US army at the time. US troops were relentless, and in spite of Black Hawk's brilliant feints and redirections to enable their families to retreat, most of the Sac and Fox were killed, including most of their elders and children. The US government compelled them to sign a second treaty ceding most of their land and removed the remained of the tribe to Kansas, then forced them to cede their reservation in Kansas and move to Oklahoma, then forced the allotment of their reservation in Oklahoma, leaving the tribe largely landless and destitute. The Sac and Fox lands in Oklahoma were opened for white settlement – free land grants for white settlers as part of the Oklahoma Land Rush and similar homesteading efforts there. Some of the Sac and Fox ran to Mexico to seek refuge. Some returned to Iowa and by selling baskets and crafts eventually got enough money to purchase land in Tama where they reestablished the Meskwaki settlement that remains there today.

Typically, the second treaty with each tribe usually involved a huge and punitive land cession, imposed after military conquest. Tribal members had to move from the newly ceded territories. Their lands were freely opened for white settlement. Even after tribal members became US citizens, they had no right to settle or homestead for free like white citizens. Citizenship was extended to native Americans piecemeal. Some became citizens via treaty. Native veterans of World War I were allowed to apply for citizenship by an act of Congress. General citizenship was conferred by act of Congress in 1924.[5]

Over and over, government agents escalated surveillance on tribes and tribal peoples. They performed a census during each treaty signing and used the information obtained to exercise increasingly onerous control over native people. Many

---

[4] Ibid., 189–191.
[5] Treuer, *Everything You Wanted to Know about Indians*, 189–191.

tribes had consensus-based governance systems, and treaty processes were usually at odds with Indigenous ways of doing things. As native people got wise to American ways of treating them, many boycotted treaty signings, believing that nothing could be sold without their consent. For example, the communities of Ponemah, Roseau, and Warroad in Northwestern Minnesota were all populous Ojibwe villages when the Americans first arrived in the area.[6] They refused to sell their land or treat with the Americans. The American government signed a treaty with Ojibwe leaders from Red Lake and Redby in 1863 and obtained their signatures on the Nelson Act in 1889. No Ojibwe people from Ponemah, Roseau, and Warroad signed those agreements. But most of their land was sold and excluded from the new reservation at Red Lake. They were alienated from the hunting and trapping resources. The timber was clearcut and sold by white settlers and corporations. They consented to none of those actions, but the agreements signed with other natives were considered binding agreements upon them.

American officials were all too happy to work the more cooperative chiefs who did show up or those they could manipulate, but the pattern was always well-informed through the surveillance tactics of military intelligence, government census work, and civilian land and legal system expansion. This happened with divided factions of the Sac and Fox, Lakota, and many other tribes. Soon the government had excellent information on who the "stand around the fort Indians" were and who had to be taught a lesson.

By sowing the seeds of conflict not just with tribes, but between tribes, the US government had reliable (though expensive) way to get the land. Manifest Destiny was the talk of the time. It was America's destiny to expand from one sea to the other. The method by which this expansion would be orchestrated relied upon carefully calculated manipulations of the tribes they encountered. The government had to surveil the tribes and pull defeated warriors into the ranks of the US army to serve as scouts in campaigns against their former native enemies (enemies often made through US government manipulations during the treaty period). The Crow and Pawnee, for example, served as scouts in the US army when it fought the Lakota.

As the government subjugated tribes one at a time, they also established reservations with the best intelligence about how to maximize white control of valuable resources and minimize tribal wealth and military resistance. Washington, Oregon, and Oklahoma have many reservations that became home to more than one tribe, who were forced to consolidate and confederate, or die. Often the combined tribal groups were former enemies, and by combining them, the government succeeded in having much of their animosity about the mistreatment of tribal peoples vented laterally against one another rather than together against the US government. The goal was to keep them subjugated and eventually eliminated. Military genocide was

---

[6] Anton Treuer, *Warrior Nation: A History of the Red Lake Ojibwe* (St. Paul, MN: Minnesota Historical Society Press, 2017).

openly acceptable to America's white Christian majority when the Indians were doing harm to whites. But as the treaty period gave way to the reservation era, genocide had to be accomplished by other means, and predictably, surveillance was at the heart of the policy shift.

In 1910, there was still a band of Shoshone and Bannock hiding out in the mountains.[7] They had never signed a treaty, never surrendered, and never came in to a reservation. Outside of American surveillance they were free. They were self-sufficient. They were healthy and independent of US government rations. But in 1911, their presence became known to whites. As white settlers killed off most of the lowland game and settlers began to travel and forage at higher elevations, the Shoshone had trouble finding food. They came out of the highland and shot a settler's cow. A vigilante posse was formed and soon accompanied by police officers. They sought out the natives and immediately opened fire on them. The natives returned fire, but had bows and arrows and were quickly overwhelmed. The vigilantes killed all the adult members of tribal group. If you were native American and were not settled on a reservation, counted, surveilled, disarmed, and forced into dependency, you were likely to be killed.

In 1914 and 1915, a group of Ute had a similar experience to the Shone and Bannock.[8] They too had not signed any treaties or moved to reservations. US marshals, local sheriffs, and a vigilante posse, rode out and attacked the peaceful Ute camps. The Ute defended themselves, and the US army sent a detachment under command of General Hugh Scott. Scott eventually convinced 160 of the Ute to submit to American control and surveillance by settling at the Ute Mountain Reservation. White law enforcement officers continued to round up "renegade" Ute who refused to come to the reservation until 1921. In 1921, the remaining Ute stalwarts were, according to US law, without tribal citizenship or American citizenship. They had no land rights and no land. They had to come to reservations to settle and submit or could purchase land somewhere else and move there as nonnative people.

Every single tribal member had to be identified and listed on tribal rolls, lists of tribal members for treaty signings and payments. Unlike the broader US population which was enumerated by census and which had certain privacy protections, tribal members had to have every facet of their identities recorded or they were denied payments from land sales, a place to live on reservation, and food annuities. Tribal enrollment, which was administered by the US government, not by tribal leaders, soon embraced the emerging "science" of eugenics. To be eligible for tribal membership and any meager benefits attached to enrollment, prospective members had to prove a certain pedigree, or percentage of tribal blood. The system was fraught with errors, and money was on the line, especially when the US government

[7] Treuer, *The Indian Wars*, 298–299.
[8] Ibid., 300–301.

began to allot tribal lands within the reservations. Allotment was a policy enabled by the Dawes Act, which passed in 1887. It enabled the US government to break up the land inside reservations. Each tribal member was supposed to be given a small homestead within their reservation and then the remaining reservation lands were opened for white settlement. Most of the Oklahoma land rushes took place within the borders of reservations on allotted tribal land. Today, reservations like Leech Lake (an Ojibwe reservation located in Northern Minnesota) have only 4 percent of the reservation in native hands; the rest is owned by private white citizens or government agencies.

Tribal enrollment and surveillance of the US government enabled the new taking. On the White Earth reservation in northern Minnesota, for example, the allotment policy began with a protection for tribal members – they were not allowed to sell their allotments for twenty-five years. So the government began to chip away at the protections, passing legislation that allowed the sale of allotments if there was timber on the land and also legislation that allowed mixed-bloods to sell. The idea was that mixed-bloods were part white therefore part competent and could sell. The reality is that this was an enabling mechanism for more land shenanigans. All but 9 percent of the White Earth reservation fell into nonnative hands through allotment.

The White Earth case is a perfect example, and it was investigated and litigated, so we have lots of information about the debacle.[9] A tribal enrollment list was generated in 1916 (adopted in 1920) to determine the number of full-bloods. Because American law stipulated different treatment of land rights for native Americans based on the percentage of their blood that the US government designated as native, this coding system was critical in the alienation of native people from their own land. Initially, all natives were protected in allotment law. They could not sell their land for twenty-five years after receiving their own land parcel through allotment.

---

[9] Information on allotment litigation at White Earth, the Jenks and Hrdlicka tests, and tribal rolls is taken from Records of the United States Attorney, US Department of Justice, "Land Allotment Fraud Cases at White Earth, Deposition Testimony," NA (Chicago Regional Branch), 11; Ales Hrdlicka, "Anthropology of the Chippewa," *Holes Anniversary Volume: Anthropological Essays* (Washington DC: 1916), 198–227; Albert Jenks to William Folwell, May 21, 1926, William Watts Folwell Papers, Minnesota Historical Society Archives; "Professor Jenks Returns to the University," *University of Minnesota Alumni Weekly* 15, no. 21 (1916): 12; Ranson J. Powell to Albert Jenks, November 16, 1914, Powell Papers, Minnesota Historical Society Archives; "Popular Picture of Indian Upset by Investigation, Eagle Beak Nose Belongs Not to Red Man, but to Fiction," *Minneapolis Journal*, April 9, 1916, 3; *Minneapolis Journal*, May 1 and 5, 1918: 12; *Minneapolis Tribune*, November 1 and 13, 1920. For reliable secondary sources, there is a fantastic article on the eugenics testing and compilation of blood quantum records at White Earth in David L. Beaulieu, "Curly Hair and Big Feet: Physical Anthropology and the Implementation of Land Allotment on the White Earth Chippewa Reservation," *American Indian Quarterly* 8, no. 4 (1984): 281–314. See also William Watts Folwell, *A History of Minnesota*, 4 vols. (St. Paul, MN: Minnesota Hisotrical Society Press, 1956 [1921]), vol. 4, 291–293.

The Burke Act was passed in 1906 and eliminated the twenty-five-year trust period on Indian allotments only for mixed-bloods, which meant that mixed-bloods could sell their allotments immediately but full-bloods had to wait twenty-five years to sell. Therefore, full-bloods might be entitled to compensation for the allotment swindles, but not the mixed-bloods. Dr. Ales Hrdlicka of the Smithsonian Museum and Dr. Albert Jenks of the University of Minnesota performed a series of cranial measurements, scratch tests (where Indians were scratched and if the mark was red or pink, he was declared a mixed-blood), and tooth examinations to determine the blood quantum of individuals asking for compensation. The tests were outrageously unscientific. Comparative sample was taken of some of the Scandinavian settlers in the area that actually showed some of them to be more native than the natives. Albert Jenks reported that Indian "Noses are coarse and crudely molded rather than finely chiseled. Contrary to popular opinion, the pure Indian has slight, delicate hands and feet, the natural form of people who do little manual labor."[10] Ranson Powell wrote to Albert Jenks during the testing process about a particularly dark Indian that he wanted stricken from the full-blood list:

> I beg to hand you herewith a copy of the testimony given by Dr. Ales Hrdlicka relating to the characteristics of the pure-blood ... I note that he calls attention to the fact developed [by] his observations, that the whiskers of the pure-blood are likewise straight. Judging by the standard the darker of the two Indians I had before you the other day would be doubtful as to his blood status because of the fact that the whiskers of his is [sic] pretty curly.[11]

The *Minneapolis Journal* headlined a subsequent article: "1,000 Lands Titles Hang by a Hair, if Curly Indians Lose."[12] There can be no doubt about the financial motivations of the surveillance, classification, and eugenics work. The *University of Minnesota Alumni Weekly* reported on Albert Jenks's work:

> So far 90% of the 300 Indians examined show unmistakable evidence of mixed-blood. The results of the government suits so far tried with aid of anthropological evidence are decidedly favorable to the citizens of Minnesota; if the defendants continue to win their cases, farming lands now valued at more than 1,500,000 will it is conservatively estimated within ten years increase in value by improvements four hundred percent. They will be worth more than 6,000,000 and taxable by the state.[13]

The entire process was a sham. In the end, the fraudulent eugenics tests verified 126 of White Earth's 5,173 Indians were full-bloods. No land was given back to natives and little compensation was made. Not surprisingly, when Albert Jenks was

---

[10] Records of the United States Attorney, U.S. Department of Justice, "Land Allotment Fraud Cases at White Earth, Deposition Testimony," NA (Chicago Regional Branch), 11.
[11] Ranson J. Powell to Albert Jenks, November 16, 1914, Powell Papers, MHS Archives.
[12] "1,000 Land Titles Hang by a Hair, if Curly Indians Lose," *Minneapolis Journal*, June 24, 1915, 1.
[13] "Professor Jenks Returns to the University," *University of Minnesota Alumni Weekly* 15, no. 21 (1916): 12.

questioned about his racist version of human origin and eugenic typing, he replied, "I accept the physical origin of man as animal ... [for] some people's ancestors but probably not mine."[14]

The "science" is comical by modern standards, but the net result was that they recorded only 126 full-bloods at White Earth. Everyone else was denied remedy for the land theft. And their surveillance notes, field records, and scientific tests are still the basis for tribal enrollment at White Earth today. And today because the blood lines are so thin from these records that the tribe has a high birth rate of 4.4 children per household, but a declining enrollment rate. It is ongoing genocide by surveillance. And the US government has created a labyrinth of laws and rules that have inhibited the tribe's recent efforts to change the criteria for tribal enrollment. For example, even though White Earth is an independent self-determined native nation, they are also part of an organization called the Minnesota Chippewa Tribe (MCT). The MCT's constitution is the constitution for White Earth. Several years ago, White Earth developed a new constitution for their tribe. The new constitution would have eliminated blood quantum as the criterion for tribal enrollment. But the MCT did not approve of the new constitution and their reform effort was invalidated. Blood quantum still determines eligibility for enrollment at White Earth today.

It was dangerous for native people to have the government know who they were, and effects were catastrophic.[15] In the late 1800s, the US government made school attendance for native children compulsory, but the tribes had few schools that satisfied the government's definition of a formal education. By the thousands, native children were therefore removed from their homes and sent to boarding schools, usually far from home. At these boarding schools, they received harsh physical punishment, forced conversions to Christianity, horrible living conditions, and poor nutrition. One-third of the children developed trachoma, a painful eye disease caused by poor hygiene. Malnutrition was widely reported. Sexual abuse of children was also widely reported. At Haskell (Kansas) and Carlisle (Pennsylvania), the schools kept cemeteries for the children, and buried them by the hundreds in some years. Parents did not get their children's bodies back for burial or have say over the religious decisions around the burial of their children. Most of the grandparent generation today have been through these schools. For the survivors, the impacts on tribal languages, community cohesion, and substance abuse were directly driven by the US government's education policy and the surveillance tactics that informed the roundup of native children.

Even as the boarding school era slowly started to give way to day schools after World War II, social services maintained a close surveillance of native children.

---

[14] "Popular Picture of Indian Upset by Investigation, Eagle Beak Nose Belongs Not to Red Man, but to Fiction," *Minneapolis Journal*, April 9, 1916, 3.

[15] Treuer, *Everything You Wanted to Know About Indians*, 257–262.

From then to now, fully one-third of native children are removed from their birth homes and placed into foster care or adopted. Even today, after passage of the Indian Child Welfare Act of 1978, the majority of the adopting and foster parents are white.[16]

The operating problem with surveillance is the way it objectifies human beings. They become numbers, data sets, tools to be manipulated or controlled. While many native people experience a special pain with invisibility and marginalization, they simultaneously experience a lot of hypervisibility. That hypervisibility is rendered possible through the constant information gathering and branding of native peoples. Their cars often show a tribal license plate. Like many people of color, many natives look darker than white Americans, and it all serves to make them easier to surveil and to treat differently. On a per capita basis, this makes native Americans the racial group most likely to be shot by police and incarcerated.[17] Police officers and judges have a lot of discretionary power, and the application of that discretion can be done with implicit bias or even prejudice. As a result, the police do not do stop-and-frisk searches on college campuses in spite of the high percentage of college kids who report regular use of marijuana and other drugs. But there has been and remains an ongoing history of stop-and-frisk searches or intense police presence in communities of color, including reservations. The intense surveillance there leads many native people to call the activity "the occupation." It started with the genesis of the United States of America and it has never ended.

Remedies are not easy to engineer. But we need a change in consciousness first to drive the policy changes that will structurally interrupt America's long history and culture of surveilling native people. More training for professionals in social services, police, and courts to interrupt implicit bias is a critical need. More privacy protections for native people are long overdue as well as an overhaul of tribal enrollment practices, with an eye on eliminating the US government's paternalistic oversight and the more self-governance empowerment to the tribes. And for all Americans, we have a responsibility to understand this history and make informed choices as we navigate forward. It's our best hope to make sure the next 500 years are different from the last.

---

[16] Ibid., 213–216.
[17] Ibid., 285–288.

12

In a Most Excellent and Perfect Order

Surveillance, Racialization, and Government Practices in Colonial Canada

Scott Thompson

ALMIGHTY God hath created and appointed all things, in heaven, earth, and waters, in a most excellent and perfect order... In earth he hath assigned and appointed kings and princes, with other governors under them, in good and necessary order ... Every degree of people, in their vocation, calling, and office, hath appointed to them their duty and order.
    An Exhortation Concerning Good Order and Obedience, The Book of Common Prayer, 1559

Every effort should be made to aid the Red man in lifting himself out of his condition of tutelage and dependence, and that is clearly our wisdom and our duty, through education and every other means, to prepare him for a higher civilization by encouraging him to assume the privileges and responsibilities of full citizenship.
    Annual Report of the Department of the Interior, 1876

In 1953, a man holding the position of "Indian Councillor" at Sarnia Indian Reserve #45 stood up. Government officials had been sent to his reserve to speak to the "Indians" and explain to them how being given the right to vote in elections, and the ability to purchase alcohol legally under Canadian law, would "help" his band properly develop into good "civilized" Canadian citizens. Having listened, he responded simply: "We were the first settlers on this continent. Then, the whites came and *made us Indians*."[1] This short statement eloquently summarizes two centuries of surveillance-focused law and social policy targeting First Nations, Inuit, and Métis peoples in Canada. It expresses two key components of Canadian/British Imperialism; first, the creation and enforcement of an imposed and unwanted racial category of "Indian," and second, the construction and assertion of an expected "education," and cultural development, tied to this racial

---

[1] Select Committee on Indian Affairs, "Second Fact Finding Tour of the Legislature's Select Committee on Indian Affairs," 1953, RG 49-132, file D-53. Archives of Ontario, Toronto, Canada (emphasis added).

identity. This chapter demonstrates the tight relationship between colonial systems of surveillance, social sorting, and the racialization of populations. Starting from an understanding of race as the social product of people's adoption of specific systems of classification and technosocial interpretations of individual identity performances,[2] and drawing on evidence from historical cases of state surveillance in Canada, this chapter argues that the surveillance-focused colonial programs that targeted the First Nations, Inuit, and Métis peoples promoted the adoption of specific cultural practices that were meant to develop "Indian" peoples into productive British subjects and Canadian citizens. In doing so, these programs produced a race-based understanding of what it was to be an "Indian" – an understanding of "Indian-ness" that existed exclusively from, and in contrast to, British white-settler-subjects. Moreover, this understanding of what it was to be an "Indian," also worked to identify strongly where "Indian" people were to fit within Canadian society and what role they were to play. As such, surveillance was crucial to the affirmation of colonial understandings of race, the racialization of populations within the assumed Canadian jurisdiction, and the cultural development of the content of the "Indian" racial category in Canada.

In making this argument it should be very clear that I am not using a uniform, or singular, cultural understanding of First Nations, Inuit, and Métis peoples in Canada. The cultures are unique, and their histories varied. I do, however, take the position and argue that the blanket, or inclusive, application of state surveillance-focused colonial technologies to *all* those legally categorized as "Indians" within the Canadian sociolegal jurisdiction worked to mediate, or selectively shape, the identity performances and understandings of these peoples in a unified way. Government programs imposed a specific, and uniform, racialized understanding of who "Indians" were. That is, this chapter argues that there are important complexities and uniqueness to the multiplicities of cultures of the First Nations, Inuit, and Métis peoples that inhabit North America; yet state colonial surveillance practices are a shared history for those living within the assumed Canadian jurisdiction, and that this uniformity worked, and continues to work, to make *all* these peoples "Indians."

As noted in the other chapters of this volume, surveillance was, and remains, a crucial component in colonialism. Surveillance systems gather data on populations, measure these data against a desired outcome or progression, and then take actions to assure that the sought-after goals are attained.[3] In regards to race,

---

[2] Scott Thompson, "Making Up Soldiers: The Role of Statistical Oversight and Reactive Path Dependence in the Effectiveness of Canada's WWII Mobilization Program 1940–1943," *Surveillance & Society* 12, no. 4 (2014): 547–565; also see Scott Thompson, "I am Zombie: Mobilization in WWII Canada and Forced 'Zombie' Performances 1939–1947," *Canadian Journal of Sociology* 41, no. 4 (2016): 465–492.

[3] Scott Thompson, "National Security, Surveillance, and the Reproduction of Colonial Understandings of Aboriginal Sovereignty in Canada," in Mitch Daschuk, Carolyn Brooks,

Browne[4] uses the term "racializing surveillance" to explain how surveillance practices press categories of difference onto colonial others while also working "to structure social relations and institutions in ways that privilege Whiteness." This chapter takes up a similar understanding of race and racialization. Yet, it also draws from Foucauldian literature, which proposes that categories of race are central in establishing hierarchical relationships of domination and subjugation, and in designating conduct as prohibited or allowed.[5] This chapter also understands surveillance technologies as the techniques, skills, and methods, designed to bring specific rationalities into being by shaping behavior.[6] In this way, surveillance is never neutral, as it always pushes the development of the social toward a specific goal or purpose, which corresponds directly to how specific surveillance systems categorize populations.[7] To understand how surveillance racializes populations and (re)produces the cultural content of applied racial categories, the surveillance practices directed at controlling the behaviors of "Indian" classified peoples within the assumed jurisdiction of Canada provide an excellent example. Colonial surveillance practices in Canada were specifically designed, have worked, and continue to work to do just that – to (re)produce the content of racial categories, as well as to mediate the identity performances of racialized peoples.

I am also conscious of not taking voice from First Nations, Inuit, and Métis peoples. The stories of how surveillance was applied, how communities responded to them, and how these communities came to understand these actions, is not the focus of this work. Rather, it is the focus of this chapter to demonstrate instances of uniformity within state surveillance practices directed at "Indian" populations, as a means of depicting how the government of Canada racialized these peoples and sought to direct their cultural development. After reviewing the British cultural understandings, or rationalities, which informed the development of colonial practices and the sorting of peoples within the territories claimed to be under British/

and James Popham (eds.), *Critical Perspectives on Social Control and Social Regulation in Canada* (Halifax: Fernwood Publishing, 2020), 385–409; Thompson, "I am Zombie," 465–492; Thompson, "Making Up Soldiers," 547–565.

[4] Simone Browne, "Race and Surveillance," in Kirstie Ball, Kevin Haggerty, and David Lyon (eds.), *Handbook on Surveillance Studies* (New York: Routledge, 2012), 72–79, 73.

[5] Ann Laura Stoler, *Race and the Education of Desire: Foucault's History of Sexuality and the Colonial Order of Things* (Durham, NC: Duke University Press, 1995).
Kim Su Rasmussen, "Foucault's Genealogy of Racism," *Theory, Culture and Society* 28, no. 5 (2011): 34–51, https://journals.sagepub.com/doi/10.1177/0263276411410448.

[6] Jan Peter Bergen and Peter-Paul Verbeek, "To-Do Is to Be: Foucault, Levinas, and Technologically Mediated Subjectivation," *Philosophy & Technology* 33, no. 4 (2020): 325–348, https://link.springer.com/article/10.1007/s13347-019-00390-7; Michael C. Behrent, "Foucault and Technology," *History and Technology* 29, no. 1 (2013): 54–104, www.tandfonline.com/doi/abs/10.1080/07341512.2013.780351.

[7] David Lyon, *Surveillance Studies: An Overview* (Cambridge, MA: Polity Press, 2012); Melvin Kranzberg, "Technology and History: Kranzberg's Laws," *Technology and Culture* 27, no. 3 (1986): 544–560, www.jstor.org/stable/3105385; Oscar Gandy, *The Panoptic Sort: A Political Economy of Personal Information* (Boulder, CO: Westview Press, 1993).

Canadian jurisdiction, this chapter identifies key colonial surveillance programs that targeted "Indian" peoples, focusing particularly on a case study that explains how surveillance practices surrounding the sale of alcohol worked to impose racial boundaries, and further embed a component of alcohol abuse within Canadian understandings of the "Indian" racial category. In short, this chapter demonstrates how colonial surveillance programs in Canada worked to racialize and *make* certain classified peoples "Indians."

BRITISH UNDERSTANDINGS OF COLONIALISM AND SOCIAL SORTING BY "RACE" IN CANADA

In its time of colonization, empire, and settlement, British Imperial colonialism fit the motto: "Make the world England" – expressing that the goal of colonial expansion was the conversion of land, labor power, and culture into forms that were compatible with European economies and British social order. For those living within the claimed jurisdiction of the Canadian Dominion, this meant reconceptualizing the First Nations, Inuit, and Métis peoples of North America within a racialized and differentiated societal position, that carried a role in the colonial process that was distinctive from white-settler-subject/citizens. As noted by the Aamjiwnaang First Nation man from Sarnia Reserve #45 above, this practice of social sorting required attributing the ordering and restrictive sociolegal category of "Indian" to these peoples. Within the Canadian context, imperialist and colonial rationalities can be traced to the British understanding of the interconnection between social order, economic productivity, and racial conflict. Together these beliefs contributed to the conceptualization of European peoples and settlers as biologically, and culturally, superior to other racialized groups they encountered. This ideology established British cultural and economic colonial governance as not only the "natural" order of things, but also as a God-given task, serving for the benefit of *all* peoples – even those who faced the subjugation and reordering required under colonialism. Understanding the interconnection of these core concepts of colonialism in Canada – social order, economic productivity, and racial conflict – are crucial as they are embedded in, and are formative of, the racial category of "Indian" that was taken up by Canadian government policy, and with this category, the racializing colonial practices of surveillance.

British imperial rationalities stem from a particular understanding of social order, (re)produced through a series of Church of England religious sermons, or homilies, that the state required to be delivered and taught to the peoples of England starting in 1547. As explained in An *Exhortation Concerning Good Order and Obedience to Rulers and Magistrates*,[8] every individual was understood to be

---

[8] Church of England, "An Exhortation Concerning Good Order and Obedience to Rulers and Magistrates," in *Twelve Homilies Selected from Those Appointed to be Read in Churches in the*

born into a particular position within a strict, hierarchically ordered, and rigid society. Those at lower levels were to defer to and serve those above them, receiving protection and guidance in return. Within this understanding of society, God decided the place and role of each individual, and in his infallibility, placed each person in their proper and rightful place. God's ordering was understood as perfection, thought to be executed in accordance with his plan and the covenant with man, in which human piety and obedience were exchanged for prosperity. As a result, every individual was called on to strictly adhere to this "natural order" of selected birth into a hierarchical society and to the fulfillment of their ascribed social roles. By doing so they would keep to God's plan and necessarily ensure prosperity for all people. As the Church of England's homily on order notes:

> ALMIGHTY God hath created and appointed all things, in heaven, earth, and waters, in a most excellent and perfect order...In earth he hath assigned and appointed kings and princes, with other governors under them, in good and necessary order... Every degree of people, in their vocation, calling, and office, hath appointed to them their duty and order. Some are in high degree, some in low; some kings and princes, some inferiors and subjects; priests and laymen, masters and servants, fathers and children, husbands and wives, rich and poor; and every one have need of other. So that in all things is to be lauded and praised the goodly order of God: without the which no house, no city, no commonwealth can continue and endure; for, where there is no right order, there reigneth all abuse, carnal liberty, enormity, sin, and Babylonical confusion.[9]

That is, strict adherence to this "natural order," which placed people in high or low degree, meant that vocations identified who should command and who would obey. Moreover, and more importantly, it brought prosperity in the form of economic productivity – as long as everyone played their role and followed God's plan.

As the English took up colonialist practices, this rationality established it as the duty, and even the burden,[10] of colonialists to bring this "natural order," and its links to prosperity through economic productivity, to the unorganized spaces of "abuse, carnal liberty, sin and Babylonical confusion" in the world. With regard to British classification and racialization of the people's whose lands they were actively colonizing, bringing God's order meant proclaiming British values, social

---

Time of Queen Elizabeth of Famous Memory (London: The Prayer-Book and Homily Society, 1854), 66–77.
[9] Kate Aughterson, *The English Renaissance: An Anthology of Sources and Documents* (New York: Routledge, 1998), 93.
[10] Kipling would later go so far as to depict this order–productivity–racial superiority link to colonial rationalities as "The White Man's Burden," lamenting, some argue facetiously, that it is the unwanted, daunting, and burdensome, task of the white race to subjugate, rule, educate, and civilize the peoples of the world. Rudyard Kipling, "The White Man's Burden," *McClure's Magazine* 12 (1899): 290–291.

organization and economic production. As Hobson[11] notes of early British imperialism and colonialism:

> when British authority has been forcibly fastened upon large populations of alien race and colour, with habits of life and thought which do not blend with ours ... [w]e are obliged in practice to make a choice between good order and justice administered autocratically in accordance with British standards, on the one hand, and delicate, costly, doubtful, and disorderly experiments in self-government on British lines upon the other, and we have practically everywhere decided to adopt the former alternative.

This need to reorder racialized societies and lands found expression in the British legal application of *terra nullius*,[12] the legal classification of "nobody's land," or lands unclaimed, that existed without legitimate legal ownership and were subject to *Discovery*.[13] In the colonial period the idea of unclaimed land was applied not only to lands without inhabitants, as it had been historically, but also to lands that were uncultivated according to European agricultural standards, that existed without permanent residences or settlements (thus excluding the "legitimate" use by any nomadic peoples), and that were under the use of peoples who held no allegiance to a Christian Crown. The expansion of the category of unclaimed land worked to open up new spaces for the application of God's order through European "discovery," colonization, and settlement.[14] As noted by Deherme,[15] colonialism linked discovery with production and racial subjugation, since:

> the most important result of colonization is to increase world productivity. It is at the same time a great social force for progress. The earth belongs to humanity. It belongs to those who know best how to develop it, increase its wealth and in the process augment it, beatify it and elevate humanity. Colonization is the propagation of the highest form of civilization yet conceived and realized, the perpetuation of the most talented race, the progressive organization of humanity.

In this way, colonial control and imposed governance was understood to be in no way oppressive, dictatorial, tyrannical, or self-serving, but instead a humanitarian act

---

[11] John M Hobson, *Imperialism: A Study* (New York: Cossimo, 2005 [1938]), 118, 122.

[12] *Terra nullius*, from the Latin for "nobody's land," is a legal term that originated in Roman Law and was later taken up by the European common law traditions. It refers to lands in which there is no legitimated land title or continuous use, and it was historically applied to lands without inhabitants (see Leslie Claude Green and Olive Patricia Dickason, *Law of Nations and the New World* (Edmonton: University of Alberta Press, 1981), 141, 180, 233, 249).

[13] The legal concept of *Discovery*, enabled Europeans to claim uninhabited lands as having been "discovered" for a given sovereign. Once land was "discovered," European sovereigns then had the legal right to exert ownership over that land, and occupy it. See Andrew Porter, *European Imperialism, 1860-1914* (Hampshire: Macmillan, 1994), 357.

[14] Ibid., 357.

[15] Cited in Alice L. Conklin, *A Mission to Civilize: The Republican Idea of Empire in France and West Africa, 1895–1930* (Stanford University Press, 1997), 56.

that fulfilled the duty of those of higher racial and social degrees to bring the natural order of God's will to the benefit of all the peoples of the world. For Canada, British expansion of economic and production practices were conceptualized as bringing prosperity, peace, and most importantly, productivity to the "lesser" races as well as to the "unordered," and "misused," spaces of North America, elevating the capacity of both peoples and land to produce useful goods and services compatible with European economies.[16]

As scientific discourses progressed, they too contributed to this colonialist vision of the betterment of "lesser" peoples through the conversion to Western productive practices. Drawing on the "evidence" of white supremacy through the perceived success of colonial expansion into the spaces of differentially racialized peoples,[17] these arguments tied discourses of race struggle and Social Darwinism together, arguing that colonial expansion was "rooted in nature, and human nature," and that it was a positive, progressive, and natural force.[18] Thinkers of the day argued that it:

> must go on ... It has been the prime condition and mode of progress in the past, therefore it is desirable it should go on. It must go on, it ought to go on ... This genuine and confident conviction about "social efficiency" must be taken as the chief moral support of Imperialism. Human progress requires the maintenance of the race struggle, in which the weakest races shall go under, while the "socially efficient" races survive and flourish: we are the "socially efficient" race. So runs the imperialist argument.[19]

As a British Dominion, and a place in which people were legally British subjects until after World War II, early Canadian governments and government policy drew strongly on British colonial and imperial discourses of order–productivity–racial superiority, envisioning themselves as a central player in world affairs. As Levitt[20] notes, "glorifying the Anglo-Saxon race made good sense because it increased pride in British heritage and made it possible to envisage a greater Canadian role in world politics as a 'linchpin' connecting the British and the Americans." In its application of colonial policy this meant the maintenance of Eurocentric economic production, the settlement and capitalist cultivation of land, and a focus on making the inhabitants of Canada good British subjects. A key impediment to this colonial dream was the sovereignty of Aboriginal peoples and how this sovereignty manifested in acts of resistance to take up British cultural and productive practices. At the time, this

---

[16] Douglas L. Cole, "The Problem of 'Nationalism' and Imperialism' in British Settlement Colonies," *Journal of British Studies* 10, no. 2 (1971): 175, 178. https://doi.org/10.1086/385614.

[17] Royal Commission on Aboriginal Peoples, *The Report of the Royal Commission on Aboriginal Peoples*, vol. 1: *Looking Forward, Looking Back* (Ottawa: Government of Canada, 1996), 113–116.

[18] Hobson, *Imperialism: A Study*, 155.

[19] Ibid.

[20] Joseph Levitt, "Race and Nation in Canadian Anglophone Historiography," *Canadian Review of Studies in Nationalism* 1 no. 8 (1981): 1–16, 4–5.

asserted sovereignty and its acts of disordering resistance to British/Canadian colonialism, were referred to collectively within government as the "Indian Problem."[21]

At the time of confederation in 1867 the federal Constitution of Canada (the British North America Act 1867) placed the jurisdiction over "Indians, and lands reserved for Indians" under the federal government. Before that time, "Indian" policy fell under the legal jurisdiction of the British Colonial Military due to the centrality of peace and allegiance in early treaties, while governance was later passed on to the separate colonial governments, with specific legislation having existed in what would become the Canadian provinces of Nova Scotia starting in 1762, Ontario in 1839, and Québec in 1850, though the western provinces which later joined the confederation had no such legislation. Also, at the time of confederation, Canada inherited a series of British Crown/First Nations treaties that had transferred land rights to the British Crown in exchange for gifts, annual payments, and in many cases education, among other specified things.[22] These treaties resulted in the restriction of the sovereignty of First Nations peoples spatially to designated reserve lands, and politically, in their establishment of exclusive relations with the British Crown.[23] With the treaties and development of colonial policy, a legal racial category of "Indian" was needed in order to distinguish the laws and rights of a given individual within the Dominion. The treaties asserted First Nations rights to treaty gifts and access to reserve land, while colonial law also clearly established that "Indians" did not hold the legal rights of British white-settler-subjects – particularly in regards to land ownership, political participation, or the production and sale of goods and services. In 1850 the category of "Indian" was defined as:

> First. – All persons of Indian Blood, reputed to belong to the particular Body or Tribe of Indians interested in such lands, and their descendants. Secondly. – All persons intermarried with any such Indians and residing among them, and the descendants of all such persons. Thirdly. – All persons adopted in infancy by any such Indians, and residing in the Village or upon the lands of such Tribe or Body of Indians.[24]

By 1876, the racial definition of "Indian" took up a strict patrilineal model, where only those born of "Indian" fathers would carry the legal classification. Here, the legislation of the Indian Act also specifically separated the legal classification of "Indian" from that of British subjects, noting that a rights-holding "person" under

---

[21] Duncan Campbell Scott, *Notes on the Meeting Place of the First Parliament of Upper Canada and the Early Buildings at Niagara* (Ottawa: Royal Society of Canada, 1914), 662.

[22] Government of Canada, *Indian Treaties and Surrenders from 1680–1902* (Ottawa: Kings Printer, 1905).

[23] Jim Aldridge and Terry Fenge, *Keeping Promises: The Royal Proclamation of 1763, Aboriginal Rights, and Treaties in Canada* (Montreal: McGill-Queen's University Press, 2015).

[24] An Act for the Better Protection of the Lands and Property of the Indians in Lower Canada 1850, c. 42, s. 5.

Canadian law was defined as "an individual other than an Indian."[25] In contrast to the "drop of blood" mode of racial classification used to identify black persons in the United States, the goods, services, and benefits legally due to treaty signatories and their people, created a situation where the government of Canada desired, and took steps, to limit and strictly manage who was a legal "Indian." Policy was to push "Indians" toward becoming good British subjects, which included cultural change, but also legal change, extinguishing their legal status as "Indians" entitled to treaty benefits, through a process known as "Enfranchisement." Initiated in 1857, the enfranchisement process was first laid out in An Act to Encourage the Gradual Civilization of Indians (1857). The Act allowed "Indians" to achieve the status of British subjects under Canadian law, giving them rights to vote, own property, purchase and possess alcohol legally, and receive a lump sum of land and money taken from their treaty group.[26] Originally thought to be something all Indians would want to obtain, enfranchisement had to be applied for, and it required the applicant to be "able to speak readily either the English or French language, of sober and industrious habits, free from debt and sufficiently intelligent."[27] In its first nineteen years, only a small number of individuals applied, and of those, only one individual willfully accepted enfranchisement.[28] This lack of Colonial success, led to the rewriting of enfranchisement laws to remove Indian status now *without* the individual's consent for an increasing number of reasons, including: marriage,[29] education,[30] birth out of wedlock,[31] leaving a reserve for a period of more than five years,[32] and living off the reserve.[33] These circumstances were taken as indicators that a given "Indian" had become sufficiently civilized, had surpassed their racial group, and was able to take up the freedoms and responsibilities of British subjects.

In the post-military governance period when authority was shifted to the colonies and later a confederated Canada in 1867, colonial governance pursued the elimination of the "Indian Problem" though the elimination of "Indian" peoples. As Wolfe[34] notes, this "logic of elimination" envisioned Indigenous sovereignty as a

---

[25] Indian Act 1876, c. 18, s. 10.
[26] John Milloy, "The Early Indian Acts: Developmental Strategy and Constitutional Change," in Ian L. Getty and Antoine Lussier (eds.), As Long as the Sun Shines and the Water Flows: A Reader in Canadian Native Studies (Vancouver: University of British Columbia Press 1983), 58.
[27] Act to Encourage the Gradual Civilization of Indians 1857, c. 26 s. 4.
[28] Milloy, The Early Indian Acts, 61.
[29] An Act for the Gradual Enfranchisement of Indians, the better management of Indian Affairs, and to Extend the Provisions of the Act 31st Victoria, Chapter 42 1869, c. 6, s. 6.
[30] Indian Act 1876, c. 18, s. 86.
[31] Ibid., s. 3a.
[32] Ibid., s. 3b.
[33] Indian Act 1918, s. 6(122a)1.
[34] Patrick Wolfe, "Settler Colonialism and the Elimination of the Native," Journal of Genocide Research 8 no. 4 (2006): 387–409.

threat to the acquisition of lands and the establishment of colonial governance. Taking up a policy of "assimilation," the goal was to convert "Indians" to good British subjects, and later good Canadian citizens, through the means of extinguishing "Indian" values, beliefs, means of production, and race – to "take the Indian out of the child."[35] In practice, this meant coercing "Indians" to take up British social organization and adopt labor practices that fit a European focused economy – mostly in the form of European agricultural practices. In the words of later legislation, government policy was to encourage "the progress of civilization among the Indian Tribes in this Province and the gradual removal of all legal distinctions between them and Her Majesty's other Canadian subjects."[36] Although the language of assimilation did exist in different forms over time, there is continuity in the affirmation of the order–productivity–racial superiority found in British imperial and colonial rationalities.[37] In 1828 Upper Canada, the preconfederation province with the most comprehensive "Indian" policy, the stated goals for governance of those classified as "Indians" were:

> 1st to collect Indians in considerable numbers, and settle them in villages with a due portion of land for their cultivation and support. 2nd To make such provision for their religious improvements, education, and instruction in husbandry as circumstances may from time to time require. 3rd To afford them such assistance in building their houses; rations; and in producing such seed and agricultural implements as may be necessary, commuting when practicable a portion of their presents for the latter.[38]

Just prior to confederation, the Canadian Bagot Commission (1842–1844) resulted in the identification of a set of similar goals into "Indian" management, development, and assimilation, including: centralization of control policy; formalization of Indian land use rights; licensing of timber; issuance of deeds on Indian lands; teaching techniques of European land management, and providing tools for agriculture; and teaching the concepts of individual ownership and Christianity.[39]

In order to more effectively and uniformly approach "Indian" identification, governance, and assimilation after confederation, the government of Canada consolidated its "Indian" policy under a single piece of legislation in 1876. Entitled The Indian Act (1876), this overarching law worked to unify under centralized federal department the governance of "Indians" and the shaping of "Indian" policy. The government noted that:

---

[35] Macdonald cited in Chris Benjamin, *Indian School Road: Legacies of the Shubenacadie Residential School* (Halifax: Nimbus Publishing, 2014), 29.
[36] An Act to Encourage the Gradual Civilization of Indians 1857, c. 26, preamble.
[37] Wolfe, *Settler Colonialism*, 387–409. Also see Lorenzo Veracini, *Settler Colonialism: A Theoretical Overview* (New York: MacMillan Palgrave, 2010).
[38] Duncan Campbell Scott, "Indian Affairs, 1867–1912," in *Canada and Its Provinces*, vol. 7, pt. 4 (Toronto: Glasgow, Brook & Company, 1914), 333.
[39] *Report on the Affairs of the Indian in Canada 1844*, Appendix EEE.

our Indian legislation generally rests on the principle, that the aborigines are to be kept in a condition of tutelage and treated as wards or children of the State. . . . [T]he true interests of the aborigines and of the State alike require that every effort should be made to aid the Red man in lifting himself out of his condition of tutelage and dependence, and *that is clearly our wisdom and our duty*, through education and every other means, *to prepare him for a higher civilization* by encouraging him to assume the privileges and responsibilities of full citizenship.[40]

Ultimately, Canadian colonial policy and surveillance practices ensured that Indian peoples were identified racially. Further, it ascribed a social position to them that was below British white-settler-subjects and gave "Indians" an expected developmental trajectory and goal to be enforced by a specified government Department of Indian Affairs. Hired to oversee this developmental change to the "Indians," Indian affairs officials were charged by Duncan Campbell Scott, then deputy superintendent-general of Indian affairs, to continue the programs of genocidal assimilation "until there is not a single Indian in Canada that has not been absorbed into the body politic, and there is no Indian question, and no Indian Department."[41] By 1880, this consolidation had standardized and stabilized colonial surveillance practices that governed the actions of "Indians" for the next seventy-one years.[42] The following sections take up how this rationality of order–productivity–racial superiority, and policy of "Indian" tutelage, found expression through state surveillance practices.

KEY CANADIAN SURVEILLANCE PROGRAMS TARGETING "INDIANS" (INDIAN AGENTS AND RESIDENTIAL SCHOOLS)

In post-confederation Canada, the primary surveillance actors regarding "Indians" were "Indian Agents." Indian Agents were government officials given the duty to oversee and manage the application of policy and law on reserves. Though the British relied on a series of trader/agents since the mid-1700s, following French colonial practice, Indian Agents' duties and responsibilities were formalized post-confederation in the Indian Act (1876).[43] These Agents would distribute treaty gifts

---

[40] *Annual Report of the Department of the Interior* 1876 (emphasis added).
[41] Brian Titley, "W. M. Graham: Indian Agent Extraordinaire," *Prairie Forum* 1 (1983): 25–41.
[42] The Indian Act went through significant revisions in 1951, and with it, policy, governance, and surveillance practices also went through important changes. See Douglas Sanders, "The Rights of the Aboriginal Peoples of Canada," *The Canadian Bar Review* 61, no. 1 (1983): 276.
[43] The duties and legal authority of Indian Agents expanded in scope significantly from 1876 until "Indian" laws and policy were significantly reorganized in 1951. After the 1951 reorganization, the majority of Indian Agents were retired, though agents remained active in isolated reserves until 1969. See Robin Brownlie, "Man on the Spot: John Daly, Indian Agent in Parry Sound, 1922–1939," *Journal of the Canadian Historical Association* 5, no. 1 (1994): 65–67; Olive Patricia Dickason, *Canada's First Nations: A History of Founding Peoples from Earliest Times* (Don Mills: Oxford University Press, 2002), 196; Milloy, *The Early Indian Acts*, 62.

In a Most Excellent and Perfect Order 243

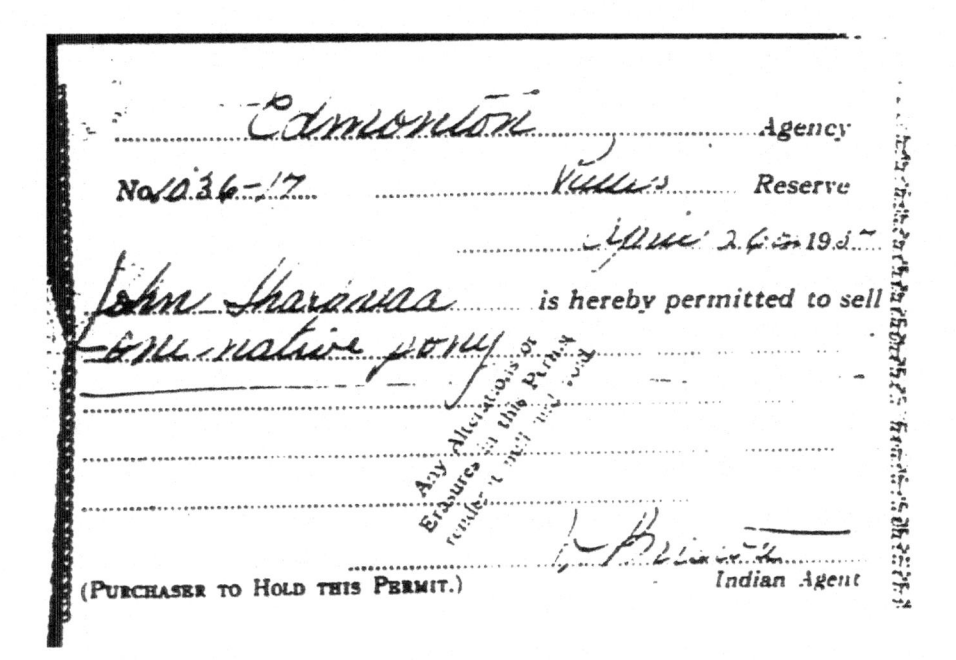

FIGURE 12.1 Indian Agent Permit Form (1937)
Permits were issued by Indian Agents for a wide variety of reasons. The above permit form gives permission for John Tharpnaa of the Paul Reserve in Alberta to sell a pony to someone off reserve. Indian Agent, 1937, "Permit – To Sell Native Pony," H2c 156B Control of Indian Reserves by Indian Agents, Catalogue #H89.55.13, Royal Alberta Museum.

and rations, act as judge and jury for legal cases involving "Indians," administer relief, oversee health conditions, manage fishing and hunting practices, and direct political life. Moreover, their word was law for those living on the reserves under their supervision.[44] Indian Agents were to watch over every aspect of life on reserves and work to enforce the government's colonial policy of assimilation. In addition to the technology of reports sent to the head office in Ottawa, "Indians'" legal position as wards, or children of the state, meant that they could not hold bank accounts, buy or sell goods, or rent or auction off reserve land; these decisions were to be made by the Indian Agent, in coordination with colonial policy. As a means of ensuring that Indian Agent directives were followed, and to communicate the approval of actions by the Agent to other British subjects, Indian Agents deployed the use of a highly detailed surveillance technology known as the "Permit System." (See Figure 12.1.)

[44] Dickason, *Canada's First Nations*, 267, 286, 299, 307–308; Laurie Barron, "The Indian Pass System in the Canadian West, 1882–1935," *Prairie Forum* 13, no. 1 (1988): 28; Sarah Carter, "Controlling Indian Movement: The Pass System," *NeWest Review* (May 1985): 8–9; Brownlie, "Man on the Spot," 65–67; Dorothee Schreiber, "'A Liberal and Paternal Spirit': Indian Agents and Native Fisheries in Canada," *Ethnohistory* 55, no. 1 (2008): 87–118.

Permits were needed for, and tracked, most aspects of reserve life – from the sale of goods to the harvesting of crops. They established the actions of Indians as being in line with applied policy and made visible to the head office the local actions of people classified as "Indians." As one individual existing under this system noted, with slight hyperbole, "you needed a permit for everything, you needed a permit [from the Indian Agent] to take a shit."[45] The application of Indian Agent control extended to cultural practices as the law forbade traditional ceremonies, dances, and gatherings – these actions not fitting with the project of assimilation to British ways of life. The Permit System was supplemented in the western provinces with a Pass System, formally in place between 1882 and 1941, where the off-reserve movements of "Indians" were monitored and restricted even though this was known within the government to be an illegal violation of treaty rights to hunt, fish, gather, and travel.[46] With permits and passes Indian Agents monitored many aspects of daily life. However, the vision of surveillance and control found its most invasive expression in the pilot program of "Model Villages" in the early 1900s. In these instances, Indian Agents chose not only the design and organization of "Indian" settlements, how labor power was to be applied, and when and how produced goods were to be used or sold, but also who should be married and have children.[47] These actions were taken in hopes of (re)producing the desired Britishness within "Indian" classified peoples both in action and appearance.

Coupled with the surveillance-focused Indian Agent system, post-confederation legislation under the Indian Act (1876 and revised 1920) required that all individuals classified as "Indian" children, later defined as ages 7 to 18, were to be educated in the British manner. The goal of this colonial project was again the extermination of First Nations, Inuit, and Métis cultures, values, and language by targeting assimilation policy at children.[48] Although these "schools" were originally voluntary, by 1894 the Indian Act had been amended to make attendance compulsory; by the 1920s, compulsory attendance was actively enforced. The "Residential School" system, as it was called, was consciously designed to render visible the social interactions of children, to observe and correct their behaviors, and to sever family ties to the parent and elder generations. As one of the program's designers noted:

> if you wish to educate these children you must separate them from their parents during the time that they are being educated. If you leave them in the family they may know how to read and write, but they still remain savages, whereas by

---

[45] Anonymous, *Recordings of Interviews with an Elder, 1956. Blood Indian Agency*, 11788 Box 2, 77, 9–15, Royal Alberta Museum, Edmonton, Canada.

[46] Barron, *The Indian Pass System in the Canadian West*, 25–42; Carter, *Controlling Indian Movement*, 8–9.

[47] Dickason, *Canada's First Nations*, 299; Titley, W. M. Graham, 25–41; "Indian Students Forced into Marriage, Farm Life," *Globe and Mail*, December 10, 1990.

[48] John Milloy, *A National Crime: The Canadian Government and the Residential School System, 1879–1986* (Winnipeg: University of Manitoba Press, 1999).

In a Most Excellent and Perfect Order 245

FIGURE 12.2 Pencil issued at a Northern Ontario Residential School
Pencil issued to First Nations children at a Northern Ontario Residential School predominately states that "misuse is abuse," making reference to the importance of avoiding the "misuse" of resources by "Indian" peoples. "A Tribe Without Freedom," *Indian Record*, XXV, no. 5 (1962): 3.

separating them in the way proposed, they acquire the habits and tastes – it is to be hoped only the good tastes – of civilized people.[49]

As such, the "schools" were purposefully built away from settlements or lands traditionally associated with seasonal gathering or hunting in order to separate children from their communities. Many children had no option but to reside within these spaces throughout the school year, while strictly enforced laws would often imprison parents for not sending their children to these places or even for visiting them.[50]

The Residential School system relied on rendering the behaviors of vulnerable children visible and actionable to colonial governance. Supervisors and administrators watched these children day and night and drummed into them the order–production–racial superiority rationality of Canadian colonial policy through the design of its teachings and the organization of classroom structure – with students staying within teachers' lines of sight. Within the schools, native languages were forbidden and cultural practices strictly prohibited, as students were strictly monitored for acting in ways associated with "Indians."[51] (See Figure 12.2.)

Instances of abuse and experiences of suffering in these spaces cannot be overstated, and the damage caused to individuals and culture was, and remains, a major challenge moving forward.[52] Conditions within these "schools" are recorded as being horrific, with inadequate resources to meet the most basic needs of the

---

[49] Hector-Lewis Langevin, "Indian Industrial Schools," Canada, House of Commons Debates (May 22, 1883), 1376.
[50] Nuu-chah-nulth Tribal Council, *Indian Residential Schools: The Nuu-Chah-Nulth Experience Report of the Nuu-Chah-Nulth Tribal Council Indian Residential School Study, 1992-1994* (Canada: Nuu-chah-nulth Tribal Council, 1996), 42; Agnes Grant, *No End to Grief: Indian Residential Schools in Canada* (Winnipeg: Pemmican, 1996), 189–190.
[51] Truth and Reconciliation Commission of Canada, *Honouring the Truth, Reconciling for the Future: Summary of the Final Report of the Truth and Reconciliation Commission of Canada* (Ottawa: Truth and Reconciliation Commission of Canada, 2015).
[52] Ibid., 135–318; Patricia Monture-Angus, *Journeying Forward: Dreaming First Nations' Independence* (Halifax: Fernwood Publishing, 1999); Eduardo Duran, *Native American Postcolonial Psychology* (Albany, NY: State University of New York Press, 1995); James Rodger Miller, *Skyscrapers Hide the Heavens: A History of Indian-White Relations in Canada* (University of Toronto Press, 1989).

children. Officials within these spaces applied physical and psychological abuse to children as a means of pressuring them towards assimilation of British ways of life and values.[53] In addition to physical, emotional, sexual, and psychological abuse, a government analysis from 1909 showed that between 35 and 60 percent of all the children taken in to these "schools" died from mistreatment, malnutrition, disease, or exposure.[54] In this way, the government of Canada used the surveillance-intensive Residential School system as a means of (re)producing British ways of life within "Indian" populations – to detrimental effects.[55]

ALCOHOL SURVEILLANCE AND THE (RE)PRODUCTION OF THE "INDIAN" RACIAL CATEGORY

Though the above section identifies key colonial surveillance practices directed to socially sort and shape the assimilation and extermination of First Nations, Inuit, and Métis cultures, beliefs, and peoples within Canada's claimed jurisdiction, this section specifically takes up colonial surveillance practices relating to alcohol consumption as a means of demonstrating: (i) how exactly it is that the legal category of "Indian" enabled the surveillance and social sorting of peoples; and (ii) how these systems worked to racialize classified peoples by mediating – that is, pressuring and shaping – the types of identity performances that "Indians" were able to take up, to give content to, and (re)produce. In short, how the "Drunken Indian" racial stereotype was supported and (re)produced through government surveillance practices and technologies. In Canada, the idea of the "Drunken Indian" or "firewater myth" – which proposes that First Nations, Inuit, and Métis peoples are "more prone to develop an inordinate craving for liquor and to lose control over their behaviour when they drink"[56] – is sadly still held by many, even though links between alcoholism and race have long since been disproven.[57] Nonetheless, this

---

[53] Grant, *No End to Grief*; Celia Haig-Brown, *Resistance and Renewal: Surviving the Indian Residential School* (Vancouver: Tillicom, 1988).

[54] Peter Bryce, Letter to the Superintendent-General of Indian Affairs, November 5, 1909. Department of Indian Affairs, RG 10, DIA Archives, doc. #AW 1-353988. Library and Archives Canada, Ottawa, Canada. Also see Kevin Annett. *Hidden From History: The Canadian Holocaust: A Summary of an Ongoing Independent Inquiry into Canadian Native "Residential Schools" and their Legacy* (Vancouver: The Truth Commission into Genocide in Canada, 2001).

[55] See Government of Canada, *Regulations Relating to the Education of Indian Children* (Ottawa: Kings Printer, 1908); Truth and Reconciliation Commission of Canada, *Honouring the Truth*.

[56] Joy Leland, *Firewater Myths: North American Indian Drinking and Alcohol Addiction* (New Brunswick, NJ: Rutgers Center of Alcohol Studies, 1976), 1.

[57] See J. E. Trimble and F. Beauvais (eds.), *Health Promotion and Substance Abuse Prevention among American Indian and Alaska Native Communities: Issues in Cultural Competence* (Washington DC: Department of Health and Human Services, 2001), 3; Peter Mancall, *Deadly Medicine: Indians and Alcohol in Early America* (Ithaca, NY: Cornell University Press, 1995), 6; Manuella Adrian, N. Layne, and R. T. Williams. "Estimating the Effect of

link to alcohol abuse remains a part of the discursive content of the category of "Indian."[58] As this section demonstrates, the link between First Nations, Inuit, and Métis peoples and alcohol abuse can be traced to the way colonial policy was built into the surveillance technologies of liquor control in Canada, specifically in the way in which these technologies worked to mediate social interactions and identity performances surrounding alcohol consumption. In short, colonial social sorting surveillance practices racialized First Nations, Inuit, and Métis peoples classified as "Indians" in a way that pushed them to take up identity performances related to either abstinence or problem drinking in relation to alcohol.

Early reports of First Nations and Inuit contact with alcohol do not fit the "Drunken Indian" myth. Some noted that "Indians had no natural craving" for alcohol, while others asserted that they "spat out booze in disgust when it was first offered to them."[59] Like any other cultural groups, drinking behavioral practices vary considerably among individuals with First Nations, Inuit, and Métis heritage, making any generalization based on this factor inaccurate or disingenuous. It has, however, been shown that in pre-confederation Canada, alcohol was consciously used as a tool of trade, for the formalizing of allegiances, and as a means to manipulate communities.[60] It is also well-documented that early fur traders and government officials, in some instances, did work to promote binge drinking and unhealthy relationships with alcohol among First Nations, Inuit, and Métis peoples.[61] In regards to colonial surveillance practices, alcohol was a key indicator through which racial boundaries were policed – as early enfranchisement legislation had called for "Indians" to prove that they were of "sober and industrious habits" in order for them to attain full rights as British subjects.[62] Moreover, early trade laws sought to use racial alcohol prohibition to ensure that "Indians" would not urbanize,

---

Native Indian Population on County Alcohol Consumption: The Example of Ontario," *The International Journal of the Addictions* 25 (1990–1991): 5A–6A.

[58] Mariana Valverde, "A Postcolonial Women's Law? Domestic Violence and the Ontario Liquor Board's 'Indian List,' 1950–1990," *Feminist Studies* 30, no. 3 (2004): 567–568.

[59] Craig Heron, *Booze: A Distilled History* (Toronto: Between the Lines, 2003), 17.

[60] Craig MacAndrew and Robert Edgerton, *Drunken Comportment: A Sociological Explanation* (Chicago, IL: Aldine, 1969), 133; Edwin Rich, *The History of the Hudson's Bay Company: 1670–1870* (New York: Macmillan, 1967), 130; Paul Phillips, *The Fur Trade*, vol. 2 (Norman, OK: University of Oklahoma Press, 1961), 110, 127; Robert Allen, *His Majesty's Indian Allies: British Indian Policy in the Defence of Canada* (Toronto: Dundurn Press, 1993), 48–51.

[61] Aborigines' Protection Society, *The Hudson's Bay Company, Canada West and the Indian Tribes* (1865), PAMPH 1865 no. 15 (Archives of Ontario, Toronto, Canada), 14; Scott, *Indian Affairs, 1867–1912*; Reuben Thwaites, *The Jesuit Relations and Allied Documents: Travels and Explorations of the Jesuit Missionaries in New France, 1610–1791* (Cleveland, OH: Burrows Brothers, 1896); Ben Spence, *Prohibition in Canada* (Toronto: Dominion Alliance, 1919); Reginald Smart and Alan Ogborne, *Northern Spirits: A Social History of Alcohol in Canada* (Toronto: Addiction Research Foundation, 1996).

[62] An Act to Encourage the Gradual Civilization of Indians 1857, c. 26, s. 4.

and instead would continue to work remote trap lines[63] as a means of maintaining European focused productive practices.[64] In the post-confederation period, the Canadian government legally barred the sale to, and possession of, alcohol for all those classified as "Indians" under the Indian Act (1876).[65] This legislation also reasserted liquor purchasing and possession as one of the legal rights granted to any "Indian" who gave up their status and treaty rights and become enfranchised. Alcohol consumption was seen as a destabilizing force for "Indians," corrupting them, and impeding their learning of the productive practices required of them within British colonial rationalities.

When the piecemeal, province-by-province, and in some cases city-by-city, prohibition on alcohol ended in Canada in the 1920s and 1930s, surveillance technologies were brought in to control the drinking of both British subjects and "Indians."[66] Though each province within Canada had separate liquor legislation and policy, "Indian" drinking was a federal matter, and it was the federal Indian Act that maintained it as an offence to sell liquor to any individual who was classified as an "Indian," or to possess alcohol if one was classified as an "Indian." In post-prohibition Canada, the ability to purchase liquor was not a right for any individual, but instead required a government permit, as driving today requires a state issued driver's permit or license. Alcohol surveillance at this time relied on these personal liquor permits as well as highly detailed point-of-purchase forms. These technologies recorded each and every purchase and made past sales visible and able to be reviewed. At the time, all liquor purchases had to be made at government-run liquor stores, and legislation specified that past purchases were to be thoroughly assessed by government officials for overconsumption before any new sales could be made. (See Figure 12.3.)

The purpose of these technologies was to enforce "a kind of prohibition" in which the state knew "exactly who is buying and how much, and what disposition is being

---

[63] Traplines are identified geographical areas, or routes through these areas, that are exclusively allocated to individual fur trappers, single families, or an Indigenous group. Traplines became registered under Canadian provincial laws to identify legal exclusivity to trap animals along these routes, while this type of land-use exclusivity was also employed in the pre-colonial period to ensure that there was no overharvesting of particular animal types. See David M. Finch, "The Registered Trapline System in Northern Ontario," *Ontario History* 112, no. 2 (2020): 178–190.

[64] Renisa Mawani, "In Between and Out of Place: Racial Hybridity, Liquor and the Law in the Late Nineteenth and Early Twentieth Century British Columbia," *Canadian Journal of Law and Society* 15, no. 2 (2000): 27; Ken Coates, *Canada's Colonies: A History of the Yukon and Northwest Territories* (Toronto: James Lorimer, 1985), 187; Derek Smith, *Canadian Indians and the Law: Selected Documents, 1663–1972* (Toronto: McClelland and Stewart, 1975), 26; Spence, *Prohibition in Canada*.

[65] Indian Act 1876, c. 18, s. 2.

[66] Scott Thompson and Gary Genosko, *Punched Drunk: Alcohol, Surveillance and the LCBO 1927-1975* (Halifax: Fernwood Publishing, 2009), 15.

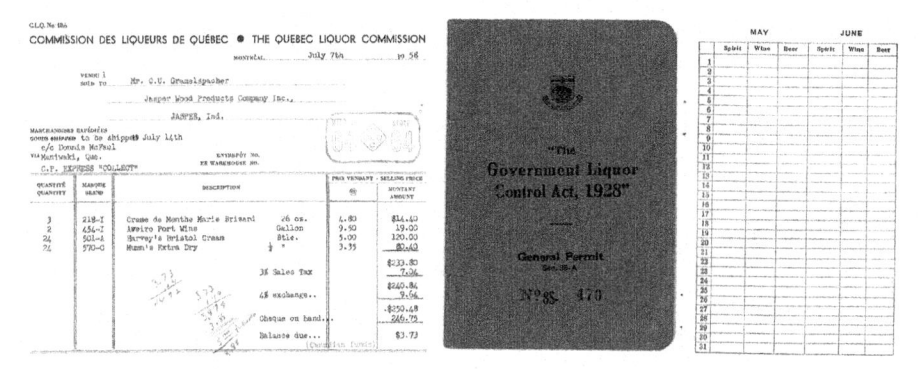

FIGURE 12.3 Purchase Order Form (Québec 1958) and Liquor Permit Book (Manitoba 1928)
The above examples are from the provinces of Québec and Manitoba, though permits and point-of-purchase order forms were in place in all Canadian jurisdictions (Thompson and Genosko, Punched Drunk, 15).

made of it."[67] The idea was not only to restrict the sale of liquor, but to control it. By "controlling it along lines that as the years go by and we carry on active educational methods we may not only eliminate the abuses and the excesses that are frequently indulged in, but that we may change the attitude of our people on the use of alcoholic beverages altogether."[68] Even though the sale of liquor had been legalized in the 1920s and 1930s, prohibition remained a popular political movement in Canada. The temperance and prohibition movements in Canada in the early 1900s had been effective in promoting the idea that liquor sales were exploitative, taking advantage of the weak-willed and the poor people who were racially or morally prone to alcohol abuse.[69] As a result, the politicians who brought in the new liquor laws stressed that consumption would be strictly controlled, while it was widely understood that "if the Government was expected to be returned at the next and succeeding elections they had to make their law effective" in controlling the drinking of weak and vulnerable populations.[70] This imposed "kind of prohibition" was also to specifically include "Indians."[71]

Under liquor control legislation, any "overindulgence" or "overspending," based on a review by liquor board government officials of purchases, coupled with the individual's income and occupation, would result in permits being cancelled and individuals' names formally added to the list of "known drunkards," called the

[67] George Howard Ferguson, *To the People of Ontario, 1927, Papers Concerning the Temperance Question in Ontario 1907–1929*, Howard Ferguson Fonds F 8, MU1029. File: Ferguson, George Howard Papers, Archives of Ontario, Toronto, Canada, 1.
[68] Ibid.
[69] "Welcome Page," Woman's Christian Temperance Union, https://web.archive.org/web/20090117033011/http://wctu.org/; Heron, *Booze*, 149, 217.
[70] John Willison, "Alberta Liquor Act; One Woman's View," *Ottawa Journal*, September 5, 1924.
[71] Ferguson, *To the People of Ontario*.

"Interdiction List."[72] Those listed would be barred from legally purchasing liquor from any stores or drinking establishments. Additionally, their names and likenesses would be circulated to local police services, drinking establishments, and stores, along with the statement that this person was on the Interdiction List and a warning that to serve them would be an offence. (See Figure 12.4).

Interdiction legislation existed in all provinces and established a nationwide legal category of "known drunkards," or "Interdicted" individuals, to whom the sale and possession of liquor was prohibited. In Ontario, as in the other provinces, those selling liquor were legally responsible for not selling liquor to those on the Interdiction List as well as those who were legally "Indians." As such, this surveillance system sorted these two groups into one single category for the purposes of enforcement – as it was explained by Head Office to those selling liquor, all "Indians" were to be conceptually added to the Interdiction List.[73]

This system of surveillance and social sorting relied on prototypical,[74] or stereotypical, means of determining "Indian" status. At the time, the Canadian government had no widely issued means of determining "Indian" status, and as such, an individual's appearance was used by liquor sales staff to racially sort those who came to purchase alcohol and to determine if their purchase would be declined as a result of them being on the Indian/Interdiction List for being an "Indian." As officials within the system explained:

> in view of the technical difficulty of deciding whether an Indian may come under the prohibitions of the *Indian Act*, whether he is a non-treaty Indian, or whether he may have become enfranchised and occupying the status of a white man, vendors, permit issuers and all other concerned are instructed to *refuse all applications for permits by persons of Indian Blood*.[75]

Another instruction to employees selling liquor explained this further, noting that vendors were to deny all those who were "looked upon by the people of the locality as Indians," even if "for one reason or another are not on the membership lists."[76] Due to this institutional policy that amalgamated with "Indians" with "known drunkards," the Interdiction List quickly became known within popular parlance as the "Indian List," linking these two previously historically separate legal categories (Indian and Interdicted) under a single racialized name.[77]

---

[72] Thompson and Genosko, *Punched Drunk*, 87–115.
[73] Ibid., 178–180.
[74] Eleanor Rosch, "Cognitive Representations of Semantic Categories," *Journal of Experimental Psychology* 104, no. 3 (1975): 192–233.
[75] Liquor Control Board of Ontario, Circulars nos. 1-4816. 1927–1963, AO: Administrative Records of the General Manager of the Liquor Control Board of Ontario, RG 41-3, boxes: 2, 7, 8, 9, no. 526 1928 (emphasis in original).
[76] Ibid. no. 63 1927.
[77] Thompson and Genosko, *Punched Drunk*, 174–181; Valverde, "A Postcolonial Women's Law?"

In a Most Excellent and Perfect Order 251

```
                              FILE COPY

 CABLE ADDRESS
"DISPENSONT"
   TORONTO

               LIQUOR CONTROL BOARD OF ONTARIO
                        55 LAKE SHORE BLVD. EAST
                        TORONTO 2, CANADA
                              July   th, 19  .


      NOTICE to all License Holders in: Armstrong, Savant Lake, Nakina, Longlac
            LCBS: #332, 245        AGENCY STORES #10, 14
            R. C. LEGIONS, BRANCHES #80, 116, 213

      RE:- (28) Mr. ██████████, ████████, Ontario
           (29) Mrs. ██████████, #██████ Band, █████████, Ontario
           (30) Mrs. ██████████, #██████ Band, █████████, Ontario
           (31) ████████████, ████ Band, ████████, Ontario
           (32) Mr. █████████, #██████ Band, █████████, Ontario
           (33) Mr. █████████, ██████, Ontario
           (34) Mr. █████████, #██████ Band, █████████, Ontario
           (35) Mr. █████████, #██████ Band, █████████, Ontario
           (36) Mr. █████████, #██ Whitesand Band, █████████, Ontario
           (37) ████████████, ████████, Ontario

                  Pursuant to the provisions of the Liquor Control
           Act and the Regulations, you are hereby prohibited to sell, serve
           or otherwise supply intoxicating liquor to the above named, for a
           period of TWELVE MONTHS FROM THE ABOVE DATE.


                              LIQUOR CONTROL BOARD OF ONTARIO.

                                   [signature]

      NAB:MR                  Chief Commissioner.

      Copy to Hotels in: Armstrong (1), Savant Lake (1), Nakina (1), Longlac (1)
           Hotel Inspector
           Chief Inspector, ██████████, O.P.P.
           R. C. Legions, Branches #80, 116, 213
           Stores as above
```

FIGURE 12.4 Interdiction notice identifying newly listed individuals (Ontario) Interdiction Notices, like the one above, were issued to all places which sold liquor in the local area, to police services and other organizations. In addition to conceptually adding all "Indians" to the list, individuals with First Nations heritage were also formally listed by Liquor Control Boards and Commissions in Canada on the Indian/Interdiction List, as seven of the above nine people added to the list in the example above are identified as Indian Band members. Liquor Control Board of Ontario 1929–1975, "Interdiction List," AO: Interdiction Records of the Liquor Licence Board of Ontario 1929–1990, RG 36-13, boxes: 194, 7, 6, 5, 4, 3, 2, 1-R, 2-R, 512, 1-D, 1, 551.

In regard to the mediation of identity performance, this meant that those who were, or looked, "Indian" faced social processes of racialization, including heightened surveillance and exclusion from legal and safe drinking places and practices. That is, one could avoid the prohibition of this system of surveillance if one could pass as a "non-Indian" – making the government's "kind of prohibition" applicable only to those who took up identity performances associated with "Indianness." Those who looked "Indian" faced the full force of liquor surveillance practices designed to identify and exclude those who misused or abused alcohol. In this way, all those on the Indian/Interdiction List for identified cases of alcohol abuse *and* those "on the list" for being an "Indian" were met with staff who adopted the identical policy and actions used to mediate, or shape and control, performances related to the consumption of alcohol. Those seeking to drink while listed were required to take up similar identity performances as a result of surveillance practices – (i) drinking in public spaces, since interdiction made it illegal to drink in one's home and the Indian Act made alcohol possession and use on reserves illegal; (ii) substitution to unregulated home-brewed liquor or alcohol designed for non-consumption purposes like rubbing alcohol or alcohol used in treating wood; (iii) purchases from bootleggers; and (iv) being subject to additional public and police scrutiny. Although this system did not succeed in completely restricting alcohol consumption by First Nations peoples, it was effective in shaping social relations and spaces in which people classified as "Indian" drank. As Maracle[78] notes:

> the law didn't stop or prevent Indians from drinking, but it did change the way they drank – for the worse. Since Indians were forbidden to buy liquor, they frequently resorted to drinking other far more dangerous intoxicants. More ominously, Indians also had to guzzle their beer, wine or liquor as quickly as possible to keep from being arrested.

A comment made to the Ontario Legislature's Select Committee on Indian Affairs by a Sioux Lookout, Ontario man in 1953 also supports the above statement, noting that after prohibition, "'firewater' ha[d] been coming in ever since," and that "we are not able to stop it."[79] In his comments he furthermore stressed the relationship between liquor surveillance, control practices, and identity performances related to drinking – asking of the government officials present:

> would [First Nations peoples] not feel better if they could go in the front door like men rather than creep like thieves to get liquor from the bootleggers? They go to a bootlegger and pay $5 and $10 for home brew, poisonous stuff. A few drinks of it will make you crazy, but you have held the Indian down so that they have to do that.[80]

---

[78] Brian Maracle, *Crazy Water: Native Voices on Addiction and Recovery* (Toronto: Viking, 1993), 44–45.
[79] Select Committee on Indian Affairs, "Second Fact Finding Tour," 521–522.
[80] Ibid.

Many individuals classified as "Indians" have lived experiences which include being arrested for public intoxication while sober,[81] while multiple Canadian legal cases have found, and established precedent, that "Indians" both appear drunk in the way that they walk and that they are prone to alcohol abuse.[82] This direct cultural link between alcohol abuse and "race," also applied to those with unhealthy drinking behaviors. In some cases of those investigated by Liquor Control Board, some individuals reviewed to be added to the Interdiction/Indian List argued that they could not possibly have an alcohol problem since they were "Caucasian."[83]

Importantly, liquor control relied on a policy of racial identification based on stereotypes, and then worked to mediate, or actively shape, the identity performances of those "Indian"-looking peoples choosing to drink alcohol. In this way, placing First Nations peoples on the Interdiction/Indian List linked the types of performances that they could take up to behaviors culturally associated with "known drunkards" – pressing them to either avoid governmental racial classification, or drinking in more public spaces off-reserve, drinking dangerous alternatives, and associating with those breaking the law to get liquor. In linking the Interdiction and "Indian" categories under the title of the "Indian List," these practices became associated with prototypical understandings of "Indianness" – creating a feedback loop where only those who identified as "Indians" were made to take up behaviors which fitted this stereotype, and only those who fitted the stereotype were racially classified as "Indians." In this instance, surveillance practices that linked the prototypical understandings of the categories of "known drunkards" and "Indians" would have an overweighted effect in shaping perceptions and cultural understandings.[84] That is, public perceptions of the prototypical "Indian" were not produced through knowledge of a representative sample of First Nations peoples' behaviors, but instead were only influenced by those who fitted a process of classification that now necessarily included performative acts associated with drunkenness.

CONCLUSIONS

To understand the link between surveillance and racialization, colonialism is rich with examples and case studies. In Canada, as in other places, the rationalities which were imbedded into colonial surveillance technologies are clear, as are the impacts and legacies of these programs. The rationality of order–productivity–racial superiority of British colonialism can be seen in the surveillance-focused assimilation practices employed by the Indian Agent, Residential Schools, and Liquor Control Boards – organizing the work of identifying, sorting, and assessing, while also

---

[81] Ibid., 92.
[82] Valverde, "A Postcolonial Women's Law."
[83] Liquor Control Board of Ontario, Interdiction List.
[84] Rosch, "Cognitive Representations of Semantic Categories."

pushing the development of "Indians" in a particular direction. It is important to note that the mediation, or shaping, of identity performances that came as a result of the colonial surveillance practices identified above, not only impacted personal experience and identity formation, but also had implications to the construction and ordering of technosocial spaces, and in the development, and persistence, of specific public perceptions about First Nations, Inuit, and Métis peoples as racial others. Each of these cases mentioned, though the liquor control section in particular, demonstrate how colonial surveillance practices sorted and racialized populations, contributing to the reproduction of a racialized and disparaging category of "Indian" within culture.

This chapter demonstrates a need to conceptualize the sociolegal category of "Indian" in Canada as being of colonial origin, and its content, and stereotypes, a product of racializing colonial surveillance practices. It also identifies a need to see the racial category of "Indian" as distinctive from the many cultures and peoples of the First Nations, Inuit, and Métis of Turtle Island, though its application to these peoples did work to uniformly shape technosocial spaces and mediate identity performances. As noted by the Aamjiwnaang councillor who begins this chapter, colonial surveillance practices *made his people "Indians."* For those of us who study surveillance and race, this insight stresses the importance not only of ensuring that we do not decouple the racial categories that we use from the specific rationalities, technologies, and histories (in this case alcohol), that gave them content, direction, and applied them to a population. We need also to be aware that conceptualizing colonial racial categories in this way presents clear grounds for disruptive political action.

13

Surveillance and Public Schools

Policing, Desegregation, and the Criminalization of Minority Youth in Charlotte-Mecklenburg Schools

Erica L. Nelson and Tracey A. Benson

YOUTH IN CHARLOTTE-MECKLENBURG SCHOOLS

This chapter reveals how the concept of policing and surveillance of urban spaces has extended to K–12 schools. Comparing the initial intent of the use of police officers in schools to the ways in which police are deployed in the present day, empirical evidence shows that the espoused intent of improving the relationships between law enforcement and youth has quickly evolved into increased criminalization and incarceration of young, school-aged children for noncriminal activity, especially in K–12 schools where a majority of the student body is Black or Hispanic and White students are absent or in the minority. While policymakers have used random mass shootings, perpetrated almost exclusively by young, White males who attend suburban schools, as a major reason for increased hiring of police officers to patrol the schoolhouse, the ill-effects of the use of school resource officers (SROs) plague majority Black and Hispanic schools.

In this chapter, we begin by tracing the history of SROs in K–12 schools. We discuss how White violence, specifically the rise in mass school shootings, has increased federal and state support for SROs. We then discuss how the proliferation of school policing has transformed the once safe space of the schoolhouse into a venue where minority youth behavior has become increasingly criminalized often leading to early incarceration. We conclude by analyzing the effectiveness of school policing, examining the use of SROs in the Charlotte-Mecklenburg School District, and offering specific policy recommendations to improve the safety of K–12 schools.

THE PROMOTION OF SCHOOL RESOURCE OFFICERS

Logic tells us that an increased police presence and surveillance in a given city, township, or neighborhood should result in lower levels of crime, be it by deterrence via increased police visibility, or by criminal apprehension and arrests. However, empirical research shows that there is no direct correlation between increased police surveillance and a unilateral decrease in crime.[1] Police surveillance has been shown to reduce specific types of crime, mainly property crimes and burglary.[2] Yet despite the ongoing debate about the effectiveness of police surveillance as a form of crime reduction, city and town governance continue to fund and maintain local law enforcement agencies.

This philosophy of utilizing police surveillance as a method of crime reduction has been employed by many school districts across the United States, through increased use of full-time police officers serving as SROs on campus during the school day. According to the National Center for Education Statistics the percentage of schools employing a sworn law enforcement officer jumped from 36 percent in 2006 to 48 percent in 2016.[3] However, during roughly the same time period, 2005–2015, the rate of school-related youth homicides only decreased by one student, from twenty-one[4] to twenty students,[5] and the rates of students who reported carrying a weapon to school only decreased by 3 percent, from 19[6] to 16 percent.[7] With the negligible decline in on-campus violent crime and criminal possession of weapons by students, the national debate about the effectiveness of police surveillance on crime reduction also extends to our K–12 school system.

According to The North Carolina Department of Public Safety, an SRO is "a certified law enforcement officer who is permanently assigned to provide coverage to a school or set of schools."[8] In school districts across the United States, the increased focus on student safety has resulted in the proliferation of these professionals being hired to surveille students on campus. The use of SROs grew in popularity in the 1990s with the passing of the 1994 Safe Schools Act and the federally funded COPS grant; but that is not where this program originated.[9]

The first SRO program began in Flint, Michigan in the 1950s under the guise of "improving the relationship between the local police and youth" and to "serve as

---

[1] John E. Eck and Edward R. Maguire, "Have Changes in Policing Reduced Violent Crime? An Assessment of the Evidence," *The Crime Drop in America* 207 (2000): 228.

[2] Hope Corman and Naci H. Mocan, "A Time-Series Analysis of Crime, Deterrence, and Drug Abuse in New York City," *American Economic Review* 90, no. 3 (2000): 584–604.

[3] National Center for Education Statistics, "Indicators of School Crime and Safety: 2017," *U.S. Department of Education / U.S. Department of Justice office of Justice Programs*, https://nces.ed.gov/pubs2018/2018036.pdf.

[4] National Center for Education Statistics, "Indicators of School Crime and Safety: 2006," *U.S. Department of Education / U.S. Department of Justice office of Justice Programs*, https://nces.ed.gov/pubs2007/2007003.pdf.

[5] National Center for Education Statistics, "Indicators of School Crime and Safety: 2017."

[6] National Center for Education Statistics, "Indicators of School Crime and Safety: 2006."

[7] National Center for Education Statistics, "Indicators of School Crime and Safety: 2017."

[8] Resources for School Resource Officers (n.d.), www.ncdps.gov.

[9] Nathan James. "Community Oriented Policing Services (COPS): Background and Funding," Congressional Research Service (Washington DC), February 6, 2014.

teachers and counselors."[10] It appears the initial SRO programs were seen as successful and therefore encouraged other cities and school districts to take similar measures.[11] As the American Civil Liberties Union notes, after the 1954 Supreme Court ruling in Brown v. Board of Education declared that segregation of the nation's schools was unconstitutional,[12] school policing significantly increased as mandatory desegregation began and school segregation decreased.[13] As students of color and families integrated predominantly White schools and neighborhoods, the presence of SROs were intended to increase student accountability and foster positive community relationships.[14] The continued increase in the use of SROs throughout the 1970s, came soon after the settling of the 1971, Swann v. Charlotte-Mecklenburg Board of Education decision,[15] and coincided with public proclamations of escalating fears of racial mixing and interracial dating as a result of school desegregation.[16] This rhetoric fueled the belief that increased police surveillance in schools would maintain the racial order in schools and ensure White student safety.

In Charlotte, North Carolina, the history of SROs follows a prototypical storyline. The Charlotte-Mecklenburg School District, like many school districts across the country, was legally segregated by race prior to the Brown v. Board of Education Supreme Court decision. However, the Brown v. Board of Education decision, and the subsequent Swann v. Charlotte-Mecklenburg Board of Education case, initially brought in a federal district court in 1965 and ultimately decided by the US Supreme Court in 1971, accelerated desegregation efforts throughout the city.[17] It was during the same time of increased desegregation that the first full-time SROs were placed in schools in the Charlotte-Mecklenburg School District.

In 1970, sworn security officers were hired to establish the Security Department of Charlotte-Mecklenburg Schools in order to maintain a safe environment on school grounds.[18] In 1971, the Supreme Court ruled that the Charlotte-Mecklenburg Schools (CMS) busing program was constitutional and could be used to speed up

---

[10] Spencer C. Weiler and Martha Cray, "Police at School: A Brief History and Current Status of School Resource Officers," *The Clearing House: A Journal of Educational Strategies, Issues and Ideas* 84, no. 4 (2011): 160–163.

[11] The limited research about the origins of school resource officers makes it difficult to trace the initial spread of the program. Additional research in needed in this area.

[12] *Brown v. Board of Education*, 347 US 483 (1954), Appeal from the United Sates (1974).

[13] Megan French-Marcelin and Sarah Hinger, "Bullies in Blue: The Origins and Consequences of School Policing," *American Civil Liberties Union* (2017), www.aclu.org/sites/default/files/field_document/aclu_bullies_in_blue_4_11_17_final.pdf.

[14] Ibid.

[15] George Hodak, "April 20, 1971: School Busing Gets the Green Light (US Supreme Court Affirmed Brown v. Board of Education Decision in Swann v. Charlotte-Mecklenburg Board of Education)," *ABA Journal* 93 (2007): 72.

[16] James T. Patterson and William W. Freehling, *Brown v. Board of Education: A Civil Rights Milestone and Its Troubled Legacy* (Oxford University Press, 2001), xviii.

[17] Hodak, "April 20, 1971."

[18] Charlotte-Mecklenburg School District, "About Us," www.cms.k12.nc.us/communications/aboutus/Pages/History.aspx.

the desegregation of schools.[19] The timeline of CMS desegregating schools and the start of the SRO program follows the national trends in the increasing criminalization of minority youth. Being one of the largest school districts in the state of North Carolina that experienced widespread, court-mandated desegregation, the CMS district is a useful case study that reflects similar patterns of other large school districts that increased the use of SROs in tandem with increased school desegregation.

While the nation was moving towards police in schools, the federal government followed suit making it easier for schools to hire SROs. The 1994 Safe Schools Act along with the federally funded COPS grant created an atmosphere and expectation that the nation's schools were not safe without police surveillance.[20] The federal government provided increased funding for police surveillance in schools but left it up to state and local boards of education to develop the guidelines and policies to determine how these police officers would behave in schools and with school administrators, students, teachers, and the community.

The influx of SROs across the nation came with the idea that these officers would build relationships with the community and keep schools safe. The Law Enforcement Management and Administrative Statistics (LEMAS) survey began collecting data detailing how many law enforcement officers were employed by schools and school districts in 1997. The survey data show a consistent increase in the hiring of law enforcement officers by school districts from 1997 to 2003, with a slight dip from 2003 to 2007.[21] The total number of SROs employed by local law enforcement agencies increased over 50 percent, from 23,500 in 1997 to 38,000 in 2007.[22] This sustained increase in the use of SROs shows that school districts and law enforcement agencies continue to strengthen their partnerships and maintain the belief that police surveillance in schools is necessary.

According to the National Association of School Resource Officers (NASRO) management manual, secondary schools were the focus for SROs because these schools "brought in children from several different schools with a variety of backgrounds thrust together with several classrooms and several teachers. With no one to really identify with, and coupled with their puberty development, the need for SROs was greatly needed at that educational level."[23] The theory behind increasing police surveillance in schools was that if schools have SROs who are able to make arrests, protect and encourage a safe school environment, and foster relationships with youth and the community, then students will feel safe, crime will decrease, and

---

[19] *Swann v. Charlotte-Mecklenburg Board of Education*, 402 US 1 (1971).
[20] Weiler and Cray, "Police at School."
[21] Nathan James and Gail McCallion, "School Resource Officers: Law Enforcement Officers in Schools," *Congressional Research Service*, June 26, 2013, https://sgp.fas.org/crs/misc/R43126.pdf.
[22] Ibid.
[23] SRO Management Symposium Course Manual (2006), www.nasro.org/clientuploads/resources/NASRO-Protect-and-Educate.pdf.

teachers and administrators will be less burdened with poor student conduct and criminal behavior.

This theory of action has not necessarily correlated with increased safety for all students, however. Since the deadly Columbine High School shooting in 1999, the number of deaths and frequency of school-related shootings has been steadily on the rise, especially in predominantly White, suburban schools. In 2000, there were four separate school shootings, claiming the lives of two students. Six years later in 2006, there were eight school shootings, claiming the lives of eight students. And, in 2012, there were another eight school shootings, including the tragic school shooting at Sandy Hook Elementary School, this time claiming the lives of a total of thirty-four students.[24] However, during this time of significant increase in suburban school shootings, police officers were still most likely to be found in schools in urban neighborhoods with high poverty.[25] In fact, only 24% of schools with between 25–50% of students eligible for free and reduced lunch employ a SRO, while 38% of schools with between 75–100% of students eligible for free and reduced lunch have a full-time SRO on staff.[26]

WHITE VIOLENCE AND POLICE SURVEILLANCE OF BLACK SCHOOLS

This increase in the use of funds from COPS program to hire SROs was in direct response to the two White male students involved in the 1999 Columbine High School mass shooting and the fear of an increase in mass school shootings.[27] Despite the rise in the use of SROs, the number of random school shootings by White males has only increased. However, the SROs on duty at the time of the 1999 Columbine High School[28] shooting as well as at the shooting at Stoneman Douglas High School,[29] nearly twenty years later, did not stop the student shooters or prevent the massive loss of student lives.

---

[24] Jason Cato, "Here's a List of Every School Shooting over the Past 50 Years," Trib Live, Safety and Discipline, February 16, 2018, https://triblive.com/news/education/safety/13313060-74/heres-a-list-of-every-school-shooting-over-the-past-50-years.

[25] Sussman, Aaron, "Learning in Lockdown: School Police, Race, and the Limits of Law," UCLA Law Review 59 (2011): 788.

[26] National Center for Education Statistics, "Indicators of School Crime and Safety: 2014," U.S. Department of Education/U.S. Department of Justice office of Justice Programs, https://nces.ed.gov/pubs2015/2015072.pdf.

[27] Chongmin Na and Denise C. Gottfredson, "Police Officers in Schools: Effects on School Crime and the Processing of Offending Behaviors," Justice Quarterly 30, no. 4 (2013): 619–650.

[28] Amanda Terkel, "Columbine High School Had Armed Guard during Massacre in 1999," Huffpost, Politics, December 23, 2012, www.huffingtonpost.com/2012/12/21/columbine-armed-guards_n_2347096.html.

[29] Avery Cotton, "Stoneman Douglas SRO Talks about Why He Did Not Go Inside School," News Channel *, National, June 5, 2018, www.wfla.com/national/stoneman-douglas-sro-talks-about-why-he-didn-t-go-inside-school/1219095986.

Between 1982 and February 2018, there were ninety-seven recorded school shooters in the United States.[30] Of these shooters, 58% were White and 97% of them were male, with the next highest racial demographic being Black at 16% and Hispanic and Asian tied at 7%.[31] From 1982 to 1991 most of the gun violence in K–12 schools was nonrandom, aimed at a specific target, took place mainly in inner-city schools, involved predominantly students of color, and was committed with handguns.[32] However, from 1992 to 2001 only one random shooting has occurred in schools located in major metropolitan areas, while twenty-two random shootings were committed by White students in suburban schools using rifles.[33] Even with overwhelming evidence that White males in suburban schools are the main perpetrators of random, mass school shootings, the Federal Bureau of Investigation (FBI) insists there is no profile of a school shooter and perpetuates an inflated association between Black and Hispanic inner-city schools and the propensity for violence.[34]

When the national media grapples with the increase in shootings in suburban schools, the popular storyline about school violence as a problem primarily associated with the violent tendencies of Blacks and Hispanics in urban schools has transformed into a narrative about the delinquency of a lone White individual (rather than a community). In this "lone wolf" narrative, individual, psychologically unstable, White, middle-class boys are not seen in the same way as Black and Latino students.[35] White males as a group have managed to evade the categorical criminalization assigned to certain minority populations, mainly Black and Latino boys, even though data overwhelmingly identify Whites are significantly more likely to be involved in criminal behavior.[36] White high school students are more likely than Blacks to have used cocaine, smoked crack, used LSD, tried heroin, and used crystal methamphetamine.[37] Whites are also 34 percent more likely to sell drugs, binge drink, drive drunk, and bring weapons to school.[38] Even with these staggering statistics detailing White youth involvement in criminal behaviors, the likelihood

---

[30] Statista, "Number of Mass Shootings in the United States between 1982 and February 2018, by Shooter's Gender," *The Statistics Portal*, www.statista.com/statistics/476445/mass-shootings-in-the-us-by-shooter-s-gender.

[31] Statista, "Number of Mass Shootings in the United States between 1982 and February 2018, by Mass Shooter's Race and Ethnicity," *The Statistics Portal*, www.statista.com/statistics/476456/mass-shootings-in-the-us-by-shooter-s-race.

[32] Michael S. Kimmel and Matthew Mahler, "Adolescent Masculinity, Homophobia, and Violence," *American Behavioral Scientist* 46, no. 10 (2003): 1439–1458.

[33] Ibid.

[34] Tim Wise, "School Shootings and White Denial," *Multicultural Perspectives* 3, no. 4 (2001): 3–4.

[35] Kimmel and Mahler, "Adolescent Masculinity."

[36] Wise, "School Shootings and White Denial."

[37] Ibid.

[38] Ibid.

of arrest or incarceration is most prevalent among youth in predominantly poor Black and Hispanic schools.[39]

Even with continued incidents of school shootings on campus, overall crime has decreased over time in all K–12 schools.[40] However, in majority Black or Hispanic urban schools, hostile police practices and zero-tolerance policies have increased incidence of youth criminalization among students of color due to harsh discipline practices for noncriminal offenses.[41]

POLICE SURVEILLANCE AND YOUTH CRIMINALIZATION

In Wake County, North Carolina the tide is shifting after a Black female Rolesville High School student was caught on video being slammed to the ground by the SRO while breaking up a fight, leading some around the nation to question the role of police in schools.[42] This criminalization of adolescents in our schools and the long-term repercussions of this has led researchers to look at how schools with and without resource officers handle discipline. Zero-tolerance policies and the "lock them up" mentality combined with the presence of full-time police officers in the schoolhouse has led to an increase in the number of youths being prosecuted in juvenile courts for misconduct that was previously handled informally without legal intervention.[43]

Research by Matthew T. Theriot found that having an SRO on campus dramatically increases the rate of arrests for disorderly conduct, the most subjective, situational, and circumstantial of all charges.[44] This supports the American Civil Liberties Union's claim that having police on campus has a negative impact on school climate and increases the criminalization of student behavior.[45] To further support this claim, Na and Gottfredson analyzed data from the US Department of Education's School Survey on Crime and Safety and found that "schools in which police were placed ... had higher recorded rates of each type of crime than schools without police" and that having the SRO in the building "increases the likelihood that students are arrested at school without increasing the reporting."[46] So while SROs are intended to create a safe environment and prevent crime, these studies

---

[39] Russell J. Skiba, Suzanne E. Eckles, and Kevin Brown. "African American Disproportionality in School Discipline: The Divide between Best Evidence and Legal Remedy," NY Law School Law Review 54 (2009): 1071.
[40] Sussman, "Learning in Lockdown."
[41] Ibid.
[42] T. K. Hui, "Deal Keeps Police in Wake County Schools, But Some Are Unhappy," The News & Observer (Raleigh, NC), June 22, 2017, www.newsobserver.com/news/local/education/article157549694.html.
[43] Sussman, "Learning in Lockdown."
[44] Matthew T. Theriot, "School Resource Officers and the Criminalization of Student Behavior," Journal of Criminal Justice 37, no. 3 (2009): 280–287.
[45] French-Marcelin and Hinger, "Bullies in Blue."
[46] Chongmin Na and Denise C. Gottfredson, "Police Officers in Schools."

show the opposite. Not only do SROs increase the number of youths arrested in schools but they do not prevent crime or increase the reporting of crime.

For example, in the Charlotte-Mecklenburg School District, in the 1997–1998 school year, there were 7,543 reported acts of possession of a controlled substance in violation of law, assault on school personnel, and possession of a weapon, at a rate of 6.3 per 1,000 students.[47] In school year 2016–2017, there were over 2,000 more (9,834) reported acts in the same categories, at a rate of 6.48 per 1,000 students.[48] Over this ten-year span, even with sustained deployment and support for SROs in schools, the incidence of school-related crime has continued to increase. In addition, in school year 2015–2016, of the 333 referrals to law enforcement in the Charlotte-Mecklenburg School District, 59% were for Black students, 17% for Hispanic students, and 16.5% for White students.[49] Referrals to law enforcement for Black students exceed their representation in the CMS school district while this is not so for Hispanic or White students. Student enrollment in CMS in 2015–2016 were 40% Black, 22% Hispanic, and 29% White.[50] Comparing referral rates to percentage of students enrolled, Black students exceeded their enrollment rates to referral to law rates by 19%. However, Hispanic and White students were under their enrollment rates by 5% and 12% respectively.

Deploying SROs in schools is not the only way to decrease student misconduct on campus. There are several methods which do not involve law enforcement that have shown to be effective. A 2002 study provided evidence that improving family involvement and community engagement significantly decreased the number of student conduct infractions in elementary as well as secondary schools.[51] Research-based practices such as School-wide Positive Behavior Support[52] and Restorative Justice Programs[53] have also shown evidence of reducing poor student conduct without the involvement of SROs or referrals to the juvenile justice system. With many proven systems of reducing student misconduct, districts may question if spending resources on employing SROs is the best method of reducing minor student infractions and incidents of violence.

---

[47] Public Schools of North Carolina State Board of Education Department of Public Instruction, "Annual Report on School Crime and Violence" (Annual Report, Raleigh, NC, n.d., 1-141).
[48] Public Schools of North Carolina State Board of Education Department of Public Instruction, "Report to the North Carolina General Assembly," (Annual Report, Raleigh, NC, 2018, 1-179).
[49] United States Office of Civil Rights, "Charlotte-Mecklenburg Schools Discipline Report," (Annual Report, Washington DC, n.d., n.p.).
[50] Ibid.
[51] Steven B. Sheldon and Joyce L. Epstein, "Improving Student Behavior and School Discipline with Family and Community Involvement," *Education and Urban Society* 35, no. 1 (2002): 4–26.
[52] Robert H. Horner, George Sugai, and Cynthia M. Anderson, "Examining the Evidence Base for School-Wide Positive Behavior Support," *Focus on Exceptional Children* 42, no. 8 (2010).
[53] Jeff Latimer, Craig Dowden, and Danielle Muise, "The Effectiveness of Restorative Justice Practices: A Meta-Analysis," *The Prison Journal* 85, no. 2 (2005): 127–144.

DOES POLICE SURVEILLANCE WORK?

Law enforcement continues to struggle to consistently identify reliable warning signs to stop potential school shooters,[54] as evidenced by the consistent trend of annual school shootings across the United States. A study conducted in 2014 of mass shootings in the United States found "there is absolutely no evidence that more armed guards or armed citizens reduced or stopped any of the 73 mass shooting studied."[55] A similar study found that while the presence of police officers in schools increased arrests for disorderly conduct, their stationing at schools has not yielded an increase in arrests for weapons possession.[56] These studies highlight that the presence of police surveillance in schools does not necessarily increase early detection of possible school shooters, reduce or stop mass shootings, or increase the seizing of firearms on campus.

Though funding for the COPS Hiring Program has been significantly reduced since the $1.7 million high in 1998,[57] the US federal government continues to provide grants and general guidance for the hiring and training of SROs.[58] Some states, like Massachusetts, have developed state policy requiring placement of SROs in schools around the state,[59] while other states, like North Carolina, leave it up to the local school board to decide whether or not to utilize SROs.[60] Inconsistent local and state policies and funding structures add to the problems of measuring the efficacy of SROs and codifying best practices for school district partnership with local law enforcement.

FEDERAL AND LOCAL SRO POLICY

While the federal government continues to support, and even encourage, police surveillance in K–12 schools, there is no federal policy guiding states as to implementation of SRO programs. In North Carolina, General Statute 115C-47 gives local boards of education the power to allow SROs in schools:

---

[54] International Association of Chiefs of Policy, "Guidelines for Preventing and Responding to School Violence," *Department of Justice* (Alexandria, VA), November 3, 1999.
[55] Frederic Lemieux, "Effect of Gun Culture and Firearm Laws on Gun Violence and Mass Shootings in the United States: A Multi-Level Quantitative Analysis," *International Journal of Criminal Justice Sciences* 9, no. 1 (2014).
[56] Theriot, "School Resource Officers and the Criminalization of Student Behavior."
[57] James, "Community Oriented Policing Services (COPS): Background and Funding."
[58] Community Oriented Policing Services, "COPS Hiring Program School Resource Officer Scholarship Opportunity for NASRO Training," US Department of Justice Office of Community Oriented Policing Services (Washington DC), September 2014.
[59] 190th General Court of The Commonwealth of Massachusetts, General Laws, Part I, Title XII, Chapter 71, Section 37P, https://malegislature.gov/Laws/GeneralLaws/PartI/TitleXII/Chapter71/Section37P.
[60] North Carolina General Statute, 115C-47, Section 47 (2005).

To Provide a Safe School Environment. – Local boards of education may enter into an agreement with the sheriff, chief of police of a local police department, or chief of police of a county police department to provide security at the schools by assigning volunteer school safety resource officers who meet the selection standards and criteria developed by the head of the appropriate local law enforcement agency and the criteria set out in G.S. 162-26 or G.S. 160A-288.4, as appropriate.[61]

This statute leaves interpretation and implementation up to local boards of education. In the Charlotte-Mecklenburg School District, the board of education policy KLG-R section V outlines relations with law enforcement agencies. In section V of the Charlotte-Mecklenburg School Board Policy the board defines an SRO and states:

School resource officers ("SROs") are certified law enforcement officers with local law enforcement agencies who are assigned to schools to help ensure safety and to prevent truancy and violence in schools. SROs are encouraged to have daily, informal, interaction with students and staff. The rules set forth in these regulations pertain only to formal interviews of students by police who are not SROs or child protective workers and are not intended to restrict or otherwise hinder this daily interaction. The rules set forth in this section are also applicable to officers of the CMSPD in their daily interactions with students.[62]

Lack of concrete policy from both the state and district level creates a gray space with a vague understanding at the school level as to the responsibility of SROs. Moreover, since SROs do not report to and are not supervised by school administrators, they are not required to follow the directives of or cooperate with building principals, teachers, or support staff. The lack of policy allowing building leaders to oversee the conduct of SROs can create problems, mainly for the students SROs are in schools to protect.

POLICE SURVEILLANCE IN CHARLOTTE-MECKLENBURG SCHOOLS

In the Charlotte-Mecklenburg School District, SROs in the city are contracted through the Charlotte-Mecklenburg Police Department (CMPD). This contracted service covers forty-nine SRO positions in middle and secondary schools. However, with seventy-nine secondary schools in the district, the school district must contract with county police departments outside of CMPD to cover the remaining schools. In a district the size of CMS, which serves over 127,000 students, the lack of a detailed and uniform SRO policy has been problematic. A CMPD official states that "each SRO is an employee of his or her law enforcement agency and is bound

---

[61] Ibid.
[62] Charlotte-Mecklenburg School Board Policy, KLG-R, section V (2009).

under their own agency's policy and directives,"[63] directives not available to the public. While a lack of policy governing SROs is problematic, the cost of employing such a robust school police force is also quite significant.

For the forty-nine SROs employed through CMPD, the 2015–2016 CMS budget included $4.7 million for SRO salaries, $1.8 million for benefits, $5.7 million for purchased services, and $250,000 for supplies and materials.[64] In North Carolina, per-pupil spending has dropped over $500 since 2008.[65] With this decreased spending, schools are being forced to do more with less. However, even with decreased funding for teachers, counselors, and school support personnel, the Charlotte-Mecklenburg School District spends more than $12 million a year on SROs.

The Charlotte-Mecklenburg School District, like many large school districts around the nation, has chosen to forgo hiring teachers, counselors, and support staff in order to hire full-time police officers to patrol the school house. According to the National Bureau of Labor Statistics, the 2017 median pay for police officers is $62,960.[66] In North Carolina, the average starting salary for teachers in 2017 is $37,514.[67] This means, in the state of North Carolina, school districts can hire nearly two teachers for every one SRO. More teachers mean smaller class sizes, and smaller class sizes have shown to boost student achievement, increase student engagement, and decrease off-task behavior, especially among students from low-income homes.[68] Conversely, adding an SRO to the building has shown no evidence of increased student performance, academically or socially, but instead increases the likelihood of early incarceration and criminalization, particularly within low-income, majority Black and Hispanic schools.[69]

IS POLICE SURVEILLANCE NECESSARY IN K–12 SCHOOLS?

Following the 2018 mass school shooting at Stoneman Douglas High School, a collection of students, parents, and community activists developed a comprehensive call to action to make schools a safer place. Their plan calls for:

---

[63] Catina Odom (Police Sergeant) in discussion with author, October 6, 2017.
[64] Charlotte-Mecklenburg Board of Education, "2015–2016 Proposed Budget Recommendation" (Budget Proposal, Charlotte, NC, 2015, 1-289).
[65] Lindsay Wagner, "Starving the Schools: Teacher Assistants, Textbooks, Services Slashed as Per-Pupil Spending Plummets," NC Policy Watch, May 31, 2018, www.ncpolicywatch.com/2015/12/08/starving-the-schools.
[66] United States Department of Labor Bureau of Labor and Statistics, "Police and Detectives," Occupational Outlook Handbook, Washington DC, www.bls.gov/ooh/protective-service/police-and-detectives.htm.
[67] National Education Association, "2016–2017 Average Teacher Salaries by State," Teacher Salary Database, www.nea.org/home/2016-2017-average-starting-teacher-salary.html.
[68] Jeremy D. Finn, Gina M. Pannozzo, and Charles M. Achilles. "The "Why's" of Class Size: Student Behavior in Small Classes," Review of Educational Research 73, no. 3 (2003): 321–368.
[69] Skiba, Eckles, and Brown, "African American Disproportionality in School Discipline."

- a ban on assault-style weapons, high-capacity ammunition clips, and products that modify semiautomatic firearms to enable them to function like automatic firearms
- universal background checks to screen for individuals with a history of violence to themselves or others or those suspected of terrorist activity
- allowing for short-term protection orders allowing for the recovery of firearms by law enforcement when violence is imminent
- a standard, universal practice of assessing school climate and maintaining safe schools, including both physically and emotionally
- increased staffing of service providers who can deliver coordinated mental health services for those with violent risk factors, including counselors, psychologists, and social workers
- the adoption of discipline practices that "foster positive social, behavioral, emotional, and academic success" along with the reduction of exclusionary practices in school discipline
- programs to allow mental health, school, and law enforcement officials to conduct threat assessments, including interventions to support individuals who pose a threat, once identified[70]

In the Stoneman Douglas call to action, they request policies to allow law enforcement officials to conduct threat assessments, not the placement of more police officers in schools. This may be because the police officer assigned to Stoneman Douglas refused to enter the building to engage the active shooter, or because there is research-based evidence that the key to reducing mass school shootings is through increased student supports, easier access to mental health services, and improving school climate. This call to action specifically requests SROs focus their time and energy on identifying and minimizing potential threats, not criminalizing behaviors of school-aged youth.

If SROs are to remain in K–12 schools, it is imperative that state and district policy be created to provide SROs, school administrators, students, and staff with guidelines and role descriptions. SROs should also receive specialized training focused on working with youth, de-escalation, bias, mental health, use of force, and student constitutional rights. By requiring and mandating the training for officers who are placed in schools, these officers would be better equipped to work in conjunction with, instead of parallel to, the school-level personnel. Finally, school-level discipline must be examined monthly opening the lines of communication and looking for trends in race, economic status, assigned consequence, and the criminal charge assigned to student behavior.

---

[70] Interdisciplinary Group on Preventing School and Community Violence, "Call for Action to Prevent Gun Violence in the United States of America" (Call for Action, NP, 2018), 1–5.

14

Surveillance and Preventing Violent Extremism

The Evidence from Schools and Further Education Colleges in England

Joel Busher, Tufyal Choudhury, and Paul Thomas

Since 2001, the British state has increased its powers of surveillance for the purposes of countering terrorism. Much of this has been through expansions of the powers of police and security services to engage in covert surveillance and access the personal data of those suspected of involvement in terrorism. Alongside this, however, the last decade has also seen the development of more diffuse practices of monitoring and surveillance as part of efforts to identify and provide support to those deemed 'vulnerable' to being drawn into terrorism. Under Prevent, the UK government's strategy for preventing violent extremism (PVE),[1] much of the responsibility was initially placed on the police and on the communities identified as having particularly high levels of vulnerability, which in practice meant Britain's Muslim communities.[2] Subsequently, however, responsibility for PVE has increasingly been shifted onto a broad swathe of professionals engaged in the delivery of public services, including social workers, youth workers, health-care workers, prison staff, school teachers, and college and university lecturers.[3]

The culmination of this 'responsibilisation' of frontline professionals,[4] for the time being at least, has been the introduction of the Counter-Terrorism and Security Act 2015 (CTSA 2015). Popularly referred to as the 'Prevent duty', this placed a legal duty on schools, colleges, and other stated authorities to show 'due regard to the need to prevent people from being drawn into terrorism'.[5] The statutory guidance accompanying this duty set out two primary areas of responsibility for schools and colleges.

---

[1] *CONTEST: The United Kingdom's Strategy for Countering Terrorism* (London: HM Government, 2018); Prevent does not apply to Northern Ireland, which is judged to have a different terrorism threat.
[2] *Preventing Violent Extremism: Winning Hearts and Minds* (London: Department for Communities and Local Government, April 2007).
[3] Paul Thomas, 'Changing Experiences of Responsibilisation and Contestation within Counter-Terrorism Policies: The British Prevent Experience', *Policy and Politics* 45, no. 3 (2017): 305.
[4] Ibid.
[5] CTSA 2015, s. 26.

First, they were required to identify individuals considered vulnerable to radicalisation, and refer them to Channel, the UK government's counter-radicalisation mentoring programme. Second, they were required to actively promote 'fundamental British values' – defined by the government as 'democracy, the rule of law, individual liberty and mutual respect and tolerance of different faiths and beliefs' – on the grounds that this would reduce students' 'vulnerability' to extremism.[6]

In this chapter, we discuss how the introduction of the Prevent duty has shaped surveillance and monitoring practices in schools and colleges in England, and how such practices intersect with the politics and practices of race, religion, and difference. The discussion draws on the emerging academic and grey literature on this topic, as well as on our own original empirical data from fieldwork conducted in the duty's initial implementation phase in 2016 and 2017. These data include seventy in-depth interviews with educationalists in fourteen schools and colleges in London and West Yorkshire, eight interviews with local Prevent practitioners from across England,[7] a national online survey of school and college staff (n=225), and discussions of emergent findings with six stakeholder groups.[8]

THE PREVENT STRATEGY: ITS EVOLUTION AND CRITICS

In order to discuss how the Prevent duty has shaped surveillance and monitoring practices in schools and colleges in England, it is first necessary to provide some context, both in terms of the evolution of the Prevent strategy and the debates that preceded and surrounded the introduction of the Prevent duty.

Intended 'to stop people becoming terrorists or supporting terrorism',[9] Prevent was first included in the UK government's overall counterterrorism strategy (CONTEST) in 2003, as one of the strategy's four strands.[10] It came to prominence in the UK context, however, after the 7 July 2005 London bombings as policy concerns about 'home-grown' terrorism came to the fore. Since then, similar preventative strategies have been adopted by many other Western states,[11] and have

---

[6] Department for Education, *The Prevent duty: Departmental Advice for Schools and Childcare Providers* (London: Department for Education, 2015); Revised Prevent Duty Guidance for England and Wales (April 2021): www.gov.uk/government/publications/prevent-duty-guidance/revised-prevent-duty-guidance-for-england-and-wales.

[7] Local government-based Prevent staff (funded by the national government's Home Office) who support Prevent implementation at the local level.

[8] For a detailed discussion of research methods, see Joel Busher et al., *What the Prevent Duty Means for Schools and Colleges in England: An Analysis of Educationalists' Experiences* (Coventry: Centre for Trust, Peace and Social Relations, Coventry University, 2017), https://pureportal.coventry.ac.uk/en/publications/what-the-prevent-duty-means-for-schools-and-colleges-in-england-a.

[9] Her Majesty's Government, *Prevent Strategy*, Cm 8092, 2011, 6.

[10] The others being Pursue, Protect, and Prepare.

[11] Didier Bigo et al., *Preventing and Countering Youth Radicalisation in the EU* (Brussels: European Parliament, 2014), www.researchgate.net/profile/Francesco-Ragazzi/publication/

become a key pillar of EU[12] and UN counter-terrorism strategies,[13] leading the UN Special Rapporteur on the promotion and protection of human rights and fundamental freedoms while countering terrorism to observe that the discourse on preventing and countering violent extremism is now 'pervasive in political, legal and policy settings'.[14] Advocates for Prevent and similar programmes internationally have argued that they prevent terrorism, with Neil Basu, the national head of the UK's Counter Terrorism Police, saying that the Prevent programme is the 'best chance' of reducing the terrorism threat.[15]

The Prevent strategy has, however, from its inception faced considerable criticism from civil society actors,[16] parliamentary committees,[17] and international observers.[18] Of particular relevance to this chapter, one of the most prominent of these criticisms has been that Prevent has effectively extended surveillance powers and securitised a growing set of community relations through the imposition of reporting requirements.[19] The UK government has rejected such claims and in its response stressed that Prevent does not criminalise those subject to interventions.[20] Nonetheless, a parliamentary inquiry was unable to rebut the claims of Prevent's critics, and instead called for an independent review while urging the government to take 'urgent steps

273661763_Preventing_and_countering_youth_radicalisation_in_the_EU/links/55082eadocf26ff55f8026a4/Preventing-and-countering-youth-radicalisation-in-the-EU.pdf?origin=publication_detail.

[12] Council of the European Union, The European Union Counter-Terrorism Strategy, 14469/4/05 REV 4, 30 November 2005.
[13] UNGA A/RES/60/288 (20 September 2006).
[14] Fionnuala Ni Aolain, Human rights impact of policies and practices aimed at preventing and countering violent extremism: Report of the Special Rapporteur on the promotion and protection of human rights and fundamental freedoms while countering terrorism, UN Doc. A/HRC/43/46, 21 February 2020.
[15] Neil Basu, 'Prevent Is Our Best Hope against Terror Threat', Counter-Terrorism Policing News, 7 August 2019, www.counterterrorism.police.uk/neil-basu-prevent.
[16] Muslim Council of Britain, The Impact of Prevent on Muslim Communities: A Briefing to the Labour Party on how British Muslim Communities are Affected by Counter-Extremism Policies (London: Muslim Council of Britain, 2016) http://archive.mcb.org.uk/wp-content/uploads/2016/12/MCB-CT-Briefing2.pdf.
[17] See House of Commons Communities and Local Government Committee, Preventing Violent Extremism: Sixth Report of Session 2009–10 (London: The Stationary Office, 2010); Parliament Joint Committee on Human Rights, Counter-Extremism, 2nd Report of session 2016/17 (London: The Stationary Office, 2017).
[18] See Committee on the Rights of the Child, Concluding observations on the fifth periodic report of the United Kingdom of Great Britain and Northern Ireland, UN Doc. CRC/C/GB/CO/5, 12 July 2016; Mania Kai, Report of the Special Rapporteur on the rights to freedom of peaceful assembly and of association on his follow-up mission to the United Kingdom of Great Britain and Northern Ireland, UN Doc. A/HRC/35/28//Add.1, 8 June 2017.
[19] Arun Kundnani, Spooked! How Not to Prevent Violent Extremism (London: Institute of Race Relations, 2009); 'Government Anti-Terrorism Strategy "Spies" on Innocent', The Guardian, 16 October 2009, www.theguardian.com/uk/2009/oct/16/anti-terrorism-strategy-spies-innocents.
[20] See, e.g., the evidence of Charles Farr, Director of OSCT to the Parliamentary Inquiry on Prevent, House of Commons Communities and Local Government Committee, Preventing Violent Extremism, Ev. 76. Q374.

to clarify how information required under Prevent does not constitute "intelligence gathering" of the type undertaken by the police or security services'.[21]

Alongside this, there have been claims that a disproportionate focus by Prevent on Muslims and Muslim communities has contributed to transform Muslims into a 'suspect community'[22] – claims which have been consistently rebutted by the UK government, particularly since a review of Prevent in 2011 explicitly directed attention towards all forms of extremism (see below), but which have persisted.[23]

A further set of criticisms have focused on the science underpinning the strategy's approach of requiring front-line workers to identify individuals 'vulnerable' to radicalisation but not yet involved in terrorism.[24] Here, critics point to the fact that there is little academic consensus over what comprise reliable indicators of vulnerability to radicalisation.

A major review of Prevent, undertaken after the Conservative–Liberal Democrat coalition government came to office in 2010 and published in 2011, resulted in a significant refocusing of Prevent, albeit this did little to quell criticism of the strategy. Three aspects of this refocusing are particularly significant for the purposes of this chapter. First, while it made clear that 'the majority of our resources and efforts will continue to be devoted to preventing people from joining or supporting Al Qa'ida, its affiliates or related groups', it spelled out that 'Prevent will address all forms of terrorism'.[25] Second, the scope of Prevent was substantially broadened from a focus on countering 'violent extremism' to include challenging 'extremist (and non-violent) ideas that are also part of the terrorist ideology',[26] defined by the government as 'vocal or active opposition to fundamental British values'.[27] Heavily influenced by the thinking of then Secretary of State for Education, Michael Gove,[28] who had previously linked terrorism to broader Muslim community practices and dispositions,[29] this laid the foundations for the promotion of 'fundamental

---

[21] Ibid., 63.
[22] Christina Pantazis and Simon Pemberton 'From the 'Old' to the 'New' Suspect Community: Examining the Impacts of Recent UK Counter-Terrorist Legislation', *British Journal of Criminology* 49 (2009): 646.
[23] Paul Thomas, 'Britain's Prevent strategy: Always Changing, Always the Same?', in Joel Busher and Lee Jerome (eds.), *The Prevent Duty in Education: Impact, Enactment and Implications* (Basingstoke: Palgrave Macmillan, 2020).
[24] Leda Blackwood, Nick Hopkins, and Steven Reicher, 'From Theorizing Radicalization to Surveillance Practices: Muslims in the Cross Hairs of Scrutiny', *Political Psychology* 37, no. 5 (2016): 597; Rik Coolsaet, *All Radicalisation Is Local: The Genesis and Drawbacks of an Elusive Concept* (Brussels: Egmont, 2016); Arun Kundnani, *The Muslims are Coming!* (London: Verso, 2014).
[25] HM Government, *Prevent Strategy*, 6.
[26] Ibid.
[27] The government definition of extremism also included 'calls for the death of members of our armed forces, whether in this country or overseas', HM Government, *Prevent Strategy*, 107.
[28] Sayeeda Warsi, *The Enemy Within: A Tale of Muslim Britain* (London: Allen Lane, 2017).
[29] Michael Gove, *Celsius 7/7* (London: Weidenfeld and Nicolson, 2006).

British values' to become an integral part of PVE in Britain. Third, funding for community-based Prevent work, previously administered via the-then Department for Communities and Local Government (DCLG), was removed and policy responsibility was centralised within the Home Office; a move which also prepared the ground for a subsequent shift in responsibility for frontline PVE policy delivery from communities to professionals working in the delivery of public services.

The new policy approach mapped out by the 2011 Prevent Review evolved further still as a result of three subsequent developments. First, following the murder in 2013 of off-duty soldier Lee Rigby by two young British Muslim converts, a report by the prime minister's task force on tackling radicalisation and extremism led the government to conclude that local authorities and other public bodies were not contributing robustly enough to support the Prevent strategy.[30]

In 2014, the UK government interpreted efforts by socially conservative elements of Muslim communities in Birmingham to utilise faith to improve educational attainment in a number of Muslim-dominated state schools as evidence of broader 'extremism' – often referred to as the 'Trojan horse' affair.[31] This resulted in the Office for Standards in Education, Children's Services and Skills (Ofsted), placing greater emphasis on the requirements of schools and colleges both to reduce the risk of radicalisation through the promotion of fundamental British values and to 'safeguard' students identified as being at risk of being drawn into processes of radicalisation. The potential significance of this change for schools and colleges was brought home as early as 2014, after one London school found itself placed in 'special measures' following an Ofsted inspection in which its quality rating was downgraded from 'Outstanding' to 'Inadequate', largely due to shortcomings in its safeguarding policies related to Prevent.[32]

Around the same time, public and policy perceptions of the need to upscale PVE efforts were also accentuated by the deepening Syria crisis and the fact that several hundred Britons travelled to the Middle East (or attempted to do so) to join the so-called 'Islamic State'.[33] This included significant numbers of young people in education, thereby further consolidating calls for educational institutions, as well as other public services working with potentially vulnerable young people, to be given a greater role in the fight against violent extremism.

The CTSA 2015 can be seen therefore as a product both of the evolution of thinking within government, and as a response to external pressures and challenges.

---

[30] Her Majesty's Government, *Tackling Extremism in the UK: Report from the Prime Minister's Task Force on Tackling Radicalisation and Extremism* (London: Cabinet Office, 2013).
[31] Shamim Miah, *Muslims, Schooling and Security: Trojan Horse, Prevent and Racial Politics* (Basingstoke: Palgrave Pivot, 2017).
[32] Richard Adams and Sally Weale, 'Church of England School Taken Aback by Ofsted Rating Amid Extremism Row', *The Guardian*, 20 November 2014, www.theguardian.com/education/2014/nov/20/church-england-school-john-cass-ofsted-downgraded-extremism.
[33] 'Who Are Britain's Jihadis', *BBC News*, 12 October 2017, www.bbc.co.uk/news/uk-32026985.

When the duty came into force in July of that year, it was shrouded in controversy, with much of the debate around the duty reflecting long-held concerns about the impacts of Prevent. Some teachers and school/college leaders, as well as prominent academics, the National Union of Teachers (now the National Education Union), and civil society organisations, initially expressed multiple concerns: that shifting previously existing counterterrorism responsibilities onto a statutory footing placed undue pressure on educational institutions and teachers; that many educators may not have the skills or confidence to facilitate the type of discussions that the duty appeared to entail; that the pressure to report terrorism-related concerns might contribute to the 'securitising' of education and could have a 'chilling effect' on free speech in the classroom; that the Prevent duty may deepen stigmatisation and suspicion of British Muslims; and that the new measures might even intensify feelings of suspicion towards the state, thereby playing into the hands of those seeking to recruit young people into terroristic activities.[34] The human rights organisation Liberty went so far as to warn that the duty risked turning teachers and childminders 'into an involuntary army of spies'.[35]

During the first year of the duty, these criticisms were given further fuel by a sharp rise in the number of young people referred to Channel, and a number of media reports of cases, some bordering on the absurd,[36] in which students, almost always of Muslim background and some as young as four years old, were questioned by the police after seemingly quite innocent comments made in the classroom.[37] In 2016, David Anderson QC, then the Independent Reviewer of Terrorism Legislation, reported a strong feeling in Muslim communities that the Prevent duty entailed 'spying' on them.[38]

The Home Office and Department for Education responded by arguing that the duty 'doesn't and shouldn't stop schools from discussing controversial issues',[39] and

---

[34] 'PREVENT will have a chilling effect on open debate, free speech and political dissent', *The Independent*, 10 July 2015, www.independent.co.uk/voices/letters/prevent-will-have-a-chilling-effect-on-open-debate-free-speech-and-political-dissent-10381491.html.

[35] Robert Mendick, 'Anti-Terror Plan to Spy on Toddlers Is "Heavy Handed"', *Daily Telegraph*, 4 January 2015, www.telegraph.co.uk/news/uknews/terrorism-in-the-uk/11323558/Anti-terror-plan-to-spy-on-toddlers-is-heavy-handed.html.

[36] See, e.g., Ben Quinn, 'Nursery "Raised Fears of Radicalisation over Boy's Cucumber Drawing"', *The Guardian*, 11 March 2016, www.theguardian.com/uk-news/2016/mar/11/nursery-radicalisation-fears-boys-cucumber-drawing-cooker-bomb.

[37] Open Society Justice Initiative, *Eroding Trust: The UK's PREVENT Counter-Extremism Strategy in Health and Education* (New York: Open Society Foundations, 2016), www.opensocietyfoundations.org/reports/eroding-trust-uk-s-prevent-counter-extremism-strategy-health-and-education.

[38] Joe Watts, 'Muslims See Anti-Extremism Scheme Prevent as a 'Spying Programme', Admits Terror Law Watchdog', *The Independent*, 6 October 2016, www.independent.co.uk/news/uk/politics/muslims-prevent-scheme-seen-as-spying-says-terrorism-law-watchdog-a7347751.html.

[39] Rachel Williams, 'School Heads Raise Alarm over New Duty to Protect Students from Extremism', *The Guardian*, 9 June 2015, www.theguardian.com/education/2015/jun/09/schools-duty-police-extremism-anti-terrorism-laws.

repeatedly emphasised that the duty applies to all forms of extremism. They also urged educationalists to think of the duty largely as an extension of existing policy and practice. The requirements around the identification and referral of individual students deemed vulnerable to radicalisation were framed as an extension of existing 'safeguarding' responsibilities,[40] a concept increasingly used by welfare and education professionals over the past three decades in relation to 'vulnerabilities' to social problems such as child abuse and neglect, child sexual exploitation, gang violence, and drug use. The requirements to reduce vulnerability to extremism through the promotion of 'fundamental British values' were also framed simply as a re-emphasising of existing responsibilities. Over time, government also put in place significant training and guidance resources to support schools, colleges, and other 'specified authorities'.

The extent to which this response by the government has assuaged criticism of and concerns about the duty remains unclear, however. On the one hand, there is evidence that a substantial portion of staff working in schools and colleges have broadly accepted the government's framing of the duty as an extension of policy and practice that pre-dated the introduction of the duty[41] – a theme to which we return below. On the other hand, criticisms of the duty have persisted, particularly from a number of academics[42] and civil society organisations,[43] and the relative absence of criticism of the duty from educators has been interpreted by some observers not as a sign that the duty is unproblematic, but that the monitoring and surveillance that it entails has simply been normalised and therefore no longer attracts the kind of opposition and resistance that might otherwise have been expected.[44]

MONITORING AND SURVEILLANCE PRACTICES UNDER THE PREVENT DUTY

We can turn now to the core questions of this chapter, about how the Prevent duty has shaped practices of monitoring and surveillance within schools and colleges, and how these practices of monitoring and surveillance have intersected with the politics and practices of race, religion, and difference. We organise this discussion around two key themes to emerge from our research. The first of these concerns a

---

[40] HM Government, *The Prevent Strategy*, 84.
[41] Joel Busher, Tufyal Choudhury, and Paul Thomas, 'The Enactment of the Counter-Terrorism "Prevent Duty" in British Schools and Colleges: Beyond Reluctant Accommodation or Straightforward Policy Acceptance', *Critical Studies on Terrorism* 12, no. 3 (2019): 440.
[42] Alice Ross, 'Academics Criticise Anti-Radicalisation Strategy in Open Letter', *The Guardian*, 29 September 2016, www.theguardian.com/uk-news/2016/sep/29/academics-criticise-prevent-anti-radicalisation-strategy-open-letter.
[43] Jamie Grierson, 'Human Rights Groups to Boycott Government's Prevent Review', *The Guardian*, 16 February 2021, www.theguardian.com/uk-news/2021/feb/16/human-rights-groups-to-boycott-government-prevent-review.
[44] 'Prevent', *Liberty*, www.libertyhumanrights.org.uk/fundamental/prevent.

tension in the data and the wider existing evidence regarding the extent to which the monitoring and surveillance undertaken under the auspices of Prevent does or does not constitute a continuation of prior professional practice. The second concerns the extent and ways in which these practices of monitoring and surveillance continue to focus disproportionately on Muslim students.

Professional Continuity vs New 'Cultures of Vigilance'

Before the Prevent training, it is fairly easy going: things would be on trust and yeah, the old days of being able to walk round the building. ... [But] with instructions from Prevent, you now start to walk round and look at people and look at sites and places and think, 'well where is the risk, how is the risk being managed?'

R13, Estates Director, College, Yorkshire

All of the schools and colleges in which we undertook fieldwork had put in place a series of measures in order to meet their new statutory obligations. Existing safeguarding policies and governance structures had been revised and updated to ensure compliance with the new requirements; the staff had received or were about to receive training to enable them to identify the signs or indicators of possible vulnerability to 'being drawn into terrorism' – under the Prevent duty, schools and colleges are required to ensure that all members of staff, including teaching, managerial, and support staff receive basic Prevent training – and were being encouraged to be alert to these signs at all times. In most schools and colleges there had also been renewed emphasis placed on online safety, with software introduced that would block access to presumed extremist content on the Internet and alert safeguarding staff when students entered words or phrases deemed to be of concern.

But to what extent did these new monitoring and surveillance practices constitute a departure from or a continuation of existing practices? After all, schools and colleges were already environments increasingly saturated with surveillance and concomitant practices of discipline. Recent decades have been marked by a significant expansion in surveillance technologies and practices to identify, verify, categorise, and track school students: technologies and practices that some argue are today an integral part of how such institutions train students to think and behave in ways that, it is believed, will both help them to flourish and enable them to make a positive contribution to society.[45] The picture that emerges from our study is far from straightforward.

On the one hand, across all of the schools and colleges in which we undertook fieldwork, it was clear that Prevent-related monitoring and surveillance was intimately intertwined with wider safeguarding practices and processes. As indicated

---

[45] Emmeline Taylor, *Surveillance Schools: Security, Discipline and Control in Contemporary Education* (Basingstoke: Palgrave MacMillan, 2013), 7.

above, Prevent-related responsibilities were incorporated within existing school/ college safeguarding policies and, while in some cases existing safeguarding teams were expanded in recognition of the increased workload that the Prevent duty entailed, in every institution oversight of Prevent-related activities sat within the institutional safeguarding team. Similarly, Prevent training was in most cases delivered as part of, rather than separate to, annual training to renew safeguarding competencies, and reporting of Prevent-related concerns followed existing safeguarding reporting pathways.

The overlap with existing safeguarding monitoring and surveillance practices was also evident in the basic technologies of surveillance: in the schema used by staff to identify which behaviours and which individuals warrant attention and the techniques through which such behaviours are observed and recorded, such as electronic logs of any concerns about individual students. As respondents repeatedly pointed out, and as often emphasised in Prevent training, there is considerable similarity between what were deemed the signs and indicators that a young person is being drawn into terrorism and the behaviours that they had previously been trained to identify and be alert to as indicators of vulnerability to other safeguarding issues, such as sudden changes in behaviour, appearance, and friendship groups.

It is unsurprising therefore that many of the educationalists we interviewed emphasised the continuity with existing practice:

> I see it as a wider viewpoint of taking care of the kids, and I don't particularly think of it as being any different to looking out for abuse or anything else that the children might, or grooming or, it's just another facet to the whole child protection remit in my opinion. [R60, Learning Resource Centre Manager, High School, London]

Indeed, in our survey data, 86 per cent of respondents agreed or strongly agreed with the statement, 'The Prevent duty in schools or colleges is a continuation of existing safeguarding responsibilities.' This broad finding has now been replicated across multiple studies,[46] and there is little doubt that this 'narrative of continuity', equating the Prevent duty within existing safeguarding requirements, helped to soften possible opposition to the duty among educators.[47] It certainly helped education professionals to see the high attrition rate within the referral system as unproblematic, even as this has comprised one of the main concerns of Prevent's critics. In 2015/16, the academic year after the duty's introduction, for example, only 14 per cent of referrals were deemed suitable for further consideration by a Channel Panel, and only a third of those considered by the Panel led to a Channel intervention. Thus, from the 7,631 safeguarding Prevent referrals made in 2015/16 (one-third of

---

[46] See Joel Busher and Lee Jerome (eds.), *The Prevent Duty in Education: Impact, Enactment and Implications* (Basingstoke: Palgrave Macmillan, 2020); Suraj Lakhani, 'Social Capital and the Enactment of Prevent Duty: An Empirical Case-Study of Schools and Colleges', *Critical Studies on Terrorism* 13, no. 4 (2020): 660.

[47] Busher, Choudhury, and Thomas, 'The Enactment of the Counter-Terrorism "Prevent Duty"'.

which were from the education sector), only 381 (5 per cent) resulted in an intervention through the Channel programme.[48] While critics of Prevent have often seized on this as evidence of the disproportionality of the duty, when seen through a safeguarding lens, such a ratio of referrals to interventions becomes normal, and indicative that the referral system is working as it should.

Yet we also found evidence of four key ways in which the monitoring and surveillance associated with the Prevent duty differed from pre-existing practices of educational monitoring and surveillance.

First, we found evidence that the Prevent duty had contributed to an important refocusing of pre-existing monitoring and surveillance practices. While most of what were understood as the potential indicators of vulnerability were broadly similar between Prevent-related concerns and those relating to other safeguarding issues, Prevent-related monitoring and surveillance focused particular attention on the expression of ideas that could be deemed extreme, and signs that could be considered indicators of some form of crisis of belonging. As such, reflecting some of the criteria set out in the framework used within the Channel programme to assess an individual's level of risk of radicalisation, alongside low self-esteem and a desire for adventure and excitement, school and college staff also saw explorations of identity, faith, and belonging as potential indicators of vulnerability to radicalisation.[49]

What also contributed to this refocusing of surveillance practices was the emphasis placed on the teaching of 'fundamental British values' as a way of building 'resilience to extremist ideas'.[50] For several respondents, this translated into a requirement to identify or 'listen out for' expressions of opinions, ideas, and ideologies that were deemed 'inappropriate' or that 'we didn't think were healthy' (R33, Head of Year, High School, Yorkshire). As one teacher explained, 'it's basically listening out for anything that doesn't sound quite in line with British Values' (R8, Senior Leader, High School, Yorkshire).

Second, for some respondents the introduction of the Prevent duty was associated with an intensification of monitoring and surveillance in comparison with pre-existing forms of monitoring and surveillance. While Prevent was widely described as a safeguarding issue, respondents often identified it as a safeguarding issue that

---

[48] Home Office, *Individuals Referred to and Supported through the Prevent programme, April 2015 to March 2016*, Statistical Bulletin 23/17, https://assets.publishing.service.gov.uk/government/uploads/system/uploads/attachment_data/file/677646/individuals-referred-supported-prevent-programme-apr2015-mar2016.pdf.

[49] Her Majesty's Government, *Channel Vulnerability Assessment Framework*, 2012, 2, https://assets.publishing.service.gov.uk/government/uploads/system/uploads/attachment_data/file/118187/vul-assessment.pdf.

[50] Rachel Pells, 'Children Must be Taught British Values at School to Develop Resilience against Terror, Says Ofsted Chief', *The Independent*, 23 June 2017, www.independent.co.uk/news/education/education-news/children-taught-british-values-school-reslience-terror-ofsted-chief-amanda-spielman-a7804656.html.

required particular vigilance. This was partly a product of the perceived severity of the risk, not just to the student and their family but also to the member of staff and the school/college if one of their students did become involved in acts of terrorism, and particularly if they as an institution were identified as having failed to spot signs that the student was at risk. Multiple respondents spoke about the emotional and moral pressure that they felt under given the high stakes, often citing the intense scrutiny placed on decisions made or not made by schools and colleges where current, or even former, students travelled to Syria.

> [W]hen the families were disappearing to Syria, and I felt schools were always blamed for everything. They seem to be pointing at the school, like, 'Why didn't they know, why hadn't they spotted anything?' And that's a concern, I think ... we've done blanket emails to staff to cover things ..., I emailed, 'Remember to listen out for extremism in any form, and if you do hear anything, just listen carefully. Log it, and let us know what's going on, and then we can take it on.' And we're doing it that way, it's ears to the ground, really, as much as anything. [R8, Senior Leader, High School, Yorkshire]

This perceived need for extra vigilance was also a product both of the apparent difficulty of detecting the threat, and its apparent ubiquity. Government guidelines emphasised that 'there is no single way of identifying an individual who is likely to be susceptible to a terrorist ideology' – presumably in part as a way of heading off criticisms about stereotyping – but in doing so they also made the threat feel much more difficult to detect.[51] This was compounded by concerns among some respondents that 'genuine' cases would likely be well-versed in how to avoid detection – a view informed both by warnings in the guidelines that those 'at risk of radicalisation may display different signs or seek to hide their views',[52] and by high-profile cases in which one or more students had been radicalised, and in some cases travelled to Syria, without apparently displaying any signs that this was happening.

At the same time, the seemingly mundane nature of some of the vulnerability indicators – sudden changes in behaviour or friendship groups are hardly unusual among teenagers – also made the threat feel ubiquitous. As several respondents observed, 'the things that you are looking out for could apply to a whole range of things' (R32, Teacher, High School, Yorkshire). The ubiquity and opacity of the indicators – when combined with beliefs that 'the smallest sign can lead to something bigger' (R63, Head of Subject, High School, London) and that 'not all radical extremists are bad people – it can happen to anybody and it's just, it's a kind of, it's a situation anyone could find themselves in' (R24, Teacher, High School, Yorkshire) – made the threat feel constant and seemingly all-encompassing, yet at the same time uncomfortably easy to overlook. Once one adds in the possible repercussions of

---

[51] Department for Education, *The Prevent Duty: Departmental Advice for Schools*, 6.
[52] Ibid.

'missing something',[53] this provided a powerful motivation for the adoption of what multiple respondents described as an approach of 'better safe than sorry'.

> Now every single little thing we report back because we also need to cover ourselves. We don't want to happen [to us] what happened to Bethnal Green [an East London school that faced particular scrutiny after three female students travelled to join ISIS]. They are saying that 'we had no idea', when there were probably lots of signs there. [R50, Designated Safeguarding Lead (DSL), school, London]

> There was absolutely nothing to be concerned about, but I think what the Prevent agenda does, is, as a teacher it makes you feel anxious and that you will miss something in some way, that you will get into trouble because you'll miss something. [R5, Senior leader, High School, Yorkshire]

Quite what this additional vigilance looked like varied across institutions and individuals. For some, it was about going beyond putting in place technical solutions to achieving cultural change – cultivating what one respondent described as 'an ethos inside the school of flagging conversations that are concerning' (R63, Head of Subject, High School, London). For some, the fact that students who were becoming radicalised were likely to seek actively to avoid detection meant that staff had to find ways to 'listen more carefully to what the child is saying to someone else [other than members of staff]', and to 'listen to their conversations with peers to see what comes out of that' (R30, Teaching Assistant, Primary School, Yorkshire), whether that was through listening in to conversations among students or encouraging students themselves to be aware of and willing to report signs of radicalisation. For others it was about inculcating a 'culture of vigilance' around security issues more broadly on the basis that if people are aware of and report on 'something not quite right or suspicious' there is always the chance that 'it could be a Prevent issue as well' (R6, Deputy Head, High School, Yorkshire).

Several respondents described how their appreciation of these apparent risks had translated into a tendency to err on the side of caution and report concerns even where they suspected there was, in fact, little risk on the grounds that 'it's not serious, but it could be serious' (R55, Deputy Head, High School, London). In such a situation, creating a paper trail to audit if something did happen served at least to limit their exposure to such risks. As one respondent recalled:

> so even though I actually kind of put, as my opening sentence [in the referral notes], 'I realise this is very vague, but', and then just trying to put the conversation that I'd had with this little boy, because it might be absolutely something and nothing, but at least that's saying on that particular date that was flagged up. [R28, Teaching Assistant, Primary School, Yorkshire]

---

[53] See quotation below.

As another respondent explained:

> I know there needs to be that element of confidentiality, but at the end of the day, whenever something happens, nobody questions why people shared information; they always question why they didn't. [R29, Deputy Head, Primary School, Yorkshire]

Third, and following on from the previous point, the perceived seriousness of the risk and need for extra vigilance also appears to have contributed to a hardening of responses by some staff to student resistance to the practices of surveillance. Student resistance to practices of surveillance in educational settings is likely as old as educational settings themselves. As Taylor notes,[54] there are multiple ways in which students resist the expansion of surveillance in educational settings today, including repositioning security cameras, placing gum on them or showing awareness of the areas that are free of camera surveillance. Crucially, she also notes that acts of resistance are often not considered serious misbehaviour by students, but are rather understood as a form of mischievousness.

Our interviews found numerous examples of students, aware of being watched and observed for indicators of radicalisation, engaging in acts that can be interpreted as forms of resistance to Prevent-related surveillance. We found students playing on the fear and concerns of teachers, reproducing the indicators as a way of winding up school and college staff and testing the boundaries of the policies. In one school, a student downloaded software to enter words flagged by IT monitoring filters into the search engines on school computers with such frequency that in the end, the terms used had to be removed from the list of banned words. In another school, knowing that staff had completed their Prevent training and had obligations to report on any concerns about support for terrorist groups, students walked around the school whispering 'ISIS' as they passed staff members.

Interviewees recognised that, for some students, Prevent provided a further arena in which to test the boundaries of what was permissible and possible – in which to engage in 'mischief':

> But I think for some they just say it as a joke also. Everyone wants, it just that part of the anti-establishment vibe isn't it? Just inherently hilarious. 'Don't say anything the police are going to get us', it's just a bit of a joke. [R45, Teacher, High School, London]

While many instances were treated as examples of mischief, we also encountered instances of harder institutional responses. In one institution such actions were met with warnings to students about potential police involvement:

---

[54] Taylor, *Surveillance Schools*, 18.

R1: ... But [students] do make jokes about it. They will say things and they know it's inflammatory and they know it will get them into trouble. Another boy ... who is very difficult. When he is in a situation he doesn't want to be in he will make comments ... He will say things like, 'I want to blow this place up, but don't report me to the police'. ... [I]t's become ... a joke badge of honour. It's quite difficult to unpick what you report and what you don't report. And what you do about that because it's not serious, but it could be serious.

INT: How do you handle that?

R1: We tell them don't be silly with that. ... [Y]ou will end of with the police knocking on your door. And they are like no I didn't mean it ... I am just being stupid, I am just joking. [R55, Deputy Head, High School, London]

We also encountered examples where staff had determined that the actions or comments of students did not comprise a serious or 'genuine' concern, but nevertheless took further action. In some cases, this was explained in terms of an underlying didactic reasoning: the student was apparently reported in order to help them understand the parameters of 'appropriate' and 'inappropriate' behaviour. In one such example, a student made comments during a class in front of the staff and students that they should pray for him, as he would soon be in Syria. Further discussions with the student led the school to determine that this was just a student playing up, trying to upset the staff in the class and that there was no concern that the student had a serious intention to travel to Syria. However, the school still decided to bring the parents in for a discussion:

R: In speaking to that child it became really apparent really, really, quickly that they were winding the TA [teaching assistant] up. I could have said that's a child who is just being naughty. But I wanted to make the point for the child that actually what you say matters.

INT: So it's actually a didactic line.

R: Yes. What you say matters. People are listening to you, every single thing that you are saying, and they will make judgements about you based on what is coming out of your mouth. Then we got the parents in and his dad wasn't happy with him. ... his dad was thinking you see why the school has done this and he was saying yes, I can see why. ... [V]ery quickly he was saying I am sorry, I will apologise to the TA. I was saying, 'okay I get that, but what if you do that and then I find out that in six months' time that you have left home and you are in Syria. What do I do now? How does that play out?' [R49, Deputy Head, High School, London]

The most striking example of this was a case in which a Muslim student had made a video with friends in which, at some point during the video, they had pretended to be promoting ISIS, telling viewers that if they wanted to join ISIS they should call them on the number or click on a link that would appear at the end of the video. It was clear to staff at the school that this was supposed to be a joke – apart from anything else the number at the end of the video was a false number and there was no link to follow. However, the case still entered the referral pathway. It led to the involvement of the Safer Schools police officer, the local Prevent team and, at some point during this process, the parents of the student were called in. When asked about why the case had been handled in this way, the respondent explained,

> I knew it was a joke but I thought they need to know that certain things are not funny and that you can't put certain things on YouTube like that. So, I looked at it and I thought, okay funny but not funny ... I was more concerned not because I think they were going to be radicalised in any way. I was more concerned about their understanding of why that was not appropriate. [R65, support worker, school, London]

In both examples, the staff viewed themselves as protecting the students by making them aware of how their actions would be interpreted in the wider world given their Muslim identity and Islamophobia in society. For the school and college staff, these were important lessons for Muslim students in avoiding 'risky identities' and performing 'safe identities'.[55] It suggests that a safeguarding policy, introduced to protect people from being drawn into terrorism, has been stretched to protect Muslim students from provoking racialised suspicion and discrimination. However, teaching Muslims to avoid actions, even jokes, that could be misconstrued as an indicator of extremism, actually reinforces a moderate/extremist binary, and in doing so legitimatises the need for surveillance of Muslim religious practices and identities for signs of extremism.

Fourth, the other way in which the monitoring and surveillance practices associated with Prevent appeared to diverge from those associated with other safeguarding issues was how difficult it was to access information with which to develop a realistic assessment of local risk. As respondents observed, in other areas of safeguarding, such as Female Genital Mutilation (FGM) or youth 'gang' violence, the relevant authorities could provide risk assessments that often included local prevalence data. Such information was used by safeguarding leads to inform their own judgements about what comprised a proportional response to those issues within their own institutions.

This was not the case with Prevent, however. Some institutional safeguarding leads had been told that they were in a 'priority' area or a 'category one' area, but these categories themselves had been left unexplained, and neither could they access comparative data for neighbouring areas. In the absence of such information,

---

[55] Gabe Mythen, Sandra Walklate, and Fatima Khan, '"I'm a Muslim, but I'm Not a Terrorist": Victimization, Risky Identities and the Performance of Safety', *British Journal of Criminology* 49, no. 6 (2009): 736.

some respondents arrived at the conclusion that maybe such designations were simply based on the size of the local Muslim population, after all.

> With Prevent, I mean, there's no data available, there's no, it's all secret squirrel. We're a category two, or category one borough, so it's a high-risk borough, but low referrals under eighteens, very low. I don't know what the over eighteen referral rate is, do you know? And there's no comparative data so you can't compare it to other boroughs: it's very, it's all quite clandestine so I can't tell you if things are better elsewhere. ... What is the actual risk? Like, we know, for example with female genital mutilation we know how many, up to about three years ago, two years ago, were affected in [name of borough]. So like, wow, you know, it's huge, so we've got to sort this out, you know? But we don't know how many are affected [in terms of Prevent-related concerns], I don't know how many are affected, and all I know is that we're category one, or whatever, but there's no, I can't find a ..., there's ..., no-one's given us a description of what that is. Well, why is it a category one? What is it? I think it's just based on the number of Muslims, but I don't know. Is it? [R61, DSL, secondary school, London]

The picture that emerges then is one in which, while the monitoring and surveillance practices undertaken in response to the Prevent duty were intertwined with and understood in the context of wider safeguarding practices, there is some evidence at least of important ways in which the introduction of the Prevent duty also refocused surveillance practices and further foregrounded ideas about the need for vigilance.

The Surveillance of Muslim Religious Practice and Identity

As described above, since the launch of the Prevent duty, the Home Office, Department for Education and assorted Prevent practitioners have been keen to emphasise that the Prevent strategy and duty apply to all forms of extremism. This was also emphasised during interviews in all of the schools and colleges in which we undertook fieldwork. Indeed, mindful of the widespread public perception that Prevent is primarily about AQ/ISIS-inspired extremism, and keen to ensure that Muslim students did not feel as though they were being singled out,[56] staff often described measures that they had taken to avoid such outcomes. This included the foregrounding of democracy, active citizenship, equality, and anti-racism in classroom activities designed to address the Prevent duty; seeking out materials that foster a balanced understanding of the threats posed by extremism, terrorism, and radicalisation; emphasising to students that AQ/ISIS-inspired terrorism should in no way be seen to be representative of Islam or Muslims; introducing students to some of the Prevent training materials that they believed conveyed that the duty was not 'targeting'

---

[56] Our research report (Busher et al., *What the Prevent Duty Means for Schools*, 55) identified that 57% of survey respondents thought that the Prevent duty was 'considerably more likely' or 'more likely' to stigmatise Muslim students in general.

Muslims; and some of the Designated Safeguarding Leads (DSLs)[57] described working closely with colleagues to help them to feel confident in their own professional judgement in order to reduce the number of unnecessary referrals.

Yet, in spite of these efforts, we still found evidence that Muslim students were a particular focus of attention, and that there were subtle and unintentional, yet significant, differences in surveillance practices with regards to Muslim and non-Muslim students. A crucial part of surveillance is, as John Fiske observes, the 'coding' of that which is 'normal' and that which is 'abnormal' or 'dangerous'.[58] Our data suggest that the indicators of vulnerability outlined through Prevent training and, ironically, during efforts by staff to protect students from perceived public prejudice towards Muslims (see above), often served to make Muslim students 'hyper-visible'.[59]

The Prevent strategy, as well as the training and guidance around the Prevent duty, attempts to draw a distinction between signs of extremism on the one hand and the expressions of conservative religious views on the other, with policymakers placing particular emphasis on the argument that Prevent is not about policing conservative religious views. However, our interviews point towards the difficulties that arise in trying to draw such clear distinctions. There were frequent and numerous examples in which (Islamic) religious practices, beliefs, and views of students, or their ethnic background, drew the attention of school and college staff and prompted further investigation and questioning.

A Muslim teacher in one school recalled, for example, receiving Prevent-related training where he was given a sheet explaining key Islamic terms like *Shahada* and *Sharia*. He understood this to be a list of words they needed to listen out for. A member of support staff with responsibility for monitoring the use of computers remembered seeing images and unfamiliar Arabic words on a screen that a student was viewing:

> I thought that word, I don't even know what that word means, but I thought it had negative connotations and it was a Muslim girl. [R60, Learning Resource Centre Manager, High School, London]

In another school, religious practices identified as signs of possible 'extremism', sufficient to warrant further investigation or monitoring, included opposition from parents to a student playing musical instruments:

---

[57] Designated Safeguarding Leads are the senior members of staff within a school or college with responsibility for safeguarding and liaison with external welfare agencies. In most instances, staff would report their concern to the DSL.

[58] John Fiske, 'Surveilling the City: Whiteness, the Black Man and Democratic Totalitarianism', *Theory, Culture & Society* 15, no. 2 (1998): 67, 72.

[59] Tina G. Patel, 'Surveillance, Suspicion and Stigma: Brown Bodies in a Terror-Panic Climate', *Surveillance & Society* 10, no. 3/4 (2012): 215. See also Fahid Qurashi, 'The Prevent Strategy and the UK "War on Terror": Embedding Infrastructures of Surveillance in Muslim Communities', *Palgrave Communications* 4, no. 17 (2018): 1.

[Y]ou're aware, that it's insane, because it might be signs that things are going on, but it might be signs that the dad's beliefs are so strong that he doesn't want him to learn to play a musical instrument. [R28, Teaching Assistant, Primary School, Yorkshire]

The same teacher recalled hearing a young male Muslim student mention his father's absence from home and began to consider whether the father had travelled to Syria as a foreign fighter. As the interviewee acknowledged, 'my mind did make a massive leap, that it sounded really strange and maybe he had gone to Syria, but also maybe he was in prison'.

In fact, the interview data point toward the potential for even mundane expressions of student 'Muslimness', Islamic signifiers, or practices to be sufficiently unfamiliar from the norms of the teacher that they are seen to require further consideration and information. One interviewee described how young Muslim men growing a beard 'in a particular way' could be a trigger for suspicion:

[W]e do have boys who come to school and suddenly turn up and they have grown a bit of a beard. So we kind of question that but we haven't really got anywhere to go ... we have become much more vigilant because when I do see a boy who is growing a beard and he is only fifteen or fourteen, it does make me a bit suspicious. When it is worn in a particular way. So, we do sort of keep an eye on them and we do have chats with them and we do try and sound out what their thinking is. [R50, Deputy Head, High School, London]

One of the DSL's interviewed recalled receiving a referral from a member of staff because 'one lad were [sic] learning Arabic because he wanted to learn the Quran in its original language and that were flagged' (R12, Student Well-Being and Safety Lead, College, Yorkshire). In another school, writing *Allahu-akbar*, a phrase used in daily prayers by Muslims, in an exercise book triggered concern and further investigation. Another respondent revealed their concern in seeing a female student suddenly come to school wearing a headscarf:

[W]hat you feel is, you know, you're honestly looking at the situation thinking, you've got a girl who has a half-Pakistani heritage, and yet you're deeming her at risk of radicalisation because she's exploring that part of her culture. That feels, you almost feel racist for thinking that. Do you see what I mean? Thinking that you'll get it wrong, and yet, your overriding concern is that you'll miss something. ... [B]etter to be vigilant and make that mistake, and find out ... that there was absolutely nothing to be concerned about. ... [I]t makes you feel anxious and that you will miss something in some way. [R5, Head of Year, High School, Yorkshire]

In this instance the respondent clearly wrestled with concerns that this added vigilance, based on the student's ethnicity, might be 'racist', but seems to resolve these concerns with reference to what is presented as the overriding importance of not 'miss[ing] something'.

All of these examples emphasise the way in which Muslim religious practices can become marked as signs of danger: not out of malice or active prejudice, but because they are different and unfamiliar to many school and college staff, the overwhelming majority of whom are white non-Muslims. A lack of understanding around Islam, and a lack of confidence in assessing risk, contribute therefore to a culture of reporting onwards anything that leaves doubt in the mind of the member of staff, and issues that could have been addressed by the classroom teacher to activate internal Prevent referral processes.

Staff experiences of responding to concerns about far-right extremism provide an interesting point of comparison. Our interviews indicate that some educationalists, at least, have a more nuanced and self-assured approach to far-right extremism, a finding supported by subsequent educational research.[60] They were confident in identifying and acting on racist comments which they believed could be addressed through lessons on equality and diversity that made it clear to all students that racism and racist language is unacceptable. The upshot of this was that they would be less likely to flag concerns because they felt more confident in their own professional judgement. As one respondent summarised:

[W]e focus on Muslim extremism, and possibly because the White extremism, far-right extremism feels more commonplace, and I suppose we don't assume that there will be any action from that, that maybe not all of us take that as seriously. ... And also, if you're being realistic, the demographic of our teaching staff is white, and so any extremism from the far-right, although it might be uncomfortable, it's more within your experience, and you feel better placed to judge how extreme you feel that is and whether you need to report it on. ... Whereas maybe the Muslim extremism, you would feel like you had to report everything on ... I feel that if a white child made extremist comments about Muslims, black people, they would be less likely to be reported than a Muslim student who made a comment ... that was seen as extreme and anti-white culture. Because the right-wing extremism seems more commonplace. [R5, Head of Year, High School, Yorkshire]

The comments here suggest then that the lack of familiarity with Muslim cultural practices and norms among a largely non-Muslim and white teaching profession contribute to generating differentiated institutionalised Prevent practices in responding to the actions of Muslim students compared to non-Muslim white students. And the suggested increased likelihood of referrals for Muslim students compared to non-Muslim white students points to the risk of discrimination.

Of course, our interview data comprise a relatively small sample. However, such findings are given a certain amount of credence by Home Office data on Prevent referrals. Of particular interest here are the data regarding the ratio between the

---

[60] Suraj Lakhani and Natalie James, '"Prevent Duty": Empirical Reflections on the Challenges of Addressing Far-Right Extremism within Secondary Schools and Colleges in the UK', *Critical Studies on Terrorism* 14, no. 1 (2021): 67.

number of referrals made and the number of cases that are then assessed to require a Channel intervention. These data indicate that professionals involved in making Prevent referrals are more effective in identifying cases of right-wing extremism compared to Islamist extremism. In 2019–2020, 1,487 referrals for concerns related to Islamist extremism resulted in 210 individuals receiving Channel support, but only 1,387 right-wing extremism referrals were needed to identify 302 individuals.[61] Thus, for every case of Islamist extremism adopted for support through the Channel programme there were seven Prevent referrals. By contrast, for every right-wing extremism case adopted for a Channel intervention there were 4.5 Prevent referrals. In other words, the rate at which right-wing extremist referrals are found to justify and require Channel interventions are almost 60 per cent higher than for Islamist referrals.

Such findings also help to explain how, while most of our survey respondents accepted surveillance and monitoring as part of safeguarding practice, and while the overwhelming majority (82 per cent) accepted that the duty ostensibly related to all forms of extremism, many nevertheless still had concerns that the Prevent duty would in practice be focused on Muslim students and that this could both negatively transform the relationship between (white) educationalists and students, and stigmatise and alienate Muslim students and their families, particularly if 'done badly' by the institution.[62] This finding points to an acute dilemma described by many of our respondents: aware of their professional obligation to enact the Prevent duty and broadly accepting of the importance of preventing young people being drawn into terrorism, but also aware of its potential for racialised surveillance, and associated stigmatisation of their Muslim students.

CONCLUSION

Surveillance and monitoring of students in English educational settings is inherent to Prevent and the enactment of the Prevent duty. While Prevent has been expanded to cover all forms of extremism, it has not been able to escape its own origins as a programme that began with a focus exclusively on Muslims and in which, our research data suggest, Muslim students remain in practice a focus of attention. This chapter shows that the implementation of Prevent has increased the scrutiny by school and college staff of the actions, behaviours, and expressions of Muslim students in particular. Furthermore, expressions of religious identity, practice, and belief have become coded as potentially suspect, requiring further attention and inquiry to determine whether they signify real threat. Aware, perhaps of

---

[61] Home Office, *Individuals Referred to and Supported through the Prevent Programme England and Wales, April 2019 to March 2020*, Statistical Bulletin: 36/20 (London: Home Office, 2020), 14.
[62] Busher, Choudhury, and Thomas, 'The Enactment of the Counter-Terrorism 'Prevent Duty''', 18.

how society may (mis)read the actions of Muslims who may be seeking to resist and subvert the surveillance they face, school and college staff teach their students vital lessons on how to enact appropriate 'safe' identities. While our research has provided some insight into how school and college staff are interpreting, implementing, and understanding the Prevent duty and the surveillance it entails, further empirical research is needed to understand the views and perceptions of students, especially Muslim students, themselves.

15

Resistance and the Politics of Surveillance and Control

Anthony E. Cook

INTRODUCTION

Black resistance movements are among the most surveilled social movements in American history. From slave insurrections to Jim Crow and Black Lives Matter mobilizations, the government and its accomplices have long worked to monitor and control these movements. This chapter explores the history of Black surveillance and control, elaborating on the impact new technologies and shifting demographics have had on Black resistance movements and their strategies to counter this surveillance and control.

RESISTANCE AND TECHNOLOGIES OF SURVEILLANCE AND CONTROL IN THE ABOLITIONIST ERA

The institution of slavery survived for over 200 years with the government, business, and citizen sectors working together to maintain it. Slavery was not relegated to the plantation we customarily envision as its exclusive domain. At least 15 percent of all slaves were urban slaves, owned by slave masters living in and around major cities. Other slaves were town and country slaves, moving back and forth between rural plantations and cities as laborers rented out by their masters. This arrangement required a system of passes and permissions, surveillance, and control, to ensure mobile Blacks posed no real threat to whites or the system of slavery.

Frederick Douglass was a prime example. Douglass, as a slave and later fugitive from slavery, constantly encountered the surveillance apparatus of slavery. As a slave, his mobility was circumscribed and monitored through a system of plantation overseers and patrolmen enforcing the pass system, which allowed for close monitoring of the movement of slaves off the plantation. If stopped without a legitimate pass from their masters, slaves could be severely punished. This punishment was often required by state law.

As a fugitive, life was a constant looking over one's shoulder for bounty hunters paid to retrieve the escaped "property" of the master and return the fugitive to the plantation. Even in Boston, Douglas's final destination after escaping the Covey plantation in Maryland, Douglas and many of his fellow fugitives had to reckon with this fear. Even for Blacks who had never been slaves, had been freed by their masters, or whose freedom had been purchased, the possibility of being kidnapped back into slavery was a real one. This overpolicing and surveillance of Blacks – slave, fugitive or free – was something Douglass constantly encountered and engaged. Thus, Douglass understood the surveillance state from the perspectives of a slave on the Covey plantation, an escaped fugitive from that plantation living in Boston and abroad to avoid recapture and a Black whose freedom was purchased by abolitionists but for as long as slavery existed, might see him illegally kidnapped and returned to slavery.

Not only did he produce profits for his plantation owner, but when rented out, Douglass increased the profits of those businesses as well, by lowering labor costs. Why pay free white labor to do the work a hired slave could do for half the wages? It was through this rent-a-slave system of labor, commonly called "hiring-out," that southern buildings and infrastructures were constructed and local businesses, colleges, and government institutions thrived. To be sure, some city governments, colleges, and universities owned slaves directly, but many hired out or outsourced labor needs to sustain their operations.

Douglass's owner rented him out to shipbuilders in Baltimore, where he worked as a ship caulker, waterproofing vessels. Slaves were hired out as field hands, blacksmiths, and masonry, mine, construction, domestic, and sex workers. Some of the revenues generated from these activities paid for the administration of a system of surveillance and control; their labor paid the salaries of plantation overseers, civilian patrol forces, official law enforcement, and bounty hunters. These surveillance and control workers were financially and psychologically invested in the defense and maintenance of slavery – no less than the banks, textile mills, transport companies, and countless small businesses sustained by the slavery ecosystem and its cash crop, cotton.

The surveillance and control industry, however, was on the front line. Plantation owners had to monitor and control slaves, lest resentments toward master and system fester into rebellion. Slaves were watched by overseers, neighborhood watch patrols, and fellow slaves. Meetings, ceremonies, religious services, and gatherings were monitored, particularly in the wake of slave revolts in the eighteenth and nineteenth centuries. Fellow-slaves betrayed Denmark Vesey's uprising in 1822, resulting in Vesey, 130 Blacks and 4 whites being charged by Charleston authorities. Thirty-seven were hanged, including Vesey. In 1831, Nat Turner engineered the largest slave revolt in US history in South Hampton County, Virginia. The bloody insurrection left over sixty whites dead – men, women, and children. After two months of hiding out in the woods near his old plantation, two slaves exposed Turner's location. Along with fifty-six others, Turner was hanged. He was skinned and mutilated, bits of his body distributed as keepsakes to those in attendance. Resistance has a high cost, not merely for those who resist, but for the innocents caught in the backlash. In the wake of Turner's insurrection, over 100 Blacks, slave and free, were killed and/or mutilated by militias and mobs.

State legislatures passed strict laws in the wake of the insurrection. Because Turner was a literate slave preacher, the Virginia General Assembly made it unlawful to teach slaves, free Blacks, or "mulattoes," a slang term used to describe biracial or multiracial individuals, to read or write. The law also restricted Blacks from holding religious meetings without the presence of a licensed white minister. Of course, these measures could only be so effective. Many slaves, like Douglass, found clever ways to convince even adversaries to help them learn to read and write. Others, possessed with a phonetically gifted ear and memory, pieced together sounds, words, and sentences to teach themselves and others over the span of years.

The point here is that the deadly backlash of white citizen militias, supplemented with regressive state legislation and slave owner reprisals, was typical of the punch–counterpunch, reform–retrenchment, one-step forward–half-a-step back, cycle of Black resistance. Government, business, and social sectors benefited from slavery, and they also shared in its administration, including doling out retribution for transgressions like escapes and insurrections.

Intensifying surveillance technologies and protocols was always part of the response to the threat posed by rebellion and escape. The pass system, mentioned previously, required slaves to have a written pass authorizing movement between separate plantations, individual plantations and cities, and one section of the city and another. However, slaves courageous enough to impersonate the person referenced on the pass always threatened the system. They simply needed to know the name written on the pass, so they could respond accurately when queried about the name.

In some states, like South Carolina, whites adapted their surveillance and control technology to include physical descriptions and distinguishing features on passes, which made it more difficult for slaves to impersonate others: height, complexion, facial features, and scars. However, literate slaves who could read and write figured out which passes they could use and which they could not. In addition, being able to write, they could forge their own passes and freedom papers as well. Again, some states adapted their surveillance and control technology accordingly. They used printing presses to standardize the paper stock on which passes were written, making counterfeit passes and papers easier to identify. This adaptation, combined with detailed descriptions of both freed slaves and those authorized to pass, made forgery much more difficult.

In any era, and no less during the days of chattel slavery, technological innovation proved to be a two-edged sword, used against and by resistance movements. The advent of the penny press and the capacity to mass-market newspapers to a broad audience accelerated the growth and impact of the abolitionist movement of the 1830s. But while William Lloyd Garrison's *The Emancipator* benefited immensely from this innovation, so did the surveillance and control apparatus of slaveholding states. The mass circulation of print reduced the cost of forgery-proof passes, facilitated the dissemination of All Points Bulletins (APB) to expedite slave recapture, and exponentially increased the circulation of pro-slavery propaganda.

The dynamic role of technology in the cycle of Black resistance and white repression did not diminish in importance during the twentieth-century progressive and civil rights eras following slavery.

RESISTANCE AND TECHNOLOGIES OF SURVEILLANCE AND CONTROL IN THE PROGRESSIVE AND CIVIL RIGHTS ERAS

The Second Industrial Revolution that began in the 1870s and ended around the start of World War I is also known as the Technological Revolution.[1] This period encompasses the Progressive era of American history, a time characterized by rapid industrialization, immigration, and urbanization. In slavery, both Black resistance and the surveillance and control of Black resistance were limited by technological constraints. During this post–Civil War period, a range of innovations markedly changed the landscape of resistance and surveillance: energy (electricity, oil, and gas), transportation (automobile and airplane), communication (telephone and radio), and human identification (Bertillon facial measurement and fingerprinting).[2] Combined with a slightly later invention – the television, introduced in the late 1920s – these innovations tremendously impacted the future of Black resistance and the government's capacity to monitor and control that resistance.

---

[1] Alfred W. McCoy, "The US Surveillance State Dates Back to the 19th Century," *Mother Jones*, July 15, 2013, www.motherjones.com/politics/2013/07/surveillance-state-nsa-history. "The origins of this emerging global surveillance state date back over a century to 'America's first information revolution' for the management of textual, statistical, and analytical data—a set of innovations whose synergy created the technological capacity for mass surveillance ... By 1900, all American cities were wired via the Gamewell Corporation's innovative telegraphic communications, with over 900 municipal police and fire systems sending 41 million messages in a single year."

[2] Richard Farebrother and Julian Champkin, "Alphonse Bertillion and the Measure of a Man: More Expert than Sherlock Holmes," *Significance* 11, no. 2 (2014): 36–39, doi:10.1111/j.1740-9713.2014.00739.x. Alphonse Bertillion, a Paris police clerk, developed a system for identifying and organizing thief descriptions. "The system [Bertillion] came up with took 11 measurements from each individual. No other person in the world would share that set of measurements. From the body he took the height, the width of the outstretched arms, and the sitting height. He took the length of the head, its breadth, the distance between the cheek bones and the length of the right ear. The length of the left foot, the left middle and little fingers, and of the left arm from the elbow to the tip of the outstretched middle finger completed the total. ... Bertillion ... calculated that the chance against all 11 points being repeated in any two individuals was 268,435,456 to 1. ... His system had been adopted by police forces everywhere [by 1888]."

As already discussed, slavery's overseers and patrols walked and rode on horseback to enforce various iterations of slavery's pass system. Other than the information contained in the pass and whatever personal knowledge they may have had about the bearer of the pass, they had limited intelligence at their disposal. As the twentieth century advanced, so did the pass system. Officers patrolled their jurisdictions in cars and enforced pass laws restricting Black mobility outside of the new plantation system of Jim Crow segregation: segregated ghettos, schools, railcars, hospitals, water fountains, and lunch counters.

These overseer patrols used new written pass modalities that combined all the innovations of slavery's pass system with modern technological advances. "Show me your pass (license)," the overseer (officer) demands of Douglass. Douglass complies, and the officer now has a high degree of confidence that Douglass's pass is not forged because it contains the imprint of a new master, the Jim Crow state, on specialized paper. The pass improves on the biometric markers used in the old slavery passes – scars left by the whip, a deformity inflicted by nature or punishment, height, and weight. The new pass likely contains Douglass's picture as the central biometric marker.

Having cleared the preliminary hurdle, the officer might still have suspicions. After all, walking and driving while Black in the Jim Crow era, as it was in slavery and still is today in many places, automatically makes a Black man suspect.[3] Except now, this seemingly simple interaction has become more complicated and stressful for the Black man. The officer can use a two-way radio, yet another technology not available to his slave-era counterparts, to call a centralized dispatcher – who by the late 1960s had the capacity to check a national database put in place by Herbert Hoover's FBI and made available to local law enforcement across the nation. The national criminal database maintained by the National Crime Information Center (NCIC) allows the officer to retrieve information on criminal records, outstanding warrants, stolen property and other possible infractions. Douglass comes up in the database: a warrant was issued for his arrest in Maryland for a long list of charges, including theft, assault, and battery, and the attempted murder of a white man named Edward Covey, a former employer. A fugitive from justice, Douglass is hauled off to jail, convicted, and sentenced to life without the possibility of parole. In the blink of an eye, history is forever altered.

These technological changes were made possible, indeed, necessitated by the urbanization of America, a process that slowly grew from the First Industrial Revolution (1760–1830) and then at warp speed during the Second Industrial Revolution (1880–1920). The integration of technology and policing became ever more urgent as cities experienced an influx of white ethnic immigrants and, later,

---

[3] D. Marvin Jones, "New Slaves: Walking While Black, Shopping While Black, Working While Black, and Learning While Black in Urban America" in *Dangerous Spaces* (California: Praeger, 2016), 37.

Black migrants fleeing the lynching, repression, and lack of economic opportunity in the South.

The Impact of White Ethnic Immigration on Surveillance Technologies and Practices

Industrialization, concentrated in and around cities, promised a new and better life for many, attracting waves of foreign immigrants. Over the period of the Second Industrial Revolution, the number of Americans in cities grew from 10 million to 54 million, with half of the American population now living in urban areas. During this period, the first-generation immigrant population increased from 7 to 14 million. By 1920, over one-third of the American population was either first- or second-generation immigrant. The impact was even greater in the major cities of the Second Industrial Revolution, where three-quarters of the populations were composed of immigrants and their children.[4]

Growing immigrant populations in American cities, coupled with America's entry into World War I, fueled a paranoia that heightened the need for security and surveillance. Congress enacted the Espionage Act of 1917 and the Sedition Act of 1918. The Espionage Act made it unlawful for individuals to express or publish opinions that would interfere with the US military's efforts to defeat Germany and its allies. The Sedition Act, an amendment to the former, got even more specific. The Act made it illegal to use disloyal, profane, or abusive language to criticize the US Constitution, the government, the military, the flag, or the uniform. More than 2,000 people were arrested and over 1,000 were convicted under this vague, catch-all of a law. Many were immigrants.

The Bolshevik Revolution of 1917 and the growth of socialism in Europe intensified paranoia and led to the Red Scare. In 1919, the Justice Department, under the leadership of A. Mitchell Palmer and his assistant, J. Edgar Hoover, launched a crusade notoriously known as the Palmer Raids. The Justice Department rounded up thousands of foreigners who were thought to be communists, socialists, anarchists, labor reformers, agitators, and just plain enemies of the state.

This period of rapid demographic, cultural, and technological change was unsettling to many. The government was implementing a surveillance apparatus it had incubated during slavery then improved with new technologies during its occupation of the Philippines in 1898. America's pacification campaign against a decade of Filipino resistance was eventually brought home and used against American citizens. In the Philippines, the US army compiled detailed information on thousands of Filipino leaders, ranging from physical appearance and kinship ties to financial

---

[4] Charles Hirschman and Elizabeth Mogford, "Immigration and the American Industrial Revolution from 1880 to 1920," *Social Science Research* 38, no. 4 (2009): 897–920, https://doi.org/10.1016/jssresearch.2009.04.001.

profiles and political networks. This intelligence operation was supported by a police force, put in place by the US army, who deftly used the information to blackmail and extort those who posed a threat to American interests and power.[5]

The architect of this intelligence operation was Colonel Van Deman, who brought the capability to America's World War I domestic campaign, creating the US army's Military Intelligence Division (MID). Van Deman collaborated with the FBI and expanded the reach of MID into a citizen spy network, the American Protective League. The League included over 350,000 citizen-operatives. The network compiled over a million pages of surveillance reports on German-Americans and others in a little over a year. It was this dark alliance between government and citizen-sector intelligence operations that made surveillance and control of Black resistance in slavery so difficult to overcome. Now, the same alliance, bolstered by advances in technology and expanded beyond police and military into property laws, was facilitating Palmer raids and other strategies to undermine and quash domestic dissent.

If these tactics and strategies sound eerily familiar, they should. COINTELPRO was short for the FBI's Counter Intelligence Program. It targeted Civil Rights, Black Power, Women's Rights, antiwar and labor leaders in the 1950s and 1960s and was a direct descendant of slavery, colonial, and World War I intelligence capabilities. The most significant differences from era to era were the growing sophistication of the intelligence-gathering apparatus made possible by changes in technology and the enhanced capacity of the modern surveillance state to deploy these technologies against its own citizens.[6]

The Impact of Black Migration on Surveillance Technologies and Practices

Blacks migrated from the rural South to cities during a period known as the Great Migration (1915–1960). By 1930, 1.3 million Black southerners had migrated to cities outside the South. In the 1940s, the demand for workers generated by the wartime defense industry and postwar economic boom attracted 1.4 million Blacks. A little over 1 million Blacks migrated in the 1950s, and another 2.4 million migrated in the

---

[5] Electronic Privacy Information Center (EPIC), "Iraqi Biometric Identification System," updated August 17, 2021, https://epic.org/privacy/biometrics/iraq.html. Similar surveillance tactics are still being used by the US military, and when they were stationed in Iraq and Afghanistan. "Since at least 2007, U.S. troops have been using mobile scanners to take fingerprints, eye scans, and input other personal data from Iraqis (and more recently, Afghans) at checkpoints, workplaces, the sites of attacks, and door-to-door canvasses. This information is being used to build an unprecedented identification database of Iraqis that is administered by the U.S. military."

[6] Darren E. Tromblay, "Political Context," in *The U.S. Domestic Intelligence Enterprise: History, Development, and Operations* (London: Taylor and Francis Group, 2016), 13–66. See for an overview of the evolution of the political context for intelligence capabilities in the domestic setting.

1960s and 1970s. In total, over 6 million Blacks migrated to urban centers in the North, Midwest, and West during this period.[7]

A combination of push–pull factors precipitated white flight to the suburbs in the postwar period (1945–1980), eventually resulting in concentrations of Blacks in inner cities: racially restrictive covenants and other forms of housing discrimination steered Blacks into inner-city ghettos; discriminatory Federal Housing Administration (FHA) financing for white homeowners financed their pursuit of the newly minted suburban dream; a postwar economic boom and highway system connected cities to outlying areas, permitting commutes back into the cities to work.[8]

In the six largest metropolitan areas for 1946–1947 alone, over 62 percent of all home construction occurred in suburban areas. Between 1950 and 1960:

> central city populations in the 25 Standard Metropolitan Statistical Areas (SMSAs) increased by just over 3%, while total suburban populations increased by well over 60%. While the total populations of the nation's largest central cities stagnated, the number of Blacks in the central cities increased substantially, indicating an urban depopulation by whites migrating to the suburban fringes. The suburbs remained largely white despite tremendous growth, and the cities became increasingly nonwhite.[9]

Once the concerns of World War II dwindled, the focus of surveillance and control was shifted from European immigrants to Blacks in inner cities. Over the course of the Great Migration, inner cities became the locus of new forms of political organization and resistance, increasing concerns among white law enforcement and intensifying surveillance and control measures against this new population of urban dwellers. Hoover placed W. E. B. Dubois and the National Association for the Advancement of Colored People (NAACP), an organization he insisted was communist-backed, under surveillance.[10] Hiring the Bureau's first Black agents,

---

[7] James N. Gregory, "The Second Great Migration: An Historical Overview," in Joe W. Trotter Jr. and Kenneth L. Kusmer (eds.), *African American Urban History: The Dynamics of Race, Class and Gender since World War II* (University of Chicago Press, 2009), 22.

[8] Leah Platt Boustan, "Was Postwar Suburbanization 'White Flight'? Evidence from the Black Migration," *Quarterly Journal of Economics* 125, no. 1 (2010): 417–443, https://doi.org/10.1162/qjec.2010.125.1.417.

[9] Eric Bickford, *White Flight: The Effect of Minority Presence on Post-World War II Suburbanization* (Berkeley, CA: University of California, 1997). Bickford cites a Bureau of Labor Statistics survey for home building in the six largest metropolitan areas for 1946–1947.

[10] Alvaro M. Bedoya, "The Color of Surveillance," *Slate*, January 18, 2016, https://slate.com/technology/2016/01/what-the-fbis-surveillance-of-martin-luther-king-says-about-modern-spying.html. "Many people know that during World War II, innocent Americans of Japanese descent were surveilled and detained in internment camps. Fewer people know that in the wake of World War I, President Woodrow Wilson openly feared that black servicemen returning from Europe would become 'the greatest medium in conveying Bolshevism to America.' Around the same time, the Military Intelligence Division created a special 'Negro Subversion' section devoted to spying on black Americans. Near the top of its list was W.E.B. DuBois, a 'rank Socialist,' whom they tracked in Paris for fear he would 'attempt to introduce socialist tendencies at the Peace Conference.'"

Hoover successfully infiltrated the 1920s Black Nationalist movement led by Marcus Garvey. After years of investigation and counterintelligence, he mounted a dubious mail fraud prosecution that resulted in Garvey's imprisonment and later deportation.

Hoover's obsession with the potential disruption of Black resistance is present throughout his tenure with the FBI. Coupled with this obsession, Hoover's hostility and refusal to protect Black crime victims established a pattern and practice that was followed by local law enforcement and even influenced President Roosevelt, who refused to support antilynching legislation in the 1930s, in part because Hoover objected to it so strongly. For Hoover, civil rights activism and disloyalty to the nation were the same.[11]

While the new technologies employed by the state certainly hampered Black resistance movements, the latter did find creative ways to use the technologies to their advantage. For instance, it is difficult to imagine a modern civil rights movement before these innovations. The Great Migration between the wars was made possible by advances in job-creating factory innovations and transportation: buses, automobiles, and planes. The concentration of Blacks in urban centers, both in and outside the South, created the critical mass that made the Montgomery bus boycott, Greensboro sit-in, Birmingham campaign, Selma to Montgomery march, and so many more protest activities, possible. The capacity to organize and mobilize these campaigns was facilitated by transformations in communication like the telephone and walkie-talkie.

Most importantly, perhaps, it is difficult to imagine how a southern-based movement might have captured the hearts and minds of the nation and world as quickly without television. The medium may have been decisive in creating the moral, financial, and citizen support necessary to overcome the half-century status quo of Jim Crow – a system maintained by a reign of home-grown terror, state-sanctioned and citizen-enforced, against the Black community.

The nightly images of Birmingham police unleashing attack dogs and turning fire hoses on peaceful protesters – using excessive force, even against pregnant Black women – proved too much to tolerate. Television helped sear these images into the public consciousness in ways Douglass's stirring oratory or Garrison's editorial page could never fully replicate during the abolitionist era. What was seen could not be unseen. Television would again and again prove to be an invaluable tool in swaying the court of public opinion: the murder of four innocent Black girls in the bombing of the 16th Street Baptist church only weeks after the televised March on Washington and King's "I Have a Dream" speech;[12]

---

[11] Ivan Greenberg, *Surveillance in America: Critical Analysis of the FBI, 1920 to the Present* (Lanham, MD: Lexington Books, 2012), 58.

[12] Carolyn Maull McKinstry, *While the World Watched: A Birmingham Bombing Survivor Comes of Age during the Civil Rights Movement* (Carol Stream, IL: Tyndale House Publishers, 2011). On September 15, 1963, a Klan-planted bomb exploded in the 16th Street Baptist Church in Birmingham, Alabama. Four young girls, who were in a bathroom near the blast, were killed.

Freedom Riders battered, bus torched, running for their lives;[13] the tortured and murdered bodies of civil rights activists Goodman, Chaney, and Schwerner exhumed from an earthen dam outside Philadelphia, Mississippi;[14] Bloody Sunday on the smoke-clouded Edmund Pettus Bridge.[15]

The movement was fortunate to have a young, charismatic, made-for-television leader, Martin Luther King, Jr., who understood the power of television and was extremely adept at maximizing its impact. Strategies and tactics, from the time of year various protests should take place to the selection and training of demonstrators, were all meticulously planned to maximize impact and messaging. Through symbols, words, and action, the movement tried to communicate the cause in a way the country could digest and support. It proved difficult to derail, even with modernized technologies at Hoover's disposal.

Hoover used infiltrators and informants to undermine the movement. He identified donors and supporters, compiled incriminating opposition files on them, and selectively used the information to choke off financial support. His counterintelligence apparatus covertly funded other less threatening leftist groups to divide and conquer the left and undermine those he believed were most dangerous, like King. He exploited the rift between the followers of King and Malcolm X, between the Student Non-Violent Coordinating Committee (SNCC) and the Southern Christian Leadership Conference (SCLC), and even between Eldridge Cleaver and Huey P. Newton within the same Black Panthers organization.[16]

Hoover's surveillance included wiretapping King's phones and bugging his hotel rooms, forging misleading documents, and circulating them to staff to sow seeds of dissension. He sent recordings to King's wife of his extramarital affairs, threatening to

---

[13] Raymond Arsenault, *Freedom Riders: 1961 and the Struggle for Racial Justice* (Oxford University Press, 2006). In 1961, Freedom Riders, a group of Black and white civil rights activist volunteers, traveled from Washington DC through the Deep South to challenge Jim Crow laws and fight for racial justice. They rode interstate buses into segregated Southern states and encountered many angry mobs along the way. One of the most widely known instance of violence happened in Montgomery, Alabama, where the Freedom Riders were brutally beaten by an angry white mob.

[14] Seth Cagin and Philip Dray, *We Are Not Afraid: The Story of Goodman, Schwerner, and Chaney and the Civil Rights Campaign for Mississippi* (New York: Macmillan Publishing Company, 1989). Also known as the Freedom Summer murders, the abduction and murders of Chaney, Goodman, and Schwerner, three civil rights workers, sparked national outrage. The three men were attempting to register Mississippi residents to vote. The Ku Klux Klan orchestrated the attack.

[15] Robert A. Pratt, *Selma's Bloody Sunday: Protest, Voting Rights, and the Struggle for Racial Equality* (Baltimore, MD: John's Hopkins University Press, 2017). On March 7, 1965, then 25-year-old John Lewis led over 600 civil right activists on a march across the Edmund Pettus Bridge in Selma, Alabama. The activists were met by oncoming state troopers who brutally attacked them. Footage of the violence rocked the nation and invigorated the fight against racial injustice.

[16] Ward Churchill and Jim Vander Wall, *Agents of Repression: The FBI's Secret Wars Against the Black Panther Party and the American Indian Movement* (Boston, MA: South End Press, 2001), 40.

expose him to the world as a fraud. Hoover and his staff plotted how they might support the rise of a successor to King, someone less threatening and easier to control. In a version of psychological warfare, the FBI consistently contacted King, threatening to expose him, even suggesting he take his life by a certain date to avoid embarrassment and humiliation to his family and tarnishing of his legacy.[17]

The measures took their toll on the psychological well-being of King and the movement. Perhaps it took away even more from King and the movement, and we will never know. The same tactics were used to a lesser or greater extent on the SNCC, Black Panthers, antiwar protestors, and the labor and women's movements. The breadth and depth of COINTELPRO are indeed staggering, and it set the stage for the next phase of the epic battle between Black resistance movements and state technologies of surveillance and control.

RESISTANCE AND TECHNOLOGIES OF SURVEILLANCE AND CONTROL IN THE ERA OF SYMBOLIC AND INSTITUTIONALIZED RACISM

If the ghetto, symbolically speaking, was the new plantation system of the Jim Crow era, the mass incarceration of Blacks in prisons and jails was such for the post-Civil Rights era. This was the era of symbolic and institutionalized racism. It is not that symbolic and institutionalized racism did not already exist; they certainly did. The white power structure has always attempted to control Blacks who were neither slaves during slavery nor residents of a Jim Crow state during segregation – trying to create slaves without masters and gaining consent to inequality without coercion. Symbolic and institutionalized racism – colorblind racism, covert and unspoken, implicit bias wrapped in the garb of custom and tradition, cumulative white privilege claiming to be the natural order of things – always played a role in nurturing conformity to an unjust status quo. Its role simply became more prominent during this era.

The year 1968 was a watershed. Martin Luther King, Jr. and Bobby Kennedy, the bright lights of America's progressive future, were assassinated. King's assassination sparked a series of urban riots that accelerated white flight from cities, turning them even more into predominantly Black enclaves. Surveillance of the Black community intensified. In its Ghetto Informant Program, the FBI placed informers in stores and institutions, establishing human listening posts throughout Black inner-city communities. Between 1968 and 1972, the program grew from 3,248 informants to 7,500.[18]

---

[17] Ward Churchill and Jim Vander Wall, *The COINTELPRO Papers: Documents from the FBI's Secret Wars Against Dissent in the United States* (Boston, MA: South End Press, 2002), 99.

[18] Ivan Greenberg, *The Dangers of Dissent: The FBI and Civil Liberties since 1965* (Washington DC: Lexington Books, 2010), 77. The army and CIA were also involved in spying on the Black community during this time. Michael Geary, *National Security and Civil Liberty:*

Kennedy's assassination all but assured Richard Nixon, who had already lost to Bobby's brother in 1960, would win the 1968 general election. Nixon campaigned on a law-and-order platform designed to appeal to disaffected southern whites in the Democratic Party – the Goldwater–Wallace Democrats and Dixiecrats rebelling against the urban unrest sweeping the country between 1964 and 1968 and the social movements of the 1950s and 1960s: Black and women's rights, antiwar, and peace.

Nixon's southern strategy relied on symbolic and coded racism. It utilized the surveillance and control tactics he had signed off on and benefited from over a long career of collaboration with Hoover and the FBI. Eventually, these tactics – secret recordings, disinformation campaigns, surveillance, blackmail, and break-ins – would lead to his downfall. But before it did, the symbolic, rhetorical, and public policy implications of constructing Black people as public enemy number one in a War on Crime would set the tone of national politics and the discourse on race for the next half century.

Ronald Reagan perfected the southern strategy and the skills of symbolic and coded racism in his campaign of 1980, consolidating a political party realignment in the South and Midwest that resulted in decades of Republican Party hegemony at every level of state and national government. Launching his 1980 campaign from Neshoba County, Mississippi, the site of the slain civil rights workers – Goodman, Chaney, and Schwerner – Reagan's Campaign constantly evoked slogans of states' rights and limited government. He projected images of Black "welfare queens" and "strapping young bucks" exploiting the system, evidence of the morally corrupting influence of the welfare state.

Reagan's War on Drugs picked up where Nixon's War on Crime left off. It ushered in the era of Black mass incarceration, the militarization of local police forces and the use of ever-more sophisticated technologies of surveillance and control. Prisons, the new plantation systems of the late twentieth century, saw an unprecedented growth in population and financial investment under both political parties. Even democratic president, Bill Clinton, brandished his "get tough on crime" credentials. He sponsored the 1994 crime bill that fueled mass incarceration, while pronouncing the era of big government was over (largely understood as a welfare state that robbed hard-working white workers of their earnings to redistribute to undeserving Blacks and other minorities).

After the election of Ronald Reagan, the nation's prison and jail population rose to 2.2 million people, a 500 percent increase between 1980 and 2015.[19] This was the highest incarceration rate in the world, surpassing Russia and China. The vast

A *Chronological Perspective* (Durham, NC: Carolina Academic Press, 2014), 202–212. Geary describes the army CONUS using over a thousand undercover soldiers scattered in hundreds of field offices from coast to coast and the CIA'S operation CHAOS, creating a database, HYDRA, of over 300,000 American citizen activists containing a range of personal data.

[19] The Sentencing Project, "Felony Disenfranchisement," updated April 2014, www.sentencing project.org/wp-content/uploads/2015/12/Felony-Disenfranchisement-Laws-in-the-US.pdf.

majority of this increase was due to prosecutions for drug offenses – a direct result of the War on Drugs campaign waged by Reagan and reenforced by subsequent administrations.

This increase in mass incarceration is rife with racial inequities, as police are more likely to target, stop and frisk, arrest, prosecute, and sentence more harshly Blacks than whites for the same offense. Black men are six times more likely to be incarcerated than white men and Black women twice as likely than white women. Latino men are twice as likely and Latino women slightly more likely to be incarcerated than their white counterparts. Staggeringly, one out of every three Black men and one out of every eighteen Black women are incarcerated at some point during their lifetimes. People of color are not more violent or more likely to commit crimes. They are incarcerated at a higher rate because they are surveilled and controlled at a higher rate than their white counterparts.

These disparities are magnified by the increasingly disparate impact on voting – a federal and local tag-team partnership in the surveillance and control of Black and Latino populations. For instance, thirty-five states prohibit persons on parole for committing a felony from voting. Thirty-one prohibit felony offenders on probation from voting as well. Four states continue to deny franchise rights even after individuals have completed their sentences. Slightly less than 8 percent of Black adults are disenfranchised, compared to 1.8 percent of the non-Black population. In Florida, Kentucky and Virginia more than one in five Blacks is disenfranchised, and given the current rates of incarceration discussed above, "three in ten of the next generation of Black men can expect to be disenfranchised at some point in their lifetime. In states that disenfranchise ex-offenders, as many as 40% of Black men may permanently lose their right to vote."[20] Had surveillance and control of people of color been proportional to that of white people, it is likely that a drastically lower number of individuals of color would face the loss of their voting rights."

This prison industrial complex that disproportionately profiles and captures Black people like a fugitive slave system is well financed. State expenditures on corrections increased from $6.7 billion in 1985 to over $56.9 billion in 2015. States with the highest incarceration rates are Louisiana, Oklahoma, Alabama, Mississippi, and Arizona – predominantly Red States. States with the lowest are Maine, Massachusetts, Minnesota, and Rhode Island – predominantly Blue States. The race-baiting Southern Strategy of the Republican Party, along with Democratic Party complicity and partnership, has had dire but predictable consequences.

An incarceration apparatus with this level of efficiency and of this magnitude requires incredible coordination at every level of government, including logistical and financial support for law enforcement at every level. The militarization of police force SWAT teams by the federal government has resulted in the transfer of billions of dollars in money and equipment to state and local police forces. This has taken

[20] Ibid.

place under the aegis of the Department of Defense's 1033 Program,[21] the Department of Homeland Security's grants to local law enforcement agencies, and the Department of Justice's Edward Byrne Memorial Justice Assistance Grant (JAG) Program.[22] Under the 1033 Program, for instance, 500 law enforcement agencies have received Mine Resistant Ambush Protected (MRAP) vehicles built for the battlefields of Iraq and Afghanistan – not the neighborhoods of Ferguson, Missouri – capable of withstanding armor-piercing roadside bombs.

In short, we have witnessed over the past forty years high levels of assistance from the federal government in establishing and maintaining this plantation apparatus of control – constant intimidation, the show and use of excessive and deadly force, mixed with a disproportionate rate of Black and Latino incarceration. Pulled from their intended use for dangerous hostage, mass shooting and terrorist scenarios, these heavily militarized SWAT units are now most often used in routine drug cases in which police are merely serving paper warrants and rarely against white targets. These SWAT units are most often used in routine drug cases in which police are merely serving warrants. These heavily militarized units have typically been used in hostage, mass shooting and terrorist scenarios – rare incidents largely involving white targets. Bringing such a show and use of deadly force to routine drug matters, like issuing a warrant, greatly increases the intensity of police intimidation and assures that the targets will be predominantly Black and Latino people. According to an ACLU study, "42 percent of people impacted by a SWAT deployment to execute a search warrant were Black and 12 percent were Latino. In deployments in which all the people impacted by the SWAT raids were minorities, 68 percent were in drug cases."[23]

Again, the War on Drugs becomes a wrongfully labeled "colorblind" front behind which intimidation and violence are routinely inflicted on communities of color. Thus, even when the War on Drugs is not incarcerating, it is playing an important role in the politics of surveillance and control. It reinforces the symbolic and institutionalized racism that Blacks and Latinos are inherently criminal, violent, and, therefore, justifiably treated as second-class citizens. It creates both a symbolic and quite real war zone in their neighborhoods, inflicting an ongoing post-traumatic stress disorder that impacts families and communities in ways too numerous to track.

---

[21] State of New Jersey Office of Emergency Management, "Law Enforcement Support Organization (LESO) – 1033 Program," http://ready.nj.gov/programs/leso-1033-program.shtml. "The U.S. Department of Defense (DoD) 1033 Program permits the Secretary of Defense of the United States of America to transfer excess DoD supplies and equipment to state, county, and local law enforcement agencies across the country for use in performing their law enforcement duties. This property is procured at little to no cost to the law enforcement agency obtaining the equipment. Any property obtained can only be used by law enforcement officers for law enforcement purposes."
[22] American Civil Liberties Union, "War Comes Home: The Excessive Militarization of American Policing," ACLU 2014, www.aclu.org/sites/default/files/field_document/jus14-warcomeshome-text-rel1.pdf.
[23] Ibid.

SUMMARY AND CONCLUSIONS: WHERE DO WE GO FROM HERE? SURVEILLANCE, CONTROL, AND BLACK RESISTANCE STRATEGIES IN THE TWENTY-FIRST CENTURY

As we have seen, Douglass, in the era of slavery, might have had a better chance of evading overseers and patrol and making his way to freedom than in the late Jim Crow era. As counterintuitive as it seems, his chances of success under Jim Crow may have been better than in the era of omnipresent symbolic and institutionalized racism following the Civil Rights movement. The prison industrial complex flourishes in this era, under the banner of colorblind law and justice, and one out of every three Black men spends time in this latest iteration of the plantation system – American prisons and jails. Might Douglass have been the one of the three, again, the imprisonment of his genius forever altering history? Before dismissing the comparison out of hand, consider there were 1.68 million Black men under state and federal criminal justice supervision in 2013 – prison, jail, probation, or parole. This was 800,000 more than the Black men enslaved in 1850.

Late twentieth century and twenty-first century technologies are now ever-changing and upgrading, poised for new breakthroughs in robotics and artificial intelligence. On the biogenetics front, the mapping and manipulation of the human genome may soon put us in the driver's seat of human creation and evolution. These technologies make the capture, processing, and analysis of mega data unparalleled in the history of the world. If Douglass carries a smartphone or any device or item possessing a GPS radio, including the one that may soon be implanted in his body, his every move can be digitally recreated and tracked. If his image has ever been captured in the form of a driver's license, bank card, or social media platform, it can be broken down into such minute biometric components that cameras, now everywhere, can capture images subjected to nanosecond calculations by high-powered computers that identify him in large crowds. Biometric data have expanded from retina and facial recognition to capillary structure, thermal imprint, smell, and other biomarkers distinguishing us from each other. The implications of these developments for Black resistance and the surveillance and control of that resistance are profound.

Recent lawsuits have exposed the domestic surveillance capabilities and activities of the NSA, FBI, and CIA. In the case of Black Lives Matter, for instance, the very technologies used to organize and mobilize resistance – social media platforms, smart phones, and computers – create electronic data trails that permit government to track and often predict activists' every move. An investigation by the American Civil Liberties Union (ACLU) in California found that police departments were using data from the country's most popular social media platforms – Twitter, Instagram, and Facebook – to track Black protesters. The report showed that "500 law enforcement agencies used a data-aggregating site, Geofeedia, to sift through and organize social media posts."[24] Social media companies often sell data to corporate advertisers, so they can contour advertising to specific users. But Geofeedia, funded by the CIA, used the same data to create detailed profiles of activists that they then funneled to law enforcement agencies as surveillance intelligence.[25]

The sophistication of state surveillance and control of people of color, thus in turn the Black resistance movements in which many participate, has only grown more powerful in the post-civil rights era, again, due to changes in technology and, in no small part, demographic shifts likely to make whites a minority by the middle of this century. The technologies of the information revolution have made possible the capture, processing, and storage of information about everything knowable. And it has even expanded our capacity to know the unknowable.

Our age has plucked the forbidden apple from the tree of life and bitten deep into its core, using technology to unveil information once not even acknowledged as tangible information. The universe stands naked before us in all its splendor and chaos. Knowledge is indeed power, but Einstein was right too: imagination is more important than knowledge. For only moral imagination can convert knowledge to power in a way that is both humane and just. Resistance movements led by persons of color are inherently disadvantaged in the struggle against the hegemonic use of knowledge by the corporate state due to the enduring history of surveillance and control of these communities. But as this chapter makes clear, technology is a double-edged sword, and opportunities for meaningful resistance to this surveillance do present themselves from time to time. We must be prepared to seize them, if democracy is to survive the politics of surveillance and control.

---

[24] Lauren C. Williams, "Police Surveillance of Black Protesters Won't Stop the Movement," thinkprogress.org, October 14, 2016, https://archive.thinkprogress.org/surveillance-wont-stop-black-activists-9008acb3944b/.
[25] Ibid.

16

Surveilled Subjects and Technologically Mediated Law Enforcement

Reflecting on Relational Concerns

Alana Saulnier

INTRODUCTION

Law enforcement is increasingly reliant on technology to automate encounters with the public, identify persons to be targeted for further scrutiny, and document interpersonal interactions. As a result, public contacts with police are transitioning from traditional interpersonal interactions to interactions that are increasingly technologically mediated. This chapter reflects on that transition and speculates on the ways in which police–community relations, particularly relations with some racial minority communities, may be affected by this transition. A central argument in favor of technologically mediated law enforcement (e.g., automated license plate readers, facial recognition software, body-worn cameras) is that this new style of policing has the ability to ensure equal protection under the law, enhancing police legitimacy, and mending poor community–police relations. Some see the introduction of technology into law enforcement encounters as a solution to resolving mistrust associated with fractured relations between police and the communities that they serve, particularly for some racial minority communities. A key question that is theoretically explored here is whether the subjects scrutinized by these technologies see them as improving community–police relations. To this end, this chapter considers the theoretical utility of relational models of procedural justice, reflecting on whether technologically mediated law enforcement addresses or disregards relational concerns. The central argument of this chapter is that techno-fixes will not, in themselves, solve underlying issues of fractured community–police relations. While technologically mediating law enforcement has some qualities that may strengthen community–police relations, this is not a determined outcome. In particular, enhancing community–police relations, particularly strained relations with racial minority communities, requires attention to the importance of relational concerns associated with the administration of law enforcement, which technological mediation does not necessarily attend to.

This chapter begins with a brief historical positioning of the strained nature of community–police relations with racial minority groups in the USA, with a particular focus on Black persons' experiences and perceptions. The increasingly technologically mediated quality of law enforcement is then acknowledged, with this transition partly attributed to accountability concerns but also characterized as a product of the broader transition to intelligence-led policing. With these foundations established, the procedural justice literature is then summarized, highlighting the relative importance of *process* (treatment during an encounter) and *outcomes* (the result of an encounter) in shaping public perceptions of police, and speculating on the influence of technological mediation in this regard. The effects of authority's disregard for relational procedural-justice concerns are a particular area of focus, with implications for subordinate self- and group-identity underscored (and especially pertinent for members of groups with historically poor relations with police). Collective reflections on several key areas are then provided, including: the promises and pitfalls of technologically mediated law enforcement framed through the lens of relational models of procedural justice, concerns associated with the transition to technologically mediated law enforcement in general and for marginalized racial minority groups in particular, and suggestions for future research directions.

POLICING, SURVEILLANCE, AND RACE

Race is a variable that is central to better understanding police-community interactions. In fact, Wesley Skogan asserts that, in the American context, race is the starting point for *all* research exploring public perceptions of police.[1] Historical context is influential in this regard. While policing is a public service that is now officially expected to be equitably distributed across social groups in democracies – with no social group receiving significantly better or worse treatment and outcomes than others – this has not always been the case. An element of early policing systems was the explicit control and subordination of racial minorities, with the historical abuse of African Americans being particularly well recognized.[2] The history of Black persons' relations with law enforcement in the USA includes "organized slave patrols and bounty hunters for runaways,"[3] followed by a more general subjection to extraordinary policing based on widespread assumptions of the inherent

---

[1] Wesley G. Skogan, "Asymmetry in the Impact of Encounters with Police," *Policing and Society* 16, no. 2 (2006): 99–126.

[2] Lyndsey P. Beutin, "Racialization as a Way of Seeing: The Limits of Counter-Surveillance and Police Reform," *Surveillance & Society* 15, no. 1 (2017): 5–20; Simone Browne, "Getting Carded: Border Control and the Politics of Canada's Permanent Resident Card," *Citizenship Studies* 9, no. 4 (2005): 423–438; Stuart Hall et al., *Policing the Crisis: Mugging, the State and Law and Order* (London: Macmillan, 1978).

[3] Simone Browne, "Everybody's Got a Little Light under the Sun: Black Luminosity and the Visual Culture of Surveillance," *Cultural Studies* 26, no. 4 (2012a): 545.

criminality of Blackness.[4] While beliefs about Blackness and criminality have permeated American society broadly, research demonstrates that this racial prejudice was also pronounced in members of police organizations throughout the 1970s to early 1990s.[5] These facts indicate the genuine historical differences in relations between Black Americans and police compared to White Americans.

Relations between police and racial minority communities (compared to White persons) are recognized as relatively poor in general, but relations with Black communities have historically been, and remain, particularly strained. For instance, research continues to reveal that Black persons encounter disproportionately high levels of policing.[6] Further, racial minorities in general report being less satisfied with police than White persons.[7] Some might attribute findings such as these entirely to the motivations of police, believing that overtly racist officers target Black persons, which leads to both the overpolicing of Black persons as well as the generation of particularly negative sentiments toward police among Black, compared to White, Americans. However, a deeper social condition perpetuating these realities requires acknowledgment: Black persons, especially Black men, have been socially cast as suspicious and potentially criminal.[8] Such persistent accusatorial gazing, whether conducted by other community members or police, has negative effects on the relations between the social groups subjected to, and those perceived as engaging in, this treatment. In particular, perceiving oneself as a target of scrutiny diminishes perceptions of trust between watchers and watched subjects.[9]

Trust is quintessential to the operation of successful policing. When community members and police do not trust each other, police work is made more difficult, and police presence is a concern rather than a comfort to community members. Undoubtedly associated with the historical legacies and contemporary disparities described above, trust is a particularly strained aspect of minority–police relations.

[4] Hall et al., *Policing the Crisis*.
[5] Ben Bowling, Alpa Parmar, and Coretta Phillips, "Policing Ethnic Minority Communities," in Tim Newburn (ed.), *Handbook of Policing* (Cullompton, Devon: Willan Publishing, 2003), 528–555.
[6] Scott Jacques, "'A Run-in with the Cops Is Really Few and Far Between': Negative Evidence and Ethnographic Understanding of Racial Discrimination by Police," *Sociological Focus* 50, no. 1 (2017): 7–17; Patrick A. Langan et al., *Contacts between Police and the Public: Findings from the 1999 National Survey* (Washington DC: US Department of Justice, Bureau of Justice Statistics, 2001); Skogan, "Asymmetry."
[7] Bowling, Parmar, and Phillips, "Policing Ethnic Minority Communities."
[8] Colin Holbrook, Daniel M.T. Fessler, and Carlos David Navarrete, "Looming Large in Others' Eyes: Racial Stereotypes Illuminate Dual Adaptations for Representing Threat versus Prestige as Physical Size," *Evolution and Human Behavior* 37, no. 1 (2016): 67–78; Maria R. Lowe, Angela Stroud, and Alice Nguyen, "Who Looks Suspicious? Racialized Surveillance in a Predominantly White Neighborhood," *Social Currents* 4, no. 1 (2017): 34–50.
[9] Tom R. Tyler, Jonathan Jackson, and Avital Mentovich, "The Consequences of Being an Object of Suspicion: Potential Pitfalls of Proactive Police Contact: Potential Pitfalls of Proactive Police Contact," *Journal of Empirical Legal Studies* 12, no. 4 (2015): 602–636.

The race-based gap in trust is substantial, longstanding, and continuing.[10] In general, racial minorities report lower levels of trust in police than Whites; however, Black communities report especially low levels.[11] Additionally, Black Americans show little variance in attitudes towards police across other key demographic variables (such as socioeconomic status) which have been demonstrated to predict attitude variation for White Americans, highlighting the "master status" of race for Black Americans' relations to police – meaning that "race ... seems to override other factors in their relationship with police."[12] Contemporary world events also warrant the consideration of how a comparable "master status" affects community–police relations for persons of Middle Eastern, South Asian, and Arabic heritages. Muslims, particularly Muslim men, have taken increasing priority as suspicious persons requiring diligent scrutiny.[13] Akin to Black persons' experiences, the heightened attention of community members and police to Muslims is producing similarly strained community–police relations.

The central principle of equality that guides law enforcement in the USA necessitates a solution that would satisfyingly eliminate race-based differences in treatment and outcomes. Public perceptions of disparities in law enforcement not only affect trust in police, but also the perceived legitimacy of police.[14] Strong community perceptions of police legitimacy are central to the success of policing in democracies.[15] Some see technologically mediated law enforcement as the solution to standardizing community–police interactions and outcomes.

A TECHNOLOGICAL SOLUTION

Technologically mediated data collection is increasingly an aspect of law enforcement, being used to assist in identifying and assessing persons as well as providing a

[10] Tom Tyler, "Police Discretion in the 21st Century Surveillance State," *University of Chicago Legal Forum* 2016, no. 1 (2016): 579–614.
[11] Tom Tyler, "Procedural Justice and Policing: A Rush to Judgment?," *Annual Review of Law and Social Science* 13, no. 1 (2017): 29–53.
[12] Skogan, "Asymmetry," 101.
[13] Bowling, Parmar, and Phillips, "Policing Ethnic Minority Communities," 528–555; Adrian Cherney and Kristina Murphy, "Being a 'Suspect Community' in a Post 9/11 World – The Impact of the War on Terror on Muslim Communities in Australia," *Australian & New Zealand Journal of Criminology* 49, no. 4 (2016): 480–496; Tina Girishbhai Patel, "Surveillance, Suspicion and Stigma: Brown Bodies in a Terror-Panic Climate," *Surveillance & Society* 10, no. 3/4 (2012): 215–234.
[14] Lorraine Mazerolle et al., "Procedural Justice and Police Legitimacy: A Systematic Review of the Research Evidence," *Journal of Experimental Criminology* 9, no. 3 (2013): 245–274; Jason Sunshine and Tom R. Tyler, "The Role of Procedural Justice and Legitimacy in Shaping Public Support for Policing," *Law & Society Review* 37, no. 3 (2003): 513–548.
[15] Charles H. Ramsey and Laurie O. Robinson. *Final Report of the President's Task Force on 21st Century Policing* (Washington DC: Office of Community Oriented Policing Services, 2015); Tom R. Tyler, *Why People Obey the Law: Procedural Justice, Legitimacy, and Compliance* (Princeton University Press, 2016).

record of interactions. Some herald technologically mediated law enforcement as an accountability solution. From border crossings to traffic stops, individual discretion has been the subject of considerable controversy due to concerns associated with explicit and implicit biases. Technologically mediating interactions (e.g., using biometric identification at airports or intelligent transportation initiatives on roadways) provides a means of addressing concerns associated with individual-level discretion.[16] Further, some have championed image-capturing technologies (e.g., CCTVs and their recent reinvention in body-worn cameras) as a way to ensure police accountability and administer reprimands for inappropriate conduct.[17] As a counterpoint, it should also be noted that examples exist in which video evidence yielded little to no accountability.[18] However, the contemporary emphasis on technology as a means to standardize treatment and outcomes of encounters with police masks other long-standing rationales underlying the adoption of technologically mediated law enforcement.

The transition from *reactive* policing (focused on responding to calls for service) to *proactive* policing (focused on preemptive interventions) was instrumental to the adoption of technologically mediated law enforcement. As identifying and intercepting *risk* became a substantial aspect of the police mandate – forcing law enforcement to adopt an increasingly proactive orientation[19] – technology became central to the control, management, and regulation of persons.[20] In this pursuit, technology was (and arguably is) more so a tool to identify risk than ensure equality in law enforcement. Acknowledging this influence (as well as the influence of calls for accountability) offers a more holistic understanding of the trajectory of technologically mediated law enforcement. Managing persons rather than eliminating conditions of abjection has long been a key objective of technological mediation.[21] Commenting on early indicators of the technologically mediated direction in which law enforcement was moving, Gary Marx worryingly described a forthcoming "maximum security society."[22] Three decades later, as the era of intelligence-led

---

[16] Elizabeth E. Joh, "Discretionless Policing: Technology and the Fourth Amendment," *California Law Review* 95, no. 1 (2007): 199–234.

[17] Michael D. White, *Police Officer Body-Worn Cameras: Assessing the Evidence* (Washington DC: US Department of Justice: Office of Justice Programs Diagnostic Center, 2014).

[18] Beutin, "Racialization"; Colin Webster, "Deadly Injustice: Trayvon Martin, Race, and the Criminal Justice System," *Ethnic and Racial Studies* 40, no. 8 (2017): 1383–1385.

[19] Richard V. Ericson and Kevin D. Haggerty, *Policing the Risk Society* (University of Toronto Press, 1997); Richard Sparks, "Perspectives on Risk and Penal Politics," in Richard Sparks and Tim Hope (eds.), *Crime, Risk and Insecurity: Law and Order in Everyday Life and Political Discourse* (London: Routledge, 2000).

[20] Kevin D Haggerty, "Technology and Crime Policy: Reply to Michael Jacobson," *Theoretical Criminology* 8, no. 4 (2004): 491–497.

[21] Kevin D. Haggerty and Richard V. Ericson, "The Surveillant Assemblage," *British Journal of Sociology* 51, no. 4 (2000): 605–622; Torin Monahan, "Regulating Belonging: Surveillance, Inequality, and the Cultural Production of Abjection," *Journal of Cultural Economy* 10, no. 2 (2017): 191–206.

[22] Gary T. Marx, *Undercover: Police Surveillance in America* (Berkeley, CA: University of California Press, 1988).

policing (ILP – a proactive policing strategy that advocates aggressive data collection for the purpose of optimal police resource distribution) gains footing, the objectives and outcomes of this new policing style require continual assessment and critique to keep such a society at bay.

This is not to suggest that ILP should be characterized negatively. The strategy holds the potential to guide police to be more efficient and effective in assisting the communities they serve. However, when conceptualized as the primary strategy used to guide police activities, ILP may be damaging to community relations – particularly given the concern that bias continues to emerge in algorithmic policing.[23] ILP prioritizes crime fighting, by means of preventative and proactive interventions made possible through extensive data collection and analysis, as central to the police mandate.[24] While adopting a strong applied focus, ILP is a strategy with little regard for more critical questions[25] – questions concerning the impact of technological mediation on community–police relations generally, or, the way in which communities with preexisting poor police relations might be more specifically affected by a focus on aggressive data collection and preemptive interventions. Many scholars have expressed concerns that bias is expressed in algorithms.[26] This position questions the assumption that technologically mediated law enforcement ensures equality in treatment and outcomes or, thereby, improves community–police relations. These are important considerations given the centrality of: (1) technology to ILP,[27]

---

[23] Lyria Bennett Moses and Janet Chan, "Algorithmic Prediction in Policing: Assumptions, Evaluation, and Accountability," *Policing and Society* 28, no. 7 (2016): 806–822; Oscar H Gandy Jr., "The Algorithm Made Me Do It! Technological Transformations of the Criminal Justice System," *The Political Economy of Communication* 7, no. 2 (2020): 3–27.

[24] Martin Innes et al., "Seeing Like a Citizen: Field Experiments in 'Community Intelligence-Led Policing,'" *Police Practice and Research: An International Journal* 10, no. 2 (2009): 99–114; Jerry H. Ratcliffe, "Intelligence-Led Policing," in Gerben Bruinsma and David Weisburd (eds.), *Encyclopedia of Criminology and Criminal Justice* (New York: Springer, 2014), 2573–2581.

[25] Nick Tilley, "Modern Approaches to Policing: Community, Problem-Oriented and Intelligence-Led," in Tim Newburn (ed.), *Handbook of Policing*, 2nd ed. (New York: Routledge, 2008).

[26] Bennett Moses and Chan, "Algorithmic Prediction in Policing"; Lucas Introna and David Wood, "Picturing Algorithmic Surveillance: The Politics of Facial Recognition Systems," *Surveillance & Society* 2, no. 2–3 (2004); Osonde Osoba and William Welser, *An Intelligence in Our Image: The Risks of Bias and Errors in Artificial Intelligence* (Santa Monica, CA: RAND Corporation, 2017).

[27] Nina Cope, "'Intelligence Led Policing or Policing Led Intelligence?': Integrating Volume Crime Analysis into Policing," *British Journal of Criminology* 44, no. 2 (2004): 188–203; Carrie B. Sanders and Stacey Hannem, "Policing 'the Risky': Technology and Surveillance in Everyday Patrol Work: Technology and Surveillance in Everyday Patrol Work," *Canadian Review of Sociology/Revue Canadienne de Sociologie* 49, no. 4 (2012): 389–410; James Sheptycki, "Organizational Pathologies in Police Intelligence Systems: Some Contributions to the Lexicon of Intelligence-Led Policing," *European Journal of Criminology* 1, no. 3 (2004): 307–332.

(2) ILP to the future of policing,[28] and (3) strong community–police relations to successful policing.[29]

In some ways, policing strategies that advocate increases in the technologically mediated quality of law enforcement might be detrimental to public perceptions of police. In the case of ILP, the priority placed on crime-fighting relative to positive relationship development is concerning (but this is not to suggest that an ILP approach cannot be successfully coupled with strategies focused on enhancing community–police relations). Research demonstrates that positive community–police relations are much more influential on public evaluations of police than instrumental concerns (e.g., crime rates).[30] However, on its own, ILP prioritizes instrumental concerns, advocating a proactive policing style that might harm community–police relations by communicating to members of the public their status as untrustworthy objects of police suspicion – as targets, not partners, of policing.[31] The effects of such a message might be particularly damaging to historically disenfranchised groups, including racial minorities.[32] Furthermore, while it is easy to characterize technology as the harbinger of equality,[33] research suggests that "officers often utilize technologies to legitimize the policing of the 'usual suspects',"[34] demonstrating that technologically mediated law enforcement does not inherently resolve issues of inequality in treatment or outcomes that contribute to poor community–police relations. While ILP and its accompanying technologically mediated approach to law enforcement are sometimes credited with enhancing police effectiveness and accountability,[35] little work has explored how technological mediation might impact community–police relations.[36] The procedural justice literature provides a foundation for speculating on this relationship.

---

[28] Jerry H. Ratcliffe, *Intelligence-Led Policing* (Routledge, 2016); Grant Wardlaw and Jennine Boughton, "Intelligence-Led Policing: The AFP Approach," in Jennine Fleming and Jennifer Wood (eds.), *Fighting Crime Together: The Challenges of Policing and Security Networks* (Sydney: University of New South Wales Press, 2006), 133–149.

[29] Sunshine and Tyler, "The Role of Procedural Justice"; Tom R. Tyler and Cheryl J. Wakslak, "Profiling and Police Legitimacy: Procedural Justice, Attributions of Motive, and Acceptance of Police Authority," *Criminology* 42, no. 2 (2004): 253–282.

[30] Tyler, "Police Discretion."

[31] Dennis P. Rosenbaum, "The Limits of Hot Spots Policing," in David Weisburd and Anthony Braga (eds.), *Police Innovation: Contrasting Perspectives* (Cambridge University Press, 2006), 253–254; Tyler, Jackson, and Mentovich, "The Consequences of Being."

[32] Tammy R. Kochel, "Constructing Hot Spots Policing: Unexamined Consequences for Disadvantaged Populations and for Police Legitimacy," *Criminal Justice Policy Review* 22, no. 3 (2011): 350–374; Eugene McLaughlin, *The New Policing* (London: SAGE, 2006).

[33] Beutin, "Racialization."

[34] Sanders and Hannem, "'Policing 'the Risky'," 389.

[35] Jerry H. Ratcliffe, "Knowledge Management Challenges in the Development of Intelligence-Led Policing," in Tom Williamson (ed.), *The Handbook of Knowledge-Based Policing: Current Conceptions and Future Directions* (Chichester, UK: John Wiley & Sons, Ltd, 2008), 205–220.

[36] Joh, "Discretionless Policing"; Alana Saulnier and Scott N. Thompson, "Police UAV Use: Institutional Realities and Public Perceptions," *Policing: An International Journal of Police Strategies & Management* 39, no. 4 (2016): 680–693; Helen Wells, "The Techno-Fix Versus the

THEORIZING IMPLICATIONS: RELATIONAL MODELS OF PROCEDURAL JUSTICE

Theories of justice offer some insight on how targets of technologically mediated law enforcement might perceive and react to those interactions. While justice-oriented research started with exploring the effects of the *outcomes* of interactions on public sentiments, the *procedures* used to reach outcomes have been found to wield the greater influence on public perceptions of authorities.[37] As such, procedural justice theory in legal scholarship has focused on how the *administration* of law by various agents (e.g., police officers and judges), affects public perceptions of an interaction and its outcome as well as behavior.[38] A central contention of procedural justice theory applied to law enforcement is that the treatment that an individual receives during encounters with legal authorities heavily influences her perceptions of, and reactions to, these authorities.

There are two explanations for why people are concerned with procedures: instrumental and relational. Instrumental explanations suggest that procedures matter to people out of a desire to wield control over the outcome produced;[39] specifically, that a person values having control over a process in the interest of producing a more favorable outcome for herself – the focus is ultimately on the outcome of the procedure. Alternatively, relational explanations maintain that procedures matter to people because treatment communicates messages of value and status – apart from any instrumental motivations, a person appreciates treatment by others that indicates that he is a respected and valued person.[40] Instrumental explanations once dominated the literature, but research demonstrates that relational concerns are more influential on perceptions of procedural justice.[41] A series

---

Fair Cop: Procedural (In)Justice and Automated Speed Limit Enforcement," *British Journal of Criminology* 48, no. 6 (2008): 798–817.

[37] E. Allan Lind and Tom R. Tyler, *The Social Psychology of Procedural Justice, Critical Issues in Social Justice* (Boston, MA: Springer US, 1988); Tyler, "Police Discretion"; Tom R. Tyler and Heather J. Smith, "Social Justice and Social Movements," in Daniel T. Gilbert, Susan T. Fiske, and Gardner Lindzey (ed.), *Handbook of Social Psychology* (New York: McGraw-Hill, 1997), 595–629.

[38] Jeff Latimer, Craig Dowden, and Danielle Muise, "The Effectiveness of Restorative Justice Practices: A Meta-Analysis," *The Prison Journal* 85, no. 2 (2005): 127–144; Tom R. Tyler, "What Is Procedural Justice?: Criteria Used by Citizens to Assess the Fairness of Legal Procedures," *Law & Society Review* 22, no. 1 (1998): 103–135; Tyler and Wakslak, "Profiling and Police Legitimacy."

[39] John Thibaut and Laurens Walker, *Procedural Justice: A Psychological Analysis* (New Jersey: Lawrence Erlbalm Associated, 1975); John Thibaut and Laurens Walker, "A Theory of Procedure," *California Law Review* 66, no. 3 (1978): 541–566.

[40] Ben Bradford, "Policing and Social Identity: Procedural Justice, Inclusion and Cooperation Between Police and Public," *Policing and Society* 24, no. 1 (2014): 22–43; Lind and Tyler, *The Social Psychology*; E. Allan Lind, Tom R. Tyler, and Yuen J. Huo, "Procedural Context and Culture: Variation in the Antecedents of Procedural Justice Judgments," *Journal of Personality and Social Psychology* 73, no. 4 (1997): 767–780.

[41] Sunshine and Tyler, "The Role of Procedural Justice," 513–548.

of relational models of procedural justice have focused on the same core set of antecedents.[42] Specifically, perceptions of procedural justice are based on a subordinate evaluating her interaction with an authority as: (1) unbiased and consistent, (2) trustworthy, (3) respectful and dignifying, and (4) as offering opportunities to provide input (voice). Empirical research demonstrates that legal authorities' attention to these relational concerns wields important effects.

A wealth of research reveals the consistency of these effects. Specifically, procedures, their outcomes, and their administrator(s) more generally are all perceived as more acceptable,[43] satisfying,[44] and legitimate[45] when treatment demonstrates attention to the aforementioned relational concerns. The production of legitimacy ("a property of an authority or institution that leads people to feel that that authority or institution is entitled to be deferred to and obeyed")[46] is particularly important for legal authorities. Perceptions of legitimacy are linked to a host of advantageous outcomes for law enforcement, including greater adherence to the law in general,[47] as well as greater compliance with the instructions of legal authorities during specific interactions.[48] This research demonstrates that public perceptions of police legitimacy accompany positive community–police

[42] Tom R. Tyler, "The Psychology of Procedural Justice: A Test of the Group-Value Model," *Journal of Personality and Social Psychology* 57, no. 5 (1989): 830–838; Tom R. Tyler and Steven L. Blader, "The Group Engagement Model: Procedural Justice, Social Identity, and Cooperative Behavior," *Personality and Social Psychology Review* 7, no. 4 (2003): 349–361; Tom R. Tyler and E. Allan Lind, "A Relational Model of Authority in Groups," in Mark P. Zanna (ed.), *Advances in Experimental Social Psychology* (Elsevier, 1992), 115–191.

[43] Mazerolle et al., "Procedural Justice and Police Legitimacy"; Tom R. Tyler and Peter Degoey, "Collective Restraint in Social Dilemmas: Procedural Justice and Social Identification Effects on Support for Authorities," *Journal of Personality and Social Psychology* 69, no. 3 (1995): 482–497.

[44] Lorraine Mazerolle et al., "Procedural Justice, Routine Encounters and Citizen Perceptions of Police: Main Findings from the Queensland Community Engagement Trial (QCET)," *Journal of Experimental Criminology* 8, no. 4 (2012): 343–367; Kevin W. Mossholder, Nathan Bennett, and Christopher L. Martin, "A Multilevel Analysis of Procedural Justice Context," *Journal of Organizational Behavior* 19, no. 1 (1998): 131–141.

[45] Sunshine and Tyler, "The Role of Procedural Justice," 513–548; Tom R. Tyler, Peter Degoey, and Heather Smith, "Understanding Why the Justice of Group Procedures Matters: A Test of the Psychological Dynamics of the Group-Value Model," *Journal of Personality and Social Psychology* 70, no. 5 (1996): 913–930; Tyler and Wakslak, "Profiling and Police Legitimacy."

[46] Sunshine and Tyler, "The Role of Procedural Justice," 514.

[47] Jonathan Jackson et al., "Why Do People Comply with the Law?: Legitimacy and the Influence of Legal Institutions," *British Journal of Criminology* 52, no. 6 (2012): 1051–1071; Kristina Murphy, "Procedural Justice, Legitimacy, and Policing," in Gerben Bruinsma and David Weisburd (ed.), *Encyclopedia of Criminology and Criminal Justice* (New York: Springer New York, 2014), 4024–4034; Tyler, *Why People Obey*.

[48] Tal Jonathan-Zamir, Badi Hasisi, and Yoram Margalioth, "Is It the What or the How? The Roles of High-Policing Tactics and Procedural Justice in Predicting Perceptions of Hostile Treatment: The Case of Security Checks at Ben-Gurion Airport, Israel: Roles of High-Policing Tactics and Procedural Justice," *Law & Society Review* 50, no. 3 (2016): 608–636; Tom R. Tyler and Yuen J. Huo, *Trust in the Law: Encouraging Public Cooperation with the Police and Courts* (New York: Russell Sage Foundation, 2002).

relations. As such, the procedural justice literature is useful for better understanding strained community–police relations.

Given the poor treatment that has historically, as well as contemporarily, been documented during police interactions with Black Americans in particular, it is not surprising that there is a long-standing and continuing race-based gap in public perceptions of police legitimacy.[49] The issue of racial profiling has been central to these poor relations.[50] Focusing on the procedural justice literature dedicated to social identity and group membership offers a fuller understanding of the relationship between poor treatment and understandings of the self in relation to police.

Identity, Group Membership, and Community–Police Relations

Perceptions of relational procedural justice concerns influence understandings of social identity – particularly the self in relation to others. The concept of "group membership" – referring to personal identification with groups ranging from very small (e.g., family networks) to very large (e.g., nation-state affiliations)[51] – is central to this relationship. Group identification shapes one's social identity, and relational concerns (i.e., respect, trust, neutrality, and voice) affect one's identification with a group.[52] While the symbolic message of inclusion is communicated through procedures attentive to relational concerns, exclusion is communicated through procedures that are not. Evaluations of group membership influence attitudes and behaviors, including sentiments such as group pride and actions such as cooperativeness.[53] For example, the extent to which an interaction with a police officer satisfies relational concerns influences a person's perceptions that he has been treated in a way that: (1) is procedurally just, (2) demonstrates he is a person that this officer values, and (3) indicates he is an included ("in-group") member of the larger social group that the officer represents (ranging from a local region to the nation). In turn, these evaluations will influence a person's compliance with the specific instructions of that officer as well as support for and compliance with the institution(s) the officer represents more broadly. In short,

---

[49] Wesley G. Skogan, "The Police and Public in England and Wales: A British Crime Survey Report," *Home Office Research Study*, No. 117 (London: HMSO, 1990); Tyler, "Police Discretion"; Tyler, Jackson, and Mentovich, "The Consequences of Being".

[50] Tyler and Wakslak, "Profiling and Police Legitimacy."

[51] Lind and Tyler, *The Social Psychology*; Tyler, "The Psychology of Procedural Justice"; Tyler and Lind, "A Relational Model."

[52] Ben Bradford, Kristina Murphy, and Jonathan Jackson, "Officers as Mirrors: Policing, Procedural Justice and the (Re)Production of Social Identity," *British Journal of Criminology* 54, no. 4 (2014): 527–550; Tyler and Blader, "The Group Engagement Model"; Tyler, Jackson, and Mentovich, "The Consequences of Being."

[53] Tom R. Tyler and Steven L. Blader, *Cooperation in Groups: Procedural Justice, Social Identity, and Behavioral Engagement* (New York: Psychology Press, 2000); Bradford, "Policing and Social Identity."

social identity is an important aspect of explaining why perceptions of procedural justice impact behavior. "What is at stake in experiences of policing is ... people's relationship with, and tendency to categorize themselves as members of, the group police represent."[54] Treatment that is evaluated as procedurally just promotes "ingroup" identification with the officer and the social group(s) he represents, as well as perceptions of legitimacy, not only in that specific interaction, but also to legal authorities more broadly.[55] Coupling this understanding of the effects of relational concerns with the historically strained relations between Black Americans and police suggests that Black Americans may be more likely to perceive themselves as "out-group" members relative to police (and the group(s) police represent more broadly, such as the nation), resulting in diminished perceptions of police legitimacy amongst other undesirable consequences.

Interactions with law enforcement present opportunities for identity construction. Furthermore, persons who feel marginalized or are uncertain of their group standing relative to superordinate groups may be particularly observant of these messages.[56] For this reason, police attention to relational concerns may be particularly significant in interactions with Black Americans, as well as members of other marginalized groups more generally. Concerns associated with racial profiling continue to be especially problematic in this regard, communicating messages of suspicion, subordinate status, and alienation.[57] Alongside communicating harmful relational messages, such treatment also creates barriers to the successful administration of law enforcement in that it compromises public perceptions of legitimacy and, thereby, cooperative behavior. The work of law enforcement is made easier when the public can be relied on as partners.[58] In fact, policing that prioritizes aggressive tactics at the expense of relational concerns can even bond stigmatized members of the public together, fostering the creation of groups that collectively stand against law enforcement.[59] These poor community–police relations need to be resolved, and an important aspect of that resolution is eliminating discriminatory law enforcement practices. A key strategy to reducing discriminatory law

---

[54] Ben Bradford, "The Dog that Never Quite Barked: Social Identity and the Persistence of Police Legitimacy," in Mary Bosworth, Carolyn Hoyle, and Lucia Zedner (eds.), *Changing Contours of Criminal Justice: Research, Politics and Policy* (Oxford University Press, 2016), 4.

[55] Bradford, Murphy, and Jackson, "Officers as Mirrors"; Tyler, Jackson, and Mentovich, "The Consequences of Being"; Tyler and Wakslak, "Profiling and Police Legitimacy."

[56] Tyler and Blader, "The Group Engagement Model."

[57] Badi Hasisi and David Weisburd, "Going beyond Ascribed Identities: The Importance of Procedural Justice in Airport Security Screening in Israel: Airport Security Screening," *Law & Society Review* 45, no. 4 (2011): 867–892; Joh, "Discretionless Policing."

[58] Robert J. Sampson, Stephen W. Raudenbush, and Felton Earls, "Neighbourhoods and Violent Crime: A Multilevel Study of Collective Efficacy," *Science* 277, no. 5328 (1997): 918–924; Skogan, "Asymmetry"; Tom R. Tyler, "Enhancing Police Legitimacy," *The Annals of the American Academy of Political and Social Science* 593, no. 1 (2004): 84–99.

[59] Clifford Stott and Steve Reicher, "How Conflict Escalates: The Inter-Group Dynamics of Collective Football Crowd 'Violence'," *Sociology* 32, no. 2 (1998): 353–377.

enforcement is better managing police interactions with the public.[60] The question is: How is that best accomplished?

Technologically mediated law enforcement offers the promise of standardizing interactions in the interest of ensuring equality before the law, but such practices also dovetail nicely with the strategic transition to ILP. Some suggest that technological mediation is a means to address procedural concerns that can arise during interactions with police by standardizing processes.[61] However, others raise concerns about the potential of such technologies to produce perceptions of exclusion.[62] Ultimately, the existing procedural justice research provides a good understanding of the importance of relational concerns to policing, but, the way in which these concerns function and are potentially addressed in the new era of technologically mediated law enforcement remains largely unexplored. The remainder of this chapter considers the promises and pitfalls of technologically mediated law enforcement framed through the lens of procedural justice theory.

TECHNOLOGICALLY MEDIATED LAW ENFORCEMENT: FOR, OR OF, PEOPLE?

As the literature reviewed demonstrates, strong community–police relations are highly desirable for the successful enactment of law enforcement, but relations between police and racial minority communities tend to be strained, with relations between police and Black communities tending to be particularly strained. These poor relations are arguably, in part, the product of experiences with and perceptions of procedurally unjust treatment that communicates messages of exclusion. As such, police attention to relational concerns may be especially critical for mending relations with racial minority communities. The trend towards technologically mediated law enforcement is, in part, intended to address accountability concerns. However, the extent to which technologically mediated law enforcement is attentive to relational concerns or genuinely addresses the crisis of poor community–police relations requires thoughtful reflection and empirical research.

Technologically mediated law enforcement greatly increases the scope of surveillance scrutiny to which the public is subjected, which may negatively impact targeted persons' perceptions of procedural justice during encounters with law enforcement. Surveillance can communicate messages of belonging (when one feels protected by the process) but can also communicate exclusion (when one feels targeted by the process).[63] Empirical work demonstrates that surveilled subjects describe feelings of inclusion or exclusion associated with surveillance encounters

---

[60] Bowling, Parmar, and Phillips, "Policing Ethnic Minority Communities"; Tyler, "Police Discretion."
[61] Hasisi and Weisburd, "Going beyond Ascribed Identities."
[62] Monahan, "Regulating Belonging."
[63] Browne, "Getting Carded."

(in the context of airport security) in terms of relational concerns (i.e., respect, trust, neutrality, and voice).[64] Furthermore, emerging evidence suggests that targets of surveillance remain attentive to relational concerns in technologically mediated law enforcement encounters, but that "out-group" members relative to police respond less positively to technologically mediated encounters than "in-group" members. Specifically, Saulnier, and Sivasubramaniam demonstrate that in the context of border crossings, interactions with a security agent that are technologically mediated (i.e., in which an automated kiosk directs a traveler to secondary screening), perceptions of relational concerns as well as surveillance acceptability were significantly greater in an "in-group" condition (i.e., the traveler was described as a resident of the country in question and of the same racial heritage of the country's dominant racial group) relative to an "out-group" condition (i.e., the traveler was described as a nonresident of the country in question and not being of the same racial heritage of the country's dominant racial group).[65] Nonetheless, with major projects underway by the USA's federal government to extend the use of technology in various law enforcement contexts (e.g., Future Attribute Screening Technology;[66] Intelligent Transportation Systems on roadways),[67] it is reasonable to anticipate that technologically mediated, or even automated, law enforcement will be increasingly common in the future.

The procedural justice literature reveals that the nature of police interactions with the public greatly impact evaluations of public satisfaction with and support for police, as well as the legitimacy of legal institutions more generally. Technological mediation is one way of altering, regulating, and standardizing these interactions. However, understandings of how the public evaluates technologically mediated law enforcement remain limited. Relational procedural justice concerns may be relevant to technologically mediated encounters with police as well as interpersonal encounters. As such, careful attention needs to be dedicated to the relational messages communicated in a technologically mediated encounter. This assertion requires empirical validation but can begin with theoretically speculating how the antecedents of procedural justice (i.e., neutrality, trust, respect, and voice) might operate in technologically mediated interactions.

---

[64] Alana Saulnier, "Surveillance as Communicating Relational Messages: Advancing Understandings of the Surveilled Subject," *Surveillance & Society* 15, no. 2 (2017): 286–302.
[65] Alana Saulnier and Diane Sivasubramaniam, "Procedural Justice Concerns and Technologically Mediated Interactions with Legal Authorities," *Surveillance & Society* 19, no. 3 (2021): 317–337.
[66] Dawn M. Sweet, Christian A. Meissner, and Dominick J. Atkinson, "Assessing Law Enforcement Performance in Behavior-Based Threat Detection Tasks Involving a Concealed Weapon or Device," *Law and Human Behavior* 41, no. 5 (2017): 411–421.
[67] Muhammad Alam, Joaquim Ferreira, and José Fonseca, "Introduction to Intelligent Transportation Systems," in Muhammad Alam, Joaquim Ferreira, and José Fonseca (eds.), *Intelligent Transportation Systems* (Cham: Springer International Publishing, 2016), 1–17.

The transition to technologically mediated law enforcement flaunts the particular allure of neutrality – a highly appealing quality given contemporary concerns associated with discriminatory policing. Technology is often conceptualized as lacking bias,[68] and this attribute proves particularly valuable in law enforcement, "where allegations of bias may lead to a sense of injustice or a loss of public confidence in police services."[69] "Techno-fixes" offer the promise of consistent and neutral treatment, establishing the foundations for interactions that should always be procedurally just.[70] However, technologically mediated law enforcement can still convey harmful relational messages, as the example of automating the administration of traffic offenses (e.g., through the use of automated license plate readers) illustrates. Although responding to traffic violations with complete consistency, empirical research demonstrates that tickets administered through a technologically automated process communicate stigmatizing messages to the ticket recipient, specifically, their status as a member of a criminal "out-group."[71] While establishing complete neutrality, perceptions of the encounter specifically and law enforcement more generally do not improve as a result of the technologically mediated quality of the encounter in this example, a fact that Tyler attributes, in part, to the dissonance that results from being labelled in a non-law-abiding out-group. The topic of neutrality will be interrogated further shortly; however, it deserves emphasizing here that we ought not to prioritize neutrality at the expense of other relational concerns. Envisioning technologies as inherently neutral lays the foundation to neglect other relational concerns (i.e., trust, respect, and voice) that may also be important to better understanding technologically mediated law enforcement.

It is reasonable to anticipate that technological mediation will affect both the extent to which surveilled subjects trust police and the extent to which these subjects feel trusted by police. Enhancing police accountability is an ideal outcome of increasing police use of technology; for instance, technology may provide a factual record of interactions (e.g., body-worn cameras) or reduce the influence of individual bias (e.g., randomized computer-generated selection for additional screening at airports). This accountability is somewhat akin to trust; specifically, investing trust in technology and away from human agents of surveillance might enhance perceptions of trust.[72] However, this arguably does not genuinely enhance public trust in police, but only artificially constructs trust when technology is present – an outcome that

---

[68] Martin French and Gavin J. D. Smith, "Surveillance and Embodiment: Dispositifs of Capture," *Body & Society* 22, no. 2 (2016): 3–27; Carrie B. Sanders and James Sheptycki, "Policing, Crime and 'Big Data'; Towards a Critique of the Moral Economy of Stochastic Governance," *Crime, Law and Social Change* 68, no. 1–2 (2017): 1–15.
[69] Sanders and Hannem, "Policing 'the Risky'."
[70] Wells, "The Techno-Fix."
[71] Tyler, "Police Discretion."
[72] French and Smith, "Surveillance and Embodiment."

does not genuinely resolve the crisis of fractured community–police relations. In addition, the transparency (or lack thereof) of the procedures and outputs of technology used for law enforcement may be an issue for the public.[73] Without clear answers to questions such as "what data is the technology collecting," "where will it be stored," "who will use it," "how might it affect me in the future," and so forth, technological mediation may undermine rather than improve public perceptions of trust in law enforcement. Furthermore, changes to the style of law enforcement that communicate more generalized suspicion may diminish public trust in police.[74] As such, the increasing uptake of technology by law enforcement (which casts a wider and more constant net of scrutiny), might actually *generate* relational issues, undermining trust by implying that trust only exists in environments of constant observation and scrutiny.

Finally, technologically mediated law enforcement may affect public perceptions of respect and voice. Perceptions of respect are central to public evaluations of police attention to relational concerns.[75] Respectful treatment is associated with perceptions of procedural fairness.[76] Some forms of technologically mediated law enforcement arguably scrutinize and regulate officers' behavior alongside citizens; as such, the introduction of some technologies (e.g., body-worn cameras) might help control the emotional state of human agents in ways that enhance perceptions of respect and voice. However, the public may perceive more automated forms of technological mediation (e.g., automated license plate readers) as unable to display the important relational qualities of respect and voice by virtue of technology's (in)ability "to demonstrate respect, respond politely or provide the ears necessary for an individual to feel that their voice has been heard."[77] While technologically mediated law enforcement may reduce exposure to aggressive or actively impolite treatment (though it also does not guarantee that), it may also render encounters emotionally flat in ways that eliminate perceptions of voice or administrator empathy. Having reflected on how technologically mediated law enforcement might affect general public sentiment based on the existing procedural justice literature, the next section continues this consideration while also specifically reflecting on race.

---

[73] Rosamunde van Brakel, "Pre-Emptive Big Data Surveillance and Its (Dis)Empowering Consequences: The Case of Predictive Policing," in Bart van der Sloot, Dennis Broeders, and Erik Schrijvers (eds.), *Exploring the Boundaries of Big Data* (Amsterdam: Amsterdam University Press, 2016), 117–131.

[74] Tyler, "Police Discretion."

[75] Jackson et al., "Why Do People Comply"; Tyler, "Police Discretion."

[76] Lorraine Mazerolle et al., "Shaping Citizen Perceptions of Police Legitimacy: A Randomized Field Trial of Procedural Justice: Shaping Citizen Perceptions of Police," *Criminology* 51, no. 1 (2013): 33–63; Elsa Saarikkomäki, "Perceptions of Procedural Justice among Young People: Narratives of Fair Treatment in Young People's Stories of Police and Security Guard Interventions," *British Journal of Criminology* 56, no. 6 (2016): 1253–1271.

[77] Wells, "The Techno-Fix," 801.

Technologically Mediated Policing and Race

There is hope that technologically mediating law enforcement will enhance public perceptions of police legitimacy, particularly the gap that exists between perceptions of Black Americans relative to White Americans. This hope is based on the belief that technological mediation will change the "style" of policing – the way in which police interact with the public. Changing the style of policing is important to seeing improvements in public perceptions of trust and legitimacy, particularly for racial minority communities.[78] Some perceive technologically mediated law enforcement as key to ensuring a long-awaited equal protection under the law. For instance, the ushering in of body-worn cameras in the USA was founded, in part, on a platform of police accountability (particularly during interactions with Black Americans). However, while technology offers the promise of neutrality, it does not determine this outcome.[79] The American context – one in which officers have not been found guilty despite damning video evidence of abuse against Black persons, such as the filmed beating of Rodney King by a group of officers in 1992 – is not one in which greater surveillance has unequivocally led to greater police accountability. Critical reflections on the application of surveillance in general prompt similar concerns. Surveillance tends to (re)produce exclusion and marginality rather than diminish it.[80] As such, a significant concern associated with technologically mediated law enforcement is that it will mask, rather than eliminate, asymmetries of power.

Relational models of procedural justice offer some insight into the subjective component of this concern, suggesting that a surveilled subject's evaluation of the neutrality of a surveillance technology is linked to their perceptions of the legitimacy of the administrator of that technology. In other words, persons who perceive law enforcement as more legitimate in general may have more favorable attitudes towards encounters with technologically mediated law enforcement, evaluating the technology as benign, neutral, and enhancing their protection. Alternatively, persons who tend to have lower appraisals of the legitimacy of law enforcement, such as Black Americans, may see the introduction of technology merely as an extension of an illegitimate authority, enhancing the extent to which they can be targeted and scrutinized. If this is the case, technology might be more accurately understood as a proxy for trust because users of the technology are only trusted when acting alongside technology. If the technology is absent or fails, will the human agent administering the procedure still be trusted? If not, has the technology genuinely enhanced perceptions of trust in police, and relatedly, police legitimacy? To address these questions empirical work is necessary. Ultimately, without addressing the deeper relational concerns connected to legitimacy, technological

---

[78] Tyler, "Police Discretion."
[79] Beutin, "Racialization"; Autumn Womack, "Visuality, Surveillance, and the Afterlife of Slavery," *American Literary History* 29, no. 1 (2017): 191–204.
[80] French and Smith, "Surveillance and Embodiment"; Monahan, "Regulating Belonging."

mediation may serve to avoid, rather than resolve, fractured community–police relations, perhaps even intensifying those poor relations by expanding the scope and ubiquity of law enforcement surveillance as well as the life of the data collected. This last point draws attention to how technologically mediated law enforcement also has the potential to be objectively harmful, with members of marginalized groups, including racial minorities, potentially disproportionately affected.

Technology is not inherently neutral.[81] Technology does have the potential to regulate the behavior of biased individuals, but, unless carefully scrutinized, it is more likely to normalize rather than correct structural inequalities.[82] In law enforcement contexts, this may manifest as Black bodies being evaluated as inherently more threatening and in need of greater use of force than White bodies, which may manifest in forms such as higher risk classifications assigned by automated decision-making (e.g., identity verification during border crossings) or greater false positive rates for non-White faces by automated facial recognition software (e.g., when used in conjunction with drones surveilling crowds). These examples illustrate ways in which the individual is subjected to greater (technologically mediated) surveillance scrutiny but not empowered by it. Technological mediation does not inherently produce neutrality; it can, in fact, engage a discriminatory process with particularly negative consequences for marginalized persons.[83] Repeated exposure to such processes (including rational discrimination, in which algorithms rely on a predictor – such as race – without an acknowledgment of context) produces the experience of cumulative disadvantage, whereby one's life chances and opportunities are negatively impacted (see Gandy, Jr. for a detailed description of the applied aspects of this process and the way in which they disproportionately affect Black Americans).[84] In a climate where racialized surveillance is well-documented,[85] it is not unreasonable to speculate that technologically mediated law enforcement may amplify, rather than diminish, the exposure of some persons to scrutiny based on factors over which they have no control.

Future Research Directions

Empirical work assessing the promises and pitfalls of technologically mediated law enforcement in varied contexts is sorely needed. In general, "empirical studies of

---

[81] Geoffrey C. Bowker and Susan Leigh Star, *Sorting Things Out: Classification and Its Consequences* (Cambridge, MA: MIT Press, 1999); Langdon Winner, "Do Artifacts Have Politics?" *Daedalus* 109, no. 1 (1980): 121–136.

[82] Oscar H. Gandy, Jr., "Engaging Rational Discrimination: Exploring Reasons for Placing Regulatory Constraints on Decision Support Systems," *Ethics and Information Technology* 12, no. 1 (2010): 29–42.

[83] Sanders and Hannem, "Policing 'the Risky'"; Sanders and Sheptycki, "Policing, Crime and 'Big Data'."

[84] Gandy Jr., "Engaging Rational Discrimination"; van Brakel, "Pre-Emptive Big Data."

[85] Simone Browne, *Dark Matters: On the Surveillance of Blackness* (Durham, NC: Duke University Press, 2015); Lowe, Stroud, and Nguyen, "Who Looks Suspicious?"

technology-in-use [are] essential in order to appreciate their true influence."[86] The existing procedural justice literature offers a sound theoretical starting point from which to explore this topic empirically. However, it is important to acknowledge that the existing procedural justice research operates largely in the context of interpersonal encounters (see footnote for exceptions).[87] As interactions with law enforcement take on an increasingly technologically mediated quality, exploring the effects of this transition through a procedural justice lens may be very important to better understanding community–police relations.

"Little is known about how technology undermines, preserves, or enhances the nature of people's interactions with police."[88] Technological mediation may enhance the effectiveness and accountability of law enforcement. However, the policing literature, in general, has tended to concentrate on the effects of police strategies on crime rates, while overlooking their effects on public perceptions of legitimacy in evaluating police "effectiveness."[89] "Before you can ask 'what works?' you have to ask 'what matters?'."[90] The procedural justice literature has unequivocally demonstrated that *treatment* matters in evaluations of police in the context of interpersonal interactions. It is essential to explore if and how the introduction of technology in law enforcement encounters affects public perceptions of treatment, the communication of relational messages, and police legitimacy. "The policing literature has done little to identify factors that may work alongside procedural justice in promoting (or impeding) its expected desirable outcomes,"[91] and technology is a key factor that needs to be considered in this regard. The perspectives of the targets of police surveillance are essential to the empirical exploration of this topic; yet, these perspectives have received little attention.[92] Furthermore, bearing in mind the substantial disparities that exist in the experiences and opinions of different social groups in relation to law enforcement, it is critical that we consider and explore intersectional considerations in such analyses.[93]

---

[86] Haggerty, "Technology and Crime Policy," 493.
[87] Joh, "Discretionless Policing"; Wells, "The Techno-Fix."
[88] Edward M. Maguire, "Police Organizations and the Iron Cage of Rationality," in Michael D. Reisig and Robert J. Kane (eds.), *The Oxford Handbook of Police and Policing* (Oxford University Press, 2014), 85.
[89] Tyler, "Procedural Justice and Policing."
[90] Ben Bowling, "Fair and Effective Policing Methods: Towards 'Good Enough' Policing," *Journal of Scandinavian Studies in Criminology and Crime Prevention* 8, no. 1 (2007): 23.
[91] Jonathan-Zamir, Hasisi, and Margalioth, "Is It the What or the How?," 613.
[92] Cynthia Lum et al., "Discretion and Fairness in Airport Security Screening," *Security Journal* 28, no. 4 (2015): 352–373; Saulnier and Thompson, "Police UAV Use"; Wells, "The Techno-Fix".
[93] Simone Browne, "Race and Surveillance," in David Lyon, Kevin Haggerty, and Kirstie Ball (eds.), *Handbook on Surveillance Studies* (New York: Routledge, 2012b), 72–79; Alana Saulnier, "Racialized Borders: Hypothesizing the Diasporic Implications of Discriminatory Surveillance at Canadian Borders," *Journal of Borderlands Studies* 30, no. 2 (2015): 227–245; Webster, "Deadly Injustice."

CONCLUSION

This chapter has reflected on the topic of technologically mediated law enforcement, contemplating how this change in the style of policing might affect public perceptions of police with specific attention to the experiences of Black Americans. Even the perception that persons are treated differently by police on the basis of race is incredibly damaging to police legitimacy and community–police relations. Some position technologically mediated law enforcement as the solution to the perceptions and realities associated with this long-standing problem, but more fully acknowledging the motivations for a transition to technologically mediated law enforcement includes reflecting on its value to ILP. While ILP, and its accompanying technologically mediated approach to law enforcement, have been demonstrated to enhance police effectiveness in terms of crime fighting, the impact of technological mediation on community–police relations requires greater attention. For this, the existing procedural justice literature offers some direction. In particular, the extent to which technologically mediated law enforcement addresses relational concerns and communicates identity-relevant information, as well as the role that race plays in these relationships, are key areas for future empirical inquiry. The extent to which the trend towards technologically mediated law enforcement is attentive to relational concerns or genuinely addresses the crisis of poor community–police relations, particularly for communities with strained relations, requires empirical research to promote the development of evidence-based policy.

In summary, technological mediation may be able to be used by law enforcement as a tool that promotes the achievement of legitimacy, but it is imperative that technological mediation does not come to serve as a substitute for trust. Legitimacy is perhaps the most important issue for policing in democracies in the twenty-first century. In that pursuit, technologically mediated encounters with law enforcement may enhance public trust and confidence in some ways. However, "techno-fixes" will not solve underlying issues of fractured community–police relations. True reform requires establishing bonds of trust between communities and police that acknowledge the importance of treatment attentive to relational concerns, which may be supported by, but are not dependent on, technological mediation.

Printed by Printforce, United Kingdom